Norman Lewis Omnibus

NORMAN LEWIS was born in London. He has written thirteen novels and nine non-fiction works. He relaxes by his travels to off-beat parts of the world, which he prefers to be as remote as possible, otherwise he lives with his family in introspective, almost monastic, calm in the depths of Essex.

NORMAN LEWIS OMNIBUS

A Dragon Apparent

Golden Earth

A Goddess in the Stones

PICADOR

A Dragon Apparent first published 1951 by Jonathan Cape Ltd

Golden Earth first published 1952 by Jonathan Cape Ltd

A Goddess in the Stones first published 1991 by Jonathan Cape Ltd
and published in paperback 1992 by Picador
in association with Jonathan Cape Ltd

This omnibus edition first published 1995 by Picador
in association with Jonathan Cape Ltd

This edition published 1996 by Picador
an imprint of Macmillan General Books
25 Eccleston Place London SW1W 9NF
and Basingstoke

Associated companies throughout the world

in association with Jonathan Cape Ltd

ISBN 0 330 33780 7

1 3 5 7 9 8 6 4 2

A CIP catalogue record for this book is available from
the British Library

Typeset by CentraCet Limited, Cambridge
Printed and bound in Great Britain by
Cox & Wyman Ltd, Reading, Berkshire

Contents

List of Illustrations

A Dragon Apparent

Saigon street scene
Saigon waterfront
The Cao-Daïst cathedral at Tay Ninh
Water-peddlers on the Chinese creek
Cochin-China: fishing in rice-fields – and in mud
The wife of the M'nong chief ignores the camera
Only the baby dares to peep
A long-house at Buon Dieo
Buon Ročai, showing jars housing tutelary spirits
Mang-Yang: the last French post
Pleiku: the sacrifice
Pleiku: a drink from the sacred jar
Prak, whose name meant 'money'
The M'nong Gar woman shows typical Moï indifference
Saigon: incense spirals in the Cantonese pagoda
Vietnamese theatre: the Chinese ambassador declares
   his love
Pnom-Penh: procession of the twenty-five spirits
The sinister smile of the Bayon
A corner of Angkor Vat
Free drinks for the bonzes
Laotian dancers amused by the camera
Audience in Angkor
The fantastic landscape of northern Laos
Meo woman
Pagoda at Luang Prabang
Cochin-China: the search for small fish

Golden Earth

The Shwedagon Pagoda
Night at the Shwedagon Pagoda
Clown actress at a pwè
The last of the Burmese puppet shows
Lake and pagoda at Mudon
Mon fisherman in the Altaran River, Moulmein
The Arakan pagoda: guardian figures taken at the
    sacking of Ayuthia
By the walls of Mandalay
Old man (race unknown) met in Maymyo market
Child beggar in the market at Maymyo
On the road to Lashio; a Shan beggar
The Kachin headman's womenfolk
A corner of the Nam Hkam market
Pot-sellers at Shwegu
Night market at Kyaukmyaung
Nat-ka-daws – wives of the spirits
Possessed by the buffalo-spirit
Rangoon: at the Shwedagon Pagoda

A
DRAGON
APPARENT

*Travels in Cambodia,
Laos, and Vietnam*

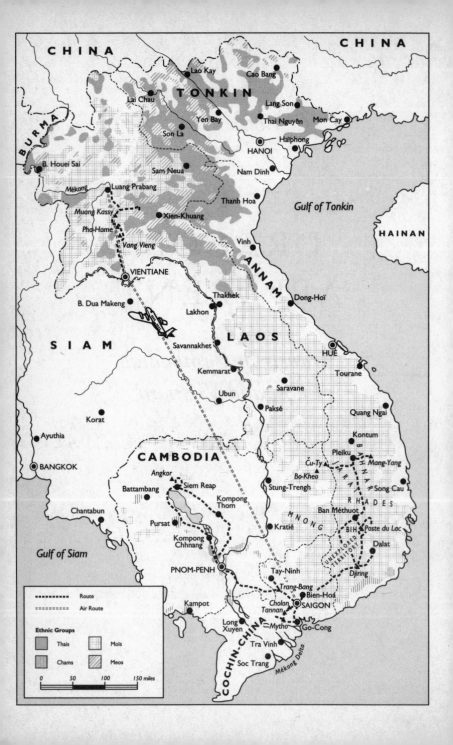

Contents

Preface to the 1982 Edition

The ancient civilizations of Vietnam, Cambodia, and Laos were already falling into decay when I travelled through South-East Asia prior to writing this book. Inevitably degeneration had followed contact with the West, and the invasion and subsequent colonization by the French; yet much of the charm and the grandeur of the past had survived in these countries, protected by their remoteness and the dense rain-forests and mountain ranges covering half their area.

The central plateau of Vietnam was peopled largely by tribes of Malayo-Polynesian origin, living in spectacular long-houses, whose existence had barely been noticed until the coming of the Japanese. These Moïs, as they were called, were living as their ancestors had probably lived for thousands of years when I visited them, and although the French had carried off some hundreds for forced labour in the tea-plantations, they had otherwise been left alone, to live their complicated, highly ceremonial, and – to an outsider like myself – idyllic lives. The long-houses accommodating a whole village, shown in this book, no longer exist. They were bombed to nothingness by the B52s in the Vietnam War, and such of the population who survived were forced into the armies fighting the Nationalist Viet-Cong, who were revenged on them in due course when the US abandonment of the country took place.

With the exception of these gracious and endearing people, the population of Vietnam, Cambodia, and Laos were Buddhist, and therefore in essence gentle, tolerant, and addicted to pleasures and satisfactions of a discriminating kind. Just as in Japan, popular excursions would be made in certain seasons to admire trees in blossom. There were night-scapes in Saigon to be visited only when the moon was in a certain phase, and rich mandarins – still existing in those days in what remained culturally a province of China – would pay for white herons to be released across the sky when the party was seated in readiness for this aesthetic experience. At

5

five in the evening, when one took the breeze on the waterfront in Saigon, stalls were put out with soft drinks of many colours, and one chose refreshment as much for its auspicious colouring as its taste. There was a right way in Vietnam to do everything, a gentle but persuasive protocol, full of subtle allusions, and nuances in gesture and speech that evaded the foreign barbarian. The Europeans corrupted but failed to barbarize Indo-China, and many of them who lived there long enough were happy enough to go native and cultivate what they could of the patina of the old civilization. Laos was considered the earthly paradise of South-East Asia, although Cambodia ran it a close second. So much was this realized by French officialdom that the competition for a posting to either country was strenuous. Many a wily administrator manoeuvred his way to a position in Ventiane or Luang Prabang, where he instantly married a Laotian wife, set up a shrine with joss-sticks to the lares of his house, and spent much of his leisure decking out Buddha caves with fresh flowers.

Both of these oases of decorum and charm were to be devastated and debauched in the Vietnam war, when as many bombs were showered among the shrines and the pagodas of these small countries as were expended in all the bombings put together of the World War in Europe.

Protocol demanded that visits be made to the rulers of these countries. I was warned to present myself at the palace of King Norodom Sihanouk, who later demoted himself to prince, and succeeded in holding the French, and after them the Americans, at bay for so many years. He was a gentle, softly spoken young man, and we sat side by side on a sofa, deploring the inroads made by the West on the traditions of his country. In that year, despite his protests, a cinema had opened in Pnom-Penh, and his subjects who flocked thither to see *Arsenic and Old Lace* forsook the ancient shadow play for ever, while temple dancers ceased to have appeal for those who had been entertained by Fred Astaire and Ginger Rogers in action.

Some dignitaries were more formal in style. The Emperor Bao-dai liked visitors to crawl into his presence, or at least make a token obeisance by falling on one knee, but these were experiences I managed to evade. Many surprises awaited the traveller. A reputedly ferocious war lord could find nothing to talk about but the cultivation of chrysanthemums. An ex-governor of South Vietnam received me with what was regarded as charming informality while seated upon a close-stool ornamented with dragons. The Pope of the Cao Daï, the universal religion which included Joan of Arc, Victor Hugo, and the Duc de la Rochefoucauld among its saints, appeared briefly in an entourage of white-robed twelve-year-old girls, said to have formed his harem.

General des Essars was in command of French troops in Cambodia, and I had two meetings with him, the first a formal one at his headquarters, and the second totally informal in the romantic and justly famous opium den run by Madame Shum, where he was accustomed to settle his nerves by smoking two pipes of an evening. Whereas on the first occasion the General had been brimming with confidence and euphoria, on the second, sedated and perhaps somewhat dispirited by his two pipes, he saw a vision of the future that left him no better than resigned in his frame of mind. He had two thousand five hundred Cambodian troops under his command, and he accepted the fact that nothing would ever turn them into fighters. Their religion, he said, had knocked all the aggression out of them. What could you expect in a country where every man-jack of them had done a year in a monastery, where they taught you that 'thou shalt not kill' had to be taken literally?

At the root of the trouble, said the General, lay the fact that Buddhism deprived the people of South-East Asia of the motives we Westerners understood and admired. If the aim in life was nothing more than to acquire virtue, what was the point of any form of competitive endeavour? If people only bothered to gather possessions for the spiritual benefit of giving them away, why then work hard? Why go to war?

And this was largely true. There were pagodas everywhere, full of monks who lived by begging, each of them holding a five-day festival once a year. A festival was always going on somewhere to provide villages in search of virtuous poverty with an opportunity for showering gifts on all comers, and shedding their burden of surplus wealth. Pnom-Penh must have been the world's only city where a man taking a taxi sometimes found himself offered a tip by the driver.

It was, of course, improper to take life in any form, however lowly. Devout Cambodians allowed mosquitoes to feast on their blood and handled leeches tenderly when they fastened on them in the rice-paddies. A monk once reproved me for crushing a cockroach underfoot, with the warning that this might have been my grandfather in reincarnation.

Villages obliged to live by fishing got round moral objections by 'rescuing the fish from drowning', and it was agreed that if they subsequently happened to die there could be no harm in consuming their flesh. All along the banks of the Mékong one saw the live fish laid out for sale, tied with decorative ribbons, often fanned by conscientious sellers, occasionally even solaced by the music of a bamboo flute.

Even in the gently melancholic autumn of those days there were guerrillas in the jungles and mountains, who had gone there to take up arms against the French, but they caused little inconvenience to the pacific traveller. The Issarak (freedom fighters), as they were called, went into action with guitars slung on their backs, involving themselves in not particularly bloody clashes, reminiscent of the ceremonial wars between Italian city states, when a day of battle might produce a single casualty. Travelling along jungle trails in areas known to be under Issarak control, I was careful to restrict such movement to the hours of the afternoon, when they could be relied upon to be taking their siesta. At the lengthy festival of the New Year, the fight was called off, and everybody went home for a week or so to worship at the ancestral shrines, engage in ritual gambling, feed the monks, and to sleep.

Later the real war was unleashed, to be conducted in secret by radio through the US Embassy in Pnom-Penh. South Vietnam was already a wasteland, deluged by high explosives, poisons, and fire. Mr Kissinger had said that the dominoes were falling, so now it was the turn of Cambodia and Laos, delivered to the greatest holocaust ever to be visited on the East. It consumed not only the present, but the past; an obliteration of cultures and values as much as physical things. From the ashes that remained no phoenix would ever rise. Not enough survived even to recreate the memory of what the world had lost.

What could these people have suffered to have transformed the sons and brothers of General des Essars' reluctant conscripts, formed in the ambulatories of monasteries rather than on the barracks square, into those terrible and implacable warriors who flocked to the standards of the Khmer Rouge?

Norman Lewis, 1982

Background

Indo-China lies immediately to the south of China proper and to the east of Burma and Siam. On a world-map it is no more than a coastal strip, swelling out at its base – the rump of Eastern Asia. It is purely a political entity: originally the French colonial possessions corresponding to the conquered Empire of Annam, and its tributaries. This temporary union is in the process of dissolution.

The Indo-Chinese countries contain the scattered remnants of as many races as those of Europe, but they are inextricably jumbled up in a jigsaw of racial islands and enclaves, from which only three nations emerge: Vietnam, Cambodia, and Laos. Of the total population of twenty-five millions, seventeen millions are Vietnamese. The Cambodians and Laotians are peoples in monastic retirement; non-participants, as followers of a contemplative and renunciatory religion, in the march of progress. The population of the whole of Indo-China is concentrated in a few fertile valleys and deltas, leaving the greater part of the country unpopulated, jungle-covered, and looking much the same as China itself must have looked several thousand years ago, before the deforestation began. The interior is neither completely mapped, nor completely explored. It abounds with game: elephants, tigers, deer, and many kinds of cattle, which, having known only hunters armed with crossbows, may be closely approached and slaughtered with the greatest ease from cars on the jungle tracks.

Pacification of the Moïs of central and southern Vietnam – those bow and arrow tribes which in the early part of the last century were believed to be the only human beings with tails – was only undertaken in 1934. Certain tribes of the remote interior have not yet submitted to French authority.

The early history of Indo-China is that of primitive aboriginals – Mongolians in the north and Malayo-Polynesians in the south – coming respectively under the influences of their great civilized neighbours, the

Chinese and the Indians. From the latter union two brilliant and neurotic civilizations were created: those of the Khmers and the Chams. Both of them, after much precocious accomplishment, overtaxed their strength in wars and collapsed. The Chams were first compressed and then absorbed by the southward movement of conquerors from China – the Vietnamese; while the remnants of the Khmers, listless and degenerate, were crowded back by the same people to the Siamese frontier. Scrupulous Vietnamese peasants still burn paper rent for the benefit of the spirits of long-vanished peoples, whose land they now possess.

The first Europeans to arrive in Indo-China – the missionaries and traders officially classified by the Vietnamese authorities as 'red-haired barbarians' – were dazzled by the people's virtues and enchanted by their hospitality. 'Whereas all the other Eastern Nations,' said the Jesuit Borri, writing in 1622,

> looking upon the Europeans as a profane people, do naturally abhor them, and therefore fly from us when first we come among them: In Cochin-China it falls out just contrary: for they strive who shall be nearest us, ask a thousand Questions, invite us to eat with them, and in short use all manner of Courtesie with much Familiarity and Respect ... This loving and easie Disposition is the Cause of much Concord among them, they all treating one another as familiarly as if they were Brothers, or of the same Family ... and it would be look'd upon as a most vile action, if one Man eating any thing, tho' never so little, should not share it with all about him, giving every one about him a bit.

Borri and his successors, however, soon found causes for criticism. As a sign apparently that 'something was rotten in the state', the devil frequently manifested himself, under horrific forms. Once called out with crosses, Agnus Deis, and relics to confront him, Borri was only a matter of instants too late and saw three prints of his feet 'above two spans long, with the Marks of a Cock's Talons and Spurs'. The laws, too, were shockingly severe. Men and women received sound thrashings in the streets for slight breaches of good manners and then knelt to thank the mandarin who had ordered the punishment. A high official found guilty of delaying the presentation of a petition to the Divine Emperor was beheaded on the spot. But in other ways there was a barbarous penal insufficiency, of which the newcomers were equally unable to approve. The maximum prison sentence was three years, which, if the prisoner had aged parents to look after, could be served under some kind of parole system at home; while thieves who pleaded dire necessity were sometimes pardoned.

It was to correct these moral weaknesses that proselytizing pressure was brought to bear, and when the Vietnamese showed themselves intractable, the principle of religious tolerance was imposed by force of arms. In 1858, after a gradual extension of their influence over fifty years, the French began the outright conquest of the country. The annexation of Vietnam – at that time known as Annam – was followed by requests from Cambodia and Laos to be taken under French protection. The Cambodians' decision is said to have been much influenced by the French assurance that they would be allowed in future to keep for themselves all the white elephants they captured – animals of peculiar sanctity which previously they had been obliged to surrender to the Vietnamese Emperor.

During the last war the Japanese were allowed to occupy Indo-China without opposition, and the French collaborated with them until March 1945. At that time, after observing the success of allied arms in the West, the Japanese decided to intern the French authorities and to set up a puppet Vietnamese state headed by the Emperor Bao-dai. This government collapsed with the defeat of Japan and was replaced by a purely nationalist one, the Viet-Minh, headed by Ho Chi-minh. The Emperor Bao-dai abdicated and, after remaining for a short time as 'adviser' to the Ho Chi-minh government, finally left the country. Shortly after, a French expeditionary corps disembarked at Saigon, and the present war began.

After five years of fighting the French have re-occupied most of the large towns, the major part of the Tonkinese rice-growing delta in the north, and about half that of Cochin-China in the south. The Viet-Minh control about four-fifths of Vietnam and the coastline of Cambodia, by which the free passage of arms is assured between Siam and their Southern Army, in Cochin-China. Although the strength of the army of the Viet-Minh is unknown it is believed to amount approximately to one hundred thousand men, and to be slightly numerically inferior to the French forces which oppose it. It is increased by an incalculable number of partisans who are to all intents and purposes inoffensive peasants during the daytime hours. The Viet-Minh is well supplied with small arms and automatic weapons, mostly purchased in Siam and the Philippines, and has recently obtained up-to-date artillery from China.

In 1949 'independence within the French Union' was granted to the three countries of Indo-China, and the ex-Emperor Bao-dai, recalled from self-imposed exile, was created head of the French-sponsored Vietnamese State. It is now apparent that this move has not been successful in its intended effect, which was to rally Vietnamese dissidents under the banner of the Emperor, and thus put an end to the war.

After four years of virtual stalemate, the military situation is again fluid. Viet-Minh leaders assured me in the spring of 1950 that by the autumn of that year they would launch an all-out offensive in an attempt to drive the French from the country before the rains broke in June 1951. When, in January 1951, the proofs of this book were being corrected, the promised offensive was already four months old, and in the north the Viet-Minh, having occupied most of Tonkin, were closing in on Hanoi. It seems certain that before the book appears further important changes will have taken place.

CHAPTER ONE

Saigon and the Vietnamese

IN 1949, a curtain which had been raised for the first time hardly more than fifty years ago in China came down again for a change of scene. Low-grade clerks in air and shipping offices all over the world were given piles of leaflets and told to stamp the word 'suspended' over such place names as Shanghai, Canton, and Kunming. Later they used the 'service discontinued' stamp. If you had wanted to go to China it was too late. You would have to content yourself with reading books about it, and that was as much of the old, unregenerate China as you would ever know. At this moment the scene shifters were busy, and they might be a long time over their job. When the curtain went up again it would be upon something as unrecognizable to an old China hand as to Marco Polo. And when this day came you had a feeling that curious travellers might find themselves restricted to state-conducted tours, admiring the marvels of reconstruction – the phoenix in concrete.

Now that China had passed into the transforming fire, it seemed that the experience of Far-Eastern travel, if ever to be enjoyed, could no longer be safely postponed. What then remained? Which would be the next country to undergo this process of change which was spreading so rapidly across Asia, and which would have to be seen now, or never again in its present form? I thought that Indo-China was the answer, and it was all the more interesting because, compared to the other Far-Eastern countries, so little had been written about it.

In the middle of January 1950, deciding to risk no further delays, I caught an Air France plane at Paris, bound for Saigon.

*

On the morning of the fourth day the dawn light daubed our faces as we came down the skies of Cochin-China. The passengers were squirming in their seats, not sleeping and not waking, and the air-hostess's trained smile came stiffly. With engines throttled back the plane dropped from sur-alpine heights in a tremorless glide, settling in the new, morning air of the plains like a dragonfly on the surface of a calm lake. As the first rays of the sun burst through the magenta mists that lay along the horizon, the empty sketching of the child's painting book open beneath us received a wash of green. Now lines were ruled lightly across it. A yellow pencilling of roads and blue of canals.

A colonel of the Foreign Legion awoke uneasily, struggling with numbed, set facial muscles to regain that easy expression of good-fellowship of a man devoted to the service of violence. Becoming interested in something he saw below, he roused a friend, and they rubbed at the window and peered down. We were passing over a road that seemed to be strangely notched at intervals. 'The defence towers,' murmured the Colonel, smiling with gentle appreciation. A few minutes later there was another moment of interest as we passed above that gauzily traced chequer-board of fields and ditches. Down there in the abyss, unreal in their remoteness, were a few huts, gathered where the ruler-drawn lines of roads crossed each other. From them a wisp of incense curled towards us. To have been seen so clearly from this height it must have been a great, billowing cloud of smoke. There was a circle of specks in the yellow fields round the village. '*Une opération*,' the Colonel said. Somehow, as he spoke, he seemed linked psychically to what was going on below. Authority flowed back into the travel-weary figure. With the accession of this priestly essence he dominated the rest of the passengers.

Beneath our eyes violence was being done, but we were as detached from it almost as from history. Space, like time, anaesthetizes the imagination. One could understand what an aid to untroubled killing the bombing plane must be.

It was a highly symbolical introduction to South-East Asia.

*

In air travel, first impressions are stifled in banality. At Saigon, the airport – a foretaste of the world-state, and as functional as a mortuary – was followed by a bus trip down Napoleonic boulevards to an internationalized air terminal. Then came the hotel, an unpalatial palace of the kind that looms across the road from French railway stations. So far the East was kept at bay. Grudgingly conceded a room, I flung open the shutters for a first impression of the town from a high vantage point, flushing as I did a covey of typical London house-sparrows.

Saigon is a French town in a hot country. It is as sensible to call it – as is usually done – the Paris of the Far East as it would be to call Kingston, Jamaica, the Oxford of the West Indies. Its inspiration has been purely commercial and it is therefore without folly, fervour, or much ostentation. There has been no audacity of architecture, no great harmonious conception of planning. Saigon is a pleasant, colourless, and characterless French provincial city, squeezed on to a strip of delta-land in the South China Seas. From it exude strangely into the surrounding creeks and rivers ten thousand sampans, harbouring an uncounted native population. To the south, the once separated China-town of Cholon has swollen so enormously as to become its grotesque Siamese twin. There are holes in the urban fabric roughly filled in with a few thousand branch and straw shacks, which are occasionally cleared by accidental fires. The better part of the city contains many shops, cafés, and cinemas, and one small, plain cathedral in red brick. Twenty thousand Europeans keep as much as possible to themselves in a few tamarind-shaded central streets and they are surrounded by about a million Vietnamese and Chinese.

I breakfasted, absurdly, but after a twenty hours fast, on a long, saffron-coloured sole; pleased that the tea served with it should have a slightly earthy, hot-house flavour. This finished I went out into the mild, yellow light and immediately witnessed a sight which compensated one for Saigon's disappointingly Westernized welcome. There was a rapid, silently swirling traffic in the streets of bicycle rickshaws mixed up with cycles; a bus, sweeping out of a side-street into the main torrent, caught a cyclist, knocked him off, and crushed his machine. Both the bus driver and the cyclist were Chinese or Vietnamese, and the bus driver, jumping down from his seat, rushed over to congratulate the cyclist on his lucky escape. Both men were delighted, and the cyclist departed, carrying the wreckage of his machine and still grinning broadly. No other incidents of my travels in Indo-China showed up more clearly the fundamental difference of attitude towards life and fortune of the East and the West.

But still impatient with Saigon's centre, I plunged quickly into the side-streets. I was immediately arrested by an agent of the customs and excise, well dressed in a kind of tropical knickerbockers, who told me politely that from my suspicious movements he believed me to be trafficking in foreign currency. Marched discreetly to the Customs House I was searched and then, when no gold or dollars were found, shown registers by the disappointed and apologetic officials to prove by the great hoards recently recovered that they rarely misjudged their man.

From this happening it was clear that Europeans rarely leave the wide boulevards where they belong, that if they sometimes take short cuts they do so purposefully, and that to wander at haphazard looked very much to the official eye like loitering with intent. For all that, it was my intention to spend my first day or two in the Far East in just such aimless roamings, collecting sharp first impressions while the mind was still freshly receptive; before the days came when so much would no longer surprise, would be overlooked, would be taken for granted. The business of organizing the journey through the country could be attended to later.

It was clear from the first moment of picking my way through these crowded, torrid streets that the lives of the people of the Far East are lived in public. In this they are different from people in almost any other part of the world. The street is the extension of the house and there is no sharp dividing line between the two. At dawn, or, in the case of Saigon, at the hour when the curfew is lifted, people roll out of bed and make for the pavement, where there is more space, to perform most of their toilet. Thereafter they eat, play cards, doze, wash themselves, have their teeth seen to, are cupped and massaged by physicians, visit fortune-tellers; all in the street. There is none of the desire for privacy that is so strong in Europe and stronger still in the Islamic countries. Even the better houses seemed to consist on the ground floor of one large room in which the family lived communally while visitors drifted in and out through the open doors.

People took small snacks at frequent intervals, seating themselves at wayside booths decorated with painted glass screens that had perhaps been imported from Japan, as the subjects were Japanese: scowling Samurai and winged tigers. Great store was set by the decorative presentation of food. Diaphanous baby octopuses were suspended before acetylene lamps. There were tasteful groupings of sliced coxcomb about cured pigs' snouts on excellent china plates. Roast chickens and ducks, lacquered bright red, were displayed in heraldic attitudes, with gracefully arched necks, or completely flattened out, like kippers. There were segments of pigs, sundered with geometrical precision, which, after the denaturalizing art to which they had been submitted, seemed with their brilliant, glossy surfaces as unreal as the furnishings of a toy butcher's shop. Here the appetites were solicited under frivolous rather than brutal forms.

One wondered about the origin of some of the delicacies: the ducks' heads fried in batter and the webbed feet of some wading bird or other. Were they the fruit of a laborious empirical process, appealing to palates of extraordinary refinement, since in either case fleshy sustenance was practically non-existent? Or were they, as a Vietnamese suggested, along with such traditional Chinese dishes as edible birds' nests and sharks' fins, the last resort of famine-stricken populations who gradually developed a taste for what, in the original emergency, they probably ate with the greatest repugnance? If this hypothesis is correct some of the results show an ironic twist. Bears' paws, once probably thrown to the beggars by the hunter, are now only within the reach of millionaires in the most exclusive Chinese restaurants. Saigon merchants have to pay about £50 per kilogram for first-quality sharks' fins, imported from West Africa, and the birds' nests harvested from the islands of the Vietnamese coast contribute notably to the cost of the arms bought by the Viet-Minh, within whose territory this source of wealth is located.

Many people when making their purchases preferred to gamble for them with the merchants, and for this reason a bowl of dice was at the disposal of customers on most stalls. A double-or-quits basis was employed, with the odds arranged slightly in the merchant's favour. Housewives are said to gamble consistently for their shopping on days shown as favourable in their horoscopes, which means that on slightly more than fifty per cent of such occasions they return home empty handed and with the house-keeping money gone. Even the children gambled for their sweets, using miniature dice in charmingly decorated bowls. Before making a throw the child usually invoked good luck in a musical phrase, consisting, as it happened, of the first four notes of the 'Volga Boat Song'.

Gambling is the besetting sin of the Vietnamese. It is a national mania, assuming at the great feast of the New Year almost a ritual aspect, since a day is set aside upon which the Vietnamese of all ages and ways of life gather together to stake their possessions on the fall of the dice. The underlying motive seems to be religious in character; an act of submission to destiny and with it a sacrifice; a propitiation and an expression of faith.

Since the belief in the uncontrollable gods of Fortune seems uppermost among Vietnamese credences, there is a universal demand for revelation of the future. There was an amazing variety of arrangements by which this demand was catered for. After the bashful and hesitant European tribute to the sciences of prediction, with its association of afternoon tea and church fêtes, this display of the seemingly innumerable methods of augury was an astonishing spectacle. There were any number of splendid mountebanks, unbelievably endowed to play their parts, with wise, ancient faces and the straggling white beards of Chinese sages. Before them on the pavement were set out the instruments of their art, the cards, the curiously shaped stones, the bowl of sand, the mirrors of catoptromancy, the divining bird. Behind them the walls were spread with backcloths covered with astrological charts, diagrams of the fateful parts of the human body, the bald heads and childishly drawn faces of phrenologists the world over, the signs of the Zodiac, and the equally picturesque Chinese years which are symbolized by animals.

But to these legitimate methods of advertisement a new and, to me, improper element had, in many cases, been added; one that involved a confusion of function and an inexcusable distortion of the very essence of prognostication. This was the implication, in pictorial form, that fate can be cheated. There were warning sketches of the misfortunes that awaited those who failed to patronize the fortune-teller. Calamity had been brought up to date, for these wretched persons were being blown to pieces by a significantly mushroom-shaped explosion. Those on the other hand who had taken the precaution to keep informed of what the fates had in store for them seemed to have been able to do something about it, since they were to be seen clasping members of the other sex under a token moonlight, or riding in what were recognizably American cars. It all seemed most illogical. If the future has been decided, then we will be atomized or achieve life's crowning success in the shape of an American car. One can't have it both ways. But perhaps a soothsayer dealing in such immutabilities would lose his business through his competitor, installed no more than three or four yards away along the street, who could show that there was some way of rubbing out the writing of destiny and that one could avoid the bombs and have the car, even if one's horoscope had arranged for it to be the other way round.

The Vietnamese are fascinated by dentistry, and I should imagine that the dentist's is one of the most crowded professions. Hard by the charts of the fortune-tellers, and at first sight easy to confuse with them, were those of the dentists; heads shown in cross-section, macabre and highly coloured, with suggested arrangements of gold teeth. Few races can resist embellishing the jaw with gold, and to the Vietnamese a good number of gold teeth, arranged according to accepted standards, are a discreet evidence of prosperity as well as showing a proper pride in one's appearance. The fact is that teeth left in their natural white state have always shocked Vietnamese susceptibilities by their resemblance to the fangs of animals. Until quite recently – and even now in some country districts – they were camouflaged with black enamel. One of the old emperors, receiving in audience a European ambassador, is said to have exclaimed in ungovernable horror, 'Who is this man with the teeth of a dog?' This mild phobia provides innumerable citizens with an artistic means of livelihood. Sometimes the teeth of both jaws are completely framed in gold, and neat shapes, often playing-card symbols, are cut in the front of the framing of each tooth, thus laying bare a minimum expanse of the original bone.

In order of popularity after the dentists come the portrait photographers. It is interesting to observe that the beautiful Vietnamese ladies, shown as specimens of the photographer's art, are less oriental than caucasian. By local standards their lips are thin and that slightly prognathous appearance, so noticeable throughout the Far East, is avoided. Only the narrow, shallow-set eyes with the Mongolian fold of the lids reveal the origin of these faces. One wonders whether those features of the oriental appearance which we regard as most typical, and perhaps least attractive, are also least attractive to them ... or whether this is yet another instance of the all-powerful effect of the cinema for standardization.

There is no doubt that here, as elsewhere throughout the world, the films have been devastating in their influence. In these streets cinema posters had been plastered up wherever a space could be found. The subjects were bloody and horrific; a torture scene with the victim's bowels being wound out on a windlass; soldiers being hacked to death on the battlefield or blown to pieces by bombs. Always blood. Rivers of blood. When a more domestic setting was depicted, it was with a sexual motive, the male being shown in full evening dress, the woman or women in cami-knickers. These were the products of Eastern studios. The imported products, as I learned later, were nearly all wild-westerns and their description has so much affected popular imagination as to have become almost synonymous with the movies themselves. The tendency now is not to say, 'I'm going to see a film' but, 'I'm going to see a far-western' or, as it becomes in Vietnamese or Chinese, a *pá-wé*. Buffalo Bill and his successors have been exhumed, or perhaps remade, to satisfy this local taste. One's eye is constantly assaulted by scenes of Far Western pseudo-history, interpreted by a Far Eastern imagination, in which ferocious cowboys, armed with the tommy-guns the white man is always supposed to have possessed, do terrible slaughter among small, slant-eyed, and rather Vietnamese-looking Indians.

The variety of the scene was endless, and in the end exhausting. Retiring to a Chinese café, I was received by a waitress who advanced with a damp towel, held in a pair of forceps. This I took and, following the example of the other patrons, wiped my face and hands with it. I ordered beer and was served a bottle with a snarling tiger on the label. It was very weak and slightly perfumed. The young lady left the change, a small pile of filthy notes, on the table. I learned later that particularly dirty notes are given to encourage customers to leave them as a tip. She then returned and joined the rest of the staff who were listening respectfully to the radio playing 'When Irish Eyes are Smiling'. This was sometimes overwhelmed by the penetrating soprano of a Chinese crooner, broadcast from the gramophone shop over the way. Looking in its window a few moments before I had noticed among the portable gramophones and the saxophones several neatly fitted crocodile cases containing silver-mounted opium sets for the chic smoker. Many small pink lizards, with black, bulging eyes, dodged about among this splendid window display.

While I sat in the café a funeral passed. It was preceded by a man with a flute and another with a drum. The hearse was so enormous that it passed with difficulty through this narrow street. The children of the family played happily about the coffin and the principal mourners in white robes were half carried and half dragged along behind. Among the officiants was a man carrying a bowl of cigarettes for the benefit of passing spirits. Apart from the funeral the traffic in this street was limited to ponies and traps on their way to market, with bundles of ducks hanging from their axles, their heads gently stroking the surface of the road.

A yard or so from the café door a herbalist had set up a stall and was selling the small, ugly, dried-up corpses of such animals as lizards, anonymous organs hideously pickled in bottles, desiccated insects, a great selection of animals' teeth, and horns of all shapes and sizes. He also had bottles of mixture, cough cures and elixirs. The advantages of taking these were illustrated in series of pictures, on the comic-strip principle. Patients with chronic coughs were shown as deserted by all. Romance in Vietnam seemed to be as insecurely founded as the makers of dentifrice believe it to be in Europe. And only with his cough cured was the sufferer seen once again in the arms of his loved one. There was a medicine too that seemed to cure mediocrity, because a course of this turned the investor from a loafer into a public speaker at the microphone.

It was all very entertaining to a stranger completely fresh from the West, but from the experiences of these few hours I had learned one disturbing thing. This was that as a European I had been invisible. My eyes never met those of a Vietnamese. There was no curious staring, no gesture or half-smile of recognition. I was ignored even by the children. The Vietnamese people, described by early travellers as gay, sociable and showing a lively curiosity where strangers were concerned, have now withdrawn into themselves. They are too civilized to spit at the sight of a white man, as the Indians of Central America do sometimes, but they are utterly indifferent. It is as if a general agreement has been reached among them that this is the best way of dealing with an intolerable presence. Even the rickshaw coolie, given, to be on the safe side, double his normal fee, takes the money in grim silence and immediately looks away. It is most uncomfortable to feel oneself an object of this universal detestation, a mere foreign-devil in fact.

CHAPTER TWO

The Universal Religion

THE FIRST IMPORTANT TASK of the visitor to Saigon on a journalistic or literary mission is to present his credentials at the Office of Information and Propaganda. The reason for this is that only through the sponsorship of this office will he be able to move about the country, as tourist accommodation rarely exists in the hinterland and, in any case, a circulation permit is required before any journey can be made.

On the second day after my arrival I therefore presented myself at the office in question and was received by the director, Monsieur de la Fournière. I was prepared for a certain amount of official discouragement of a project which involved travelling over as much as I could of a country where a war was in progress. At best I hoped for permission to visit one or two of the larger towns, travelling possibly by plane. At worst I feared that I might be told quite flatly that I could not leave Saigon. I was therefore amazed to find this interview going entirely contrary to my expectations. The consistent contrariness of travel is one of its fascinations, but usually it is the other way round. The difficulties and frustrations turn out to be worse than one had feared.

The director was young, expansive, and enthusiastic. I had hardly begun to outline my hopes before he took over. Far from being surprised that anyone should want to travel about the country at such a time, he seemed to find the idea both reasonable and praiseworthy. Taking up a firm stance before a wall map, he began to demolish distances and dangers with bold, sweeping gestures and in rapid idiomatic English. The outlines of the journey were sketched in, in a few firm strokes.

'Laos first, I suggest,' said the director. 'An earthly paradise. Can't imagine it if you haven't been there. I say, first, because you want to get there before the rains wash the place away. Probably be just in time. Otherwise you might find yourself stranded.'

'Mean travelling by plane,' I suggested.

'No,' the director said. 'Planes can't take off. More likely to find yourself cut off until they rebuilt the bridges at the end of the year. That is, unless you could get to the Mékong. That's why it's better to go now. No point in taking unnecessary chances.'

The director drew a short, firm line on the map with his pencil. 'First stage – Dalat. Centre of the elephant-hunting country. Go and see the Emperor. Might get him to take you on a trip. Better to go by convoy though. You're sure to find it more interesting than by air. Attacks getting infrequent these days. Anyway, nothing venture, nothing have.'

I agreed, enchanted with the breathtaking novelty of this attitude in an official. The director plunged on confidently through half-explored jungles towards the central plateaux. 'You aren't looking for a luxury tour I suppose? That is, you don't mind pigging it with soldiers occasionally?'

We hovered over Kontum. 'Malarial,' the director said. 'Rather nasty type too. Nothing to worry about though, if you keep moving. Normal hazards, that is ... The Viet-Minh? – Well naturally you'll inform yourself on the spot. No sense in putting your head into the lion's mouth.'

We now turned our faces to the west. The director thought that it wasn't advisable to go further north, as some of the tribes hadn't made an official submission, and, in any case, the country wasn't accurately mapped. Of course, one might jolly one of the local administrators into getting up a little expedition on the side. He hesitated, evidently toying wistfully with the prospect, before putting it, reluctantly, from his mind and turning a Balboan eye to survey the few hundred miles of jungle and swamps separating us from the border of Siam.

'We want to get to the Mékong River somehow or other. Probably find a soldier or professional hunter going somewhere, in a jeep. What we call a *moyen de fortune* ... Paksí, now, that's an idea.' With a wave of the hand the director vanquished the many bands of vulgar pirates, as the French call them, which infest that area. 'Or if not Paksí, Savannakhet?' Soaring above the degrees of latitude separating these alternatives, the director whisked us back to our crossroads in central Annam and set us off in another direction, clearing with an intrepid finger a track subsequently described as *digéri* by the jungle. 'Once you get to Mékong——' The director shrugged his shoulders. The adventure was practically at an end, for only a thousand miles or so in a pirogue had to be covered before reaching Saigon again. 'Unless you happen to hit on a *moyen de fortune* going north to Vientiane. Then, of course, if you felt like it, and the opportunity came along, you could get across country to Xien Khouang in the Meo country ... perhaps from there up towards the frontier of Burma or of Yunnan.'

It was evident that the director was loth to return from these exciting prospects to the drab dependabilities of Saigon, where the *moyen de fortune* had no place.

Moyen de fortune. The phrase was beginning to touch the imagination. It was one that rang continually in my ears from that time on. It became the keynote of my journeyings.

It was the duty of a subordinate, a Monsieur Ferry, to clothe the director's flights of creative fancy with the sober trappings of organization. Ferry's first glance at the suggested itinerary produced a pursing of the lips. As for the *terra incognita* to the north and west, he couldn't say. No doubt the director knew what he was talking about. It was his job to see that I got to Dalat, where a Madame Schneider would take charge of me and pass me on to a Monsieur Doustin at Ban Méthuot. After that – well – it would all depend upon the direction I chose, and, of course, local conditions.

Monsieur Doustin, a very knowledgeable man, would see to all that. Ferry presented me with the three maps of the country, physical, ethnographical, and geological, that are given to all official visitors and journalists. These were followed by a collection of publications; special numbers of French magazines devoted to Indo-China and government papers on the contemporary economic and political situation. It was a highly intelligent and efficient method of presenting the French point of view, and I was mildly surprised to find that such a breadth of interests was taken for granted in the visitor.

Above all it was reassuring to gather that any aspects of this journey that might have savoured of the conducted tour looked like disappearing as soon as one was a reasonable distance from Saigon, to be replaced by the fickle and planless dispositions of fortune.

Ferry went with me to the office of the bus company that ran the service to Dalat. He was disappointed to find from the seating plan that all the best places had been sold. The choice seats were those that flanked the interior aisle, because, if the convoy happened to be attacked, you were protected in this position, to some slight measure, by the bodies of those who sat between you and the windows. I had a corner seat at the front of the bus, which afforded an excellent field of vision, accompanied, of course, with the maximum vulnerability on two sides.

Since I would have a few spare days in Saigon, Ferry had an attractive suggestion to put forward. On the following day, Monsieur Pignon, the High Commissioner and foremost French personality in Indo-China, was to pay an official visit to the Pope of the Cao-Daïst religion, at his seat at Tay-Ninh, some fifty miles away. For this occasion, a strong military escort would be provided, and as it was a great opportunity to escape the boredom of life, hemmed-in in Saigon, anyone who could possibly do so would get themselves invited. For a journalist, it was only a matter of applying.

From Ferry's description, Cao-Daïsm sounded extraordinary enough to merit investigation. There was a cathedral, he said, that looked like a fantasy from the brain of Disney, and all the faiths of the Orient had been ransacked to create the pompous ritual, which had been grafted on an organization copied from the Roman Catholic Church. What was more to the point at the present time was that the Cao-Daïsts had a formidable private army with which they controlled a portion of Cochin-China. The French tolerated them because they were anti-Viet-Minh, and therefore helped, in their way, to split up the nationalist front. There

were also militant Buddhist and Catholic minorities among the
Vietnamese, all of whom scrapped with each other as well as the
Viet-Minh, but these lacked the florid exuberance – and the power –
of the Cao-Daïsts. Ferry thought that it might help in extracting the
maximum benefit from the experience if I spent a few hours reading
the subject up. He, therefore, presented me, on behalf of his office,
with a work entitled *Histoire et Philosophie du Cao-Daïsme* (*Bouddh-
isme rénové, spiritisme Vietnamien, religion nouvelle en Eurasie*), by a
certain Gabriel Gobron, whose description as European representative of the faith sounded, to my mind, a faintly commercial note.
Gobron was also described as having 'quitted his fleshly envelope of
suffering in 1941'.

I returned to the hotel at about seven thirty, switched on the
enormous ceiling fan, and went to open the window. The square
below was brightly lit and the sky was still luminous with the
aftermath of sunset. As I pushed open the window, there was a
momentary, slight resistance, and a violent explosion thumped in my
eardrums. Across the square an indolent wreath of smoke lifted
from the café tables and dissolved. Two figures got up from a table,
arms about one another's shoulders, and reeled away like drunkards
who have decided to call it a night. Other patrons seemed to have
dropped off to sleep with their heads on the tables, except for one,
who stood up and went through a slow repertoire of calisthenics. A
passer-by fell to his knees. Now, after several seconds, the evening
strollers changed direction and from all quarters they began to move,
without excitement, towards the café. I went down to see if there
was anything to be done, but already the wounded were being
tended in their cramped attitudes and the discipline of routine was
taking charge. Waiters snatched the seemingly wine-stained cloths
off the tables. A boy with a stiff broom and pail came out and began
scrubbing at the spotted pavement. An officer, one hand bound up
in a napkin, sat clicking imperiously for service with the fingers of
the other. Within ten minutes every table was full again. This hand-
grenade, one of eight reported to have been thrown that evening,

caused fifteen casualties – a Saigon record to date. The mortar-fire in the suburbs did not start until after ten o'clock.

Before going to sleep, I set myself to the task of extracting the doctrinal kernel in Gobron's book from its formidable husk of metaphysical jargon. I learned that Cao-Daïsm was officially founded in 1926, originating among one of the many groups of Cochin-Chinese spiritualists. The favoured congregation were informed, through the agency of an instrument known in English as the planchette, or in French as *la Corbeille-à-bec* – a platform-like device carrying a pencil upon which the hand is rested – that they were in touch with Li Taï-pé, sometimes known as the Chinese Homer, who, in the Tang Dynasty, after 'the burning of the books', re-established Chinese literature.

Li Taï-pé began by announcing that he was the bearer of a most important message to mankind from the Lord of the Universe. He explained that he, Li Taï-pé, in his capacity of Minister to the Supreme Spirit, had at various epochs and in different parts of the globe founded Confucianism, the Cult of the Ancestors, Christianity, Taoism, and Buddhism. (In later messages Islam was added to this list.) The establishment of these religions, the sage said – each of which took into consideration the customs and psychology of the races for which they were separately designed – took place at a time when the peoples of the world had little contact with each other owing to the deficient means of transport. In these days things were very different. The whole world had been explored and communi-cations had reached a stage when any part of the globe was only a few days removed from any other part. The time had clearly come, through his intervention, to bring about an intelligent re-organiz-ation, a syncretism of all these only superficially diverse creeds in a harmonious and cosmopolitan whole. The divinely inspired amalgam was to be called after the name Cao-Daï, by which the Founder of the Universe had stated that he now wished to be known.

At this early period the objects of the religion, as summarized by Li Taï-pé, were 'to combat heresy, to sow among the peoples the love of good and the practice of virtue, to learn to love justice and resignation, to reveal to men the posthumous consequences of the acts by which they assassinate their souls'. It seems later to have been realized that the combating of heresy was an anomaly in a religion aiming at a fusion of existing doctrines, and it was abandoned.

A calendar of saints, while in the process of formation, is still meagre. It includes Victor Hugo, Allan Kerdec, Joan of Arc, de la Rochefoucauld, St Bernard, St John the Baptist, and the Jade Emperor. These frequently communicate by spirtualistic means with the Cao-Daïst leaders, giving their rulings on such important matters of ritual as the offering of votive papers on ancestral altars. It would seem that in oriental spiritualism a curious prestige attaches to 'guides' of Western origin, paralleled, of course, by the Indian chiefs, the Buddhist monks, and the Chinese sages, that play so prominent a part in equivalent practices in Europe.

From the philosophical point of view, Cao-Daïsm seems to be encountering some difficulty in its efforts to reconcile such contradictory tenets as original sin and redemption with the doctrine of the soul's evolution through re-incarnation. The prescribed rites are strongly oriental in character: regular prostrations before an altar, which must include ritual candlesticks, an incense burner, offerings of fruit, and a painting showing an eye (the sign of the Cao-Daï) surrounded by clouds. Occidental converts are excused by the Pope from ritual prostrations, which 'for the moment may be replaced by profound reverences'.

In Cochin-China it is a respected convention that all organized movements of persons shall start well before dawn. The intelligent intention behind this practice, which has been remarked upon by all travellers in the past, is to permit as much of the journey as possible to be covered in the coolest hours. What happens in practice, at least in these days, is that various members of the party cannot find transport to take them to the agreed place of assembly and have to be fetched; while others are not awakened by the hotel-boy, who may not have understood the arrangement, or may, on the other hand, be employing this means of passive resistance towards the hated European. In one way or another, the precious minutes of

coolness are frittered away and it is dawn before one finally leaves
Saigon. In this case further delays were introduced by the many
security measures, the halts at road-blocks, the slow winding of the
convoy round obstacles, the waiting for telephone reports of conditions ahead from major defence-posts on the route. While we
dawdled thus the sun bulged over the horizon, silhouetting with
exaggerated picturesqueness a group of junks moored in some
unsuspected canal. For a short time the effect of the heat was
directional, as if an electric fire had been switched on in a cool room.
But the air soon warmed up and within half an hour one might have
been sitting in a London traffic block in a July day heat-wave.

The convoy was made up of about twenty civilian cars and was
escorted by three armoured vehicles and several lorries carrying
white-turbanned Algerians. The foreign visitors had been carefully
separated. I rode in a Citroën and was in the charge of an English-
speaking functionary, a Monsieur Beauvais, whose task it was, I
gathered, to provide a running commentary of the trip, throwing in,
occasionally, in accordance with the official line of the moment, a
few words in praise of Cao-Daïsm. In this he was somewhat
frustrated by a colleague sitting in the front seat, who, being unable
to speak English and assuming that I did not understand French,
contributed an explosion of disgust, salted with such expressions as
merde and *dégueulasse*, whenever he overheard a mention of the
words Cao-Daï. However, even from the French point of view it did
not really matter, as the official attitude was just then in the process
of switching round once more. Beauvais, too, soon stopped worrying
about his official job. What he was really interested in was English
literature and in particular English civilization as presented by John
Galsworthy, which contrasted so nostalgically with the barbarous life
of a government employee in Cochin-China.

As soon as the convoy was really under way it began to travel at
high speed. Except where we were forced to slow down for road-
blocks the Citroën was doing a steady 60 m.p.h. The deserted paddy-
fields through which our road ran were the colour of putty and the
sunshine reflected blearily from the muddy water. As we passed,
congregations of egrets launched themselves into the air, rising

straight up in a kind of leap, assisted with a few indolent wing-beats, and then settling down uneasily in the same place again. There were distant villages, raised on hillocks above the water, and solitary villas – Mediterranean-looking, with their verandas and flaking stucco, except for the china lions in the garden, grinning at us absurdly, and the roof with its facetious dragon or sky-blue ceramic dolphins. Sometimes such houses had been burned out. There were no signs of human life. The populace had evidently received orders, as for the passage of the Son of Heaven, or of one of the Divine Emperors, to keep indoors. Sometimes, at what I suppose were considered danger points, lines of Vietnamese auxiliaries stood with their backs to the road, rifles at the ready. At short intervals we passed beneath the watch-towers; squat structures, made of small Roman-looking bricks, shaded with Provençal roofs, and surrounded with concentric pallisades of sharpened bamboo staves. In theory, the whole length of the road can be swept by machine-gun fire from the towers, whose defenders are also supposed to patrol the surrounding area. These pigmy forts lent a rather pleasant accent, a faintly Tuscan flavour, to the flat monotony of the landcape.

After about thirty-five miles we entered Cao-Daï territory, in which, according to my official guide, complete tranquillity had been restored. His friend said something about bandits and rats, and spat out of the window. I asked why the towers were even closer together and why machine-gunners squatted behind their weapons which were pointed up every side-road. Monsieur Beauvais said there was no harm in making sure, sighed, and brought the subject back again to the amenities of upper-class rural England.

Our first Cao-Daïst town was Trang-Bang, where a reception had been arranged. There seemed to be thousands of children. For miles around, the countryside must have been combed for them. They had been washed, dressed in their best, and lined up beside the road, clutching in one hand their bunches of flowers of the six symbolical colours and giving the Fascist salute with the other. The spontaneous acclamations were tremendous and the children, who all looked like jolly china dolls, were, I am sure, enjoying themselves enormously, without having the faintest idea what it was all about. Monsieur

Beauvais seemed much embarrassed by the Fascist salute, from which his friend, however, derived grim pleasure.

The notables of Trang-Bang, dressed in their best formal silks, were on the spot to mix with the visitors. In this country, which owes all its civilization to China, the best years of one's life are its concluding decades. The dejection that encroaching age stamps so often in the Western face – the melancholy sense of having outlived one's usefulness – are replaced here with a complacency of spirit and a prestige that increases automatically with the years. Cao-Daïsm was founded by retired functionaries and professional men, who see to it that no one who is not a grandfather ever manages to get his foot on the bottom rung of the ladder. Going up to one of these happy old men, I complimented him on the appearance of the children, who were still cheering and saluting. The old man's face crinkled in a smile of ineffable wisdom. He explained that it was the result of a vegetarian diet. Vegetarianism, he explained, was one of the tenets of the Cao-Daïst faith.

'Of course, we don't insist on our converts making a sudden break with their bad habits. We start them off with a meatless day a week and gradually improve them until a full release is attained.'

'And have all your people attained a full release?'

'Almost miraculously, yes,' said the old man delightedly. 'They turned their backs on the squalid past, almost overnight. Why, even five-year-old children implored their parents never to let them see meat or fish again. It was a wonderful experience.'

We chatted pleasantly for some time. My friend informed me that he was a fourth grade official of the Cao-Daïst Legislative Corps, a lawyer with the rank of Bishop, and that he expected shortly to be promoted to Inspector-General of the third grade, carrying the dignity of Principal Archbishop. After that the way remained clear to the final attainable splendour, the culmination of all the efforts of his mature years, the rank of Cardinal-Legislator – only five grades removed from the Pope himself. There would be many more austerities to be practised before that glittering goal could be reached, but what did it matter? At his age one could do without almost anything. That was the best of it, the old man pointed out, smiling gleefully. All those abstentions – the renunciation of relations with one's wife, for instance – they came into force only in the higher grades. The turn of the screw was put on gently, so that by the time you had to give things up for the Kingdom of God, you were pretty well ready to give them up anyway. It was all so humane.

It might have been, but what about the children with all this voluntary abnegation, practised almost as soon as they were out of the cradle? The answer was given by a Cao-Daïst doctor of the ninth grade and a member of the Charity Corps, in which he had reached the rather low rank of *fidèle-ardent*.

'We suffer from malnutrition in all its forms,' he said. 'Just look at the children. Look at the condition of their skins. Covered from head to foot with sores, most of them.'

I told him that those I saw looked the picture of health.

'Well, naturally,' the doctor said. 'You don't expect them to put the pellagra cases in the front line, do you?'

Beauvais was embarrassed once more, before we left. There was a burst of heavy mortar-fire. Beauvais thought it was miles away and that the wind was carrying the sound in our direction. But there was no wind in Cochin-China – at least while I was there.

At Tay-Ninh we were first received by the administrator, dressed in a gorgeous old mandarin's coat of dull blue silk, on which the yellow flowers and medallions were seen rather faintly, like the watermarks on superior stationery. The administrator had a small, aged face which, in the local manner, he kept under conspicuous control. Whenever he smiled, which in the course of his duties he did frequently, he laid bare a row of ivory hearts in the background of his gold-framed teeth. Having welcomed, with unquenchable vitality, each member of the visiting party – a task occupying at least half an hour – he darted away, and reappeared with an amateur ciné-camera with which he exposed a few feet of film on each of the principal French dignitaries. Champagne and biscuits were now served, and as polite interest in one's surroundings seemed to be encouraged, I wandered through the ground-floor rooms of the administrator's typically European villa.

The administrator had thought fit to advertise the modernity of his outlook by furnishing his house in Western style. The tables, with their Liberty runners, the chairs, the Indian rugs, the thick, greasy glaze of the pottery, recalled a Tottenham Court Road showroom. But progressive Easterners of this type find it almost impossible to prevent a dash of the local flavour intruding itself into the flat and tasteless 'good taste' of their European décor. Even when the interloper is without other merit, I find it at least piquant. In this case the administrator had decorated one of his otherwise impeccable Heal walls with the pictures of the four vices. Here, where the reproduction Van Gogh sunflower should have been, were the stern warnings, to be seen on sale in all Saigon art shops, to the gambler, the drunkard, the opium smoker, and the voluptuary. The administrator had probably been taken in because the technical production of these masterpieces was typically Western and curiously photographic in its flat, bluish monochrome. But the subjects themselves, gentle, contemplative almost, and not in the least horrific, were as Vietnamese as pictures of Highland cattle are English. The only detail I can remember of these somnolent transgressions was the fine mosquito-net with which the bed in the last scene was equipped. Vietnam needs a Rowlandson or a Hogarth to deter its sinners. Gin Lane in oriental guise would sell a million copies.

The next item on the programme was a visit to the cathedral, where, according to the description of the ceremonies I read in the next day's paper, His Holiness, Pope Pham Cong-tac, whose name means 'the Sun shining from the South', awaited us, beneath the golden parasol, attired in his uniform of Grand-Marshal of the Celestial Empire. He was carrying his Marshal's baton, at the sight of which, according to Cao-Daïst literature, all evil spirits flee in terror.

Physically, the Pope looked hardly able to support the weight of his dignity. He was a tiny, insignificant figure of a man, with an air of irremediable melancholy. His presence was, in any case, overshadowed by the startling architectural details of the cathedral, for the design of which he himself had been responsible.

From a distance this structure could have been dismissed as the monstrous result of a marriage between a pagoda and a southern baroque church, but at close range the vulgarity of the building was so impressive that mild antipathy gave way to fascinated horror. This cathedral must be the most outrageously vulgar building ever to have been erected with serious intent. It was a palace in candy from a coloured fantasy by Disney; an example of fun-fair architecture in extreme form. Over the doorway was a grotesquely undignified piece of statuary showing Jesus Christ borne upon the shoulders of Lao-Tzu and in his turn carrying Confucius and Buddha. They were made to look like Japanese acrobats about to begin their act. Once inside, one expected continually to hear bellowing laughter relayed from some nearby Tunnel of Love. But the question was, what had been Pham Cong-tac's intention in producing a house for this petrified forest of pink dragons, this hugger-mugger of symbolism, this pawnbroker's collection of cult objects? Was he consciously catering to the debased and credulous tastes of his flock? Or could it be that visible manifestations of religious energy on the part of men who have lived lives entirely divorced from art must always assume these grotesque forms?

In support of the latter theory it is significant that the founders and directors of this movement were all men who had spent most of their lives in the harness of a profession or in the civil service. To have been successful as they had been in these walks of life would have left them little time to cultivate taste, if they happened to have been born without it. I was interested, subsequently, to note in the ensuing ritual that, although the Governor of South Vietnam kowtowed energetically before the altar, no attempt was made to induce Monsieur Pignon, the High Commissioner, to do so. Profiting by the experiences of even the Emperors of China and Annam with foreign ambassadors, the Cao-Daïsts have recognized the seemingly congenital disinclination of Europeans to performing the kowtow, so that Western converts are excused this form of devotional exercise. Monsieur Pignon did, however, consent to hold lighted joss-sticks between his clasped fingers and incline his head, even if somewhat distantly, before the massed symbols of Lao-Tzu, Confucius, Buddha, and Jesus Christ.

The siting of the Cao-Daïst Rome at Tay-Ninh was by no means accidental. A few miles from the town a single symmetrical mountain humps up suddenly from the plain, rising from what must be practically sea-level to three thousand feet. As there is not another hillock for fifty miles in any direction to break the flat and featureless monotony of Cochin-China, this darkly forested plum-pudding silhouette is quite remarkable. In a part of the world where every religion has its sacred mountain, such an eminence is obviously irresistible. Consequently it has been since dimmest antiquity a place of revelation. Its slopes are said to be riddled with caves, both natural and artificial, housing at one time or other the cult objects of numerous sects. It was most unfortunate from my point of view that the holy mountain itself was possessed not by the Cao-Daïsts but the Viet-Minh. This prevented a most interesting visit, although it was in any case improbable that revolutionary iconoclasm had spared the relics of those ancient beliefs.

But there were other survivals of Tay-Ninh's notable past to be seen in the streets of the town itself; pathetic-looking groups of Chams in the penitent's robes of the rank and file of the Cao-Daïst faithful. At the end of the Middle Ages the Annamese, moving southwards from China, had overwhelmed, absorbed, digested the brilliant civilization of Champa. Now only a few particles of that shattered community remained. They were scattered about in a few isolated villages in Cochin-China and Cambodia, and here they had clung to their holy place.

These Chams were aboriginal Malayo-Polynesians, the only group of that race to have accepted the civilization of Indian colonizers in the remote past. They made a great impression upon Marco Polo, but judging from the account of the Dominican Gabriel de San Antonio, who visited them in the sixteenth century, there was a nightmarish element in their civilization. It was brilliant but unbalanced and psychopathic, like that of the Aztecs. The Chams could place themselves in the vanguard of the technical achievement of their day, devise new agricultural methods, undertake vast irrigational projects, encourage the arts and sciences. And yet one half of the racial mind never developed. Stone Age beliefs, like grim Easter Island faces, were always there in the background. On certain days, San Antonio says, they sacrificed over six thousand people, and their gall was collected and sent to the King, who bathed in it to gain immortality.

These degenerate survivors of that glittering, sinister past were Brahmanists or Muslims, or both combined. The metaphysical appetite of South-East Asia is insatiable and its tolerance absolute. The modern Chams find no difficulty in worshipping the Hindu Trinity, the *linga*, the bull of Siva, a pythoness, Allah – who is believed to have been an eleventh-century Cham king – plus Mohammed and a number of uncomprehended words taken from Muslim sacred invocations and regarded as the names of deities, each with its special function. They are inclined to give their children such names as Dog, Cat, Rat to distract from them the attentions of evil spirits. For this reason there were several Cham kings named Excrement. One assumes that the Chams will have little difficulty in adding to their already enormous catalogue of rituals and credences those few new ones imposed by the Cao-Daïsts.

From the newspaper account I learned that on leaving the cathedral, 'preceded by a unicorn, a dragon, and a band playing *une marche précipiteuse*, escorted by a numerous suite carrying the car of the Buddha, the portraits of Sun Yat-sen and Victor Hugo, and the statue of Joan of Arc', we marched to the Vatican. The streets, said the account, were lined with adepts dressed in togas of red, blue, yellow, and white. In the general commotion I must have missed some of this. I should have much enjoyed the processional unicorn, which I failed to see either then or at any other time. I recall, however, the dragon; a fine capering beast which on its hind legs leaped up into the air and tossed its head most desperately to the

jerky rhythm of fife and drum. The report failed to mention a guard
of honour of the Cao-Daïst army, equipped with well-made wooden
imitation rifles. When I mentioned the matter of the toy guns, I was
told that it was out of respect for the sanctity of the surroundings.

The Vatican was the administrator's villa all over again, except
that His Holiness had an evident liking for grandmother clocks.
Fanned by turkey's feathers, hosts and guests exchanged lengthy
platitudes of goodwill, which at random were broken off for a stroll
in the garden, or a visit to the champagne bar, and then renewed
without the slightest embarrassment, as if no interruption had taken
place.

At the banquet which followed, I sat next to a Cao-Daïst colonel,
who informed me, with a secret, knowing smile, that he was head of
the secret police of this Universal Religion of the Age of Improved
Transport. The meal was vegetarian and although the French visitors
had been told that they could order eggs if they wished, no one
dared to do so. There were seven courses, six of which were based
on soya, which I first mistook for some kind of overstewed and
tasteless meat, that had, somehow or other, been served by mistake.
The Colonel and I got on very well together and helped each other
liberally to soya. Although intoxicants are equally forbidden to the
Cao-Daïst faithful, I noticed many of the dignitaries present stretching the point, and the Colonel, himself, had several helpings of red
wine, after which he genially discussed the technique of his
profession.

On my left was a young man who asked me if I was familiar with
the works of Victor Hugo. I nodded, without emphasis, barely
remembering the first lines of a poem beginning: '*Mon père, ce héros
au sourire si doux*—'

'I am a re-incarnation of a member of the poet's family,' the
young man said. I congratulated him and asked if he also wrote.
The modest reply was that he would have considered it an
impertinence to do so after the tremendous reputation of his
kinsman, who, after all, was generally admitted to be the greatest
poet who ever lived. Did I, by the way, realize that the master's

sublimest works had been written after his death, or, as he put it, since dis-incarnation? My informant then went on to explain that he was the official editor of Victor Hugo's posthumous work, a task simplified by the fact that only certain of the highest ranking members of the hierarchy were permitted mediumistic contact with such saints as Li Taï-pé, Joan of Arc, and the poet. All Victor Hugo's communications were given in verse and this, plus his life's work, would ultimately form a corpus to be memorized by candidates for high office. Much intrigued by this adaptation of the old Chinese system of literary examinations for the mandarinate, I asked for a sample of the poet's most recent production and was given the account of the Creation as described in a seance to the Ho-Phap, or Pope. I reproduce a few lines.

HO-PHAP (*referring to Victor Hugo's use of the word 'water' in his description of the creation*):
Est-ce bien la forme de l'eau parlée dans la genèse chrétienne?
VICTOR HUGO:
Oui, c'est cette sorte de gaz qu'on appelle hydrogène,
Plus ou moins dense qui fait la partie la plus saine,
Dire que l'Esprit de Dieu nage au-dessus des eaux,
C'est à ce sens qu'il faut comprendre le mot,
Avec son astral qui est de lumière,
Il anime par sa chaleur ces inertes matières,
Une couche d'oxygène produit, se met en action,
Le contact des deux gaz donne une détonation.
– Mais vous avez, Ho-Phap, une crampe à la main,
Renvoyons notre causèrie pour demain.

At the very hour when these junketings were in progress at Tay-Ninh, French troops were under fire from Cao-Daïsts in the Province of Mytho, about seventy miles to the south. The French said that the Cao-Daïsts had turned to banditry and that a battle had developed when they had called upon them to give up their arms. The Pope,

Pham Cong-tac, promptly repudiated all responsibility, pointing out that the insurgents had left his fold and joined one of the eleven schismatic sects that refused to recognize his authority. The schismatic sect can be as politically useful to the Cao-Daïsts as a racial minority elsewhere.

CHAPTER THREE

Sunday Diversions

BACK IN SAIGON I had a day to spare before the real journey began. It was Sunday, and in the morning I walked slowly to the Jardins Botaniques. Clusters of Vietnamese beauties on bicycles were bound in the same direction, floating, it seemed, rather than pedalling, as the trains of their silk gowns trailed in the air behind them. The robes worn by Vietnamese ladies recall those of ancient China, before the sumptuary laws imposed by the Manchus. White silk is the material preferred, and as Vietnamese girls are always utterly immaculate and addicted to swan-like movements, the whole effect is one of unearthly elegance. The park was full of these ethereal creatures, gliding in decorous groups through the shady paths, sometimes accompanied by gallants, who, in their cotton shirts, shorts, and trilby hats, provided a sadly anti-climactic spectacle. The girls thus arrayed belonged to the classes which included shop assistants and all ranks above. Domestic servants, or *boyesses*, as they are pleasantly known by the French, were dressed just as charmingly, but more simply, in pyjamas only. It is curious that members of the lower social strata are permitted to protect themselves from sunstroke by conical straw hats, whereas the bourgeoisie, although employing every hair-style, from an uncontrollable torrent of tresses reaching to the waist to a permanent wave, do not allow themselves a head-covering. In passing it should be observed that the kind of coolie-straw that a girl wears for her best is a beautifully made piece of headgear, of lacquered, semi-diaphanous material, lightly stitched over a framework of circular ribs. It is held in position for Sunday strolling with a strap of silk with a bow at each end and a third bow under the chin. The result is extremely coquettish and I felt sure that the shop girl or typist must regret being prevented, by her social position, from wearing such a becoming adornment.

Photography is a popular excuse for these decorous *fêtes-champêtres* of Saigon. There were several accepted backgrounds for portraiture which were in constant use. The archaeological museum is housed in a pagoda-like building and a group of legendary maidens loitered constantly in the vicinity, awaiting their turns to be photographed, caressing the snout of one of the decorative dragons. Another favoured site was the lake verge. The water had dried away leaving a few inches of liquid coated with a patina of scum, through which unsupported lotus flowers thrust a yard into the air. There was a punt, a standard photographic property, which could be set adrift only with great difficulty, in which the lady to be photographed balanced herself, looking mysterious and rather forlorn, while the photographer camouflaged the painter with lotus leaves before taking his shot. The moment the exposure had been made, the punt was hauled in, another lady floated into photogenic position, while her predecessor drifted away at the side of her escort.

The natural history of the Jardins Botaniques is charming rather than exciting. One does not look for sinister manifestations of nature-in-the-tropics in a public park, but I was surprised at the absence of all troublesome insects, such as wasps or flies. A few undistinguished butterflies fluttered about, looking like those to be seen on any English heath. There were few flowers, but sprays of purple blossoms, with thick velvet-looking petals, sprouted from the trunk and thicker branches of one of the trees. Since it was a local tree, there was no way of discovering its name. The only trees labelled were exotic specimens from Dakar and Madagascar, so presumably one would have to go to these places to study the vegetation of Indo-China. Cranes were building their nests in the topmost branches and a beautiful and very Chinese sight they made, with the sun shining through the lavender-grey plumage of their wings against the pale green foliage. Somewhere, too, just above my head, wherever I went, but always invisible, a bird produced tirelessly a single mournful note. It was as if a cuckoo had flown into a great hollow jar and there repeated incessantly the first note of its call. This was a sound which later I was to realize is hardly ever absent from the background of Indo-China.

The deportment of the Vietnamese in such places is beyond reproach. There is a gently repressive, Sunday-school atmosphere. Docilely, the visitors admired the caged deer; threw dice for ice-cream – folding the paper containers and stowing them in their pockets; viewed in silent satisfaction their choice of the eight original films of Charlot, shown by a 9.5 mm., hand-cranked cinema contraption, rigged up on a bicycle; patronized the fortune-tellers, who counted their pulses and examined their eyeballs with magnifying glasses before disclosing the edicts of the fates; bought tributes of artificial flowers from a kiosk bearing on its pale blue awning, for decorative purposes only, the words, 'EMPLOYEZ LE PÂTÉ ET SAVON DENTIFRICE DE ...' the manufacturer's name having been removed.

It was all very delightful and civilized.

Down by the river, where I went in the afternoon, the feeling was very different. Half the Vietnamese population of Saigon lives on the water and whenever I happened to be in Saigon, and had an hour or two to spare, I used to go there to enjoy the spectacle of the vivid, turbulent life of the common people. In my many walks along the river bank, I never, except within fifty yards of the *Cercle Nautique*, saw another European.

The original reason for taking to the water must have been that it was just as cheap to build a small sampan as a hut, the risk of fire was lessened, and there was no question of ground rent. Moreover, if one liked an occasional change of scene, nothing was easier than to move. The temperature on the river is quite a number of degrees cooler than in the town and one can take a dip whenever one feels like it. The laundry problem is facilitated for the womenfolk, and by keeping a few lines in the water one can occasionally catch a fish. All in all, there seems to be no real excuse for living anywhere else. Owing to the immense population now living in sampans on the Chinese Creek and its tributaries, numerous floating services have come into being to cater for them. There are sampan-restaurants, with cauldrons of noodle soup; water sellers who carry drinking water in the white-enamelled bottoms of their boats; shops of all kinds; and, of course, river-borne magicians.

To reach the quay-side meant a walk of not more than five minutes up the main street, the Rue Catenat. It was five o'clock, and by this hour possible to risk the sun and walk out in the open, along the water's edge, where the dockers were loading and unloading cargoes. A quarter of a mile away, across the river, was no man's land. One could go there during the daytime, but at night the Viet-Minh sometimes appeared and fired mortar-shells into the centre of the town. Previously, the further bank had been clustered with huts, but the French had cleared them away, thus aggravating the refugee problem. At about this time the dockers had their evening meal and the owners of the eating booths had accordingly set a long line of tables. On each table stood three bottles, one of Tiger beer flanked on each side by brilliantly coloured mineral waters. Awaiting the customers, in bowls of attractive designs, were semi-hatched eggs with small apertures cut in their sides to allow of choice in the degree of incubation.

I walked on to the waterfront café at the Point des Blageurs and sat down to enjoy the scene in comfort. The animation with which I was surrounded was, in its way, different from and more intense than anything I had experienced before. One has been accustomed to crowds, to the spectacle of vast gatherings of people in the streets, in places of entertainment, in railway stations or restaurants. But such crowds have all been, more or less, engaged in a similar kind of activity. Here it was the diversity of occupation that was so remarkable. There must have been many hundreds of people in sight, all busily living their own lives and most of them independently of the actions of others in their immediate neighbourhood.

There were several junks moored just off-shore. They had gardens on their decks, with domestic pets, a few cocks and hens, a canary in the cage, and flowers growing in packing cases. Somebody was constantly pottering round these deck-gardens, watering the flowers or looking to see if the hen had laid an egg. Through openings in the junks' sides one could observe incidents from the domestic routine. Occasionally a naked child came flying through in an attempt to land on top of another child, splashing about in the water beneath. There were people sprawled about under the canopies of fifty sampans, playing cards, dicing, chatting, sleeping. People came ashore and exercised pigs on leads along the waterfront. A score of anglers drooped motionless over their lines, the most singular of these being one who tried his luck through a manhole cover in the street. Professional fishermen worked from sampans, lowering into the water large triangular nets at the end of levers. One would have expected this process occasionally to produce a spectacular fish; but not so. I never saw anything longer than three inches come out of the water. The prawn fishers seemed to have better luck. They worked up to their knees in black slime, groping about with their wicker baskets in the mud. It was filthy work, but they at least caught prawns. Women, if they were not cooking, were washing themselves, leaving no part of their persons unvisited, but completing the process in such as way that not an unwonted inch of their form was displayed. For no particular reason that one could see, people fidgeted continually with junks and sampans, shifting them here and there, and then replacing them in exactly the same position as before. In doing so they narrowly avoided collisions with lightermen who were ferrying passengers to and from the ships in the port. Hawkers passed incessantly, drawing attention to their wares with melodious cries or the beating of appropriate gongs. They were ignored by innumerable loafers who hung about, giving advice on a dozen gambling games that were in progress. In the background musical-comedy river-boats thrashed slowly past. They had triple decks and tall narrow funnels, their balustrades were as ornate as the balconies of New Orleans, and they were smothered in red Chinese characters.

CHAPTER FOUR

A Convoy to Dalat

THE DALAT CONVOY left at 5 a.m. Suspecting – as indeed proved to be the case – that the hotel boy would not call me, I lay awake most of the night, perspiring gently, listening to the occasional explosion of distant mortar-bombs and to the rumble of army trucks patrolling the streets. I was travelling in a shirt and shorts, and my bag was packed with the bare essentials for a journey of unknown length: a pair of long trousers and a jacket for formal occasions (if any), a mosquito net, anti-malarial tablets, insect-repellent cream, and a camera. A French acquaintance had suggested, in all seriousness, that I should carry a pistol; not so much for self-defence as to be able to Save The Last Bullet for Myself, should I fall into the hands of the Viet-Minh. This suggestion I had rejected. I was carrying a travelling permit obtained for me by the Office of Information, importantly styled 'Ordre de Mission', in which I was described as 'Lewis Norman, Écrivain Anglais, habilité par MM. Jonathan Cape, Thirty Bedford Square'. This paper had to be frequently renewed, the description suffering in consequence both compression and distortion. In the end I became 'Louis Norman Thirsty Bedford', and it was under this agreeable title that I finished my journeyings.

At four thirty, feeling not particularly refreshed, I got up, dressed quickly, and went down into the square to find a *cyclo*. As usual, there were three or four, drowsing over their handle-bars, outside the hotel. I sat down in the chair, arranging my bag awkwardly under my legs, and we pushed off. As *cyclos* are not supposed to understand French one does not give them verbal directions. They just pedal straight ahead and one flaps with either hand when the time comes to turn.

We found the civilian part of the convoy in the process of assembly behind the red-brick cathedral. The spectral figures of my fellow-passengers lurked by the bus, leaving it until the last possible moment before getting in. I was the only European present and no one took the slightest notice of me. In these times the whites preferred to travel by air.

The bus was equipped internally to carry about twice the number of passengers one would have supposed from its external dimensions. This had been achieved, quite simply, by fitting seats that would have accommodated a ten-year-old child in comfort and by arranging it so that one's legs were clenched firmly by the seat in front. I thanked heaven, in the circumstances, that I was travelling with the silent and introverted Vietnamese and not, for instance, a busful of excited Arabs. The travellers were dressed in their workaday clothes of black calico, except for the driver, who wore black satin pyjamas embroidered with the Chinese characters for good luck, and a most expensive looking golden-brown velour hat. He was about five feet in height and weighed, perhaps, eight stone; physically somewhat ill-endowed, it seemed, to control this overloaded juggernaut. Very sensibly, I thought, watching him hauling on his mighty wheel, a notice pinned to his back asked passengers, in two languages, not to distract his attention by talking to him.

Sitting next to me was a well-preserved lady in middle age. Her hair was arranged in a complicated chignon, set off with jewelled pins in the form of small daisy-like flowers. Having neglected her fine set of teeth, the white bone was showing slightly through their coating of black enamel. She was heavily perfumed with jasmine and as most of the female passengers showed a predilection for such pungent attars, the atmosphere of the bus was soon heavy with a funereal sweetness. My travelling companion carried a small box, like a powder compact, from which, shortly after we moved off, she selected betel nut and began to chew. At quite long intervals she leaned over me and shot a thin stream of juice through the window. When later we stopped I noticed that the wind-carried splash of orange betel against the blue side of the bus was, in its way, not undecorative.

Before and behind us the convoy stretched as far as the eye could see. It seemed to be composed entirely of the lorries of Chinese merchants. They looked like motorized covered wagons with their tops of plaited bamboo. Their sides were painted with the usual Chinese characters for good fortune, peace, longevity, and riches. It was a bad thing in an attack, they said, to be sandwiched between Chinese lorries, which were said to panic in the most unphilosophical manner at the first shot fired. At each end of the convoy there were armoured cars, and on the rare occasions when the road was wide enough they came fussing along the line of the convoy, like hens marshalling nervous chicks. The trouble was that the road rarely permitted the passage of two vehicles abreast and, naturally enough, it was in the narrow sectors, where the convoy might be spread out over five miles of road, with the armoured cars wedged in immutable position, that the ambushes took place.

For the first thirty or forty miles out of Saigon we were still in the flat, rice-growing country. We passed many solitary villas by the roadside – the 'big-houses' of Cochin-China, with dragons of smoky-blue china undulating like sea-serpents across their roofs and a menagerie of ceramic lions and elephants in their gardens. Vietnamese animal figures are never intimidating in their aspect. Their expressions are always genial, even flippant, and one suspects that the intention is humorous as well as ornamental. The rooftops seemed to be the favourite place to assemble china figures of all kinds; perhaps because they would be silhouetted in this way to the best possible effect. The best examples included jovial, bearded philosophers in the act of beating tambourines, with one leg skittishly raised, or else ogling ladies who enticed them coquettishly. Souvenirs of family visits to the seaside perhaps. Who knows? At all events most of the houses were deserted, or had been requisitioned by the military; but where the family remained there was invariably a platform on a pole placed somewhere near the front door with offerings to the spirits: a bowl with rice, a pot of tea, joss-sticks, even a packet of cigarettes.

This was the Borri country, where the first Jesuit missionaries had set out upon their labours, enchanted with the civility of their reception, although perturbed by the prevalence of devils. 'They walk about the Cities so familiarly in human Shapes, that they are not at all fear'd but admitted into Company.'

The villages were stockaded, with strong points at the angles of the fortifications. Inside there were towers and *miradors* as they are called locally; structures like oil derricks supporting a machine-gun post. Sometimes truncated towers had been built into the roofs of the larger houses. It was said that one could enter these villages with safety only in daytime, and some of them, not even then, unless in convoy. The surface of the road here had been ruined by the habit of Viet-Minh sympathizers of digging trenches across it. For miles on end convoy speed had to be reduced to a walking pace as we bumped across the endless corrugations produced by this rustic sabotage. The landscape on the village outskirts was peaceful enough, with the ancestral tombs scattered about and taking up, incidentally, a great deal of cultivatable space. The more imposing tombs had been built on what slight eminence could be found and great attention had been paid, for the benefit of the ancestral shades, to the view they afforded. It was evident that a certain amount of landscape gardening had occasionally been attempted in the vicinity. The tombs themselves were of pleasantly weathered stone, sometimes charmingly tiled. Often it looked as though a group of villas had been engulfed by some terrestrial convulsion, leaving only the flat roofs with their ornamental balustrades above the ground.

Our first stop was Bien-Hoa, where all the passengers got out and bought food. I had not yet reached the stage when I was able to fall in with the scheme of things and buy myself a bowl of Chinese soup or a dried and salted fish, so I went hungry. I was soon to be cured of this reluctance of self-adaptation to a new environment, for I never remember any subsequent journey during the whole of my travels in the country when the hour of departure was late enough to permit me to get breakfast, or rather *petit déjeuner*. It would not, in any case, have been easy to eat in comfort at Bien Hoa as a whole tribe of beggars came out of the village and performed a mournful pilgrimage down the convoy displaying their ghastly sores. Among these were many cases of elephantiasis. The presence of these beggars seemed, by the way, to disprove the French allegation that the Vietnamese never give alms.

It was here too that I noticed that the telephone wires had been colonized by innumerable spiders, which had woven their strands about the wires in such a way as to incorporate them in an enormous, elongated web. At evenly spaced intervals a four-inch spider watched over the territory allotted to it in this vast co-operative enterprise, but as no flies were caught within my sight during the half-hour we waited at Bien-Hoa, I was unable to draw any Bruce-like inspiration in support of collective effort.

Soon after Bien-Hoa we plunged into the forest. For many miles it had been cleared for perhaps a hundred yards on each side of the road. Then suddenly the jungle returned, pressing about us so close that the slender, bowed-over bamboos stroked the bus's roof as we passed beneath them. When faced with the tropical forest the problem of the writer and painter is alike. The forest is fussy in detail, lacking in any unifying motive and tends to be flatly monochromatic. There is a baroque superabundance of forms, which, unfortunately, do not add up to a Churrigueresque altar-piece. In the depths of our jungle there may have been superb orchids and even certain flowers indigenous to this part of the world whose blooms are several feet across. But all we could see was a dusty confusion of leaves like one of those dense and often grimy thickets cultivated by people in England to safeguard their privacy.

There was a single moment of excitement, when a colossal boa constrictor slithered across the road ahead of us. It was a serpent of the kind one has always seen coiled motionless in the corner of its cage at the zoo. Now it was quite extraordinary to see one in such purposeful motion. Somehow the driver missed it, stopped, reversed, and was just too late to run over its tail, which was withdrawn with a mighty flexing of the muscles. Behind us the following Chinese lorry went charging into the fernery to avoid us. There were none of the bellowing recriminations one comes to expect at such times.

The Chinese lorry was driven out under its own power and on we went.

The midday stop was at a village rather romantically named, I thought, Kilometre 113. There was a ring of the frontier outpost about this that stirred the imagination. We were still in the forest, which had thinned out a little, and we were perhaps a thousand feet above sea-level. Strewn about all over the place were huge, smooth, mysterious looking boulders. Some of them had huts built on the top with ladders leading up to them, and others even small forts. It was here that I saw for the first time a sight imagined by many Westerners to be extremely typical of South-Eastern Asia – the uncovered female breast. There was a Moï village somewhere close by and several Moï girls were hanging about the garrison's sleeping quarters. They were thin and under-nourished looking, with, how-ever, the invulnerable torso of the Polynesian, wreathed in this case only by garlands of small violet-coloured flowers. Several groups of Moïs of both sexes padded past down the road while we were there. They looked dirty, degenerate, and miserable, the inevitable fate, as I later learned, of these tribes when they come into contact with civilization. Several of them, with grotesque effect, wore British battledress tops but had bare posteriors.

There was an eating place in the village that was serving pork and peas – take it or leave it – and where you could buy weak beer at the equivalent of five shillings a bottle. Here, too, the frontier atmosphere was very marked and obviously enjoyed by the soldiers who waved aside the eating utensils and preferred to manipulate their victuals with a clasp knife and a chunk of bread. However, the French are poor hands at licentious soldiering, being, perhaps, a little too close to the polished sources of our civilization for this. The restaurant with all its faults and at its toughest would probably have been like the salon of a Habsburg Pretender compared with any pub in Gibraltar with a Yankee warship in port.

Setting out again we found that we had acquired an escort – a Vietnamese soldier with a tommy-gun, who was followed into the bus so closely by a white butterfly that it might have been his familiar spirit. He sat down beside the driver and went to sleep with the butterfly flapping in his face. We were now entering the most dangerous phase of the journey, where a year before most of the vehicles had been burned in an attack and there had been several hundred casualties. A couple of spotting planes circled overhead ready, if necessary, to radio the alarm. After attacks, parachutists are usually dropped but it takes an hour or two for them to get to the scene and by that time it is all over. The Viet-Minh who usually attack in strength have their will with the convoy, and by the time the relieving force arrives they have disappeared.

The road mounted slowly and the vehicles lumbered painfully round the hillsides, so that seen from a bend, the convoy looked like the severed segments of a caterpillar. Gradually we freed ourselves from the dense vegetation, emerging finally into a savannah of coarse grass with occasional clumps of deciduous trees that looked like cork-oaks but were sparingly adorned with pale lemon flowers. The heat was terrific. Having been designed for service in some far northern clime, the bus's windows could only be forced down a few inches and as the sun's decline in the sky began, the bus was flooded with an incandescent glare, from which there was no escape. Slowly we ground our way on towards Dalat. Our passage out of the Valley of the Shadow was marked by our escort's waking up, uncocking his gun, and stopping the bus to get out. Now I noticed that the trees had rid themselves of their coverings of parasites, that the swathings of creepers were no more, and that lianas ceased to drip from the branches. The road widened and began to look like a corniche in embryo. Pines made their appearance. We were driving into Dalat.

Dalat is the playground of Indo-China and has a fair share of the dreariness so often associated with places thus advertised. Taking full advantage of an altitude of three thousand feet and the pine forests, a forlorn attempt has been made to encourage a sub-alpine atmosphere, but it remains nothing more than an uninspired imitation; a not very magnificent failure. Even imitations, if carried to sufficiently daring lengths, sometimes generate a fascination of their own. But the spuriousness of Dalat was cautious and hesitant. It looked like a drab little resort in Haute Savoie, developed by someone who had spent a few years as vice-consul in Shanghai. Of Dalat, though, one thing must be admitted; that life there, even in peacetime, is not entirely divorced from adventure, since there is a chance, one in a thousand perhaps, of knocking into a tiger if one strolls in the streets after dark.

We skirted a sad little lake, with edges cropped like a pond on Hampstead Heath, and wound up the main street past the Salon de Thé, the Crillon Grill, a *dancing*, the Chic Shanghai Bar, and into the square. We had covered two hundred and fifty miles in thirteen hours. Now a problem arose. I had been told in Saigon to contact a Madame Schneider, who held some important, but undefined, post and was responsible for foreigners. Madame Schneider would be able to find me a room in a town which might be overflowing with visitors and would make all necessary arrangements for the next stage of my journey, to Ban Méthuot. Her address? Well, as far as anybody knew, she didn't have one. If it came to that, no one in Dalat had addresses, certainly not important people like Madame Schneider. The first person one met in the street would be able to point out where she lived.

As a telegram had been sent from Saigon to warn Madame of my arrival, I half hoped to see either her or her representative awaiting me at the bus terminus. But no; one by one the passengers were claimed by their relations, the crowd thinned and melted away. It was after six, the streets were deserted, and the daylight was waning. The local taxi-cab service consisted of tiny traps drawn by the Indo-Chinese equivalent of the Shetland pony. Only one of these remained and I approached the small Vietnamese boy in charge of it.

NL: Est-ce que vous connaissez Madame Schneider?
SMALL BOY: Moi connaisse.
NL: Où est-ce qu'elle habite?
SMALL BOY: Là-bas. Moi connaisse. (*A vague sweep of the arm towards the darkening pine-clad slopes.*)

NL: Mais, elle habite en ville?

SMALL BOY (*impatiently*): Oui, oui. Moi connaisse. Madame Slé-lé.

It seemed pointless to continue the interrogation in the face of the child's rather surly assurance. I got in, the pony's head was turned towards the wilds, and we set off. We had reached the town's outskirts when the trap stopped outside a small grocer's shop. 'Madame Slé-lé,' said the boy.

It seemed unlikely that this Vietnamese lady could be the object of my search, and indeed, after I had pronounced the name very slowly and, as I thought, distinctly, half a dozen times, the light dawned. Of course, it was not she, Madame Slé-lé, I wanted at all. It was Madame Sné-dé. The important and celebrated Madame Sné-dé. '*Oui, bien-sûr. Moi connaisse! Moi connaisse!*'

Having received the most graphic description of the route to be taken, we set off again. It seemed that neither the street Madame Schneider lived in, nor her villa itself, possessed a name. But following the instructions it would be impossible to go wrong. Unfortunately the outer suburbs were hilly and our pony, not much larger than a good-sized St Bernard dog, was tired. On slight gradients we got out and walked. Uphill we had to help with the pulling. In the gathering twilight we found an avenue that seemed to fit the description, although all the avenues and villas were practically identical, with unmade dust roads, crazy paths, and overhanging eaves, designed to give protection from the snow that could never fall. I worked my way along the avenue going from villa to villa, but no knock was ever answered. Sometimes I caught sight of Vietnamese servants lurking at the house's rear, but the moment they realized I had seen them, they slipped quietly away and disappeared. Eventually I found a French woman, the first I had seen in this outwardly French town. Leaning out of an upstairs window she pointed in the dim direction of the villa where she thought Madame Schneider lived. So once again, I left the trap, cut across a garden coated with pine needles, and managed to steal up on an elderly Vietnamese domestic, who seemed to be a cook, as I caught him in the act of scouring out some pots. Placing myself between him and the back door, so as to cut off any attempt to escape, I began an interrogation.

It is necessary at this point to refer to the existence of pidgin-French and to explain its nature, since this was the occasion when I realized the urgency of mastering its essentials. Pidgin-French, or petit-nègre as it is called, lacks the gay fantasy of its English equivalent, but is, by compensation, far less complex. Its vocabulary is limited to perhaps a hundred words. Verbs are used in the infinitive except where this is difficult to pronounce, when a special pidgin form is devised; thus connaître becomes connaisse. There are adaptations in the way of pronunciation too. The Vietnamese will not bother with difficult foreign consonants. They cannot pronounce r, and f in the Vietnamese language contains a strong element of p in its pronunciation. Thus, for example, bière de France becomes bí' de Pla' or bí' de Pa'; or, to take a sentence, 'Je veux du fromage Roquefort', is translated, 'Moi content po'-mo' Lo'-po'.'

It was only as my conversation with the cook progressed that I began to realize the existence of these difficulties.

NL: Madame Schneider, est-ce qu'elle habite ici?

COOK: Moi pas connaisse.

NL (*with exaggerated distinctness and quite useless emphasis on final r*): Schnaydair-r-e, Madame Schnaydair-r-e.

COOK (*smiling faintly with recognition*): Sé-dé?

NL (*after great imaginative effort*): Oui.

COOK: Oui.

NL: Est-ce qu'elle est à la maison?

COOK: Moi pas connaisse. (*I do not understand.*)

NL (*beginning to learn lesson*): Madame Sé-dé ici?

COOK: Madame partir.

NL (*refusing to surrender to the finality of the tone*): Madame va venir?

COOK: Oui.

NL: Quand?

COOK (*employing the indefinite future offered in appeasement to foreigners the world over, meaning, in ten minutes, tomorrow, next week*): Maintenant.

NL (*unappeased*): Mais où est-elle allée?

COOK: Moi pas connaisse. (*This time, either I do not understand, or I do not know.*)

NL (*doubtful now whether this is the right lady*): Madame, elle est mariée?

COOK: Oui.

NL: Elle a un mari, donc?

COOK: Non.

NL: Alors, elle est veuve?

COOK (*in a desperate effort to make the whole thing crystal clear*): Monsieur pas mari, Monsieur médicin. Madame venir, Madame partir. Monsieur venir attend Madame venir. Monsieur, Madame manger.

With a few more hours' practice I should have readily understood from the lucid account of the Schneider family activities that Madame had already been home and had popped out again, probably for a cocktail with a neighbour, that her husband, who was a doctor, would shortly be arriving and that they would have dinner together at home. As it was the conversation dragged on fatuously. I gathered in quick succession that Madame was in the administration, that she was a doctor, that she was both, that she was on holiday, had returned to France, was shopping in town, and no longer lived there.

My driver, whose attempts to be helpful had only added to the insane confusion, now tired suddenly of the whole business, demanded in pellucid French sixty piastres, the equivalent of one pound, and rattled off, a small Asiatic charioteer, into the gloom. Finally the cook, too, retreated inside, leaving me standing there alone, a prey to mosquitoes and to noisy blundering insects like monstrous May-bugs which struck me repeatedly in the face. It was then that a lorry drove up and deposited Madame Schneider and her husband. They were much surprised to find me awaiting them and told me that they had sent a telegram to Saigon to say that a room had been reserved for me at the Baliverne Hotel and fixing an appointment for me at the Mairie next day. Although quite unprepared for my visit they insisted that I should stay to dinner. Asked how long I expected to stay in Dalat, I replied that I wanted to leave as soon as possible. Madame wanted to know when I wished her to try to arrange an audience with the Emperor Bao-dai, whose villa was just down the road. It seemed that I had passed it without paying it any particular attention. To this are come the Emperors of Annam!

Although there had been some hints at Saigon of the possibilities of an imperial hunting trip, I had never supposed that an official audience was taken so much as a matter of course and I said something to the effect that I hadn't given much thought to the matter. The Schneiders seemed surprised. This was my first experience of the fact that writers and journalists travelling in the Far East are supposed to be anxious to interview any crowned heads that happen to be within reach, and that to neglect to show much anxiety is considered a little oafish – even a breach of good manners. It is really extraordinary that these august persons should be wounded in their self-esteem when some insignificant traveller fails to express a desire to be received by them. In any case, my hostess thought, the matter of an audience could quite well wait for a day or two as there was little likelihood of my being able to leave Dalat in under a week. It was further explained to me that I would have to return along the Saigon road to a point about seventy-five miles south where it joined the main road to Ban Méthuot. There was a convoy due to leave Saigon for Ban Méthuot next morning, but I should almost certainly fail to make the connection. The next convoy would leave in about a week's time. I thought it strange that the people in Saigon should have arranged, in that case, for me to travel to Ban Méthuot via Dalat, and Madame Schneider said that they had probably taken the map too literally. There were two jungle tracks that cut across country from a village called Djiring, about thirty miles away, but one was the Emperor's private hunting track and his permission would have to be obtained to use it, while as for the other, which had only been completed two years previously, it might be months before – but suddenly Madame had an idea; hadn't there been some talk of a gendarmerie officer going to Ban Méthuot in the next few days? Picking up the telephone she got through to the gendarmerie, and sure enough, by a really remarkable chance, a Lieutenant Suéry was leaving next morning. He had a seat to spare in his car and would be pleased to call for me at the inevitable hour of 5 a.m.

The doctor ran me over to the Baliverne Hotel. It was a pretentious building, externally a bad example of timid functionalism tempered with would-be Hispanic swagger. My reception was a good example of Vietnamese passive resistance. It started off with the doctor confidently announcing that he had reserved a room for me by telephone. The Vietnamese male receptionist consulted a list and shook his head. The doctor asked him to make sure and the receptionist went carefully through the rooms, one by one, apparently checking the name of each occupant. No, there was no reservation in that name. Much embarrassed the doctor turned to me. 'It's absolutely extraordinary. I telephoned myself.'

'Would you mind making one final check?' he asked. The clerk shook his head. 'No room has been reserved.'

'Well then let me speak to the manager.'

'The manager is not here.'

In desperation the doctor asked, 'And have you no rooms of any kind?'

'Certainly we have rooms.'

'Then why didn't you say so before?'

'You asked if there was a reservation, and I told you there was none.'

Tired but relieved I signed the register. The reception clerk seemed to remember something.

'At what time will you be leaving in the morning?'

'At five o'clock.'

'Will you require breakfast before leaving?'

'Well – if it won't be too early—'

'Yes, it will be too early.'

While waiting for my luggage to be taken up I saw one of the most amazing sartorial sights I have ever seen. An American car drove up and in came a party of wealthy Chinese. The girls were dressed in rolled-up tartan trousers and cardigans. With them was what seemed to be a Vietnamese mandarin in a flowered silk gown, but wearing a flat tweed cap. A foretaste of the mysterious East to come!

My room was furnished with the cheapest of modernistic furniture, there was a smelly lavatory and an empty water bottle. The page-boy refused five piastres (1s. 8d.) and demanded ten. Huge lethargic mosquitoes floated about the room, but they were so slow in flight that I picked them all out of the air in five minutes. I was glad that my stay in Dalat would be limited to one night.

Awaiting sleep I considered the matter of the extraordinary accessibility of the oriental potentates of our times. Having with me Crawford's *Journal of An Embassy to Cochin China*, which gives a fascinating account of the country at the time of his visit, in 1822, I turned up the passage referring to his vain attempts to be received in audience by the Emperor of Annam – an ancestor of the present sovereign. Crawford, who was kept kicking his heels for two months, never achieved his purpose because it was objected that the Embassy was undertaken on behalf of the Governor-General of India and not of the King of England himself. His experiences throughout show a marked similarity to those of envoys sent in various abortive attempts to establish diplomatic relations with the Emperor of China.

Crawford soon found that although the Cochin-Chinese were hospitable, cheerful, scrupulously polite and entirely lacking in the rapacity of the Siamese, they were 'extremely ceremonious and partial to display and parade in little matters to the extent of ostentation'. In his preliminary conference with a deputation of mandarins of Saigon, eight hours were spent in consideration of the wording of the letter he carried from the Governor-General to the Emperor. While agreeing that the intentions were probably respectful, the mandarins pointed out that it would be contrary to the laws of the country to present it in its original, barbarous form.

For example, the sentence, 'His Excellency sends certain presents in token of his profound respect and esteem for His Majesty the Emperor of Cochin-China.' 'This was not to be endured, because, as the matter was explained to us, profound respect and esteem must be considered as a matter of course from anyone that addressed His Majesty of Cochin-China.'

At the suggestion of the mandarins, the passage was rendered as follows, 'I send Your Majesty certain presents because you are a great King.' Exception was also taken to His Majesty being addressed as 'Sovereign of Laos and Cambodia', 'in recognition of the fact', as Crawford says, 'that he had just conquered a great part of these two countries. The mandarins informed me that it was no honour for the King of Cochin-China to be styled "a King of slaves".'

At Hué, the capital, the Chinese translation of the amended document came in for further criticism. The mandarins were horrified by the crudity of the Governor-General's reference to the death of the late Emperor, who 'ought to have been represented as not dead, but merely gone to Heaven'. 'This tedious matter' (the further alterations) 'occupied from ten in the morning until five in the evening . . .'

But it was all to no purpose. The Cochin-Chinese continued to be infallibly polite and most sympathetic.

'"It is natural enough," said the mandarin with a smile, "that you should employ every expedient in your power to attain the honour of being presented to so great a king."'

A hint was dropped of certain indiscretions committed by a predecessor, a Mr Roberts, who on the occasion of his mission in 1805 had included in the customary presents 'a series of prints representing the capture of Seringapatam, and the death of Tippoo Sultaun'. A Chinese merchant sent them word that in his belief the Court 'desired no intercourse whatever with them . . . the Cochin-Chinese looked upon the men with red hair and white teeth – that is to say Europeans – to be as naturally prone to war and depredations as tigers'.

Crawford struggled on with his losing battle, but there was nothing to be done. He was entertained and banqueted, noting in one instance that they were served with three bowls of eggs on which hens had been put to sit ten to twelve days previously. By way of consolation he was told at the time of his dismissal that five years before a similar mission from the French King had met with the same rebuff and that the Emperor had refused to accept the presents accompanying it.

The comparison with my own subsequent experiences gives some measure of the decline in the prestige of the Indo-Chinese kingdoms.

CHAPTER FIVE

Région Inconnue

HAVING BEEN WARNED of the Lieutenant's liking for punctuality I was waiting, shivering slightly, in the hotel's grandiose drive soon after four thirty. The trouble in the *Hauts Plateaux* of Indo-China is that while the temperature may reach 90° in the shade soon after the sun rises, it usually feels like a mild December day in England just before dawn. Above the creaking of cicadas I could hear the occasional bark of a stag. On the stroke of five came the distant rattling of a car and the jerky reflection of headlights among the trees. The Citroën came juddering up the road and Lieutenant Suéry got out and introduced himself. He was in his forties, a Provençal with a fine melancholy face; one of those southerners who contradict the accepted Mediterranean pattern with their coolness of manner, their reserve, and their taciturnity. Suéry had a worried look and I suspected him of suffering from stomach ulcers. Only his rapid, sing-song speech, which I found almost impossible to understand, gave a clue to his origin.

The car rattled badly. No car could stand up for long to these terrible roads. The chauffeur was a Vietnamese corporal called Nha – pronounced *nya*. He was the first genial member of his race I had met and he smiled continually. Suéry sat beside him in front and criticized his driving and I was in the back seat surrounded by the luggage. It was still quite dark and after a while a short circuit developed causing the lights to bump on and off. Suéry nagged at the chauffeur about this and after a while Nha told him cheerily that he couldn't find the short in the dark and in any case he wasn't an electrician. I could understand every word Nha said but had great difficulty with Suéry's high-pitched, buzzing replies. Suéry asked me if I had a gun in my baggage, and I said, 'No, why?' Suéry said it would be an extraordinary thing if we did not see at least one tiger or leopard on the track. Viet-Minh patrols? – no, not a chance. We were thirty miles from the regular frontier of their territory, and where we were going it was real no man's land – no man's land in the sense that, so far as anybody knew, there was no population at all. Two hundred miles of unexplored jungle without a single village, it was believed. You didn't find the Viet-Minh wandering about in that kind of place. They couldn't live on air any more than anybody else. Anyway the corporal had a rifle and if we came across a tiger we would take a pot at it, just for luck. Of course he couldn't countenance hunting on a duty tour, but we would call that self-defence.

We reached Djiring in a chilly dawn. It was nothing more than a line of shacks on each side of the road. This was where I had been hoping to find a place to get some coffee. But it was too early. A few Moïs were wandering about the street pulling on their long silver pipes. They were wrapped in blankets worn with toga-like dignity, a fold flung over the left shoulder. The blankets were woven at the hems with some fine intricate pattern.

We were on the jungle track when the sun came up. It showed a path hardly wide enough in most places for two cars to pass, with an earth surface varying in colour from orange to brick-red. We were passing through unexplored country; a succession of low mountain ranges with peaks reaching a maximum of three and a half thousand feet. Our world was clothed in frothy vegetation, which, on the more distant mountains, looked as close-textured as moss. Lit up by the bland morning sun it was a cheerful, spring-like aspect. As we plunged down into the valleys the landscape closed in on us, till at the lowest levels we practically tunnelled through the bamboos, which seemed to have choked to death all other forms of growth. At slightly higher altitudes we passed between evenly spaced ranks of trees. Their absolutely smooth trunks went straight up without any projection to the roof of the forest, where they put out a parasol of branches. From their bases to the height of perhaps twenty feet the trunks were bastioned with thin strengthening-vanes. There was no way that any of the hundred forms of parasitic growth could take hold. Each tree, it seemed, laid claim to a certain area for its growth, and I saw one with its trunk wrapped almost completely round an intruder of a different species.

There were other trees which had not adapted themselves to the social environment of the jungle and they were loaded with parasitic ferns that had established themselves in the crevices of the rough bark, while lianas, orchids, and creepers cascaded from their branches. There was a curious regularity of shape to be observed about some of these parasites, particularly in the case of a chaplet of fleshy leaves fastened about vertical branches, from which there spilled, as from an over-filled basket, green, fretted patterns, repetitive in design as the torn newspaper of the cinema-queue busker. At this season, in early February, there were no flowering orchids, but sometimes in the valley-bottoms, half extinguished among the bamboos, we caught a glimpse of the fiery smoke of flamboyant trees. A flower, too, grew abundantly by the roadside which looked like willow herb, but was lavender in colour. These were visited by butterflies of rather sombre magnificence – typical, I suppose, of dim forest interiors. Usually they were black with splashes of green or blue iridescence. They did not settle, but hovered poised like fruit-sucking birds, probing with probosces at the blooms. They fluttered in their thousands above the many streams and once, passing through a savannah, we came across what proved on investigation to be the mountanous excretion of an elephant. At first nothing could be seen of it but the glinting of the dark, splendid wings of the butterflies that had settled upon it.

I was intrigued by the process by which some day the jungle would probably re-claim the track – a digestive action which had already begun. Since most of the trees were without low-level branches, there was little lateral pressure; no remorseless closing-in of the walls of vegetation on both sides. What had happened was that plants had seeded themselves in the track itself and had already reached the stage when they could have been potted-out for the embellishment of all the boarding houses of England. There were many aspidistra- and laurel-like varieties, throwing out new leaves that were often curiously veined, hairy, mottled, or lacquered. Some bore small orange-blossom-like flowers and spiders had increased the nuptial illusion by draping them with gauzy bridal veils. I saw several familiar birds including bee-eaters, kingfishers, and shrikes, and we once passed a peregrine falcon perched most uncomfortably on a slender swaying bamboo. The lieutenant was mortified that no tiger had appeared and said that now the sun was well up it was unlikely that we would see one. However, a troop of gibbons dropped from the trees into our path, awaiting our oncoming in petrified astonishment. At the last moment, when the chauffeur was already braking hard, they departed with fine acrobatic flourishes. Jungle-fowl frequently appeared ahead. They were as small as bantams and nearly as sprightly on the wing as blackbirds. It seems that the polygamous habit of the farmyard exists in the wild state – though on a lesser scale – since a cock was never without his two or three hens. The chauffeur Nha groaned in horror at these wasted opportunities but the lieutenant would not relax discipline even when we saw a huge boar in the track, at right angles to us, lethargic and indifferent, its head hanging down and snout practically touching the ground. It remained a perfect, unmissable target, until we were within a few yards of it, when, without looking up or making any preliminary movement, it seemed suddenly to vanish, as if de-materialized.

By the afternoon we had left the jungle and entered a region of *forêt-clairière* – patches of woodland alternating with coarse-grass savannahs. This phenomenon might have been caused by extreme variations in the natural fertility of the soil, or by the destructive cultivation of the region in the past by primitive tribes. There would be a few miles of grassland, followed, as the soil improved, by clumps of fern, bushes trimmed sedately with what looked like wild roses, and then, finally, the jungle again, a bulging explosion of verdure. The Lieutenant said that these parts swarmed with all kinds of game, particularly elephants, tigers, and gaurs – a large species of buffalo of legendary ferocity in Indo-China, which provides all local hunters with their most hair-raising escape stories. We saw none of them.

For several hours, it seemed to me, the Lieutenant had been showing signs of irritation. This took the form of constant criticism of the chauffeur's driving. It was no mean feat to drive a car along this track, with its ever loose surface, its acute bends, its gradients, the patches of freshly grown vegetation through which we were obliged to crash implacably. I thought that Nha was doing very well. We had had no nasty turns, so far. I was well content to relax and look at the scenery. Not so the Lieutenant. He began to indulge in the most acute form of back-seat driving, which included a regular flow of instructions. It went something like this:

'All right now – gently out of the bend. Now accelerate hard – all you've got. No, don't change up. Why change up when you'll have to change down again straight away? Keep your foot on the throttle, now swing her across – bottom gear – there you are, you left it too late: stall the engine that way. Never change down after a corner like that, change before. Now give her full throttle – hey, slow down! What on earth are you doing? My God, you'll have us over the top before we know where we are. There you go now – I told you you'd stall the engine.'

It was evident that Nha was getting rattled. After he had followed Suéry's instructions as best he could, thereby twice stalling the engine on a hill, Suéry asked him if he was tired and would like a rest. Nha got out without a word and came round to the other side and Suéry took the wheel. Suéry's driving was dynamic. We roared up gradients on full throttle in each gear, snaking gently on the soft surface. Bends were taken in Grand Prix style. It was quite exciting.

After about ten minutes of this we happened to be coming down a hill with an easy gradient. There was a drop of about a hundred feet into a ravine on the left and a bank on the right. The road had widened out and Suéry thought he could take the bend at forty. I had a glimpse of a flock of small green parakeets leaving the top of a tree growing in the ravine, but was unable to follow their flight owing to the swinging away of the landscape. One moment I was looking at the birds flying up from the top of the tree, then the landscape shifted round and I saw the road – also slipping away – and a steep bank coming up at us. I heard Suéry say, '*Mon Dieu,*' three times very quickly and I wedged my feet up against the seat in front and pushed away hard. There was a crash and something hit me on top of the head and we seemed to bounce up into the air and go backwards. We did fifteen yards back-first down the road in the direction we were going, with all the car doors open. I fell out first and I saw Nha and Suéry fall out on opposite sides. Nha sat in the road with his head in his hands and Suéry got up and walked backwards a few steps. His face was covered with blood which was already dripping down his shirt. There was a ringing in my ears but I knew that I was not badly hurt. Nha got up and sat on the running board and said, '*Oh malheureux,*' as well as something in Vietnamese. He then grinned and we both went over to look after Suéry. Suéry had a deep, ragged wound over his eye and a lot of small cuts on his face and arms. He had broken the steering wheel with his chest. I wiped the worst of the blood off him with a clean handkerchief and got some plastic skin out of my bag and squeezed it over his cuts.

In half an hour everybody was feeling well enough to look at the car. It was a wreck, one of the front wheels folded half underneath the chassis. By the best possible luck we had covered all but about thirty kilometres of the distance to the first military post, but it was going to be dark in two hours' time. Suéry seemed to think that it wouldn't be a good thing to spend the night in the car and Nha explained why, later. We had our second piece of good luck when Nha remembered the existence of a hut used by the Moï guard, which, he thought, couldn't be more than a mile or two from where we were. Taking what we could easily carry, we set out and in about half an hour came to a shallow clearing in the jungle with a plaited bamboo hut raised on piles. Two young Moïs in army tunics and loincloths peered out at us through the door-opening. They seemed as pleased to see us as if we had been disreputable relations. A brief, dubious scrutiny, and they both turned away, hoping that by ignoring our existence we might be persuaded to leave them in peace. Nha called and one of them came and stood at the top of the step-ladder. Nha beckoned to him and he turned away as if to appeal to the other. Finally the pair of them with the clearest possible reluctance came slowly down the ladder. Suéry gave Nha fussy details of what he was to say to them and Nha, who said he only knew a few words

of the language, started, as best he could, with the interpreting, while
the Moïs stood there, fidgeting and unhappy. They were gentle,
girlish-looking lads of about twenty years of age. Following local
custom they had had their front teeth knocked out and wore their
hair in a bun. They had a few narrow brass bracelets round their
wrists, and a silver churchwarden pipe protruded from the pocket of
each army tunic. Nha first explained that Suéry was an officer and
they must consider themselves under his orders. Did they realize
that? There was a doubtful assent.

'Very well,' Suéry said, 'ask them what arms they have.'

The Moïs said they had two rifles.

'Tell them to go and get them,' Suéry said, looking a trifle
relieved.

The Moïs went trotting off and reappeared with the rifles, carried
smartly at the trail. Suéry took each gun, opened the breech
mechanism, inspected it, and looked along the barrels. He seemed
pleased.

'Ask them how many rounds of ammunition they have between
them.'

Nha translated this and the Moïs shook their heads. They had
none.

'My God,' Suéry said, 'well what have they got to defend
themselves with?' The Moïs said they had a crossbow apiece. 'Any
arrows?' Suéry wanted to know, with sarcasm. The Moïs said, yes,
they had arrows and also *coupe-coupes*. 'Very well,' Suéry said. 'Tell
them to go and bring the *coupe-coupes*.' The Moïs came trooping
back with the *coupe-coupes* over their shoulders. They had heavy,
curved blades, as sharp as razors, about eighteen inches long, and
could be used as knives or axes. 'Good,' Suéry said. 'Now tell them
they are to set out for Dak-Song immediately; get there as quickly
as they can and bring help. I'll give them a note for the *Chef de la
Poste*.'

While Nha was trying to put this into their language you could
see the Moïs' faces cloud over. They just said they didn't understand.
This was the line they took and they stuck to it. The simple, polished bronze faces, until now good-natured and rather bewildered,

suddenly emptied of expression. The light of comprehension went out, or rather, was switched off.

Suéry accepted defeat. He knew that nothing in the world would get those Moïs to walk along that jungle track in the dark. He asked Nha if he would go with one of the Moïs and Nha, looking slightly sick, said yes. But when the proposition was put to the Moïs they prepared a second line of retreat by saying that their sergeant had ordered them to stay there until he came back. And where was the sergeant? He was wounded and had gone away, where, they didn't know. It was days, perhaps weeks since it happened, but he had told them to stay where they were, and stay they would. Did they not realize, said Nha becoming indignant, that a lieutenant was more important than a sergeant and that his orders would over-ride any they had received? Once again the Moïs did not understand.

The Lieutenant got up and said he would sleep in the hut.

The idea of spending the night in a Moï hut filled Nha with revulsion, as he told me as soon as the Lieutenant was out of hearing. A hut that had been occupied by savages – imagine the smell. Well – I would soon see for myself. And there was another angle that had to be considered. Supposing bandits – or pirates as they were invariably called – happened to find the wrecked car. This would be the first place they would think of to look for us. Didn't I realize that the Lieutenant had been thinking of pirates when he decided against sleeping in the car? Only a few hours away there were several villages and the junction of various cross-country routes. Just the kind of place, in fact, where pirates could always be expected to hang about. He wasn't thinking so much of the Viet-Minh as of *pirates vulgaires* mixed up with Japanese deserters. That's what the Moï guards were there for. Naturally the pirates didn't bother about such small fry; but if they knew we were here – *oh malheureux!* These dolorous exclamations of Nha's were always accompanied by a bright smile. I'm sure that he wasn't particularly impressed by the hazards to which we were exposed, but enjoyed, as people do, making the most of them. The next peril he produced was tigers, remarking with a gay conviction that, *'les tigres vont causer avec nous ce soir'*. I pointed out that the Moïs were still alive. He said that although the Moïs were disgusting savages they knew how to deal with tigers and we didn't. Nha had all the distaste of the conservative, plains-dwelling Vietnamese for everything that had to do with forests or mountains and their inhabitants. The Vietnamese, like the Chinese, prefer their landscapes to possess the comfort of the familiar rather than the mystery of the unknown. Nha was already sickening for the ditches and rice-fields of Cochin-China.

Nha's prejudices were, of course, unjustified. The Moï hut was spotless and contained no odours of any kind. It had been made in sections of plaited-bamboo, tied with lianas over a framework. Inside it felt very insecure. At every pace you felt as though your foot were going through the floor. The whole structure creaked and swayed. A large circular earthenware tray on the floor served as a hearth and Suéry wanted to light a fire to keep off the mosquitoes. Nha asked him if he thought we should advertise our presence. Suéry said it was either that or being eaten alive by the mosquitoes, and this was a bad area for malaria. They had a rare kind of mosquito up here that bred in running water, the *Anopheles minimus*. There was none deadlier.

When we lit the fire we nearly choked ourselves with the smoke, but the Moïs re-arranged the logs and the smoke died down leaving a faint odour of incense in the room. I went out and stood by the door. It was not quite dark. There was a huge owl flapping backwards and forwards across the clearing and near by, in the undergrowth, a bird sang with a powerful nightingale-like song. I pulled the door across the opening, tied it in position with a length of liana, and went to lie down.

Suéry had told Nha to have the Moïs take turns at a watch; but once again comprehension lapsed. No sooner had we stretched ourselves out by the fire than they stole past us and went into a partitioned-off section of the hut, and we saw them no more. I was sure they were thoroughly miserable at our presence, which was probably most offensive to the tutelary spirit of the hut, whom they lacked the means to placate by sacrifice.

Lying as close as I could get to the fire I was hot down one side and chilly on the other. The cool night air came up through the bamboo floor and, however I lay, projections in the bamboo stuck into my back. Finally I began to doze lightly but was continually awakened, sometimes by somebody getting up and setting the hut asway; sometimes I was not sure by what. But then as I lay trying to collect my wits I would hear animal sounds, not loud and menacing, but casual, confident, and none the less sinister; a cough, a sigh, or a soft, restless whining.

I came to painfully, somewhere about dawn, realizing that I had been listening through increasing degrees of consciousness to what I had dreamily accepted as the noise of a shipyard at work. There was a regular industrial crash, made, as I had supposed, by a piledriver or a riveting machine. With consciousness fully returned and with it the realization of where I was, it seemed unreasonable that this clamour should not stop. Nha was already awake. It was a bird, he said. I thought of a hornbill with the habits of a woodpecker. But no, Nha said, this was the cry of a bird and not the concussion of a gigantic bill against a hollow tree. It was a mystery I was never able to solve, as, however the sound was caused, I never heard it again. Familiar, though, from that time on was another form of salutation of the dawn, a huge demoniacal, whistling howl that started in first one and then another corner of the jungle until the air resounded with the rising and falling scream of sirens. These were screaming monkeys. They kept up the lunatic chorus for half an hour each morning.

We washed in some greenish water from a nearby stream. There was nothing to eat or drink; no evidence, in fact, to suggest the Moïs bothered about regular meals. Nha raised the question and one of the Moïs offered to go and shoot a monkey with his crossbow. We thanked him and prepared to leave. Suéry told Nha to stay with the car while he and I walked to Dak-Song. Owing to Nha's perpetual grin, I could not see that he was not pleased with the prospect of being left behind, but Suéry knew him well enough to be able to tell. He asked Nha if he was afraid to stay by himself and Nha said, no, not if he didn't have to stay the night. If he had to stay the night, well then – *Oh malheureux!* Suéry promised that whatever happened he would see to it that he was relieved by nightfall. Nha then asked Suéry if he would like to take the rifle – 'in case you see any boars'. Suéry refused this very gallant offer and having presented the Moïs with a few cigarettes to cut up for their pipes, we started out.

I was glad of this opportunity to walk to Dak-Song, having felt that I wanted to form a closer contact with this unspoiled and unexplored forest than was possible in a closed-in car. It was like a splendid May morning in England, a little cool at first in the shade of the trees, but I knew that once the sun was high enough to shine on the road it would be very different.

The forest was as full of tender greens as an English woodland in early spring. It was temperate in its forms, placid almost, with occasional exuberances that, unsated by excess, one was able to appreciate. The air resounded with the morning songs of birds which were quite unlike any I had heard before. In the gardens of Saigon one was haunted by a monotonous piping. Here the birds produced more complicated melodies than the warblers of the West, impressing me not so much as in the case of our blackbird or nightingale, by the quality of a limited repertoire of notes, as by the variety and range of the melody, which in some cases could have easily been fitted into a formal musical composition. It was as though a collection of mocking birds had been taught European music by a Vietnamese artist on a bamboo flute. And besides these musical performers there were many more producing sheer noise; the rattling of a stick along iron railings, the escape of steam from a boiler, the squealing of brakes, a single muted stroke on a gong. I never heard these bird sounds and songs again. Elsewhere in Indo-China great destruction is done to wild-life by indiscriminate burning of the forests by the tribes, and birds are, of course, hunted for food. It is possible that in this supposedly unpopulated area, marked on French maps as *Région Inconnue*, birds and animals exist which are not to be found elsewhere.

Unfortunately there was little to be seen. A few small honey-sucking birds fluttered about the lavender willow-herb and we frequently saw a species rather smaller than a lark, black in colour and with a tail which looked like a single feather at the end of an eighteen-inch long hair. It was difficult to understand, as we watched it threading in and out the thick jungle foliage, how its evolution could have been assisted by this unhandy appendage. Once only we saw a hornbill, sombrely splendid in black and yellow, launch itself from a tree top and go swooping through a glade in a dashing, easy flight. On the wing there was nothing incongruous about its immense bill.

We were about five miles from Dak-Song when we had a very bad moment. For hours under the sun's nearly vertical rays the jungle had become tamed and silent. Plodding through the red, shadeless dust, we were dirty and sweat-soaked. Suéry's shirt was spattered with brown bloodstains. I had a bad thirst but still not bad enough to risk a drink out of a stream. Just ahead the track turned sharply to the left to avoid a small, low hill that was very densely wooded. From this as we approached there suddenly came a huge, shattering, calamitous sound. It seemed in some way incongruous, improper to this tranquil atmosphere of an overgrown corner of an English wood on an afternoon in a heat-wave. I judged the sound to be produced by two tigers quarrelling, perhaps, over a kill. The snarling intake of breath followed by the furious, coughing roars was unmistakable. Suéry looked as if he wanted to pretend that he had heard nothing. That was half the trouble, there was something ridiculous, as well as alarming, about the situation. Either of us alone might have retreated up the road as quickly as we could, but together we were obliged to go on. It would have been no more seemly to show alarm than at the casual approach of a bull while crossing a field in either of our native lands. As we strode on I began to calculate the number of steps (thirty) that it would take us to reach the point of maximum danger and the number (two hundred) before we could start to breathe easily again.

But now a distressing complication awaited us. We reached the corner and turned left, but the track, instead of going on straight ahead, curved immediately to the right. The chilling sounds broke out again, very close now, and it was quite evident that my two hundred yards, instead of taking us to safety, would be fully employed in skirting the base of the hillock and that during that time we should be at roughly an even distance from the tigers. And this was how it turned out. We walked on round the hairpin bend expecting at every moment to see the animals come bounding down into the road in front of us. Every few seconds there was another outburst of roars. Our preoccupied silence was the only indication that we realized that anything unusual was happening. Glancing from side to side for a possible way of escape, I confirmed what I already knew, that the trees were as unclimbable as the columns of a Gothic cathedral. Perhaps half a mile further on Suéry broke the silence. 'They never attack in daytime,' he said.

This, it seemed, was one of the accepted fallacies of bush-life in Indo-China. The republican guard at Dak-Song when we arrived said the same thing. 'I hardly ever drive along the track without seeing one. Shot some beauties. They never attack you in daylight. Rarely attack human beings at all.'

The latter assertion is probably correct but I was only allowed two days in which to delude myself with the former. At Ban Méthuot one of the first French officials I met had been mauled by a tiger while coming out of his garden in the town at midday. The tiger was probably old and decrepit as it only ripped up the man's thigh in a desultory fashion before making off down the main street in the direction of the municipal offices and the church.

Dak-Song was a sun-scorched forest-clearing; a few Polynesian huts, and a pile-raised long-house used by Moï conscripts as a barracks. A strange face in such a place is an extraordinary event and Moï children ran screaming to their parents at our approach. The republican guards in charge of the post lived dismally in the huts. There were no amenities of any kind, no shop, canteen, or bar. At more or less weekly intervals the convoy to Ban Méthuot passed through, and the checking of vehicles and passes, occupying perhaps one hour, was their only routine activity. They had endless time to devote to the sad reflections that are the occupational disease of colonial soldiering. The staleness of existence couldn't be imagined, the *Chef de la Poste* said. The only thing you could do was to go out and shoot a tiger or a gaur, or something like that. Even then you couldn't call it sport. They were too tame. They came and gave themselves up. Committed suicide. The other day he had seen a herd of gaur in a clearing near by. He had just driven up to them in his jeep, picked out the biggest one, and shot it like that. The *Chef* sighed, thinking perhaps of weekend partridge shooting in France.

Our host apologized for a splendid lunch of wild poultry, the flesh of which was very white and sweet, and Suéry said that he would try to let him have some tinned stew next time he came through. The drinks were, of course, warm. It always surprised me that the Frenchman in the tropics lacking ice never made an attempt to cool liquids by keeping them, as the Spanish do, in porous vessels.

There was a sawmill at the post and the manager came over for coffee. He had the gentle, humorous cynicism of a man who, having started out with a fund of ideals, has found them not quite sufficient to cover all life's opportunities. Since heart-burnings were the order at the guard's table the manager contributed to the tale of frustration by a description of some of his difficulties. The forest was full of sao, a quite remarkable wood, impervious, as he put it, to destructive agents, and favoured by the Chinese of old for the manufacture of their war-junks. There the wood was, enough to make one's fortune ten times over, and yet there was no way of getting it down to Saigon. 'A hundred logs,' said the manager, 'and I'd leave you fellows to rot where you are and clear off back to France.' One of the guards said that it only meant waiting a short time now, 'till the roads are open again'. After that he could ship all the wood in Dak-Song. But the manager laughed. It would be no good at all if the roads were open. That would bring prices right down, only spoil things. What he wanted to find was some way to get the wood down there with the roads closed – like they did with the rice round Saigon. He'd have to find a smart Chinese that could take care of it for him with the Viet-Minh.

After lunch the *Chef de la Poste* showed us round and we happened to be there when a party of unusually handsome Moïs arrived. Instead of being dressed as those of Dak-Song were, in tattered

European shirts, these were splendid in tasselled loincloths, earplugs, and necklaces of beads and teeth. They had with them a pretty girl of about sixteen, with small, sharp breasts and the everted top lip of a child. One of the guards made discreet enquiries about her, but on learning that she was married, lost interest. They were members of a local tribe called M'nongs, a mysterious people the *Chef* said, who had only made their submission in 1939, since when they had assassinated eight administrators who had gone to live among them. Why? The *Chef* shrugged his shoulders. Nobody seemed to know. The M'nongs were quiet, well-behaved people but it was easy to upset them in some way or other without realizing it. You did the wrong thing and you disappeared. For an administrator it must have been a bit like living in one of those police-states, except that there was no clue as to what was expected of you. You would be getting on like a house on fire, a tribal bloodbrother; you might even, as he had heard some of them did, marry two or three native wives. And then you slipped up in some way and nobody ever saw you again. By the way, the *Chef* added, they had one custom here it might interest us to hear about. The men were considered the property of the women, so that a mother bought a husband for her daughter from a woman who had a son to sell. The price in these days, the *Chef* said, was about eight hundred piastres, so that in the case of a woman with a dozen sons, '*Elle reçoit du fric – n'est ce pas?*'

If the Vietnamese had been indifferent, these M'nongs were oblivious. They did their business, which seemed to consist of paying a tax in rice, through one of the tame Dak-Song Moïs. We walked round them looking at their ornaments but none of them so much as glanced at us. We might have been transparent. It was a coincidence that after this first encounter with the noble savage of Indo-China as he is when practically untouched by Western influence, only ten minutes should pass before I was given the opportunity of seeing the other side of the medal. The native guards brought in a half-crazed creature in rags who had escaped from one of the plantations. After having been severely beaten by one of the overseers he had run away and had made a journey through the jungle of three days and three nights to get here. The Frenchmen treated the man kindly and told the Moïs to give him food and shelter. I gathered that it was part of their duty to see that he was sent back, but they said that they had no intention of doing so. This was the general attitude of the lesser French officials I met. They had no use whatever for the plantation owners and would not lend their authority, unless they were compelled to, to the support of any abuse.

Sometime in the early evening a breakdown truck arrived from Ban Méthuot in response to the radio SOS that had been sent. Suéry went off in it and, as it had been arranged that I should continue my journey on the convoy that was coming through later that evening, we said goodbye. I was sorry to part company with Suéry. He was the only Frenchman I ever saw a Vietnamese treat with affectionate respect, so that there must have been something exceptional about him. Suéry thought more of Nha's comfort than he did of his own and he told me that the thing that upset him most about wrecking the car was that it might maroon them both in Ban Méthuot and thus prevent Nha from going back to Saigon to spend the New Year with his people – a terrible misfortune for any Vietnamese. He was most anxious to relieve Nha before nightfall and to be able to take him a good meal.

The *Chef de la Poste* had been on tenterhooks ever since the night before about the convoy's non-appearance. It was now twenty hours late and, as the telephone lines had been cut, they had no news. Soon after Suéry left a message came through to say that it had been attacked. The first few trucks that arrived knew that there had been an attack but could give no account of what had taken place. The drivers sat stiffly in their seats, dazed with fatigue and mantled with yellow dust. The *Chef* said he would put me on the first of them that had a seat to spare, but in each case the passengers were crammed so tightly in the driver's cabin that it was difficult to see how he could twist the steering wheel or change gear. The backs of the lorries were jammed with merchandise.

After five or six of them had passed through the check-point in this way the *Chef* decided that he had found a lorry with a hole in the cargo large enough for a human being to crawl into. He made one of the cabin passengers get down from the front and climb into this crevice, telling me to take his place. I did not like the idea of doing this, and said so, but the *Chef* waved aside such objections saying that I had better take the chance while I could, because if the convoy had been badly shot-up there wouldn't be many more lorries to come. I therefore swallowed my scruples, put my bag in the back, and climbed in, although feeling most uncomfortable about the whole affair. The lorry started off, bucking and crashing over the most appalling road I have ever travelled on. It was extremely difficult to stay in one's seat. The vehicles in front had raised a pall of yellow dust which, as it grew dark, the headlights were quite unable to penetrate. Shutting the windows hardly reduced the density of the cloud that swirled into the cabin but was quite effective to hold in the terrible heat generated by the engine roaring in low gear. I felt my presence keenly resented. So much so that I spoke to the driver intending to offer to change places with the man who had been sent to ride in the back, but I got no reply. He looked in fact so grim that I began to feel a little nervous, catching, incidentally, several venomous, sidelong glances from my fellow passengers. After a while the driver took to muttering to the man who was sitting next to him, crushed in between him and the door. A suggestion seemed to have been made and the man nodded in agreement. He opened the door and swung outside, peering back, evidently to see if another vehicle was in sight. Looking, as I thought, intently in my direction he made a sign to the driver who put the gear lever in neutral and pulled the lorry up. I thought that the chances were no better than one in four that they were going to throw me out. However, the driver's friend jumped down and went to the back of the lorry, after which he came back, got in, and we went on as before.

At about 11 p.m. we got into Ban Méthuot. The driver suddenly asked me in good French where I wanted to go. I told him the Mairie. He said, 'We've passed it. I'll go back.' I told him not to trouble, that I could easily walk, but he put the lorry in reverse and backed down the street till we came to the Mairie. I asked him how much I owed him, getting out a hundred-piastre note; he said, 'Nothing,' and pushed the money away. Thanking him I held my hand out and felt much relieved when he took it, smiled, and said, *'Au revoir.'*

I stood there for a moment looking after the lorry as it lurched away up the street. There were one or two street lamps and as it passed under them the curved canopy painted over with Chinese characters reminded me of an old-fashioned Chinese lantern.

CHAPTER SIX

Ban Méthuot

MONSIEUR DOUSTIN, chief representative, in the temporary absence of the Resident, of the French civil authority in the province, accepted the time and manner of my arrival with the imperturbability of a true diplomat. To judge from his manner nothing could have been more normal than my appearance at his door filthy and dishevelled, about thirty hours after I had been expected. When, shortly afterwards, seated before a meal of great complication, my plans were discussed and I mentioned my hope of getting across country to Paksé, there was no exasperated raising of the eyes. In the presence of such lunatic hopes Monsieur Doustin allowed himself only the faintest of sardonic smiles. The trouble with the people at Saigon, of course, was that they just didn't know what was happening; which, said Doustin severely, was a little surprising considering that they were the official source of information. Ban Méthuot to Paksé! The sardonic smile deepened a little. No one had done the trip for a year or two. It wasn't even known whether the track was practicable, or whether it had vanished into the jungle by now. In any case, nothing whatever was known about the state of security of the region. These people that stuck to their offices in Saigon were carried away by their imaginations. There wasn't much traffic leaving Ban Méthuot in any direction, and unless one had a positive mission it was just as well to be philosophical and go wherever the first *moyen de fortune* happened to be going. Even that might mean quite a few days cooling one's heels. And why not? There were few more interesting areas in Indo-China, or the Far East, if it came to that. An anthropologist's paradise, Doustin said. And one that was passing away before your very eyes. I had arrived, in fact, just in time.

There was another important point to remember, the *Chef de*

Cabinet said. In the Darlac province, he personally would guarantee my safety; but once I passed beyond the frontiers of his jurisdiction, ah, that was another matter. Pirates everywhere. People who called themselves nationalists, or freedom fighters, but who really took to piracy just as their ancestors before them had done, because it was the easiest way of making a living. This brought up the convoy attack and Doustin said that he had heard that eight vehicles had been destroyed out of the thirty-odd that made up the convoy. The conversation turned to the tranquillity of life in our respective home countries. Doustin had memories of service in England with the Free French, spent in what I had always thought of as drab provincial towns, but where, according to him, all the problems of existence had been solved. I was continually being invited by French officials to share a nostalgia for such unlikely places as Birkenhead or Dover – Peterborough was Doustin's choice – seen now across the years of fierce, sunny exile as congeries of quaint pubs, full of tenderly acquiescent maidens, and wrapped in a Turner sunset. It is extraordinary, too, the experiences that people can succeed in remembering with affection. Doustin had even come to believe that he had liked Naafi tea.

A room had been prepared for me in the Residence. It was not a large building, but conceived in the grand manner, with a wide ambassadorial entrance and a flight of steps worthy of an Italian customs house. Sentries ensconced in the bougainvillaea woke up and slapped their rifle-stocks furiously at our approach. As soon as we entered the house white-clad Moï domestics with tamed, empty faces flitted at our heels.

'Tomorrow morning,' announced Doustin with the voice of decision, 'you will be tired. Very well, breakfast at eight o'clock. An English breakfast, naturally, with an omelette. You don't take beer before eleven, do you? Ah, the English light ale!'

And now came the moment of efficient unbending – efficient, because Doustin could not be otherwise. 'If you want anything, don't stand on ceremony. Just stand at the window and holler. *Poussez un grand coup de gueule.*' A light, saloon-bar slap on the back and I was dismissed for the night. The quick, confident footsteps receding down the marble corridor. The yelp of the guard-commander. The sharp acceleration of a car being driven competently, dashingly, away. I put out the light and opened the windows. My cheeks, ears, chin were brushed by soft, disgusting contacts. Hundreds of moths were coming in.

As I was not to see Doustin before ten in the morning, I spent an hour or two before that looking round the town. There was not much to see. Before 1946 there had been a native town, but it had been burned down in the trouble with the Viet-Minh. Now there were a few French villas on each side of a dust road, a sluttish-looking hotel built of wood and green-painted, and a Vietnamese market with a few shack-lined alleys leading off it.

The Vietnamese shops sold a great collection of improbable rubbish; celluloid dolls and soap-boxes, plastic belts, calendars with pictures of Chinese girls playing hockey, spurious rhinoceros horn used as an aphrodisiac, and fake tigers' teeth as a medicine. There were dried and salted flat-fish no bigger than five-shilling pieces. Thousands of them. They were strewn about on counters mixed up with haberdashery and bottles of blood-coloured lemonade. There were innumerable hideous Ali-Baba jars, brown and green and with a glaze like toffee. These are made by the Vietnamese and sold to the Moïs for use in their drinking ceremonies. The most popular personal ornament on sale was an enamel brooch depicting a Flying Fortress. For the house one could buy a picture of Sun Yat-sen in a mother-of-pearl studded frame, a landscape decorated with artificial flowers and grass, or a mirror painted with planets with aeroplanes encircling them. The most popular utensil, and undoubtedly the one of greatest utility in the East, was the jerrycan. Bicycle repairing was the most popular industry represented in the market. After that came portrait photography; particularly booths which offered a large number of different poses – photomaton style – for a fixed sum. The Vietnamese trotted in and out of them continually. Few Moïs were to be seen but I saw one ultracivilized Moï woman, probably a convert of some kind, wearing nothing above the waist but a ridiculously inadequate brassière, and carrying a blue plastic handbag.

Frangipani trees grew in the market place. They were leafless
with polished, swollen-looking branches, and bore sprays of white
thick-petalled flowers. Hundreds of house-sparrows perched in
them.

At exactly ten o'clock I was shown into Monsieur Doustin's office.
He awaited me poised beneath a wall map, ready to organize my
movements in the period immediately ahead. I was harangued
briefly on the military situation, which was presented, as far as I
could see, with complete frankness. Doustin was too subtle to
indulge in crude propaganda. He would have considered this
inefficient, preferring to expose some of the weaknesses as well as all
the strength of his side. The Viet-Minh were devils incarnate and
the French, well, sometimes they lost patience – went a bit too far.
What could you expect with men fighting in these terrible conditions? A couple of years out in the bush and always seeing the
same half a dozen faces. How would you like it yourself? Doustin
also thought that there was far too much loose, anti-colonial talk
about. In this part of the world France had nothing to be ashamed
of. They were doing good work and he wanted me to see some of it
for myself. So, as there was not much chance of being able to get
away from Ban Méthuot for a week or two, he was going to arrange
a side-trip for me through the most interesting part of the Moï
country. It was all arranged. I was to start tomorrow, and a young
administrator and an inspector of schools would be going with me.

Although there was an ominous suggestion of the conducted tour
in this, it did not, in fact, work out that way. Whether at heart
Doustin was really as confident of being on the side of the powers of
light as he seemed, I don't know. My opinion is that whatever his
doubts he cast them out, counting them as weakness. He was almost
the last of his kind that I met among the French. The rule thereafter
was an ability to see two sides to any question, leading to a Hamlet-
like infirmity of purpose and sometimes to the darkest of pessimism.

*

Doustin produced a final suggestion. Before visiting the Moï country he thought I should see a Doctor Jouin, who had lived among the tribes for many years and was considered the leading living authority on their customs. Doctor Jouin was the head of the medical services of that nebulous enclave in Vietnam of undiluted French authority: Les Populations Montagnardes du Sud Indo-chinois, and the author of several weighty anthropological works, published under the dignified auspices of the Musée de L'Homme.

I found him at a table cluttered with the charts and mathematical figures that seem to enter so much these days into what one would have thought the least mathematical of sciences. He was white-haired and gentle, his face permanently illuminated with the Buddhistic peace generated by complete absorption in an urgent and valuable task. From the inside information available to him in his official position, the doctor informed me, he had decided ten years ago that this engaging race was doomed in quite a short time to disappear from the earth. He had therefore set to work to learn what he could of their attractive if primitive civilization before it was too late. In the beginning the task had seemed simple enough and, in any case, he had not intended to probe too deeply. But then he had made exciting discoveries and had been lured on into an unknown country where the horizons constantly receded. Every attempt to clear up some limited aspect of his subject had uncovered endless others. And now he found himself in a trap. He had committed himself to labours which could never be finished. And time and the conditions of the country were against him. It needed a dozen workers like himself to occupy themselves with the still enormous volume of material available which, however, was melting away and which in a few years would be lost for ever.

We started talking about the Moïs in the early afternoon and it was evening before I left the doctor's villa, carrying with me various monographs as well as the manuscript of a work in progress. From these and from our conversation much of the following information has been extracted.

CHAPTER SEVEN

The Moïs

IN THE EARLY PART of the last century the Moïs seem to have been regarded as articulate animals rather than human beings. European traders did their best, but without success, to acquire specimens for zoological collections in Europe. In 1819, Captain Rey of Bordeaux, who carried a cargo of fire-arms to the Emperor of Annam, was assured by no less a dignitary than the Mandarin of the Strangers, of the existence of 'Moys, or wild men'. The Mandarin had seen many of them when commanding a corps of elephants in the interior. They had tails, he said, and he had managed to capture one and bring it back with him to the capital as a present for the Emperor. Rey was interested enough to take this up with the French mandarins at the court, when he visited them, and they confirmed all he had been told, beyond possibility of doubt. 'My respectable friends ... had never seen these extraordinary creatures; but they had so often heard their existence affirmed by men of character and probity, that they knew not how to disbelieve the report. The tail was said to be in length about eight inches and a half. Although endowed with speech as well as with the human figure, the mandarins seemed, I thought, to conceive them to be only irrational animals.' With the foregoing exception, Rey said, concluding his report of the fauna of Cochin-China, all its abundant variety of animals could be found in the adjoining countries.

Before the end of the century, these opinions had to be modified. The explorer Mouhot – discoverer of Angkor Vat – had published an account of his visit to the Stieng tribe. The Moïs were officially conceded souls and some theorists even began to raise the matter of the lost tribes of Israel. However, until the colonial era with its census-taking, and head-taxes, these newly promoted human beings remained inaccessible, and still fairly mysterious, in their forests.

The Moïs, it seems, are well aware of the unsatisfactory state of the technical side of their civilization and usually seek to excuse themselves to strangers who allude to it by citing one of their self-deprecatory legends. A favourite one describes the tactical disadvantages suffered at the creation, when the Moïs were last to crawl out of the holes in the ground and found everything worth having already appropriated. Then again, the matter of illiteracy, they say. What could you expect? When the Great Spirit told all the nations to bring writing materials, on which their alphabets would be inscribed, the Moïs with typical improvidence, instead of providing tablets of stone or even wood, turned up with a piece of deer-skin, which later, complete with alphabet, was eaten by the dogs.

There are supposed to be about a million Moïs distributed over the mountainous areas of Indo-China. The exact number is unknown, as a few remote valleys have not even made their official submission. But whatever it is, it is dwindling rapidly, as in the districts most affected by Western penetration some villages have lost half their number in a single generation. They are a handsome, bronze-skinned people, of Malayo-Polynesian stock, related to the Dyaks of Borneo, the Igoroths and Aétas of the Philippines, and to the various tribes inhabiting the hinterlands of such widely separated parts as Madagascar and Hainan Island, off the coast of China. They hunt with the crossbow, being particularly noted for their skill in the capture and taming of elephants, which they sell as far afield as Burma. A clue to the extent of their culture's diffusion is given by their use of the sap of the Ipoh tree for poisoning their arrow-tips. The utilization of this poison, although the Ipoh tree grows in many other areas, is limited to Malaysia, Indo-China, a small easterly strip of Thailand and Burma, Borneo, and Timor. The poison's effect is intensified, as necessary, according to the size of the game, by adding to it a strychnine-containing decoction from broial root and extracts of the fangs of snakes and scorpions' stings. A scratch from a weapon dipped in this appalling concoction – the use of which is hedged about with many semi-religious prohibitions – produces death in the case of human beings in a few minutes.

The Moïs cultivate rice by the 'dry' method, which is to say that they burn down parts of the forest just before the beginning of the rainy season, drop their rice seed into the holes in the ground and leave the rains to do the rest. The name Moï is Vietnamese for 'savage'. The Moïs have been enslaved by all the technically superior races, Siamese, Laotians, and Cambodians, among others, who have come into contact with them. Far from having derived any benefit from this association with their superiors, the greater degree of external influence the more deplorable the condition of the Moïs who have suffered it.

The free survivors seem to the casual observer to lead gay and sociable existences, much occupied with gluttonous feasting and the consumption of rice-spirit. This hearty manner of living is said to depend upon and be proportionate to the tribe's inaccessibility. Unless compelled to, Moïs do not work for wages and their civilized neighbours are shocked by what they consider their incurable sloth. Village labours, however, such as the erection of houses or the clearing of the forest, are undertaken communally and with great zest. The Moïs are art-collectors, and wealth consists in the possession of gongs, drums, and jars, some of which are of ancient Chinese or Cham origin and therefore of great value, even in the West. Occasionally such museum pieces are wheedled out of them by Europeans who tend to remain in ignorance of the treasure they have stumbled upon, under the impression that they have acquired nothing more than an interesting example of Moï artisanship.

Apart from being used to store rice-wine, jars are accumulated in the hope that spirits will take up their residence in them. When a spirit moves into a jar, the fact is revealed to the owner in a dream, but official recognition is only accorded after an examination by experts for certain external signs. The jar thus honoured is not necessarily an antique, although the spirits usually show artistic discrimination. In any case the jar becomes a valuable piece of property and may be sold, complete with spirit, for a large number of buffaloes. As the spirit, or talismanic virtue, is thought of in some way as being divisible, a handle is frequently broken off when a jar is sold, and worshipped in the same way the complete jar was before. A considerable inter-tribal trade exists in such jars, and expert appraisers and negotiators carry out the transactions. They are said to exact large profits.

According to scientific investigators, such as Doctor Jouin, the most extraordinary thing about the Moïs is their unique racial memory. It is even suggested that a concerted study of their sagas (which are on the point of perishing), might throw an unprecedented light on man's existence in prehistoric times. The Rhadés, one of the least degenerate of the tribes, possess, according to the doctor, a name for and a description of the mammoth and the megatherium as well as the hippopotamus – which has been extinct in the Far East in the historic epoch.

The unique value, it would appear, of the Moï saga resides in the fact that it is ritual and sacrosanct. It may be recited only in certain specified circumstances, and without the slightest modification. Even if words and phrases have lost their meaning, are mutilated or incomplete, no attempt, under powerful religious sanction, must be made at restoration. The sagas, therefore, although involving great interpretational difficulties, have remained a treasure-house of information relating to the remote past. Events of the last thousand years or so seem to have made little impression on the Moï imagination. The brilliant Indianized civilizations of the Khmers and the Chams are hardly referred to. Angkor Thom is the work of 'strangers recently arrived in the country'. The sagas describe the Moïs' own establishment in Indo-China after leaving their island homes at an unknown period, which must antedate the fifth century BC, since at that time they are already referred to in the annals of the kingdom of Fu-Nan.

The non-scientific visitor appears to be most impressed by the innumerable rituals with which the Moïs surround their existence. The most onerous of these are concerned with death. Those which are associated with good health are the least important and tend to be quite perfunctory because to die of sickness is a sign of the spirits' favour and ensures a comfortable hereafter in the bowels of the earth. Doctor Jouin had the greatest difficulty in persuading the

Moïs to accept any kind of medical treatment, as they pointed out to him that he wanted to deprive them of the chance of a 'good' death, exposing them therefore, when cured, to the possibility of a 'bad' death by accident or violence. Such a 'bad' death condemns the ghost to wander in eternal wretchedness in the heavens.

Lepers are regarded as having been born under a lucky star, as they do no work, are fed by the tribe, and are certain of an exemplary end.

The death rites, on the contrary, are prolonged over two years and are so costly that a single death may exhaust the equivalent of the village income for one month, whereas an epidemic, by causing it to use up in sacrifices the whole of its reserves, is certain to bring starvation in its train.

In arranging their ceremonies the Moïs pay great attention to the type of death the defunct has suffered. There are specially compli-cated and expensive rites for those who have died from various kinds of violence, who have died in a foreign country, have disappeared and are presumed dead, for young children, lunatics, and, of course, for women dead in childbirth who are believed to turn into revengeful demons. The village is surrounded by open tombs, the occupants of which are 'fed' daily and kept informed of all family affairs.

From the sheer multiplicity of the rites, all of which require alcoholic consumption, the intriguing side-issue emerges that respect-ability and drunkenness are allied. The upright man gives evidence of his ritual adequacy by being drunk as often as possible, he is respected by all for his piety, a pattern held up to youth. The words *nam lu* uttered in grave welcome to the stranger in a Moï village, and meaning let us get drunk together, have all the exhortatory value of an invitation to common prayer. Moï villages are said to be one of the few places in the world where the domestic animals, dogs, pigs, and hens, having fed in the fermented mash from the sacred jars, are to be seen in a state of helpless intoxication. Conviviality is the rule; a norm of polite conduct. Passers-by are begged to join in Moï orgies of eating and drinking and it is bad taste – that is offensive to the spirits – to eat or drink less than is provided by the fearsome liberality of the hosts. To prevent any possibility of the visitor's unwittingly committing this kind of discourtesy, or remaining in a state of disreputable sobriety, an attendant squats at his side keeping a careful check on his consumption and ensuring that he drinks at least the minimum measure of three cow's horns.

The other aspect of the Moï way of life that seems to have created the greatest impression upon those who have studied them is that, although, by occidental standards, crimes are few, the conceptions of right and wrong seem to be quite incomprehensible to them. In their place, and incidentally governing conduct by the most rigid standards, are the notions of what is expedient and what is inexpedient. The Moï is concerned rather with policy than justice. Piety and fervour have no place in his ritual observations. Contrition is meaningless. There is no moral condemnation in Moï folklore of those who commit anti-social acts.

All this as well as the elaborate ceremonials accompanied by their ritual drunkenness is explained by the Moï conception of a universe dominated by a number of powerful spirits who, together with the manes of their own ancestors, control their destinies. The relationship is a contractual one; the spirits and the manes appearing rather in the light of strict and exacting creditors. Broadly speaking there is nothing either particularly benevolent or hostile in the attitude of these ghostly autocrats towards their human feudatories. All they claim are their just debts – the ceremonies. No more and no less than these. As long as they are scrupulously paid, all goes well with the individual, the family, and the tribe. Drought or deluge, 'the bad death', epidemics – in fact, misfortunes of all kinds – are merely indications that the rites have been violated, and the only remedy lies in finding the offender, and compelling him to put the matter right by providing the prescribed reparation.

The view taken of human conduct and its effects is totally opposed to the religious teachings of the West, which accept that the wicked man prospers and that the moral debts of those who break all but the eleventh commandment are settled in another existence. Among the Moïs retribution is swift and terrestrial. The wicked – that is, the ritually negligent man – is quickly ruined. If he continues to pile up spiritual debts he is certain of a sudden death – the invariable sign that the ghostly creditors, becoming impatient, have claimed his soul for non-payment.

The thing works out in practice much better than one might expect. Crimes against the individual, such as theft or violence, are viewed as contravening the rites due to the plaintiff's ancestral manes. The aggressor, however, is seen as no more than the instrument of one of the spirits who has chosen this way to punish the victim for some ritual inadequacy. The judge, therefore, reciting in verse the appropriate passage of common law, abstains from stern moralization. Both sides are in the wrong, and rather illogically, it seems, the aggressor is sentenced to make material reparation and also – what is regarded as far more important – to provide the animals and liquor necessary for the ritual reparation to be paid to the offended spirits. The ritual reparation, of course, takes priority, and in cases of hardship may be paid for in instalments. The offender is compelled by law to take part in this feast which provides as a secondary function the means of reconciliation of the two parties.

There is no distinction among the Moïs between civil and criminal law and no difference is made between intentional and unintentional injury. If a man strikes another in a fit of temper or shoots him accidentally while out hunting, it is all the work of the spirits and the payment to be made has already been laid down. No eyebrows are lifted. It is just another human misfortune to be settled by a drinking bout at which the whole village gets tipsy. The Moïs do not apply the death penalty, since otherwise the community would expose itself to the vengeance of the ghost of the executed man. Two of the greatest crimes are the theft of water and of rice, which are under the protection of powerful spirits. Owing to the sacrilegious nature of such an offence, which exposes the community to the resentment of the spirits involved, the offender in this case is banished for life.

The white colonist, in his treatment of the Moïs, has been at once both sentimental and predatory. The smaller administrators, disinterested – since they have nothing to lose whether the Moïs work or not – tend to regard them as delightful children. An outstanding example of this attitude was the celebrated Sabatier who refused to allow missionaries in his territory, had the bridges demolished when he heard that a high official was on his way to investigate the labour problem, and is said to have married three Moï wives.

After seeing the first effects of white encroachment in the Moï country, he went even further than this, advocating complete withdrawal and allowing the Moïs to live their lives in their own way. But the government found it impossible to refrain from meddling, from suppressing tribal warfare, judging, counting, taxing, and above all – and fatally – making labour compulsory for the requirements of Europeans. It was the action of the planters who were determined to have labour for their plantations that defeated Sabatier.

The planters are a very small group of men; a few families who possess Indo-China's richest fortunes. Their attitude towards the Moïs is probably identical with that of any of the old slave-owning aristocracies towards the producers of their wealth. It is one of utter contempt, without which effective exploitation would probably be impossible. In the past they have employed labour recruiters, paying high premiums for each man who could be induced or tricked into signing on for three or five years – a period of indenture which the labourer rarely survived. Coolies were kept under armed guard and thrashings were liberally administered. Sometimes they were re-sold and transported to the Pacific Islands. Recent attempts to temper these conditions have met with the most resolute opposition, the planters asking, pertinently as they believe, what after all is the purpose of a colony?

Thus the conflict between administrator and planter continues, and whatever mitigations of the Moïs' lot may have taken place, the principle of compulsion persists. For the privilege of having the white newcomers in his country each adult male pays a tax in rice and must give up a number of days annually for labour on the plantations or roads. It is the infringement of the Moï's liberty which is the fundamental vexation. For fifty days he is prevented from performing the rites, therefore compromising him heavily with the spirits, who demand to be repaid. There enters also the factor that in a finely balanced economy the loss to him and his family of this amount of time may make the difference between sufficiency and ruin. Moï society recalls that of Islam or the pre-Columbian civilization of America in that every action of the individual from birth to death is rigidly controlled. It is a tightly unified system which has shown itself fairly successful in dealing with the internal life of the tribe, but brittle and without resistance to external shock. Moï customary law and the rites deal with every eventuality, and take into account every situation but one. The Moï has not been permitted the initiative to meet an attack from an unexpected quarter. If someone offends the village's tutelary spirit, the thing can be put right without much trouble. But if a timber-cutting company with a concession comes along and cuts down the banyan tree that contains the spirit, and takes it away, what is to be done? It is the end of the world.

CHAPTER EIGHT

Darlac

THE WHOLE DISTRICT of the Dak Lac is seen as if through dark glasses. There is not a great deal of colour. It is a study in smoky blues, greens, and white. The light has a cool Nordic quality and the lake itself is an Icelandic *vatyn* with the mountain reflections blurred in the dim sparkle of the frosted surface. The islands seem edged with ice, but this edging is a packed fringe of egrets and when an eagle drops among them the ice dissolves as the egrets rise, to reform again as they settle. One's views of the lake seem always to be obtained through the spare branches of the frangipani or the *lilas de Japon* – negligent brushstrokes on silk, with a sparse adornment of white blossom.

In the morning the mountains float above a cauldron of mist in which islands slowly materialize, and along the near shore, below the administrator's bungalow, the topmost branches of the trees are elegantly supported upon layers of vapour. Later the scene solidifies and the lake is seen to be encircled by mountains, covered to their peaks by a tight webbing of jungle. The water's edge is feathered by bamboos. As the sun drops in the sky, its light is no longer reflected from the moss-like sheath of vegetation on the distant highlands which, instead of glowing with yellow light, as they would in northern climes, turn to the darkest of smoky blue. Fishing eagles turning against this dark background show their white underparts and the end of their dive is marked by a fountain rising from the water. At this hour the butterflies appear and fly down to the lake. They are black, slashed with lemon, and as big as bats. Egrets pass in drifts on their way to roost. The last movement is a curved line of cranes, with black, heraldic silhouettes against the darkening sky. All day and all through the night the cool sound of gongs comes over the water from unseen Moï villages.

The administrator's bungalow was built on a prominence by the lake's verge. Standing on the balcony you could look down at the groups of white herons mincing through the shallows beneath, and flapping their wings in a sudden flurry of panic to free themselves from the entangling weeds just below the surface. The bungalow was surrounded by a defensive pallisade and there was an inner belt planted with sharpened staves, their foot-long protruding points hidden in the grass. Below was a military post with a few Moï conscripts. The post stands at the head of a pass guarding the way to Ban Méthuot. At the other – the eastern end – of the winding, marshy valley is the coastal town of Nha Trang. But long before Nha Trang, and not very far, in fact, from the post at Dak Lac, are the first outposts of the Viet-Minh. Up to the present the Viet-Minh have not troubled to come up into the mountains. But one day my friends supposed they would and when they did it would certainly be up that valley, where every morning we could hear the schools of monkeys howling at the dawn.

Apart from the huts the Moï guards and their families lived in, there was only one other human habitation in sight. This was the Emperor's new shooting box, in the process of completion, which crowned a pinnacle still higher than that of the administrator's bungalow. It was less than imperial in style; a cubic structure of vaguely Germanic inspiration. There was more of the pill-box than the pleasure-dome about it, and unconscious reflection, perhaps, of the unhappy times. A steam-roller – a truly amazing apparition in such an environment – was flattening the surface of a well-laid asphalt road leading to the summit when I visited the site. It had been chosen, they said, so that His Majesty, when not actually hunting, could have the satisfaction of watching herds of wild elephants from his windows. On the occasion when I made free with the imperial view-point, it goes without saying that there were no elephants to be seen.

My friends at the post were Ribo, the administrator, and Cacot, an inspector of schools, who was spending a short holiday with him.

Ribo had one hundred and eighteen Moï villages, with a population of about twenty thousand, under his jurisdication. Both of these young men were well under thirty, genial, expansive, optimistic by temperament and pessimistic by conviction. The post turned out to be not only an outpost of French colonial domination but of existentialism. On my first evening there, after a full-scale French dinner, with two wines and a liqueur, I was expected to make an intelligent contribution to a discussion on Marcel Aymé's *Le Confort Intellectuel* which had just arrived from Le Club Français du Livre.

Before this, however, we went out shooting on the lake in a Moï pirogue. The pirogue was very long and narrow. To avoid upsetting it, it was necessary to sit or crouch perfectly still in whatever position one elected to adopt. Cacot, whose intellectual pessimism never extended to such matters as hunting, proposed to return with the pirogue's bottom covered with duck, but I was beginning to realize by this time that this kind of luck was not to be expected when I formed one of a hunting party.

The pirogue slid over the water, its rounded bottom stroking the matted aquatic plants that lay just below the surface. The mountains had now put on their featureless mantle of dusky blue and brilliant white clouds bulged up from behind them. Swallows kept us company, zigzagging around us, and eagles wheeled in the sky. Large fish jumped occasionally and brought fishing hawks swooping over their position. A village somewhere was playing the gongs – two slow and four fast beats repeated over and over again.

The Moï spotted a large number of duck, lying like a heavy pencil-line, drawn near the lake's horizon. Cacot became very enthusiastic and suggested that we should go crocodile hunting after dinner. He thought we might get a few deer, too, while we were about it. The Moï was manœuvring the pirogue towards the duck, taking advantage of the cover provided by the islands and the reeds. We cut lanes through the lotus-beds spreading from the islands and this slowed us up. Cacot could not see the necessity for this, as he said that no one ever went shooting on the lake, so the birds would be tame. We were within about a hundred yards of them when they took off, with a twittering noise, like a flock of frightened finches.

They were ferruginous ducks, which I only knew from illustrations. There were about two hundred of them and curiosity was their undoing because the whole flight suddenly turned towards us and passed over our heads, with Ribo and Cacot blazing away at them. Several of them dropped like stones into the lake, but the weeds were so thick that we only picked up one that fell by the pirogue. It was a handsome reddish-brown bird, a little smaller than a mallard, with slate-blue bill and legs. We nosed about the lake for another hour but the ducks would never let us get anywhere near them again. Cacot said that he thought that the Emperor had been shooting there.

Determined to go home with some sort of a bag he now concentrated on the only other birds on the lake which he thought might be edible. These were isolated black-winged stilts, elegant and fragile-looking, which, seeming never to have come under fire before, let us get within a few yards of them. Cacot shot several. They were very tenacious of life and, although severely damaged at close range, dived and remained below the surface for so long a time that it seemed as if they were determined to drown rather than be captured. They were found with great difficulty by the Moï, groping about among the under-water weeds. In flavour they were much inferior to duck.

After supper we went out hunting in Ribo's jeep. Fortunately Cacot had been talked out of the crocodile shooting expedition on the grounds that we should all get malaria in the swamps. Cacot had a powerful light, like a miner's lamp, attached to his forehead, carrying the battery in a haversack. We drove along one of the Emperor's private hunting tracks and Cacot turned his head from side to side trying to pick up a reflection from the eyes of game. Finally this happened. Five pairs of luminous pin-pricks shone in the depths of a clearing, belonging, Cacot whispered hoarsely, to deer. Jumping down from the jeep he plunged into the long grass, the beam of light jerking and wavering in front of him. At the end of the glade the deer could finally be made out, awaiting his coming, heads and necks above the grass, immobile as dummies in a shooting gallery. The light steadied, there was a red flash and charging echoes. The deer's going was not to be seen. The clearing was suddenly emptied. Cacot came back and got into the jeep, saying that he was feeling tired. On the way home he brought down a small skunk-like animal with a long difficult shot. It had coarse, bristly fur, which Cacot seemed to think was of some value. After it had lain in the garage under the bungalow for a day it began to stink and the driver was told to bury it.

That night I was awakened by a prolonged slithering sound in the room, followed by a click. It was not a loud sound by any means but there was a suggestion of danger about it, which evidently impressed the subconscious mind. There was no electric light and it did not seem a very good idea to me to get up and look for the matches, because although I could not account for the click the slithering sound corresponded in my imagination to the noise a large snake would make in crossing the floor. I, therefore, lay quietly under the mosquito net, which I hoped would prove a deterrent to any exploratory reptile. The sound was repeated several times and then stopped. I went to sleep.

Almost immediately, it seemed, I was awakened by a truly hideous outcry, very definitely in the room and coming from a point not more than six feet from where I lay. This was a gurgling peal of ghastly hilarity, ending in the cry *jeck-o* repeated several times. Although in the stillness of the night I ascribed this to some kind of predatory monster, it turned out next morning to be no more than the house's tutelary jecko lizard, a large and repulsive monster of its kind which liked to lurk during the daytime in an angle of the bookcase, switching its tail angrily over the volumes of Jean-Paul Sartre. The jecko, it seems, is only dangerous to the extent that it defends itself vigorously when attacked and is regarded as fateful by the Vietnamese who draw auguries from the number of times it repeats the concluding bi-syllable of its call.

I was never able to account for the slither and the click.

The sun was well up when we drove out next morning. Out of respect for the conventions of the country there had been some talk of making a dawn start, but many civilized delays had spun out the time. It was a genial morning. We dropped down the spiral road past the shore of the lake, which was still peeling off its layers of mist. There were a few Moïs out fishing in their pirogues, floating, it seemed, in suspension. Moïs were pottering about in the streams running down to the lake, setting fish-traps or washing out their kitchen pots – a job they were very particular about.

Our path was beaten across fairly open country. There were rice-fields on both sides, but the rice had been harvested a month or two before and now they were deserted except for buffaloes mooching about looking for mud-holes, and a few storks. The Moïs, who had nothing much to occupy themselves with at this season, were wandering about trying to find some way of using up the time between one drinking bout and the next. There were families sauntering along the path who looked as if they intended to walk a mile or two until they found a suitable spot for a picnic. The mother would be carrying a fat section of bamboo, with the food packed inside, while the father had a jar of rice alcohol slung on his back. The children ran about loosing off their crossbows unsuccessfully at any small birds they happened to see.

We passed fishing parties, organized *pour le sport* more than with serious intent, since a little effort was diluted with much horseplay. The method in favour was for a number of persons to stir up the water of a stream or pool until it became thoroughly muddy and presumably confusing to the fish. Then they stabbed into it at random with a kind of harpoon shaped like a bottle but much larger and made of wicker, with a sharp circular edge at its open bottom. Both sexes took part and the fishing provided an excuse for endless practical jokes, involving duckings. These people were M'nongs, belonging to the same tribal group as those I had seen at Dak-Song, and one of the main divisions of the Moïs, who occupy a large, vague area to the south of Ban Méthuot. They are supposed to be slightly less advanced than the Rhadés whose territory begins a few miles away to the north and who are the strongest and most numerous of the Moï tribes. You could always distinguish the M'nongs by the large ivory cylinders they wore in their earlobes. The ones who still lived by hunting and, occasionally, raiding were supposed to carry poison for their arrows in one of these hollow cylinders and the antidote in the other.

We stopped at the village of Buon Dieo where there was a new school to be inspected, one of the five in the territory. At a distance Buon Dieo looked like an anthropologist's scale model in an exhibition, a perfect example of a village in some remote and unspoilt South-Seas civilization. It was all so well ordered that one expected to find litter baskets, and notices saying 'a place for everything and everything in its place'. There was not a scrap of refuse nor a bad smell in the village. If the long-houses had been a tenth part of their size you could have described them as arty and crafty, with their technical-institute pattern of woven bamboo walls. And the clean, new images at the head of the step-ladders up to the houses, the geometrical patterns on the well-scrubbed sacrificial posts and the strings of dangling figures cut out of paper. It was all so much of an exhibit – rather too clean and lifeless – the ideal M'nong village arranged for the benefit of visiting students. But the scale of the thing saved it and made it real. That and the seven thousand foot peaks of the Annamite Chain that formed the background. Some of the best *cases* were a good sixty yards long. The village was lifeless because the people were keeping out of sight until the chief could be brought, and the chief was hastily putting on the European sports-shirt he wore as a badge of authority.

The chief of Buon Dieo had the sad, old, wizened face of a highly successful Levantine shopkeeper with a tendency to stomach ulcers. Besides his sports-shirt he wore a dark-blue turban, a loincloth beautifully woven with a fine design of stylized flowers, and an ornament in the form of a pair of tweezers suspended from a chain worn round his neck. Ribo had visited the chief only a few days before, so that it was hoped that the ceremonial forms to be gone through would be much less involved than usual. We first visited the school which the whole village had combined to build in ten days. Ribo said that you only had to appeal to the Moïs' imagination to get them enthusiastic over a project, to make them believe that it had their spirits' approval, for them to be filled with this kind of

Stakhanovite fervour. One of the villagers, who had been in the army and was therefore considered a man of culture, would give three days a week as a teacher. The school had just been inaugurated with the sacrifice of a buffalo and there were a few gnawed bones lying about on the floor. Ribo's severe criticism of this seemed to me unfair in this model village from a colonial exhibition. In embellishment of the otherwise bare classrooms were several posters of Monte Carlo.

The commonroom of the chief's house was furnished with impressive simplicity. There were benches round the walls, carved out of some ebony-like wood, and clean rush matting on the floor. There was such a complete absence of household odds and ends that one had the impression of his wife going round tidying up after each visit. The principal objects were a battery of gongs of various sizes together with several drums, the largest of which, a massive affair hung with bells, the chief said was worth at least ten buffaloes. Not, of course, that he would ever think of selling it, in view of its sentimental associations. It had been in his wife's family for several generations, and was only struck on occasions of great solemnity such as the appearance of a comet. The main beams of the house were sparingly decorated with what upon inspection proved to be advertisements and cartoons cut from French and American illustrated journals.

There were seven jars attached to a framework in the centre of the room and as soon as the chief's sons-in-law had arrived and hung up their crossbows on the beam over the adventures of Dick Tracy, they were sent off with bamboo containers to the nearest ditch for water. In the meanwhile the seals of mud were removed from the necks of the jars and rice-straw and leaves were forced down inside them over the fermented rice-mash to prevent solid particles from rising when the water was added. The thing began to look serious and Ribo asked the chief, through his interpreter, for the very minimum ceremony to be performed as we had other villages to visit that day. The chief said that he had already understood that, and that was why only seven jars had been provided. It was such a poor affair that he hardly liked to have the gongs beaten to invite the household god's presence. He hoped that by way of compensation he would be given sufficient notice of a visit next time to enable him to arrange a reception on a proper scale. He would guarantee to lay us all out for twenty-four hours.

This being the first of what I was told would be an endless succession of such encounters in the Moï country I was careful to study the details of the ceremony. Although these varied in detail from village to village, the essentials remained the same. The gong-orchestra starts up a deafening rhythm. You seat yourself on a stool before the principal jar, in the centre, take the bamboo tube in your mouth and do your best to consume the correct measure of three cow-horns full of spirit. Your attendant, who squats, facing you, on the other side of the jar, has no difficulty in keeping a check on the amount drunk, since the level is never allowed to drop below the top of the jar, water being constantly added from a small hole in the side of the horn, on which he keeps his thumb until the drinking begins. After you have finished with the principal jar, you move to the right of the line and work your way down. There is no obligatory minimum consumption from the secondary jars. At frequent inter- vals you suck up the spirit to the mouth of the tube and then, your thumb held over the end, you present it to one of the dignitaries present, who, beaming his thanks, takes a short suck and hands it back to you. In performing these courtesies you are warned to give priority to those whose loincloths are the most splendid, but if, in this case, the apparel oft proclaims the man, age is a more certain criterion with the women.

The M'nongs are matriarchal and it is to the relatively aged and powerful mothers-in-law that all property really belongs. Although the women hold back for a while and it is left to the men to initiate the ceremonies, the rice-alcohol, the jars, the gongs, the drums, and the house itself are all theirs. It is, therefore, not only a mark of exquisite courtesy but a tactful recognition of economic realities to gesture as soon as possible with one's tube in the direction of the most elderly of the ladies standing on the threshold of the common- room. With surprising alacrity the next stool is vacated by its occupying notable to allow the true power in the house with a gracious and impeccably toothless smile to take her place. This toothlessness, of course, has no relation to the lady's great age and arises from the fact that the incisors are regarded by the Moïs as unbearably canine in their effect and are, therefore, broken out of the jaws at the age of puberty.

The chief's wife at Buon Dieo possessed, in spite of her years, a firm and splendid figure. She wore a gay sarong, probably obtained from a Cambodian trader, and in the intervals of drinking smoked a silver-mounted pipe. Her ceremonial demeanour was slow and deliberate as befitting her station and it was some time before the wife of another dignitary could be invited with propriety to join the party. A small group of these awaited their turn and at their backs hovered a row of solemn, Gauguinesque beauties, the chief's daughters, whose husbands, if any, being of no account in the social hierarchy of the tribe, had been sent about their business while such important matters were being treated. No more than seven or eight leaders of Buon Dieo society separated us from these bronze Venuses, but each one would have to be entertained with protracted urbanity.

With a great effort, the two or three dowagers were disposed of, and we were down to the nursing-mothers, who, removing their babies from the breast and passing them to onlookers, tripped lightly towards us. Although the rice-alcohol, with its queer burnt-cereal taste, was weaker than usual, my friends said, it was beginning to take effect. The Moïs had slipped into an easy-going joviality and the nursing-mothers received some mild familiarities, for which they exchanged good-natured slaps. Their capacity for alcohol, though, was greater than that of the elder ladies, and they were not to be deceived by a mere pretence of drinking on our part. Calling for beakers they sucked up the alcohol, spat libations, syphoned off liquor until the beakers were filled, and presented them to us. Taking stock of the situation we saw that we had drunk our way to within two nursing-mothers of those perfect young representatives of the Polynesian race, the chief's daughters, who flung us occasional glances from between sweeping lashes. But we were all flagging, dizzy with the alcohol and the stunning reverberation of the gongs. And the morning was wearing on. It would have been difficult to imagine our condition by the time we had drunk our way down to an interesting social level. The Moïs encouraged us with smiles and gestures, but we could do no more.

It was at a village in the vicinity of Buon Dieo where two years previously an extraordinary affair had taken place. A family of eight persons were suspected of magic practices to the detriment of the village. According to local custom a representative was chosen as accuser and a trial by ordeal arranged. This consisted of the villagers' champion and the head of the accused family plunging their heads under water, the first to withdraw his head, in this case the accused, being held to have lost the day. According to the rulings of customary law governing this rather unusual case the charged persons were found to be possessed by certain minor demons, located in each case in a bodily organ. The general attitude thus was a sympathetic one. The prisoners were regarded as dangerously sick and only curable by the removal of the affected organ. After this was done they would be once more regarded as entirely normal members of society. The fact that death quickly followed the operations was entirely incidental and most sincerely regretted by all concerned. This was all the more so since the eight were regarded as having, quite accidentally, died the 'bad' death and therefore certain to be converted into revengeful ghouls unless propitiated by the most costly sacrifices, spread over a period of two years. In conformity with this obligation every animal in the village was soon slaughtered and the rice reserves converted into alcohol. The villagers then borrowed from neighbouring communities until their credit was completely exhausted, after which they settled down to starve.

It was at this point that the affair reached the administrator's ears. As a result eight of the principals in the case were tried in the French court and received thirty years apiece. No Moï, of course, could ever understand the justice of this, and it would be impossible to convince him that the appalling fate of the prisoners, all praiseworthy men in their eyes, is anything more than the revenge of the spirits of the eight who died. It is because their sacrifices were insufficient. If only their resources hadn't given out, all would have been well. And there is something in the last suggestion, because it was only the exhaustion of the food supplies that caused the administrator to hear about the affair.

Beyond the model villages of the M'nong R'lams lay the country of the less evolved M'nong Gars. The villages of the M'nong Gars were built along the banks of the Krong Kno in the shallows of which the villagers seemed to spend most of their day bathing or inspecting and re-setting their fish-traps. The Krong Kno was a swift, yellow current, divided by sandbanks on which unconcerned M'nong Circes sat in groups, arranging their tresses.

Buon Ročai, where Ribo had business, had been the headquarters of a well-known French anthropologist, who had been determined to live as a M'nong, eschewing all the aids of Western civilization. Some time before our visit he had been reduced by various maladies, including beri-beri, to a condition when he could no longer walk, and the M'nongs, foreseeing the possibility of having to arrange the expensive burial ceremonies prescribed when a stranger dies in the village, got a message through to Ban Méthuot, asking for him to be taken away. He seemed to have been well liked. The hut in which he had lived for a number of months had been declared taboo and everything in it was exactly as he had left it. The table was still littered with the papers he had been working on, with his fountain pen lying among them. There was an uncorked bottle of French gin, a miniature camera, and several films. Ribo said that he used to exchange legends with the M'nongs and that their favourite was the story of Ulysses and the Sirens which much resembled one of their own, dating from the days when their ancestors, contemporaries perhaps of the Homeric Greeks, had been a seafaring people. In this village there were several sufferers from *tukalau*, a fungoid disease of the skin only found in Polynesia and among certain South American tribes. The M'nong Gar long-houses were not raised on posts like all those we had seen until now.

At Buon Ročai we were joined by the chief of a canton of M'nong

Gar villages. He was importantly dressed in a thick black coat, a vest, and carpet slippers, worn over several pairs of woollen socks. A Turkish towel was wound, boating-style, round his neck, and to complete this ensemble – which did not include trousers – he wore a ten-gallon cowboy hat with a chin-strap. The chief's face was stamped with the rodent expression of an Oriental who has had too much to do with Europeans. He smiled frequently showing a row of gums that had been badly damaged in a too-conscientious effort to remove all the evidence of teeth. The chief was evidently not a man to be afraid of ghosts, as according to Ribo he had committed two murders, but was too valuable for administrative purposes to be put out of circulation – an unusual concession to expediency in so stern a moralist as Ribo.

It was decided to stop next at Buon Lê Bang, where the anthropologist's fiancée lived, so that Cacot, who would shortly be passing through Saigon on his way back to France, could call at the hospital with news of her. When we arrived the village was in the middle of a ceremony. A buffalo had been sacrificed that morning and now bleeding collops of flesh, complete with hide and hair, were hanging up all over the village. Brillat-Savarins were industriously engaged in chopping up meat and compounding it with various herbs, according to their secret recipes. Frameworks had been put up outside all the houses on which brilliant red strips, attached at regular intervals, were drying like chilli peppers in the sun. Scintillating, metallic looking flies spiralled about them.

The villagers were in a hilarious state. They had already been at the alcohol for four or five hours and there was a deafening clamour of gongs from the principal house. The ceremonial stiffness had long since worn off and we were assailed on all sides with offerings of raw meat and alcohol in Bakelite cups. We went into the common house, in which, until they had outgrown it numerically, the whole village had lived. There was none of the strict division here of the M'nong R'lams, with the partitioned-off family apartments which it was incorrect to enter, and the commonroom, with its neatly arranged ceremonial objects, where the visitors were received. This, instead, was a low, single chamber, perhaps fifty yards in length, lit by the two entrance apertures at each end, and a certain amount of light that filtered through the woven bamboo walls. The space occupied by each family was marked off by the formal arrangement of the family's possessions. This was applied even to the cooking pots, suspended from the wall, each in its place and exactly level with the neighbour's identical cooking pot. The jars, too, formed unbroken ranks from one end of the house to the other. It was an astonishing display of a passion for order, which had arisen, apparently, from the exigencies of sharing the limited available space. One imagined some senior personality, in the role of orderly officer, running his eye along the line of pots on his daily tour of inspection, with a critical frown for the occasional improperly folded blanket.

Cacot asked to see the anthropologist's fiancée and she was instantly produced along with a couple of young relations. She was a splendid creature with large black eyes and a deep yellow, but by no means unpleasing, complexion. The removal of her teeth had been clumsily done, resulting in permanently swollen gums and a slight displacement of the top lip. Although slightly tipsy she managed to retain a pleasantly demure manner and many Bakelite cups had to pass from hand to hand before she could be persuaded to raise her eyes. The two younger Gauguin models sat twisting their hands, heads averted, and faces, as far as one could see, masked with fright, having quite sobered up under the effect of our terrifying presence. It appeared that the all-powerful old women of the tribe were sufficiently drunk by now not to require propitiation, so Cacot asked without more formality if any of the girls were available for marriage. The fathers immediately appeared, clearly delighted. Both the younger girls were ready at any time, and their mothers would pay a high price in jars and gongs for approved sons-in-law. Unfortunately the older girl was already promised. In the case of a good-looking girl like that the competition was bound to be strenuous, and no wonder a European had fallen for her. Being a divorcee, the father pointed out, she was exceptionally well off, as, according to law, she had kept all her husband's property when he had left her home. Cacot said he would decide on the younger of the remaining pair and marry her, with a holocaust of buffaloes, when he came back from France. He gave the girl a few promissory pats about the torso, and she did a painful best to look pleased. Whether this was taken seriously or not, I don't know. Probably not. The Moïs enjoy leg-pulling as much as anybody else.

After leaving Buon Lê Bang we were on the Emperor's new hunting track. Moïs were hacking this out of the virgin forest with implements that looked like garden hoes. They were paid six piastres a day, the piastre being worth fourpence officially, or about three-halfpence on the blackmarket, and they were lucky to be able to work off their fifty days, compulsory labour in this way and not on a plantation. When this road was finished, the Emperor would be able to drive in his specially fitted-up jeep, with a wooden platform built up, throne-like, in the back, right into the heart of what is supposed to be the richest hunting country in the world.

It was a mysterious landscape with mountains like thunder-clouds threatening from the horizon. Clumps of bamboo spurted up from low, boiling vegetation. For the first time I saw the miracle of a peacock in flight, that Cacot fired at hopelessly, soaring with trailing plumage to the very top of a fern-swathed tree. The country was over-run with tigers and all the M'nongs' stories were of them. Local wizards were reputed to specialize in tiger-taming and obtained their hold upon the villagers by allowing themselves to be seen riding upon the back of a muzzled tiger. Ribo was quite convinced that this took place; but even the most unimaginative European becomes infected with local credences in such places as this. There were a thousand inadvertent ways, too, of calling up a tiger, always ready, it seemed, to appear, like an uncomplaisant genie at the rubbing of ring or lamp. Most solecisms and lapses of table manners were reputed to have this unfortunate effect. It was particularly disastrous to scrape rice from a pot with a knife. Ribo said that the prestige of the tiger and their supposed human accomplices had risen so high that the M'nongs were becoming afraid to hunt them. After a recent hunt in which the tiger was killed, all the dogs who had taken part were found dead next day. Poisoned by a sorcerer, he thought. It was two of these tiger-men that the *Chef de Canton* had done away with. There was something curiously symbolical about the victory of this puny creature in his collection of cast-off Western clothes against the men in the tiger-skins.

The last village reached that day was Buon Choah, belonging to a small and exceptionally interesting tribe called the Bihs. When Doctor Jouin had visited the valley, two years before, they still retained their ancient burial customs which, he said, were identical with those of the Hovas of Madagascar. For two years the dead were exposed in open coffins in the trees. After that the bones were taken down and thoroughly cleaned, and before final burial, the skull was carried round the fields by an old woman of the family, and offerings were made to it. Doctor Jouin's photograph of the elevated coffin, which he needed for a book on Moï funeral customs, had been destroyed during the Japanese occupation and I promised to take another for him. But I was too late. In the two years since Jouin had been there American evangelical missionaries had been to the village, persuaded the Bihs to give up such customs, and by way of giving something in exchange had taught one of the village boys to play the harmonium.

We had been spotted on the outskirts of Buon Choah and by the time we walked into the village an extraordinary spectacle was taking place. Women were scrambling in lines down the step-ladders of the long-houses, like cadets coming down the rigging of a training ship. They then formed up in two rows – one on each side of the path, standing fairly smartly to attention. They wore white turbans and navy-blue calico blouses and skirts. The chief came hurrying to meet us, carrying under his arm a copy in English of the Gospel of St Mark and the usual diploma awarded for meritorious service to the Japanese.

Ribo and Cacot seemed faintly displeased and said something to the chief, nodding in the direction of the women. The chief snapped out a word of command and the blouses began to come off. When the women weren't being quick enough, the chief and the heads of families shouted at them in stern reproof. In a few seconds the reception parade was ready and we made our way to the chief's house between two score or so of freely displayed Balinese torsos. I believe that Ribo and Cacot thought that the blouses, too, were the work of the pastor, and felt that the moment had come to draw the line.

At Cêo-Rêo, not far from Buon Choah, are located the villages of those enigmatic personages, the Sadets, of Fire and Water, whose fearsome reputation is widespread throughout Indo-China. It is astonishing to realize that from the remotest antiquity the Kings of Champa, Laos, and Cambodia – that is, the temporal powers between which Indo-China was divided – all paid tribute to the formidable spiritual authority of these two poor Jarai tribesmen.

The Sadet of Fire is the guardian of a fabulous sword; a primitive, crudely hewn blade, according to report, which is kept wrapped in cotton rags. The mere act of half drawing this weapon – to which the aforementioned kingdoms all lay claim – would be sufficient to plunge the whole of living creation into a profound slumber; while to draw it completely would cause the world to be devoured by fire. Until the reign of the present king of Cambodia's grandfather, a caravan of elephants bearing rich presents was sent annually to the Sadet of Water.

Both the Sadets seem to be regarded as the incarnation of supernatural beings, possessing involuntary and apparently uncontrollable powers, which are malefic rather than benevolent. The Sadet of Water is associated, in some obscure way, with epidemics, and is a kind of spiritual leper, surrounded with the most awesome taboos. When he travels through the country, shelters are specially erected for him outside the villages, and offerings are placed in them. Neither Sadet is allowed to die a natural death. As soon as one is considered to be mortally ill, he is dispatched by lance-thrusts, and a successor is chosen by divination from the members of his family. The mantle of this relinquished authority is said to be assumed with much reluctance by the person designated.

CHAPTER NINE

The Rhadés

NEXT MORNING we reached the country of the Rhadés, who are said to be the most advanced of the Moï tribes. Like all the others they are great talkers and topers and have the familiar self-depreciatory humour ('our women are the ugliest in the world'), but they have not yet been infected with that sense of doom, that listlessness in the face of threatened extinction that seems to beset most members of the animal species after they have passed a certain stage on the downhill path. It has also been found that the Rhadés will accept slight modifications in their way of living if such innovations can be represented to them as approved by the spirits.

Ribo had sent word calling the personalities of the village of Buon Plum to a palaver. Their village had been selected as the guinea-pig for the social experiment that was his pet project. The idea was to introduce agricultural innovations and anti-malarial measures. Buon Plum was to become a model village; an object lesson to all its neighbours, who, it was hoped, would be anxious to follow suit. That was how it went in theory. But it was clear that Ribo could not convince himself that it would really work out that way. There were so many factors to be taken into account; some, I thought, that as a French official he felt unable to specify. However, Ribo had gone so far as to persuade the people of Buon Plum to put in a great deal of work, clearing an area of forest and planting a communal orchard and vegetable garden. They were to plant maize and manioc, which they wouldn't know how to turn into alcohol. As a result, he hoped (but doubted), they would eat more and drink less. This time he was going to talk to them about anti-malarial measures.

We were met, outside the village, by the chief accompanied by the heads of families, each carrying leaves of tobacco and a small bowl containing cooked rice and an egg. It was correct to take a leaf of tobacco from each, and to symbolize acceptance of the food by touching the egg. The chief had the fine, pensive face and the curving nostrils and lips of the best type of Yemeni Arab. (Do anthropologists still go about taking cranial measurements and if so, what could they make of the diversity of the Moïs?)

The chief and his notables were all turned out in their best turbans, jackets, and loincloths. Every man held ready for inspection a Japanese diploma or a certificate of service with the French-raised militia. Ribo, alarmed by the formal atmosphere, decided to ask the chief, at this stage, for the ceremonies preceding the palaver to be cut to a strict minimum. The chief bowed gravely in agreement but pointed out that as a newcomer – myself – was present, a brief rite inviting the protection of the various spirits could not be avoided. Ribo shrugged his resignation and we accordingly went up into the commonroom of the chief's long-house, where my friend's pessimism deepened at the sight of the lined-up alcohol jars. The arrangement of the room was almost identical with that of the M'nong R'lams; the benches running round the walls, the battery of gongs, and the great buffalo-hide drums. On the beams, hung with leather shields, crossbows, and drinking-horns, were the art treasures I was coming to expect: a daringly sporting Vietnamese calendar showing a bathing beauty, a car-chassis oiling chart, a Tarzan cartoon.

At a sign from the chief I took up position on a stool opposite the principal jar but with my back to it. The gongs struck up but I could see nothing of what was happening, as all the activity was going on behind me. I was alone in the middle of the room facing a blank wall awaiting my formal presentation to the spirits before I could be allowed to join the ceremony. Someone came and stood behind me and began a low-voiced incantation, barely audible above the clangour of the gongs. I was told afterwards that this was the sorcerer, who had come in with a white cock, had bathed its feet in water, and was now waving it over my head. As soon as the incantation was complete the sorcerer turned me round on the stool and handed me the bamboo tube from the tall jar. At the same time the chief's wife, the only woman in the room, took a thin, open-ended copper bracelet from one of the jar handles and fastened it round my left wrist. This conferring on the welcome stranger of the copper bracelet must be a custom of extreme antiquity, since it is practised by Moï tribes all over Indo-China, most of which have lived in separation in historical times. It carries with it temporary tribal protection and a number of minor privileges, which vary in detail from village to village, such as the right to touch certain of the sacred drums. There is a fuller degree of initiation which is undertaken by some Europeans wishing to take part in the more closely guarded ceremonies such as those accompanying the removal of the front teeth at puberty. In this case the initiate pays for the sacrifice of a pig, and a little blood drawn from his foot is mixed in alcohol with that of the pig and drunk by all present. On such occasions a thicker bracelet is conferred, on which is engraved a secret mark. Further sacrifices are indicated by additional marks, the bracelet serving thus to record, for all to see, its wearer's services to the community, and is the equivalent on the spiritual level of the Japanese diploma or the French certificate of military service. Many Europeans are to be seen wearing half a dozen or so of the thinner bracelets. They are one of those mild affectations, like tying on the spare wheel of one's car with liana, which mark the old Indo-China hand.

Having by this time taken part in several Moï ceremonies, I was beginning to appreciate some of the fine points which at first I had overlooked. Thus, I had noticed that when beginning to drink from each fresh jar a polished ritualist like Ribo spat a libation through the loosely woven bamboo floor, doing so in a most grave and deliberate manner. Following this practice for the first time, I noticed that although the spiritual essence of the libation may have been accepted by the tutelary spirits, the physical presence was received with acclamation by eagerly guzzling ducks, which, attracted by the sound of the gongs, had marshalled themselves under the floor, directly beneath the jars. The row of notables seated opposite nodded benignly at this gracious performance. Their spirits were beginning to pick up, under the belief, probably, that a full-blown ceremony was going to develop after all. Attendants were hovering hopefully in the background with titbits of raw meat on bamboo skewers, and others who had been surreptitiously sent down to the river were now arriving with tubes full of water and waited in expectation of the order to top up fresh jars. The boys seated at the gongs were beating out a frenzied rhythm. But Ribo was looking at his watch, and as soon as the minimum three cows horns had been accounted for, he asked the chief for the palaver to begin.

The Moïs, in the way of most so-called primitive peoples, put themselves to great efforts to be polite to strangers. Although there was no doubt about the general disappointment at this breaking up of what had looked like being a good party, there was a great show of understanding of the importance of the occasion, and every village male able to attend was immediately sent for. Within a few minutes they were all lined up like a photographer's group along one wall of the commonroom, as earnest looking as theological students in the presence of a cardinal. Not an eye strayed in the direction of the jars from which the neglected drinking-tubes curved despondently. There was a dead silence and as soon as Ribo began to speak every man and boy was clearly straining his ears, although no one understood a word of French. It was curious that none of the matriarchs was present.

Ribo began with a familiar gambit. 'Tell them, Tuón,' he told the interpreter, 'that the spirits are angry with the Moï people. Tell them that when the people of Buon Plum were counted, twenty years ago, there were eighty-six adult males. Now there are forty.' Tuón put this into Rhadés and Ribo said that, although unable to speak the language, he understood it enough to know that the plain facts were being clothed in the poetic eloquence which the Rhadés, with their reverence for the spoken word, would expect of their administrator.

'The Rhadés will vanish from the Earth,' said Ribo, warming to his subject. 'The Annamites will come to Ban Méthuot as they came to Dalat. They will cultivate the rice-fields of the Rhadés and their dogs will scratch up the bones of the Rhadés' ancestors.' In a lugubrious voice Tuón rearranged this Jeremiad for local taste. The Arab-looking chief seemed depressed. Ribo belaboured his hearers shrewdly with threats of post-mortuary horrors unless they helped themselves before it was too late. 'Do you want to keep out the Annamites?' he asked. 'Do you want to keep the country for your children and grandchildren to be able to perform the rites for your spirits?' There was a brief roar of assent. Ribo explained that the only way this could be done was to increase their numbers by combating the malaria that was killing them off. This could be done by buying medicine and mosquito nets with the money earned by the sale of surplus fruit and vegetables. Was that agreed? It was. And would the chief see to it that the new wealth wouldn't be turned, as usual, into jars and gongs? The chief gave his word.

With this the palaver was at an end and we were about to go when the interpreter told us that a meal had been prepared for us. Among the Moïs it is disgracefully rude, and offensive to several powerful spirits, to refuse an offer of food. Such an offence would in theory be compoundable only with a sacrifice of alcohol. A great effort should also be made to eat all that is offered. Ribo was alarmed again. The Moïs are the most omnivorous race in the world, and he warned us that a delicate situation might arise if, for instance, we found ourselves served with a dish of the highly prized variety of maggots that are cultivated by some tribes for the table.

However, we underestimated the sophistication of the chief of Buon Plum. A rickety table and three chairs were carried into the commonroom. The first bowl arrived and we saw, with relief, that it contained only plain rice. There followed a dish of roasted wild poultry, and – a culinary surprise about the equal of being served an elaborate French sauce with one's fried fish in an English café – a saucer of *nuôc mâm*, the extract of fermented fish whose truly appalling odour is so strangely divorced from its flavour. There were ivory chopsticks provided and dainty Chinese bowls. The whole village in its undissolved photographer's group looked on in entranced silence. As we picked up our chopsticks the chief made a sign and one of their number came forward and began to play on a flute.

*

The interpreter Tuón was an *évolué*. This in Indo-China is the usual designation for one who has forsaken the customs of his or her race, dresses in European cast-offs, wears an habitually subservient expression, and is sometimes privileged, by way of compensation, to ride a bicycle. True to type, the evolved Tuón looked like a beachcomber, but perhaps his evolution was not complete, since he had not yet acquired a fawning smile. Ribo had noticed that some of the people of Buon Plum had been taking him aside, as it seemed, to discuss some private matter, and he asked what they had been saying. Tuón said evasively that they weren't pleased about something. Weren't pleased about what, Ribo insisted. About the people who had been sent to the plantation and hadn't come back, Tuón said. And what was to stop them, Ribo asked. If they had wanted to come back, they would have done so.

But Tuón grumbled in a most un-evolved manner. I was beginning to see him in a loincloth again. He was tactless enough to tell Ribo that the men were being kept by force on the plantation, and the villagers had told him that not only could they not carry on with the orchard and the vegetable garden, they would have to reduce the area of their rice-field if these men were not released. Ribo said that we would go to the plantation and look into the matter for ourselves.

Two days later, when on our way back to Ban Méthuot, the investigatory visit was paid. The plantation was one of a number in the country supplying rubber to manufacturers of motor-car tyres. It continues to prosper because of its location, where it is temporarily out of reach of the Viet-Minh, although the administrative buildings were burned down in an attack in 1946. Most of its competitors in the south have been put out of business by the desertion of their labour, or by their too close proximity to the fighting zones.

There was something feudal in the spaciousness of these great Romanic buildings of the plantation, a contemptuous patrician setting of extremes of grandeur and wretchedness. Crouching peons squatted in their rags at the foot of splendid stairways and humped bales of rubber in its various stages beneath colonnaded arches. The *colonus* was fetched from some central domestic lair, emerging to meet us through the kitchens. It was difficult to place his origin with any certainty although he was undoubtedly a European. He looked younger than he was and moved fussily in a perpetual effort to use up some of his too great store of vitality. He was dressed like a townsman, wore a talisman against the evil-eye on his wrist-strap, and a religious medal, which he sometimes fumbled with, suspended from a fine gold chain round his neck. I imagine that he lived in patriarchal intimacy with his family and his servants. He was probably abstemious, experienced intense, narrow loyalties, and was quite implacable. He smiled a great deal.

We were shown into a huge room, which the director probably disliked, and seated round a most elaborate cocktail cabinet. With the technique of a cabaret tart the director poured out large shots of whisky for us, serving himself with what was probably a little coloured water. Two henchmen came in and sat down; enormous, pink-faced fellows who mopped their faces, and, in imitation of their chief, smiled incessantly. They were like the pictures one has seen of trusties in an American penitentiary, and there was something about their inarticulate and rather sinister good humour that provided a perfect foil for the dapper geniality of the director.

Ribo asked if that month's renewal contracts had been prepared for the men who would be working another year. The director said they had. Good, Ribo said, in that case they could now be signed in his presence. The Italian said they had been signed already. How was that, Ribo asked, when he had made it most clear that he wanted to be present at the signing. The director was charming, repentant, conciliatory. How really extraordinary! He had quite misunderstood. Still, there would be plenty of future occasions. Monsieur the administrator must realize perfectly well that all he wanted was to co-operate. This was just a little more convincing than the patently insincere regrets of the receptionist in a high-class hotel. The director bathed us in his smile. Very well, said Ribo, coolly, we would go and talk to the signatories, now.

The director was delighted. With a flood of protestations he asked that it should be remembered that he never demanded better than to be given the chance to show any of his good friends round. The whole of the plantation was wide open to them at any time. He had nothing to hide. He turned to his trusties for moral support, and they grinned back gleefully at him. There you are, the director seemed to say, by his look. He waved the bottle of whisky at us. He was never happier than in company. And now we were here he was going to take the opportunity to show us over his model establishment, the fine, up-to-date workers' huts, the infirmary . . . After that he insisted that we come back to dinner.

It was a good two hours before Ribo, battling against the tide, got what he had come for. We were taken into a yard where about fifty Moïs were lined up awaiting us. These were the coolies whose contracts had been due for renewal, and of them only three had refused to sign and were being sent back to their villages. They were as miserable looking a collection of human scarecrows as one could have seen anywhere, and suddenly I realized that in the villages I had never seen a poverty-stricken Moï. Ribo checked their names off against a list he had, while the director, as if to forestall the possibility of any criticism, launched an offensive of his own. Calling Tuón, he told him to ask this ragged assemblage if they were satisfied with the treatment they had received. There was no reply to the question and the director seemed much surprised. Ribo now took a hand. 'Tell them to speak up,' he said. 'If they are dissatisfied with their contracts, let them say so. There is absolutely nothing to be afraid of.' The two bodyguards looked on cheerfully with folded arms. The director went up to one of the dejected figures and prodded him cautiously with his finger. 'Ask this man if he is satisfied.' Tuón spoke to him and, with averted eyes, the man mumbled a reply. 'Well,' said the director confidently, 'and what does he say?' 'He says that he is satisfied,' Tuón told him.

The director turned with a spreading of the hands. Only a moment's respite was allowed for this to sink in before he was pressing his advantage. 'Now ask them all – I say all of them, if they have not received the premium of one hundred and fifty piastres. You, you, and you,' said the director, permitting his fingertip to approach to within an inch of the rags, 'have you or have you not received your premium? If not, you have only to tell me now and I myself will give you the money.' There was a prestidigitatory flourish and a wad of clean notes appeared in the director's hand, and were waved under a line of apathetic noses. 'They have all received the premium,' Tuón said.

A sunny smile broke easily in the director's face and the bundle of notes described a last, graceful arc before disappearing into his pocket. 'What did I tell you? They have all received the premium. A generous advance on their wages. Money to send to their necessitous families.' The thing was clearly concluded. The director was afraid that he was being victimized by certain invidious persons he preferred not to name who put themselves to a lot of trouble to spread silly reports about him. There was one way only to deal with that kind of thing and that was to expose it to the light of day, and, foo! – some imaginary object was blown away with a light puff of the director's breath, and the director's palms were brushed quickly together in brisk gestures of exorcism. He turned now, awaiting the visitors' pleasure. Had they seen enough yet? If so ... The Frenchmen, dour, almost stolid beside this Etruscan mime, were reluctant to be persuaded. Tuón was more depressed than ever. The Rhadés had let him down. He drooped in his convict's garb. The fifty solemn coolies stared at their feet. The director and his men were on good terms with all the world.

Ribo made a last attempt, while the director arched his eyebrows and rolled his eyes in humorous tolerance. 'Tell them we came to see them because we heard that they were dissatisfied. Now we know that this was not true. They have chosen of their own free will to work for the company. We shall go back and tell their people that they are happy.' A voice in the rear rank mumbled something and Tuón went towards it. The two strong-arm men, still smiling, although now incredulously, moved forward. Two Moïs were blotted out in the towering bulk of each of them. The director was looking at his watch again. Ribo asked what the man had said. 'He says he was forced to sign,' Tuón told him. There was no sign of triumph in the colourless voice.

How was he forced to sign, Ribo asked. The big men were making for the dissenter who was looking from side to side, as if for a way of escape. Ribo followed them. 'Tell him to speak the truth,' Ribo said, 'and I promise no harm shall come to him.' Tuón spoke to the man again. He had the rather womanly good looks one finds so often among the Jarai tribes to the north, and it was hard to believe that he came of the same stock as the semitic-looking chief of Buon Plum. His legs and arms were covered with scars which showed up a pale, ugly pink against the dark bronze of the skin. He said that he had been kept a prisoner until he agreed to put his thumb-mark on the paper. The two trusties stood over him as he mumbled out this revelation, barrel chests thrust out, grinning down at him. Their attention was only distracted when another voice was heard. A second man had found the courage to tell the administrator that he had been taken and his thumb forced on to the contract. There was a growing murmur as this extraordinary rebellion spread. Others joined in to say that they had only found out at the end of their fifty days' obligatory service that they had been tricked into putting their thumb-mark on a contract for a year. They were always having to put their thumb-mark on something or other, like receipts for the tools they were given to work with. Tuón was going from man to man up and down the lines. He came back to say that only three of the coolies would stay of their own free will.

But now Ribo was faced with a new problem. It was one thing to badger the company into releasing a few workers who might be held there by force or trickery, but quite another, as it seemed clear would happen, if this were followed up, to attempt to deprive a powerful and wealthy concern like this of the whole of its labour. Ribo knew that, traditionally, administrators were broken for attempts of this kind. The thing was too big. It had got out of control. The genie he had summoned up could not be appeased by a trifling reform. Either the company must be allowed to continue to get its labour by fraud or force – since it was evident that this was the only way it could be got – or it would go out of business. It was as drastic as that. And then, with the company no more, and the untended plantations reverting to the jungle, where would the tyre companies get their rubber, and ultimately the French motorist his tyres? It seems, in fact, since there is no reason to suppose that other rubber plantations in Indo-China are run on Christian principles, that this commodity which is regarded as essential to the conduct of our civilization is often only to be obtained by turning a blind eye to illegalities and oppression, and that there is little difference in practice between the secret gangsterism of these days and the open slavery officially abolished in the last century.

There was only one course open to Ribo: to withdraw as gracefully as he could after promising the Rhadés that the whole matter would be investigated. The director was not in the slightest degree shaken. He would probably have preferred to avoid this unpleasant incident, because he was affable and expansive by nature, liked to get on with people, and did not enjoy scenes. But he knew perfectly well that Ribo could do nothing to him, that is to say, nothing serious, without challenging the purpose of the colony itself. A Resident himself, whose power was far greater than Ribo's, told me later that all he could do was to put a brake on the activities of the planters. 'We snap at their heels, like curs – that's all it amounts to. If it wasn't for us they'd go into the villages after the labour and bring the men back at the point of the gun.'

And now I knew why Ribo, Doctor Jouin, and all the rest of them were so sure that there was no hope for the Moïs. They always told you that it was the malaria, although it didn't make sense that it was only in our time, after all those centuries of resistance to malaria, that it should begin to finish them off. Ribo might succeed, with his model villages, in checking that downhill plunge, in holding the level of the population of Buon Plum or even in setting it on the uphill climb again. But while, beneath the show of solicitude on the part of men of science and low-level officials, the real purpose of the Moï village as seen from above was to provide forced labour, there could be no real recovery.

CHAPTER TEN

The Vanishing Tribes

BAN MÉTHUOT was dull enough after the Dak Lac. I was promptly re-installed by Doustin among the silent splendours of the Residence, and told, once again, to '*pousser un grand coup de gueule*' out of the window if I wanted anything. Doustin thought that there was little hope of leaving Ban Méthuot yet awhile, in any direction, and mentioned that the convoy which had left Ban Méthuot, following mine, had been badly shot up. However, one would see – one would see, and smiling secretly he withdrew, to the crashing of the sentries' salute. I felt that he had something up his sleeve.

In the cool of the later afternoon I visited the local missionaries. Having heard something of their activities in the Dak Lac area, I was curious to see these people who taught their Moï converts to sing in harmony from Sankey and Moody and distributed woollen berets, as a sign of grace, to their children.

Mr Jones, the missionary, was a spare, bearded American, who looked like a New England farmer out of a picture by Grant Wood. His expression was one of severe beatitude, and his wife, too, gave the impression of being the happy possessor of a simple formula which had relieved her from doubts and misgivings of any kind. I do not believe that either of the Joneses had ever wrestled with an angel, nor would they have seen any point in the pessimistic attitude of most of the prophets. The practice and propagation of their religion was to them a pleasant and satisfying activity, offering, moreover, plenty of scope for self-expression. They lived in the best villa in Ban Méthuot, and were aided in their tasks by two cars and a plane.

Tha pastors of the American Evangelical Mission do not agree with a diet of locusts and wild honey. It is normal for them to arrive in a country, I was told, with several tons of canned foodstuffs, calculated to last the length of the stay. Referring to the luxurious appointments of his villas, Mr Jones went out of his way to assure me that they were normal by French colonial standards. Moreover, he said, he and his wife often slept in the bush. He went on to say that they both liked and admired the French immensely and did their best to co-operate with them in every possible way. They were in better odour, in fact, than the French Roman Catholic Mission, which had been banned from some areas for its political activities. By this the pastor supposed they had taken some sort of interest in the natives apart from their spiritual welfare – a thing the American Evangelical Mission never did. I waited in vain for the quotation beginning, 'Render unto Caesar', and refrained from telling the pastor that the missionaries are universally thought by the French authorities (I believe them to be wrong) to be political agents of Washington. In this the French show a lack of understanding of the American mind, arguing with Latin simplicity that as the missionaries make few converts – in the Buddhist parts of the country, none at all – why, otherwise, keep them there?

In reply to my enquiry after the progress of his labours the pastor said that they were making some headway against unbelievable difficulties. To take the language problem alone. Like most of these Far-Eastern languages, it was barren in abstractions, which provided the most appalling difficulties when it came to translating the Holy Writ. To give just one example, he cited the text, 'God is Love'. In Rhadés there was no word for God. In fact these people didn't get the idea at all without a great deal of explanation. Also there was no word for love. So the text came out in translation, 'The Great Spirit is not angry'. It got over that way, he supposed, but not as he would have liked it.

You could imagine, he said, the kind of effort that went into the preparation of his address when he visited a new village for the first time. 'Before starting in on them, we had to build a prayer-house of our own. We told them that we wouldn't go into any of their houses that had been tainted with the blood of heathen sacrifices. After we got the place built, and it cost us plenty – in commodities like salt, I mean – we went right in there and endeavoured to preach the Christ crucified and risen, to all that attended.' The pastor said that they always took pictures of the crucifixion, to give away, having learned that the natives were interested in the technique of any new blood-sacrifice. Some of the natives used to turn up expecting a ceremony with what the pastor called 'that damnable alcohol of theirs', and when they didn't see any jars about the place they went away again. 'However, we didn't give up the fight. There was nothing so sweet to my ears as to have one of these poor, ignorant, deluded souls we had struggled and prayed for, come to us and say, "When I die you will plant a cross on my grave and not a buffalo skull." That was victory indeed,' said the pastor, and for a moment there was a true pioneering gleam in his eyes.

I asked if he had ever found the tribes intolerant of his preaching, and the pastor said, no, on the contrary. The trouble was that the natives were only too ready to accept any message but wanted to be allowed to fit in the new revelation among their own idolatries. He just couldn't make them understand that God was a jealous god. That was another term that they didn't have in their language, and he had to spend hours explaining to them. A typical attitude after hearing the gospel was to offer to include the new spirit in their pantheon along with the spirits of earth, water, thunder, and rice. This usually went with the suggestion of a big ceremony, to be provided by the pastor, at which a number of buffaloes and jars would be sacrificed and the new spirit would be invited to be present. 'We just can't get them to see how foolish and wicked these sacrifices are. Why, only today we saw some natives drinking in a field and when they saw us in the car they came running over to offer us alcohol. Can you imagine that? We actually recognized people we had already given instruction in their own language out of a little manual we produced.' The pastor put a book in my hand. It contained, said the title page, thirty hymns, a section on prayer, an explanation of twenty-six religious terms, a short summary of the Old and New Testaments and a Church manual, with duties of preachers, elders, baptism, the Lord's Supper, dedication, the marriage service, and the Apostle's Creed. And all this was written in the Rhadés language with its lack of such words as God, love, hate, jealousy. A formidable accomplishment indeed!

Bringing up the matter of the plantations and their effect upon his endeavours – since coolies working thirteen hours a day and seven days a week would obviously be unable to attend Divine Worship – the pastor drew in his horns immediately. He was concerned only with the natives' spiritual welfare, and their material conditions were no interest of his whatever. One thing could be said in favour of the plantations, in fact, and that was that a man working there was at least put out of the way of temptation. His view was that it didn't really matter what happened to a man in this world so long as he had acquired the priceless treasure of Faith. When Jesus said that 'He that believeth in me shall be saved' he was not referring to this life. Naturally, if one of his Christians got into trouble he would try to come through for him, so long as it didn't annoy the French. I realized quite sharply that the pastor was totally uninterested in the natives as a whole, but only in 'our Christians (we love them like children)'. He collected souls with the not very fierce pleasure that others collect stamps.

It is curious that a twentieth-century Evangelist should join hands in this belief in the unique and exclusive value of faith with his first missionary predecessor, the seventeenth-century Jesuit, Borri. Borri was scandalized and depressed at a display of most of the Christian virtues on the part of a people who had not benefited by conversion.

Others profess Poverty, living upon Alms; others exercise the Works of Mercy, minist'ring to the Sick … without receiving any Reward, others undertaking some pious Work, as building of Bridges, or other such thing for the Publick Good, or erecting of Temples … There are also some Omsaiis (priests) who profess the Farrier's Trade, and compassionately cure Elephants, Oxen and Horses, without asking any Reward, being satisfy'd with anything that is freely given them … insomuch that if any Man came newly into that Country, he might easily be persuaded that there had been Christians there in former times; so near has the Devil endeavour'd to imitate us.

There was, however, a remedy for this distressing state of affairs, for

> This is that part of the Earth call'd Cochin-China, which wants
> nothing to make it a part of Heaven, but that God should send
> thither a great many of His Angels, so S. John Chrysostom calls
> Apostolical Men, and Preachers of the Gospel. How easily would the
> Faith be spread abroad in this Kingdom ... for there is no need here
> of being disguis'd or conceal'd, these People admitting of all Strangers
> in their Kingdom, and being well pleas'd that every one should live
> in his own Religion ... nor do they shun Strangers, as is practis'd in
> other Eastern Nations, but make much of them, affect their Persons,
> prize their Commodities, and commend their Doctrine.

Borri had his wish. The Angels, Apostolical Men, and Preachers
of the Gospel arrived in great numbers, and it was under the pretext
of protecting them from Annamese oppression that the French
conquest of the country was undertaken.

That evening I went mistakenly to a restaurant that masqueraded
under a European name. I believe it was the Restaurant something or
other. In this part of the world one is always at the mercy of the Far
Eastern peoples' broadmindedness and ingenuity in matters of food,
and consequently there sometimes arises a craving for something
simple, definite, and nameable. The Restaurant fell badly between
two stools. Although a juke-box groaned gustily in a corner, the
screen that only partially excluded the kitchen details was ominously
decorated with dragons, and the remnants of a meal that had been
eaten with chopsticks were snatched from my table as I sat down.
Without my being given a chance to express my preference, a moody
Vietnamese waiter now arrived with a plate of eggs, which might
have been laid by thrushes. They looked like highly coloured and
greatly magnified frog spawn and were bathed in green oil. This was
followed by the *plat du jour* for Europeans, described as a *Chateau-
briand maison*, a huge slab of bluish-grey meat, undoubtedly cut from

the haunches of some rare, ass-like animal that had been shot in the local forest. '*Et des pommes Lyonnaises*,' said the sombre-faced waiter arriving again, and releasing over the plate a scoopful of fried, sliced manioc. This was accompanied by a bottle of perfumed beer.

Since it was an odd day of the month, and therefore lucky, my neighbour, a French soldier, following the example of several other patrons, decided to play for his dinner. The system favoured was *Tai-Xiu*, in which three dice are used and the house wins when the score is under ten, besides taking as its percentage any bet when triple threes come up. None of the players seemed to realize that the luck of odd days is universal and not one-sided. Chanting most dolefully, the waiter shook the dice in the bowl and threw them on the table. My neighbour lost and paid double his bill. The house soothsayer now arrived and took his hand, informing him after a brief study of its lines and for a small payment, that he had offended a minor demon and that the time was unpropitious for him to travel by elephant, to build a house, or begin clearing a rice-field.

For the further diversion of its patrons this restaurant had fixed to its wall a large glass-fronted box, housing white rats. A brain sharpened by a study of the problem of perpetual motion had devised a system of miniature treadmills which kept the rats continually on the move. Only rarely was one allowed to perch for a few seconds on a narrow ledge before being dislodged and plunged into hectic activity again by the arrival of one of its companions. It was an hypnotic spectacle and one felt sure, especially in the throes of digestion of one's ass-steak, that somewhere arising out of this was to be drawn a cruelly Buddhist moral.

I strolled back to the Residence in the failing light, hoping that it was not too dark to see a tiger before it saw me. Green fire-flies were pulsating in the shrubberies. Owls had taken up positions on garden gateposts, not so much as budging as I passed them, and occasionally as a breeze stirred I caught the fine-drawn wailing of a distant gramophone or the brief spate of notes of some strong-throated Eastern nightingale. As I turned into the garden of the

Residence a Moï guard materialized, like Herne the Hunter, against a tree-trunk, pushed a bayonet towards me, and shouted a challenge; a whiplash of monosyllables in some unknown language. This was a recurrent embarrassment. There was nothing to be done but to stand there, with occasional blossoms drifting between us, and say anything in English that came into my head. After a few moments, embarrassment touched the Moï, too, the bayonet drooped, there was a slurred-over drill movement, and he sank back, his face screened in aerial roots.

Within a few minutes of my return Doustin was tapping at my door, smiling his controlled smile, and mildly triumphant. It appeared that an important politician, a French Deputy, had just arrived and would be leaving at three o'clock in the morning for Pleiku, which was about two hundred miles to the north. Did I want to go? I did.

The Deputy, who was an ex-Governor of Cochin-China, was travelling with his secretary and a chauffeur, and the whole party, as usual, was armed to the teeth. Outside the towns in the central plateaux of Annam it is really no man's land, and Viet-Minh patrols probably use the roads as much as isolated French cars. It was always assumed that the Viet-Minh were regular in their habits and did not travel at night. The Deputy was going to make the best of this night journey by shooting game, if he saw any. He had a splendid new gun, a five-shot repeater, and both the Deputy and his secretary said that they would be very surprised if they didn't get at least one leopard.

We were held up for some time on the outskirts of Ban Méthuot through taking the wrong track. The big soft American car nosed its way through the bamboo thickets, its headlight beams trapped, as if in a thick fog, a few yards ahead of the car. At night the sameness of the forest was immeasurably intensified. In the end the driver found the right track and we plunged forward confidently into the tunnel of bleached vegetation. The Deputy and his secretary, wrapped as if for grouse-shooting on the moors, sat with tense gun-barrels poking through the windows on each side. There was a single moment of excitement when we saw, swinging before us, a cluster of pale lamps. The driver braked and doors were half opened but it was only the tossing eyes of a herd of domestic buffalo, which now, fully revealed in the headlights, turned their hindquarters to charge from us, plunging noisily through the solid walls of bamboo.

In the early dawn we had still shot nothing and the Deputy, with failing eyesight but unimpaired enthusiasm, had to be restrained from opening fire on more buffaloes, a group of Moïs on the horizon, and finally upon piles of elephant droppings in the road. Our final and profitless exploit was a great advance through thorny bush after the will-o'-the-wisp sound of screaming peacocks, which could always be heard in the trees fifty yards ahead. After this rifles were put aside and the shooting members of the party relapsed into a gloomy coma as we climbed out of the hunting country into the pleasant sunlit plateau of Pleiku.

It was a wide, Mexican-looking landscape, a great, rolling panorama of whitened elephant grass with the worn-down and partly wooded craters of ancient volcanoes in the middle distance, and a blue ribbon of peaks curled along the horizon. Elegant white hawks with black wing-tips circled above us. Occasionally we saw a few Moïs of the handsome Jarai tribe, marching in single file and in correct family order; the young men first, carrying their lances, then the women, and finally an old man – the head of the family. Before reaching a village this little procession would halt to allow the old man to take his ceremonial place at its head. The Jarais carried their household goods in wicker baskets of excellent workmanship, slung on their backs. They smoked silver-ornamented churchwarden pipes and wore necklaces of linked silver spirals.

Pleiku was an authentic frontier town, with military notices on all sides. Pine trees grew in the bright red earth, but there was no grass – only the red soil and the pines. The smart, Mediterranean-looking villas were set back from the road and surrounded by spiked pallisades. A few cars with armoured windscreens were running about, and civilians as well as the soldiers carried rifles. We passed a strong-point at the crossroads, and I was charmed to see that warning was given by beating a gong. Hairy, long-snouted pigs, indistinguishable from wild boars, dashed about the streets. I noticed that the urbanized Jarais had discarded their fine wicker baskets and jars, replacing them with jerry-cans. All Pleiku resounded with the same powerful nightingale song which I had heard, only in rare bursts, in Ban Méthuot.

The cross-country journey into Laos, which at Saigon had sounded so simple and reasonable, and at Ban Méthuot had taken on a more problematical colour, was now at Pleiku·beginning to look like a hopeless proposition. Laos, as one approached it, seemed to exert a powerful anti-magnetic repulsion. At Saigon there were vague memories of many cross-country trips, dating perhaps from pre-war days. In Ban Méthuot professional hunters were thought to have sometimes made the journey. But in Pleiku the information was uncompromisingly definite. No one went there at all, said Monsieur Préau, the Resident, and the most he could promise to do, in the most favourable circumstances, would be to get me to Bo-Kheo, about halfway to Stung Treng, in Laos, and after that it would be up to me.

But even the Pleiku–Bo-Kheo section of the journey would call for careful organizing, because it was a year or two since anyone had done it, and therefore the bridges might be down. From Bo-Kheo to Stung Treng, Préau said, there used to be a regular lorry service run by the Chinese. Regular, but on what days? It was important to be in possession of all the facts, because there were no Europeans in Bo-Kheo, and nowhere to stay; therefore one's arrival had more or less to coincide with the lorry's departure. And, said Monsieur Préau, he would have to see me quite definitely on the lorry and the lorry in motion, before turning back, because Chinese lorries had a habit of breaking down and sometimes it took several weeks to get spare parts – several months in Bo-Kheo perhaps since how were they to get there?

Then again there was the question of the security of the Bo-Kheo–Stung Treng area. By that, he meant whether or not there were bandits about, and if so what kind, and how many. All this information would take a few days to get and Préau suggested that I might like to fill in the time visiting some of the outlying military posts in his territory. He was sending a man next day for a report to Mang-Yang, their furthermost outpost in the East, and I was welcome to go with him.

Doustin had sent an official telegram to Préau, advising him of my arrival, but in addition to this I carried a personal letter from Ribo and Cacot, from whom I had parted on the best of terms. The three men had been in the Colonial Service together in Mauretania. Préau evidently wanted to do all he could, but had I known at the time what he was up against in Pleiku, I should have hesitated to trouble him with my presence. A few days before, Viet-Minh groups had visited most of the villages in the zone and had requisitioned rice. They had also set up their own posts, some of which the French were still trying to find. At this moment when it was thought necessary to press every available Moï into the militia, the planters had suddenly brought pressure to bear for the increase of the supply of labour to the plantations. Préau was between the devil and the deep, but I only learned this, a little at a time, in the days that followed.

Next morning we set out for Mang-Yang. Among the Resident's many troubles was a chronic shortage of transport. That morning the jeep we were to use broke down as soon as it was started up, and the driver spent the time, until Préau arrived to find out what had happened, shooting at pigeons with a crossbow. In the end we had to go off in the Resident's Citroën, leaving him only a lorry for use in emergency. Mang-Yang was about eighty miles away, nearly half-way to Qui-Nhon, on the coast, which, with a belt of territory of uncertain width, was solidly in Viet-Minh hands.

My companion, Préau's secretary, was an excessively peaceful-looking young man. He sat beside me in the back of the car, with a sporting gun on one side and a Sten on the other. Our road wound around the great eroded stumps of volcanoes, and it was in these bare surroundings, quite out of their normal element, that we suddenly saw ahead of us a group of seven or eight peacocks. They were sauntering in the road and paid no attention whatever to us. It would have been possible to run them down. My friend fired and the birds, without signs of alarm, trooped away into the grass, all but one, which fell sprawling in a ditch. The driver went to pick it up. There was something that was rather shocking about the ungainly posture of this bird in its shattered dignity. It was slightly indecent. Searching in the stiff screens of plumage, the driver could find no injury, there was no dappling of blood, the muscular legs struck out, and when released the wings beat down strongly. Whichever way the bird was held, its head curved up towards us fixing us reproachfully with its eyes. The secretary told the driver to kill it, and the man looked embarrassed. He made some incomprehensible excuse, speaking in Jarai. Nobody, it seemed, cared to kill the bird and it was stowed away in the back of the car. I felt uncomfortable about this and the secretary probably did so too, as he talked about taking the bird back and keeping it as a pet. When later in the day we opened the back of the car to inspect it, the secretary was horrified to find that all the bird's fine feathers had been quietly plucked out at some time when we had left the car unattended.

At Dak Ayun a yellow fortress bristled in the plain, a log-built affair with bamboo palisades in place of barbed-wire entanglements. Patrols would have to walk round it, and it could hold off an attack by a company of not too resolute infantry, but the first field-gun would blow it to matchwood in a few minutes. The machine-guns of Dak Ayun protected the survivors of four Bahnar villages which had been concentrated beneath its walls. The Bahnars, a somewhat lowlier tribe than the Jarais or the Rhadés, had suffered Viet-Minh reprisals for giving information to the French. A party of Viet-Minh tommy-gunners had arrived, judged the notables concerned, and executed twelve of them on the spot with their own lances. The secretary had to report on the condition of the refugees.

The senior NCO in charge of the fort took us to see them. He was as pale as if he had come from watching an execution, and had a black Landru beard. The Bahnars were living in wretched shelters of leaves and branches. They were filthy, diseased, ragged – and probably starving, since they had lost their animals. The tigers were attacking them, the NCO said. Tigers were so bad in these parts that his men had orders never to leave the fort unless in pairs and carrying their arms. Among this stench and misery I noticed a woman weaving cloth strikingly patterned with stylized monkeys. Her weaving frame was carved with almost Persian intricacy. This was the fate of Moïs who defied the Viet-Minh by giving information to the French. Later I learned that even severer punishments awaited those who offended the French from fear of the Viet-Minh.

Leaving these tragic people, we started off for Mang-Yang. The pale-faced NCO asked to come with us. It was a great treat for him, he said, to be able to leave the confinement of his stronghold, and he added that as mortar-fire had been reported that morning in the Mang-Yang sector, we might just possibly run into a Viet-Minh fighting patrol, in which case an extra Sten in the car might make all the difference. It was true that from that point the road showed more signs of border affrays. We passed a burned-out car with a grave beside it, a deserted and partially demolished Moï village and a wrecked bridge, now being rebuilt under the eye of a crouching machine-gunner.

At Mang-Yang we had come to the extreme limit of the territory held, however tenuously, by the French. This ultimate outpost, temporary or otherwise, of the colonial possessions in Central Annam was held for France by a slap-happy sergeant from Perpignan, a cabaret-Provençal, who roared with laughter at the thought of his isolation, and poured us out half-tumblers of Chartreuse, which was all he could get to drink. Every morning, with teutonic regularity, the Viet-Minh fired five or seven mortar-bombs at them from over the crest of the nearest hill. They replied with their trench-mortar and that was the end of hostilities for the day. There was nothing to stop you going out if you wanted to, and he himself used to make short expeditions to collect butterflies. The only other excitement was produced by the occasional passage of a herd of elephants. He used to fire at them with the Bren, but so far without results.

Laughing loudly, the sergeant made us climb to the top of a tower where he kept his butterflies, his Bren, a row of French pin-ups, and his store of Chartreuse. His view was superb. A patch of the forest was still smouldering where the morning's mortar-shells had fallen.

The sergeant said it was a pity we hadn't come earlier and suggested we stayed the night, when we could be sure to see some action in the morning. We asked him how he got on with the Moïs, and he said that he was lucky to be where he was and not down in Cohin-China in command of Bao-Dai Vietnamese. Down there it was nothing for a fort to be sold out to the Viet-Minh, but the Moïs had never done anything like that so far. They didn't seem to know the value of money. That reminded him, he said, his men had caught a tiger-cub the day before, and we must see it before we went. He called one of the guards and told him to fetch the cub, but the man said something and shook his head. The sergeant burst out laughing again. 'Well, what do you think of that? Ah, *mince alors* . . . they've eaten it.'

That ubiquitous tiger! I never saw one, except for a single specimen at Dalat, hanging, as large as a pony, from a tree, to be skinned, while a brace of Vietnamese doctors bid excitedly against each other for the teeth and the valuable medicinal portions of the intestines. Even the Evangelical pastor at Pleiku, with whom I dined that night, had only to go for an hour's moonlight drive in order to see one, and had actually found one in his front garden a few evenings before.

It was from the pastor that I learned, quite accidentally of course – although this was boldly confirmed later by a French official – what happens to Moïs who fail to advise the French of the presence of the Viet-Minh in their neighbourhood. He told me that he had just come back from Kontum where he had been visiting one of 'our Christians' who had been put in prison for this omission. Quite casually the pastor mentioned that this Christian, who had been three months in the prison, couldn't use his arms yet. I asked why, and the pastor said, as if it followed as a matter of course, that they had been disjointed at the interrogation. Were there any more than his Christian involved? Why, yes, about eighty had been arrested, of which he guessed that no more than twenty had been strung up. And who had done this? The pastor mentioned the name of a military commandant I had already met. Both he, and his wife, he said, found him in their personal relations a very charming man. In fact, he treated them so well they found it hard to believe that he could be, well – kind of rugged, when it came to such disciplinary matters.

There was a well-known tea plantation not far away, and the French officials, as usual, had not been afraid to let me know, in a roundabout way, what they thought of it, and of the methods of the planter. But the missionaries had nothing but praise for the Algerian that ran the place, and it turned out that he had given them their furniture. There was something quite extraordinary in this situation that, while French colonial officials privately condemned what was ultimately the colony's *raison d'être*, and if admitting the use of torture turned their backs in distaste upon the torturer, these men of God shut their eyes to abuse, and would even accept gifts evidently designed to ensure their good will and perhaps co-operation. It should be emphasized that in the small conventional details of conduct, they were, like Brutus, honourable men, patterns of American small-town society, clean looking and clean living, hospitable, friendly, and married to wives who might have been voted second most likely to succeed in whatever had been their particular collegiate class-year.

But one began to wonder whether a whole catalogue of easy, short-range virtues had not been outweighed by some gigantic, fundamental shortcoming – which might have been that they had added respectability to the three original virtues of Faith, Hope, and Charity, and had made it greatest of the four. If unpleasant things like lynchings at home and torturings abroad happened, it was best to ignore them; most respectable to pretend they didn't exist. To do otherwise would be to 'meddle with politics', a form of activity much disapproved of by Pontius Pilate. I repeat that the American Evangelical missionaries were the happiest looking people I have seen in my life.

It so happened that I soon found myself visiting the plantation whose director the missionaries had found so generous. Strangers in Indo-China soon find out that the great plantations are thought of by the colonists as the principal show-places the country has to offer; only slightly less spectacular, perhaps, than Mount Fuji from one of its accepted viewpoints, Niagara Falls, or the Grand Canyon. In actual fact I cannot conceive of anything less exciting, since in the ends of efficiency a plantation is governed by an order that is wearisome in the extreme. Usually only one type of bush or tree is cultivated and the fact that there may be hundreds of thousands or even millions of them does nothing in my opinion to lessen the tedium.

The plantation we visited had roads along which we did 50 m.p.h. for mile after mile in a jeep, seeing nothing but dull little bushes of absolutely uniform size and spacing. We were taken to a height from which there spread out beneath one a peerless landscape, across miles and miles of which it was as if a fine-tooth comb had been drawn, producing a monotonous warp of close-drawn lines. The director scorched along in his car through this vast and boring domain, showing us with pride the barrage he was building, designed to produce some fantastic kilowattage, and with sorrow the ruins of splendid seignorial buildings that had been gutted by the Viet-Minh. There were three millon tea plants and only a thousand coolies, which was a desperate state of affairs, the director said. They suffered, too, from the chronic idleness of the natives' disposition. The government saw to it that they handled them with kid-gloves – they were paid a fixed rate of five piastres for a working day of twelve hours, plus eight hundred grams of rice and an allowance of salt – but whatever was done for them they showed no signs of realizing how well off they were.

At the plantation house we found why the official who took me to the plantation had been sent for. The Deputy with whom I had travelled up from Ban Méthuot awaited him. There had been a little luncheon party in the Deputy's honour, and the Deputy and the planters now got my friend in a corner and formed a ring round him, faintly menacing beneath the post-prandial geniality. In the meanwhile the lady of the house discussed literature. She had just been reading, in translation, Mr Graham Greene's *The Heart of the Matter*, and found it too terribly depressing – quite the most depressing book she had ever read. Did British colonials really lead those awful existences? And, besides that, as ardent Catholics, both she and her husband did not know whether they approved of the theme. She sighed and looked round her, doubtless reassured, after Greene's harrowing account of the bungaloid crudities of West Africa, by the infallible heritage of Latin civilization in her surroundings.

Meanwhile voices at the other end of the room were raised. The Deputy was laying down the law. The plantation had to have more labour, and he had come up from Saigon to see that it got it. The local authority said that there was absolutely nothing to be done. Every available man had already been drained from the villages in the neighbourhood. If the villages were to survive an irreducible minimum of able-bodied men had to be left in them. The Deputy told him that three hundred more men were needed, and they were going to have them by hook or by crook. My friend pointed out that between military service and labour in the plantations they had practically exhausted the man-power of the Jarai tribe. This gave the Deputy an idea. Military commitments up here in the plateaux were unimportant, he said. If necessary the three hundred men could be transferred from the *Garde Montagnarde*. It was at this point that the administrator gave up. Three hundred soldiers would be withdrawn from the forts and set to work picking tea-leaves at a time when enemy infiltrations were more frequent than ever before. Thus, assuming that it was in France's interests to keep its hold in Indo-China, were the nation's interests sacrificed to the short-term ambitions of a small, powerful group of its citizens.

Putting down the book which depressed her so much, the director's wife had an idea. The perfect solution, she thought, would be if the government would allow them to employ the Chinese nationalist internees, who were being held in the Tonkinese camps, instead of leaving them there to eat their heads off in idleness. She was sure that the Chinese would be only too pleased to have the chance to work. All those present agreed with her, and the Deputy said that he would raise the matter in Saigon.

'The plantation', said the administrator, on our way back, 'will burn – and they know it. It is only a question of time. But before that happens they are determined to squeeze out the very last drop of blood.'

CHAPTER ELEVEN

Central Annam

THERE IS A SCHOOL at Pleiku for the children of the Jarai and Bahnar tribes in the neighbourhood. With some difficulty, and by putting pressure on the chiefs, the children are persuaded to come and sit in its classrooms, where they learn a few words of French and acquire higher education embracing a nodding acquaintance with Napoleon's campaigns and the names of the principal rivers of France. As it happens, the European idea of education as a process quite separate from other aspects of living and occupying most of a child's energies until, say, at least the age of fourteen, is quite incomprehensible in its wastefulness, from the Moï's point of view. A Moï cannot be persuaded that there is any virtue in knowledge which cannot be applied. At six years of age the Moï child is introduced as a matter of rigid tribal custom to certain light tasks in the rice-field; he learns a little carpentry and receives preliminary instruction in the arts of gathering food. He is usefully employed, for his labours are integrated with the village economy, and they increase in usefulness in proportion to his growing older. These serious activities are, no doubt, far more enjoyable than learning lessons in a classroom. However, it has been decided that if the Moïs are to be turned into valuable colonial citizens they must be educated according to Western standards. So to the schoolroom they go.

The recruiting campaign for scholars having gone well at Pleiku, it had been found necessary to build an annexe. But at this stage tribal custom was too strong to be ignored. The children's parents would not allow them to occupy the new building unless it had first been consecrated for use; that is, put under protection of the tribal spirits by an appropriate sacrifice.

A sacrifice of this kind must be made as soon as possible after sunrise, as it takes several hours to prepare the flesh for the subsequent feast. At seven o'clock, then, in the cool morning, when the pines threw long shadows over the red earth, a young buffalo was dragged into the schoolyard and tied to the sacrificial stake.

The buffalo is regarded by the Moï as spiritually more than an animal, and hardly less than a human being. It is therefore entitled – unlike other animals, which are simply knocked on the head – to a slow and highly ceremonial death. This is always accorded it. As a further sign of respect, the animal is presented before the sacrifice, as in this case, with a generous drink of rice-alcohol from one of the sacred jars.

It was held by a rope of rice-straw round the neck and was terrified by some mysterious animal premonition. In the background had been set up ritual masts, their stems ornamented with stylized geometrical designs; suns, moons, toucans' beaks, flies' wings, buffaloes' teeth, and their tops sprouting artificial branches of frayed bamboo, from which hung streamers and carved plaquettes. These masts are the Moïs' equivalent of flagpoles. They are highly artistic and their intention is to attract the visual attention of the spirits to be invited to the ceremony, just as they are summoned audibly by gongs. After the sacrifice the masts are planted about the villages as a permanent decoration, providing thus a perpetual gala effect. The sacrificial stake, too, often subordinates solidity to art. It sometimes breaks, allowing the buffalo to escape. However lamentable its condition, no attempt is made to recapture it, since this would conflict with the spirit's evident wish.

As soon as the buffalo had been attached, a group of pupils, carrying gongs and dressed in sombre, handsome blankets, appeared. With a slow, mournful beating of the gongs they began to circle about the buffalo which, more alarmed than ever at these sinister preliminaries, made panic-stricken efforts to break free. Four more pupils joined the death procession. They carried a huge drum supported on a framework of poles, which had been borrowed from a local chief. This drum, I learned, was valued at fifteen buffaloes and there had been a great deal of fussy admonition on the chief's part before he could be persuaded to let it go. A few minutes later, the chief himself, who had been worrying about his property, turned up, and, wearing a military medal on the breast of a new, white sports-shirt, took his stand in the front row of the audience to make sure that there was no culpable negligence. When beaten, the drum gave out a most important sound, a muffled growling, agreed by those present to be irresistible to the spirits, however aloof.

What followed was a most distressing spectacle. Two of the fathers stood out. Carrying *coupe-coupes* (the Moï weapon which is half knife and half axe), they approached the animal from behind. They succeeded after several false attempts, when the heavy knife struck home with a hideous chopping sound, in hamstringing first one leg, causing the animal to hop about on a single back leg in a frantic effort to avoid the blows, and then the second leg, when it collapsed on its hocks, its rear legs bent uselessly under it. This frightful disablement failed to prevent it from shuffling with desperate energy round the post, while, like minor bull-fighters that have fulfilled the role assigned to them, the men with the *coupe-coupes* retired, and two others, armed with lances, stepped forward. The subsequent tragedy was long drawn-out and incomparably bloodier than a bull-fight, when until the last moments of its life the bull is majestic and incalculable. About this grotesquely shuffling bulk there was squalor and humiliation in which we were all involved. No particular technique, it seemed, was demanded of the killers, and they had a a good half-hour in which to pursue their prey with desultory proddings and stabbings. Finally, with a frightful shuddering groan – the first sound that it had uttered – the animal expired, was immediately dragged away and thrown on a brushwood fire, where it was left to scorch superficially for about fifteen minutes. No attempt has ever been made to reform or modify cruel sacrifices of this kind, and this is the end which awaits every buffalo in the Moï country. One is told by the French that it is part of their policy to respect the religious customs of the natives. In such matters as this there is much official susceptibility where the natives' freedom of action is concerned.

In the early afternoon we came back. There were thirty-seven jars of alcohol lined up with a number of bamboo tubes protruding from each, and every Moï in Pleiku, including all the pupils, was exeedingly tight. Politely, following the Resident's example, we took our place for a few seconds before each jar, rejected the baskets of chopped raw meat, and nibbled with slight nausea at skewers with tit-bits grilled *à la kebab*. This token participation was obligatory, otherwise the Resident risked having the heads of the families declare the ceremony null and void and refuse to allow the children to attend school. After a few minutes we arose to go, but the Jarai schoolmaster spotted our intention and came reeling towards us to beg the Resident to wait a moment. There was a surprise arranged for us and, raising his arm, he shouted a command. The thirty-seven pupils rose unsteadily from their jars and, leaning upon each other for support, formed a swaying line. There while we faced them rather sheepishly across the blood-splashed earth and beneath the buffalo skull, now scraped clean and shining and impaled on a spruce ritual post, they burst into 'Auld Lang Syne', rendered to the words, *'Faut-il nous quitter sans espoir – sans espoir de retour?'* They wanted to show us that their school years had not been spent for nothing.

The remainder of the day was spent in an official visit to the Vietnamese community of Pleiku. To guard against any fifth column activities on behalf of the Viet-Minh, all the Vietnamese in the district had been concentrated in the single village of Phu-Tho, which was guarded by a French fort. The purpose of the Resident's visit was to offer official congratulations on the eve of the feast of Têt, the Chinese and Vietnamese New Year; originally celebrated with the abandonment of all endeavour for the first three months of the year – a period which it has now been found convenient to reduce to a week.

The attitude of the Resident towards his Vietnamese minority was one of uneasy tolerance. I had now, in unbroken succession, met four French administrators who were all highly intelligent, broad-minded, and well intentioned. They recognized evil, and as far as they could without risking their positions, they fought it where they saw it. At least one of them, although he would not openly admit it, was a fervent anti-colonialist. Yet none of them could ever find a good word for the Vietnamese. They conceded that there was a special charm in the way of living of the Laotians and the Cambodians. The Moïs, of course, were children, lazy and improvident but delightful. But the Vietnamese – well, you never knew where you were with them, they suffered from an inferiority complex, concealed their true thoughts or feelings, were cruel and had no religion to speak about, were 'not like us'. It is unsafe to discuss the Vietnamese in a French audience, because a reproving voice will always be raised to tell you to wait until you have lived thirty years in the country before you talk of fathoming this muddy psychological pool. The most intelligent Frenchman seems to be influenced subconsciously in this matter by the sheer dead-weight of prejudice of his uncritical compatriots. I am reminded of the British interpretation of the Chinese character as portrayed in the popular magazines of the period following the Boxer rebellion, when for a generation the Chinese supplied us with villains of fiction who were obnoxious in a two-faced and totally un-English way.

To me this suggests that the French like the Laotians and the rest of them because they do not fear them. They can relax their defences in the comfortable knowledge that these are harmless and declining peoples, and with this their good qualities become, rather nostalgically, apparent. They are like the Spanish conquerors of the West Indies who delayed official recognition that the Caribs had souls until their extermination was almost complete, or like the Americans who are sentimental about their vanishing Indians, forgetting the massacres of the last century when the only 'good Injun' was a dead one. The Vietnamese are a subject people who refuse to go into a graceful decline. There are seventeen millions of these 'bad Injuns' and nothing is too bad for them.

The manner of my friends, therefore, when we were received by the notables of Phu-Tho, was courteous but not genial. It seemed that we had arrived a little sooner than expected because a dignitary, meeting us with clasped hands and low bows at the flower-decorated arch of entry, begged us to wait until the official drum was fetched. This arrived a few minutes later, carried on poles by a scampering group of notables, who gravely lined up before us and, hoisting their pennants, conducted us with slow and solemn pomp to the pagoda.

There is more poetry in a Vietnamese village but less art than in a Moï one. Under magic compulsion the Moïs carve the objects dedicated to the spirits with designs which have come to have a secondary, artistic value. There is little of this kind of art about poor Vietnamese villages. Unlike the Moï, who is non-specialized and self-sufficient, the Vietnamese belongs to a money society, and is a market for manufactured products, most of them shoddy; although he may have one or two good pieces of pre-war Chinese porcelain about the house. He does not object to living in a hovel provided that it contains a vase of flowers and the essence of the perfect household represented by the bright and blossom-decked niche dedicated to the ancestral spirits. The Vietnamese is fortunate in that his household lares do not suffer from the fussy obsession for order of their Moï counterparts.

The pagoda of Phu-Tho, then, was nothing more than a wooden shack, with a corrugated-iron roof – the most valuable part of its construction – which would have disgraced any Moï village. For all that, it was gay with jonquils, narcissus, and chrysanthemums, coaxed into choice and grotesque shapes by the devoted cunning of these serene-faced patriarchs. One wall of the pagoda could be opened up completely, and before this opening we sat on a row of chairs, while joss-sticks were lighted and gongs reverently thumped. An official presented us with a rectangle of vermilion paper apiece, excellently painted with Chinese ideograms for conventional New Year's greetings. Mine read 'five felicities under the same door'. These Chinese New Year's greetings are much prized throughout Indo-China, particularly in remote districts of Cambodia and Laos where there are no Chinese. Here the meanings of the ideograms are unknown and the consequent element of mystery enhances their magic virtues. One sees them pasted on most doorposts in some villages, where they are carefully preserved the year round.

Our visit to the pagoda was in deference to a principle no different from that followed in Moï villages. We were being presented to the tutelary spirit. The pagoda of a tutelary spirit is to be found in every

Vietnamese village, and sometimes there are two or more. In the past the ancient cult has been modified by the system of Confucius and by Buddhism, but now the driving force in the two great philosophies has faltered and waned, and the cult still survives. The tutelary spirit was once some outstanding village personality, or even its founder, for whom, in return for services rendered, has been created a sort of spiritual baronetcy. In Phu-Tho there was nothing particularly colourful related of the character of this semi-divine distinguished citizen, but at another village I visited he had been a thief of quite extraordinary prowess. For the annual feast some meritorious person was granted the privilege of representing him in a ceremony which consisted in the representative's breaking into the pagoda at night and carrying off the sacred tablets. He was then chased, caught, pelted with mud and refuse by the indignant villagers, and received a ritual beating to which every tax-paying male was allowed to contribute his blow. Having recovered from this treatment, he became the guest of honour at the subsequent feast.

It was inevitable that the presentation of the pagoda should be followed by the Vietnamese equivalent of the alcohol jar. Unfortunately the civilities of the morning had provoked in the case of each of us a severe attack of the kind of indigestion that follows an excess of rice-alcohol. We were alarmed, then, when, cramped with heartburn, we were led into the Spanish-type patio of the *Chef du conseil*'s house, and observed a table laden with bottles of sweet, heavy, French aperitifs. We took our seats at the table, eyeing the bottles dully, while the notables filed slowly in, and stood in a cricle facing us, round the walls. They were dressed in black coats and turbans and white trousers. There was a moment of confusion when it was realized that someone had usurped the Resident's chair of honour, distinguished by a towel that had been hung over the back, but this was soon put right, and the *Chef du conseil* standing forward, with head bent slightly and clasped hands, delivered a fairly long speech of welcome in Vietnamese. As soon as this was over the notables advanced implacably with cakes of rice, honey, and nuts, stamped into the shapes appropriate to the season, others arriving with cups of tea, while yet others resolutely uncorked the bottles – chosen, I was certain, for their colour, as they were all red – and poured out a white Bakelite mugful of Cap Corse, Suze, or Campari – whichever happened to be nearest. Our attendants then took a respectful pace back to allow us to drink. There was a moment of hesitation while the notables looked on anxiously, then the Resident, abstemious by nature but conscientious in his duties, raised his glass. Murmurs of approval came from the onlookers and now, to our consternation, we saw that bottles of champagne were being uncorked. But the notables were all smiles and highly delighted with the miniature explosions of the popping corks, reminding them, no doubt, of celebratory firecrackers, and therefore highly suitable to the occasion. For the champagne the white Bakelite mugs were removed and replace in the interests of colour-harmony with pale blue ones.

At last, although from a glance at a side-table it was clear that more colour-combinations of liquors and mugs had been intended, the Resident seized an opportunity to rise. The ceremonial drum was rushed into position, the banners elevated, and off we went, at a rapid if unsteady shuffle. But it was not back to the Resident's Citroën that we were led. Instead the procession stopped before another house, a replica of the first, with the Spanish patio, the towel-draped chair, the felicitous cakes, the encircling notables, and a startling vision of a liquor called Eau de Violette in lemon-coloured containers. This, we found, was the house of the religious head of the community, who was, if anything, more important than the mayor, and we should have been taken there first but for the fact that our host had been caught unprepared by our premature arrival.

Next day the awaited news had come from Stung Treng, and it was discouraging. Cambodian bandits, displaced as I learned later by operations against them in central Cambodia, had arrived in the area. It was a good spot for bandits, removed as far as possible from the centres of authority and yet populated by many prosperous fishing villages along the Sré-Pok and Sé-San rivers; tributaries of the Mékong, between which the road to Stung Treng ran. The Resident said that he had business with the chief of the Jarai village of Ču-Ty, which was a good way along my road. This man was also chief of a *secteur* of villages and his jurisdiction ran as far as Bo-Kheo, being in this direction, at the native level, co-extensive with that of the Resident himself. The Resident said we should be able to get up-to-date information from him of the situation on the borders of Cambodia and Laos.

Accordingly we set out in the Resident's lorry, accompanied by a schools inspector from Pleiku who wanted to visit the school at Ču-Ty, and an entirely Europeanized Jarai interpreter, who wore handsome French clothes and the latest fashion in plastic belts and wrist-straps. This young man, who was in his early twenties, was the first successfully Westernized Moï I had seen. He looked like a minor French film star and was indistinguishable from a southern European, except, perhaps, that he smiled more. The Resident happened to mention that he was a young man of exceptional intelligence, adding that it was a further testimony to the inherent mental capabilities of primitive peoples that he knew of another Jarai boy who had left his village for the first time when nine years old and had just been commissioned in the army after having passed out of the officer's school with the highest marks of his class.

It was clear that the road westwards to Ču-Ty was regarded as of strategic value, because Jarai labourers were hard at work clearing the forest to a depth of about a hundred yards on each side. The vast bonfires they had started gave rise to a strange phenomenon. Millions of winged insects fleeing the conflagration were being chased by certainly thousands of birds offering a wonderful opportunity for a naturalist interested in the ornithology and the insect life of South-East Asia. Some of the birds were trim and tight-looking; flycatchers, perhaps, successfully engaged in a normal routine. Others, managing with difficulty their spectacular plumage, extracted less profit from the holocaust. Sometimes, absorbed in the chase, birds came floundering into the lorry and disgorged a half-swallowed butterfly before taking off. There were other predators, too, that benefited. The elegant hawks of the plateau of Kontum had gathered to feast upon those whose caution had been dulled by excess.

The village of Ču-Ty was built imposingly on a hill-top, and its chief awaited us at the head of the steps leading to the veranda of his long-house. He was a huge, grinning villain; a Jarai Henry the Eighth, whose name, Prak, meant money. He possessed five elephants, three wives, several rice-fields, and a jeep, given to him by the planter of Pleiku, who was reported to pay him ten piastres for each man supplied to the plantations, in addition to the half-piastre paid by the government. Prak was one of those energetic, scheming rascals, who could have been in other times a king among his people, but had sold himself for a trifling sum.

There were none of the elaborate Moï courtesies forthcoming where Prak was concerned. He had learned Western forthrightness in such matters, and awaited us on his veranda, dressed in a single-breasted jacket, while a servitor stood at his elbow with a quart of brandy and a breakfast cup to serve it in. Prak was not the man, either, to worry about ritual offerings of eggs and rice or tobacco leaves. He made a sign and a member of his retinue picked up a piece of wood, dropped from the veranda, and fell upon a passing piglet. There was a light-seeming but practised blow, the pig fell shuddering, and the man set fire to a nearby pile of brushwood and threw the corpse in the flames. The whole thing was done in perhaps two minutes. The sow wandered up and sniffed nostalgically at the gout of blood left by her offspring on the scene of the tragedy. We went into the long-house whilst Prak snapped out a few orders, sending his minions scurrying in all directions to line up alcohol jars and fetch water.

While the sacrifice was in preparation we strolled over with the inspector to visit the school. It seemed very large for the size of the village. There were about thirty children in a classroom decorated with their own drawings of jeeps and man-faced tigers. As we entered the room the children stood and began to sing what was perhaps the school song, consisting of a repetition of the words 'Bonjour Monsieur, merci Monsieur'. The inspector praised the Jarai master for the attendance and the master told him that when any child failed to attend regularly Prak sent for the father and beat him.

The schoolmaster was petrified by the importance of the occasion. When the inspector told him to let us see the physical culture class in action, the only thing he could think of getting them to demonstrate for our benefit was breathing exercises. We stood there watching the small chests inflating and deflating hundreds of times, as it seemed, before realizing that the schoolmaster intended the repertoire to go no further than this. Finally the inspector, whose eyes were beginning to bulge, could stand it no longer. 'Surely that's not all they've been taught?' The schoolmaster explained that he had thought best to perfect one thing at a time and that they had tended to concentrate, until now, on rhythmical breathing. His scared voice could hardly be heard above the busy intake and expulsion of breath. The inspector went over to tell them to stop but although the children showed the whites of their eyes at the approach of the fierce, pale face, they could not be made to understand. 'Well, for God's sake get them to do something,' the inspector said. 'Don't have them stand about like this. Get them on the move. They have got legs, haven't they?' Prak looked on, wiping the palms of his hands together and leering ferociously at the schoolmaster who, in desperation, managed another order, and the boys formed a line and began to run round in a circle. When asked by the inspector what they called that, the schoolmaster said, correct running. The inspector swore and we walked away, leaving the pupils and future citizens of Ču-Ty to their correct running, which they continued until we were out of sight.

In spite of the informality of Prak's reception his conduct of the ensuing ceremony was exemplary, and it was an interesting one, preserving possibly more of its ancient character than any I had previously seen. The Resident was seated before the jars with his right foot placed on the customary copper bracelet, which itself rested on an axehead and contained some cotton and pieces of pork cut from the recently slain pig. A bowl containing the pig's heart and its four feet was placed on the ground so that the Resident faced it while the sorcerer went through the familiar manipulations with a white cock. Prak's wealth was, of course, displayed in an impressive battery of gongs, and when these struck up they raised a din which brought the domestic animals scurrying from far and near for their share in the libations. Prak's alcohol, too, was stronger than I had tasted, the principal jar being hardly weaker than proof whisky. None of the members of the harem appeared, but it was soon evident that they were conducting a ceremony of their own, for a strange sound was heard from the interior apartments. It was a gramophone, playing sambas and rumbas; the favourite, 'Maria de Bahia', being played some half-dozen times while we were there. The interpreter, who had been sitting apart, his face graven with a smile of resolute tolerance, told me that such Latin-American popular recording was the only type of Western music popular with the Moïs.

The afternoon's entertainment was concluded when Ču-Ty's leading elephant hunter gave a demonstration of his skill with the crossbow. Having heard much of Moï aptitude with this weapon (for example, they kill even elephants with an enormous bow loaded by two men), I was ready to be shown marvels. With suitable reverence we stood by while the great man was handed his bow, selected from a quiver a two-foot length of untipped bamboo, and slipped it, with professional unconcern, into the notch. One half expected a cruel piece of eccentricity of the William Tell order, which would have to be sternly discountenanced by the Resident, or, failing that, the splitting of a wand at thirty paces after the manner of Sherwood Forest. Our marksman, however, requested from Prak, and was granted, permission to aim at a fairly stout sacrificial mast from about half this distance. The bolt was discharged with such terrific force that I did not see it in the air. However, to the great satisfaction of the onlooking villagers, it missed the mast. The second bolt went home and it took two men to pull it out again.

The Resident now asked Prak for information about the road to Stung Treng and Prak told him that there were bandits in and around Bo-Kheo itself, and that shooting had been heard in this village on the previous day. Further conversation followed in private;

it probably had to do with the demand for three hundred more men for the plantations. When this subject happened to come up I asked one of the Resident's staff what would happen to a man who ran away from the plantation and went back to his village. The answer was that the chief, who had received a premium for him, would undoubtedly send him back again. If, on the other hand, the man left his village to avoid labour or military conscription, he would be breaking customary law, since it was an offence for a man to leave his village without the chief's sanction. One could imagine the fate of any fugitive who threw himself on Prak's mercy.

When we left Prak escorted us part of our way in his jeep. With great difficulty he was levered into the seat next to the driver, half tipsy and humming through his nose 'The Lady in Red'. Behind him sat the elephant hunter, having substituted a Sten gun for his bow. Thus the cortège set out for Pleiku. As we passed the school the pupils were lined up at the roadside waving tricolors and chanting, '*Bonjour Monsieur, merci Monsieur*', which, as it sounded extremely like something by Ketelby, seems to suggest that this composer's inspiration was sometimes more truly oriental in feeling than most of us have supposed.

Back at Pleiku we discussed over a dinner of roast peacock – which was rather like tough veal – the possibility of my getting through to Stung Treng. Once again the Resident told me that he would willingly take me to Bo-Kheo, but thought that it would be extremely ill-advised to make the journey. I formed the opinion that he was secretly worried at the idea of my going so far, even as Bo-Kheo, because, as he later confessed, apart from any responsibility he felt over me, he frankly didn't want to lose an almost irreplaceable car. This being a very reasonable and understandable attitude, I felt that I could not trespass any further on the Resident's kindness. The original intention, as suggested by Monsieur de la Fournière at Saigon, had been to take advantage of any lifts I could get with people who in the ordinary course of their duties were travelling across country. But the people didn't exist, and it had never been any part of my intention to inveigle administrators, hard pushed as they were, into making special journeys, involving risk to their personnel and vehicles, on my behalf. I therefore told Monsieur Préau that I had decided against attempting to make the cross-country journey to Laos and would return, as soon as an opportunity offered, to Saigon.

The Resident then suggested as an alternative that I might go further north to Kontum, the ultimate town in French occupation. Kontum is the centre of the Bahnar country, where Bahnar villages are still to be seen, not as I had seen them in wretched degeneration at Mang-Yang, but unspoilt, with their amazing communal houses with steepled roofs and their primitive communism which is carried to such lengths that a single chicken will, if necessary, be divided into fifty parts. It was an attractive idea, but I felt that this delay might endanger the visit to Laos, which might be cut off by the rains before I could get there. When opportunities of this kind turned up one always had to think, not so much about the time expended in the actual journey, as the time one might have to waste, stranded somewhere, awaiting some means of getting back. The Resident then made another suggestion. He was obliged to make a routine visit to the village of Plei-Kli, which was one hundred miles on the road to Ban Méthuot. If I wanted to take this opportunity to get back to Ban Méthuot, he would come with me, as it would provide him with a good excuse to get away for a couple of days. This suggestion I naturally fell in with, only too relieved to find that I should not have to lose a week or two in Pleiku before an opportunity arose of getting away.

Our arrival at Ban Méthuot coincided with the first day of the feast of Têt. All activity in the town was paralysed. The shops were shut and there was nobody about. For the Vietnamese this was the combination of all the religious feasts of the Western world, and, since there is no Sabbath in the East, it was the only holiday of the year. Just before midnight a ceremony had been staged in each Vietnamese house to take leave of the household spirit of the expiring lunar year, which is believed to return at this time to the

Jade Emperor with a detailed report of the family's actions, for good or for evil. The departing spirit had been provided, in addition to a lavish send-off meal, with money for the voyage, mandarins' shoes, a winged bonnet of the kind that only spirits and mandarins are entitled to wear, and the legendary carp on which the spirit would ride to heaven. The feast would serve also to welcome the incoming spirit and to invite the ancestral spirits to participate in the ensuing New Year's festivities. The day of our arrival would be dedicated to visits exchanged by families and friends, the Scottish custom of 'first footing' in reverse, as there is some competition to avoid being the first to cross a threshold at the New Year, since to do so is to carry the responsibility for any misfortunes which may fall on the family during that year.

Monsieur Doustin was, of course, not at all surprised to see me again, but did not know how he was going to get me back to Saigon. The whole country would be in the catalepsy of the Têt for a full week, and, even after that, he had no idea when a convoy would be formed. The recent attacks had thrown the merchants into a panic. Ban Méthuot, it seemed, was effectively sealed off by solemn feasting and by war. Back in my old room at the Residence I resigned myself to a prolonged appreciation of the view from my window, which looked out over a gracious garden with a peach tree in bloom. It seemed that one or two young couples had succeeded in evading the festive confinement and had made a pilgrimage to admire the classic distortions of the branches and to have themselves photographed against a background of blossom.

Perhaps twenty minutes of reflection were allowed to me before Doustin re-appeared. The Emperor Bao-dai's plane was arriving in half an hour, and if it were to be returning to Dalat or Saigon he saw no reason why he shouldn't ask for a lift for me. We therefore jumped into his car and shot out to the airport, arriving there just as the plane had touched down. It was a Dakota, and I was truly delighted to see that a dragon had been painted on the fuselage.

The Emperor was the first to alight, followed by a young lady in black velvet robes, whom from her carriage, which was even more regal than that of most Vietnamese girls, I stupidly presumed to be the Empress. I was later informed that she had been Miss Hanoi 1949, and had accepted the position of air-hostess on the Emperor's plane. Several French officers and civilians followed but there were no Vietnamese in the imperial entourage. I was presented to the Emperor who shook hands with reasonable vigour, while I recalled that up to the reign of his grandfather an even accidental physical contact with the Son of Heaven would have involved strangulation, although if the offender had committed the breach of taboo with the intention of protecting the Divine Emperor from some danger, he would have been posthumously promoted to a high rank in the mandarinate and furnished with an expensive tomb.

Although thick-set for a Vietnamese, Bao-dai was not, as American newspapers have described him, 'pudgy'. In contrast to the experience of some newspaper correspondents who told me that he always seemed bored when interviewed, I found him cheerful enough, possibly at the prospect of a hunting-trip. He asked me if I hunted and I said that I did not. (I had been warned that it was not a good thing to be invited to join a Bao-dai hunting party.) The reply surprised the Emperor and the well-arched imperial eyebrows were raised slightly higher. I explained that I lived in England where game was neither plentiful, varied, nor spectacular. The Emperor said that I should try elephant shooting and that there was no better place to make a start than Ban Méthuot. Doustin then asked the Emperor if he would be returning to Dalat or Saigon, as if so I would like a lift, and the Emperor told him that he was going hunting for a few days, but that I was welcome to fly back with him after that. In fact he might decide to send the plane back the next day, in which case the pilot could take me.

But not two hours later I was disturbed once again in the contemplation of my peach tree and the strolling Vietnamese beauties. Doustin came to report that two officials from Dalat who had been staying in the town had just been given permission by Bao-dai to return by way of the Emperor's private hunting road, and I could go with them if I liked. They were leaving immediately and would stay at the Poste du Lac in readiness to make the usual small-hours start in the morning.

We were received with the exuberant melancholy of the true existentialist. While the two hunters got out their various weapons, fussed happily with them, and deluded themselves with a mirage of false hopes for the morrow, I retired to the veranda and thumbed over the latest selection to arrive from Le Club Français du Livre. Whenever I raised my eyes it was over an impeccable landscape. Eagles were shattering the ice-blue mirror of the lake and a flight of white birds, far off against the dim mountains, were no more than particles of glittering metallic dust.

Thus night descended. At dusk we heard the motor of the electric generator start up and my host smiled with cautious satisfaction. Light pulsated in the filaments of the electric bulbs for perhaps thirty seconds before failing. As on every previous evening the engine had immediately broken down. We lit the lamps and settled down to an evening's reading. But there was a sudden alarm. Somewhere below us in the forest, we heard a car accelerating uphill, and peering through the window we could see headlights shining through the trees. The car was coming in our direction. There could be only one explanation of this extraordinary event – the approach of the imperial hunting party. It seems that taken thus by surprise, our host felt himself ill-prepared to receive a visit from the most august personage in the land. At all events the lights were quickly extinguished – a cautionary measure which was quite successful, for we heard the car stop and depart.

Those who follow the mystery of the hunter know not the lassitudes affecting ordinary mortals. The Emperor's hunting trips, which last all night, are said by those who have taken part in them to involve the most appalling risks and exertions. Fortunately the Vice-Mayor and the Chief Justice's wish to make a start before dawn was frustrated by our host's civilized horror of such excesses. As a compromise, breakfast was served to the howling of monkeys at daybreak. Ten minutes later we were out on Bao-dai's hunting track. On all occasions when the Emperor travels by road between Dalat and Ban Méthuot, this is the way he comes and I think that there may be some significance in the strange fact that no escort is required, although the track is far nearer the territory continuously occupied by the Viet-Minh than the main road where attacks are so frequent. This ties up perhaps with the fact that there had never been an attempt on the Viet-Minh's part to assassinate the Emperor, and it is not an original hypothesis that the Emperor's role in relation to the French may be similar to that now claimed for Marshal Pétain *vis-à-vis* the Germans. Some secret understanding may in fact exist between the Emperor and the extreme nationalists.

The road, narrow and winding, affords many a sickening glimpse of a fern-clad precipice through the screen of lianas and bamboos. On this morning it was bitterly cold and only the heights were free from a thick, clammy mist. Suddenly, without warning, we would emerge from this, while climbing, into the brilliant sunshine, so that the mist lay spread out below us like the surface of a steaming lake, with islands of rock and vegetation. Once a silver pheasant came winging up through the surface like a gorgeous flying-fish, and flew on to settle in one of the tree-top islands. The Vice-Mayor and the Judge shot several wild-cocks that, however maimed, clung to their lives with the frightful tenacity of their kind. Five peacocks, surprised in the deserted Moï rice-field, flew vertically to the topmost branches of a tree, and there were slaughtered – perfect targets sitting sihouetted against the sky. But this was the total bag, and a mighty wild boar absorbed at close range a charge of ball-shot and departed with no sign of inconvenience.

We stopped to collect some orchids for the Vice-Mayor's wife. They were white and orange like tiny jonquil flowers and hung in clusters on waxen stems. While the Vice-Mayor was up the tree, I took an interest in some of the insects. There were huge dragonflies that came darting up and remained stationary at a distance of a foot or so, accompanying me as if inquisitive. Their wings, which were without the usual sheen, moved with such rapidity that their bodies seemed to be unsupported in the air. Another large winged insect was equally happy in at least two of the elements. On alighting, its wings were folded away with great deliberation into a protective case, after which, streamlined, and without impeding projections, it scampered off to forage among the fallen leaves and grass-roots.

At midday we stopped to cook a meal of tiny eggs. This part of the forest was intersected by many small streams and the damp earth sprouted an endless variety of ferns, from all the small recognizable ones of Europe to some as large as palms and others that looked like bracken but were the colour of the brightest beech-leaves in autumn. After the early morning, for some reason or other, one did not expect to see game, but there were plenty of large inedible birds about, and the frequent appearance of a *coq de pagode* which looked like jungle-fowl but had a long tail and could have only been eaten, said my friends, by a starving man, sent them several times scrambling vainly for their guns.

It was near here that we saw, in the distance, the last of the Moï villages, and decided that it would do our digestions good to walk to it. We crossed over a bridge of twisted lianas and walked perhaps half a mile along a path through rice-fields. The village was a M'nong Gar one, with the houses built on the earth itself. In the distance it was a pleasant enough sight, with its yellow thatched roofs, the sacrificial masts with their streamers, and the children playing in the clean, open spaces. We passed the mounds of several abandoned graves and others which were still open, with miniature houses built over them containing the personal possessions of the defunct; his clothing, blankets, necklaces, jars, drums, the rice-bowls that are replenished daily, and the horns of the buffalo sacrificed at the funeral.

By the time we reached the village it was deserted. There was a single woman left alone, sifting herbs outside her hut, but she paid not the slightest attention to us. Three of our party of four were armed, and we wondered whether the sudden appearance of armed men in their midst had caused the villagers to disappear like this. At the other end of the village we found more signs of life. Two men were at work making *coupe-coupes* in a primitive forge, while a boy worked the bellows made from two thick sections of bamboo, filled with wooden pistons. These also ignored us, but one of the men suddenly got up, with face averted, and went away towards the entrance to the village. The Vice-Mayor suspected that he might be going to organize an ambush in case we committed any hostile action. He thought that it was best to act in a natural and unconcerned way, so we picked up various half-finished *coupe-coupes* and put them down again, and wanted to take an interest in the woman's occupation, but she had gone. The Judge rather overdid his nonchalance – much to the alarm of the Rhadés chauffeur – by fingering the ornaments on one of the sacrificial masts. The Rhadés chauffeur who only knew a few words of French, said he could not speak the local dialect. The village, he said, was forbidden and we must go immediately. He could give no explanation for this opinion and when questioned drained his face of intelligence and took refuge in '*Moi pas connaisse*'.

There was something a little sinister about this village that was deserted even by the domestic animals. No sooner had we left the forge than it became silent. The imagination, too, was affected by the framework supporting buffalo skulls, flanked by two Easter-Island figures that had been stained by sacrificial blood. As we reached the outskirts we heard the slapping of naked feet behind us. The man who had stayed behind in the forge was running after us. He stopped a few paces away and bowing his head respectfully took his right elbow in his left palm and came forward to touch hands with each of us in turn. He was the chief, we found, and seeing that we intended no harm he had had an attack of bad conscience at his shocking breach of good manners in letting us go like that. Now, said the chauffeur, who had suddenly recovered his wits, he had come to invite us back to the village to broach a jar of alcohol with him.

CHAPTER TWELVE

Cholon and Cochin-China

AIR-FRANCE planes from Dalat were booked up three weeks ahead. By what I thought at the time was a miracle I got a seat on a plane run by a small company without any delay. It turned out later that there was not much demand for this plane as the company had had one or two crashes on the run. There was not much hope of a successful forced-landing in those jungles.

While waiting to take off, I chatted with a fellow passenger, a Vietnamese student, who wanted to know what I was doing in the country. I told him, and the conversation immediately took a political turn. Which Vietnamese intellectuals had I met? I confessed that I had met none. The student didn't see how I could form any objective opinion of the conditions of his country when the only opinions I listened to were those of French colonialists. This reasonable point of view had already occurred to me and I said that the chief reason why I had made no contacts among the Vietnamese was that, judging from their manner, they would be difficult to approach. The student said that this was natural enough, as I would be taken for a Frenchman. He persisted so strongly that I should meet certain intellectuals that I was sure that he was about to suggest how this could be done when the plane took off. We were seated on loose camp-stools and as soon as the plane began to lurch in the hot air-currents we were thrown about rather badly. My friend, who was flying for the first time, was violently ill and I did not have the chance of speaking to him again.

Saigon was as rumbustious as ever, with lorries full of Algerians patrolling the streets and the cafés full of German legionnaires. I dined at a Chinese restaurant on the main road to Cholon. This was outside the European quarter and I enjoyed the district because of the turbulent processes of living that went on all round me. Although I noticed in my newspaper that this restaurant advertised itself as having *emplacement discret*, the walls were much scarred from a bomb which had been thrown in it the previous night. Perhaps for this reason it was crowded, in deference to the theory that two shells do not burst in the same crater. The waiter said that they hoped to have a wire-grille fitted by the next day, which would keep the grenades out. Their little incident had only contributed two casualties to the grand total of seventeen for the night. But a colleague had been one of the unfortunate pair. His condition, said my waiter, was very grave, and curiously enough, all this had been foretold by the resident fortune-teller, who I now observed to be approaching my table carrying the tools of his trade and smiling in anticipation of the grisly predictions he would unfold for suitable payment.

I had happened to read that a Vietnamese nationalist newspaper had been suppressed and this gave me an idea. Next day I called at the paper's office and asked to see the Editor. He was not there. When would he come? Nobody knew. Well, would he ever come? I was trying to pin down one of the blank-faced employees to commit himself to a definite statement, but, without knowing it, I was a beginner engaging in a verbal ju-jitsu with masters of the art, whose forebears for several generations had schooled themselves to meet force with evasion. Too much directness on my part only produced a '*pas connaisse*', and while still trying to talk my way out of this fog of non-cooperation I found myself manœuvred out into the street. A Vietnamese was walking on either side but in a casual and non-committal manner, as if they were going somewhere on their own account and they happened by chance to find themselves walking at the same speed as myself. Refusing to talk anything but the pidgin-French which allowed for maximum of misunderstanding, they suggested that I might like to disclose, without reserve, the full nature of my business with the Editor. There was nothing for it but to tell them. Others joined them, friends it seemed, particles broken haphazardly from the great anonymous crowd, and I was invited to repeat my story. While we strolled thus, separated continually by boys on bicycles, beggars, animals, and children playing with toys, the thing was considered and at last – it was hinted at, rather than announced – I gathered that if I called back that afternoon I might, or might not, see someone who would interest me.

I was naturally not surprised when I returned that no one I recognized was there. The faces of that morning were not to be seen, and when I called across the counter to one of the much abstracted clerks, I got the '*pas connaisse*' that I expected. There was a flight of stairs at the end of the room and I went up them into a first-floor room. A young man came out from behind a partition, and said in English, with a good accent, 'Are you the Englishman?' He wore thick spectacles and had a grave, studious expression. In starting to introduce myself I spoke French, and he asked me, a trifle sharply, to speak English. I told him the reason for my presence in the country and that as until then I had been exposed solely to French propaganda from the other side. This remark was not considered funny. With a sternly reproving glance the young man told me that all Vietnamese patriots were members of the Viet-Minh and that if I really wanted to see Vietnam, I should not bother with French-occupied territory but cross the lines to the Democratic Republic. I told him that I should be delighted to do so, if given the opportunity. He then asked to see any documents that might help to establish my bona fides, and I showed him my passport and various letters. The application, he said, would have to be submitted to the branch of the army of the Viet-Minh which dealt with such matters. He thought that it would take several weeks to get an answer and to make arrangements for 'crossing over'. I asked whether he thought permission would be granted and he said yes. He regretted being unable to give me his name and told me that I should be unable to get in touch with him again, but he would find means to contact me when the moment came.

This was the first of such political experiences, and that night the second occurred in the most improbable way.

I had been invited to spend the evening with a French journalist and his Vietnamese mistress. It was evident from the start that it would follow the standard pattern: dinner at the Chalet, followed by an excursion to Cholon for a visit to the gambling casino and one or more of the night-clubs. Cholon is a purely Chinese city, about three miles from Saigon, which it overshadows in almost all activities. For some reason or other it is supposed to be more 'typically Chinese' than the great seaports of China itself, and one is told in proof of this that the city shots in some Hollywood epic of life in China were taken in its streets. There is a great, swollen wartime population of perhaps three-quarters of a million, most of whom live wretchedly, and an exceptional proportion of millionaires whose number is continually added to by black-marketeering triumphs arising out of the present war. The Chinese are go-betweens for both sides. They sell food from the rural Viet-Minh areas to the French towns, and the dollars smuggled in from France, which are needed to buy arms, to the Viet-Minh. As they are not affected by causes, either good or evil, they prosper exceedingly.

Cholon capitalizes, to some extent, its exotic attraction for Europeans, but this is offset by the necessity at the same time to provide titillation for the rich Chinese, who form the bulk of the patrons at the places of amusement. The result is an astonishing pastiche. Our first visit on this particular occasion was to the 'Van Canh Nightspot', at which a certain Ramona was billed to appear each evening, '*dans ses danses exotiques*'. The band was Philippine and played with great feeling such revived classics as 'September in the Rain'. Ramona, who was stated to be 'direct from Mexico City' but who, I noticed, spoke Italian to her partner, performed a hip-rolling fantasy of her own devising, inspired undoubtedly by the Bosphorus rather than the China Seas. The clientèle was composed in the main of elderly Chinese rice-merchants, who danced with Chinese and Vietnamese taxi-girls.

After this, my friend was lured by his girl into the 'Parc des Attractions', where she, but not he, was frisked at the entrance for concealed weapons. Like most Vietnamese, she was a victim of the passion for gambling, and by limiting herself each day to a certain sum which she placed on well-known exceptionally lucky combinations, her losses were regular but not disastrous. On this occasion, influenced by her interpretation of a dream, she lost in record time. This was one of Cholon's two great gambling dens, and here, in a cheerful fun-fair atmosphere, the wealth of the Vietnamese people, both high and low – since all incomes are catered for – drains steadily away into the coffers of the Chinese, who, of course, are made to pay very dearly by the French authorities for the facilities thus afforded.

We finished up at the 'Paradis', and it was here that the amazing circumstances happened. The Paradis is favoured by the Chinese, who are attracted by the discreet indirect lighting, which is lowered as often as possible during sentimental numbers. Most of the girls – at least, the Chinese ones – who act as hostesses are supposed to have been sold into glittering servitude by their impoverished parents, and it is a polite convention to refer to this as soon as possible over the champagne, and to press one's temporary partner for details of this romantic aspect of her past. A celebrated crooner, Wang Sue, was at the microphone, but it was 'September in the Rain' again, and while the powerful sing-song voice intoned 'the leaves of brown came tumbling down' my friends went off to dance leaving me to the mercy of the 'taxi-manager' who arrived with *une girl* they had secretly ordered for me. (Why had English been chosen as the lingua-franca of such pleasures?) The fourth member of our party had the fragile aristocracy of manner of most Vietnamese dance-hostesses. Her features, powdered chalk-white, wore a kind of death-bed composure. She was sheathed in the traditional costume, in this case of white silk, had incredible fingernails, and every hair on her head was, I am quite sure, in place. The only human touch in this total of geisha perfections was a man's wrist watch which bulked enormously on that lotus-stem wrist.

The two girls were evidently old friends, probably colleagues. They chatted happily, and once, from the oriental, fan-screened glances I intercepted, it seemed that I was the object of their remarks. When the other two got up again, the girl said, 'You are English, aren't you? Do you think that we Vietnamese are as civilized as the French?' Somewhat surprised by this first sample of small-talk in a Saigon night-club, I replied, yes, that I thought they were. From this point on the conversation followed the lines of that with my chance acquaintance on the Dalat plane, although as the circumstances were more favourable, it was carried to a more profitable conclusion. It was through this girl that I was put in touch with the leading Vietnamese revolutionary-nationalists in Saigon.

A message left next day at the hotel invited me to call at a certain address at a certain time. I went there and found that the address given was a luxurious-looking villa. There were several expensive cars outside. A group of Vietnamese, who were at first reluctant to give their names, awaited me. Among them was a prosperous lawyer, a bank director, and an ex-member of the Cabinet of the Governor of Cochin-China. All these people were members of the wealthy, land-owning class, and all were whole-hearted supporters of the Viet-Minh, which, if, as it is said to be, under communist control, would supposedly dispossess them as soon as it came to power. One of this group was actually known to be a high-ranking member of the Viet-Minh, but was left unmolested in Saigon by the French as providing an unofficial diplomatic contact, which could be used whenever the occasion necessitated.

It would be tedious to describe the conversation that followed, but it may be summed up by saying that these people made it clear that the Vietnamese would never be satisfied with anything less from France than India had obtained from England. The 'Independence within the French Union' conceded a year before was described as a bad joke, since it left France's control of all the key positions unaltered. The publication by the Viet-Minh of a secret report prepared in 1948 by Monsieur Bollaert, the previous High Commissioner, for submission to the Prime Minister, had not helped. A great deal of publicity had been given to the sentence which might be roughly translated, 'It is my impression that we must make a concession to Viet-Nam of the term, independence; but I am convinced that this word need never be interpreted in any light other than that of a religious verbalism.'

And that was how it worked out in practice, my informants said. To take the example of the police force. A great show had been made of turning over to the Vietnamese of the Sureté headquarters in the Rue Catinat. But all the French had actually done was to leave the incoming officials an empty building and open up themselves again at another address under the title of Sureté Fédérale. As the Sureté Fédérale had kept all the archives, the Vietnamese organization was disabled from the start. Then again, French troops would be withdrawn from Vietnamese soil, but, somewhat vaguely, 'when the opportune moment arrives'. And, of course, extra-territorial rights were retained, by which persons other than Vietnamese nationals were tried in mixed courts presided over by a French judge. This meant that Cambodians and Laotians, as well as French, were not subject in Vietnam to Vietnamese law, while all matters relating to security came before a French Military tribunal.

Thus, I was informed, was independence interpreted. But there were other and more sinister French manœuvres which envisaged the possibility of the Vietnamese independence becoming real and took steps accordingly. Certain districts such as the Hauts Plateaux and the areas occupied by various tribal groups in Tonkin had been declared racial minority zones and separated entirely from Vietnam. And now, at the assembly of the Union Française the Cambodians, who had never raised their voices before, had been worked upon to demand the return of their old provinces in Cochin-China as well as legal right of access to the port of Saigon. Militant religious sects such as Cao-Daïsm and the Hoa-Hao, originally banned by the King of Cambodia and the Emperor of Annam, had been encouraged as potential separatists and aided in the formation of private armies. In this way, Vietnam, even fully independent, would be weakened in every possible way.

And now after this revelation of rankling injustices and huge-scale political manipulations, a curious complaint was made, the *cri du coeur* of the Asiatic's injured ego, a single comparatively insignificant fact, but significantly disclosed at the end of the list of oppressions: the French were as insultingly exclusive as ever – 'the *cercle sportif* does not admit Vietnamese'. Perhaps, if the French – and the English – had been gentler with their colonial subjects' *amour-propre* in the matter of such things as club memberships, their position in the Far East might have been a lot less precarious than it is.

Planes to Laos were infrequent and the earliest seat I could get was for a fortnight later. In the meanwhile, a French acquaintance, who was trying to sell British Land-Rover cars to the Cambodian army, mentioned that he was sending a sample car to the army head-quarters at Pnom-Penh and asked if I would like to go with it. I accepted the offer, with great pleasure, especially as my friend would be making the journey by plane and suggested that we might spend a few days together in Cambodia. He had lived for several years in the country and knew it as well as any European could.

There were four days to spare before the car went to Cambodia and I filled in this time by going on one of the more-or-less standard excursions round the re-conquered part of Cochin-China arranged for foreign correspondents by the French army. These trips could be quite exciting if one ran into action, and this made the French a little chary about them, because sometimes correspondents saw more than they were supposed to see, and sent back a batch of unfavour-able telegrams. Bob Miller, of the United Press, for instance, was in an armoured barge going up a canal at ten o'clock one night when three sampans were picked up ahead by the searchlight. Two of them failed to stop and were riddled by machine-gun fire. The third gave up and three peasants – an old couple and their son – were brought aboard. They were carrying rice, travelling by night probably to avoid the exactions of local officials. Their cargo was tipped into the water. The boy, who tried to escape by jumping over the side, was killed by a hand-grenade thrown in after him. The officer in command was exceedingly young, charming, and co-operative. He was convinced that the peasants had not been partisans of the Viet-Minh, but they had broken the curfew regulations, and what followed was the logic of warfare. In a country where they were enormously outnumbered by a hostile populace, it was only by making people understand that breaches of regulations would be punished with extreme severity that they could hope to keep the upper hand. But this kind of logic is apt not to be so apparent to non-combatants, including newspaper men, who sometimes protest that it was the attitude of the Nazis in occupied countries.

The scenes and sensations of the next four days followed each other so thick and fast that the memory of them is a photo-montage, a jumble of hardly separable images; the enemy strong-point seen through the bamboo palisade – irresponsive to the machine-gunner's provocation; the thump of the armoured barge nosing through the sedges, ibises rising up from its bows; the soldiers in isolated posts, reining-in their minds with spinsterish occupations, mat-making or knitting; the resigned homage of the notables of fifty villages; the cannonading at night heard from the dim, daemonic interior of a mandarin's palace.

Luong Hoa stands out. There was a Catholic church with a statue of an Annamese saint standing before a junk, and a remarkable grandfather clock which might have become a cult-object, since the priest bowed slightly in passing it. The clock was covered all over with those rather sickly illustrations which usually accompany religious texts, but it was evident that this was local work as a few Chinese lanterns had been fitted in among the roses and angels. Ever since the Jesuits first went to China, the Far East has been bombarded by clocks, and the palaces of most oriental potentates are as cluttered with them as a French municipal pawnshop. But this, if only on account of sheer size – it must have been nine feet tall – was certainly a worthy object of the villagers' pride. Luong Hoa had recently suffered forty casualties in a battle with the Viet-Minh.

The French senior officer commanding in this section who showed me round was a man in his middle fifties who bore an astonishing resemblance to the French film actor Raimu. He was a typical *père de famille*, bluff-natured and mildly eccentric, who liked to have a drink with the sergeant in charge of any post we visited. Dogs took to him wherever we went, and hung about snuffing affectionately at his boots. He carried a tin of condensed milk in his pocket and every now and then would pour out a dollop for them to lick up. It seemed impossible to associate this man with the bloody happenings that must have occurred within the zone of his command, and perhaps by his orders.

We went stumping together through the next village on foot. It was a delightful place, with half the village fishing in a stream by the side of the road and brightly painted houses with good quality coffins displayed for the neighbours' benefit outside most of them. Bougainvillaea exploded streakily across the ceramic-tiled front of a pagoda; a benign dragon writhed across the roof-top, and a dancer, embarrassed by trailing robes of porcelain, waved her cymbals across the gables at a jovial savant facing her. The Commandant patted the heads of Vietnamese children and said that to attempt to drive through the village after dark, let alone walk, would be certain death. He was another of those French officers who remembered with affection some dingy jumping-off point in England for the invasion of Europe, and we were joined from the first moment by the bond of our common experience of Ellesmere Port.

Our road threaded continually through Catholic and Cao-Daïst areas which were said to war incessantly with one another. The local Cao-Daïsts, although in some way schismatic, recognized the Pope at Tay Ninh, even if they did not subject themselves wholeheartedly to his authority. The Commandant said that they specialized in piracy on the waterways with which the province was networked. It had always been Cao-Daïst policy to attempt to duplicate French administration with their own exact counterpart on the ecclesiastical level, but now, he said, they were trying to extend this principle to their military organization, and only the other day a complete Headquarters' Staff arrived from Tay Ninh to be attached to his own HQ at Tanan. He sent them packing.

The Catholics, said the Commandant, with no diminution in cheerfulness, were an even worse menace. Some of them hadn't had an ordained priest since the missionaries were expelled in the early part of the last century, and they spent their time raiding other villages, gathering in their church for two hours every evening to howl the canticles, after which they raped their female captives. Every village we passed was surrounded by double or triple stockades, and sometimes a moat, and overlooked by *miradors*. Some of these structures, said the Commandant, were so rickety through neglect that they would topple over if anyone tried to climb up them.

And this was the state to which the Jesuit Borri's 'near heaven' had come.

That night we dined in the officers' mess at Tanan. On the previous night one of the hand-grenades, which I succeeded always in just missing, had come in through the window and wounded an officer. This time the Commandant had posted sentries so that we should all have a nice quiet evening. But no sooner had we taken our seats than there was a series of explosions. The defence-towers on the outskirts of the town were being attacked by mortar-fire. A few minutes later the French twenty-five-pounders joined in. One after another the officers were called to their posts. By the time the entrée was served the Commandant and I faced a very junior officer across an otherwise deserted table. Soon the light failed and we decided to call it a night.

Of the next day, I remember that we visited the exemplary village of Than Phú, whose state of grace was due to the fact, the French thought, that except for fifteen nominal Catholics the village was a Buddhist one, without Cao-Daïst converts. Than Phú possessed a historic pagoda, the only building, the French said, that had been spared when the Viet-Minh burned the place. It contained a bell in which about a hundred and fifty years ago Gia-Long, the last of the great Emperors, had hidden when fleeing from the rebellious Taysons. To prove that this could be done the bonze crept into the bell. But he was a tiny, wizened old fellow and it was very evident that Gia-Long's descendant, the present Emperor, would have little hope, if the need arose, in emulating his ancestor's feat. The real interest in this pagoda lay in a great cautionary fresco depicting the respective fates in the hereafter of the blessed and the damned. The old bonze, who by the way was much respected by the Commandant, was very proud of this, and there was a smile of gentle satisfaction on his face when the time came to show it off.

The rewards of evil-doing were portrayed with great fidelity to detail across the whole of one wall. Minor crimes that had escaped detection in life were punished here according to their gravity with the four prescribed degrees of chastisement: the facial mark, removal of the nose, amputation of the foot, and castration. The duplication in hell of a felon's death began with the mere strangulation by devils of those who had erred, perhaps, rather than sinned, and included the varieties of slow death prepared for the perpetrators of such atrocious crimes as grossly unfilial conduct. Fiends worked on these offenders with knives marked with the bodily member to be sliced, drawn at random, according to the ancient penal practice, from the lottery sack. Tigers devoured others, and yet others, who had probably in their lifetimes questioned the heavenly mandate of the divine Emperor, were being dismembered by the elephants specially trained to inflict capital punishment. Demon executioners stood apart, in corners, practising their aim on bamboo stalks, marked according to tradition with betel lines.

All the victims concerned were neatly dressed for the occasion, and did not appear to despair; a reflection perhaps of the Annamese custom of encouraging the condemned to meet their ends with as much dignity as the circumstances permitted, and insisting indeed on a show of composure which included the elegant performance of the five ritual prostrations in taking leave of the accompanying relations.

On the opposite wall the blessed were shown in their bliss. But as beatitude is less keenly felt than suffering, the rewards of virtue were insubstantial, even insipid. Heaven was one of those briefly sketched Chinese landscapes; a few misty, not altogether credible peaks, pine trees, a stream, a bridge. It was the heaven of the poet and the artist of one of the early Chinese dynasties, and the Annamese souls in glory wandered through it disconsolately and somewhat out of their element. The old bonze, too, was soon bored with this and lured us with gentle insistence back to the vigorous scenes of damnation, pointing out to us obscure refinements of torture that we had missed.

That a Buddhist pagoda could be decorated in this way, of course, was a measure of the distortion that the religion had suffered in the course of its slow propagation through India and China and finally into Cochin-China. Nirvana had become a picnic excursion to the hills, and the sorrows of the soul bound to the wheel of incarnation, a series of vulgar episodes in the torture-chamber. An illustration, indeed, of the barbarism that infects the great religious systems in their decline.

There was never, by the way, any cause for embarrassment in going boldly into any pagoda in Indo-China, prying curiously among its shrines, watching the rites, and even photographing them. The officiants, on the contrary, were delighted at any manifestation of interest. It is part of a genial Confucian tradition, which has spread to all the other cults. 'The Master having gone in to the Grand Temple, asked questions about everything. Someone remarked: "Who says that the Son of the citizen of Tsou (Confucius) has any knowledge of ceremonial observances? He comes to the temple and asks about everything he sees." Hearing the remark, the Master said: "This in itself is a ceremonial observance."'

Later, when alone, I would make a trifling donation to the pagoda funds, which would be enthusiastically acknowledged by the beating of a great gong and the burning for my benefit of a few inches of one of the great spiralling coils of incense suspended from the roof. And sometimes the old priest would throw in a minor piece of divination, shaking into my hand one of a jarful of what looked like spills, but which were assorted prophetic utterances from the classics, written on slips of screwed-up paper. Coming to my help with the elegant but inexplicable ideographs he would clearly indicate by his gleeful, congratulatory smile that at last Fortune was about to open wide its arms to me.

Than Phú, the exemplary village, was followed by the ideal French post. It had been the work of a *sergent-chef* who, like the Commandant, would shortly be returning, demobilized, to France, where it was obvious that they would both spend the rest of their days in a Kipling-esque nostalgia for Indo-China. And yet, much as the colonies had become his spiritual home, and depressed as he was at the thought of his repatriation, the *Sergent-chef* was extremely proud of the fact that he had made his post a Corner of France. And at what a cost. He had imported bulbs by air-mail and there had been a painful sprouting of tulips, dragged inch by inch from that ochreous soil, their heads now hanging a little wearily in the nooses that attached them to their supporting canes. Over them reared up exuberant ranks of canna, grown only to afford shade for the European importation. A native hut, too, had been pathetically camouflaged as a *bistro*; a *rendezvous des sports* for the benefit of visiting NCOs. Anything to shut out for a while the hateful sight of bamboos, the memory of which would become so dear in a few months' time.

The *Sergent-chef* also kept a boa-constrictor in a cage. It was fed monthly with a live duck, a ceremony which collected appreciative crowds. He said that the snake refused to interest itself in food that was not alive.

A new Vietnamese village had formed like a series of cells round the ideal post. In their tragic situation, the prey of every kind of gangster and bandit, the peasants' one craving is for protection and stability. Their village destroyed in military operations, they live uncomfortably dispersed in temporary shelters and eat the shrimps and undersized fish caught in the irrigation ditches. As soon as a military post goes up in their neighbourhood they are naturally attracted to it, and under the cover of its machine-guns they rebuild their huts, plant their vegetables, establish a market. They are encouraged to do this, and tragedy only happens when the Viet-Minh, first terrorizing the villagers, use its cover to attack the post. Massacres have occurred in the subsequent reprisals, which, since by this time the Viet-Minh have left, are directed against the villagers.

The new village without a name was, temporarily at least, prospering. The *Sergent-chef* had appointed himself unofficial mayor and was insisting on European sanitary standards, which, to his surprise, were scrupulously carried out. He held a daily inspection of the streets and market place, made vendors mark the prices on their goods, awarded certificates of merit for the best kept houses. He helped to fit up a town-hall and a theatre – the two essentials of Vietnamese communal life – and presented the information centre with a frivolous dragon which he found in a deserted ruin. The Vietnamese, who had probably seen their last village blown off the face of the earth, were as surprised, no doubt, as they were gratified. It was a pity, the *Sergent-chef* said, that we had not been there the day before, because he had helped the villagers to celebrate the Têt by organizing a regatta, with sampan races for both sexes and all ages, and he had taken the liberty of offering a few tins of army rations as prizes. The Commandant nodded in benevolent approval.

This, I believe, was the average French soldier's attitude. If given half a chance he would make a kind of pet of anyone who was dependent upon him – even Vietnamese peasants. He soon began to feel as responsible for their welfare as the administrators I met did for that of the Moïs. The soldiers had none of the civilian prejudices towards the Vietnamese. I asked the *Sergent-chef* if it was a fact that they had no sense of humour, and he was staggered by such an absurd suggestion. I wondered how the Commandant and his NCO would have reacted if called upon to put into practice paragraph four of the military proclamation which says, 'every native quarter situated in the immediate neighbourhood of a point where an important act of sabotage has been committed, will be razed to the ground'.

The situation at Binh Long Dong was less favourable. I was in another zone of command now, and the familiar warring factions in the neighbourhood had been overshadowed by a partisan-chief, an unsmiling mountain of a man, who had been decorated with the Croix de Guerre, and lived in a magnificent fortified villa, full of paddy and streamlined furnishings. The main piece of furniture, however, in the reception room was a rack, an intelligent adaption of the umbrella stand, on which guests hung their weapons. The room was gay with the most expensive artificial flowers of cloth and paper, and we were offered champagne and sweet biscuits. This man was a rare sport of nature, the archetype of a Vietnamese pirate turned Governor, or a Chinese War-Lord. One wondered if whatever factor it was that had produced all this bone and muscle from the slender Vietnamese stock had also created the fierce, resolute character. He was quite illiterate, but had recently begun to interest himself in the choicer rewards of success, and had built pillars of precious wood into his house, specially brought from Tonkin, at a cost of three thousand piastres each.

About half the land of this community was owned by big proprietors who had been finding it practically impossible to collect their rents. If they put the screw too hard on the peasant farmers, they were liable to be kidnapped by the Viet-Minh and receive a period of 're-education' and an enormous fine before being released. Nowadays they could hire bodyguards from the partisan-chief who specialized in protection for prominent citizens and industrial enterprises. But even this, they were beginning to realize, wasn't doing them much good, as the farmers had got into the habit of telling them when they called for the rent: 'Too late, I've already had to pay it to the Viet-Minh.'

A ferry nearby provided a racket for yet another petty regional boss. There he stood by the shore in his uniform of a lieutenant in the Bao-Dai army and bright yellow boots, prepared, for a *concussion* (most descriptive word), to grant priority to any vehicle not wishing to take its turn in the queue. If no *concussion* was forthcoming you waited in the line, perhaps an hour, perhaps half the day. The village at the ferry, overtopped with its crop of *miradors*, looked like a mean Siena, but rose-coloured pastors instead of starlings crowded sociably on the roofs. While we awaited the ferry-boat a partisan patrol passed, complete with their wives. Several of them carried bird-cages as well as rifles.

There was an undercurrent of artistic feeling in these harassed villages of Cochin-China that the quilting of poverty could not entirely suffocate. A tree grew in the garden of a fisherman's hut. The leaves had been stripped off and replaced by small, silvery fish, which from an aesthetic quirk he preferred to dry in this manner. Sometimes a lamp had been planted outside a hovel, graceful yet solid, like a reduced version of a London lamp-post, but with a golden-scaled dragon curled on the top. Or perhaps the usual platform set upon a post with offerings to the wandering and neglected spirits had been elaborated into a tiny pagoda, containing, say, along with the tea-cup and the incense-sticks, a packet of Craven A. There were wayside food stalls everywhere, and as much attention, one felt sure, was paid to the matching of the colours of the food displayed in the bowls, as to the flavour itself.

The sky above all these villages was full of grotesque and meaningful kites. Like miniature balloon-barrages they hung there, as if designed to frustrate the surprise attacks of fabulous aerial monsters.

The zone of French occupation in Cochin-China is shapeless and unpredictable. There is a small squid-like body which thrusts out groping tentacles into a vast no-man's-land of canal-patterned paddy-fields and swamps. On a larger scale the country is hugely segmented by the mouths of the Mékong which leave great ragged tongues of land projecting into the sea. The enemy is everywhere; in full strength and with complete organization in one of the great estuarial peninsulas, and split into skirmishing groups in the next. Defence towers garrisoned by Bao-Dai troops control the main roads, but only in daylight hours. Traffic is withdrawn before sundown and only starts again at eight in the morning.

During the night hours, the defence towers, too, go out of business and their defenders lie low, while the Viet-Minh patrols pass by on their way to collect tolls or impose retribution, conducting their activities even in the suburbs of Saigon. There are supposed to be live-and-let-live arrangements, and sometimes, perhaps when these breakdown, the Viet-Minh arrive in force and lay siege to a few towers, which may or may not be prepared to hold out to the last bullet. In this pacified zone you can sleep in the towns at night, so long as you do not go out after dark, but you cannot stay in the villages, some of which it is better to keep away from even in daytime. The enemy includes the regular army of the Viet-Minh, tough and brilliant in guerrilla tactics, but lightly armed; innumerable partisans who follow respectable occupations in the daytime, but turn into guerrillas at night; and, as well, all that farrago of dubious allies, including the religious armies, who accepted French arms in order to live by near-banditry, but who are ready and willing to administer a stab in the back and will go over to the other side as soon as the moment seems right. As for friends – they are probably few, since the logic of modern warfare involves the destruction of the guilty and the innocent, and friends along with enemies. On the anniversary of the signing – a year before – of the agreement with Bao-dai for Vietnamese 'independence', the French declared a holiday and, blundering on in a quite un-Gallic but wholly Teuton fashion, ordered spontaneous demonstrations of joy. The police would see to it, newspapers warned, that flags were hung out. Can it have been the influence of German occupation? Or is it the circumstances and not the race that make the Nazi? To be fair to them, the French themselves, reading this in their papers, were either amused or horrified. The day came, the celebrations were ignored, the streets were empty, no flags flew. And the police did nothing about it.

It was at the house of one of the remaining allies, a high official of the Bao-dai government, that the banquet was given on the last night of my Cochin-China interlude. There had been no warning of this glittering occasion. I was caught in a state of total unpreparedness, my change of clothing, when I made an inspection, being nearly as grimed with yellow dust as those I wore. And now to my alarm I found myself seated at the right hand of the Vietnamese provincial Governor, facing the *décolletée* lady of the Colonel and a row of senior officers and officials in gleaming sharkskin. But the French are a genial people, little troubled by starchiness and the rigours of social self-defence. Besides that, the nature of the banquet was in itself an all-out, frontal attack on the citadels of dignity. Formal deportment is shattered and devastated by the manipulation of Vietnamese food, and although some people might have been merely embarrassed, the French headquarters' staff at Mytho and their womenfolk were prepared to treat the thing as a gastronomic romp. Undoubtedly in placing bowls and chopsticks before his guests, the *Chef de Province* knew his types.

Vietnamese cooking, like most aspects of Vietnamese culture, has been strongly influenced by the Chinese. By comparison it is provincial, lacking the range and the formidable ingenuity of the Pekinese and Cantonese cuisines. But there are a few specialities which have been evolved with a great deal of dietetic insight. The best known of these is *Chà Gió*, with which we were served as an entrée. *Chà Gió* consists fundamentally of very small, highly spiced meat-rolls, which are transferred easily enough with chopsticks from the dish to one's plate. But this is nothing more than a preliminary operation, and many dexterous manipulations follow. Two or three kinds of vegetable leaves are provided as salad, plus minute spring-onions. A leaf of each kind is picked up and – this is not so easy – placed in superimposition on one's plate and garnished with an onion, ready to receive the meat roll in the middle. And now comes the operation calling for natural skill, or years of practice, since the leaves must be wrapped neatly round the narrow cylinder of minced meat. The *Chà Gió*, now fully prepared, is lifted with the chopsticks and dowsed in the saucer of *nuóc-mâm* at the side of one's plate, from which, according to Mr Houghton-Broderick, an odour resembling that of tiger's urine arises. The total operation takes the non-expert several minutes and involves as many contretemps as one would expect. On this occasion, the Europeans soon gave up the struggle, throwing dignity to the winds, and dabbled happily with their fingers. A spirit of comradeship was noticeable, a democratic kinship born in an atmosphere of common endeavour, frustration, and ridicule.

When travelling I make a sincere effort to throw overboard all prejudices concerning food. Consequently after a brief period of struggle I had already come to terms with *nuóc-mâm*, about which almost every writer on Indo-China since the first Jesuit has grumbled so consistently. I felt indeed that I had taken the first steps towards connoisseurship, and it was in this spirit that I congratulated the Governor on his supply which was the colour of pale honey, thickish,

and of obvious excellence. *Nuóc-mâm* is produced by the fermentation of juices exuded by layers of fish subjected to pressure between
layers of salt. The best result as in viniculture is produced by the
first drawing-off, before artificial pressure is applied, and there are
three or more subsequent pressings with consequent deteriorations
in quality. First *crus* are allowed to mature like brandy, improving
steadily with age. The Governor told me that he thought his stock,
which he had inherited, was over a hundred years old. All the fierce
ammoniacal exhalations were long since spent, and what remained
was not more than a whiff of mellow corruption. Taking a grain of
cooked rice, he deposited it on the golden surface, where it remained
supported by the tension – an infallible test of quality, he said.

After the *Chà Gió* came a flux of delicacies, designed undoubtedly
to provoke curiosity and admiration and to provide the excuse for
enormously prolonged dalliance at the table, rather than to appease
gross appetites. The Vietnamese picked judiciously at the breasts of
lacquered pigeons, the sliced coxcombs, and the tiny diaphanous fish,
while the Europeans ate with barbarian forthrightness, finding their
chopsticks useful to illustrate with fine flourishes – since shop-talk
had crept in – the feints, the encirclements, the annihilation. The
Governor had been presented with a remarkable lighter, an unwieldy
engine, which commanded admiration by producing flame in some
quite unexpected way. How this was done, I have forgotten, but I
know that it was not by friction on a flint. Throughout the meal he
could hardly bear to put this away and fiddled continually with it
between the courses, while his guests stuffed themselves with the rare
meats he hardly touched. For me there was an allegory in this scene.

The night of the return to Saigon I went with Vietnamese friends
for the second time to the Vietnamese theatre. The first visit had
been an appalling fiasco, although cruelly funny in its way; a pathetic
attempt at a wild western musical, inspired perhaps by reports of
Oklahoma. It was acted by fragile, slant-eyed beauties in chaps,
wearing ten-gallon hats and toting six-shooters, their cheeks heavily
incarnadined in representation of occidental plethora. The cowboys
had coloured their top lips and chins bright blue to suggest a strong
Western growth of beard. Provided with guitars which they were

unable to play, they shrilled a strident oriental version of hillbilly airs, which someone in the orchestra accompanied on some Vietnamese stringed instrument, punctuating the lines with a vigorous clashing of cymbals.

This second experience was a great improvement. It was a traditional play describing the tragic courtship by a Chinese Ambassador of an unattached medieval Empress of Vietnam. The costumery was the most gorgeous and obviously expensive I have ever seen. There was none of the dreamy symbolism of Cambodia and Laos in this performance. The acting was literal and never relapsed into ballet. When, for instance, the Ambassador and his rival the Chief Mandarin fought a duel, the fight was meant to be a real one; a dazzling display of traditional swordsmanship, and not a set *pas de deux* with each performer releasing symbolical thunderbolts. The culminating point was reached when, with a mighty cut, the Ambassador's arm was hacked off. Much blood flowed, some of which the Ambassador staunched with his handkerchief which he tenderly presented to the Empress. Afterwards, holding his severed right arm in his left hand, the Ambassador acted an energetic death-scene, lasting half an hour, finally expiring, still upright, in the arms of his followers. The dramatic high spots of the scene were accentuated by an orchestral supernumerary on a special perch who beat a cymbal.

Extreme despair at the Ambassador's fate was registered by all the company, including the Empress, hurling themselves to the ground and then performing a kind of frantic gyration. This was the moment when the curtain should have been rung down, but unfortunately it stuck halfway. The orchestra had worked up to a deafening finale, with the cymbals man lashing out as if fighting for his life and the human Catherine wheels whirling, with peacocks' feathers and brocaded panels flying in all directions. And then the cast had had enough. Leaping as one man to their feet, the Ambassador still clutching his arm, they caught at the edge of the curtain and pulled it down. It was an exciting performance in the zestful tradition, I thought, of an essentially northern people, whose culture had remained completely uncontaminated in their long sojourn in the south.

CHAPTER THIRTEEN

Into Cambodia

THE LAND-ROVER bounded westwards over the road to Cambodia. It was the only road of any length in the country open to unescorted, daytime traffic, although it had been closed for a fortnight before the day we left, 'owing to damage caused by the weather'. We plunged through a bland and smiling landscape, animated by doll-like Vietnamese figures, and mud-caked buffaloes that ambled across the road, lowering their heads as if to charge when it was too late. Children dangled lines from bridges, while their elders, gathered in sociable groups, groped for fish, waist-deep in liquid mud. The kites, floating over the villages, were pale ideographs against a deeper sky. There were miles of deserted rubber plantations.

It was better, said the driver, not to stop between the towers, and his method was to accelerate to about 65 m.p.h. until a tower was about two hundred yards away. He would then relax speed until we were past, and about the same distance on the other side. This confidence in the towers seemed not altogether well founded. The papers had recently published an account of an attack by one of the garrisons on a car straggling behind a convoy in which the driver was shot dead and a lady passenger's finger was almost bitten off in an attempt to rob her of a ring. We frequently found that ditches had been dug across the road by Viet-Minh sympathizers, and subsequently filled in with loose earth. A series of such semi-obstacles taken at full throttle was a fun-fair sensation, even in the Land-Rover. At one point we passed a newly burned-out car from which a tracery of smoke still arose.

*

Cambodia. It was a place-name always accompanied in my imagination by tinkling, percussive music. Although the Vietnamese had been encroaching for centuries upon Cambodian land, there were signs of a true physical frontier at the present border. We came to a wide river; on one side was Cochin-China – which had once been Cambodia too – with the neat, busy Vietnamese, the mosaic of rice-fields and the plantations. Across the river was the Cambodia of present times, and what, too, must have been some early frontier of the ancient Khmer state, since everything changed immediately. It was not only the people, but the flora and the fauna. A cultural Great Divide; a separation of continents. On one bank of the river were the ordinary forest trees, which, as amateurs of natural history, the Vietnamese would spare if not compelled to clear them for rice-fields or plantations. The other bank bore sparse clumps of coconut palms – the first I had seen in my travels – and beyond them, a foretaste of the withered plains of India.

The bamboos and the underbrush had gone, and with them the dark-winged, purposeful butterflies of the Vietnamese forests. Here only trivial fritillaries fluttered over the white prairie grass. Great pied kingfishers as well as the large and small blue varieties encrusted the edges of yellow pools and ditches that served no economic purpose. There were no rice-fields. Cambodians lounged inertly about the rare villages that were no more than a few squalid African huts. In one village some women with dirty, handsome faces were pouring earth into some of the worst holes in this terrible road, while a group of bonzes stood by, watching them with saintly detachment. The trim pyjamas of the Vietnamese had given way to the dreary weeds of India; a drab, sarong-like skirt, pulled, in the men's case, into the shape of breeches by bringing the waist-sash through the legs. There might be, in addition to this, a jacket of some dingy material and a rag wound round the head as a turban. It was curious to reflect that under the barrack-room discipline of their spirits, the aboriginal Moïs – when left alone – were the best dressed and best housed people in Indo-China. After them came the Vietnamese, in their brisk, work-a-day turnout – you never saw a ragged one – and their flower-decked shacks. And last of all were these descendants of the great Khmer civilization, who quite clearly didn't care in the slightest how they lived or dressed.

But the Cambodians had one enormous advantage over the others. There were no plantations to be seen on this side of the river. So far, the Grendel of colonial capitalism had been kept at bay. The Cambodians are practising Buddhists, and every man, including the King, must spend a year of his life as a mendicant novice in a Buddhist monastery. And the strength of this second of the world religions lies in the fact that it has produced a tradition, a permanent state of mind, which makes its followers neither adept as exploiters nor amenable to exploitation. The Cambodians, like the Burmese, the Laotians, and others, no doubt, of the South-East Asiatic peoples, are, by their own design, poor, but supremely happy. In these rich and comparatively underpopulated countries there is no struggle for existence, and this provided the ideal atmosphere for the practice of the gentle faith in which their people have been reared.

The Vietnamese, whose Buddhism is diluted almost to the point of non-existence, has a competitive soul, is a respecter of work for its own sake, and strives to increase and multiply. As he will work hard for himself, he can be made to work hard for others, and is therefore the prey of the exploiter. There are a few uneasily conducted plantations in Cambodia, and while I was there, in fact, there was a serious revolt in one of them. But Cambodia has no surplus population and no proletariat. Every man can have as much land as he can cultivate. As far as I know no Cambodian has ever been shipped in the hulks to end his life toiling in some depopulated South-Sea island.

Spurred on by thoughts of what the French call isolated acts of piracy we reached Pnom-Penh, the capital, early the same afternoon. It is approached through unimposing suburbs: several miles of shacks among the trees, most of them reeling slightly on their supporting posts. There are a few pagodas, insubstantial looking and tawdry with gilt, which contrived to remind one of the Far-Eastern section of a colonial exhibition, and many graveyards of bonzes with tombs almost as showy as those of the cemeteries of northern Italy. The dogs of India are here, one per house; an ugly yellow variety with a petulant expression, and sometimes in a state of utter decrepitude. Together with the pigs and occasional domestic monkeys they profit to the utmost, in their slow saunterings on the road, from the Buddhist aversion to taking life. Through the open doors one sees that the houses contain no furniture, in keeping with the Cambodian's indifference to material possessions. The occupants wash, dress, and, of course, eat in public, and half-naked families are to be observed squatting round devouring the splendid fish that can be had almost for the taking away, down by the river. Refuse is thrown out of a window or pushed through the floor, collecting in massive mounds for the benefit of the kitchen-midden excavators of the future. There is none of the well-bred aloofness of the Vietnamese about these people. The Cambodians stare at whatever interests them and will giggle at slight provocation.

The centre of Pnom-Penh has, of course, been taken over by the Chinese, who have indulged in it to the limit their taste for neon signs, opened many cinemas, too many radio shops with loudspeakers blaring in the doorways, and a casino, which, started in 1949, is said already to have bankrupted half the Cambodians of the capital. However, they are supposed to be a local breed of Chinese, cheerful vulgarians raised in the country, and very much to be preferred to the arrogant immigrants from Hong Kong that lord it in Saigon.

The matter calling for first attention in Pnom-Penh was that of the journey to Laos, which I still wanted to make overland, if this could be done from Cambodia. There was a road which followed the River Mékong, which in Saigon was thought to be impassable in places. In normal times one could ascend by the river itself, which, at the height of the rainy season, was navigable up to one thousand six hundred miles from its mouth by one sort of craft or other. This was the end of the dry season when the water was at its lowest. Nor did anyone in Saigon know if boats still went up the river.

First enquiries were unhopeful in result. There were many fine old river boats, picturesque relics of the first decades of steam navigation, moored along the bank by the King's palace. But there were no signs of activity, no polishing of brasses or clanging of bells, no evidence that the greenish hawsers would ever be loosened or the anchors dragged up by their rusting chains. The crews slept out of sight or had gone away. These ships would stay there for ever, one felt, a painted riverine background to the town's flattish silhouette.

But there was one boat actually about to leave, said a Frenchman I spoke to. He pointed to the one with an eye painted on the bows that lay alongside the King's state launch, and, sure enough, a curl of smoke rose from the tall black funnel. Hastening up the gangplank I asked for the Captain and was led into the presence of an elderly gentleman in an old-fashioned Chinese gown, who half reclined on a bench in what I took to be the first-class passengers' saloon. At his side was a jam-jar containing a goldfish, which, while we talked, he prodded at absently with a fountain pen. I asked this venerable mariner when the boat was going and he answered, in good French, that it was making a journey of one night up the river. That seemed of little use, I explained, as it would take a week to get to southern Laos. Did he connect with any other service? Not that he knew of, the old gentleman replied pleasantly. And the pirate situation, I asked. Were they ever attacked? The gown was lifted for access to an inner pocket, and a bullet produced gleefully for my inspection. It had been recovered, he said, from the body of one of the crew. But such attacks were infrequent now. Until a month or two ago he hadn't been able to leave his estate and this was only his second trip down to Pnom-Penh. I now at last realized that the boat was a private one, and later I learned that its owner was a well-known Chinese millionaire.

Nor were the prospects for road travel much brighter. The Royal Hotel had a special noticeboard covered with what looked like army standing orders. They were the constantly changing regulations dealing with travel on the various roads, and the minimum degree of precaution permitted vehicles to travel in pairs, at not more than one hundred metres from each other. Each car had to carry three passengers.

The situation looked even less promising when Valas arrived on the evening plane and we went down to the *cercle* together. The first piece of news that greeted him was that a business friend had been shot dead, two miles from the town's centre, and a few minutes later we were drinking with a man who had been captured by a band of Issarak nationalists. This man, a schoolteacher, had been saved by his Sino-Cambodian chauffeur, who had convinced the Issarak, in an argument lasting several hours, that his master, quite accidentally, observed the five virtues – proved by the fact that he accepted poor pupils without payment – and should be spared. He was, therefore, held prisoner, while the Issarak went for rides in the car until the petrol was used up, when they set him free, leaving him with the car.

On the next day's programme was a visit arranged by the enthusiastic members of the local information centre to the head-quarters of General des Essars, who was in command of the French Army in Cambodia. I decided that if anyone knew what the prospects of getting to Laos were, it would be the General and that these preoccupations might, therefore, be postponed for that day.

Pnom-Penh was one of those synthetic Chinese towns with all the warm glitter so cheering to the hearts of Sunday night Coventry Street crowds. The Chinese are not interested in South-East Asian towns until they have reached on their initiative a certain level of population and prosperity. They then descend like a flock of gregarious birds, galvanizing its life with their crow-like vitality. The feeble shoots of local culture wither away and what remains is a degenerate native slum round the hard, bright, self-contained, Chinese core. Valas and I went to look for the Cambodian ballet. In addition to the King's private troupe there had been another in a fairly flourishing state as late as 1946 when Valas had lived there. We found the house, but it was empty, and neighbours said that the corps de ballet had disbanded. It evidently couldn't compete against such attractions as *Arsenic et Vieille Dentelle*, currently showing at one of the Chinese cinemas.

But Madame Shum's was still going strong. Madame Shum's is Pnom-Penh's leading opium den, or *salon de désintoxication* as they are now, with a kind of prim irony, renamed. The salon was a great bamboo shack among the trees, its empty window apertures glowing feebly with death-bed light. In these romantic surroundings the raffish élite of Pnom-Penh meet together at night over the sociable sucking of opium pipes.

We were received by Madame herself, who possessed all the calm dignity of her social position. There was evidently a certain snob-value in being on calling terms with the head of the house, comparable to the privilege of being allowed to address a well-known head-waiter by his Christian name. The rank and file of patrons were dealt with by underlings, but the socially prominent always made a point of calling at the administrative headquarters to present their compliments to Madame. We were served with highballs on the veranda while Madame showed us the latest portrait of her son, who was studying medicine in France, and of her daughter, an extremely beautiful girl of seventeen, who was at college in Saigon. They were by different French fathers, she mentioned. Valas produced the formal banter the occasion demanded, including mild, chivalrous overtures to Madame herself and a request for the daughter's hand.

One went to Madame Shum's, Valas said, first because it was the thing to do, and secondly because you met all kinds of business and other contacts there. We did in fact run into one man who hoped we might be induced to buy a certain American car from him. He had imported this car with a particular client in mind, a wealthy Chinese, who, since it was the only one of its kind in Indo-China and loaded with chromiumed accessories, was expected to jump at the chance. Before seeing it the Chinese had asked all the questions covering the essentials. Was it fitted with a radio? – Yes. Press button hood-operation? – Yes. Parking and pass-lights? – Yes. Two-tone horn? – Yes. Air-conditioning? – No, but it could be fitted.

Only at the last moment when the man was sure the sale was in the bag had he turned up with a tape-measure. He was sorry, it was too small, several centimetres shorter than a Buick he had been offered. Thus have the provincial Chinese of Pnom-Penh, separated from the mainsprings of their culture, turned away from the curious and the exquisite, and embraced the standards of taste which are impressed by fashion, by glitter, and by sheer size.

As a concession to the atmosphere at Madame Shum's patrons were supposed to remove their clothing and put on a sarong. At first one felt childish and self-conscious, like a timid experimenter, perhaps, in a nudist colony. But among all these corpulent officials, these chiefs-of-staff and under-secretaries padding to their pleasures down the creaking corridors, the feeling soon passed. It was nothing more than a casual encounter of elks in semi-regalia. There seemed to be no desire for privacy. The sarong was the badge of a temporary inward and spiritual state. One showed one's determination to go native for a couple of hours after dinner and one was expected to flop down quite unconcernedly wherever there happened to be a vacant mat.

The actual smoking, a tedious process, brought no reward, it seemed, unless persevered with. I was promised that with six pipes I could expect to be reasonably sick, which was as far as a beginner got on the first few occasions. However, the smell of the stale smoke-impregnated compartment of a 'workman's special' was enough for me. It was another convention that one stretched oneself out on a mat while the blob of opium was toasted over a spirit lamp before being transferred to the bowl of the yard-long pipe. These preparatory rites were performed by a corps of uniformly ill-favoured young Cambodian ladies, whose looks Madame excused by saying that all the pretty ones had recently been abducted by some ex-bandits newly formed into a patriotic army. Valas smoked three pipes and was ready to move. No one seemed in the slightest affected by their indulgences, despite the fact that two civil servants and a very high-ranking officer in the same room had smoked fifteen pipes and said that they would smoke thirty before leaving. Apart from the sheepish good-fellowship of shared weakness, there was nothing in their manner – I met the officer later on duty – that seemed in any way other than normal.

Valas was highly suspicious of the quality of the opium, and asked whether it was contraband rubbish from Siam. The original wrapper, marked with the government stamp, had to be found to convince him.

Valas could find no one among the opium smokers who wanted to buy the car, but there was at least news of the disbanded ballet. The girls had gone to work in the *Lap ton* dancing places. Breaking away from Madame Shum's sombre haven, we therefore got into the car and plunged back again into the vast, brazen clamour of Pnom-Penh's centre. It must have been a great day for the Chinese, who have always enjoyed noise, when the principles of electrical amplification were discovered. Here, as at Cholon, the crowds had an air of exultation, of crisis. Heralds with banners stood at the crossroads. Trumpeting loudspeakers yelled an actor's lines, their rhythm fiercely marked by the crashing of cymbals. Stone-faced men in flagging silk bowed their heads beneath the thunder of celestial drums, and sing-song girls sobbed in immense cosmic anguish from the open casements of good first-floor restaurants.

But the places where the Cambodians go to dance are quite properly a little withdrawn from all this Tartar fury. We found a quiet back street with waste paper kicked about all over its dusty surface, and a few sad yellow dogs. The noise of someone banging a drum came to us through a broken fence, on the other side of which was a kind of beer garden. There were a dozen marble-topped tables and a stage with a row of Cambodian girls sitting with their hands in their laps at the back of it. Out in front was a microphone and a band in the form of one man who was beating a drum. The centre of the stage was marked by a small table with a bunch of fleshy red blooms in a large whole-milk tin. The place was lit by the early-type, ghastly fluorescent tubes, and there were notices about minimum *consummations* in French, Chinese, and Vietnamese. All the customers were Cambodians but the Chinese who ran the place didn't even bother to put up a notice in their language. The Chinese management sat at a table right up by the stage, with their backs to the patrons, doing the accounts, while the Cambodians sipped their blood-coloured lemonade and smiled as if delighted by inner visions. The Cambodians kept arriving on bicycles that were decorated with pennants and all kinds of gadgets. They came from those shacks we had seen on the outskirts of the town and were very dapper-looking with their sports-shirts, American ties, and slicked-down hair.

Someone on the management table struck a small gong and the drummer started up again. A moon-faced young Cambodian, who had been egged on by his friends, went up on to the stage and began to croon into the microphone a Tino Rossi song called 'Gardien de Camargue'. After the first verse he was handed a pair of maracas and, still singing, began to slash out some kind of unrecognizable rhythm which the drummer did his best to follow. It was now the turn of the ex-members of the Cambodian ballet to go into action. As soon as one of them caught the eye of a patron, she got up, left the stage, went over to his table, and putting her hands together in the attitude of prayer made a solemn-faced bow. The young man then followed her back to the stage and joined her in a kind of processional dance round the centre table with the flowers in the milk-tin. The couples kept three or four feet apart, their hands and arms weaving about in the formal gestures of the *Ramayana* and their feet doing their best to conform to a rhythm which was not quite a fox-trot, a rumba, or a béguine. No charge was made for the dancing. It was all included in the price of the beer.

The girls' faces wore the frozen expressions demanded by tradition, since in the classic dances the emotions must be interpreted by a repertoire of postures. Their partners seemed to have emancipated themselves from this courtly discipline and did not mind looking as if they were having a vulgar good time. When a girl felt she had given her partner his money's worth she just turned her back while the dance was in progress and bowed to him. The pair then turned away and left each other without so much as exchanging a glance. This dance had been imported in recent years from Siam and in it were enshrined thus, on the verge of oblivion, the gestures from the mimes of the Cambodian kings.

Valas pointed out the star performer, whom he remembered from the old days. She was not the best-looking of the girls and the extraordinary mask-like effect of her features was heightened, rather grotesquely, by a red stain, the size of a five-shilling piece, caused by cupping, in the dead centre of her forehead. For all that she had the truly impressive sinuosity of a girl who had spent more than half her short life contorting her body into the strange rhythmic moulds demanded by the representation of the fabulous serpents, birds, and apes of the *Ramayana*. In the interval, the half-hour relief from the doleful conspiracy of crooner and drummer, the girls wandered off the stage. Valas caught the prima ballerina's eye and she came down to us swaying slightly as she moved through the tables, with the undulation of a charmed cobra. As she lowered herself into a chair there was the faintest tinkle of concealed ornaments. With the gesture of a drowning arm raised from the surface of an enchanted lake, a silk head-shawl was discarded. It was most unfortunate that we spoke no Cambodian and the lady knew only two words of French: *soupe Chinoise*. The soup was served and we had reached a conversational impasse. However, the universal language of art came to our aid. The controlled face relaxed in the beginnings of an anxious half-smile. A bond was to be created that would defeat the barriers of speech. Sita, the beloved of Rama, opened her plastic handbag and groped in it for a picture which she passed across the table to us. It was an indecent photograph, of the Port Said kind, vintage about 1925.

We finished the evening with a visit to a night-club called, I believe, the Florida, or something equally absurd. Valas had endured mild heart-burnings for several years over a Vietnamese dance-hostess who worked there, known as 'La Panthère'. He paid her an immense sum to come and sit at our table for about half an hour. She was immaculate, regal, and rather surly. They soon fell out over the provenance of some jewellery she was wearing, and the atmosphere became heavy with suppressed recrimination.

But the Florida was well worth a visit for a study of its patrons. A Frenchwoman in a sarong was pointed out who had married a Cambodian prince and had gone so completely native that she refused to speak anything but Cambodian. There was a Chinese millionaire of seventy, a grave little fellow, who came there every night to rumba with the same statuesque professional partner. Two representatives of distinguished Cambodian families with Portuguese names were present – descendants of Fernao Mendes Pinto's two shipmates, left behind when he escaped from slavery in the country. The owner of a small fleet of *cyclos* had come here to relax. He made the equivalent of £1000 per month from the hundred coolies who worked for him and was therefore able to spend ten months of the year in Paris. From this it was clear that a rickshaw coolie who owned his own *cyclo* could live comfortably. But on further enquiry I learned this was ruled out because only Europeans with a great deal of pull could get the licences, which were strictly limited. In any case, whatever the coolies earned, said Valas, they would only gamble it away; and the only difference as things were was that one man squandered the money instead of a hundred.

CHAPTER FOURTEEN

King Norodom's Capital

NEXT MORNING, I saw General des Essars, who was in command of French troops in Cambodia. Like all the official personalities I visited in the country, he seemed to be enjoying life, and he gave the impression of being no more than faintly amused by the preposterous difficulties of the military task.

A London newspaper had been interested to know what were the possibilities, in the event of the French being obliged to leave Indo-China, of Vietnam, Cambodia, and Laos lining up together to form an effective barrier to what was called the southwards march of communism? Put into plain language, this meant, could these three countries combine to keep out an invasion by Chinese communists? The General said that he would not wish to have his opinion quoted on such a point, and would content himself with supplying figures to give some idea of the Cambodian war-potential.

The regular army, he said, consisted of three battalions, comprising two thousand five hundred men. There was also a national guard which wasn't particularly well trained or well equipped. These short-time warriors also numbered about two thousand five hundred, and the General quoted Wellington's remark about not knowing whether or not they would frighten the enemy, but, by God, they frightened him. He felt nervous about giving them up-to-date arms, because if they had anything worth taking they would clear off – *ils foutraient le camp*. Besides this there was an officers' school with twelve students and a police force whose armoury contained one medium machine-gun and two tommy-guns. On the whole, the General said, it wasn't famous. But there you were, what could you expect in a country where every man-jack of them had done a year in a monastery, where they taught you that thou shalt not kill had to be taken literally? 'They defend themselves –

sometimes,' the General said. 'But that is about the best you can say for them.'

As for the other side of the medal, there were the Viet-Minh, who held the coastline, solidly, all the way from the frontier of Siam to Cochin-China. And then there were five bands of Issarak nationalists, all well armed with fetus amulets and automatic weapons, and they were only getting a little peace round the capital itself since the sixth band, that of Dap Chhuon, had surrendered, and Dap Chhuon himself had been given the governorship of the province of Siem-Reap. I remembered seeing propaganda pictures at Saigon of the ceremony that had accompanied Dap Chhuon's submission. It had been a well staged act of fealty. Dap Chhuon, thin and tough, with the ravaged face of an anchorite, knelt before the King, who, dressed, I believe, in the uniform of a French admiral, and smiling like a Bodhisattva, was leaning over to hand him back his carbine. This was the thing in a nutshell. You committed a single murder and you were probably shackled hand and foot, thrown into a dark hole in the ground and left to rot. You went in for large-scale slaughter, called yourself an Issarak, and managed to keep a whole skin for a year or two, and it was cheaper to buy you off. The King himself made the nation's peace with you and you got a provincial governorship. And now, with Dap Chhuon and his three hundred and fifty men keeping order, tourists could come again – for the first time for several years – to visit the ruins at Angkor Vat.

But the General pursed his lips and shook his head over future prospects. It seemed that a certain, quite unforeseen element had suddenly cropped up. It was to be feared, in fact, that Dap Chhuon was no decent, reliable, straightforward bandit after all. Either he had never been one of the old school of dependable tiger's-liver-eating thugs, or in some mysterious way he had been corrupted, being now, indeed, suspected of having turned communist. The latest news of him was that he had put one of his men in each of the villages who had presented the notables with a list of reforms to be carried out. That was the state of affairs. Apart from all the bother the Viet-Minh gave, they now had their own people, who used to be satisfied with looting pigs and rice, going in for all this silly nonsense.

The general wondered how long it would be before he had to send the planes to Siem-Reap.

It was clear that this account of the military situation in Cambodia contained the death of my hopes about the overland journey to Laos. Of the five Issarak bands still active, one, controlled it was thought by the Viet-Minh, operated on the Cambodia–Laos border. This would have been the same band that was reported in the neighbourhood of Stung Treng, when I had tried to reach Laos from Central Annam. They were mounted, the General said, well armed, and very mobile. By the time he could get planes to any district where they were reported to have been seen, it was always too late. Land operations were almost useless, because you had to fight with soldiers who expected to be fed regularly and generally mollycoddled. But the bandits didn't worry about creature comforts. While you were dragging your baggage trains about after them, they just slipped off into the mountains, or some god-awful swamp, and that was that.

General des Essars's absence of confidence in the ability of Cambodia to stand on its own feet was certainly not shared by its Prime Minister, S. E. Yem Sambaur, whom I visited next. Since the accumulation of wealth is considered rather ill-bred in post-Khmer Cambodia, there are few large fortunes and little ostentation among the Cambodians. The head of the State, beneath the King, lived in what looked like a six-roomed villa, furnished in European style with a sober good taste rarely seen in Western imitations in the Far East. I was surprised to find that although said to be about forty, His Excellency looked rather like a not too serious-minded undergraduate of about twenty-three. This extraordinary youthfulness was a thing I continually noticed about the people of Cambodia and Laos, my impression entirely contradicting that of the thirteenth-century Chinese traveller Chou Ta-Kouan, who wrote a unique account of the Khmers at the height of their power. Ta-Kouan found that the Cambodians of his day – and the race has suffered not the slightest change – aged very quickly. A Cambodian lady of twenty or thirty looked as old as a Chinese of forty or fifty. This is so far from being the case today that one wonders whether that heavy burden of glory the Khmers carried, the constant warrings and the exactions of task-masters and divine kings, may not have been wearisome to the flesh as well as a vexation of spirit. Their descendants are without a care in the world and wear wonderfully well.

Yem Sambaur had the face of a dusky fawn. He laughed continually, especially when describing the atrocities committed by the French Foreign Legion in Cambodian villages. I found it surprising that the Prime Minister should express himself with such complete lack of restraint in political matters to a foreigner and an utter stranger. It was even odder that a French official of the Information Bureau should have arranged the visit. It was all very Cambodian; the unquenchable good humour of Sambaur, and that of the Frenchman too. He had been several years in Cambodia, he said, and would never leave it, if he could help it. He was literally turning into a Cambodian before one's eyes and could have mingled quite easily with that serene group of functionaries I saw later at the Palace, and have avoided detection.

His Excellency, addressing me continually as Monsieur le Direc-teur, spoke very seriously about relations with the French, although the sharpness of his remarks never ruffled his seraphic expression. The Cambodians had refused to sign the agreement by which Cambodia became 'independent within the framework of the French Union' because of several quite unacceptable provisions. The fact that Bao-dai, the Emperor of Vietnam, had signed, did not influence them in the least. The first serious obstacle was that the minorities in Cambodia, including the French, and of course the Chinese, could not be brought before Cambodian courts – an insult to a legal code recognized as one of the most humane in the world. The second objection was that French troops were to be allowed to operate on Cambodian soil. 'We can take care of the Issarak, without French help,' the Prime Minister said. 'If the country were really indepen-dent there would be no Issarak. There would be no reason for them.' As it was the French Air Force, on the mere report that Issarak had been seen in them, bombed Cambodian villages off the face of the earth, or the Foreign Legion went into them and massacred the villagers; men, women, and children. I asked if His Excellency were referring to isolated incidents, and still smiling broadly he told me that cases were reported to him every day.

And as a result, the country people were turning to communism. Communism, Yem Sambaur thought, was singularly unsuited to the people of Cambodia, a country without industries and an urban proletariat, and with few rich landowners. But now it was being presented to the people as a way of salvation. That was why you had the phenomenon of Cambodian Issarak chiefs coming to terms with the hitherto detested Vietnamese – a totally unprecedented state of affairs. The best way to convert a villager to communism was to burn his house down and kill one or more members of his family. In this way you abolished a man's inducements to lead a quiet, respectable existence. When you cut the bonds that tied a man to the existing order, he naturally became a bandit, and if you could persuade him that the communists would fight his enemies more ruthlessly than the others, well, he would be a communist too. And that was how the Issarak bands grew, and that was also why they were quite ready to provide themselves, if the Viet-Minh suggested it, with political commissars. 'But then, of course,' said His Excellency, still smiling, 'the transition to communism is less difficult for an Asiatic, even for members of the upper classes. Perhaps we have less to lose. In any case, the prospect does not alarm us. There are times when one feels that perhaps it would be even better to be a little poorer, if at the same time one could be a little freer.'

Western architecture has always been impressed with the *kolossal*. Cities are dominated by dome, tower or turret; the acts of faith or monuments to fear. The spires of gothic cathedrals, rising cliff-like above the roofs of a medieval town, are visible in some cases from such a distance that the surrounding buildings are concealed by the curvature of the earth's surface.

In South-east Asia the motives that found their expression in this kind of building are absent, and it is only to be found in the ruined temples and mausolea of Angkor. Apart from the houses in

European quarters, all buildings must be of a single storey, since there is an ancient and universal prohibition against standing directly above another's head. This is so scrupulously observed that in Cambodia it is even illegal for a manacled prisoner to be lodged temporarily under the raised floor of the typical Cambodian house.

The Royal Palace at Pnom-Penh, then, is a single-storey affair, and quite obscured, except from the river's bank, by other buildings. It is pagoda architecture and one feels that if the pinchbeck glitter of the gilding could be subdued it would provide, perhaps, a charming and discreet lakeside ornament. We have seen buildings of this kind so often in colonial exhibitions that we have come to associate them with impermanence, and even suspect that they may be supplied in sections with simple instructions for erection. It comes as no surprise to learn that the Palace was built by the French soon after Cambodia became a protectorate. But even the ancient and notable pagodas of Luang Prabang turn out later to be not very much better as buildings, however far superior their decoration may be.

Behind the high, screening wall, the palace proved to consist of several separate buildings, all of which, except those containing the private apartments, could be visited on a set tour, for which a guide was provided. Among this cluster of lacquered, box-like edifices, their roofs curled up as if by the scorching sun, there was one of solidly incongruous stone. This was a house presented by Napoleon III to Queen Eugénie and then taken down and sent here as a gift to the Cambodian monarch of the day. It looked like the permanent administrative offices, stolid and matter-of-fact, on an exposition site, squatting among the lath and plaster which after a few months would be taken down and cleared away. The presence of the European interloper gave a clue to the contents of the pavilions themselves.

These were frankly museum exhibits of the past two centuries of royal history. Some of them were strangely revelatory. The only building which could be described as internally impressive was the Silver Pagoda, and then it was impressive rather as a curiosity. Here for the first time one glimpsed the East of the traveller's tale, prodigious, garish, and wasteful. If the kings of Cambodia had never felt the urge to build an Escorial or a Caserta they had at least floored a pagoda with five thousand blocks of solid silver, and although the aesthetic effect was no choicer than that to be had from walking on the polished deck of a battleship, there had at least been fine, profligate squandering of precious metal.

The purpose of the Silver Pagoda appeared to be to house the royal treasure, consisting principally of a great collection of Buddhas, in gold and jade and other precious materials, some with diamonds in their foreheads. Whenever a Buddha happened to be of solid gold, the guide, padding relentlessly in the rear, inevitably announced the exact weight of the metal that had gone into its construction. Below the ranks of Buddhas, with their smiles, placid, ironic, or even supercilious, were lined up rows of pawnbrokers' counters. In these, behind the scratched and dirty glass, had been assembled for inspection the gifts of foreign potentates of the past, together with what looked like nothing more than a great miscellaneous collection of family bric-à-brac.

One brooded over enormous jewelled watches, full of whimsy and misplaced ingenuity in their methods of working; Victorian compositions of wax flowers, fruit, and sea-shells under bell-jars; a miniature Buddha studded with perhaps ten thousand pounds' worth of diamonds seated uneasily on the back of a tortoiseshell hairbrush; reliquaries of cloisonné and beaten gold; an ivory backscratcher; more jewelled Buddhas; china eggs of the kind that are supposed to induce hens to lay; a string of Christmas-tree decorations – tinsel and silver balls. One imagined the Queen, or perhaps a succession of queens, making a periodical clear-out of their cupboards and then tripping down to the Silver Pagoda with all the attractive, useless things that had to be found a home somewhere. The family photographs were perhaps the most interesting thing about this magpie's hoard. There were the monarchs and their queens in faded sepia, staring of eye and stiff of pose in the European clothing into which they had just been buckled and laced for the occasion. Among them was one informal and dashing scene, probably taken by one of the courtiers, of the old King Sisowath waltzing round with a very aged lady. And sometimes, under the influence perhaps of Edward

VII, the ruler of Cambodia was displayed in knickerbockers, the oddest of all garments for an oriental potentate, possessing, one supposed, a plurality of wives.

Of the other pagodas' contents I remember less, but of the waxworks jumble of exhibits two things caught the imagination. One was the genial cynicism with which the French had sent the reigning king, when they had taken over the country, a statue of himself ... only all they had done was to find a spare statue of Napoleon III, knock the head off and replace it with one of the Cambodian monarch roughy chiselled-up from a portrait. The other thing that impressed me was the extraordinary variety of the King's regalia of State, which changed in style according to the manner in which he showed himelf. Thus there was an assortment of crowns, with varying numbers of tiers, for use according to whether his majesty was riding on an elephant, or on horseback, or being carried in a palanquin. To these there had been recently added a new form of ceremonial headgear, to meet the case of the motor car. For such public occasions he wears a bowler hat, decorated with a diamond cockade.

It was soon clear to me that the enthusiastic Monsieur Salis of the Bureau of Information, who had arranged this visit, would never rest content until he had obtained for me an audience with the King. And as he seemed to be on the best possible terms with everyone at the Palace, a man who liked Cambodians and was equally liked by them, I felt quite certain that he would succeed. However, as nothing definite had been arranged by the time we left the Palace, I went off for a walk, hoping to be able to find a booth where they sold theatrical masks, which I had seen from the car on the previous night.

Thereafter there was some similarity between my experiences and those of the French explorer Mouhot – or at least the first part of his experiences – when he interviewed the King of Cambodia in 1859. Mouhot had just arrived in the capital and his luggage had not caught up with him. However, weary and travel-stained as he was, the King sent for him. To quote his account, 'I objected that I could not visit him in my travelling dress. "Oh, that is nothing, the King has no dress at all, and he will be delighted to see you," was the reply.' When, after an hour or so's chase round Pnom-Penh, Monsieur Salis finally found me, with the news that the interview had been arranged, these were practically the words he used. The temperature was at least a hundred in the shade, and I was wearing shorts and covered in grime and perspiration, but it was nothing, Salis said. The people at the Palace were all *'des braves gens'*, and they expected a traveller to look like one. We would go up there right away.

In Mouhot's account, the ancestor of the present King is shown rather in the light of one of these comical stock-figures of an African paramount chief. '"Good brandy," said the King in English (the only words he knew of that language)' and, 'His majesty then displayed to me his European furniture, mahogany tables covered with china vases and other ornaments of a commonplace description; above all, he pointed out, as worthy of notice, two old looking-glasses in gilt frames, a sofa and various similar articles. "I am but beginning," said he; "in a few years my palace will be beautiful."'

The present King appeared to me to be of a quite different calibre.

Salis led the way up the steps to the anteroom of the audience chamber and introduced me to the members of the royal staff. We had hardly shaken hands before the King skipped into view through an open doorway on the right. He was wearing the smile that one saw in the photographs, and it was considerably less complaisant than that of any of the Buddhas in the Silver Pagoda. The King shook hands vigorously and we went into the audience chamber together and sat down on a settee.

King Norodom of Cambodia is spiritual and temporal head of his people, the ultimate possessor of all Cambodian land – which, however, he bestows freely upon the petition of those who wish to cultivate it – and the inheritor of all who die intestate. He is the only person in the kingdom entitled to a six-tiered parasol, and, being semi-divine, and above the law, his privileges include the right to contract incestuous marriage with an aunt or a half-sister. In return for his prerogatives he performs the many ancient ceremonials in use since the days of Angkor, such as the ablutions of the Brahmanical idols, which assure the wellbeing and prosperity of the people. Being without debts, free of crime or bodily blemish, he was permitted to serve the customary year as a mendicant novice in a Buddhist monastery. My only previous interviews with royal personages had been with Arab princes, and the King of Cambodia in his informality was like somebody whose acquaintance one had just made in a bar, by comparison. The personal splendour of the past had been reduced to mere sartorial impeccability, in the form of a well-cut grey flannel suit.

Norodom, who is a man of thirty and looks twenty-one, is said by some of the French to be the most intelligent Cambodian. It was, in fact, quite astonishing how easily he brushed aside all the polite generalities accepted on such occasions, to embark without further ado on a competent half-hour lecture on Cambodian politics. It was much the same story as Yem Sambaur's, but couched in less forthright terms. Sambaur's bloody massacres became 'incidents of violence'. It was difficult to associate the King's gentle manner with harsh, uncompromising words like murder. The King's thesis, to which he returned continually, was that the French continually lagged behind the times. '*Ils ne marchent pas à la tête des évènements; ils se laissent dépasser par les temps.*' As King of Cambodia and a Buddhist gentleman he would engage his word that French commercial interests would remain untouched if only they would get out – just as the English had done in India. France had failed in its engagements as the protecting power when the Japanese had been allowed, without resistance, to overrun the country. The old treaties were therefore invalid, and in future Cambodia would prefer to protect herself. France, said the King, could not boast of having brought civilization to Cambodia. The phrase '*l'œuvre civilisatrice de la France*' was an insult to their ancient culture, especially when the Cambodian country folk who made up nine-tenths of the population could only judge this civilizing task by what they saw of the Foreign Legion.

When it was clear that the interview had run its normal and

reasonable course, there was an awkward moment. The conversation lagged and the King's smile became a little fixed. The time had come to withdraw and I waited for the King to indicate, by rising, that the interview was at an end. But it was becoming evident that innate politeness was too strong for the conventions of royal deportment. Forming the conclusion that if I did not make the first move we should both be condemned to sit there indefinitely, exchanging painful smiles and trying to think of something to say, I got up. I am sure that His Majesty was grateful.

That evening, which was my last at Pnom-Penh, I had an extraordinary piece of good luck. In the course of my travels I was coming to accept that wherever I was I was fated to experience a sub-normal amount of the customary activites. The theatre would be closed, the custom abolished, the service discontinued, the road cut by bandits, the tiger invisible, the season just over – or not yet started. But at Pnom-Penh, I was in luck. I went out of the hotel at about five in the evening and walked right into the most rampageous of Chinese celebrations – the procession of the twenty-five spirits, which the police had done their best to prevent and which had now broken loose, providing as fair an example of the medieval Chinese idea of a good time for all as it would have been possible to see in these days.

There is an alien northern vigour about such Chinese divertisse-ments which is quite outlandish in the languorous and debilitating tropics. Moreover, a century or two's sojourn in the deep south had done nothing to calm the Chinese temperament, nor caused them to envelop any relish for the sedate posturings of Indonesia. When the Chinese dance, they leap and twirl, a spectacle I had observed before at the Mardi Gras *comparsas* in Havana, when the Chinese com-munity decided to participate, suddenly appearing on the streets with their dragon, and startling even the bloodshot-eyed negroes of Cuba with their exertions. Wherever there are Chinese communities such celebrations as the twenty-five spirits tend to be discounte-nanced, as they disrupt all activities while they are in progress, and produce a state of exaltation which sometimes ends in riot. There had been an official attempt at interference with the Pnom-Penh procession which should have accompanied the Chinese New Year, and it was some two weeks delayed.

By five o'clock the non-Chinese citizens had long since given up trying to go about their business and had resigned themselves to calling it a day. All the cars were taken off the roads and the shops were shut, while the twenty-five spirits, incarnated in their human representatives – both male and female – were carried round and round the town, in palanquins, on thrones, and on stages accompanied by their altars and cult objects from the various pagodas. Each spirit was preceded by a dragon, a rabble of standard bearers, and a horde of attendants running amok with gongs and drums. The spirits themselves looked like the old-fashioned idea of Chinese pirates, even to the sashes tied round their foreheads. They kept up a lusty howling, twirled their swords, and frothed at the lips. Occasionally a particularly energetic spirit would make a flying leap from his throne or platform, seize a bystander, and join with him in a frenzied Tartar dance, while the surrounding cult devotees clashed their cymbals and howled like damned souls. Other spirits confined to their palanquins swayed from side to side in the throes of cataleptic seizure, pausing only to inflict slight self-mutilations with their knives or to thrust skewers through their cheeks. I was told that the celebrants had all drugged themselves with hypodermic injections before setting out, five hours previously; but now it was evident that some of the effect was wearing off, as, under the strain of carrying the altars and palanquins, some of the bearers were beginning to collapse. When this happened a spirit would be thrown into the crowd with even more violence than he bargained for.

At this stage the rickshaw coolies were beginning to reap the harvest. They lay in wait in the side-streets ready to pick up the victims of syncope, self-inflicted wounds, and various types of seizure. By the time the procession had disintegrated they had done a roaring trade. That night half the coolies in Pnom-Penh were gambling in the casino and owing to a temporary hold-up in the workings of the laws of average, a lot of them actually won. For the first time in its short history the syndicate found themselves down on the evening. This shocking circumstance was followed next day by the dismissal of all those girl croupiers who intone so melodiously the winning numbers; not because they were suspected of cheating, but because they were unlucky.

CHAPTER FIFTEEN

Angkor

I GOT A LIFT on a French military lorry that was going to Siem-Reap, the nearest town to the ruins of Angkor Vat; arriving there without incident – by courtesy of Dap Chhuon – on the evening of the same day.

Siem-Reap was another slumbering Shangri-La, perfumed slightly with putrid fish-sauce. In a palm-shaded river meandering through it both the sexes bathed all day long, lifting up their garments with extreme modesty as they allowed their bodies to sink below the level of the milk-chocolate-coloured water. When they had had enough of bathing they sat on the bank and caught occasional fish with lengths of cotton and bent pins.

With the ingeniousness of clever, lazy people, the Cambodians had worked out an irrigation system that looked as if a comic artist had had a hand in its construction. There were hundreds of great, rickety water-wheels turning slowly all day and splashing tumblers-full of water into conduits, that in their turn ran into a crazy network of bamboo tubes and finally reached the pocket-handkerchief-sized gardens that people bothered to cultivate. It was all very inefficient and wasteful and probably only a quarter of the water taken out of the river eventually got to the gardens. Some of the scoops only scooped up a thimbleful of water and others were set in the wheels at such an angle that they missed the collecting chute and the water went back into the river again. But all the open bamboo channels leading to the gardens had a trickle running through them and until that dried up no one would be disposed to worry.

There were many baleful-looking dogs, like miniature hyenas, with wrinkled snouts and foreheads; almost hairless and sometimes tail-less. Each house possessed one of these small, ugly creatures, which seemed to lay claim to a certain area round the house and therefore advanced with a hideous snarling and yapping when one entered it. One was then escorted with furious menaces to the boundary of the next cur's territory and so passed on down the road. The dogs never barked at Cambodians.

Everywhere the air was filled with the sweet creaking sound of the irrigation wheels mingled with the song of some bulbul that sang like a blackbird. The houses were the normal Cambodian shacks, standing on piles above their refuse. Besides each was the usual receptacle raised on a post with the offerings for wandering and neglected spirits – those who had no descendants on earth left to provide for them. But in this custom the Cambodians had bettered the Vietnamese, furnishing as a temporary sanctuary for these ghostly paupers most elegant little multi-tiered pagodas.

I found that the girls of a Cambodian country town were liable to smile at and even address strangers, especially if their courage was fortified by numbers. Dressed in sarong-like skirts of plain colours, with a blouse hardly reaching the midriff or perhaps just a scarf concealing the breasts, they would come sauntering out of the most squalid hovels, clean, bright, and pretty, and with a ready smile of welcome. It was strange to see one of these gliding shapes suddenly galvanized into efficient action at the sight of a cow in her vegetable garden, which she chased out, throwing sticks at it with an accuracy and force that no Western woman could ever hope to emulate.

Valas had told me that when in Siem-Reap it was more important to see the Cambodian theatre than Angkor itself, because the ruins would wait. But once again it was too late. The Chinese had been granted a month's licence to run a gambling casino and they had taken over the theatre for this purpose. Anyway, I was told, it was doubtful if the theatre would open again. They were arranging for weekly cinema shows and who would be bothered with going to watch people they had known all their lives dressed up as gods and devils, when they could see a *pa-wé* for the same money?

But I was at least lucky in one small thing. I had noticed in the

King's audience room a curious decoration consisting of a delicately fretted-out scene from some well-known episode of the *Ramayana*. The intricate lacing of motives looked, until the rear-illumination was switched on, as if it had been punched out of brass; but when lit-up it proved to be semi-transparent and was actually made from treated hide. The King mentioned – and it surprised me that an oriental sovereign should have any appreciation for the arts of his country – that this was a typical pattern used in the old shadow plays, and that they could still be found in Siem-Reap. And in Siem-Reap, despite the fact that I was assured that the workshop had long since gone out of business, I tracked it down. There were the artists, squatting on the ground, dressing the leather, marking the surface out with chalk, and punching out the traditional patterns. No more orders would be forthcoming for the shadow-theatre, of course, but a few private persons still bought their work for decorative purposes. They sold me their show-piece, a delightful Lokesvara, for about fifteen shillings. I learned later from a visit to the Musée de L'Homme at Paris that this art is still practised, though in a less finished way, in Siam and in Java.

Although the basis of Cambodian art is Indonesian and there are many recognizable affinities between the decorational motives of Cambodia and of all those countries where the Indian artistic influence has at some time been paramount, the Cambodians have undoubtedly added a flourish of their own, a recognizable style, generated in their aboriginal past, that asserts itself above the general pattern. Unfortunately, as Monsieur Henri Marchal, Conservator of Angkor has said, the Cambodian aristocracy, who were the only patrons of Cambodian art, have abandoned it in the last half-century in favour of European importations. After the loss of their independence rich Cambodians developed an inferiority complex about everything their country produced. European cannons were more effective than the sacred and invincible sword of Cambodia; therefore nothing Cambodian was worth having. The mandarins dismissed the goldsmiths and the sculptors who formed part of their normal households, and bought themselves gilt mirrors and Victorian tasselled furniture.

Perhaps the two most valuable and altruistic works the French have done in the Far East have been the creation in 1930 of the Institut Bouddhique at Pnom-Penh (after Catholic missionaries had succeeded in several years in making only one convert), and the establishment in the same city of the École des Arts Cambodgiens. The latter institution has made a desperate and successful attempt to save the situation, by encouraging the production of goods of high artistic value that can be sold in the ordinary way of commerce. The utmost difficulty was experienced in reassembling the artists with whom the old traditions would have died. They had returned to their villages and taken up the cultivation of rice, or fishing. When they were tracked down, it was found that some of them, who were already ageing, had not touched a tool for a quarter of a century. However, the happy fact is that the effort was made just in time, and that the Khmer arts which were on the point of vanishing for ever were given a vigorous artificial respiration and are now in fairly good shape. Naturally enough, they are now directed to commercial ends, and are largely applied to the rather banal objects demanded by the tourist and export trades. It is a stimulating reflection that the imaginative verve and faultless technique of modern Cambodian art at its best is considered by experts to rival that employed in the ornamentation of Angkor, and that this creative ability is now placed within the reach of a wide public in the form of such articles as cigarette cases and powder boxes. According to Monsieur Marchal the present danger lies in the fact that the Cambodian is determined at all costs to be absolutely up to date, and is therefore inclined to turn his back on his own impressive artistic heritage, and allow himself to be too deeply influenced by movements in Europe, purely because they are fashionable and would-be audacious.

As there was nowhere to stay in Siem-Reap, I had to go to the Grand Hotel outside the town, which draws its sporadic nourishment from visitors to Angkor. I returned to the town – a blistering, shadeless walk of a mile – for occasional meals. In the whole of Cambodia there is not a single Cambodian restaurant. True Cambodian dishes, just as Aztec dainties in Mexico and Moorish delicacies in Spain, are only to be eaten in the market booths and wayside stalls of remote towns, which are the last refuges of vanishing, culinary cultures. While from fear of infection one dared not at Siem-Reap risk those brilliant rissoles, those strange membraneous sacks containing who knows what empirically discovered tit-bit, there was always a restaurant serving what came vaguely under the heading of Chinese food. This is, at least, light, adapted to the climate, and consequently less burdensome than the surfeit of stewed meats inevitably provided by the Grand Babylon hotels of the Far East.

The Grand Hôtel des Ruines had had several lean years. It was said that one or two of the guests had been kidnapped. The necessity, until a few months before, of an armed escort, must have provided an element of drama not altogether unsuitable in a visit to Angkor. Now the visitors were beginning to come again, arriving in chartered planes from Siam, signing their names in the register which was coated as soon as opened with a layer of small, exhausted flies falling continually from the ceiling. Perking up, the management arranged conducted tours to the ruins. In the morning the hotel car went to Angkor Thom, in the afternoon it covered what was called the Little Circuit. The next morning it would be Angkor Thom again and in the afternoon Angkor Vat. You had to stay three days to be taken finally on a tour of the Grand Circuit. Naturally in the circumstances the hotel wanted to keep its guests as long as possible. And even Baedeker would not have found three days unreasonable for the visit to Angkor.

There were many remoter temples, such as the exquisite Banteay Srei, thirty kilometres away, which the bus did not reach, as it was doubtful whether the writ of Dap Chhuon ran in these distant parts. The forces of the tutelary bandit seemed to be concentrated in the immediate vicinity. There was a sports-field under my window and every morning, soon after dawn, a party of Dap Chhuon's men used to arrive for an hour's PT. Against a background of goal posts, they failed to terrify. They were thin from the years spent under the greenwood tree and as they 'knees-bent' and 'stretched', each piratical rib could be counted. Beyond the playing-field and the gymnasts, was the forest, tawny and autumnal, from which in the far distance emerged the helmeted shapes of the three central towers of Angkor Vat.

The existence of Angkor was reported by sixteenth-century missionaries, although the ruins were not fully described until Mouhot's visit in 1859. They are probaby the most spectacular man-made remains in the world, and as no European could ever be expected to rest content with the comfortable attitude taken by the Cambodians who assured Mouhot that 'they made themselves', the details of their origins have provoked endless speculation and many learned volumes.

At its maximum extension at the end of the twelfth century, the Khmer Empire included, in addition to the present kingdom of Cambodia, parts of the Malay Peninsula, Burma, Siam, and Cochin-China, but for practical and metaphysical reasons the capital has always been in the vicinity of Angkor. There are important Khmer ruins scattered through the forests over a hundred-mile radius. The principal monuments are the colossal mausoleum of Angkor Vat, the shell of the city of Angkor Thom, with its fantastic centre piece, the Bayon, and a few scattered temples and foundations; some pyramidical, but all built on a strictly rectangular plan and carefully oriented with doors facing the cardinal points. Between these are clear open spaces, since permanence was only desired for religious edifices and only those could be built of brick and stone. All these buildings were erected between the ninth and twelfth centuries.

Savants of the late nineteenth century have argued with compelling logic that Angkor Vat took three hundred years to build, although the figure generally accepted at the present time is nearer thirty. Divergences of opinion regarding the completion dates of other monuments ranged over several centuries, and there was a similarly fierce conflict of theory over the purposes of the buildings and the identity of the statuary. The arguments have been slowly resolved and many a dogma demolished by the periodical discovery of steles, on which the monarchs of those days have left a record not only of their achievements but of their motives. Thus Udayaditya-varman II informs posterity that he built the Baphûon, which was then the centre of a city which pre-dated Angkor Thom, 'because he had remembered that the centre of the universe is marked by the mountain of Meru and it was appropriate that his capital should have a Meru in its centre'.

This statement presents one with a key to the whole situation. All Khmer building was governed by an extravagant symbolism. The first Khmer King, who, returning from Java, had thrown off the suzerainty of that kingdom and unified Cambodia under his rule, had promptly declared himself a god. Under the aspect of Siva he took the title of 'Lord of the Universe'. He was obliged, therefore, to order his kingdom, or at least his capital, along the lines of an established precedent – provided in this case by Buddhist mythology. The Buddhist universe included a central mountain of Meru, which supported the heavens and was surrounded by an ocean, and finally a high wall of rocks which formed the barrier and enclosure of space. There was a lot more in it than this, but these were the reasonable limits to which the King's symbolism could be pushed. He built his artificial hill, the wide moat round his city, and the wall. This probably helped to convince him that he really was a god. It was wishful thinking on a cosmic scale.

Yet there was a curious sense of dependence shown by these self-created divinities upon the observance of their cult by their successors and their subjects. It was a grotesque magnification of the belief underlying so many Eastern religions that the fate of the dead is in some way linked to the living, who must provide them with regular offerings if they are to remain prosperous and contented in the land of souls. This idea, lodged in the ruthlessly energetic mind of a Khmer king, was translated into action on a huge scale. The King erected temples and consecrated statues to his divinized parents while leaving behind him inscriptions which positively implore his successors to follow his example. His immortality, King Yaçovarman admits on one of his steles, depends upon the maintenance of the cult. Seen in this light these deities were not comparable to the unassailable gods of the ancient Mediterranean world, for a neglected and forgotten god-king passed into oblivion. He became no more than one of the great multitude of nameless and forgotten spirits for which the pious erect those tiny shrines outside their homes.

So the King came in time to devote the whole of his efforts to the preservation of this shaky immortality. The royal megalomania reached its height with Jayavarman VII. Ta Prohm, built to house the image and the divine essence of the Queen Mother and two hundred and sixty attendant and lesser deities, required for its service seventy-nine thousand, three hundred and sixty-five persons of whom about five thousand were priests. The gold plate used in this temple weighed five tons and the temple establishment lived upon the revenues of three thousand, one hundred and forty villages. The King's obligations to his father gave rise five years later to the erection of Prah Khan. This time, according to the stele discovered in 1939, there were four hundred and thirty minor divinities included with the old King – nobles who as a kind of promotion for meritorious services had been either granted apotheosis or raised posthumously to the divine status. The responsibility for the upkeep of this establishment fell upon five thousand, three hundred and twenty-four villages, the total number of persons involved being ninety-seven thousand, eight hundred and forty. Among the dependencies of Prah Khan was the little sanctuary of Néak Pân, built upon one of those sharply rectangular artificial lakes the Khmers were so fond of digging out. This symbolized a lake situated, according to Hindu legend, somewhere in the Himalayas, which was supposed to possess extraordinary purificatory powers. Its construction was no mere poetic conceit, but followed a formula by which it became, in essence, the original lake. In this way the Khmer King saved himself the kind of gigantic wild-goose chase sometimes undertaken by the Chinese emperors in their searches for similar legendary sites.

These are the games of children, who by a slight imaginative effort can even transform inanimate objects into living ones; a broom into a horse. But the children's games played by the kings of

Cambodia were backed by monstrous and freakish power. Néak Pân, of course, was a trifle for those days, probably not occupying more than ten thousand men for a mere three or four years.

But the King was not, and never could be satisfied. Hounded on by furious compulsions, he reconstructed his capital in such a way that the Baphûon – microcosm of Meru – was no longer in the town's geometrical centre. This called for another sacred mountain, a great extension of the moat and entirely new walls. After only ten years of his reign there were already thirteen thousand, five hundred villages comprising three hundred and six thousand, three hundred and seventy-two men at work on these projects. The new sacred mountain was the Bayon, the most singular of all the Angkor monuments. It was Jayavarman's last work, begun in about 1190, and it marked the height of the Khmer power and foreshadowed its end. From its towers sixty-four colossal faces of the King, now represented as one with the Buddha, smiled, with rather savage satisfaction, it seems, towards the four quarters of the kingdom. Even Pierre Loti, who knew nothing of the Bayon's history, found it very sinister.

With inexorable willpower at the service of mania, the Khmer kings called into being whole populations whose only ultimate function, whether directly or indirectly, was the furtherance of their insatiable cult. In the early period, the economic basis of this efflorescence was the inland sea of Tonlé Sap, close to which all the successive capitals had been situated and which contained, and still contains, so many fish that when in the dry season the waters sink to their low level, the oars of boatmen are impeded by them. The Tonlé Sap provided food for the whole populace through the exertions of a few fishermen, and the King saw to it that all the spare hours were occupied with profitable labour. An agricultural people, efficiently tilling fertile soil – and one is reminded of the pre-Columbian Mayans – can live fairly comfortably on an aggregate of forty or fifty days' labour a year. Inevitably, however, some organizing genius comes along to make sure that the spare three hundred days are occupied in impressive but largely wasteful undertakings.

With the flying start provided by the Tonlé Sap the kingdom was expanded in all directions, covered with rice-fields, nourished by a brilliant irrigational system and linked up by a network of roads, with elaborately equipped staging points providing shelter for the buffaloes and elephants used as beasts of transport, as well as their masters. The great building King, Jayavarman VII, in addition to his religious foundations and influenced perhaps by the fact that he was a leper, established a hundred and two hospitals. He did not omit to furnish on the great stele of Prah Khan the most detailed catalogue of the medicaments with which they were stocked. It was a huge piece of organization, controlled finally by a vast machine of state, with its Domesday Books and its army of accountants, to keep track of the activities of every single man in the interests of maximum production. One can be quite sure that there was a police force and that the minds of the young were carefully moulded by the priesthood to fit them for the efficient fulfilment of their duties. The Khmer Empire was nothing if not totalitarian.

A great deal of unnecessary mystery has been made about the downfall of the Khmers, followed by the abandonment of Angkor. It has often been attributed to spectacular Acts of God. The facts, simple enough, are related by the Chinese traveller Chou Ta-Kouan, who visited Angkor when its decadence was already well advanced, and when, partly because the sandstone quarries were exhausted, even the building mania had petered out. It seems that the Khmers, attacked in retaliation by the Siamese, had been obliged to apply the principles of total war. 'They say,' said Chou Ta-Kouan, 'that in the war with the Siamese, all the people were forced to fight.' One notes that Ta-Kouan speaks of compulsion, and suspects that if any were spared conscription it would have been those tens of thousands of temple servants who ministered to the royal cult. If the report is true that the Khmer army was several millions strong, it must have been by far the largest in the world of its day. But these peasants torn from their rice-fields and forced into uniform fought with little enthusiasm and the wars dragged on until final defeat.

In the meanwhile the irrigation systems were allowed to fall into ruin and the rice-fields on which the enormous, swollen population depended quicky reverted to forests. The highly productive paddy-field system was progressively abandoned in favour of that present

scourge of Indo-China, rice-cultivation in 'rays', which involves the
annual burning of the forest. It was a method, since it occupies the
minimum of labour, which must have been tempting to a nation at
war, but results are poor and decrease rapidly, and ultimately it results
in the sterilization and exhaustion of the soil. The process of decline,
once under way, could not be halted, and defeat was made absolute
by the victor's introduction of the primitive apostolic Buddhism of
the 'Little Vehicle', the religion of withdrawal, of renunciation, of
tranquillity, which was so utterly destructive to the perverted power-
cults of the divine kings. It was the subtlest of Carthaginian Peaces.

It is possible that the ruins of Angkor are in many ways more
impressive than the city itself was in its heyday. Time has wrought
wonders with the sandstone, which must have been garish enough
when freshly cut. And vandalism and the flailings of sun and rain
have done much to mute that excessive symmetry, that all-pervading
symbolism, that repetitiousness which I find irritating in Far Eastern
art. There is evidence of an obsession with the magic of numbers
and of the dignifying, under artistic forms, of primeval superstitions.
One feels that the Khmer must have reasoned that if it was a good
thing to erect one statue to Vishnu or of a Devata, then it was fifty
times better to have fifty of them. Adepts of magic never seem to be
convinced that their magical practices are completely and finally
effective. The causeway which leads into Angkor Vat is, or was,
flanked at exactly spaced intervals by pairs of nagas – seven-headed
serpents. I do not find seven-headed serpents particularly decorative,
and much prefer the lions *couchant* of which there are many
hundreds. However, they represent the serpent beneath which
Buddha sheltered. They are, therefore, in essence, protective; and it
is necesary to have as many as can be fitted in. I think that it is an
aesthetic advantage that the majority of them have been broken and
are missing.

The causeway conducts one smack into the centre of the whole
architectural composition. It could not be otherwise, since all
considerations had to be subordinated to that of symbolism; and to

have built the formal approach from any angle but this would have been to risk throwing the universe, or at least the kingdom, out of balance, by sympathetic magic. Angkor Vat, however, is best viewed from across the water from one of the corners of the moat. Immediately the tyranny of the matched-pair is broken. The towers, many-tiered like the head-dress of an Indian dancer, are regrouped in majestic nonchalance. The Vat gathers itself from the lake, raised on a long, low-lying portico. Above that the unbroken lines of the roofs rise one above the other, to be capped by the towers, which are somehow jaunty in spite of the sad harmony of the old, disintegrated colours. A lotus-broken reflection is carried on the mildewed waters of the lake.

And all the monuments of ancient Greece could be enclosed in this one building.

Within the Vat miles of goddesses and heavenly dancing girls, de-humanized and amiable, posture in bas-relief round the gallery walls. They are all exactly of the same height and physique, hands and arms frozen in one of the dozen or so correct gestures. Since Khmer art is never erotic – and one remembers de la Rochefoucauld's 'where ambition has entered love rarely returns' – they do not exhibit the development of breast and hip which is so characteristic of similar figures in Indian art.

The triumphant existence is portrayed in a series of set poses. The king or god out hunting adopts the wooden pose of a dancer to shoot a deer – in itself depicted with admirable realism. Victorious princes and warriors parade for the ascent to heaven (success being identified with virtue), heads overlapping in three-quarters profile, left hands on breasts and right on hips. Nothing, however, could be more realistic than the treatment of the defeated and the damned, who are naturally consigned to hell. The postures of these bodies being trodden underfoot by horsemen and torn by wild beasts have been observed and carefully copied from life. Only the devils are permitted a hieratic stance.

But is is when the artist is left to his own devices in his treatment of the ordinary citizen, and his everyday life, that he shows us what he can do. Gone is the processional dignity and the frigid smile of power. The peasants and fisher-folk are shown as thick-limbed and grotesque, with coarse, clownish faces. With gleeful licence the artist depicts their buffoonery as they haggle over tripe in the market, slaughter their pigs, smirkingly watch a cock-fight or visit a palmist. These are the trollish faces that medieval church-sculptors carved on almost invisible bosses as a relief from the insipidity of righteousness. The vulgar of Angkor are shown taking their pleasure on the Tonlé Sap – capering on the deck of a becalmed junk like day-trippers on the river boat to Southend, or hunched over a game of chess. With lower-class respectability most of them have put on short jackets for the occasion. Meanwhile, a boat-load of the better people passes, all seated with decorum, fashionable in their semi-nudity, facing one way, and smiling with the refined beatitude induced by the knowledge that sooner or later they will appear in the honours list as minor gods.

Cormorants and herons are shown competing with the fishermen for their catches while crocodiles menace them from the water. The Khmers made much decorative use of flora and fauna. The anarchic quality of trees is subdued and subjected to a Byzantine stylization, but the animals that lurk among them are seen in a lively naturalism comparable to Palaeolithic cave-art. And the intention that animated cave-art is roughly identical with that which produced these miles of bas-reliefs. Their object was magical and their decorative effect quite incidental. Angkor Vat was the funerary temple of Suryavaraman II divinized under the aspect of Vishnu, and this world in sculpture replaced the great funeral holocausts of earlier days. That aesthetic pleasure had no bearing upon the question is proved by the fact that many scenes have been sculpted with scrupulous care in places where they are quite invisible, or even – as in the case of the Bayon – on the building's subterranean foundations.

Ta Prohm, which Jayavarman VII built to house his mother's cult, and which occupied the working lives of seventy-nine thousand of his subjects, was scheduled to detain the thirty tourists from Siam for one hour.

The temple was built on flat land and offers none of the spectacular vistas of Angkor Vat, nor the architectural surprises of Bayon. It has therefore been maintained as a kind of reserve where the prodigious conflict between the ruins and the jungle is permitted to continue under control. The spectacle of this monstrous vegetable aggression is a favourite with most visitors to the ruins.

Released from the hotel bus, the thirty tourists plunged forward at a semi-trot into the caverns of this rectangular labyrinth. For a few moments their pattering footsteps echoed down the flagstoned passages and then they were absorbed in the silence of those dim, shattered vastnesses, and I saw none of them again until it was time to return.

Ta Prohm is an arrested cataclysm. In its invasion, the forest has not broken through it, but poured over the top, and the many courtyards have become cavities and holes in the forest's false bottom. In places the cloisters are quite dark, where the windows have been covered with subsidences of earth, humus, and trees. Otherwise they are illuminated with an aquarium light, filtered through screens of roots and green lianas.

Entering the courtyards one comes into a new kind of vegetable world; not the one of branches and leaves with which one is familiar, but that of roots. Ta Prohm is an exhibition of the mysterious subterranean life of plants, of which it offers an infinite variety of cross-sections. Huge trees have seeded themselves on the roofs of the squat towers and their soaring trunks are obscured from sight; but here one can study in comfort the drama of those secret and conspiratorial activities that labour to support their titanic growth.

Down, then, come the roots, pale, swelling, and muscular. There is a grossness in the sight; a recollection of sagging ropes of lava, a parody of the bulging limbs of circus-freaks, shamefully revealed. The approach is exploratory. The roots follow the outlines of the masonry; duplicating pilasters and pillars; never seeking to bridge a gap and always preserving a smooth living contact with the stone surfaces; burlesqueing in their ropy bulk the architectural motives which they cover. It is only long after the hold has been secured that the deadly wrestling bout begins. As the roots swell their grip contracts. Whole blocks of masonry are torn out, and brandished in mid-air. A section of wall is cracked, disjointed, and held in suspension like a gibbeted corpse, prevented by the roots' embrace from disintegration. There are roots which appear suddenly, bursting through the flagstones to wander twenty yards like huge boa-constrictors, before plunging through the up-ended stones to earth again. An isolated tower bears on its summit a complete sample of the virgin jungle, with ferns and underbrush and a giant fig tree which screens the faces of the statuary with its liana-curtains, and discards a halo of parakeets at the approach of footsteps.

The temple is incompletely cleared. One wanders on down identical passages or through identical courtyards – it is as repetitive in plan as a sectional bookcase – and then suddenly there is a thirty-foot wall, a tidal wave of vegetation, in which the heavenly dancers drown with decorous gestures.

But there are still some signs of life in the temples and mausolea of Angkor, besides the sinister and stinking presence of myriads of bats. The people now come to these once exclusive places and burn incense-sticks before the Buddhas, which probably started their existence as idealized representations of various members of the Khmer aristocracy. Parties of bonzes stroll through the ruins. They carry the inevitable yellow parasols and sometimes box cameras with which they photograph each other, for the benefit of their friends back at the monastery, against some particularly sacrosanct background such as the corpulent shape of a man who had once made a corner in fish.

My last daylight hours at Angkor were spent by the lake of Sram Srang. The Khmers were always digging out huge artificial lakes, which, if the preliminary surveying had been correctly carried out, and temples and statues were erected according to accepted precedents round their margins or on a centre island, could always be declared to possess purificatory qualities. For this reason Sram Srang was supposed to have been a favourite royal bathing place, with its grand approach, its majestic flight of steps, flanked with mythical animals, and its golden barges.

Now the lions were faceless, and the nagas had lost most of their heads. The severe rectangularity of old had been softened by subsidences of the banks, which had solidified into little peninsulas on which trees were growing. Buffaloes stood motionless in the virtuous water with only their heads showing. Sometimes even their heads were withdrawn for a few moments below the surface. Giant kingfishers flashed past, linked to their reflections; twin shooting stars in a grey-green firmament. Until forty years ago the Cambodians exported these birds' skins to China where they were made into mandarins' jackets, taking in exchange pottery and silk. And then the vogue for European goods grew up, and the industry languished.

As if from nowhere a group of boys materialized. They were selling crossbows. They were better looking and their physique was better than either the nobles or the commons on the Angkor Vat bas-reliefs, but six hundred years ago they would have worked twelve hours a day, and now they probably worked an hour a week, if at all. Three or four of them always lurked forlornly in the vicinity of the various ruins in the outrageous hope of one day selling a crossbow to a tourist.

One of them surprised me by speaking understandable French, and this was such a rarity that I asked him if he would act as a guide to one or two of the outlying monuments I wanted to see. At the same time I thought that I would be able to question him as to the existence of legends, and particularly about the legend of the leper-king which was supposed to be the only memory of the Khmer rulers that had survived. The boy said he would be delighted, but when? I said that night, as it was practically full-moon, and I believed that I could get a rickshaw in Siem-Reap to bring me out to Angkor. His face fell. He was sorry, it couldn't be managed. I asked why not? Were the ex-bandits unreliable at night? Oh, no it was not that. On the contrary they were very disciplined, and with Dap Chhuon in command you were in fact safer at Angkor than at

.Pnom-Penh. Well, then, what was it? ... the tigers, perhaps? No, it wasn't the tigers, either ... but the fact was that after dark Angkor was a very bad place for the *néak ta eysaur* and the *néak ta en* – in other words, the spirits Siva and Indra.

Thus had the powerful Brahmanical gods of the Khmer Empire shrunk and shrivelled along with the Empire itself. And now they were no more than *néak ta* – mere tree spirits to frighten babies with; of no more importance than the *khmoo pray* – the wicked dead, such women who had died in childbed; the *beisac* – the famished souls of those who have died violently, who return from hell to implore food; the *smer*, who, losing their reason, have become werewolves, and the *srei ap*, beautiful girls, who through dabbling in black magic have inadvertently turned themselves into heads, accompanied only by alimentary canals, and live on excrement. The Khmer gods have accompanied their worshippers in their decline.

A rumour existed in Siem-Reap of the survival of a troupe of heavenly dancers. At the hotel there was a knowledgeable hanger-on who had learned enough English from American visitors to describe himself as an officer's pimp. From him I made enquiries.

His first reaction was to produce the slow compassionate smile of the sensitive man who dislikes to disappoint. There were dancers, but they were very old – at least fifty – and quite ugly. On clarifying the nature of my enquiry, he said that they were not only old, but charged a lot for their services, that he did not know where they could be contacted, and that they had no proper clothes to dance in. These had to be hired from a Chinese, who 'would not be there'. It was clear that my informant's services as an intermediary would only cover the simplest arrangements and that he had now retired behind this squid-like effusion of negatives. But at this point, some of my fellow-guests became interested. Among them was an Anglo-American business executive from Bangkok, who had lived a number of years in Siam and said that he was used to tackling situations like this. The Chinese, he said, was the key to the problem. The thing was to find the Chinese ... if possible the one who hired out the costumes. There was no doubt about it that this man could make arrangements for us to see a Cambodian dance.

Down to the town, therefore, went my friend, and in due course a suitable Chinese was discovered. He was one of those octopuses of commerce that plant themselves squarely in the centre of the business life of such towns; the kind of man – Tes Heak, I believe his name was – who anyone could lead you to, and who was to be discovered unassumingly, pencil behind ear, on a sack of dry fish, surrounded by his stocks of dried milk, his cobra skins, his coffins, and his Algerian wine. Tes Heak also ran the bus services, conducted an undertaking establishment, with a hearse most lavishly equipped with miniature puppet theatres, and supplied an American car for weddings, to the wings and roof of which gilt dragons were attached. Taking in the situation with a saurian flicker of the eyelids, he produced a number of reasons overlooked by the officer's pimp why it would be infeasible to persuade the heavenly dancers to perform. He even complained that they had artistic temperaments, hastily adding, however, when it looked as though he was being taken seriously, that a performance would cost fifteen hundred piastres – about £27.

This seemed an enormous fee for a short demonstration by the five ladies, who, Tes Heak said, might be induced to go through a short repertoire. My hopes had been to arrange something that would be as spontaneous and unselfconscious as possible – perhaps in a back yard. But Tes Heak was revolted at so shoddy a proposal. Such a spectacle, he thought, should be staged in the forecourt of Angkor Vat itself, and by moonlight. It was clear that he knew his tourist, and that this negligently sown seed would probably fall on fertile soil. Just as there is a collective crowd-mentality which is a little more (or less) than the sum total of the mentalities of its individual members, so the single traveller multiplied by thirty becomes a tourist with a certain garishness of taste that he did not possess before, a kind of temporary distemper provoked by gregarious indulgence, that commits him to extravagances. The idea of a spectacle in the grand manner was, therefore, enthusiastically acclaimed.

Having easily won the first round, Tes Heak now suggested drummers, a local orchestra, and an escort of torch-bearers – at a slight extra charge, of course. This too was agreed, and finally, at a cost of three thousand piastres, the thing was arranged.

At ten o'clock that night, therefore, the hotel bus stopped at the end of the causeway leading to Angkor Vat. News of the performance had spread, and to my surprise what must have been most of the population of Siem-Reap, and probably of the neighbouring villages as well, had put in an appearance. A fiesta atmosphere prevailed with stalls selling hot sausages clamped between two slabs of bread, sugar-cane juice – crushed out while you waited – mounds of pale green jelly, and mineral waters. In addition to the hundred small shaven-headed torch-bearers, in the old style, who awaited our coming along the causeway, waving bundles of resin-soaked rags, at least five hundred of the hurrying crowd flashed electric torches as they walked, to the natural detriment of the archaic effect.

The passengers, mostly women, who had dressed with painstaking informality for the occasion, stepped down gingerly into this carnival scene. With their charming, defeated smiles, the sellers of crossbows pounced upon them and in the background a group of Dap Chhuon's men, lean from their peace-time rations and physical jerks, eyed the occidental display with the wistful sincerity of tethered peregrines.

Along the causeway the torch-bearers, descrying a European among the padding Cambodians, would gesticulate and wave their flaming rags. A small group had deserted their post and clambered down into the water where, torches aloft, they were looking for something – a living fountain-group in bronze. Shutting out half the horizon was the long, low mass of Angkor Vat, moonlight glinting feebly in its towers. There was a certain poetry in the scene, and the ridiculous march of the tourists, flinching from its wan escort of bow-sellers, was part of it.

By the time we arrived at the forecourt the Cambodians were already installed on the best vantage points, riding the mute lions and perched on the necks of beheaded serpents. The torch-bearers now broke away and stormed raggedly forward; the rearguard of a triumph. Four acetylene lamps lit up a white amphitheatre of expectant faces and a player seated himself at a semi-circular xylophone and began a discursive tinkling.

Although I had no standards by which to judge, the dancing seemed lifeless – a mime of embalmed postures. Only four dancers had appeared, and two – as we had been fairly warned – were indeed past their prime. Although no doubt perfectly correct in their rendering of such episodes as the fight between Hanuman and the Demon King, the two fifty-year-old ladies could hardly be expected to galvanize us with the impetuosity of a combat which, according to the epic, was conducted chiefly with thunderbolts, aerial javelins, and arrows of wind. But if the old ladies were lacking in vigour, their youthful pupils showed no signs of having been schooled in such elementary feats as going through fairly long interpretative passages while balancing on one leg, the other being bent backwards from the knee, and held at right angles. There were some perilous wobbles, causing on one occasion an elderly lady to animate the powdered mask in which her features were set by the most unclassical of grimaces.

But the girls came into their own soon after, deposing the heavy, multi-tiered crowns, and exchanging the stiff, hired finery for sarongs and blouses. Joined by several more girls and partners from the audience they gave a sparkling demonstration of the *lap ton*. It was a dance with a sense of humour – an extraordinary thing in these countries – particularly the version which mimicked a husband and wife quarrelling, and there was as much of Eastern grace as could be combined with the vigour of the West. There was no dead symbolism here, nor were there traces of ritual intended to assist the growth of the crops. But the performers were thoroughly enjoying themselves, skipping about and twirling their hands, evidently relieved at the release from the puppet-antics of a pre-historic tradition. These were the low-class caperings on the junk in bas-relief ... and it was soon clear that this was what the audience had come to see.

CHAPTER SIXTEEN

Bandit Country

THERE WAS AN INTREPID American girl at the hotel. She was not a member of the tourist party from Siam, but had straggled in unobtrusively from Tokio, via Macao and Saigon and many other intermediary China-Sea ports with remote and evocatory names. She was writing, and living on a small, carefully managed allowance, and appeared never to stop travelling. One of the motives for these uneasy wanderings was her connection with the *Des Moines Register*, the leading newspaper of her home town. Her assignment was to look up all the Des Moines citizens she could find living in the Far East and write a chatty, human account of their doings for the benefit of the people at home. So far she had only found one exile from Des Moines in Indo-China.

She was brave and indefatigable with an appetite for regular achievement. The spirit she enshrined, with its voracity for random facts and experiences, was rather that of the late twenties than the early fifties. I came across her continually in the ruins. Guide-book in hand, waving guides aside, she tracked down all the most obscure pieces of sculpture ('Say, have you seen Indra on a three-headed elephant?') and the isolated temples, half submerged in the jungle, that others overlooked. She was as preoccupied with numerology as the Khmers themselves, checking up on the exact numbers of gods and demons and marvelling, as the great kings would have had her marvel, at the sixty-four faces of the temples containing the sixteen images and all constructed in best selected sandstone, with the regrettable laterite patching kept well out of sight.

Now this dauntless girl, having digested all that Angkor had to offer, had decided to go on to Siam, but had no intention of going all the way back to Siagon and flying from there by the regular route. Instead she was determined to cross country somehow or other to the Siamese border, a matter of a hundred miles or so, where she could get a train to Bangkok. There was, in fact, a road through Sisophon which joined up there with the railroad, and doubled it to the Siamese frontier town, but there were no trains on this side of the frontier owing to the presence of one or more of the five bands of Issaraks who had not yet shown signs of surrendering. Nor, according to reports, was the road safe for most of its length; but she had persuaded the French Army, who were always delighted to oblige in such matters, to take her on the first military transport to go through.

I mention all this because I had to get back to Saigon fairly soon now; either to go on the trip to the Viet-Minh occupied territory or to take up the seat I had booked on the plane to Laos, and I had learned that if I wanted to return to Pnom-Penh by the safe road – the one policed by Dap Chhuon – which runs along the eastern shore of the great lake, it would mean a wait of several days for transport. But there was another way of returning more quickly, although apparently with some risk, down the west-shore road. Under some kind of *sub rosa* arrangement Tes Heak ran a bus which slipped out of Siem-Reap in the early morning hours and took this route. It occurred to me that if the American girl-journalist was prepared to take the chance in a French military car, there was no reason why I should not do so under Tes Heak's auspices, as a man with his business flair would undoubtedly have an arrangement with the bandits through whose territory we passed.

The bus to Pnom-Penh stole out of the town at four in the morning. Like all Asiatic buses it was packed solidly with passengers, and only by paying nearly twice the right fare had I been able to obtain one of Tes Heak's attractive tickets, covered in red ideographs. In the bus I was given the place of honour on the right of the driver, who was obliged to jostle me continually as he changed gear. Three distinguished citizens of Siem-Reap were squeezed in on his left and a complete row of yellow-robed bonzes sat, with cultivated impassivity of expression, immediately behind. Although vowed to lives of self-abnegation there were certain minor bourgeois affectations which they were not forbidden. One was the wearing of sun-glasses, which they and all the other passengers of distinction put on as soon as the dawn came.

The passengers carried with them strings of dried fish, just as they might have carried sandwiches. These, hung up within easy reach, filled the bus with a rich, sea-shore tang. As soon as we were underway, one of the bonzes, bothered by his parasol, leaned over and hooked it over the windscreen. The others followed suit, leaving the driver with half his normal field of vision. He paid no attention to this handicap; in any case, it would have been unthinkable to criticize the holy men.

It was a bad thing if you were in the least mechanically minded to sit next to the driver because you couldn't help noticing some of the things that were wrong with the car. In these countries cars are driven on relentlessly until under the strain something goes. Patched up with ingenious makeshifts they are put back on the road again where they carry on, come what may, until finally, with elliptical cylinders, worn-out bearings, burnt valves, crippled transmissions, flattened springs, and shattered bodies, not another mile can be forced out of them. In the meanwhile, and until this final disintegration, their drivers handle them with confidence and verve.

In this case the engine seemed to be loose in the chassis as the control pedals jiggered about quite independent of the floorboards. The driver was obliged to hold the foot-brake off by hooking his toe under it, and to drive with one hand on the gear lever, to prevent its jumping out of gear. The steering wheel turned freely through about ninety degrees before the steering was affected, and the lights went off and on as we hurtled over the bumps. None of these inconveniences seemed to worry the driver in the least. He was a small, elderly Chinese, who conducted the bus with quiet determination. Whatever happened and however terrible the road, he drove straight on at the bus's maximum speed – a bellowing forty-five miles an hour.

It seemed that we had taken a cross-country cut, avoiding the towns I had expected to pass through, because somehow or other we missed Sisophon. A few miles away over on our left would have been the shores of the great lake which, although in the present dry season was only about ninety miles in length by about twenty in width, has the habit of tripling its area and flooding many square miles of forest at the height of the rains. It is this flooding of the forest which produces the enormous annual increase in the number of fish, which are so concentrated when the shrinkage takes place that they are practically scooped out of the water, rather than fished. At this season when the waters were at their lowest (and when this great exterminatory fishing was actually going on), the water had receded from ten to fifteen miles, leaving behind sticky prairies, with temporary villages where they grew a few vegetables, and temporary roads. On the lake itself, always out of sight, was a fringe of floating villages, which moved backwards and forwards across the map with the expansion and contraction of the waters.

Soon after sunrise we found ourselves on a main road. You could tell it was a main road because, although the surface was even more awful than that of the temporary track, there were permanent villages and bridges. One modern bridge we passed over was a reconstruction of an ancient Khmer one with the remnants of a balustrade formed from the body of a seven-headed serpent. In a few places the jagged stumps of ruins rose above the ground.

We stopped at a village for breakfast, a half-circle of slate-coloured shacks with all the uprights newly plastered, as if for the visit of a circus, with vermilion Chinese New Year posters. A few day-dreaming Cambodians had found posts to lean against and there was a great collection of the hyena-faced dogs in the street, which our driver carefully avoided.

Since eating in strange surroundings is half the pleasure of Asiatic travel, the passengers all tied their dried fish to the backs of the seats, got down, and made for the dark cavern that was the local café. Two of the senior bonzes seated themselves together at a table. One got out a fountain pen and began to write a letter, while the other took a snack out of an American mess-can.

The four other junior bonzes who were travelling with us now lined up in the gutter, graded in order of height, each one holding his basin. Walking a few paces until they were opposite the first house, they stopped and left-turned. A woman came out of the house, ready as if warned by premonition, with a bowl and ladle. Facing the line for the moment, rather like a sergeant inspecting a parade, she then squatted down and raised the bowl for a moment to her forehead. Getting up again, and starting at the leading bonze, she passed briskly down the line, depositing a ladleful of rice in each bowl. This completed, the bonzes right-turned and marched in single file to the next house.

Having a fad for the interior decoration of such places, I preferred to go right into the café's forbidding interior instead of sitting outside. I was rewarded with a picture of Sun Yat-sen (Chiang Kai-shek had quite disappeared and Mao Tse-tung had not yet arrived), a badly cured tiger's skin, a collection of imitation rhinoceros's horns, and an advertisement for the Khmer National Lottery, consisting of four pictures of Cambodian family life. The first scene, shortly entitled 'Misery', showed an ordinary household, its members squatting about on the floor of their house, doing, as you would expect, nothing in particular. In the second picture the husband, struck by an idea contained in a balloon floating above his head, suggests buying a lottery ticket. In spite of their misery, the money is found for this. In picture three – they win, and, on being told the grand news, express their joy with the hand-flourishes of temple dancers. Fourth picture, 'Happiness', is refined and sedate. The wife wears a red jumper, a short skirt, and carpet slippers. Her man has put on a coat with lapels, a collar, and tie. In the ordinary way both of them would now die of heat-stroke; but the lottery has taken care of that too. They sit in front of an electric fan.

I was now more and more embarrassed by my speechlessness in such places as this. In the remote interior of Indo-China it is a good thing, for both one's comfort and one's safety, to speak a few words of one of the principal languages, Vietnamese, Cambodian, Laotian, or even Chinese. But the first and last present great difficulties, owing to their tonal system. One must be willing to sing as well as speak. And Cambodian, although poverty-stricken in words expressing abstractions, is bewilderingly rich in other respects. There are, for instance, seventeen different verbs replacing the English verb *to carry*; according to whether one carries on the head, the back, the shoulders, the hip, in the arms, suspended from a cord, etc. There are also seven forms of address, reflecting, one supposes, the old Khmer social order, which take into account both the social and moral standing of the person one is addressing – and give grave offence if improperly used. This is not a simple matter like using the polite form in a Latin language. The differences are so great as almost to divide the language into seven separate dialects.

In the case of one's food requirements, the remedy is to try to draw what one wants (my stylized sketch of a bird produced not a chicken's wing, but two fried sparrows on a skewer), or point to what others are eating – invariably Chinese soup, from which the tentacles of small river octopi tend to trail. All this gives the greatest amusement to the customers, although, with the chiding finger of several thousand years' civilization behind them, the Indo-Chinese have far too much maiden-auntish control over themselves to laugh uproariously, as Africans might. In this case one of the heads of the family was fetched, who with dignified bows invited me into the kitchen, where in the antechamber to Dante's hell I selected some brightly dyed minced meat, which was delivered to me wrapped – in Hungarian style – in a cabbage leaf. Salt was always rare and precious in these places, and one was expected, in its place, to dowse one's food in rancid sauces or to nibble between mouthfuls at salted fish. This café, however, supplied what was described in English, on the tin's label, as Ve-Tsin Gourmet Powder, a yellow and pungent spice, which, if you used enough, produced a faint salinity.

Something like a state of emergency seemed to have been proclaimed in the neighbourhood, and several members of the National Guard were mooching round looking for somewhere to sleep. One of them slumped into a vacant chair at my table, and his rifle clattered to the ground. He groped for it, picked it up, leaned it against the table, and stuck a flower down the barrel. It was an oldish weapon with a rusty bolt, but the butt had been most tastefully carved with a close, intricate design of leaves, through which a helmeted horseman charged with raised sword.

When it was time to set off again, the driver himself went round the village to look out each passenger, tracking down with difficulty some who, wanting to make the most of the excursion, had wandered off to see the local sights. We were leaving some of our fellow-passengers behind and collecting some new ones – Cambodian women who arrived carrying their belongings in beautifully woven baskets. Their good looks were subdued by the determined composure they adopted to cover all traces of excitement. The girls' hair was done up in thick, glossy chignons, but the older women wore their hair in the close, ragged crop which happened, quite by chance, to correspond to the European fashion of that time.

Leaving the village, we thundered on through dead-flat country. On each side stretched a milky slough with deep pools, the colour of pale yolk, in which buffaloes squirmed like fat grey maggots. The sky was iron-grey over this waste of tempera. For the first time I saw glossy ibises, in extraordinary partnership with eagles, paddling awkwardly in the shallows. The villages here were quite different, and for a short distance each house had a kind of totem pole with a carved wooden cock raised in front of it. The country manners, too, were informal. At a hamlet stop an exquisite lady in black knickers descended the steps of her house, and, stationing herself with her back to us, before a large earthenware jar, began her morning toilet. Properly, the bonzes averted their eyes. Across the road the building of a new house had been started – a combined village enterprise which would take three or four days – and the solemn moment of the insertion of the central pillar, flying its red banner, was being fêted with flutes and drums.

And so we went on, the driver, it seemed, feeling his way with quiet perspicacity across the gentle, sunlit, dangerous landscape, stopping sometimes to make enquiries from a peasant, and then making perhaps a detour into the white waste to avoid some doubtful village. The bus took terrible punishment. We developed electrical troubles and without slackening speed the driver sent his mate out to repair them. With the bus leaping and lurching beneath him he crawled bare-footed all over the front end, opening first one and then the other side of the bonnet, wielding his pliers to strip and join wires and insulating the joints with oblongs of tape he carried stuck to the skin of his legs. People who wanted rides were always trying to stop us. The driver took no notice of ordinary civilians, shouted polite excuses to bonzes, and stopped for soldiers.

In the early afternoon there was another pause. Once again there was a Chinese restaurant, and the family, until the invasion from the bus took place, could be seen taking their siesta on the tables in the background. It was a very enterprising concern; probably under new management. The food was served in splendid gold-edged bowls, splashed over with Chinese lettering, and stylized cocks and dragon-flies had been painted on the spoons. But in spite of its amenities the restaurant did not object to patrons bringing their own food. While I was busy with my salted prawns one of the passengers, a frugal Cambodian, sat down at my side, ordered a glass of tea, and unwrapping a banana leaf produced a small bird, looking as if it might have been fried in bread-crumbs, which, holding by the beak, he devoured in two bites. When we had both finished our meal he got up, smiled, and beckoned to me to go with him. We walked a short way down the street and he pointed to a house which consisted of a framework only supporting several intricately carved doors. There were no walls, and just as we arrived, the occupant, who had been reclining on a mat under a parasol, got up, opened one of the doors and came down the step-ladder into the street. From his dress, which included a thick black pullover and a topee, I judged him to be a man of importance. My companion grinned and said *pirate*.

This village was on a river-bank and had a market selling a great deal of fish. There was a particular species which I saw here for the first time, but continually thereafter. What was remarkable about it was that it was always displayed for sale alive; in this case neatly lined up on banana leaves with others of its sort, price tickets balanced unsteadily on the flattish tops of each head between the eyes. Sometimes the fish, which I was told lived for about three hours after being taken out of the water, would start to move unsteadily away on ventral fins that were evolving into flippers. This happened particularly when they were chivvied by dogs. They would make a yard or so's progress before being recovered and gently replaced by the Cambodian maiden in charge. When a sale was made the fish were tied up, using a length of thin bamboo, with a neat bow, and taken away suspended from the buyer's finger. The only dead fish on offer were very large, and these, by way of placation, had their jaws forced wide apart and a propitiatory prawn thrust between them. It was a village of animal-lovers, and two great pink buffaloes – the lucky kind – had the run of it and had stopped at the market for a feed of choice vegetables, while the vendors looked on admiringly.

It was here that a rather ill-boding incident took place. Three soldiers had been travelling with us and now suddenly they came rushing up, breaking through the group of passengers who waited in the shade of the bus for the driver's signal to take their seats. Scrambling into the bus they threw their possessions out of the window into the street, jumping after them – upsetting as they did so a pyramid of hens in bottle-shaped wicker baskets – and then dashed off up the road, trailing belts and bandoliers.

A clucking excitement now spread among the passengers, and some of them, following the soldiers' example, tried to unload their packages. They were frustrated by the arrival of the driver, who, abandoning his normal phlegm, and waving his arms like a goose-herd, drove them back into the bus. When I tried to follow, the way was barred and the driver explained possibly in Mandarin that some difficulty had arisen. His arguments were supported by helpful translations into Cambodian by the passengers, speaking with the exaggerated slowness and clarity which they felt sure would more than compensate for an actual ignorance of the language. The senior bonze joined in, respectfully removing his sun-glasses before beginning a low-voiced exposition of the circumstance in some scholarly lingua franca – probably Pali. The man of the restaurant clambered down, and pushing his way to the front, said *pirate* again, but this time with a sadly apologetic smile. One of the market people called to interpret, asked '*Toi parler Français?*' But when I said yes, shook his head in confusion and, having exhausted his vocabulary, was allowed to escape.

Once again the man of the restaurant was back, determined to break this impasse, while the driver cranked the starting-handle furiously. Hearing the word *pirate* again I pointd up the street to where the master of the skeleton house, whom I supposed had retired on the proceeds of Dacoity, having made a dignified re-ascent of his step-ladder and passed through his front door, was stretched out on his mat. But the man shook his head. Raising both arms he laid his eye along the sights of an invisible gun, pointed in my direction, pressed a phantom trigger, and produced with his tongue a sharp, conclusive click. Then placing a finger on each eyelid he drew them down over his eyes, sighed deeply, and gave a final puff, as if in dismissal of something, perhaps a soul. The passengers, who had all crowded over to our side of the bus, were much impressed with this piece of theatre, and shook their heads sympathetically.

The driver had now started the engine and was making gestures of impatience, but my friend persevered. From further sign language, some of which was international – such as the laying of both hands, palms together, under the cheek, to represent sleep – it was conveyed that as there were bandits ahead it would be better for me to stay in this village and to spend the night there, because if they found me on the bus, they would shoot me. This did not seem a very good idea, because I felt that if the bandits heard that I was in the village, as they probably would, they would most likely come for me, and I should be alone. Whereas if I went on with the bus and the worst came to the worst, I might be to some extent protected by the natural human sympathy, the bond of neighbourliness, however slight, that begins after a while to exist between fellow-passengers who are thrown together on such journeys. I therefore succeeded in making it clear that I wanted to go with the bus.

As soon as my determination to continue with them had sunk in, the driver, aided by several of the passengers, began a re-organization of the baggage at the back of the bus. This was piled up round a kind of priest's hole, in the opening of which I crouched in the manner of a hermit-crab, refusing to withdraw myself entirely from sight unless an emergency arose.

There followed two stifling but uneventful hours, by the end of which I was half anaesthetized by the fierce gases from the bales of dried fish. The bus then stopped again. We had come to a ferry and the driver beckoned to me to come out. It seemed that the danger point was past. But we were just on the point of embarking on the ferry barge when a young man came up. He was dressed in a new American GI uniform, and in spite of his air of easy authority, appeared to be weaponless. Going up to each of the passengers he made a collection. When my turn came, I smiled and shook my head. The young man repeated whatever it was that he had said, and I shook my head again. With an expression of slight embarrassment he then gave up and went off. '*Pirate*,' said my friend of the restaurant again, nodding his head after him.

Three days later I reached Saigon, just in time to claim my seat on the plane for Laos.

CHAPTER SEVENTEEN

Laos

LAOS FROM TEN THOUSAND FEET was a grey-green frothing seen through a heat-mist that was like a pane of dirty glass. As we came into Vientiane in the late afternoon the mist thickened and the pilot came down as if to look for landmarks. For the last half-hour bundles of rags kept whirling past the cabin. They were vultures – bad things to hit at two hundred miles an hour. We landed bumpily in a haze, as though bonfires had been lit round the field; and in this the sun wallowed – a diffused yellow disc. As the door of the cabin was opened, the heat rolled in.

In most journeyings there stands out the memory of days of discouragement, when the enthusiasm flags under the strain of petty physical discomforts. The introduction to Laos was spent in such a period. This was the earthly paradise that all the French had promised; the country that was one vast Tahiti, causing all the French who had been stationed there to affect ever after a vaguely dissolute manner. To be fair to Laos I was seeing it at the worst of all possible seasons – it was late March – when the air is burdened with the presage of storms and the landscape blighted with autumnal sadness. Heat lay like an interdict on the town of Vientiane, although the sun was wrapped until late morning in a sweltering mist. At certain hours, out of the stillness, a hot wind rose suddenly and skirmished in the streets, producing a brief, false animation, flapping huge leaves in the faces of passers-by, who were half disembodied by the swirling dust, above which they floated like genii. Sometimes the grey, swollen sky squeezed out a few drops of rain.

I was lodged in the government guest-house, a European villa – since it had two storeys – which at some time had gone native, with earthenware dragons crawling on its roof. Hornets had started cellular constructions in the window shutters and armies of cockroaches marched across the floors. Precious, expensive water was brought in large pots and left in the subdivision of the room where, using a gourd with a hole in its bottom, you could take a shower. The main advantage of having this open pot of water in the room was that it collected a gauzy layer of mosquitoes which were content to stay there in harmless concentration, unless disturbed. The Mékong could be seen from the window, a sallow strip of water across half a mile of whitened river-bed. Perhaps this drought had something to do with the town's electrical generating system, because only occasionally – and never at night – would the filament of the electric light bulb consent to glow feebly. Whenever the hot wind sprang up, stirring the trees round the house, great dry leaves as big as dishes came tumbling down and fell with a crash in the layer already deposited on the earth. It was the death-rattle of the year, which in Laos expires in croaking senility, to be reborn with the raging storms which were about to break.

Vientiane is a religious centre, one of the two ancient capitals of Laos. It abounds with pagodas, many of them deserted and in ruins, and colossal Buddhas, with dusty half-obliterated smiles, sit in the tumbled brickwork.

Since at this time, when the earth had dried up, there was no work to be done anywhere, it was the season of *bouns*, the Laotian festivals. Each pagoda holds one as a means of collecting funds. They last for three days, and although an attempt is made not to hold two *bouns* at the same time, there are so many pagodas that duplication cannot always be helped; so that every night for several weeks the sky over one or more districts of Vientiane glows with the reflection of thousands of lights, while from a distance one catches the gusty, carnival sounds of Laotian rejoicings. *Bouns* start at about eleven, and go on all night.

The first night after my arrival I went to a *boun*, which I found by following a crowd. It was about two miles from the town's centre and I passed several pagodas on the way, where carpenters were working by lamplight in preparation for a future festival.

An enclosure had been built round the pagoda in which every kind of light, from hurricane lamps to fluorescent tubes, had been concentrated in an anarchic glare. The pagoda had hired a generator for the occasion. There was no entrance fee, but young ladies with demurely lowered eyes waited just inside to accept donations, in return for which you received a candle, a posy of Japanese lilac, and two joss-sticks in a bamboo container. Among the many attractions was a free theatre show, lasting for many hours, indistinguishable, except to an expert, from the theatre of Siam. Actors remained on the stage for what seemed interminable periods, occasionally advancing or retreating a few steps. Meanwhile their babies played happily round their feet, and quite frequently a stage-hand would walk across and interrupt a scene for a few seconds to pump up the pressure in the hurricane lamps.

On a nearby platform the *lap ton* was being danced. Once again it was the major attraction, but as it was still incorrect for Laotian girls to dance in public, religious enterprise had arranged for hostesses to be brought over from Siam, just across the river. The pagoda hired the girls for three nights and lodged them in a nearby building. It cost a piastre to cavort round the stage for about fifteen minutes with one of them. They were dressed in hideous knee-length frocks, and some seemed to have permanent waves. The backward Laotian girls in their dowdy finery, their silk scarves, their skirts woven at the hem and waist-band with silver and gold thread, and their abundant jewel-decked chignons, could only look on wistfully. As I arrived the organizers were having trouble with the microphone – indispensable adjunct to any social occasion in the new Far East. A young man chanted a soft, nasal melody which could only be heard within the *boun* enclosure itself. But suddenly the electricians were successful with their tinkerings and all Vientiane was flooded with a great, ogrish baying. The electricians hugged each other, and, enchanted by the din, the audience began to drift away from the theatre and make for the dancing floor.

The second attraction in order of popularity was a love-court. A quadrangular arrangement of tables had been formed, covered by a thatched roof raised on posts decorated with woven bamboo representations of animals, weapons, and phallic emblems. Seated round the tables in the interior of the square were the girls, and their suitors sat facing them. Between the couples had been placed offerings of food, brought by the girls. Originally a tribute to some ancient, forgotten fertility god, a primeval Thai Venus, the offerings would be given, next day, to the bonzes. All through the night the bantering of witticisms, the singing and the exchange of improvised verse would go on, accompanied by the accordion-like wheezings of the kène, the Stone Age gourd pipes of Laos. Sometimes through a happy fault in the circuit the splutter and bellow of the loudspeakers would suddenly lapse, and you heard the beehive dronings of the communal love-making, the kènes, and the voice of the presiding bonze, preaching continually in an archaic, incomprehensible language from the wicker cage into which he had been fastened. The cage symbolized the protection of his religion from these earthly distractions. As soon as inspiration failed he would be relieved by the next on the rota of preachers, waiting now to take his place.

Love-courts are the accepted preliminary to the consummation of affairs of the heart, which – despite European conviction that romantic love is a Western invention – are accompanied in Laos by much versifying and mild self-imposed frustrations. When, for instance, a well-known beauty is wooed by a number of suitors, a serenading match may be arranged on the veranda of her house to permit her to test under competitive conditions the poetic and musical capabilities of each of them. Complete pre-marital freedom is recognized, but much outward reserve is maintained. There is a time and place for everything. It is incorrect, for example, to acknowledge in the street a lady with whom one happens to be on particularly good terms. These things in Laos are fraught with an etiquette which is the legacy of a highly organized society not too far gone in decay.

The charm of Vientiane lies in the life and the customs of the people. Unless one is an amateur of pagoda architecture there is little else to be seen. The Laotians have preferred to work in wood, rather than stone, and their art, confined chiefly to the decoration by religious artists of the doors, pillars, and interiors of pagodas, quickly perishes in such a climate.

Outside the town there is a great, grey, half-decayed *stupa*, built as a tomb for a hair of the Buddha. It is surrounded by a cloister, containing perhaps a thousand Buddha images, a collection of which the people of Vientiane are very proud. But even here, where the religion is practised in its purest form, there is a little degeneration, a little backsliding from the lofty philosophic conception; and the taint of magic practices shows itself. Selecting one of the numerous images as a personal tutelary divinity, the devotee subjects it to a kind of bribery similar to that sometimes practised in southern Europe with images of the saints. In this case the image's chief function is healing, and when the sufferer recovers from any complaint he hastens to the pagoda to apply gold-leaf to the part of the Buddha corresponding to that where he has felt the pain in his own body. I was interested to deduce from this practice that the people of Vientiane are much plagued by headaches – perhaps those which accompany malaria.

Standing in a corner of the sanctuary was an ancient ithyphallic statue, an old Hindu divinity, no doubt, which had been worn smooth in the appropriate parts by the feminine adoration of a thousand years. I was told that the women of the French colony who wish for a child frequently emulate their husbands' pose of Laos-ization by coming here secretly to pay their respects. I wondered whether this clandestine tribute might not be extended eventually to the Buddhas to solicit their curative powers; and if so what we should learn from it about the prevalence of disease among Europeans.

The museum of Vientiane, which I visited in the hope of learning something of the living art of the country, has also little more to show than a collection of Buddhas. There is a tranquillity, a lack of compulsion in the Hinayanist Buddhism of Cambodia and Laos – so different from the neurotic deformation practised by the later Khmer kings – which is not propitious to the development of religious art. There was no violence or drama in the life of Buddha comparable to that of Christ, and the Indian epics have been eschewed in Laos as improperly secular. It has been enough to carve Buddhas, and more Buddhas *ad infinitum*, seeking perhaps to multiply in this way the magic virtues which each image contains. The curator takes you round, explaining the characteristic postures – there are seven or eight – all of which can be appreciated in five minutes. After that there are minute differences of physique and physiognomy to be noted that reflect the influences of India, of Java, of Thibet, or of Ceylon. That is all.

By the time the museums turn to the art of the people, the grotesque animals in bamboo, the carved movable figures which are obscene to European eyes – all of which become a pagan burnt offering at the end of each *boun* – it will be too late. The microphone is an infallible sign of what is to come. Nothing of this kind will survive the era of materialism, under whatever form it arrives.

These are the sights of Vientiane, but in addition there is a spectacle which is popular with Europeans, who, remote, isolated, and living under difficulties, tend to shut themselves up within the protective social rituals of people in exile.

This spectacle is the slaughterhouse at work. I do not know whether or not it is illegal in Laotian law to kill animals, but certainly it is thought shameful, and the killing for Europeans is done at the dead of night on the outskirts of the town. The slaughterers are obliged to work by flares, which is responsible, the French think, for an unusually picturesque effect. It is 'not done' to go along while the actual killing is in progress, but shortly after, when the carcasses are suspended from hooks to be cut up, and the workers, stripped to their loincloths, and garishly splashed, paddle about in a vermilion sea. Cars are stationed just beyond the reach of the steaming odours, and one is recommended to see the thing as one views a nude in a picture gallery – that is, divorced from all but a disinterested abstraction, in this case the colour.

*

The possibilities of Vientiane, it was clear, would be quickly exhausted. Thao Nhouy, the Laotian Minister of Education, lent me his jeep to see some of the surrounding villages, but the roads were so appalling that it broke down after being driven for about five miles. He then suggested that I might like to see the local schoolgirls dancing, and when I said that I would be delighted, and asked for permission to take photographs, the girls were sent off home, on their bicycles, to get their best clothes. An hour or two later they began to trickle back, wearing their mothers' jewellery as well as their own and with their silk finery done up in paper parcels. When they had dressed and were ready they made a glittering sight. One girl wore a scarf ornamented with real gold thread said to be worth about £50 in English money. They danced under the supervision of a teacher whom I recognized as a professional actor, from the *boun*, and who occasionally intervened when a girl failed in some minor feat, such as bending her fingers back at an expressive ninety degrees from the palm.

All these girls, dressed as they were like princesses, came from shacks in the forest. Each one had a bicycle – infallibly fitted with dynamo lighting, and sometimes three-speed gears. It seems that a bicycle for his daughter is one of the essentials for which a Laotian will work. It is considered ill-bred and irreligious in Laos to work more than is necessary. The father of a family cultivates an amount of land, estimated, by a bonze who is expert in such matters, to be sufficient for his requirements. If there are six members of the family, six standard, equal sized portions of land will be cultivated. If a child is born into the family another piece of land is cleared and worked. When a member of the family dies, whether it be a baby or the grandfather, cultivation of his portion will be stopped. Just enough is produced for the family to eat and to provide a small surplus sold in the market – *with the bonze's approval* – to buy occasional strict necessities, like a silk shawl and a bicycle for the daughter. There is no social insurance and there are no poor. The old and the sick are supported by the young, or, where they are left without able-bodied providers, by the community, and the bonzes give instructions for the necessary land to be placed under cultivation for them. The accumulation of wealth which is not to be used for definite, approved purposes causes a man to lose prestige among his neighbours, just, as in the West, the process is reversed. The main difference, it seems, between Buddhism in Indo-China, and Christianity – apart from any question as to their relative merits – is that, whether we admire it or not, the former is largely put into practice.

It is a stimulating reflection that the Western millionaire, obsessed for the sake of social distinction with the amassing of enormous possessions – little of which he can personally consume – would attain the same ends of personal celebrity under a Laotian Buddhistic order of things by his priestly austerities – by embracing the most abject and prestige-conferring form of poverty.

For this reason perhaps the local Evangelist missionary and his wife have made no converts. Like all who have lived among the Laotians they are charmed with them – although, of course, disappointed at their blindness. They also deplore their immorality.

In the matter of converts the Evangelists have been no more unsuccessful than their Portuguese, Spanish, and French forerunners. The Laotians having little capacity for abstractions, either in their language or religion, cannot follow the subtlety of Western religious concepts. They have a passion for taking things *au pied de la lettre*. Being told that the basic commandment of Christianity as well as Buddhism is 'thou shalt not kill', they cannot swallow such reservations as capital punishment and 'the just war', while casuistry repels them. Moreover, a bonze, the spiritual leader of the country people among whom he lives and works, occupies, by virtue of his rigorous fulfilment of the principles of his religion, a position in their esteem accorded in the West, say, to a boxing champion. The Laotians have come to associate the prestige of sanctity with certain abstinences and uncomfortable practices. The bonze gives an example of utter renunciation which is awe-inspiring by comparison with the minor self-abnegations of the villagers. The Laotians, therefore, although tolerant in the extreme, are not impressed by the worth of a would-be spiritual leader who presents himself to them loaded with material possessions. And this negative attitude deepens into a certain aversion if, as usually happens, the holy men of the West spend most of their time hunting in a country where animals must be allowed to die of old age. I fear that where the austere Dominicans, and the Jesuits failed, there is little hope for the Evangelists.

However, the missionary was far from despondent. There were Meos in the mountains not far from Vientiane, and just as in the plateaux of Vietnam the Moïs had not rejected the Gospel, so here the primitive peoples of the mountains seemed promising material for evangelization. There would be no risk of jeopardizing conversion by hunting among such hearty amateurs of open-air sports as the Meos, and if the missionary had more of this world's goods than they – well, that was a sure sign that his *ai* (or spirit) was stronger, and it would be a good thing to imitate him. Before the Meos could trouble themselves with renunciatory religions they would have to create a comfortable and abundant civilization for themselves. There was no chance of becoming sated with prosperity at the top of their mountains.

The missionary had made one trip to the Meos and was well pleased with his reception. The Meos, he said, were delightful children. Since tribes at this cultural level are hospitable to the last degree and much given to humouring strangers' whims, the whole village seemed to have foregathered and listened most attentively while he preached. It seemed to me that if the missionary had preached in Meo it was rather an achievement and I asked him whether, in fact, he had done this, or had contented himself with Laotian, which most Meos understand. 'I did neither,' he said. 'I preached in English, and from the way my words were received I feel that we may have started something up there.'

It may be doubted that in thus boldly treating the language barrier as non-existent the Evangelist had succeeded in communicating anything of the Christian point of view to his Meo audience. But this performance was, in fact, no more than the *reductio ad absurdum* of a situation which had arisen even with the first Jesuit missionaries. The separating gulf of language, of thought and of tradition, was too wide and deep. Father Buzome, for example, the first missionary to be sent to Indo-China by the Society of Jesus at Macao, was, if possible, even less effective. The Father preached with the aid of phrases prepared in advance for him by ships' interpreters, and as a result carried out a number of baptisms. It was only by the accident of watching a farcical theatrical performance in which he saw himself represented, that he found out to his sorrow that his converts had no idea, even, of what the term Christian meant. One of the players was dressed to represent the Father, but was provided with a great artificial stomach. He had a boy as his assistant. The turn consisted in asking the boy 'whether he would go into the Belly of the Portuguese'. The boy then replied that he would, and the player stuffed him into the artificial stomach, repeating this ridiculous procedure many times to the great diversion of the onlookers.

To his horror Father Buzome realized that the invitation to enter the belly of the Portuguese was precisely the phrase he had been accustomed to use when asking potential converts if they were willing to accept Christianity. Thus, by his linguistic industry, the Father had done no more than bring his religion into secret ridicule; while the Meos, at least, are not likely to have felt anything other than slight bewilderment at the Evangelist's quite unintelligible discourse.

Laos, they said at Saigon, was happily free from those disorders that made travel so chancy in the rest of Indo-China. The only difficulty was getting to Laos. Once you got there all was well, and there was nothing to stop you going about the country as much as you liked.

This account proved to be cruelly fictitious. You left Vientiane in the same way you came – by plane. Either that, or you waited an indefinite time for the military convoy which provisioned Xien Khouang in the north and the posts between – islands in perilous seas. The only way to get to Luang Prabang, the second of the ancient capitals of the country, which was about three hundred miles away up the Mékong – or about two hundred and fifty miles across country – was by one of the occasional motor pirogues. It now remained to find out what were the possibilities of making the trip in this way.

Providing myself with a Chinese interpreter – the pirogues being, of course, Chinese owned – I went down to the river. By walking a mile or two along the thirty-foot-deep bank you came to a place where the main stream floundered over from the Siamese side, so that a few barely connected stagnant puddles lay directly beneath. In one of these the pirogue lay, cracking in the sun and seemingly abandoned. It was an ugly, shapeless craft, a small junk, with its deck-space entirely covered over with a kind of hutment, so that travellers were confined to a stinking semi-darkness for the duration of their journey. It was arranged so that air and light could be kept out by the lowering of rush-matting screens over the few apertures in the sides.

A few corpse-like figures lay strewn about the foreshore and the interpreter, raising the rags that covered one face, awoke its owner. An absurd conversation now took place, complicated by the interpreter's refusal to use any medium but pidgin-French.

NL: Is that the owner of the boat?

INTERPRETER: Yes.

NL: Tell him I want to go to Luang Prabang.

INTERPRETER (*to* BOATMAN): Him content go Luang Prabang.

BOATMAN (*in French*): Yes.

INTERPRETER: Him say yes.

NL: Ask him when he expects to start.

INTERPRETER: Yes, possible you go. Him say.

NL: I know, but when?

INTERPRETER: When? Ha! Today, tomorrow. Maybe you content to go. All right.

NL: Do you mind asking him?

INTERPRETER: (*determined not to lose face by speaking a word of Chinese, puts this into a long incomprehensible rigmarole of pidgin.* BOATMAN *replies similarly.*)

INTERPRETER: Him say engine no good. Sick. Soon he cure.

NL: When?

INTERPRETER: Today, tomorrow, maybe. You content go – you go.

NL (*converted to pidgin*): How long trip take?

BOATMAN (*in French*): Ten nights.

INTERPRETER: Fifteen nights.

NL: Why you say fifteen? Him no know?

INTERPRETER: Ten nights runnings maybe. Stoppings too.

(*Another Chinese arrives and does his best to spread confusion. He describes himself as a Hong Kong Englishman.*)

HE (*in English*): This boat good. First top-rate class. You come back tomorrow, after yesterday gone. How?

NL: Why come back tomorrow?

INTERPRETER (*suddenly falling into line with* HE, *and pointing to* BOATMAN): Him no say go. Him brother say.

NL: Him brother where?

INTERPRETER and HE: Him brother gone.

NL: When him come?

BOATMAN: Today, tomorrow, approximately.

INTERPRETER: Approximately.

CHAPTER EIGHTEEN

The Road to Xien Khouang

THE STRUGGLE with the pirogue men, which I expected would become a daily routine, was suddenly broken off by news of a convoy going to Xien Khouang. And better still there was a spare seat in a car which would leave the convoy after the danger point was passed and carry on to Luang Prabang. This was a jeep belonging to a French official called Dupont, a flamboyant, red-bearded figure I had often seen hurtling through the streets of Vientiane. Dupont had been on a mission in Vientiane and was now returning to his home in Luang Prabang.

He arrived at the villa at about 3 a.m. next morning – a tornado approach, through the foot-deep carpet of dead leaves. Shrouded in protective clothing as the driver of an early Panhard-Levasseur he could be seen through the bare frangipani branches, tooting his horn continually, and waving his arms with excited exasperation at the thought of things he had forgotten. There was a platform built between the driver's and passenger's seats on which a dog which looked like a Samoyed perched uneasily. Dupont said it was a race bred only by the Meos. In the back of the jeep a Laotian driver sat buried in luggage. He was asleep, and as we took the corners his head rolled from side to side like a freshly cut-down suicide.

So far I had met French intellectuals, soldiers, politicians, but Dupont was the man of action, although action that seemed often without motivation or relevance. He was a corsair out of his day, an adventurer who was swaggeringly going native and whose ardours Laos would tame and temper. Dupont had married a Laotian wife in Luang Prabang and said that he would never return to France. His children would probably be brought up as Buddhists, and by that time, no doubt, Dupont himself would be paying some sort of lax observance to the rites. In the meanwhile he had reached the point of respecting in a light-hearted way all the superstitions of East and West combined; sometimes perplexed when they were in conflict, as happens, for example, with Friday the 13th, since in Indo-China all odd days are fairly lucky, and the Friday is the luckiest day of the week. He carried a Laotian sorcerer's stick, engraved with signs and symbols enabling him to cast a rapid horoscope, but was only affected by verdicts in support of decisions he had already taken. Dupont was in a great hurry to get back to Luang Prabang, because his wife was pregnant and he was afraid that she would hurt herself on her bicycle, although he had dismantled it and had hidden some essential parts. We were supposed to stay in the convoy until the Xien Khouang embranchment was reached, about a hundred miles from Luang Prabang, but Dupont said that if I had no objection we would clear off on our own at the first possible opportunity. He then made some fatalistic remarks about death and predestination.

At the convoy assembly point, we found a great show of discipline. Tight-lipped officers were walking up and down examining tyres and checking guns and ammunition. Drivers were assembled and lectured on convoy discipline. A soldier's Laotian wife, being observed to be pregnant, was refused permission to travel. The infantry escort was carried in five or six lorries and as many others were loaded with supplies. A dozen jeeps were placed in the middle of the convoy, which was guarded at each end by an armoured car. Dupont was turned back when he tried to bluff his way to the head of the column behind the leading armoured car, from which position he had hoped to be able to sneak away at an early opportunity.

Although by the time we got underway it was shortly before dawn, all Vientiane was still awake. Grinding our way through the streets we passed a *boun* in full swing with its temple-dancers still traipsing round their stage, and the magnified sobbings of a crooner not quite drowned in the roar of thirty exhausts. The streets were full of torch-carrying crowds.

No sooner had we left the town than the dust, released from its covering of fallen leaves, rose up in an all-obliterating fog. It was useless to rebel, to attempt evasion, to muffle up the face and cover the mouth with a handkerchief. In the end you gave in. Dust erupted in seemingly solid cones from the wheels of the preceding cars. In an hour we were turned into reluctant millers. Dawn revealed Dupont falsely tranquil beneath a yellow mask. Our Laotian driver slept peacefully and drifts had filled in the hollows of his upturned face. The Meo dog cleared its fur occasionally with a violent muscular spasm, and, sneezing continually, spattered us with its saliva. Dupont comforted it in Laotian, which he said the dog understood, as well as some Chinese.

Beyond the veil which the convoy spread about itself, the forest took shape dimly, or rather, disclosed its leafy anarchy. Stems, trunks and flowers – if there were any – were all contained in a grey carapace of leaves. Once or twice, a silver pheasant, its plumage dulled in the haze, passed over our heads and splashed into the foliage again. Only when we stopped and the ochreous fog slowly settled could the colour seep back again into the landscape. Somewhere beyond the barricade of trees, the sun had risen and was greeted by the mournful howling of monkeys. Small, dull birds had awakened in every bush and produced a single melancholy note. The soldiers, forming dejected groups, scooped the dust from their ears, rinsed out their mouths with vacuum-flask coffee, and were professionally pessimistic about the outcome of the journey. Dupont came to an understanding with the drivers immediately ahead, and in this way improved his position in the convoy by two places. He had just found a stream in which he was about to throw his dog – the animal was terrified of water – when the officer in charge blew his whistle for the convoy to get underway.

Until midday we slithered and bumped along the track, walled in by the monotonous forest. Then at last the forest diminished and shrivelled into bush, then scrub, and finally a savannah of coarse grass. Here crouching among cyclopean boulders were the few huts of plaited bamboo which made up the first village. Into this we thumped, bursting out of our envelope of dust and swerving to avoid naked babies and senile dogs. A canopy of vultures driven into the air by thundering wheels hung in suspension above us.

This was the lunch halt. We had been eating dust for eight hours and had averaged seven miles an hour. It was from this point onwards that trouble might be expected. But I told Dupont that there would be no trouble. However many times the convoy might have been attacked previously it would not be attacked when I was travelling with it. For once I found someone in hearty agreement with me. Dupont said that the convoy system was a ridiculous waste of time. You could travel up and down this road with not much more hope of running into bandits than on Route Nationale Number Seven. Anyway, if you were craven about such things, what was wrong with travelling at night only, when bandits – especially Laotian ones – were in bed? He said that we would really have to think seriously about how we were going to get away from the convoy, because the risks we were incurring in swallowing germ-infested dust were several thousand times greater than stopping the odd bullet if we were off by ourselves.

Dupont, who refused to eat army rations while there were cooked meals to be had in the neighbourhood, led the way to the sombre Chinese hovel masquerading as a restaurant. He ordered three portions of Soupe Chinoise, one for his dog, which to his dismay was missing when the food arrived. The Chinese apologized for the poor quality of his soup, being deprived by his isolation, he said, of every accepted ingredient. He promised to send out for some tree-frogs to enrich the flavour if we could give him half an hour. Owing to the time limit set by the convoy-commander, we had to reject this offer, declining also to select for grilling one of a group of live lung-fish hastily lined up for approval.

The proprietor had not been over modest. The soup was utterly negative in flavour. We were sipping our coffee, which tasted of earth and bitter herbs, when a commotion aroused us. Hurrying from the restaurant we saw Dupont's dog busy with carrion in a nearby field, surrounded by an excited huddle of vultures for whose benefit it had been exposed there. Dupont's cries of horror were interrupted by the whistle of the convoy-commander, who this time signalled for all officers to gather round him. He told them that seventy Issaraks were reported to be in ambush, awaiting us at Kilometre 115 – about twenty miles further on. They were turned out in new American uniforms, he said, and were well armed. At Kilometre 115 a cross-country track leading from Siam into Vietnam crossed our route. It occurred to both Dupont and myself that if this report was several hours old, it was not likely that the Issarak would be in the place where they were first seen. However, the official view taken was that they would not have moved more than five kilometres down the road in our direction, because orders were given for the infantry escort to dismount from their lorries at Kilometre 110 and to precede the convoy on foot for the next five kilometres. We noticed, too, that the officer assumed that the Issarak, if they had moved at all, would have inevitably marched towards us, and not in the other direction, because, once Kilometre 115 had been reached, the danger would be officially declared at an end, and the infantry ordered back into their lorries.

We now entered a country of low, bare hills; a whitish landscape, rarely animated by wandering pink-skinned buffaloes. In the hollows there were islands of splendid vegetation – flamboyant trees, arranged as if by design, with giant ferns and feathery bamboos. Peacocks gleamed in abandoned paddy-fields, and storks, flapping away at our approach, trailed their legs in pools of yellow marsh-water. The vegetation was sensitive to quite small variations in altitude. The valley-bottoms were choked with bamboo thickets, and slender, segmented canes, wreathed in blue convolvulus, curved over our path like coachmen's whips, flicking us as we passed beneath. At this level the ditches were full of dead butterflies which seemed to have completed their lives' span while in the act of drinking. But a climb of only a few hundred feet was enough to break right out of this hot-house profusion, to pass through the curtains of liana and to reach the first pines.

Approaching the portentous kilometre, the road became steadily worse. It was only just wide enough for the six-wheelers to pass and there were frequent tyre-bursts. Whenever a vehicle was put out of action, it was manhandled off the road and left to its own devices. There was continual trouble with the bridges, which were temporary affairs, put up at the end of the rainy season and only intended to last until the weather broke again. The most rickety-looking of the bridges had to be tested first with a jeep, followed by an unladen lorry. When this precaution was neglected, a lorry loaded with supplies crashed through and fell into the river below. This meant a painful detour through the water for the rest of the convoy. Several vehicles also got stuck and had to be hauled out. Any of these moments would have provided an ideal opportunity for an attack.

The Meo dog suffered from the heat just as badly as, according to report, its original owner would have done. Its tongue lolled from its mouth and, laying its head either on Dupont's lap or on mine, it dribbled on our bare knees. It could not stand the dust, and wetted us further with its continual sneezings.

Some of the drivers were showing signs of tiredness, and probably nervous strain. The standard of driving was going down. We were once again in the bamboo thickets, and the road was no better than a ledge round the flank of a low hill. On our right was a precipice, but the vegetation was so thick that you could get no idea of the drop. Dupont, having profited by casualties in front, had now worked his way up to a position immediately behind the last of the lorries, and we were nosing our way round the hill, keeping a look-out for occasional gaps in the road left by subsidences, when the lorry ahead suddenly turned off the road and went over the side. Gently, almost, it was lowered from sight amongst the bamboos. Up till the last fraction of a second before a thousand graceful stems screened it from our view it was still upright and quite level. The soldiers in it had hardly risen from their seats and raised their arms not so much in alarm, it seemed, as to wave farewell.

Soon after, the infantry climbed down from the lorries and began their march in single file along the sides of the road in front. This manœuvre seemed to me not only useless but dangerous, since nothing could have been easier for ambushers than to let the soldiers go by then destroy the defenceless vehicles. In the spirit of one who whistles in the dark to keep his courage up, the armoured car ahead occasionally opened up with its machine-guns and 2-cm. cannon, provoking, to the great discomfort of the following cars, one small forest fire. We never heard that the enemy was other than imaginary. At five in the afternoon we crawled into the village of Vang Vieng, having done about twenty miles since midday.

Vang Vieng was just such another village as the one where we had had our midday Chinese soup, but it was set in the most staggering surroundings. Overhanging it was a range of mountains which were not very high, since the peaks only reached eight thousand feet, but which did not look like any mountains I had ever seen before. There was no visual preparation by a gently rising foreground of foothills. These were stupendous walls of rock rising four thousand, five thousand, and six thousand feet sheer out of an absolutely flat plain. We were overhung, as it were, by a huge scrabbling in the sky, which at its base had been erased by mists. Dupont said that we would pass over these mountains that night.

It was at Vang Vieng that Dupont had planned to slip away. His resolution was only slightly shaken when it was announced that the whole convoy would stay in the village overnight, owing to the presence of a small force of Viet-Minh, which the infantry would have to clear out, in a village fifteen kilometres further along the road; but as all the men were thoroughly tired this operation would be postponed till early next morning. Dupont was determined not to stay in Vang Vieng, but even he seemed to think twice about deliberately disobeying the convoy-commander's orders, and when he finally did so it was done in gentle stages, rather than in one flagrant act of insubordination. The excuse given for this phobia about Vang Vieng was that all the sleeping space would be taken up and we should find nowhere to stretch out comfortably.

We were still filthy from our travels, sweat-soaked and covered in bright yellow dust, through which the perspiration trickled down regular courses. As part of his campaign Dupont suggested that we should have a meal first and after that get permission from the convoy-commander to go for a bathe in a river, twelve kilometres

down the road, where we should still be three kilometres short of
the village with the Viet-Minh. Dupont described this river as if it
had magical curative properties. It came out of a cave not far away,
he said, and the water was icy cold. This course being agreed upon,
we went to the usual Chinese eating-house run by one Sour Hak.
Taken by surprise by our invasion, Sour Hak found himself short of
food. However, as these villages are completely cut off during the six
months' rainy season, there are always standbys for an emergency.
Reaching to the top of the cupboard he found a hunk of venison
boucané, dusted it off, and set it before us. This meat, prepared in a
manner similar to that employed by the Argentine gauchos, was
black, fine grained in texture as cheese, odourless, and tasted slightly
of liquorice. According to the usages of life in the bush, strips were
cut off it with one's clasp knife. Fortunately, Sour Hak was found,
quite mysteriously, to have a stock of first-rate burgundy, doubtlessly
bought in the belief that it was Algerian. Dupont's sudden optimism
was only lowered by Sour Hak's refusal at any price to sell a green
parakeet, which had flown in one day and attached itself to the
house. Since tasting civilization nothing could persuade this bird to
use its wings again, although like a true Laotian it enjoyed being
taken for a ride on a bicycle. Dupont's process of going native
involved a craze for collecting animals. By the time the parakeet had
bitten him several times, he was ready to offer anything for it –
including a worn out Citroën car he kept at Luang Prabang – but it
was all of no avail.

When we left Sour Hak's place there was no one in sight in the
street. Dupont said that the officers would be eating, so why worry
them? We would motor off quietly down the road, have our bathe,
and then see how we felt. So, driving quite slowly and pretending to
take an interest in the sights, we edged our way out of the village;
past the sentries, the last house, the last Laotian girl squatting on her
veranda looking into space; out into the splendid and menacing
amphitheatre of the landscape; very much alone, but invulnerable
with the good red burgundy awash in our stomachs.

The river was there, as Dupont promised, and we swam about in
it for half an hour, while the Laotian driver sat on the log bridge

holding his Sten between his knees. People always alarm you with stories of the perils, the leeches, and the parasites to be picked up from bathing in these countries, but as far as could be seen, the River Song – tributary of the Mékong – looked like any river in the South of England. The water poured with a swift, black, curling surface round the boulders and under the bridge. It was cold and there were long, flat, trailing weeds just below the surface. As we went into the water great mustard stains spread from us, were thinned and borne away. The Meo dog, yelping in protest, was thrown in over and over again.

Dupont now made mention of the next part of his programme. Since things had gone so well, why not stroll over to the village of Pha-Tang, half a mile off the road, down the river, and ask permission to sleep there? In this way we should at least get a comfortable night's sleep, and then, in the morning – if, of course, we felt like it – we could rejoin the convoy without more ado, and no one would be the worse.

Pha-Tang was a cluster of palms and thatched roofs under the high scrawled translucent mountain shapes. A flourish of cranes deserted the village paddy-fields at our approach. Dupont told the driver to wait behind as we went into the village. As a convert to the Laotian way of life he paid much attention to local etiquette; he said that we must on no account appear with arms. There were no signs of life in the village and Dupont found this disconcerting. We must keep a careful look-out, he said, for a white thread across the path, or a cross decorated with red flowers. Either would mean that the village was taboo to strangers; in the first case because of a violent death or the presence of epidemic disease and in the second because the feast of the tutelary spirit was being celebrated. It was for reasons of these periodical taboos that Laotian villages, although built as near as possible to roads, were not actually on them. The places where we had stopped that day were not true Laotian villages at all, but military posts, around which a few store-keepers, mostly Chinese, had grouped themselves.

Although Dupont could find no signs of a definite taboo, he was still very uneasy that no one had come out to greet us. The correct thing on entering a Laotian village with the intention of staying the night was to ask for the headman and obtain his permission to do so. Unless this were done it would be a grave discourtesy to enter any house. Dupont emphasized that while the Laotians were tolerant, civilized, and hospitable, there were certain indispensable forms, and as we mooched about the deserted village, he poured out information on the subject, even describing the position for correct sleeping, body stretched out at right angles to the wall containing the door, feet pointing to the door. When I suggested that we might find an empty hut and sleep in it, he was startled. Although the villagers might overlook minor breaches of custom, he said, this would be a grave one, involving them in an expensive purification ceremony before the hut could be occupied again.

I offered no more suggestions and in the end we found a rather scared-looking woman who said, when Dupont spoke to her in Laotian, that the headman was away, and was not expected back. It was quite clear now that we were not welcome, and Dupont said that perhaps it would be better, after all, not to sleep in the village. Thinking about this experience afterwards, I concluded that the villagers dared not welcome us in the usual way, being unable to guarantee our safety, with the Issarak bands and the Viet-Minh in the neighbourhood. I expected that Dupont would now resign himself and return to Vang Vieng, but he began to produce arguments for carrying on. The worst thing about the convoy, he said, was that it prevented our seeing so many things and doing so many things that we could otherwise do. Up in the mountains there were Meo villages, he said, and he badly wanted to get another Meo dog. They were rare and hard to come by, but he knew one of the Meo chiefs who would oblige him. Having found out that I was very ready to be interested in such things, Dupont produced this Meo village as a kind of gaudy enticement. The only thing that separated us from the leisurely enjoyment of such pleasures was a single village, not more than three kilometres away, which, once passed, was the last until we reached the military post of Muong Kassy, fifty kilometres away, over the mountains. Dupont's final suggestion was that we should stay where we were until about an hour after dark, then creep up to the outskirts of the village – Pha Home was its name – with lights off, switch on the lights to make sure there was no barrier, and rush through it.

At about eight thirty, then, by which time Dupont was convinced that the village of Pha Home, with its Viet-Minh visitors, would be peacefully sleeping, we started off. It was difficult to approach the village quietly, as the road was uphill all the way. Dupont stopped and tried to quieten the exhaust, by squeezing the ends of the pipe together. This certainly reduced the exhaust note to a strangled snuffling, but through it sounded too plainly the miscellaneous rattlings that nothing could stop, and as soon as the headlights were switched off there was no way of avoiding the pot-holes and the small, loose boulders, over which we crashed continually. It was lucky for us that the village lay back about a hundred yards from the road. In spite of the hour, it was full of light and animation. As we sneaked past we could see a bonfire with a group silhouetted round it. Our passing appeared to go quite unnoticed.

We reached Muong Kassy about two hours later and slept in a large barn-like Laotian building of thatch and bamboo, which served as the officers' mess. Insects had been at the bamboo and the slightest movement filled the air with a powder which had the effect of snuff. The building swayed slightly with each step, but no more when there were twenty occupants, as there were next day, than when there were only two.

Muong Kassy was the headquarters of a company of engineers whose job was the upkeep of the bridges. They were uncomfortably isolated here on top of a small hill rising only partially free of the forests, with magnificent views in all directions, which nobody noticed any longer. There was no doctor, so that casualties of any kind might have to wait several weeks for a convoy going in any direction. In the rainy season, when roads and bridges disappeared, the garrison was confined to barracks for five or six months. Outside the stockades the usual straggling collection of Laotian and Chinese huts had formed, with saloons selling 'shoum', a fire-water made from maize.

Everything was brought by convoy and was in short supply, except the shoum which was a local speciality. The store-keepers also had a stock of what was described in English on the label as 'fruit tonic'. The fruit tonic was made in Siam and was probably an industrial by-product; but the garrison had found out that shoum plus fruit tonic was more effective than either separately, and that, stunned by a good stiff early morning dose of this, the day's boredoms could be better supported. A shoum-and-fruit-tonic relaxed the nerves too. It was after we had been introduced to this Muong Kassy custom that Dupont changed his plans, and, quite forgetting about his pregnant wife, and the bicycle she might succeed in putting together, he said we would stay the day, and leave next morning.

Taking a guide from the camp, we went for a dip in the river. There was a recognized place about a mile up the river, which was free from weed and rock, and once again, because the water was deep and swiftly running, it was very cold and refreshing. We had been swimming round for an hour or so when we noticed a number of Laotian girls hanging about. They were not watching us, but sauntering backwards and forwards in twos and threes, chatting to each other. By the time there were twelve of them, Dupont, keeping well in the water, called to them and asked if we were disturbing them in any way. One of the girls came to the edge of the bank, bowed, and looking down at her feet said that it was their usual bathing time, but that there was no hurry, of course. Dupont asked the girls if they would retire for a moment, and they walked a short distance away and stood in a preoccupied circle while we got out of the water. We then dressed quickly and walked on down the path leading to their village. After about a hundred yards we looked back. All the girls, quite naked, were in the water. At that moment two bonzes were strolling slowly along the bank past them; but the girls paid no attention. The bonzes were wrapped in the mantle of holy invisibility.

When we reached the village, Dupont asked punctiliously for the headman, making the excuse that he wanted to visit the pagoda. It was quite evident that this headman was in the good graces of the garrison, and probably supplied them with labour. He was very dignified and had a fine house, with European furniture. Although barefooted, he wore a French suit. On the suggestions of the soldier from the camp he took down his trousers and showed us his legs, which from his ankles to thighs were tattooed, in the local manner, so closely that he seemed to be wearing stockings. The annual *boun* had just been celebrated at the local pagoda and a bonze was in the act of sweeping into a heap the votive offerings with which the floor of the courtyard was littered. There was a great collection of elephants, buffaloes, peacocks and tigers, all woven in basket-work, the kind of thing that Picasso produces when he is not painting, but perhaps rather better. They seemed to me to be of the greatest artistic interest. I asked the headman if it would be possible to take any, as the bonze was crumpling and smashing them vigorously with his broom. But the chief shook his head regretfully. Buddhism had degenerated in these remote provinces and was swamped with re-emergent spirit cults. These objects had been dedicated to the *phi* and would have to be burnt in a ritual fire. The *phi* would also receive the burnt essence, I noticed, of a large, very obscene, and no doubt magically valuable picture.

At about this time when the bonze was treading underfoot the village's artistic output of several months, a party of Issarak or Viet-Minh, timing their action to coincide with the convoy's arrival at Muong Kassy, had set fire to the forest just south of the post. A steady breeze was blowing from that quarter, and the fire, started over a width of about a mile and fanning out as it advanced, moved slowly towards the fort.

Coming up over the river-bank it took us some time to realize what was happening. There was a haze; but then there was always a haze in Laos, although by this time of day it should have been clearing and not thickening. And then we heard the crackling, punctuated with the sharp pops, which might have been distant rifle fire, but which were the explosions of thick stems of bamboo.

Looking up then we saw the curtain of smoke hanging over Muong Kassy, white at the top, and black at its base and streaked occasionally by lance-points of flame, which were still two miles away.

We ran to where the car was parked, started it and tried to drive down the road towards the fire. Dupont was as pleased with it as 14 July. In about fifty yards we got tangled up with the convoy and had to leave the car on the side of the road and run on. The fire was advancing on a ragged front and was as irresistible as a volcano. Black smoke was being blown before it so that at first the flames were out of sight; but when they came through they were two hundred feet high – twice the height of the tallest tree. It went forward in zigzagging rushes, eating its way quickly through the bamboo thickets, which went up like oil wells. A lane of fire had broken right out of the general advance and its spear-point was wandering up over the hillside, already level with the fort. Large clumps of green forest were being left behind or encircled and then consumed at leisure as the fire went through the bamboo. It caught at the lianas, too, and went up a tree from top to bottom in shrivelling streamers – just like Christmas decorations catching fire. The noise of the exploding bamboos was becoming deafening and the sky was covered in a cloud through which black ash streamed up like flotsam carried on flood-waters. I noticed, though, that only the tops of some of the trees had caught on the other side of the road.

Orders were given to prepare to evacuate the fort. There was a great deal of ammunition and thousands of gallons of petrol, stored in cans, and the soldiers were swarming like ants stacking it in the road and loading the lorries. Confusion developed and matured into chaos, largely caused by the arrival of half the convoy, which blocked the road and prevented the lorries being driven out of the fort. Before an evacuation could be made the convoy had to be moved on through the village, but half the drivers couldn't be found. They had wandered off to look at the fire and taken their starting keys with them.

In the meanwhile the Laotians and Chinese rushing out of their houses with their beds and bedding, and piling their stocks of groceries between the wheels of the cars, had made rapid movement impossible, even when the drivers could be rounded up. One family was actually at work taking their house down.

And then as an hour passed in struggling tumult with the convoy at last bludgeoned on through the village and safely parked on the other side, and hundreds of crates and cans loaded on to the lorries, the wind veered and the main front of the fire went by, about half a mile away. A few offshoots coming in our direction burned feebly for a while among the bamboos, and it was all over.

Next morning we left before dawn. But when daylight came there was no sunrise for us. For hours we went on climbing and dropping through the haze-dimmed mountain shapes. We were travelling at between three thousand and four thousand feet and there was no underbrush. Instead, a few trees straggled up the mountain sides, bearing sparse blossom like the flowering of an orchard in early spring. As the haze cleared a little we could see that the mountain tops bore caps of yellow grass. Dupont said that this was the work of the Meos and that it meant that we were getting into their country. Shortly we would go up to a village and try to buy a dog.

CHAPTER NINETEEN

Into the Meo Country

IN THE SENSE THAT least is known about them, the Meos are the most mysterious of the twelve principal races of Indo-China. This Mongolian people is to be found at altitudes higher than three thousand feet over the whole of Indo-China north of the twenty-first parallel of latitude. They are utterly incapable of bearing, even for the shortest time, other than cool and temperate climates. Being self-supporting, they rarely come down to visit the markets of the plains and valleys, and, when obliged to cultivate fields below the three thousand feet line, they always return to their villages to sleep.

The Meos' territorial aspirations are purely vertical. By their disastrous method of cultivation, which completely exhausts the soil in a few years, they have been forced steadily southwards from China. In migration, as in the year 1860, when they crossed the frontier of Indo-China, they will fight their way savagely and effectively across low-lying country, only to split up and disperse immediately the mountains are reached. An ethnographical map of northern Indo-China is pock-marked with groups of Meos. Since 1860 they have travelled about four hundred miles and are now filtering slowly southwards down the Annamite Chain, where from time to time a new group is reported on a mountain top. They are said to have been attacked in recent years by government forces in northern Siam, but it is unlikely that anything short of extermination can stop their slow, silent movement through the mountains. Europeans who have studied them superficially believe them to be of Esquimaux origin, a theory which is offered to explain their horror of warm climates. These authorities report that they possess legends of eternal snows and of Arctic days and nights. But the short description published in 1906 by Commandant Lunet de Lajonquière says nothing of this, and no other scientific account of the Meos has appeared.

Besides the Meos' predilection for mountain tops they have other claims to distinction. They are utterly independent and quite fearless. Their passion for freedom compels them to live in the smallest of villages and, apart from such rare events as the invasion of 1860, they will not tolerate chiefs or leaders. If forcibly brought to lower altitudes they are soon taken ill and die. They are normally pacific, but if compelled to fight are apt to eat the livers of slain enemies.

The Meos are the only people in Indo-China who are not in the slightest concerned with evil spirits, although they admit their existence. Their complete indifference to all the ghouls and devils that plague the races surrounding them has invested them with enormous prestige, which they are careful to cultivate. They like to encourage the belief, prevalent among the Thais, that they are werewolves and can turn into tigers at wish. They have no funerary cults but celebrate a funeral – or any other event providing the slightest excuse – with orgies of drinking. Husbands and wives keep their own property. Children are given the greatest degree of freedom, and sexual promiscuity before marriage – even with strangers – is general. 'Sacred groves' exist – there is a celebrated one at Dong-Van in Tonkin – to which Meo girls resort, and offer themselves freely to all comers. It is said that large-scale maps, upon which the locations of such groves have been scrupulously plotted, are the prized possessions of most French garrisons in Tonkin. Besides breeding fine white dogs, they are experts at taming monkeys and birds, particularly a kind of minah which they teach a wide repertoire of imitative sounds. The Meos will only part with their animals for an enormous price – payable in solid silver which they immediately convert into massive jewellery.

But the first village beyond the Muong Kassy, perched on a bare hilltop, and reached laboriously up a long winding path, proved not to belong to Meos but the 'black' Thais – so called from the distinctive dress of their women. It was like climbing up to an eagle's eyrie and finding crows in possession. A rare species of crow though. Checking up on the ethnographical map, you saw that these were the only black Thais in Laos, although you could follow their tracks in isolated, coloured blobs right down from the frontier of Yunnan where they had crossed over from China. The Thais are the aboriginal stock from which both the Laotian and Siamese nations developed, but the black Thais are the only tribe with a taste for the high mountains, with the hard life and the freedom.

Their village was a philosopher's retreat. Ten or fifteen huts clung to the flattened summit of the hill, silhouetted, whichever way you looked, against white mist. Ten paces away the slopes went plunging down and were dissolved in vapour. Across the sky was a wavy, unsupported line of peaks. A few ravens flapped about the thatches, and babies, peering at us through the stockades, howled with horror at what they saw.

The headman received us in his hut, which marked the village's centre. He was dressed in Chinese-looking clothes of some coarse black stuff, wore a black turban and was smoking a foot-long pipe with a bowl the size of a thimble. We had seen a number of fine white Meo dogs bouncing about in the village and Dupont, speaking Laotian, asked if he could buy one. The Chief sent out to see if anyone would sell a dog, and while we were waiting produced a large dish of roasted chicken, already dissected in the Chinese style. This provoked such a lengthy exchange of protestations that the chicken was cold before Dupont decided that we could politely eat it. He presented the Chief with some army rations in exchange, and this, too, set in motion a chain-sequence of reiterated offers and mock refusals. Dupont asked if there were any ceremonies taking place in the vicinity. The Chief replied that a marriage fair had been organized in the next Thai village, but that you had to cross a range of mountains to reach it.

This custom, widespread in mountain tribes which are split up into scattered, isolated hamlets, is practised by the Meos as well as the Thais. Once a year eligible bachelors and maidens gather at some convenient central point, and each one in turn, the boys alternating with the girls, describes in verse, to the accompaniment of kènes, their possessions, their accomplishments, or their virtues. Formal offers of marriage then follow, and according to eye-witnesses of the custom, the metrical form in no way inhibits the most banal cataloguing of articles to be included in the marriage contract.

We were still eating when the Chief's messenger came back with the only dog on offer. It was a poor forlorn animal, suffering probably from some wasting disease, and an enormous price was demanded.

As there was no dog to be had from these intermediaries, there was nothing for it but to go to the source itself, even if it meant another stiff climb on foot. Instead of turning left, therefore, at the junction of the main road to Luang Prabang, we took the right-hand fork towards Xien Khouang, which, although it led us out of our way, went right through the heart of Meo country in Laos. Shortly after, we came up with a Meo family, who were struggling up a hill loaded down like beasts of burden with their possessions. The Meos threw down their bundles and looked us over with puzzled amusement. One of them, who wore pigtails to show that he was the head of the family, came over, cut the choice centre out of a sugar cane he was carrying and presented it to us, roaring with laughter. This was typical Meo conduct. The Meo is grateful to strangers for amusing him with their clownish faces and ridiculous clothes, and his first impulse is to look round for something to give them. Shouting with joy, the children leaped into the car and were cuffed out again by their father. The woman who, if a Thai or a Laotian, would have stood apart with downcast eyes, bent down to examine Dupont's sandals. She wore several pounds in weight of solid silver jewellery round her neck and had had her head recently shaved.

Meo finery at its best is the most extravagantly colourful in Indo-China. The women are stiff with embroidery and heavy silver necklaces and chains, and are half extinguished by enormous turbans that look like Chinese lanterns. But this family was in its workaday clothes, as its head was very anxious to explain to Dupont. They had been away a week, working in their opium-poppy-fields, and now they were on their way home for a flying visit. Dupont asked about a dog, and the head of the family invited us to come up and see for ourselves, as he had no idea who was home and who wasn't.

It was a long, slow climb up to the village, although the Meos, as they skipped along by our side, seemed in no way to notice the slope, nor their huge burdens. The coarse grass – usual legacy of Meo occupation – was replaced here by a noxious thorny scrub. For miles, in all directions from the village, nothing would grow but this ultimate of austere vegetations. This village was at the last stage before it would have to be moved. The fields under cultivation were now so far away that the villagers lived dispersed in temporary shelters where they worked. Very soon they would be too far from the village to return at all and it would be moved, ten or fifteen miles, always south, leaving behind the prairie grass and scrub. It only wanted the Mans to arrive here from Tonkin – the Mans cultivate on Meo lines between one thousand and three thousand feet – to reproduce eventually in Laos the denuded wilderness of southern China.

The Meo village consisted of nothing but a few most decrepit hovels. They were the lowest and the most barbarous examples of human dwellings that it would be possible to find. Why should the Meos be the most elegantly dressed and the worst housed people in the country? They are superb at the few handicrafts they undertake, but they just can't be bothered about how they are sheltered or how they sleep. There is no compulsion; no household genie – like those of the Moïs – demanding high standards of order and cleanliness in the house; no canons of taste and refinement spreading slowly downwards from an idly exquisite aristocracy, since all Meos are kept hard at work; no spirit of bourgeois emulation, since this is total democracy, with no betters to imitate. The Meos have only themselves to please, and the result is anarchy.

In the hovel we were taken to, the contents of a thousand schoolboy's pockets lay strewn about; the lengths of string, the broken penknives, the buttons, the mirror glass, the tins, the bottles, and the burned-out lamp bulbs. Here was accumulated the jackdaw harvesting, the valuable glittering rubbish which was all a Meo wanted of civilization, and which he was free to take, while leaving the civilization itself severely alone. What foolish, generous people, these town-dwellers were!

Our host's wife, a child of fifteen, was lying with her baby on a heap of rags in the corner. The baby was sick, he said, but the only thing necessary was to keep it away from the light – and air – as much as possible. Most Meo babies die in their first two years, and one wonders what would have happened by now to the fertile land of Indo-China if they didn't.

There was a gun in the corner – a muzzle-loader of the kind it takes a Meo two years to make. They are copied from the guns first supplied by the Jesuits to the Chinese, but are turned out by an endlessly laborious process involving boring out a solid bar by twirling a white-hot iron in it. It was enormously long, like an old-fashioned Arab stove-pipe gun, and when Dupont took notice of it the Meo offered to show it to him in use. We went outside and he loaded it with powder and shot he made himself. This process took about five minutes. Before pressing the trigger he warned us to stand well away because of the muzzle blast. The target was a small banana-leaf, skewered against a bank at twenty paces. There was a tremendous bang when he fired, but the leaf remained intact. He blamed this on the maize-spirit which we had just drunk, and was quite delighted when Dupont, giving a demonstration with his American light carbine, also missed.

There were no dogs at all at this village. They were all down at the poppy-fields with their owners, the Meo said.

Luang Prabang lies at the end of a long, curling descent from the mountains and through smoking bamboo groves, on the banks of the Mékong. It is built into a tongue of land formed by the confluence with the river of a tributary; a small, somnolent and sanctified Manhattan Island. A main street has turnings down to the river on each side and a pagoda at every few yards, with a glittering roof and doors and pillars carved with a close pattern of gilded and painted designs. There is an infallible sense of colour, a blending of old gold and turquoise and of many greys; but the bonzes are continually at work, painting and carving and refurbishing, so that everything is just a little too new (an extraordinary complaint in Laos), too spruce, too odorous of freshly applied varnish. The roof finials glisten with new applied glass and china mosaic. The ancient blunted features of lions and dragons get regular scrubbings, have their teeth painted dead white and are refitted, as required, with new eyes of green glass. A year or two's neglect might greatly improve Luang Prabang.

For all the briskness with which its holy places are maintained, the silence in Luang Prabang is only disturbed by the distant, classroom sounds of bonzes chanting in Pali, and the slow, mild booming of gongs. It is the home-town of the siesta and the Ultima Thule of all French escapists in the Far East. Europeans who come here to live soon acquire a certain recognizable manner. They develop quiet voices, and gentle, rapt expressions. This is accompanied by the determined insouciance of the New Year's reveller. It is an attitude which is looked for and is put on like a false nose or a carnival hat. Laos-ized Frenchmen are like the results of successful lobotomy operations – untroubled and mildly libidinous. They salt their conversation with Laotian phrases, all of which express a harmoniously negative outlook. *Bo pen nhang*, which is continually to be heard, means no more than, 'It doesn't matter.' But said in Laotian it takes on the emphasis of a declaration of faith. Single men instantly take to themselves Laotian wives, completing their bride's happiness with the present of a superb bicycle, covered with mascots and pennants, and with chaplets of artificial flowers round the hub-caps, instead of the leather dust-removing strap one sees in Europe. Several painters have retired here to escape the world, and to produce an occasional tranquil canvas, but Luang Prabang has not yet found a Gauguin.

On the day after our arrival I was invited home by Dupont to meet his wife, whose bicycle was still in pieces when he got back. They lived in a charming Mediterranean sort of house that had nestled down well among the pagodas. It was full of animals, including a large, handsome, domesticated goat that delighted to lurk behind furniture and charge unsuspecting guests.

Madame Dupont was pretty and gay, tall for a Laotian and evidently as nearly European in type as Dupont had been able to find. They seemed very attached to each other. Dupont assured me that jealousy was quite unknown in Laos, and that his wife not only expected him to have adulterous adventures while away from home, but actually advised him in the precautions to take. He did not know whether she allowed herself similar liberties, but thought it likely that she did. At all events he didn't see how he could very well show himself less civilized about it than was she. I was sorry not to be able to understand anything his wife said, except the inevitable *bo pen nhang* which was repeated several times. In a polite effort to make me feel at home, Madame Dupont brought out the family snapshot album and we turned the pages together. There were one or two photographs, evidently taken by her husband, of not fully dressed ladies who were also not Madame. She drew my attention to these, giggling slightly.

After supper, an army officer came in with another Laotian lady. Speaking in an extraordinary whisper, he told me that she was a princess – a member of the royal family – and entitled to a parasol of five tiers. He admitted, quite frankly, that there was no shortage of princesses in Luang Prabang, and all genuine. They had been friends for fifteen years now, he whispered, although they had never troubled to marry ... why, he couldn't think. It was easy enough. Dupont agreed with him here, mentioning the case of a subordinate of his who had recently arrived. 'At six o'clock', Dupont said, 'he expressed the wish to get married. My wife went out to look for a suitable girl, and was back with one by six thirty. At seven the bonzes came and performed a marriage ceremony which took half an hour. At seven thirty we opened a bottle of champagne and drank to the health of the bride and bridegroom, and by eight they were already in bed.'

The evening was rounded off by a routine visit to the local opium den, which, probably by design, was as decrepit and sinister as a waxworks exhibit. We stayed only a few minutes in this green-lit, melodramatic establishment, but it was clear that the unprofitable puff at the pipe was not to be avoided. One had to make some show of going to the devil.

I was lodged in the minor palace of the *Conseiller de la République*, the senior French official in northern Laos, a Monsieur Leveau. The *Conseiller* was a man whose shyness and slight reserve of manner failed to mask a quite extraordinary hospitality. He never, for instance, issued a formal invitation to a meal, preferring with an air of casual assumption to say something like: 'Of course, you'll be dining at home tonight.' Monsieur Leveau was married to a Laotian wife, to whom I was not presented, and the huge official building always seemed strangely empty. We dined facing each other across a darkly gleaming wasteland of ambassadorial table. Sometimes a Laotian servant stole into the room carrying dishes; trailing behind him the distant sounds of a domestic interior. These were immediately sealed off by the closing of the door, leaving us to the vault-like silences of the huge room. As we sat there the light bulbs gave out in various parts of the room and were swiftly replaced. In Luang Prabang the electric current was switched on at the same time as the water was turned off – at seven thirty. But the result was no more than a feeble striving of the filament, and the lamp in my bedroom produced a light considerably less than that of one candle. Monsieur Leveau partly got over this difficulty by enormously over-running lamps intended for a much lower voltage, but they did not last long.

After dinner, when the *Conseiller* relaxed for an hour, he could sometimes be persuaded to talk about some of his problems. These were the chronic worries of the Issarak and the Viet-Minh. To the west of Luang Prabang the frontier with Burma started, and Burmese irregulars crossed it from time to time. Chinese opium smugglers conducted a regular trade with the Meos, and turned pirate when business was bad. But now that the communists had taken over in Yunnan there were some signs of this traffic slackening. And then the Meos themselves. They were passing like a blight through the mountains. Leveau's ambition was to change their agricultural habits. If they could be persuaded to come down to one thousand feet he could give them irrigated rice-fields to cultivate, and had offered to provide the buffaloes to do the work.

I brought up the question of the Khas. The Khas are the aboriginals of Laos and are, in fact, Moï tribes under another name. Several hundred years ago they were conquered and enslaved by the Laotian nation, and now Khas were to be seen hanging about the market places of Laotian towns and villages, utterly broken and degenerate, as helpless as the pathetic remnants of once powerful Indian tribes in North America. I asked if it was true that Laotians still possessed Kha slaves. Leveau smiled in his tolerant and sceptical Laotian way and said that it all depended what you meant by slavery. The slavery of the old West Indian plantation kind was unknown in the Far East. For superstitious if for no other reasons, the peoples of Indo-China always trod very gently when it came to oppression of others. The spirits of their ancestors had to be reckoned with, and they themselves if pushed too far might be forced to revenge themselves by the efficient occult methods strangers were always imagined to possess. He cited the well-known fact of a collective bad-conscience on the part of the Vietnamese, who conduct special sacrifices and offer symbolical rent to the spirits of the unknown aboriginal possessors of the land they now occupy. Leveau believed that slavery did occasionally exist, but that it took more the form of a racial aristocracy maintaining a subject people in a condition of moral inferiority. The fact that a labourer happened to receive no money for his services hardly entered into the question, since we were not dealing with a money society and no one in Laos worked for more than his keep.

Leveau mentioned, as I had already heard, that there is evidence that the Khas before they were over-run possessed great artistic ability. He showed me as a proof a large bronze drum he possessed. This was identical with one in possession of the Musée de L'Homme which is described as being used by the Karens of Burma in the ritual conjuration of rain. A similar one, illustrated in Maurice Collis's book *The First Holy One*, is represented as a Chinese War Drum of the Han Dynasty. The drum, which was cast by the *cire perdue* method, is decorated with an almost chaotic richness of design sometimes found in Chinese metal mirrors. It depicts in the greatest detail the activities of a primitive people, living by hunting, fishing and rice-growing. There are processions led by dancers with castanets and accompanied by musicians playing the kène. Their longhouses are depicted as crescent-shaped boats full of warriors in feathered head-dresses, carrying bows, javelins, and axes. Birds and animals are shown in profusion, and the species are recognizable. According to the information of Monsieur Victor Goloubew of the École Française d'Extrême-Orient, these drums were found in large quantities in a burial ground in Tonkin and date from the period of Chinese domination, about two thousand years ago. The same authority affirms that the art in question is related to that of the Dyaks, and of the Bataks of Sumatra, while the technique of the workmanship is Chinese. This suggests that these people together with the Moïs, the Khas, and the Karens may all once have been united in a homogeneous Bronze Age culture – strongly influenced by the Chinese – which was probably at a far higher level than their present ones.

It remains to be said that such drums as have come into the ownership of citizens of Luang Prabang, in sad and symbolical descent from their original high function, now serve as cocktail tables.

It was fitting that at Luang Prabang the impetus of travel should have spent itself. Not even convoys ever came as far as this. Groups of unfortunate men occasionally set off on foot and walked for as long as three weeks through jungle trails to relieve isolated posts. Other arrivals and departures were by a weekly DC3 plying between Luang Prabang and Vientiane. It was booked up well ahead.

Down at the river-side the story was much the same as at Vientiane. There were pirogues which supposedly made regular journeys, but no one was prepared to commit himself to positive information about them. One authority went so far as to say that it was out of the question to hope to travel north by pirogue because the river was too low at this time of the year. I had just thanked him when the engine of what looked like a totally abandoned hulk, lying in an oily pool not far away, suddenly burst into wheezy activity.

One of the crew of two said that they would be leaving in half an hour. Bound for where? – Vientiane? No ... Xieng Khong – for the unnavigable north, of course. All the space had been reserved for a body of ex-pirates who had changed sides and had now, it was said, demanded to be sent back to fight their former allies.

While I was slowly piecing together this jig-saw of information in pidgin-French, the brand-new patriots arrived for embarkation, a most apathetic looking body of men. In their ill-fitting uniforms they were standardized, deprived of individuality by a common factor of misery, an ingrained habit of expressionless stoicism. Silently they filed up the gang-plank and filled the dim interior of the pirogue. It was difficult to believe that the fire of conviction burned in any of these breasts, and I felt sorry for the French NCO who was being sent back in charge.

But Monsieur Leveau said that there would also be a pirogue going south one day, and to save me from being victimized by Chinese cat-and-mouse tactics he sent for the owner and asked him when the boat would leave. With gentle satisfaction the Chinese immediately replied that the engine had broken down. Monsieur Leveau had been as ready for this as I had been, and said that he would send a mechanic down to inspect the engine. To this the Chinese replied that the repair was already in hand, and would be done by tomorrow – approximately. (The latter word, with which the Chinese protect their flanks in argument, corresponds to an equivalent in their own language – *Ch'a pu to* – and is never out of their mouths.) And after that? the *Conseiller* asked. The Chinese thought and said that he would have to give the boat a trial. This would take another day – approximately. And then? Well, then he would have to see about getting some cargo, which, after all, depended upon other people, and not on him. Shaking his head sadly, Leveau sent him away. There was something indomitable about this clearcut determination to have no truck with Western ideas about time and organization. Leveau told him to report every day as to the progress that was being made. But each day, the news of a difficulty resolved was accompanied by another protective imponderable, and then the trump card was slyly produced: the reported lowness of the water through the rapids which might make it impossible to go as far as Vientiane. It was quite clear that nothing short of the direct action of a War Lord or a Commissar could have compelled this man to go against his national tradition and commit himself to a definite promise.

And now there were other difficulties including money ones. Through the artificial pegging of the piastre at about two and a half times its real value, Indo-China is very expensive. The further one goes from Saigon the more expensive it becomes, because all supplies have to be brought by lengthy and laborious methods of transport. At Luang Prabang the bad, weak beer which cost about two and fourpence a bottle in Saigon, had reached eight shillings after a fifteen-thousand-mile trip up the Mékong. All other prices were in proportion. I was therefore becoming uncomfortably short of money, and it was an alarming thought that I might be stranded several weeks before the force of circumstance compelled the Chinese pirogue owner to set out for Vientiane. Even when this date was fixed, and supposing that it were quite soon, there were the provisions for the voyage to be thought about. If everything went well it would take five days – or nights, as they say in Indo-China – downstream. But if a breakdown happened it might take two or three times as long. I was warned by Dupont that it would be impossible to buy anything in the Laotian villages; even to the number of eggs laid by the hens, everything was calculated so that no more than the bare essential was produced.

The other difficulty was that of a slow, progressive, and hardly perceptible decline in health; a wasting away of the energy, and a seeping paralysis of the will. Comparing each day's performance with the previous one I could not measure the increase in lethargy. But when I remembered how I had felt and what I had been able to do a month previously; how even at Angkor I had walked mile after mile through the ruins in the rabid sunshine – it was by this that I could gauge the decline. Quite suddenly my strength had gone. I could only walk slowly and welcomed with relief the hour of the siesta. The siesta was slowly eating into the day, and now tended to last all the afternoon. It was as essential as eating and I could never imagine that I should ever be able to discontinue the habit, even in England.

I first put it down to the special kind of heat, to which even the natives of these countries never accustom themselves. It has greatly affected their history. The mountain people, attracted by the easy, abundant life of the hot river valleys, came down, settled there, and with the formidable gift of leisure built, while their reserve of energy lasted, those brilliant, freakish civilizations that were never given the chance to grow up. Soon they relapsed into peaceful decadence, adopted religions which were suitable to their decline and which also fostered it, and became adepts of sleep. After the hour of the midday meal, Luang Prabang and all Laos is trance-bound. No living thing moves at this season until five in the evening.

But it was beginning to seem to me that, even allowing for the heat, something must be wrong. A hill rises sharply in the middle of the town, topped by a glittering pagoda. The climb up to this, long put off, was so thoroughly exhausting that it used up the day's supply of energy. The pagoda when I finally got there was very small and contained a collection of mouldering wooden Buddhas. The redecorating bonzes had not been able to bring themselves to climb up here, so that most of the paintwork and gilding had weathered away, to the carvings' great advantage. But there seemed to have been a recent clear-out, perhaps in preparation for a refurbishing to come. The images that were too far gone in decay had been stuffed into niches of the surrounding rocks, one of which bore a bright yellow poster which I supposed at first to have some religious significance, but which proved to be an advertisement for the Victory Brand Glorious Firecracker Company, and showed a Chinese nationalist soldier giving the V sign. The attraction of the pagoda lay in its doors, deeply carved with a graceful, swirling design of foliage, dancers, and elephants. In either direction one looked out upon a very Chinese scene of mountains and rivers barely sketched in mist. It was viewed through the bare scrawny branches of frangipani trees planted round the pagoda, and at a lower level the slopes were clouded with the flowering trees bearing the blossoms which are called locally golden flowers of Burma.

After the descent from the pagoda I actually felt the need of a pre-lunch nap, and slightly alarmed I asked a French acquaintance's advice. Characteristically, he recommended me to a Sino-Vietnamese doctor, celebrated, he said, for his almost magical cures. The readiness to put one's faith in exotic medicine is another phase of going native. I have seen it happen before in Central America where people of European origin are quite ready to have themselves treated by Indian *shimans*, excusing themselves with a 'you never know; there may be something in it, after all'. In this case I had formed the private theory that amoebic dysentery might be the trouble, which, while it exhausts the vitality, does not always produce the familiar symptoms. Should this have been the doctor's opinion I was rather hoping, for the experience of it, that he would treat me, following the well-known Cambodian method, by an extract of the bark of the *pon* tree, which is only completely effective when the patient is allowed to cut the bark himself, removing it from the tree at a little above the level of his navel.

The Sino-Vietnamese doctor practised in a well-built single-roomed shack, with a good-sized garden and a river-view. The garden trees were decorated with offerings to the water spirits which naturally predominate in such a riverine town as Luang Prabang. They were contained in miniature ships made from banana leaves, with very high prows and sterns – far higher than those of the local pirogues. Since Laotian spirits have a highly developed aesthetic sense, they had also been offered red flowers. Egg shells had been thrust into the holes and cavities of the trees, perhaps for the benefit of landlubber genii. Unless this was the work of the domestic, the doctor evidently believed in doing in Rome what the Romans did.

Dr Nam Tuan Thanh received me in his consulting-room, a curtained-off corner of his hut, which was adorned with flowers in brass vases, coloured photographs of members of his family, and several framed diplomas. The doctor was dressed with extreme professional conservatism in a gown of dark blue silk decorated with the Chinese character for longevity. A few distinguished white hairs trailed from the point of his chin and the corners of his upper lip.

The doctor's manner was sympathetic but gently authoritarian. Grasping both wrists he quickly palpated the nine pulses recognized in Chinese medicine on each, corresponding in each case to an organ or group of organs. This was followed by a brief examination of the fingernails, after which the doctor pronounced me to be a classic example of a chronic excess of *yang* over *yin* – the positive and negative bodily humours – somewhat complicated by a minor obstruction of the *k'i*, or vital fluid. The condition thus originated in the liver – the most prominent *yang* organ, which, however, sympathetically influenced the *yin* organs corresponding to it – the spleen and the pancreas. The obstruction of the *k'i*, said Doctor Tuan Thanh, with perhaps the merest hint of contempt, was of nervous or psychological origin, and would clear up of its own account. As for the lack of balance between *yang* and *yin*, it would need much treatment and he would content himself with providing me with a few pointers for future reference. I should limit myself, carefully avoiding the remedies classified as *pou*, *sheng*, *san*, *piao*, and *yao*, to the category of medicaments known as *chiang* which comprised the metallic salts and oils of oleaginous seeds. Moreover I should remember that I was dominated by the number nine and the Western direction. The spirit should be refreshed as often as possible by the contemplation of white flowers. And I could expect to feel much better in the autumn.

In the meanwhile, he said, it might help matters, if only as a temporary measure, for an acupuncture to be performed, which, however, would not be completely effective owing to the overcast sky. Instructing me to lie on my side on his couch, the doctor removed a short metal needle from a lacquered case, gazed at it affectionately, and telling me to cough, thrust it into the back of each thigh. After that I was give a dose of what tasted like Epsom salts, and the doctor, examining the eighteen pulses again, told me that I was feeling better; which, owing to the natural stimulus of the circumstance, I of course was.

In one respect, at least, I found that the doctor had fallen into line with Western usages. In Cambodia, at any rate, the fee for successful treatment – and no fee is charged unless the treatment is successful – is a length of calico, four betel leaves, an areca nut, four handfuls of cooked rice, and a wax candle stuck in a slice of bamboo trunk. The doctor had commuted such payment in kind to a simple sum in Indo-Chinese piastres.

Next day, Monsieur Leveau mentioned that he had news of a military plane which had been parachuting supplies to a post somewhere in the north and which might stop at Luang Prabang on its way back to Vientiane. At the military headquarters they told me that it was not certain whether the plane would be stopping or not, but that if it did, it should arrive at about three in the afternoon. They had not been able to establish any radio contact with it. It was not thought that any attempt would be made to land after that hour because of the deepening haze and the fact that Luang Prabang was in a basin in the mountains, which made the take-off a difficult one.

I was beginning to feel an unreasoning horror at the prospect of a long enforced idleness in Luang Prabang and this news filled me with high hopes. But at three o'clock there was no plane, and as nothing had been heard of it by four o'clock, all expectations were given up. The sun had now disappeared again, smothered in the thickening mist, and the town's edges had gone soft in the flat yellow light. One was imprisoned in air that felt like a tepid bath. Breathing was an effort.

At five o'clock a vibration crept over the sky, swelling presently into the waxing and waning of aero-engines. Within a few minutes the plane was overhead, and seemed, always invisible, to be making a slow, spiralling descent. Soon after, Dupont's red jeep came tearing up through the mist. He said that the plane was coming in to land but that if it took off again, it would do so immediately. I threw my things into the jeep and waved goodbye to Leveau, who said it was too late for the plane to leave that night, and that he would expect me to dinner. Dupont, an amateur of emergency, tore down to the

Saigon street scene

Saigon waterfront

The Cao-Daïst cathedral at Tay Ninh

Water-peddlers on the Chinese creek

Cochin-China: fishing in rice fields . . .

. . . and in mud

The wife of the M'nong chief ignores the camera

Only the baby dares to peep

A long-house at Buon Dieo

Buon Ročai, showing jars housing tutelary spirits

river-bank, hooting and gesticulating for the ferry boat. By the time we were on the river we could see the plane overhead, only a few hundred feet up, and when we reached the field, it had just landed, an ancient Junkers JU51, palsied with vibration as it lumbered up the runway, its three propellers slapping idly.

It was now a quarter to six and in just over an hour the sweltering mist would deepen into night. The *droppermen* wanted to stay, but the pilot was determined to go on to Vientiane, and with thunder rumbling like heavy traffic beyond the unseen rim of the mountains, we took off. The pilot had no idea of how things were in Vientiane, because the radio wasn't working, and there was no time to circle to make height. Instead we were going to fly straight down the gorges of the Mékong, and as long, he mentioned, as we could see the river without being forced down so low as to be caught in the down draughts, it should be all right. And so we went, charging into the heart of the mountains, which were usually veiled from us, but sometimes billowed out, grey and ugly, from the mist. There were crags and pinnacles that towered up and then suddenly sank down, leaning sickeningly away as the pilot turned steeply from them; and once we passed quite near to a shrine perched on a rock jutting out of empty space. At last a *dropperman*, looking at his watch, said that we were through the mountains. Almost immediately, it seemed, the light went out. We were shrouded in the murk of a London railway terminus approach.

We landed at Vientiane at the beginnings of a tremendous thunderstorm, the crashing overture to the rainy season. The lightning was a continuous coloured display, an idle manipulation of theatrical lighting effects, through which one saw as in a spotlight the prodigious concussion of the rain that in a few days would clear the Laotian skies again – and wash away its roads.

CHAPTER TWENTY

The Viet-Minh

I BELIEVE THAT many political conspirators derive satisfaction from self-dramatization and that this taste for situations based on fictional models often complicates their lives unnecessarily.

As soon as I had returned to Saigon from Laos I was invited to meet an agent who had just come from the headquarters of Nguyen-Binh, the General in command of the southern Viet-Minh armies. He was to be responsible for my safe conduct into Viet-Minh occupied territory. I was sure that the setting chosen for the meeting had been lifted from spy or detective fiction.

Visiting one of the Cholon dancing places in response to a note left at the hotel, I found there my dance-hostess friend. Excusing herself at the table where she had been sitting, she came over and gave me a piece of paper with an address on it. I was to go there at eleven next morning. There was no one I could ask for. She had just been given the address, and that was all she knew.

The address, I found, was that of a doctor's surgery in a crowded back street of Cholon. Soon after my arrival in Indo-China I should have been delighted by this jostling vociferous humanity; the children playing with bottle tops, the coolies limping under their loads, the rich men in sharkskin, the beggars, and the dogs; but now I was hardened and immunized. When I found that the place was a surgery, I wondered if I had been given the right address. There was a pagoda on one side and a café on the other, but no signs of any private houses. I went in and found myself in a waiting-room with oriental patients lining the walls. It was probably the first time a European had ever been in that room, and I felt awkward and conspicuous, but, as usual, no one looked up. After a few minutes a door at the end of the room opened, and a woman carrying a baby came out. A white-gowned doctor stood framed in the doorway behind her, beckoning to the next patient. He did not seem to see me. Another woman went in, and the door shut behind her.

There seemed to be nothing to do but sit down and wait. I sat down in a chair left vacant at the end of one line, after all the patients had just moved up one. The door opened again and the woman who had just gone in came out. Through the opening I saw an interior lined with gleaming gadgets. Now the doctor would come again and this time he would see me. I was already a quarter of an hour late for the appointment. When the rather stern-looking, elderly figure appeared again I made a slight gesture, but was ignored. The patient at the end got up and went in and we all moved up one. I was beginning to be convinced that I had come to the wrong address and could imagine a ridiculous situation arising when it came to my turn to enter the surgery. A few passers-by came in to chat with friends in the waiting-room, bringing with them the tremendous din of the street. After them squeezed a blind beggar with a splendid, old-fashioned Tonkinese hat, a yard across, and then came a seller of iced sugar-cane juice and a goldfish-hawker. A china cuckoo-clock 'marque jazz' shrilled the half-hour, and one or two of the patients, glancing up, began to unwrap their snacks. The surgery door opened again, and just at that moment the young man sitting next to me spoke. 'Are you the foreigner who wants to go for a walk in the country?' he said. I said yes, I was.

He introduced himself as Dinh – an assumed name, he assured me, with a wry smile. I was interested to notice, in support of a theory I was beginning to form, that for a Vietnamese he was very 'unmongolian' in appearance. He was thin-lipped and cadaverous and there was an unusual narrowness across the cheekbones. If not a Frenchman he could certainly have passed for a Slav. There had been many Caucasian characteristics about the other Vietnamese intellectuals and revolutionaries I had met, and I was wondering whether whatever physical mutation it was that produced this decrease in Mongolian peculiarities encouraged at the same time the emergence of certain well-known Western traits, such as restless aggressiveness, an impatience with mere contemplation, and a taste for action.

Dinh informed me that all the arrangements had been made for my journey and that I should be taken wherever I wanted to go in Viet-Minh territory. The only difficulty would be in crossing the lines. He could not say exactly when we should be ready to start.

A young girl who had been sitting opposite now got up and came across to join us. Dinh introduced her as Gnuyet, adding that the name meant 'moonlight'. She made a face at this disclosure and apologized for the name's being so old-fashioned. She was the most beautiful girl I had seen in the Far East, and was sixteen. Dinh said that she would be travelling with me. She had been wounded and had been given leave to come to Saigon to convalesce with her parents. Having always understood that there were no women fighting in the Viet-Minh army, I asked her how she came to be wounded. She said that she had been caught in a parachutist's raid while giving a propaganda and theatrical show in a village. She had been prevented by her costume from getting away and had been shot and left for dead and had actually heard the order given for her burial, but had managed to crawl away after nightfall. She was obviously very proud to have been wounded, and anxious to get back. Her contempt for the frivolities of Saigon was measureless.

'In the *maquis* we only eat twice a day,' she said, with austere satisfaction. 'A little fish with rice. Some of our brothers and sisters who have been used to over-indulgence find it difficult at first, but they soon get used to it. But then, the life is very healthy. We start the day at five with physical exercises. And, of course, running and hiking are very popular. It is all good for the health. People are full of joy. They are always smiling. In the liberated territory there is a great deal of music. Everyone is expected to play a musical instrument. But not decadent music, of course. Beethoven and Bach – yes. We like them very much.'

And so, breathlessly, it went on. It was a revivalism, but an Asiatic brand of revivalism. An ultra-puritanical movement is launched at the drop of a hat in these countries. The prohibition of smoking ('some of our brothers and sisters do it in secret on the junks'), of gambling, of drinking, of feminine make-up; the rough standardized clothing, the communal pastimes, the obligatory sports, the compul-

sory culture ('in our spare time we volunteer to educate the peasants')
... it is all repugnant to Western individualism and habits of
freedom. But state interference in almost every aspect of the citizen's
existence was the normal thing under the paternalistic system of
government of Vietnam before the European's arrival. A modern
communist state is libertarian by comparison with Vietnam under
Gia-long, the last of the great emperors.

Dinh's enthusiasm was more reasoned than that of the girl, and
when the girl had gone out he even allowed himself a slightly bitter
reflection. I asked in a roundabout way if Viet-Minh losses had been
very heavy, and he said that practically all those who were in the
movement from the beginning had been killed. 'All except the
intellectuals,' he then added. 'The intellectuals don't get themselves
killed.'

I asked him why the Viet-Minh permitted minor acts of terrorism
in Saigon, such as the nightly throwing of grenades into cafés and
into cinema entrances. He said that the reason for this was that the
owners had failed to pay their contributions towards Viet-Minh
funds, and were therefore made an example of. In a way, it was also
to show disapproval of such frivolities when there was a war on. He
said that jobs of this kind were done by selected 'executioners', and,
using the word, he grimaced with distaste.

These tentative arrangements fell through. It was unfortunate for
me that at this time the Viet-Minh started several small, simultaneous
offensives, the most serious of them being at Tra-Vinh, about thirty
miles south of Saigon. Nothing could be done while the battle was
going on.

After a few days I had another interview with Dinh; once again
in the doctor's waiting-room. As it seemed as though I might be
kept waiting for weeks to make the official visit to the General's
headquarters on the *Plaine des Joncs*, I asked whether something less
ambitious could be arranged. I mentioned a certain engineering firm
I had heard of, which, although working on the French account,
was actually allowed to pass unmolested in any way through Viet-

Minh territory. The engineers used to travel every day in a private car down a road where not even a French armoured vehicle would have dared to show itself, and Viet-Minh soldiers sometimes strolled up to watch them at their work. It was another of those privately organized live-and-let-live arrangements, like the one by which foodstuffs are imported by Chinese go-betweens from Viet-Minh areas into Saigon. In this case, the construction work was allowed to go on because the Viet-Minh were clearly of the opinion that it was they who, one day, would derive the benefit from it.

I now asked Dinh whether, as I knew the engineers, and they had agreed to take me with them, it would not be possible to enter Viet-Minh territory in this way, and whether he could not obtain for me a safe conduct to allow me to move about freely once I got in. But the Vietnamese are formalists and bureaucrats by tradition. They revere the written word, documents that have been properly signed, stamped, and counter-stamped, passwords, countersigns, and standing orders. Having been governed for many centuries by a civil service into which it was the ambition of all to enter, they are respectfully familiar with all the delaying devices which such a system imposes. Behind the smoke screens of his excuses I was sure that the real trouble was that Dinh would have to refer back to higher authority for a decision.

The most important objection he raised was that the suggested area was cut off from the main body of Viet-Minh territory and that I should therefore miss all the show-pieces: the broadcasting station, the arms factories, the cloth mills, the schools, the 105-mm. howitzer recently captured from the French, and, most important of all, the 're-education' centres. I told him that as funds were running out and I should not be able to stay much longer in Indo-China, anything would be better than nothing at all. He agreed to enquire what could be done, and to give me the answer in two days.

When the two days had passed the Tra-Vinh battle was still being fought. The Viet-Minh had captured a large number of defence-towers and instead of withdrawing as usual with the captured equipment, they brought up reinforcements and awaited the French counter-attack. Ambushes were laid for the French troops rushed from other areas, and further diversionary attacks were launched in neighbouring provinces. Neither the French nor Dinh knew whether any of these might not develop into the general offensive the Viet-Minh had promised before the dry season broke. It was therefore agreed that I might go with the engineers to the town in question, where I was to wait at a certain hotel, and an attempt would be made to pick me up. If the worst came to the worst it would simply mean sleeping a night there and being brought back by the engineers – who made the trip daily – next day. Viet-Minh troops and partisans in the town would be warned of my presence.

Next afternoon I left Saigon in the car belonging to a director of the engineering firm. It was driven by one of the junior employees who had just arrived from Europe, was not a Frenchman, and knew nothing whatever of the political situation. It was he who had staggered the French in Saigon by his description of how he had fraternized with a Viet-Minh patrol. He had been swimming in a river at the time and had found them waiting for him when he came out. A quite friendly chat followed, and when the patrol found out he was a foreigner they shook his hand and went off. My friend who still didn't know the difference between Viet-Minh and Vietnam believed his nationality a kind of talisman protecting him from dangers of all kinds. I told him that to a Vietnamese all Europeans looked exactly the same, but he refused to believe it. He was quite sure that his extra ten per cent of Mediterranean characteristics was universally recognizable.

After Laos, Cochin-China was harsh and brilliant. It was as if the earth had gone to rust at the tail-end of the dry season. Sometimes there was a crystalline glitter where the sunlight shattered on the tiles of a flattened tomb. Buffaloes scrambled over the parched earth, bearing gleaming crescents of horns. The lagoons had blackened in stagnant concentration, and the peasants groping for fish were stained by the muddy water so that at a distance their circular hats seemed to float like brilliant money on the water. Junks were moving hull down through the canals and rivers, and only the sharks' fins of their sails could be seen cutting across the plains. An armoured car had nosed into a clump of palms, where several white-haired, pink-faced Teutons of the Foreign Legion hid from the sun.

The town contained a single sordid colourful little hotel. You went in through a café, passing under an awning of dried fish, to mount a narrow staircase in complete darkness. The rooms had swing doors like saloons, but the town must have lived through former days of grandeur as each chamber had a bath alcove. A Chinese lady was taking a bath in mine, but she soon dressed and came out and we smiled and bowed to each other in the passage. Radio sets appeared to be going at full blast in every room, all tuned in to different stations. Soon after my arrival the proprietor came up and asked me to pay. He brought with him a bottle of cherry-brandy and presented me with a drink on the house. The change was brought by a small oriental chambermaid, who sat on the edge of the brass bed, singing, while she counted out the incredibly filthy notes which she hoped that I would return to her in disgust.

A few minutes later the proprietor was back, with a Vietnamese girl of about twelve, who, he said, had come to take me to the house of a friend. Following this child I was taken to a gloomy little palace in a back street. Here I was invited to seat myself in a carved chair that was all the more throne-like from the fact that it was raised on a low dais, and left alone. A few minutes later the little girl was back again with a glass of lemonade and then once again with a saucer of nuts. The dragons and unicorns writhing through the mother-of-pearl-studded surfaces of the furniture gradually sank into darkness. It was night.

I was dozing when Dinh arrived. He was accompanied by a rather chinless and bespectacled youth called Trang and seemed cheerful and nervous at the same time. Both of them wore dungarees and carried Stens. Dinh had brought a pair of rubber boots which he told me to put on, but they were too small. He seemed worried about my white shirt and trousers, but when we got outside we found ourselves in brilliant moonlight. The dress made no difference. If possible they were more conspicuous than I was in their black against the broad whitewashed surfaces of wall and road.

The streets were quite empty. Bao-Dai troops garrisoned two towers on the other side of the town, but Dinh said that they had orders never to leave the towers after sunset. We heard several distant rifle-shots which set the dogs barking, the barks ending in howls as the dogs were kicked into silence. We walked in the shadow of a wall; Dinh in front, followed by myself and then Trang. In a few minutes we were outside the town and scrambled down a low embankment into the rice-fields. We were on very low ground by the river, threading our way through a morass of quicksilver. Mist trailed in banks above the water. In the moonlight its surface was curiously solid. When we splashed through shallow pools a phosphorescence exploded round our boots. An enormous owl came flapping down to inspect us, and passed on with a strange, booming cry.

We reached a canal where a sampan awaited us, hidden among the water palms. Two soldiers standing in the boat held out their hands to steady us as we climbed aboard. They, too, were dressed in dark dungarees and wore Australian-type bush hats. We sat in the bottom of the sampan while the two soldiers, one standing at each end, began to row it along the canal. They rowed by a long single oar fastened to a post. After a short distance, one of them stopped rowing and tried to start up an engine. He had great difficulty, and Dinh held a torch while he took the carburettor to pieces. Trang said that the petrol was of very bad quality. They bought most of it from the Chinese who usually adulterated it with paraffin. In the end the engine was started. It was fitted with a very efficient silencing system, which Dinh said was of their own design. There were a few mechanical rattles, but no exhaust noise could be heard.

Little could be heard in fact along most of the reaches of water above the tremendous chirpings of frogs, which as we turned into narrow channels plopped into the water ahead of us in their hundreds. Twisting and turning through a maze of waterways we went on. The mosquitoes were very troublesome, biting through the three pairs of stockings I always wore, to get at their favourite area, the ankles, as well as feeding greedily on the neck, wrists, and forehead. We passed clumps of water palms where fireflies were carrying on an extraordinary display, weaving a scroll-work through the fronds like the fancy terminals of the signatures of the Victorian era. In such a clump the sampan was stopped, with the engine switched off, while the soldiers listened to heavy mortar and machine-gun fire, which sounded, allowing for the water, as if it might be two or three miles away. A few hundred yards further on we stopped again. A dark shape, silhouetted by moonlight, lolled in the water ahead. Someone on our boat switched on a small searchlight and, as this happened, large aquatic birds flustered up with a great commotion from some low bushes among the reeds. The dark object was a sampan lying low in the water. We approached it slowly with levelled tommy-guns, but it was empty and partially waterlogged. Further down still, we ran into another obstacle, a log across the water. But this was the equivalent of a roadblock, and after an exchange of passwords with unseen guards on the bank it was pulled back far enough for us to pass through.

Soon after, a plane passed low overhead. It dropped a Very light a long way from us, so that the flickering reflection hardly imposed itself on the moonlight. The machine-gun and mortar fire started again. Dinh said in English, 'Exciting.' This was one of the three English adjectives he occasionally produced, the others being 'captivating' – used to describe any aspect of life in Viet-Minh territory – and 'regrettable' – reserved for the French and all their doings.

We stopped again when we overtook a sampan full of peasants. They were ordered ashore, where one of the soldiers, who it appeared was an officer, harangued them in angry tones. Dinh said that the brother officer had criticized them for failing to obey the curfew order, summary criticism being the lowest grade of disciplinary measures. And what came next, I asked. Arrest followed by public criticism, Dinh said, although nobody wanted to be too hard on first offenders. I mentioned the old Vietnamese simple correction of thirty strokes with the rattan cane, and Dinh said that naturally anyone would prefer that, as public criticism was so much less dignified. There had never been any stigma in a beating, because the offence was purged on the spot, but a public criticism took a lot of wearing down. People tended to say, there goes so-and-so who was publicly criticized. Psychological methods, besides being less barbarous, were more effective. A typical offence in the case of which such a punishment might be awarded, said Dinh, would be the failure, after warning, to build a proper outside latrine for the use of one's family.

We landed and went in single file up a lane through the palms. The moon was sinking now and the sound of the distant firing had ceased. In Indo-China the two sides seem to have reached an informal agreement to restrict their nocturnal combats to the early part of the night. Even the relentless chirping of the frogs had quietened. A few yards from the water's edge we came to huts made of branches and palm leaves. It was the local military headquarters.

Dinh explained that the unit, which had been newly established here, was chiefly occupied with observation of enemy movements, but that all male members were fully trained for combatant duties to which they could be transferred in emergency. It was one of a number of similar posts which formed an outside screen, interlinked by radio and sending back information to the army's headquarters in the centre of the *Plaine des Joncs*. Observers were sent out from here with portable signals equipment with which they kept a twenty-four-hourly observation of troop movements in a defined territory. This information was passed on regularly to the Army signals centre where it was all pieced together and collated with the other information received, so that in theory a complete track was kept of the movement of every French patrol or operational group from the moment it left its barracks until it returned. A great deal of stress was laid upon the necessity for absolutely accurate information regarding numerical strengths and types of weapons carried. In this way Army headquarters was able to decide whether the enemy was to be attacked or avoided. This particular post, Dinh said, owing to its perfect situation, was invulnerable, except from the air. It could only be approached by small, lightly armed craft which could be blown up in the narrow waterways by mines manufactured specially for this purpose. It was screened from the air by the method of building the administrative huts into the palms, close to the water's edge. Reconnaissance planes were never fired at, however low they flew. At a later stage – quite soon now, Dinh thought – these peripheral posts would throw out offshoots, further in the direction of French-occupied territory, while they themselves would be transformed into battalion headquarters, with a purely operational function.

There was a second purpose which the post fulfilled. This was an educational and propaganda one. It was their job, for which they were allotted a certain time, to stamp out illiteracy in their area. From total literacy in the old pre-colonial days, when every man's ambition had been for his son to be able to compete in the civil service examinations, the literate minority of the population had dropped as low as twenty per cent. The people would now be educated, said Dinh, and in the interior of Viet-Minh territory where peaceful conditions prevailed it had been declared (with a touch of the old authoritarian sternness) a punishable offence to be unable to read and write. In frontier areas such as this it was left to public opinion. To be illiterate was unpatriotic, the Viet-Minh had told the peasants. And when they could read the Viet-Minh would of course supply their intellectual food.

By the time we arrived all the personnel of the post, with the exception of the duty staff, were already in bed. Dinh explained that the last meal was taken at five o'clock, and after that parties went canoeing, swimming, or walking, or to their improving labours in the villages. But for the last week they had all been virtually confined to barracks owing to the fighting in the neighbourhood. Radio warnings had been received of several marine-commando raids in their area, and once they had been obliged to send men to create a diversion when a nearby post had been attacked. We had timed our arrival, it seemed, most unfortunately.

The commander of the post now came in. He had been out watching the attack which we had heard and which had been directed against a group of towers held by Bao-dai forces. He was about twenty-five years of age, small, slight, and grave, with features blunted with deep pock marks. He carried no badges of rank, but was the equivalent, Dinh said, of a captain. Officers were not saluted and were called brother, like anyone else. 'A respect for his superiors is second nature to any Vietnamese. It could not be increased by the addition of titles.'

Apologizing for being too busy to show me round in person, the commander said that there had been a flare-up of activity in all sectors and that Bao-dai troops drafted into the area had just received orders to attack them. I asked how they knew that, and the commander smiling rather distantly said that it was their business to know. To forestall any such attack, it had, at all events, been decided to capture all the towers, and a combat team had been sent with the necessary assault equipment. Asked whether the towers would be held when captured, the commander said no, there was no point in it. They would be demolished. Two towers had been taken that night, but he thought that Army headquarters might have decided to make a daylight attack on those that remained. Where possible they liked to have a camera-man filming such actions so that the staff officers could see how the commanders in the field were doing their jobs and correct their mistakes where necessary. Films of well-organized attacks also served instructional and propaganda purposes.

I asked whether it would be possible to see such an operation, and the commander, with a trace of coldness in his manner, said he thought it was extremely unlikely. He had no authority whatever to give permission. Regretting perhaps his somewhat blunt refusal, he then said that actions of this kind were sometimes dangerous. Usually the tower surrendered without opposition at all, or only a token opposition, because they were always attacked in greatly superior force. But on one occasion recently, after a surrender had been arranged by peaceful negotiation, and at the moment when the Viet-Minh party was advancing to take over, the tower had opened fire, killing the officer commanding and a high official who had been sent to observe from headquarters. That, said the commander, was a rare example of a bungle. But it went to show that accidents did happen.

Among the statistical charts with which the room was decorated was a propaganda poster. It consisted of a map of the world with

China and the Soviet Union united in a huge red mass. Across were written words in Vietnamese, which the Commander said meant, 'These people are with you.' He added, 'Our enemies are slowly converting us to communism. If it is only by becoming communists that we shall achieve our liberty, then we shall become communists.'

We slept on bunks in the guard-hut. Mosquito nets were provided and there was a box of anti-malarial tablets open on a table. I was awakened before dawn by a bugle blowing but went off to sleep and awoke again when the sun was well up. Washing was done in a hut fitted with wooden bowls lined with sheet-metal. Large jars full of water were provided. Dinh, who was already up and came into the wash-room, said that filling the jars from the river was one of the rota fatigues, like cooking and other domestic tasks.

Afterwards he suggested a dip and we went down and swam about in a pool of warmish yellow water. Dinh mentioned that this was reserved for males only and that the ladies' bathing pool was further along the river, modestly screened, I noticed, with an unusually dense growth of water palm. There had been a period, Dinh said, when 'naturism' and mixed sunbathing had received official sanction as cultural relaxations, allotted their half-hour in the days's approved activities. But now they were viewed with disfavour, along with the composition of lyrical poetry, as unfavourable to the development of a realistic attitude towards present problems. Love affairs, too, were detrimental to efficiency and were something to be kept, like smoking, for furtive indulgence in the bottoms of junks.

At ten o'clock the first meal was served; a Quakerish affair, girls on one side of the table, eyes demurely lowered, and men on the other, all dressed in black calico. The temptation to stare at the European must have been great. Dinh said that in the interior of Viet-Minh territory some of the young people have not seen a Westerner since early childhood, and that their first experience of the fierce, red, and often bearded features of the enemy was particularly terrifying.

The meal consisted of *tit-ca* – pork stewed in coconut milk – and balls of *riz gluant*. *Gluant*, which means sticky, is exactly what the rice is not, and could not possibly be more unlike the boiled rice eaten in England. Each separate grain is firm, greyish in colour, and practically dry; but the cooking is done in such a way that the grains adhere to each other and can be kneaded into balls. There was a poor quality *nuóc-mâm* to dip it in; thin, black and powerfully malodorous. The food was eaten rapidly and in silence, fifteen minutes being allowed. It would be followed by fifteen minutes' rest and then a short period of calisthenics, Dinh informed me. The commander corrected him. Conforming to a new directive, the second morning period of physical culture had been discontinued, but could be replaced, if circumstances permitted, with community singing. A jug of water and a bowl stood at the door of the hut, and all washed their hands as they went out to their rather staid oriental version of Strength through Joy.

The post had a prisoner they were very proud of. They excused themselves by saying that they had not had the chance to send him back to the Army cage. But it was clear that they were really keeping him as long as they possibly could, and that he was regarded much as the pet boa-constrictor had been in the ideal French post – a fabulous monster which, once rendered harmless, had become a mascot, an object of amiable curiosity. He was a German legionary who had been found, more or less by accident, after his jeep had been blown up by one of their bamboo mines. The mine seemed not to have been very powerful as the other occupants of the car got away, leaving this man who had leg injuries. The Commander said that he had been found quite sympathetic to their cause, and undoubtedly had been compelled to fight for the French. He expected that after an indoctrination course and a period of observation he would be offered the chance to enlist in the Viet-Minh Army. Dinh mentioned that the loyalty of suitable candidates of this kind was tested at the end of their indoctrination, by giving them every opportunity to escape. When commando raids were made in the neighbourhood of prisoner-of-war cages, the guards dispersed, telling the prisoners to stay where they were. Those who did so received good conduct marks and some small privileges.

No guard had been placed on the hut where the prisoner lay. Apart from his leg wounds, the Commander said, neither he nor anyone could ever hope to escape through the maze of waterways. The German was small, dark, and slender; diminished, too, perhaps, by his misfortunes. He lay in the bunk in his uniform with his legs in paper bandages. When he found out that I was not another prisoner he was at first rather sullen and hostile. I asked him how he felt, and he said that his legs hurt him all the time and he would give a year's pay for a packet of cigarettes. At first he refused to give his name but later he said that it was Breczina. He was a Sudeten and had been an *Unterscharführer* in the Waffen SS – a selected man, he said – and had been wounded on the Russian and Western fronts. To my enquiry as to the treatment he had received, he said that he couldn't complain, but that the food was filth. And was it true that he had been converted to the Viet-Minh's point of view? He made a face. I could imagine what he thought of reds, he said, but if the worst came to the worst, he would sooner be an officer in the Viet-Minh Army – and they had told him that Germans from the Legion sometimes got commissions – than rot in a prisoner-of-war camp again. His fate was of little importance, since the defeat of Germany had proved for him that there was no purpose behind the universe. At the moment he was inconvenienced only by the loss of his spectacles, and his one sorrow was that what had happened to him had still further postponed the day when he would see his parents again. He had not seen them since he left school to enter the army.

Later in the day there was some air activity. A plane came over and circled the area several times, as if it were taking photographs. The temptation to fire at it must have been great as it flew very low. Dinh thought that there would have been a fifty-fifty chance of bringing it down with machine-gun fire. He said that the Viet-Minh were badly provided with anti-aircraft defence in the south and that there was a standing order that immediately a gun had been fired it had to be removed to another site. Soon after the plane appeared, a whistle was blown as a signal for all personnel to take cover, and later an order was issued that no one not on duty was to leave the huts for the rest of the day. Front-line experiences, unless with an army on the move, are very restricted in their scope, and when the sector happens to be a small island screened by walls of vegetation in a swamp, one might as well be in a submarine for all one sees.

It was arranged that we should leave as soon as it was dark, since, as there had been no daylight activity, the night was expected to be a lively one. We boarded the sampan at dusk, and from the Commander's last-minute cordiality it was clear that he was relieved to see us go.

Once again the night was of a rare and perfect brilliance, with a sky of transparent gun-metal fenced in by a tall horizon of white palms. Through shining spear-hedged lanes we thrust forward with a gondola smoothness, pulling into a bank at last, where we left the sampan and climbed a low hillock. Here once had been a village, for although the shacks housing the living had disappeared a cluster of old substantial tombs remained, a stark revelation of bone-white stone in the neutral earth. On three sides stretched out a bleached-paper jungle of palms, but ahead was clear ground. In the centre of this cleared stage, about a mile away, a tower rose up; a small, neat, medieval shape, with its low girdle of bamboo; isolated in a plain which shone with the dull granularity of an ice-rink. 'I have a surprise for you,' Dinh said, looking at his watch. 'In fifteen minutes the attack will begin.'

But fifteen minutes later nothing happened. Another fifteen minutes passed and Dinh was getting nervous. The assault party would be there, he said, but undoubtedly hidden from us by some unseen dip in the terrain. And then a faint growling could be heard, the distorted ramblings of a radio set badly tuned in, or the un-natural bass of a gramophone running down. 'The loudspeakers,' Dinh said, in triumph. The tower was being invited to surrender.

The growling stopped and there was a long silence. It was drama of a high order, its effect heightened by the setting and the strange theatrical lighting. There was the tower, a graceful, well-made toy, solid, and intact. At this moment the dozen or score of men who defended it would be cowering somewhere in its base, having crawled perhaps for extra protection, as one sometimes does in such emergencies, under quite insubstantial pieces of furniture. And at any moment this would crumple before our eyes, dissolve or fall apart in the slow-motion that always seems to attend such violent dissolution seen from a distance. It was like the moment in the bull ring when the door of the pen is flung open and one awaits the bull's onrushing entry with excitement and a faint trepidation.

There was a slight disturbance in the plain at an enormous distance from the tower, which gathered itself into a silver puff of smoke, and then lost shape again. An explosion thumped in our ears. It seemed impossible that the mortar-bomb had been aimed at the tower. Another insignificant bubble of smoke formed and floated upward. It was much nearer than the first, but still a long way away. Dinh thought that this might be an inexperienced team who were being given some practice. It was clear from the violence of the explosions that an unusually heavy mortar was being used, but it was also clear that it was hopeless for this task. A quite small gun would have blown the tower off the face of the earth in a few rounds, but unless one of the mortar-bombs could be landed fair and square on the sloping roof of the tower it was clearly useless.

And now there was a faint, distant screeching as of a heavy iron gate turning upon its hinge, and we both ducked slightly. The screeching ended in an explosion that was sharper but less heavy than that of the mortar-bombs, and the puff of smoke was nearer to the tower than the others had been. The attackers were under fire from a French twenty-five pounder. Another whistle seemed to be coming straight at us, and we crouched down behind the low wall of a tomb as black earth fanned out halfway between us and the tower. Dinh said in English, 'Exciting.' At the same moment, almost, smoke spurted at the foot of the tower, and we saw pinpoints of fire, which lasted for a few seconds and then went out. 'A direct hit,' Dinh said. 'They will surrender now.' And sure enough, we could just make out an insect movement beyond the stockade, soon absorbed in a fold in the earth. The garrison had given in. A few more twenty-five pounder shells came over, and then the silence closed in.

Asiatics could still be content, it seemed, to settle their differences, if left to themselves, with such a mild display of pyrotechnics. A whiff of powder and a face-saving show of resistance lasting half an hour, and it was all over. For the defeated it would be followed by a decent probationary period of indoctrination, and then a change of flag. All this was not so far removed from the old Sino-Annamese conception of warfare which had become so oddly picturesque now, so dilettante even, in its half-measures and grotesque chivalries, the opposing generals meeting to agree over a pullet's entrails the date and place of battle; the warriors carrying lanterns at night to give their enemies a fair chance to see them; the battle suspended while the weather cleared up; the victory conceded to the side showing greater proficiency in the beating of offensive gongs. One is reminded of the military manuals – indispensable to old-style Vietnamese warfare – of those genial fire-eaters, General Dao and Marshal Khe; with their leisurely discussion of the best way to cook rice on horseback, while on the march, and their emphasis on the value of aggressive masks – or, in their absence, of merely pulling faces at the enemy.

Victory, as Pasquier observes, in his study of the Vietnamese Army, was usually accorded, avoiding final resorts to arms, to the side recognized as possessing the moral ascendancy. It is all part of the essential pacifism and civilization – liable to crop out whenever given the opportunity – of a people who possess the proverb: 'The greatest honour any human being can possibly hope for is to return to his village with the degree of Doctor of Letters awarded at the triennial competitions at Hué. After that it is not a bad thing to come back as Marshal of the Empire, having won a great victory over the enemy.'

In the afternoon of the next day, I saw Saigon again, and for the last time.

I was driving back with the engineer. It had been a quiet night in the city, he said. That was to say, only an average number of grenades had been thrown. But he was afraid that more trouble was expected, because a shipful of Africans had arrived and the streets were full of them.

In fact, as we came into the suburbs we saw them, the Senegalese, wandering like lost children near the posts they had taken over – the black heads of processional giants carried jerkily above the oblivious Asiatic crowd.

The first strangers to arrive here, says Borri, were shipwrecked mariners, who 'took such an Affection to the Country that not a Man of them would go away; so that the Captain of the Ship was forc'd to drive them aboard with many Blows and Cuts, which he effectually did, loading the Ship with the Rice they had gather'd only by going about, crying, *I am hungry*'.

This, surely, was the end of the story; the completion of a cycle … these frightened blacks and the sullen natives of the country with their averted faces. The successors of the shipwrecked Europeans had come back in increasing numbers, preaching, trading, worming their way into the organism of the country, changing it, remoulding it, and finally taking it for their own. And now they had withdrawn again into the port of their entry, where behind this African rampart they awaited the findings of Destiny.

I wondered whether it had all been worth it – the brief shotgun marriage with the West, now to be so relentlessly broken off. Had there been, after all, some mysterious historical necessity for all the bloodshed, the years of scorn, the servitude, the contempt? Could some ultimately fructifying process have been at work? And would the free nations of Indo-China, in their coming renascence, have gained in the long run by the enforced rupture with the old, unchanging way of life, now to be replaced, one presumed, by a materialist philosophy and the all-eclipsing ideal of the raised standard of living?

These were questions, since there is no yard-stick for felicity, to which no final answer could ever be given. And even a partial answer would have to be left to an observer of the next generation.

GOLDEN EARTH

Travels in Burma

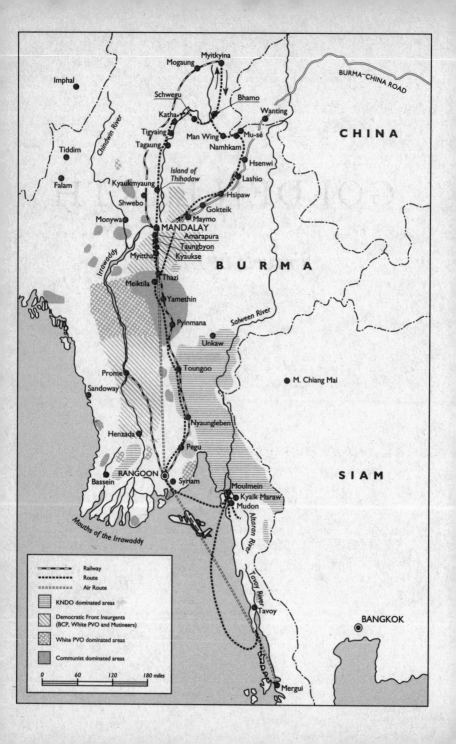

Contents

Foreword

In 1949, with the creation of the People's Republic of China, that country became as remote and inaccessible as Thibet had been of old. I believed that this policy of self-isolation might spread to neighbouring countries and, having determined to see before I died something of the Far East, I went in 1950 to Indo-China, and covered a little of the area still open to travel in that fabulous country. In that year there was no slacking in the rate at which the Far Eastern lands were passing beyond the reach of the literary sightseer. Korea was scorched off the map, and if we were embroiled with China, said the observers, the flames of this conflagration might spread to Burma where Communist guerrillas were already firmly entrenched. One of two things would then happen: either the country would pass with China behind what had been called the Bamboo Curtain, or it would be defended by the West, as Korea had been defended, and with similar results. In either case the traditional Burma, with its archaic and charming way of life, would have vanished.

In a rational plan for seeing a little of the Eastern world these grave considerations seemed to me to entitle Burma to priority. Accordingly I flew there at the beginning of 1951.

Burma was known of old as

Savarna Bhumi (the Golden Earth)

and in Burmese classical literature as

Sona Paranta (the Golden Land)

CHAPTER ONE

Rangoon

BURMA SPREAD as a dark stain into the midnight sea. Soon the inert grey of water lifted to the horizon, but the darkness that followed it was sprinkled with points of light. There was a bleared reflection from broad waterways of the wasting moon; the blinking of lamps strung out in lines, leading web-like to the centre of some unseen city; then the banal reality of that accepted wonder of the air-traveller's world, the Shwedagon Pagoda by night. The moonlight was too weak to reveal the pagoda's golden surfaces, and as it was late most of the artificial illumination had been switched off. What remained was a deserted fair-ground at midnight – a few trivial pendants of lights which sketched in, without revealing, the august shape.

At the airport, the bleak, palely lit buildings, where lines of passengers awaited their interrogation by innumerable officials, were decorated, as if by design, by groups of tiny silk-clad elfin creatures – unmistakably adult, since some nursed at the breast exquisite miniatures of themselves. And while the dreary procession of sleep-walkers dragged by from official to official, from bureau to bureau, the little silken groups sat comfortably apart, faces impeccably powdered, hair garlanded, hands in lap, watching us with unblinking eyes, no evidence of relish, and only the occasional ejaculation of a stream of betel. There seemed no answer to the riddle of their presence. They were there when first we staggered into the building and still there, squatting silent and motionless in unchanged positions, when, hours later, as it seemed, the bus took us away. Of Mingaladon Airport it could at least be said that it did not suffer from the cosmopolitan insipidity natural to airports. Here one was bathed in the essence of the country while waiting to pass through the formalities.

*

I awoke next morning feeling dazed and queasy. There had been an earthquake in the small hours – the first of any importance, the papers said, since that of 1931 – but although half awakened I had put the sensation down to a mild heart attack, or some manifestation of over-tiredness, and immediately dropped off again. Now I was aroused once more by an unfamiliar clamour. Outside the window was a courtyard, and mynas were using it for their exercises, giving out shrill, bubbling cries, indistinguishable from the gurglings of those pipes which are filled with water and used to imitate bird-sounds. There were crows as well; fine glossy Asiatic specimens, not very large, but very sprightly, their shoulders splashed with a blue iridescence. They were extremely noisy in their affable crow-like way. Above their endless cawings could sometimes be heard a shrill kitten-like mew. This came from a kite perched on a wireless aerial. It was useless to hope for more sleep.

In any case, there was a knock on the door and a smart young Indian page appeared and handed me a card on which was printed, U MAUNG LAT, EX-HEAD MASTER. Further enquiries from the boy produced nothing better than nods and smiles, so reluctantly I dressed and went down. U Maung Lat, who was sitting in the lounge, rose to greet me. He had the manner of a savant and was dressed conservatively, wearing a hand-tied turban, and the frayed jacket of the impecunious man of letters. Smiling gently, he produced a newspaper cutting which said that among the passengers to arrive on that morning's plane had been the author Lewis Morgan. The police, he said, had been able, from their records, to direct him to my hotel. It is one of the accepted humiliations of the writer that, however simple his name, no one can ever get it right. In my travels in Indo-China I had been given an identification paper describing me as Louis Norman, writer, commissioned by Jonathan Cape Ltd. of Thirty Bedford Square. By a slow process of compression and corruption I finished this journey as Monsieur Thirsty Bedford; which, as the name and description had been recopied about twenty times, I did not think unreasonable. But on the present occasion, having written out my name in full perhaps a dozen times within the past few hours, I found the distortion less pardonable.

However, U Maung Lat's smile was irresistible. 'Mr Morgan,' he said, coming straight to the point, 'I have decided my wish to place upon your shoulders the responsibility of publishing my treatise, amounting to ninety-four thousand words, on those three things for which Burma is of all countries the most famous.' The three things, said my visitor, were snake charming, the playing of rattan football, and the destruction of the invading forces sent by a Ming emperor of China. This, his lifetime's work he said, had been accepted, during the Japanese occupation, by the Domei Agency, but, alas, through subsequent events beyond their control, they had been unable to fulfil their contract.

Many other new arrivals in Rangoon, I have no doubt, must have met this charming eccentric, but on me this delightful piece of oriental dottiness, gleaned from my first non-official contact in Burma, had a tonic effect. Immediately the irritations of the night before vanished. I was full of hope for the future.

Rangoon, even in temporary decline, is imperial and rectilinear. It was built by a people who refused compromise with the East, and has wide, straight, shadeless streets, with much solid bank-architecture of vaguely Grecian inspiration. In the town one is constantly being taken back to Leadenhall Street; while down on the Rangoon river-front the style is that of the London Customs House. Within these edifices, there is something ecclesiastical in the gleaming of dark woods and brass. In passing over these thresholds the voice is instinctively hushed. There is much façade and presence, little pretence at comfort, and no surrender to the climate. This was the Victorian colonizer's response to the unsubstantial glories of Mandalay.

These massive columns now rise with shabby dignity from the tangle of scavenging dogs and sprawling, ragged bodies at their base. In recent years, the main thoroughfares, with such resolutely English names as Commissioner's Road, have acquired a squalid incrustation of stalls and barracks, and through these European arteries now courses pure oriental blood. Down by the port it is an Indian settlement. Over to the west the Chinese have moved in with their outdoor theatres and joss-houses. The Burmese, in their own capital city, content themselves with the suburbs. Little has been done by the new authority to check the encroaching squalor. Side lanes are piled with stinking refuse which mounts up quicker than the dogs and crows can dispose of it. The covers have been taken off most of the drains and not replaced. Half-starved Indians lie dying in the sunshine. Occasionally insurgents cut off the town's water supply. There are small annual epidemics of cholera and smallpox, and the incidence of bubonic plague is unlikely to decrease because the sewers of Rangoon swarm with rats, which it is irreligious, according to all Burmese and most Indians, to kill. Even when the rats have been caught alive in traps, to what end it is not clear, they have actually been released by the pious, who were ready to rise earlier than the rat-catchers, if spiritual merit could thereby be earned. Wherever there is a vacant space the authorities have allowed refugees to put up pestiferous shacks, which now flank in unbroken lines the country roads leading into Rangoon, the railway tracks, and the shores of the Royal Lake.

Amidst this fetor the Burmese masses live their festal and contemplative existences. Untouched by the decaying middens in which they live, they emerge into the sunshine immaculate and serene. The Burmese must be the best-dressed people in the world. There is no misery of the kind that manifests itself in rags and sores. In Buddhism there is a positive, tangible advantage – the acquisition of merit – to be obtained by works of charity. These are chalked up to the credit of the soul in subsequent existences. Unfortunately for the Indian immigrants this purchase of merit seems to apply somewhat less in the case of not-altogether-human foreigners.

It was Burma Union Day, one of the many public holidays when the Burmese are able to practise their aptitude for leisure in the many ingenious ways they have developed through the centuries. The streets of Rangoon, wallowing in sun, flashed and scintillated with strolling crowds, skirted in their best silk longyis. All places of public entertainment had been open since early morning. A cinema showing a Burmese film was advertising this by a full-scale orchestra, with drums, gongs, and a squealing flute, set up outside on the pavement. But the Burmese were not exacting in the matter of entertainment and the products of Filmistan – the Indian Hollywood – were being patronized with equal enthusiasm. A production called *Ekthi-Larki* had attracted long queues. It was a comedy; the posters said in English that 'when you come out you cry, because so roaring is this film'. On the whole the Orient prefers straight drama in its films, and that as sensational and horrific as possible. Such productions are known here as *se-ta*, a Burmanization of the word stunt. I later discovered that, of twenty-two films showing in Rangoon at that moment, eighteen were *se-tas*.

The Burmese cinema was, by the way, showing a South Sea Island affair; a Polynesian epic *à la* Hollywood, but orientalized to local taste. In the advertising stills the hero, a Burmese Johnny Weismuller, wore check shorts, a satin shirt, and pearl-handled pistols. For some obscure reason he carried in one hand an *Industry Year Book and Directory* for 1934. The heroine wore a sarong, of the type Miss Dorothy Lamour has described as her contribution to culture, and a brassière. She was definitely Anglo-Burman with marked Aryan characteristics, thus strengthening my theory formed by previous observation in the Far East that standards of beauty eventually accommodate themselves to the ideals set by the real possessors of power. In other words: unless and until the balance of world power swings from West to East, urban Easterners will go on trying to look like American film actors and actresses; and, in the course of centuries, the process will probably be more or less completed by natural selection. I first formed this theory when I heard that (before recent events) Pekinese young ladies of fashion were building up a modish aquilinity of feature by having an ivory wedge inserted by plastic surgery along the bridge of the nose. A further operation was practised, according to my information, upon the upper eyelids, to abolish for the very wealthy the reproach of almond-shaped eyes.

The chief Western contribution of the moment to the entertainment of Rangoon film-goers was *Anna and the King of Siam*, 'enshrouding all the Glamour and Mystery of the East'. Glamour and Mystery! Can it be that only now, when for us Cathay and the Indies have been stripped of those shadowy attributes, orientals themselves are beginning to be persuaded of their existence ... just as the natives of the Isle of Capri and Old Monterrey have accepted with enthusiasm the songs composed in their honour in Brooklyn. In the case of Anna and the King, the film had not yet started, and a tight, neck-craning circle had formed round someone who was entertaining them. A picturesque mountebank demonstrating some traditional Eastern legerdemain? Not at all. Merely a machine which for eight annas engraved your name, while you waited, on the barrel of your fountain pen.

And so with all the rest of it. What was trashiest in the only half-understood West had been found most acceptable. The Russian Balalaika night club, where respectable Burmese businessmen submitted uneasily, for good form's sake, to the fondling of Chinese hostesses and listened without appreciation to Jock d'Souza's Super Hep Swingtette; the Impatient Virgins and Hard-Boiled Virgins on the bookstalls; the useless, illegally imported American cars, which it was unsafe to drive outside the town. These were no more than the greedily snatched-at symbols of prestige.

This undigested Westernism was much in evidence, too, in the national celebrations. For several hundred years orientals have kept the West under close observation, hoping ultimately to extract the secret, to uncover the mechanism behind that mysterious supremacy in such matters as accurate clocks and automatic weapons. How was it that not even the benign interest of the heavens, as shown by the most splendid of horoscopes, could protect a man against a Western bullet? The reason clearly lay in the effectiveness of the barbarians' semi-magic rites and ceremonies; one of which, and a spectacular one, consisted of gathering in groups to practise stertorous, rhythmic breathing accompanied by the shamanistic jerking of arms and legs. Here then, in the public gardens of Bogyoke Square, was a deputation of ladies from the Karenni States, marching and counter-marching, bending and stretching, holding their breath for enormous lengths of time, before, when on the verge of asphyxiation, expelling it in geyser-like eruptions. Having come under Burmese civilizing influence, the Karen ladies had left at home their own splendid national costumes and appeared in Burmese blouses and longyis; the limit of Westernization they could decently permit themselves.

The Chinese, stamped with the uniformity of national renaissance, had gone further and donned PT kit for the celebration. Lorry after lorry roared by filled with the young adherents of Mao Tse-tung, looking very purposeful in their blue outfits, and carefully graded, lorry by lorry, according to size.

Further down the street an open-air film show reproduced scenes from the previous year's rejoicings. The Prime Minister of Burma, the honourable Thakin Nu, was shown feeding a large concourse of Buddhist monks. A Burmese prime minister feeds monks on public occasions in much the same way as the heads of other states, or their representatives, inspect troops. The procedure is intended to emphasize the spiritual and renunciatory basis of Burmese civilization, and orthodox Burmese were as much shocked by the omission by the British Viceroy of this ancient and regal custom as by any other aspect of their loss of independence.

No effort is spared by the Burmese government to underline its devotion to non-materialistic ideals. A further scene showed the Prime Minister at the head of a solemn procession and carrying a tooth of the Buddha, which was being taken in state to a shrine in the Chin country. The tooth was probably a miraculous self-reproduction of one of the originals and duly authenticated as such by the Buddhist priesthood. Such miracles are extremely rare and thus the existing teeth continue to be valued by Buddhists beyond all price. In 1560 the Burmese King offered the modern equivalent of about a million pounds to the Portuguese for one they had looted from Ceylon, but the Portuguese turned down the offer, and destroyed the tooth as an idol.

The film show ended with secular light relief in the form of a selection of dances and ceremonies by remote tribespeople. They included an amiable drinking rite carried out by some Chins which involved the transfer, in a kind of Valentino kiss, of mouthfuls of rice-liquor from the men to the women of the tribe. The original supply of liquor was contained in beer-bottles, on which the labels had been carefully preserved. When all the participants had been warmed up by these preliminaries, they linked arms and broke into what looked like – and perhaps was – the Lambeth Walk.

Across the gardens where the well-conducted oriental revels were taking place gleamed softly the inverted golden bell of the Sule Pagoda. The erection of this monument in the eighteenth century was a religious gesture on the part of Alaungpaya, one of the last great Burmese kings. Always an amateur of the grand manner, Alaungpaya's human sacrifices were the best that could be procured; so that at the foundation of this pious institution the victim was a Talaing princeling, who was buried alive with extraordinary pomp. In this way he became the spirit-guardian of Rangoon, a minor god, who is shown in effigy simpering upon a golden throne, apparently unresentful of the process by which his divinity was acquired. The spire of the Sule Pagoda is plated with gold, furnished by the devout. It is approached by four covered stairways, with a minor temple, well constructed in corrugated iron, built over each entrance. These additions have been given at various times by leading merchants of the city, who have thereby acquired great merit and probably avoided numerous reincarnations. Some, according to the inscriptions, were Hindus, at least by origin, and may, as good business men, have considered the expense no more than a reasonable insurance risk.

The sanctity inherent in the pagoda begins at the first step leading from the street pavement up to the platform under which the sacred relics are buried. It also extends to the various shops built into the pagoda's surrounding wall, some of them – including a lottery-ticket seller's – being of a remarkably secular character. Before entering any of them, as well as before ascending the pagoda steps, the shoes must be removed. One of the shops was the publishing centre of a Buddhist mission and several short sermons in English were stuck on the window. These dealt with the technique of suppressing the lusts of the flesh. I was about to go in when I caught sight of the notice – familiar in Burma – 'no foot-wearing'. Elsewhere about the pagoda (the Burmese have an affection for manufactured participles) umbrella-ing was forbidden. As I was struggling with my shoes a young man came from the back of the shop and asked me, in an Oxford accent and with the mild, well-bred manner of the dilettante shop-keeper, what he could do for me. I told him I should like to have some of his tracts and he said, 'Why, of course,' supposing, by the way, that I must be Mr Morgan. Admitting this, I said that it seemed odd to me that he should have guessed it and the young man replied that he knew all of the resident white population by sight, adding, with resignation, that he supposed his shop would have a curiosity value for a literary visitor. He was a well-known English Buddhist, and subsequently – Buddhist homilies being a noteworthy feature of Burmese journalism – I read and enjoyed several of his sermons in the Rangoon press.

CHAPTER TWO

Preparations

I WANTED TO LEAVE Rangoon as soon as possible and to travel in the interior, covering before the arrival of the wet season, at the end of April, as much of the country as I could. My ignorance of conditions in Burma was quite extraordinary. This was partly due to an efficient censorship and the fact that foreign journalists do not usually leave Rangoon. The last occasion when Burmese affairs had been strongly featured in the British press had been in 1948, when the Karen insurgents had taken Mandalay and seemed to be about to overthrow the Burmese government. Since then interest had died down, and communiqués from the country had become more and more infrequent. In July 1949, the Prime Minister had announced that peace was attainable within one year. Having heard no more I assumed that it had been attained. At all events I imagined that Burma would be as peaceful as a Friesian dairy farm by comparison with Malaya, Indonesia, or Indo-China.

When in December 1950 I saw the Burmese Ambassador to Britain to ask for permission to visit the country, my lack of information was such that I actually suggested that I might be allowed to enter Burma from Manipur in the north. With visions of a leisurely progression, in the Victorian manner, from the northern frontier to Tenasserim in the extreme south, I was prepared for austerities rather than hazards. The transport would be slow and primitive; in crowded, rickety buses and antique, but incredibly picturesque, river-steamers. Food and lodging would be no more than adequate, but always interesting. There would be many delays and minor miseries, but from these a retrospective pleasure could be distilled. This was the Burmese journey for which I was prepared in the imagination and it was for this that I had built up a reserve of philosophic tolerance. His Excellency U Ohn listened with indulgence to my suggested itinerary, and then suggested that it might be better to go to Rangoon first and make my further arrangements from there. This seemed to me a great waste of time as well as bad geographical organization. However, I found the conversation deftly changed to poetry and art, from which, while lunch lasted, it was never allowed to deviate. Never was an ambassadorial decision conveyed with more diplomatic finesse.

My delusions about the possibilities and character of travel in Burma were stripped away, in regular stages, within thirty-six hours of my arrival. On the first morning I bought a newspaper and noted with slight surprise that a ferry-boat crossing the river to a suburb of Rangoon had been held up by pirates and three members of the crew killed. Mention was made of a village, some twenty miles away, where the whole population had been carried off by insurgents. Serious fighting seemed to be going on, too, in various parts of the country as there were a few extremely vague reports about government troops capturing towns. Sometimes the towns were 're-captured', which suggested a certain aggressive capacity on the part of whoever it was the troops were fighting. In this newspaper I made my first acquaintance with that familiar Anglo-Burmese verb, to dacoit. At ten o'clock on the previous night a private car had been dacoited in the outskirts of Rangoon itself.

Further doubts about the stability of the country were aroused by an account of the experiences of a Canadian friend, employed as a specialist by the Burmese government, who had just returned from a visit to Syriam. Syriam, five miles away, across the Rangoon River, was the scene of an ambitious and revolutionary governmental experiment in land reform and was obviously chosen because it was at Rangoon's back door and therefore accessible at all times to the forces of law and order. My friend, however, had been accompanied by a formidable escort of infantry and had felt more like a Caribbean dictator than an adviser on statistical problems.

My final awakening to the true state of affairs came as a result of an interest in ornithology. A Burmese was squatting at the entrance to the Strand Hotel with a wicker cage containing half a dozen fine specimens of the Asiatic variety of the purple moorhen. They would eventually provide, he assured me, the basis of a curry. I asked where they had come from, and the man said that he had netted them in the swamps, not two miles away, across the river. The possibility of a refreshing spell of early-morning bird-watching immediately occurred to me. There would be other waders; certainly bitterns – perhaps ibises. Could he take me with him? The shake of the head was emphatic. An onlooker enlightened me. 'Across the river, they will shoot you, and no one will hesitate to consider your fate. Be sure that on sighting your near approach they will shoot at you without delaying.' It was a piece of sensationalism, a gross exaggeration, but it gave at least a hint of the sad condition of human security outside Rangoon.

Later that day I presented my letter of introduction to U Thant at the Secretariat. U Thant, the Permanent Secretary at the Ministry of Information, saw no reason why I should not go wherever I wished. Later I found that as this was his first experience of a request to travel about the country, he was not quite sure of the official procedure to be followed. However, any doubts were veiled beneath more than even the normal measure of Burmese charm. There were regular air-services to all the larger towns, he said hopefully. I replied that if I travelled by air, I should not see Burma. U Thant said that the railway service from Rangoon to Mandalay was working. It was perhaps a little inconvenient because of a break in the line. Proper arrangements were made to carry passengers across the gap in rail communications, either in lorries or bullock-carts, and if they were sometimes held up it was only to extract a kind of toll. That was to say, no violence was ever done. Where would I like to go first? Down to Mergui, I said. A coastal ship was leaving Rangoon in two days, and as such ships sailed at rather long intervals it seemed an opportunity which ought not to be missed. U Thant agreed: perhaps with relief. As long as you stayed on a ship you were out of harm's way. And now, he said, he would pass me on to

U Ba San, chief of the Special Branch Police, dealing with foreigners, who would handle the mere formality of issuing a travel permit.

U Ba San's cordiality, naturally enough in view of his office, was on a more limited scale. The permit for Mergui was made out, together with permission to go ashore when the ship put in at Moulmein on the way. Tavoy, he said, was quite out of the question, because the military situation there was uncertain. And at Mergui and Moulmein I must report immediately upon arrival to the District Commissioner and the Deputy Superintendent of Police. In the interests of my own safety, he said, I should not attempt to go outside the limits of either town. I then brought up the matter of my proposed visit to Mandalay and the Shan and Kachin States. To save any further call upon his time, could any permits required be issued there and then? U Ba San shook his head. The question of any further journeys could be gone into on my return from Mergui. But would such permits be forthcoming? I asked. U Ba San said he could promise nothing. I must understand that there were security problems involved. The authorities in the various districts would have to be warned of an impending visit to allow them sufficient time, of course, to facilitate my journey in every possible way.

After leaving U Ba San I visited the British Consulate where it was suggested that more might be discovered about travelling conditions in Burma by applying to one or two of the old English residents, particularly the executives of the big companies.

Following this advice I presented myself at the headquarters of the Burmah Oil Company. There was about this palatial building a mortuary stillness, in which might have echoed the lamentations of Hebrew prophets over mighty empires and enterprises doomed to decay. In this potential habitation of dragons and abode of owls I was received by an officer who told me that although he had been in Burma a number of years he had never managed to get to Mergui. He hoped to go one day, when he could find time. Meanwhile, he suggested, speaking as an ex-journalist, that if I wanted some journalistic copy – and sensational copy at that – I might try going up to Mandalay on one of the river-steamers that went there occasionally. As far as he knew, no European had done the trip since

1947. It might be a bit uncomfortable. Probably have to kip on deck and look after yourself for food. And then of course the boats were mortared and machine-gunned, but they kept too far from the shore for it to do much damage. On the whole, a pretty interesting trip, he thought. Lots of half-sunken craft all over the place, and always the chance of a hot reception when you tried to put in at a village which had changed hands since you called there last time.

In answer to my polite enquiries after the company's fortunes and prospects, I was told that so far as their Burma interests went, they couldn't be bleaker. The refineries had been destroyed in the war, and as for the pipeline, they once went to the trouble of counting the holes in a mile length of the pipe and found over a thousand of them. Couldn't get a new pipeline because of the steel shortage and even if they could the insurgents would knock thousands of holes through it, as, if, and when installed. Nowadays all they did was to extract just as much oil as they could sell in the area round the wells themselves. It was cheaper to bring it from Abadan to Rangoon than to ship it down the river. My informant mentioned that the Burmese government now demanded a half share in the enterprise, but as they hadn't any money, the British government was being approached for a loan to finance the transaction. The cruellest cut of all, he said, was that they weren't allowed to discharge any of their thousands of surplus employees.

CHAPTER THREE

Dramatic Entertainment

THERE WAS A CLEAR DAY to spare before the ship left for Mergui, and having heard that at this time of the year traditional Burmese pwès were to be seen in the outer suburb of Kemmendine, I went up there next afternoon. Pwès are the dramatic entertainments inseparable from the many Burmese festivals, which to the Burmese are the most important things in life. No charge is made to watch these open-air performances. They are paid for by public subscription, or out of the generosity of some citizen who feels himself temporarily in funds and in this way acquires social prestige. The streets of Kemmendine seem to have been designed with public celebrations in mind. They are enormously wide and well shaded by trees. Usually two or more pwès, with their attendant side-shows of all kinds, are going on at a time.

I happened to arrive in Kemmendine just before the necessary religious preliminaries to the rejoicings which would begin that evening. Prominent families of the district had built pavilions along both sides of the streets; small garish pagodas, bedizened with a fairground decoration of gilded cardboard, spangles, and mirror-glass. Here on carpets and at low tables friends would be entertained by feasting and music – chiefly from portable gramophones. The more pretentious pavilions contained potted trees laden with almond or peach blossom. At least, so it appeared until this inflorescence was submitted to close inspection, when the several thousand delicate blossoms proved to be made of paper. Such art, such ingenuity had gone into these creations that it was hard to believe that they were not, indeed, the vulgar and quite unacceptable real thing. There was another tree, too, a larger one, from which the unrefined foliage had been removed, and from the branches were suspended the gifts destined for the hundred and ten Buddhist monks who were the district's spiritual advisers. All the presents – mostly aluminium cooking utensils – were contained in white paper bags which had been supplied, without charge, I was told, by a local firm in exchange for permission to print upon them the firm's name, together with an appropriate text in somewhat smaller lettering.

At three o'clock precisely, the ceremonial march of the holy men was due to take place. For this moment – the culmination of the year's activities – the whole population was lined up, having that morning observed solemn fast. Not until their venerated guests had eaten would they break bread. Matrons, who had done their hair for the occasion in the most elaborate and matriarchal fashion, looked as if they were balancing shining cauldrons upon their heads. The faces of the young girls and children were faultless masks of white complexion-protecting powdered bark. From each adult mouth protruded a ceremonial cheroot of enormous length, its barrel swathed in white or scarlet paper. There was a smart tattoo of gongs, a general hiss of excitement and respect, and the leader of the saintly procession came into view. A proud Burmese citizen at my elbow told me that enough had been collected in the neighbourhood to give each of the hundred and ten pongyis a present of fifty rupees. To the gong's thudding the procession continued towards the Christmas tree with its burden of cooking pots. The distribution was made, the faces of both donors and recipients frozen by the solemnity of the occasion. After that the great moment had come when the possessors of pavilions could supplicate their spiritual lords to permit them to acquire merit by partaking of the food which had been prepared. Only when the unworldly stomachs had been filled would the family be entitled to clear up what was left.

At nine o'clock in the evening the secular celebrations began. On a raised platform two clowns were giving a slapstick performance, which was funny enough – even when not a word of the dialogue could be understood. At regular intervals an actress came in and sang and danced. She was a tiny, doll-like creature with a face that was plain and even sullen in repose. But as soon as she began to dance she became transfigured. She had all the poise and fire of a Spanish flamenco dancer, plus the snake-like head and eye movements of an Indian. To this she added the Burmese speciality of thrusting out her arms in such extraordinary positions that they appeared to be dislocated at the elbows. As she leaped and cavorted she repeatedly kicked away from her prancing but invisible feet the long skirt and train of the ancient Burmese court-dress she wore – a difficult feat which has been incorporated into the formal movements of the dance. Sometimes the clowns joined in, dancing in mimicry of the actress, who, as soon as she had finished her piece, would suddenly relapse into a set pose, turn her back on the public, and squatting on her heels, make up her face or drink tea.

This performance would go on until one-thirty in the morning, when straight theatrical shows, lasting until dawn, would begin in other parts of the pwè-ground. For over four hours these clowns would pour out a stream of extempore wit and topical allusion, while the two or three actresses of the company would wriggle and leap. Only then would this typical pantomime audience have had their temporary fill of knockabout farce and be ready to face situation and plot.

The Burmese adore comedy and although the strait-laced classical plays of neighbouring countries have been introduced in the past, they are soon so completely transformed by buffoonery as to become unrecognizable. Thus the *Ramayana*, the play of Sanskrit origin, which runs to some sixty thousand verses and takes three days to present in an abbreviated form, could never survive in Burma. There is no action, and gesture is all-important; so much so that elaborate treatises have been written on the various gestures and their meaning. When the Burmese conquered Siam they may have felt some rankling sense of inferiority, as conquerors sometimes do, in the face of what they suspect to be the more polished culture of the defeated. Something of this kind, perhaps, led to an attempted transplantation of this elephantine divertissement. But it was quite unable to survive Burmese comic genius. Burmese parodists went eagerly to work on the Sanskrit gods and goddesses, who soon appeared as pie-slinging comedians. The ancient Burmese miracle plays suffered a similar fate, degenerating into pure farce. Actors had to be threatened with magical sanctions, in the form of death from supernaturally induced diarrhoea, to restrain them from actually introducing skits on religion into their performances.

Unlike their neighbours, the Siamese, the Javanese, and the Cambodians, the Burmese have never had shadow plays. On the other hand, they have possessed since earliest times a well-developed and highly interesting puppet show. This, according to Dr Maung Htin Aung, the authority on Burmese drama, began to decay immediately after royal patronage was lost with the dethronement of the last Burmese king. In his work upon the Burmese theatre this authority says that when in 1921 a puppet performance was given at Pegu, English officials asked to be his father's guests, for although they had been some years in Burma, they had never been able to find a puppet show. In those days there were only two companies left, and in 1936, says Dr Maung Htin Aung, the puppet show definitely ceased to exist.

In view of these findings by an expert I must count myself as exceptionally lucky – particularly after missing by a hair's breadth in Cambodia, the year before, the last of the Cambodian ballets and shadow plays – to have stumbled quite accidentally on a full-scale puppet show of the type supposed to be extinct. The puppet show was being presented a few yards along the street from the clowns and dancers; that is to say about three miles from the centre of Rangoon.

During the day a large stage had been put up with a proper drop-curtain, and for about an hour before the show started a full-scale orchestra had set to work to attract an audience. The instruments consisted of a heavily carved and gilded circular frame containing seventeen gongs of various diameters and another housing as many drums. There was a large and very decorative boat-shaped xylophone, several big drums, and several pairs of cymbals. The air was sketched in by a player upon a hnè – the Burmese flute terminating in a horn, which produces notes of a singularly penetrative quality.

With goodwill and fair perseverance one can acquire a taste for this music, the keynote of which is unabashed vivacity.

Through the wide cracks in the makeshift stage-carpentry, the puppet-masters could be seen, engaged in prayer for some time before the show began. Presumably these prayers are to the thirty-seven nats, the gods of the ancient Burmese, to whom, Dr Maung Htin Aung says, they also make offerings of food – although I did not see this. When the curtain rose the senior puppet-master leaned over the low back-drop and sang to the audience a lengthy description of the drama to be presented. The curtain was then lowered, and when it was again raised, the stage was occupied by a puppet dressed as a peasant carrying a large sword, and a dragon of the Burmese or serpentine variety. After solo dances, followed by a vigorous combat, the dragon was defeated and, since to show the taking of life – even that of a mythological monster – would have been an impropriety, the Burmese St George mounted the dragon's back and rode away. This curtain raiser was followed by a dance by two genial-looking giants and then a series of dances by various birds, a white horse, and a monkey. Each of these performers had its signature tune which was crashed out by the orchestra whenever it made its appearance. The dances were extremely funny, the puppets being handled with amazing skill. In particular there was a kind of Disney stork, an animal of grotesque benevolence which opened and shut its bill and flapped its eyelids in time to the music. Everything that was essentially stork-like had been captured in this caricature. On the other hand, human puppets, when the intention was not comic, were manipulated with such fidelity to observed human postures and movements that spectators far back in the audience could easily have had the illusion that they were watching flesh-and-blood players.

After these animal interludes the main performance began, a traditional 'royal play' with the King himself, princes and princesses, the ministers, and, of course, clowns. It is interesting that the semi-divine Burmese kings did not object to these stage representations of themselves, insisting only that the court dress, manners, and customs shown should be correct in every detail. On the legitimate stage royal impersonations could not be carried to the length of wearing the golden shoes – supreme symbol of kingly authority – and breaches of this ordinance were, once again, supposed to be followed by supernatural retribution in the form of a mortal attack of diarrhoea.

Oriental crowds in a festive mood are remarkably docile. Nothing seems to disturb their poise, to unsettle their capacity for relaxation. They are prepared to compose themselves at short notice, to watch with utter absorption whatever is offered in the way of entertainment. They never find it necessary to convince themselves or others, by boisterous display, that they are having a good time. Movement is slow and languorous, the crowd's internal currents intertwining with processional solemnity. Like that of some other Far Easterners, the training of the Burmese, however great their curiosity, does not permit them to stare at the extraordinary sight of a foreigner, or to betray any interest other than the discreetest of passing glances. There is no nudging, no muffled giggle, no turning of the head. No other Westerner was to be seen in this gay but decorous concourse; nor did I ever see one on the many subsequent occasions that I visited the pwès at Kemmendine. This seeming indifference was Burmese good breeding. If I happened to be standing at the back of a crowd I could shortly expect a discreet tap on the arm and then an invitation by nods and gestures to make my way to the front. Once in a good position there would be no further overtures; but it was always possible, simply by looking puzzled, to get a description, in halting English, of what was going on. This, since the cross-talk of Burmese comedians is usually bawdy, would be bowdlerized in an attempt to befit it for Western ears. Accompanying actions sometimes made it difficult to impose this censorship. 'See, the lady and the gentleman have gone away to the wood together. Beyond the stage you shall imagine a wood ... now they are disturbed ... suddenly they return.' (A scream of laughter from the crowd.) 'They think this is funny behaving because the lady and the gentleman wear now, without realization, each other's skirts. These jokes are to please the country people who are not serious. For us, too, they are vulgar.'

The Burman's ready kindliness towards the stranger is remarkable, when it is remembered that through failure to spend a token period as a novice in a Buddhist monastery, the foreigner has never quite qualified as a human being. In the old days, indeed, the same auxiliary was applied to visitors from the non-Buddhist world as to pigs or buffaloes. Referring, for instance, to two foreigners, the Burman said, 'two (animals) foreigners'. The contemporary attitude is one of secret compassion. The alien's present incarnation has fallen only just short of success. Many acts of merit in previous existences have rescued him from rebirth as a cockroach or a pariah dog, and all that is now required to attain complete humanity is that final spark of enlightenment provided by the acceptance of the noble eight-fold path. This may be accomplished in the very next existence.

The attitude of the Burmese Buddhist is, then, less exclusive and more encouraging than that of certain Christian sects, with their final damnation through lack of faith. All living things are perfectible in this muted, archaic Darwinism. Even that symbol of all the excellences, the white elephant, had probably passed in previous existences through the condition of an intestinal worm or a sewer rat, and could still return to them – as King Mindon ruled in a specific instance – through loss of accumulated merit, as a consequence of the trampling of a groom.

Clearly the Burmese recognized the virtue which had raised me from the protozoan slime. Observing my interest in the puppet show, one of the stage-hands appeared and invited me back stage. There the puppet-masters took snacks with their families, or slept between acts. They had the grave, dedicated faces of a monkish order and were dressed with elaborate conservatism; turbans wrapped round the old-style bun of hair; longyis tied in front with a great, billowing prodigality of cloth. Their solemn and sacerdotal manner was in no way diminished by the horn-rimmed spectacles they wore. Puppets hung, in bunches like carrots, from the roof. Some of the more extravagantly decked-out specimens were detached and dangled for my admiration. One, stiff with gold thread and brocade, and with an acutely introspective expression, was introduced as 'the Princess of Wales'.

I was allowed to stand and watch over the shoulders of the showmen at their business, noting that effective control of the puppets was not the only consideration. Their hands could be seen by the audience, and these as well as each separate finger had to be moved with prescribed rhythm and exact gesture, like those of a Sanskrit dancer.

As they were by far the best of the few poor examples of Burmese art I had yet seen, I wanted to buy a collection of puppets; but enquiries were met with evasion. The puppets were not to be bought anywhere. They were made specially to the order of the troupe. Where were they made? – Mandalay. (It was always the inaccessible Mandalay to which one was directed, in response to this kind of enquiry.) A few more feelers on the subject and I realized that I had been attempting to trespass in guild preserves, and that puppets were not to be had by outsiders.

When I left I was accompanied by the senior puppet-master to the most fanciful of the nearby pavilions, a pleasure-dome of glittering unsubstantiality, in which a party of upper-class Burmese sat on chairs, thus separated by distinguished discomfort from the mass of their mat-squatting countrymen. On a wicker table – an expensive and rickety European importation – in the pavilion's centre had been placed a bowlful of sinister-looking liquid, its surface broken by lumps of black jelly. Seizing a glass, the senior puppet-master expertly wiped the rim with his fingers, plunged it into the bowl, and removing a gobbet which stuck to the outside edge, handed it to me. With severe hospitality he raised his glass in my direction before putting it to his lips. There was no avoiding this rite. Holding back the black frogspawn with my teeth I drank deeply of the warm, sweetish, iron-tasting liquid.

CHAPTER FOUR

Excursion to the Deep South

THE PROSPECT OF a sea trip to Mergui by coastal steamer was something to exercise the imagination. I had memories of such rovings, vagrant and obscure of purpose, along the Arabian and Red Sea coasts. The ships had been wonderful battered old relics, full of nautical mannerisms and impregnated with the musk of exotic cargoes. They had been laid down in ports like Gdynia, with cabins built round the boiler-room in sensible preparation for Arctic voyagings; and at the end of their lives, when long overdue for the scrap-heap, they had been picked up for a song by Arabs with sharp trading practices, renamed after one of the attributes of the Almighty, *The Righteous* or *The Upright*, and relaunched upon Arabian seas. Such ships were usually skippered by empirical navigators, captains who lost themselves when out of sight of familiar coastal landmarks. They were nearly as useless as the vessels they sailed in; drank like fishes; went in for religious mania, or for spells of mild insanity in which they were liable to stalk the bridge in the nude. The passengers, too, fitted into the general picture; sword-bearing rulers of a corner of a desert, half-crazed lighthouse keepers, broken-down adventurers scraping a living in any dubious enterprise they could smell out. There was no better way to get to know the seamy side of the seafaring life.

From first impressions down by the landing stage, nothing could have looked more hopeful. The Rangoon river-shore was encrusted with deserted junks, showing a fine tangle of masts and archaic demoded rigging, patched and variegated sails, defaced figureheads. At the water's edge there was a desultory skirmishing of pariah dogs. A few ancient gharries were grouped for hire in the shade of the riverine trees, and as their drivers, white-bearded patriarchs, dreamed, bulbuls warbled softly in the branches above them.

Somewhere a gong was being tapped intermittently, in the way that pianos are tinkled upon in English suburbs on fading Sunday afternoons. There was a lassitude in the air propitious to the embarkation upon a voyage to decaying southern ports.

I looked forward to days of enforced meditation, punctuated by meals taken with some garrulous old salt, delighted to have found so appreciative an audience for his fables. It was taken for granted that with the possible exception of a missionary, I should be the only European aboard, but I expected that at the Captain's table I should meet a Chinese merchant on his way to the Mergui archipelago to negotiate for a cargo of edible birds' nests.

From the first glimpse, however, the *Menam* discouraged further indulgence in dreams. It was larger and trimmer, I thought, than the Southern Burmese coastal trade justified. At the moment of my going aboard, a certain amount of fussy repainting was being done, but the smell of turpentine could not entirely overlay a boarding-house whiff of cooking greens. In the cabins there were notices about boat-drills, and others asking passengers to be punctual for 'tiffin'. Dinner was due to be served immediately we sailed, and to nothing less than my dismay this was heralded by one of those tinkling shipboard airs, those witless Alpine glockenspiels, that are heard on transatlantic liners as a prelude to the meal-time interruption of boredom.

On reaching the dining saloon, I made, in the absence of a steward, for the nearest table, at which, although several very obviously English people were already seated, there were a number of vacant places. Before sitting down, I asked as a matter of courtesy, if the vacant places were not reserved. To this question there was no reply although I received several embarrassed looks. I therefore left this table and went and sat down at the next, which appeared to be occupied by, what I imagined from their dress to be, Anglo-Burmese. Apparently some allocation of places had already been made – and evidently on a basis of colour and race. The *Menam* was, in fact, a little enclave of diehard Englishry. It had been years since I visited a British colony, and I had forgotten what it was like. When Burma had gained its independence it had reasonably been made illegal to attempt to exclude Burmese on racial grounds from hotels and clubs in Rangoon. In the few days I had spent there I had come to take for granted, to accept without question or thought, the mingling of English, Burmese, Anglo-Burmese, and Chinese in the hotel bars, lounges, and dining-rooms. And here, in the port of Rangoon, was this floating redoubt of the old system. About the *Menam* there was none of the seedy, globe-trotting fellowship I had hoped for. When the dining saloon was full I saw that the English were seated – with internal social grading carefully maintained, no doubt – at several separate tables. Another had been reserved for a group of Australian Catholic missionaries. At another the pure Burmese had been isolated; while at mine the Anglo-Burmese were gathered together. Soon the ship's wireless operator, an Anglo-Burman, joined us, being evidently excluded from the company of the white ship's officers at meal times. Shortly after I had taken my seat, a steward appeared and came over to ask me if I would like to change my place; but as the Anglo-Burmese seemed not to object to my presence, I decided to stay where I was.

At the shipping office I had enquired hopefully about the cooking, remembering that on very small ships you can sometimes eat the adventurous food cooked in the crew's galley. All the cooks, said the shipping clerk, were Chinese. But now I knew that my relief had been premature and the meaning of that whiff of greens was explained. Chinese cooks there were; but they had been compelled to adapt themselves to a new and strange culinary art – one in which specific gravity could matter more than flavour. 'Thick or clear soup, sir?' the steward murmured in my ear. After that came stewed meat with the boiled vegetables; then college pudding.

Fortunately we were too few and too divided for the traditional frolics to be arranged; but there were deck-quoits, and a library with a fair assortment of such titles as *Lay Her Among the Lilies*. The key was found and the volumes, bright with their dust-jacket promise of rape and murder, distributed against signature in the book. Meanwhile the flat-lands of the delta slipped past in the darkness, broken only by the wallowing passage of a junk, with lamps at its masthead, or a twinkle of illumination outlining the shape of a pagoda on the land.

I had come to be thankful for the social exclusiveness through which I found myself among the Anglo-Burmese. Hearing, with some surprise, that I was really interested in Burma, one of my fellow-diners asked if I would like to meet a Burman of some renown who was travelling in the ship, a fellow-citizen of his who was returning to Moulmein after spending some time in hospital in Rangoon. This proved to be one of the most happy contacts I made in Burma.

I was presented to U Tun Win next morning, and found him seated at table, separating the flakes of his breakfast cereal as if they had been the leaves of an incunabulum. His small, frail, aged body was animated by an extraordinary alertness, and when I or anyone else produced some piece of politely empty small-talk, he would stop with upraised spoon or fork, intent and smiling dreamily as if in appreciation of good music. Whenever he put a question he would await the answer with the nervous impatience of a terrier on guard at a rabbit hole. Then he would repeat it aloud, very slowly, dissecting it clause by clause, as if subjecting it to the arguments of learned counsel, before passing, with nods of approval, the verdict, 'Good – yes, very good.' He was prone to a materialistic over-simplification of human motives, which led him into a mistaken estimation of the reasons for the Anglo-Saxon passengers' habit of arriving for their meals up to an hour later than the advertised time. 'It is their habit to do this because they judge that in this way they can be served with superior food without arousing our unfavourable comment.'

U Tun Win was, indeed, a most delightful old man, an ex-barrister who possessed inexhaustible information about his country, and had also acquired the ability, rather uncommon in the Orient, to arrange his facts and conclusions in a logical, organized manner.

It was U Tun Win who went to the trouble of explaining the Land Nationalization Act to me, a radical piece of land reform, comparable with that carried out in China by Mao Tse-tung. Under this enactment any bona fide landless cultivator will be given ten acres of land, which is the maximum it is believed that he can work efficiently by his own labour and with one yoke of oxen. Landowners are to be compensated by receiving an amount in cash equal to twelve times the annual tax they pay on the land relinquished. This measure, said U Tun Win, was really outright confiscation, because the amount of compensation was very small and would only be paid when the government was in a position to do so – and you knew what that meant. The maximum amount of land any bona fide cultivator could hold – and he must work it himself, or with his family – was fifty acres (as compared with three hundred acres allowed in their land reforms by the government of Pakistan).

U Tun Win hastened to say that he could not approve of this measure which he regarded as little less than robbery. In defence of his opinion he quoted certain utterances of the Buddha which he interpreted, although I could not agree with him, as condoning the accumulation of property, and the capitalist order in general. U Tun Win was a Mon (as the Talaings of old are now called) and many of his people in the Tavoy, Moulmein, and Mergui districts are in revolt against the government. They would be willing to unite with the Karens in the formation of an independent Mon-Karen State, he said. It was evident from what he told me that this state, if ever it came into being, would be reactionary by comparison with the Union of Burma, and that the land nationalization measures would be abolished in Mon-Karen areas.

It is remarkable how intimate a part religion plays in the life and thought of the Burmese, when there is no attempt to canalize it into public observances restricted to one day in the week. U Tun Win attacked the Land Nationalization Act because, quite sincerely, I believe, he considered it contrary to Buddhist teaching. Thakin Nu, the Prime Minister, found it necessary to invoke precisely the same religious authority when the bill was submitted to parliament. His speech on this occasion was nothing less than a lengthy sermon, with immense quotations from the Buddhist scriptures and a searching analysis from the religious point of view of the illusion of wealth. One can imagine the consternation, the exchange of embarrassed glances, if the present Prime Minister of Great Britain took it into his head to engage in a fervent advocation of primitive Christianity, including the quotation *in extenso* of the Sermon on the Mount, during, say, the debate on the Steel Nationalization Act.

However, much as U Tun Win could not agree with the action that had been taken, he agreed that something drastic had to be done. Following in the footsteps of the English, a horde of hereditary Indian money-lenders – the Chettyars – came to Burma. With centuries of money-lending technique behind them, they found the Burmese an easy prey. Agents were sent into villages to induce Burmese farmers to accept loans. Enchanted at the prospect of being able to give parties and pay for pwès out of harvests they had yet to reap, the farmers rushed to take the money at two per cent *per month*. By 1945 sixty per cent of the petty rice lands of southern Burma had fallen by foreclosure into the hands of the Chettyars, who had increased their capital ten times since their arrival in the country. The Indian community, as a whole, owned two-thirds of Burmese agricultural land. The interests of the Chettyars were purely financial, and as the weight of custom prevented them from leaving their traditional avocation and becoming farmers, they let the lands to the highest bidder, but without security of lease. This rack-renting brought about a steady decline in the fertility of the soil, because the tenant farmer, who could not be sure of keeping his land for more than a season, took no pains to improve it, and did not even trouble to keep the bunds (water-retaining dykes) in repair. Land at Moulmein, said U Tun Win, which in the time of their forefathers had yielded sixty bags of paddy per acre, was now down to a yield of twenty-five. What was worse, free and comparatively prosperous Burmese farmers had been turned into a landless agricultural proletariat, from whose ranks the bandit and insurgent forces were readily recruited. 'Thus, if property is not given to those without property much misery is caused,' said the Buddha, in the Çakkravatti Sermon.

Still, U Tun Win would not go so far as confiscation. What should be done, he said, was to compel landowners by law to improve their land, and only if they failed to do this should the land be resumed by the government. You would get the land all the same, he said (with the suspicion of a wink), because nothing would ever make the Chettyars work, and they would have to go. But there would be no outright injustice, no flagrant conflict with religious principle.

The morning was lustrous. We were about half a mile off shore, approaching Moulmein, and the sun gleamed on a landscape brilliant with the fresh greens of marshy vegetation. There was a narrow coastal plain, with oxen feeding in the grass down by the many creeks that intersected it. Gondola-like sampans were moored at the mouths of inlets, their double sterns painted in red, white, and orange geometrical shapes. Inland four junks in line, showing only the burnt-umber triangular fins of their sails, passed shark-like along some unseen waterway. An occasional tall tree among the luminous serration of water palms by the shore was silhouetted against a soft, water-colour smear of hills. From each hill's summit protruded the white nipple of a pagoda. Butterflies came floating out to the ship; the sombrely splendid ones of the South-East Asian forests. Blown up against the deck-houses and derricks they were held there for an instant, flattened as if for exhibition, before fluttering away.

We passed a headland tipped with sand, on which egrets swarmed like white maggots. A junk reeled by in the glassy billows; a black, raffish silhouette, with delicately tapering bows, and a tiered poop with the passengers in their coloured silks crowding to the balustrade. Its great blood-red sail was carried like a banner. Had I known it, I could have had a stylish passage down to Mergui in one of these craft, and thus have avoided the stifling bourgeois atmosphere of the *Menam*.

My favourite descriptive writer on Burma, the Reverend Mr Malcolm, an American Baptist missionary, was much impressed with this prospect when, in 1835, he visited Moulmein. 'The scenery is rendered romantic and peculiar,' he notes, 'by small mountains, arising abruptly from the level fields to the height of four, five, and six hundred feet; the base scarcely exceeding the size of the summit.' The worthy man's aesthetic satisfaction is blighted, however, by another feature (which I have already mentioned) of this otherwise peerless landscape.

On the summits of many of them, apparently inaccessible to human feet, Boodhist zeal has erected pagodas, whose white forms, conspicuous far and near, remind the traveller every moment that he surveys a region covered with the shadows of spiritual death. Some of the smaller hills I ascended. My heart sickened as I stood beside the dumb gods of this deluded people ... nothing is left to prove they have been, but their decayed pagodas, misshapen gods, and unblessed graves.

I find books by early Victorian missionaries extremely readable. These vigorous men showed an unquenchable curiosity about every aspect of the countries in which they struggled for the salvation of souls. As a result they are full of exact information about the geology, the natural history, products, commerce, and customs of the people. Their pages are naturally salted with quotations from the more ferocious books of the Old Testament and they are scandalized by almost everything they see; but the main thing is that, whether they disapprove or not, they write it all down. With all their arrogant fanaticism, their stupid condemnation of all they do not understand, how much more one can learn about the country from them than from so many modern collections of impressions, with their amused tolerance, their tepid well-mannered sympathy.

Malcolm went to Moulmein to combat polygamy, establish a native seminary, and – rather remarkably – to put into practice a plan for giving English names to the native children. Although he never ceases to insist that the people of Moulmein are 'perishing in their sins' – for 'Boodhists have no idea of the remission of sins any way. Their only hope is to balance them with merit' – he seems to have come off rather well at the hands of the benighted heathen.

Wherever we stopped to eat, we entered a house freely and were immediately offered clean mats, and treated with the utmost hospitality ... they sometimes expostulated with the servant, as he was cooking our meals, that he had brought rice and fowls, instead of allowing them to furnish our table. They (the missionaries) are bountifully supplied, even where their message meets only with opposition.

On the whole the reverend gentleman seems to find this display of apparent virtue in the heathen a source of irritation. It is an imposture, he decides. 'Though, in this world, hypocrites mingle with God's people, and resemble them,' he moralizes, 'the Great Shepherd instantly detects them, and, at the appointed time, will unerringly divide them.' This comforting thought expressed, the author feels entitled to call a truce to sermonizing and launches into a most exact description of brahminy cattle.

Moulmein came into sight beyond a headland; the twin Mogul towers of a mosque rising above a spinney of masts, the receding planes of corrugated iron roofs, palms brandished like feather-dusters held at many angles, the tarnished gold of pagodas on the skyline.

As the ship approached the shore the details took recognizable shape. There were the decaying houses of vanished commercial dynasties, perhaps more noble in their decline than in their heyday. An old warehouse with a baroque eau-de-nil façade had become a cinema. On a ribbon of sand at the water's edge a few vultures spread their wings furtively over what the sea had surrendered to them. The colours of this town were old and faded, degraded and washed out: the red of rust, the greens and greys of patinas and stains. A stench of mud and decomposing vegetation lowered itself like a blanket over the ship.

It was still early morning when we tied up alongside the wharf, and about an hour later I was just about to sit down to breakfast when an exceedingly handsome young Burman came to my table and introduced himself as U Tun Win's son. U Tun Win had mentioned vaguely that he expected me to be his guest as long as the ship stayed at Moulmein, but I had taken this no more seriously than a European invitation of the 'do look in and see us any time you happen to be round our way' variety. Since the old man had gone ashore without saying goodbye, I did not expect to see him again. I now learned from his son – who told me to call him by his familiar name of Oh-oh – that the invitation had been seriously meant indeed. In fact an intensive programme of sightseeing had been arranged in the hour U Tun Win had been ashore. Beyond the wharf-gate a canary-coloured jeep awaited us. In this, said Oh-oh, we would first see the sights of the town. At eleven o'clock we were invited to a party given by a family whose son had just entered the Buddhist novitiate. Then we would breakfast, after which he proposed an excursion into the surrounding countryside, since I should naturally want to visit the principal pagodas of the Moulmein district. The suggestion of breakfasting at about midday was my first introduction to the Burmese custom of taking one's first meal of the day – universally known as breakfast – at any time between dawn and three thirty in the afternoon. Somewhat alarmed at this suggestion – although otherwise, of course, enchanted – I insisted on Oh-oh's joining me there and then at the bacon and eggs.

Moulmein was a town of strong baroque flavour. It was as if the essence of the Renaissance had finally reached it via Portugal, and after careful straining through an Indian mesh. There was a spaciousness of planning; an evidence of studied proportion about the old stone houses. Doors and windows were often flanked with heavy double columns. Much crudely stained glass was to be seen. Balconies were of wrought iron and from the eaves depended stalactites of fretted woodwork. The original roofs had been replaced by corrugated iron. It was as if an Indian architect had been responsible for this style, after spending perhaps a week in Goa. Crows alighted and perched swaying on the potted sunflowers put out on balconies. Rows of coconuts had been suspended from the eaves for the tutelary spirits' accommodation.

The Indians were here in strength and had brought with them their sacred cows, their 'medical halls', their 'select recommended gents' oriental tailors'. Business was done beneath fascia boards painted with ferocious tigers, firing howitzers, and bombing planes. The cinema with the fine old façade was showing *The Good Earth* and had distributed its advertising boards in various parts of the town. One leaned against one of the multiple trunks of a huge banyan tree, which was the home of one or more nats, for shrines were attached to it, and votive wooden horses hung from its boughs. Girls sat in a streamer-decorated shop and sewed shirts while a musician played to them on a mandolin. In the town lock-up, a little further down the street, a single prisoner balanced on one leg in a bamboo cage. At the other end of the town there had been an attempt at road repairs, but this had clearly been abandoned several years ago. Now the steamroller, which had been left where it stood, was already sunken to its axles. In a few more years it would probably have disappeared from sight, a rich find for the archaeologist of future centuries.

There was, of course, a festival going on, with booths and pavilions filling all the side streets and open spaces. Some of the citizens, anticipating the distractions of the evening, already carried hydrogen-filled balloons as they went about their business. The main street was jammed with bullock-carts and jeeps. All the latter had been vividly repainted and carried such names as 'Hep-Cat' and 'Lady for a Night'. Oh-oh's was called 'Cupid'.

Above the cheerful animation of this scene rose in majestic aloofness the fabulous, almost unearthly, golden shape of the Old Moulmein Pagoda; so hateful to Malcolm, so nostalgically romantic to Kipling. It was all that remained without change of the magnificence of the East.

The novitiate party was held over U Sein's pawnshop. Although the Burmese are less interested in money than most other races, it is usual to announce the cost of such celebrations. In honour of their son's coming of age and his automatically entering a monastery for a short period, the U Sein family had spent five thousand rupees – say four hundred pounds. The reception would last three days, and, in the biblical manner, guests were to be brought in from the highways and byways. The U Seins had also paid for an open-air theatrical show for the three nights.

It called for a high order of organizing ability to deal with the crush of guests, but when the Burmese felt like it they could be very efficient. You went in by one door and left by another, passing in the interim through the successive stages of the U Sein hospitality. Just by the entrance, the members of the family, in gorgeous turn-out, awaited new arrivals. Only the son, the *raison d'être* of the party, was not present, for he had already, with shaven head and in yellow robes, made his token renunciation of the world. In the background lurked a pair of young ladies, as bejewelled as Eastern queens, whose office it was to collect the shoes. It was at this point that the organization was so noticeable, because in exchange for the shoes you received a numbered fan, and a slip bearing a corresponding number was put in the shoes themselves. There was a room full of them, all arranged in numerical order.

The first part of the reception took place on the first floor. Here, in a room which was as big as a small dance-hall, about two hundred guests were seated on mats on the polished floor. As each new party appeared at the top of the staircase, hostesses floated towards them and shepherded them across the room to the patches of vacant floor space. These girls had developed a kind of cinema-usherette technique, signalling to each other with their hands as usherettes do with torches. Once the party was seated other lady-helps materialized, gliding up with silver trays set with the impedimenta of betel-chewing (clearly a convention, since no one chewed), and others containing saucers heaped with such Burmese hors-d'œuvres as pickled tea-leaves, salted ginger, fried garlic, sesamum seeds, roasted peas, and dried, shredded prawns. It was the accepted thing to sit round this refection for about an hour, by which time 'breakfast' would be ready.

Fortunately, orientals are not obsessed by the necessity of keeping up polite conversation. It is sufficient to contribute an occasional remark; to produce for the benefit of those sitting opposite, a smile, which, indeed, tends after a time to stiffen into the kind of grimace produced at the demand of the old-fashioned photographer. It seems, even, that the European capacity for sustained conversation is found rather wearisome in the Far East. There we sat with unexerted sociability, nibbling occasionally at the tea-leaves or prawns, speculating on the fee the principal actor would demand that evening, and admiring the furnishings of the room. One of these was a three-dimensional picture, a grotto bespangled with fragments of mirror-glass and adorned with artificial flowers in which cut-out figures knelt in adoration of the Virgin Mary. There was a coronation of King George V, charged with the flat detail and oppressive colours of such works of art, and a collection of portraits of American film stars, about a hundred of them, all stuck side by side in a frame. In the corner a Buddhist shrine had been fixed up on a platform. It was a standard commercial product put out by a Burmese manufacturing firm, and available in several sizes – of which this was the largest – all in identical style and furnishings. In addition to concealed lighting supplied by the makers, the pawnshop had added, as befitted a successful enterprise, fluorescent tubes of alternate pink and green.

Representatives of all the races of Moulmein had come to the party; Indians, Malays, and, of course, Anglo-Burmese, who wore European clothes, and with a certain difficulty forced their thoughts into an English linguistic mould. The Burmese women were resplendent as brides, with their haloes of white blossoms. I wondered how many pledges the pawnshop had temporarily relinquished to decorate for an hour those much braceleted arms, those pearl-adorned throats.

Music had been provided, so a notice said, by the New Electric Photographic Studio, which evidently sold gramophones and radio sets as well. They blasted us from several loudspeakers, playing without pause or remission a resounding medley of swing and the national music of which Malcolm said, 'it is keen and shrill ... although I never heard pleasant tunes from it'.

After the customary hour had passed, our group became a little fidgety. Oh-oh leaned across to tell me, in his hesitant English, that by this time breakfast should have been ready. It seemed that the great influx of guests had strained the organization. The sign that food was prepared for us would be given by the arrival of one of the young lady helpers, who would present each of us with a flower. Soon after, in fact, she arrived; cool, correctly aloof and imperturbable, despite the heat and the enforced speeding up of her normal pace. As promised, we received our flowers; white orchids – artificial, of course, since it would have been demeaning to the house to have offered anything so ordinary as a genuine blossom.

Trooping downstairs we presented our flowers for inspection to more helpers, who, after a glance at them, led us to our table. In a matter of seconds we were served plain and fancy cake, ice-cream and sago pudding flavoured with coconut and various seeds. Following the example of the others I added these ingredients together, stirred them up and swallowed the result with a spoon. Eating took perhaps ten minutes. After that it was in order to leave. We passed out, after showing our fans and collecting our shoes, by the exit door. On one side a maiden waited holding out foot-long cheroots. On the other stood a large tub filled with paper bags containing gifts for each departing guest. Mine was an aluminium basin.

What was left of the morning was spent in routine visits to Oh-oh's relations and friends. Such calls involved no tiresome exchange of platitudes. You just sat down, explained what you were doing there, smiled a little, waited a little. Unexplained persons drifted in from the street, or appeared from inner rooms, looked at you and went away. Usually a bottle of branded mineral water – occasionally from a precious reserve of Coca-Cola – was produced in your honour. These were the unceremonial visitings of honest country people the world over.

At the very hottest time of the early afternoon, when for a moment I thought regretfully of the naps the sahibs on the *Menam* would just be about to take under the electric fans in their cabins, I learned that we were going for a drive outside town. Seven of us – the oriental minimum of passengers – squeezed into the jeep, and we were off to visit a pagoda at a village called Mudon, a Sunday afternoon jaunt which seemed to be an institution. It now occurred to me to mention that a member of the Special Branch of the Burmese Police who had visited the ship had emphasized that on no account should I leave the town, and that to attempt to do so was to risk kidnapping or assassination. Oh-oh, replying with his calm Burmese smile, said there was no danger. We would all go to Mudon. And how far away was Mudon? Eighteen miles, Oh-oh said. Slightly alarmed by now, as I had imagined that this village was an outer suburb of Moulmein, I asked again, were there any Karen rebels in the neighbourhood? Oh-oh said there were. And did they ambush cars? He shook his head. Attack them?... An emphatic nod. So that was it. He had not understood. The word ambush had been too much. And there the difficulty lay in our communication with each other. So much of what was not understood was passed over with a smile and a nod. It was better to say yes, and let it go at that, than to admit that one hadn't understood the question.

All our party spoke English, and one, a garlanded Burmese lady with the name of Amelia Williams, actually taught it. But it was a special brand of English, based on the Old Testament and the Sankey and Moody of the Baptist missions. Those whose knowledge of the language had been gained in this way had a queer, archaic flavour about their speech. One took food, rather than ate; strove to attain rather than tried to get. People were stricken with divers sicknesses rather than become ill; from which they did not die, but succumbed, or rendered up the spirit. Into this sonorous idiom many raucous notes had been introduced, the jargon from technical books, American cinema-slang. Thus, removed from its fresh, native sources, English, still the lingua franca of much of southern Asia, was degenerating into a kind of Creole. Already, in such a simple matter as enquiring about the situation outside Moulmein, I could not quite make myself understood. There seemed to be no way of finding out just what risks were involved. Oh-oh, smiling continually, said that it was dangerous, and yet somehow not dangerous. People got shot sometimes; but this fate, mysteriously, could not happen to us. There was a tight ring of insurgents round Moulmein, but in some unexplained way we could pass unscathed through this cordon and reach Mudon.

Our road was through country which had once been jungle and would soon be jungle again. The paddy-fields had been deserted and were grown over with scrub-bush. Where villages, now vanished, had once existed, a few thinning garden flowers grew, and bougainvillaea raced like purple lightning through the thickets. A few hamlets remained, with shacks made of great dried leaves stuck over frames. Girls were strolling about wearing parakeet-crests of flowers, and in this part of Burma – I never saw them again – the bullock-carts were decorated with carvings as intricate as the figureheads on old Maori war-canoes. I tried to buy some carving and Oh-oh, who went off to make enquiries, returned with a small ivory medallion produced for the tourist trade in Mergui. There were a few of the hills which Malcolm had admired so much, geological curiosities with precipitous sides, and virgin jungle growing on the top.

At the end of our pilgrimage we found a lake, pleasantly surrounded by sparsely wooded hillocks. Here our party got down from the jeep, immediately, by way of a holiday convention, donning tinted spectacles. A few more picnicking jeeps were parked on what had been agreed upon as a beauty spot. Soldiers of the Union of Burma army strolled about with rifles slung and parasols opened. The crew of an armoured car were asleep in the shade of their vehicle and were not roused by a distant exchange of shots. The pagoda was built entirely of corrugated iron, but seen across the water the composition of striated greys and silvers was not out of harmony with its surroundings.

After dutifully viewing the pagoda of Mudon we now set off again at full speed, with the intention, it seemed, of pushing as far eastwards as we could without running into a battle. The limit was reached at the village of Kyaik Maraw, on the Altaran River, which had been the scene of a sharp fight a few days previously. From the sight of serene groups of Burmese girls in the streets it was hard to imagine that this was an outpost, with Mon-Karen insurgents on the other bank of the river. While we stood on the bank and looked across the stream to where, half a mile away, a pair of insurgent soldiers were doing something to a sampan, a fisherman came past, paddling his canoe after his net which was floating downstream at a fair speed. Sticks protruded from various points in the net, and just as it passed us one of the sticks dipped, in indication that a fish had been caught. At a cry from Oh-oh, the fisherman shot over to this place, extracted the catch, paddled back to us, and handed it to Oh-oh, in exchange for a few small coins. Then he was off again like a streak, paddling furiously to overtake his fast-disappearing net. The fish, a fine, large, regularly shaped specimen, was laid tenderly in the shade, and eyes were averted while it leaped and quivered in mortal convulsion. Fishermen, as takers of life, are much despised by the orthodox Burmese, who, occasionally, as part of a celebration, or in a moment of religious fervour, buy the contents of a net and throw them back into the river. The fishermen have always claimed in self-defence that they do not kill the fish or even damage them by the use of a hook. All they do is to put them out on the bank to dry after their long soaking in the water. If in this process they should happen to die, there can be no harm in eating them.

It proved that the bond which, with the exception of Mrs Williams, united my friends, was a common membership or ex-membership of the local Boy Scouts' troop, of which Oh-oh was scout master. Back in Moulmein, we visited each home in turn, to view the trophies accorded for scout-lore, and groups photographed at annual jamborees.

Easterners have an ostrich digestion for all that promises, however obscurely, to benefit their souls. Any association with a profession of ideals is eagerly embraced. Whether gained as Scouts, Rotarians, Masons, Rosicrucians, or Oxford Groupers, a contribution of virtue is eagerly accepted and added to the jackdaw store. When my friends spoke of camping they did so with reverence. It ranked as a kind of yoga exercise helping to quicken one's step on the road to salvation.

They had all been to the Baptist school, where, in pursuance of the policy instituted in Malcolm's time, they had been given such names as John, Michael, or Peter, which the missionaries had believed would help them in their struggle with the devil. These names had been taken, and in most cases added to those already possessed. Sometimes a surprising amalgam resulted. Amongst the members of the Moulmein Scout troop were a Sunny Jim Than Myint, an Abraham Ba Nyunt Dashwood, and an Edwin Saung Chin Stephen Min. Not all of these had become Baptists, but many of those who had, had then gone one step further and, without racial justification, described themselves as Anglo-Burmese.

*

At five o'clock I dined with U Tun Win. Dinner was on the enormous balcony of his wooden house, and the old man asked if I had any objection to his sitting cross-legged on the seat of his chair, as he could never really relax in any other position. While we toyed with the usual Burmese hors-d'œuvres, a servant swarmed up a palm in the garden and hacked off coconuts to be used in the curry. Among the dishes served was some dried fish, which attracted a handsome Siamese cat. Springing on the table, where its presence was tolerated, it waited until its master's head was turned, and then seized the tail. This, it seemed, was a morsel of exceptional succulence, which U Tun Win was not prepared to give up, and, recovering it after a short struggle, he ate it hastily.

Although U Tun Win claimed that Burmese women enjoyed absolute equality with men, and quoted long extracts from the ancient Laws of Manu in support of this contention, none of his several daughters was to be seen. According to custom they would eat in one of the inner rooms, after their father had finished his meal. The mother had been dead some years and the old man said that he relished his new freedom too keenly to contemplate re-marriage. From his account the Burmese were exceedingly liberal in matrimonial matters – though slightly less so down in the conservative south. Marriage is considered to exist, without further ceremony, when a couple are seen to eat together; although there is nothing particularly compromising about people of different sexes sleeping in the same room. Divorce takes place by mutual consent, without going to court; and if a man enters a monastery, his wife can remarry at the end of seven days. Wives and husbands retain their separate property, but infinite legal complications are introduced in divorce cases over the matter of the children's maintenance. A Christian cannot marry a Buddhist in the informal manner which is customary when both parties are Buddhists. In this case a legal ceremony is required; and if a foreigner shows preference for the custom of the country by simply living with a Burmese woman, she has the right to go before the court and demand that he be legally declared her husband.

Many Westerners, despite the evidence of the Old Testament,

cling to a smug belief that romantic love is a Western invention, dating vaguely from the era of chivalry. With this goes the equally fallacious opinion that Easterners are coolly matter-of-fact in their relations between the sexes. This view is reflected in the novelist's stock portrait of the white-man-in-exile's dusky mistress; an acquiescent shadow, who comes to life only if thrown aside, when, sinister and vindictive, she is ready with the wasting poison. This matter-of-factness does not exist. Although much sexual freedom before marriage is the rule in most Eastern races, courtship is often very prolonged and subjected to all kinds of self-imposed restrictions. In many parts eliminative contests are arranged between suitors, and there is much serenading and creation of simple poetry. An old-style Moulmein courtship took about three years, said U Tun Win, to develop through all its stages. He did not, however, mention a curious custom of the district – a Mon one – which was described to me later by a European who had married a local girl – although he denied having taken part in this ceremony himself.

All the Mon houses are built on piles, with floors about four feet above ground. On the floor of a certain room of each house there is a small hole, through which a hand can pass. About dusk each day, the admirers of a girl of marriageable age will start to collect near her residence, and as soon as it is dark, each youth will, in the order of his arrival, take his turn to go under the house and pass his hand up through the hole in the floor. The girl sits on the floor near the hole, and as the hand appears, she holds it in one of hers. Etiquette demands that she must clasp each hand, but as soon as she releases it the admirer must depart, allowing the next man in turn to take his place. Although the girl cannot see the man, and neither is allowed to speak, she is supposed to be able to recognize the various hands, and shows her favour by holding one hand longer than the rest.

In view of the extraordinary freedom existing in matrimonial affairs, it is remarkable that the law should interfere more in matters relating to property than it does in the West. The Burmese Buddhist has no testamentary powers. Upon his death his property is divided among his family in proportions laid down by the ancient Indian legal code which the country adopted in remote times. When I asked what happened if there were families by more than one wife, U Tun Win said that every contingency was provided for, but the law was so complex on such points that an exposition of it would occupy what remained of the evening.

Although U Tun Win kindly invited me to spend the night in his house, there was some doubt about the time the ship would be sailing next morning so, rather than be stranded in Moulmein for a week, I felt it safer to return. On the way to the quay I passed the procession with which the pwè would be inaugurated. First came one of the glittering manufactured Buddhist shrines, carried on a pedicab. It was lit by festoons of coloured electric bulbs, supplied from an accumulator carried on another pedicab just behind. After that came an ex-American army GMT truck which had been painted – tyres included – bright scarlet, and on which a harp had been mounted. The music plucked from the strings of this was broadcast through an amplifying system, so that every corner of Moulmein, the cabins of the *Menam* included, was penetrated by a powerful twanging.

We were later than had been expected in finishing the loading of our cargo of rubber next day. In the morning the Karen Bishop of Tenasserim came aboard and preached a sermon on moral re-armament, devoutly listened to by the Burmese and Anglo-Burmese, whether Christian or not. Meanwhile the radio had been left on, tuned into London, though the reception was weak and distorted. Sometimes it faded out altogether and the crisp voice of the overseas announcer was replaced by the wavering semitones of a vina played by someone in Colombo. The English, none of whom seemed to have bothered to go ashore, sat relaxed before their beers in comfortable boredom. One was making a rug.

We had been joined by a party of young Anglo-Burmese women who had convinced their doctors that they were in need of a bracing sea voyage; and now, released from the pressure of the suburban English life they had inherited along with their names, they exploded in an effervescence of girlish high spirits. Led by a Mrs Forbes-

Russell, a strapping sixth-former in a longyi, they romped about, discharging gushes of long-stored emotion on appropriate objects: awe at the vision of the engine-room, consternation at the notices relating to alarm signals given in emergency, delight at the huge fans, set in frantic motion at the pressing of a button. Like many provincial travellers they had been afraid of starving on the voyage and had brought with them pots filled with delicious messes of kyaw-swe – vermicelli fried in the Burmese style. Soon platefuls were being distributed to passengers in the first-class saloon – offered even, to their obvious embarrassment, to the sahibs. Fortunately, further excesses of attempted fraternization were prevented by the ship's anchors being raised, when, despite the sea's being as flat as the surface of a frozen lake, the newcomers, snatching up their bottles of eau-de-cologne, retired to be ill. At tea-time they appeared again, only to be shaken by the sight of honey on the table. In Burma this is used principally to preserve the corpses of holy men for the decent period of a year or so which must elapse before they are cremated, and even when offered for consumption is suspected of having been put to this use.

All along the river from Moulmein the banks were covered with rich, velvety turf, with clumps of water-palms kindled by the sun into glowing green fire. As soon as we reached the sea, jungle closed in over the land, tumbling down the low cliff-sides to within a few feet of the water. There were a few small islands, carrying helmets of vegetation, pierced with caves and slashed with white sand where their bases entered the sea. White cranes flew majestically in the tree-tops, and swifts came out to meet us, ringed the ship and flew back. Pagodas had been placed like follies of Hohenstaufen castles, on the sheerest, the most inaccessible spurs.

Further south the coast receded; we passed range after range of pale mountains, seen as a reflection in dark water. Here we saw shoals of flying fish and occasionally a slim, streamlined shape broke surface and skimmed away from us, propelling itself forward in a leap of twenty yards or so by violent oscillations of the tail whenever it touched the water. Finally, in the late afternoon we anchored in the Tavoy River, about twenty miles from the town. It was reported that conditions were so bad there that it was not safe to take the ship in. Lighters were waiting for passengers and cargo, and after an hour we steamed on.

That night I found I had a cabin companion; a Burmese official who had joined the ship at Moulmein. He carried a suitcase filled entirely with copies of *Tit-Bits* and *Reader's Digest*, which he read, lying in his bunk, late into the night. Reading maketh a full man, and I have no doubt that he was full of the concentrated information purveyed by his favourite journals. He was content, however, to remain as he was, without adding the attributes of the conversationalist to those of the reader. During the rest of the voyage, although he smiled when our eyes met, he never spoke. He possessed the knack of manipulating his knife and fork with great efficiency, although he held them as if they had been a chopstick held in each hand. It was evident that he was a man of some consequence, because next day, at Mergui, there was a deputation of notables to meet him. Before going ashore he dressed himself carefully in a flowered shirt and Tyrolean *Lederhosen*.

CHAPTER FIVE

Mergui

WHEN I CAME UP on deck, soon after dawn, we were a few miles short of Mergui and the ship was full of the heavy perfume of the liliaceous flowers of which floral tributes are so often composed. This fragrance of the embalming parlour reached us from jungles which were still a mile or two away. All round the ship were wonderfully complicated fish-traps; elaborate marine corrals fashioned from plaited osiers, with arched openings to permit the entrance of small junks, and narrow footways built all round them to facilitate inspection. Attached to them were rafts with sleeping quarters and the Burmese equivalent of 'mod. con.' Once these floating mazes had been constructed – and no doubt they were capitalist enterprises – there was nothing more to be done than keep up fish-collecting patrols.

Mergui emerged from behind a foreshore of shining slime, from which the ribs of ancient wrecks protruded. A few grey Dutch-shaped roofs thrust up through the mud, with a strip of mist lying among them. There was a gilded pagoda, with causeways up its artificial mound, making it look like a Mayan truncated pyramid. King Island broke off from the mainland, and slipped past on our right, with landslides of swarthy earth showing through the webbing of green. The trees growing on it were so tall that their doubtlessly stout trunks were like long spindly wireless masts. We passed, in midstream, an antique oil tanker, completely coated with rust, called *The Golden Dragon*.

If you had been set on retirement from the world in the traditional South Seas manner of the 'nineties, you need have gone no further than Mergui. Or at least, so it seemed at first sight. It was immediately clear that this place had been purged of the vulgar agitations common to most ports. The jetty had fallen into the harbour and no one had bothered to recover it. Ships anchored a hundred yards off shore, and sampans – when there were any about – unloaded passengers. They were dumped on a sloping wasteland of slime-covered boulders, up which they scrambled and slithered to reach the quay-side. Semi-wrecks lay about the harbour with vitals bursting through their rotting planks. The wharves – mostly empty – were pleasantly styled go-downs. A civil-supplies building – a place of most eerie dilapidation – had convolvulus and flowering bean plants crawling over its façade, and through the paneless upper windows you could see bats hanging from the rafters. On the quay-side a large iron tank bore the notice 'to drink', and a honey and white fishing eagle balanced on its edge, peering wistfully into the inner depths. The junks anchored along the front had small platforms built into their sterns where their guardian spirits could conveniently perch. Well-dressed young men came up and said 'Where are you going?' then walked on, without awaiting an answer.

What, too, could have been more romantic than the traditional products of this island – esculent birds' nests and pearls? True there was also a bit of rubber and some tin; but not enough of either to bring about any rise in the commercial temperature of the place. But, alas, one outstanding characteristic of Mergui eclipsed all others, and would certainly have broken the resolve of the most tenacious escapist. This was the smell. In Eastern travels one becomes so familiar with the smell of open drains that in the end it loses its power to offend. A selective mechanism comes into action. One can sniff appreciatively at the fragrances of drying tobacco leaves, aromatic resins, and incenses while ignoring that of excrement. In Mergui such a discrimination was not possible. The whole of an otherwise charming promenade down by the sea was befouled with a carpet of fish, spread out to decay sufficiently to be regarded as edible in the form of gnapi. 'Most malodorous', as the old Portuguese Father put it, with understatement. 'The common people use a variety ... which neither dogs nor cats will touch. This obviates the necessity of putting a watch over it. This class stinks so badly that people unaccustomed to such a bad smell have to hold their noses when they pass the place where it lies.' Father Manrique's observation was exact. The packs of ill-starred pariahs which infest Mergui's streets, hunting continually for the wherewithal to keep life in their hideous bodies, salute the gnapi beds continually in the usual canine way, but make no attempt to eat it.

Mergui's dog population might prove a further deterrent to the would-be South Seas recluse. There are more dogs than humans; they are a slinking, evil breed, cursed with every conceivable affliction. Their suppurating wounds, their goitres, their tumours are hideously evident on their hairless bodies. Bitches suffering from some ghastly elephantiasis go trailing morbidly swollen paps in the dust. Many were earless, partially blind, and had paralysed or dislocated limbs. There had been couplings with horrid pathological results it was impossible not to see. One dog's hindquarters were completely out of action. It could only drag itself along by its front legs and whenever it stopped, being unable to sit down, it turned round several times and then collapsed. When the final twilight of decrepitude is reached, a ring of dogs forms and, closing in upon the snapping, snarling victim, they devour it. In Upper Burma the only service the Japanese did the people was to eat most of the pariah dogs; which the Burmese will in no circumstances bring himself to kill. Perhaps even the Japanese stomach was turned by the dogs of Mergui.

The main street was Moulmein all over again. English had retained its prestige as the advertising medium. The Oriental Gents Smartman Tailors were there. You could buy an Ideal Leisure-time hat, or observe a cobbler at work under a tiger-flanked 'Shoe to repair invisible'. The pharmaceutical trade was shared by Messrs May and Baker, and Maclean, and the anonymous house responsible for that familiar Burmese specific composed of newly hatched crocodiles in a black unguent. Misguided effort had gone into the manufacture of quaint miniatures, bullock-carts and peacocks, from the mother-of-pearl obtained from the giant conches which litter local beaches.

There was one product of Mergui, famous in the old days, which I could not locate. 'There is a village called Mirgim,' said Caesar Fredericke,

> in whose harbour every yeere there lade some ships with Verzina ... which is an excellent wine ... whose liquor they distill, and so make an excellent drinke cleare as christall, good to the mouth, and better to the stomake, and it hath an excellent gentle virtue, that if one were rotten with the french pockes, drinking good store of this, he shall be whole againe, and I have seene it proved, because that when I was in Cochin, there was a friend of mine, whose nose beganne to drop away with that disease, and he was counselled of the doctors of phisicke, that he should go to Tanasary at the time of the new wines, and that he should drinke of the nyper wie, night and day ... This man went thither, and did so, and I have seene him after with good colour and sound.

In those days Mergui was a port of Siam, as it was a hundred years later when it was the scene of the activities of the English pirate Samuel White, who got himself appointed harbour-master by the Siamese government. White was a latter-day De Brito, but a man of lesser calibre since whilst De Brito set out to turn Lower Burma into a Portuguese possession, all White hoped to do was to fill his pockets as quickly as possible and get back to England. The difference between common piracy and empire-building is a matter of scale and success. If White could have held on to Mergui and facilitated its ultimate annexation to the British crown he would have been an empire-builder but, as it was, his enterprise failed; although, by robbing all who fell into his clutches he put by enough to enable himself to set up as a squire when he finally reached home.

The massacre by the Siamese that put an end to White's dictatorship at Mergui resulted in the declaration of war upon Siam by the East India Company. This was a period when the interests of a commercial faction could be openly identified with those of the nation, and a declaration of war upon a friendly foreign power need be no more than a matter of resolution taken at a board meeting of directors. Fortunately for both nations, the company had another war on its hands at the time – with Aurungzeb – and could not spare men or ships to avenge the White débâcle. The thing was allowed to fizzle out.

As the *Menam* would be continuing its voyage from Mergui down to Penang and Singapore, I had arranged to fly back from Mergui. In Rangoon the importance had been stressed of organizing the return trip so as to avoid staying a night in Mergui. Outside Rangoon, hotels as Europeans understand them do not exist. Before the war, most towns had 'Dak' bungalows, or Circuit Houses for the accommodation of officials on tour. Although equipped with monastic simplicity, they were kept clean by a caretaker, and the traveller's servant could cook him the kind of food he was used to. In this way the white man was able to maintain himself in hygienic isolation. Now, for one reason or another, the bungalows were not available; they had been bombed, had fallen derelict, or had been taken over by the military, or they were located outside the town in situations once desirable, but now undefended from dacoits.

At all events there were no lodgings to be had in Mergui, apart from Chinese doss-houses, at the thought of which even the Burmese shook their heads. In case an unexpected breakdown in arrangements compelled me to spend a night or more in Mergui, I was recommended to present myself at a Buddhist monastery, where I could always be sure of a well-swept corner, a clean mat, and a simple meal.

There was a club-room atmosphere in the office of the airline which was reached by a rickety outside staircase, at the top of which a man lay in a hammock picking at the strings of a guitar. A highly efficient-looking radio set occupied most of one side of the room. It looked like ex-army equipment and although it had probably been installed for some technical reason, passers-by dropped in frequently to twiddle the many dials, producing, with cries of admiration, a vociferous cross-section of the radio programmes of eastern Asia. A beautiful woman with golden safety-pins in her ears stood thumbing the pages of a Burmese ladies' journal dealing with romance, fashions, and the home, and called (in Burmese) *The Bloodsucker*. A further attraction was a fine, large tank of tropical fish, fitted with devices for maintaining an even temperature and aerating the water. An official, seeing my interest in this, came over and described the various types of fish, and their peculiarities. There was one specimen of the most refined and fragile ugliness which, he claimed with pride, had never before been kept alive, in Mergui. That he had been able to do so he put down to the continual noise and light.

When the matter of the plane was raised, he sighed. In the first place he had received no telegram, so no seat had been reserved. Anyway all the planes were booked for several trips ahead. He went away to confer with a colleague. There was a rattle of Burmese monosyllables in which such words as time schedule, over-booked, and Sunday plane continually occurred; fitful beams of comprehension that in some way contrived only to deepen the murk of future prospects. The Burmese language, as now spoken, is studded with English words which the Burmese find not easily translatable. All the sinister euphemisms like 'liberation' are there, and such verbs as 'to neutralize' are appropriated with joy. The official told me that it took six words to say Sunday plane in Burmese, and the same number, of course, to say Thursday plane. This also was 'over-booked'. With knotted brow he rechecked his list. On Sunday a delegation was off to stick gold-leaf on the Shwedagon Pagoda. Thursday's plane was monopolized by Rotarians. The Burmese people enjoyed travel. To be on the safe side he suggested that I should contact the shipping company. The *Menam* would be calling on its return journey in two weeks' time. Or I could more easily get a plane from Moulmein – if only there were any way of getting to Moulmein.

I went down to the police station to enquire for lodgings. Outside, a great crowd had collected to examine a travelling exhibit of photographs of traffic accidents. When fatal accidents happen in Burma the grim composition is left undisturbed until the police photographer arrives with his equipment, deftly composes the face – if any remains – of the victim, and sets to work. From these grisly tableaux I learned, by the way, that when a body is bisected by a train, the normal disposition of the parts can remain unaltered, top and bottom sections still tenuously united by the clothing.

The station-sergeant was cheerful. There was no accommodation problems in Mergui. A constable was sent along to conduct me to a reeling shack, plastered with Chinese ideographs, with a notice in English which said 'Yok Seng. Licensed under the hotel and restaurant tax act'. Yok Seng's was on the edge of the residential quarter, and surrounding buildings were made entirely from the perforated steel used by the Americans on their airfield landing strips. This, in Mergui, being airy and dacoit-proof, is regarded as choice building material. But the quality of the material is offset by a serious disadvantage. The construction of a normal wooden Burmese house is a matter of skill and connoisseurship, called for on account of the invisible thread of fortune connecting the building with its inhabitants. The building posts, according to shape, are masculine, feminine, or neuter; and the feminine ones, which swell out at the base, are – provided that all other things are equal – fortunate and honourable. A fat Burmese manual exists, giving a great number of rules for the construction of the lucky house. It goes carefully into such questions as the number of and position of the knots in the wood, and the effect on the occupiers' fortunes of the shape of the side pieces of the steps leading up to the veranda. Finally, the house-guardian, when it does not live in a coconut – as at Moulmein – occupies the south post of the house, which is adorned with leaves. There is no doubt that the terrible simplification introduced by the use of airstrip perforated-steel will produce new problems. There's no luck – and no ill-luck – about the house. Its occupants must pay for their convenience by surrendering themselves to an atmosphere of ghastly spiritual neutrality.

The ground floor of Yok Seng's place, which was open to the street, contained a few tables and chairs, and beneath them, on the beaten earth, pariah dogs and a stunted breed of Rhode Island Red chickens twitched and scuffled as vermin troubled their siesta.

After the policeman had banged his rifle a few times on a table top, a Chinese came down some stairs in the rear, wiping his hands, as he approached us, on his only garment, a bloodstained pair of white slacks. There would be no trouble in putting me up, he said amiably and in excellent English. I could sleep anywhere I liked, on the floor downstairs – the shutters were pulled down at night – and this had the advantage of privacy. Or if I liked company, he could find space on a comfortably boarded floor upstairs, where a few of his friends – all respectable merchants – were sleeping. Downstairs, of course, I could pick my own position, relax, and have the place to myself. Better still, he said, as soon as the customers were gone he would put a couple of tables together and I could sleep on those.

It was becoming clear to me that on my projected journey through the interior of Burma – if it became reality – I should not be able to look forward to anything in the matter of lodgings much better than Yok Seng's establishment. Indeed the time might soon come when I should remember its appointments with nostalgia. I therefore settled there and then for the two tables, clinching the deal with the proprietor over a formal cup of tea.

Much to my delight I found that besides running his hotel Yok Seng was in the export business, and that among the products he shipped to Hong Kong were as many edible birds' nests as he could buy, although as they were at that time out of season, he was unable to show me any. From what he told me of his own experiences of this precious merchandise, together with the information given in a printed leaflet with which he presented me, I was able to form a clearer idea than ever before of the harassed existence of my favourite bird, the *Collocalia francica*, or grey-rumped swift.

The *Collocalia francica*, which breeds in caves on islands of the Mergui archipelago, is famed in the Far East for the immaculacy by which all its acts are characterized. In the leaflet – it was published in 1907 and had scientific pretensions – I read that this excellent bird was believed to obtain its nutriment from the air. Its name in Siamese means 'wind-eating bird', and it is stated never to have been observed in the act of taking solid food of any kind. The nest, which is fixed to the most inaccessible parts of high caves, is half the size of a small saucer. It is transparent and takes, in the first place, three months to make from the fine, web-like threads of saliva secreted by

Mang-Yang: the last French post

Pleiku: the sacrifice

Pleiku: a drink from the sacred jar

Prak, whose name meant 'money'

The M'nong Gar woman shows typical Moï indifference

Saigon: incense spirals in the Cantonese pagoda

Vietnamese theatre: the Chinese ambassador declares his love

Pnom-Penh: procession of the twenty-five spirits

the bird. Its first nests are collected as soon as complete. The bird then hastily produces a second, which is regarded as an inferior *cru*; and when this is taken, a third, of which it is sometimes left in possession. These are 'white' nests, unsullied by any foreign material. A related species of bird, of less ethereal habits, produces 'black' nests, containing feathers, flies, and even droppings. These are not acceptable in Hong Kong, the chief birds' nest market; but find buyers among the less exacting Chinese of the Straits Settlements. The grey-rumped swift not only does not foul its nests, but does not permit its young to do so, although perhaps in view of its reputed feedings habits, the impulse is slight. At all events nests are as spotless and saleable after incubation as before.

It was inevitable that so remarkable a performance should have attracted the attention of those dauntless empiricists, the Chinese. In about 1750 a Chinese called Hao Yieng presented his wife, children, and slaves, together with fifty cases of tobacco to the Siamese king, asking in return to be allowed to collect birds' nests on the islands. He soon became immensely rich and was made Governor of a province. Realizing the value of the monopoly, the Crown then took over. A corps of hereditary collectors was created; officers of the Crown who were not allowed to change their employment, and who were permitted to carry firearms to guard the caves. Nest poachers were heavily fined. After an analysis conducted in the manner of their day a body of early Chinese scientists unanimously declared that the nest was composed of solidified sea-foam. It was a short step to regarding it as an essential ingredient of the elixir of life. Although the elixir remained elusive, a combination of birds' nests and ginseng is still considered by the Chinese to be the nearest thing to it ever discovered, and capable in nine cases out of ten of restoring to life a patient on the point of death.

Unfortunately, said Yok Seng, many unscrupulous practices had crept into the trade. One was the manufacture by unprincipled persons of spurious nests. Such nests were made of jellies extracted from various seaweeds, and sometimes most artfully flavoured by the addition of a trifling percentage of the real thing. And just as in the intensive agriculture of Tonkin, where human excrement is the most valuable commodity after rice itself, there are assayers able to detect fraudulent adulteration with inferior substitutes, so the merchants of Mergui employed experts to nibble judiciously at samples of nests. 'But be sure,' said Yok Seng, 'that when you order bird's nest soup in a restaurant, it is the fake you will be served.' It took a nest-eater of many years' experience to tell the difference between the genuine article and the succulent imitation which would fail to double your span of years.

It came almost as a disappointment when the necessity for submitting to the experience of the Yok Seng hospitality was removed. Unexpectedly, the *Menam* was to stay another night at Mergui, and that evening a message came from the air company's office to say that there had been a cancellation on the Sunday plane and they had booked the seat for me.

There was something of a party on the *Menam* that night. A couple of tin-miners came aboard and were entertained by friends. The Captain made his first appearance, and later came over to my table. He had heard that I was a writer, and would like to know what I proposed to write about. Burma, I told him, knowing infallibly what was to come. And what were my qualifications?... How long had I lived, or would live in the country? I had arrived a week before, and might stay a few months.

The Captain found it hard to conceal his exasperation. For twenty-eight years he had knocked about these coasts, and he seemed to feel that anyone who had spent less time in the Far East than he, had no right to write about it. The things he had seen in his days! The stories he could tell if he felt like it! And what did this rare information amount to, when finally after a few more double whiskies the process of unburdening began? A little smuggling; a little gun running; repetitive descriptions of Homeric drinking bouts in which the Captain had justified his manhood and his race against all comers; fun with Burmese 'bits of stuff'. Of this material were his Burmese memories composed.

And this was the common, almost the invariable attitude. The old hands seem to feel that they possess a kind of reluctant, vested interest in the place of their exile. Without having suffered with them the long, boring years of expatriation, it was an impertinence to have an opinion. And yet when questioned they would often boastfully display their ignorance, their contempt and distaste for everything about the country. As soon as the central streets of Rangoon were left behind there was never another European to be seen.

It has always been the same. Of all the Europeans who visited Burma, from earliest times down to the days of Symes' Embassy at the beginning of the last century, only eight troubled to give any account of the country, however brief. Hundreds of factors of the East India Company resided in Syriam, Pegu, or at Ava, yet none of them in his letters shows any evidence of curiosity about the strange life that went on around them, or that he ever thought of Burma other than in terms of 'Ellephants teeth, Pegue Plancks, Tynn, Oyle, and Mortavan jars'.

Early next morning I put my bag into a sampan which lay alongside the ship, heaving in the tide's pulse, and then, with a thrust of the oars, we were carried away, swept with the current downstream. Shorewards rose magic mountains of shining garbage, and on the beach at their base, the sea peeled off its layers of indolent water. Beyond, over the curve of the earth, rose the town's silhouette; the roofs, the mysterious towers, the minarets of abandoned factories. On a black rock a group of Burmese children, with top-knots and fringed hair, threw stones into the water, and laughed seawards. We skimmed through a marsh to land, and as the incoming tide rippled before us it lifted the flat green leaves, and the water glistened round their rims. This was the last I saw of Mergui.

The airport jeep was waiting at the appointed place and, as we went up through the woods, through the patchy scarlets of flamboyant trees, and past the tarnished gilding of pagodas, the driver chatted amiably. He wanted to talk about the scandal of the Seventeen-Days festival that was just over in Mergui. It would be my good fortune to be travelling with one of the greatest of Burmese actors, who had been playing every night and in the course of the seventeen days had been paid half a lakh of rupees – about four thousand pounds. On these celebrations the people of Mergui had spent a total of eight lakhs, say sixty-five thousand pounds, and were now reduced to temporary penury. The pawnshop had been obliged to close down on the first day, after running out of cash.

This kind of thing, said the driver, eager as the Burmese always are to condemn their national vices, was the curse of Mergui. People spent all they had on the pwès, and then just scraped along as best they could for the rest of the year. Tradition had a lot to do with it. Miserliness was one of the Burmese deadly sins, ranking in the hierarchy of crime on a level with fratricide. That was why the Indians, who regarded thrift as a cardinal virtue, were getting control of the country's wealth. The driver sighed and shook his head at such foolishness. He was dressed with suspicious plainness for the possessor of such a gadget-loaded car, and had probably gambled away most of his resources, including his silk longyis. For the next few weeks he would live on plain rice and gnapi. After that he would dress in silk again, continuing on plain fare, however, until he had redeemed his wristwatch and ruby ring. Then would follow another visit to the gambling tables and the pawnshop; and the process of recovery would start all over again.

The airport was a prairie of burnt grass surrounded by bush. Snacks were being served in a palm-leaf shack, and an official who attached himself in an informal, almost abstracted way, led me to this and ordered cups of thick sweet tea, and hard-boiled eggs, for which he would not allow me to pay. A few soldiers were hanging about, and presently these scattered to various points of the perimeter, where they took up position behind light machine-guns. An army lorry came charging up, loaded with more troops, who tumbled out and formed two ranks. They were smartly turned out in British uniforms, with knife-edge creases in the right places. Eyes were turned skywards in response to a faint throbbing and the Sunday plane came into sight, glinting distantly. Dropping down gently, as if lowered on a thread, to land, it disappeared, absorbed in the heat-haze, from which it suddenly burst forth when almost upon us. The plane, a Dakota, stopped, with its idly slapping propellers raising squalls of dust. A door opened and a military figure leaped down. Two officers ran forward, saluted and shook hands. One raised a Leica to his eye. There was a yelp of command, in traditionally unrecognizable English, followed by a smacking of butts as arms were correctly presented. A brigadier had arrived to take over operations in the south.

The normal seating equipment of the Sunday plane had been removed to allow the carriage of more passengers and freight. We sat on what looked like theatre-queue stools, with backs. The airline had a reputation for keeping its planes in the air as much as possible and the floor was littered with the debris of several previous trips. The party on their way to gild the Shwedagon spire were seen off with garlands, in the Hawaiian manner. Sensibly, as the temperature in the plane must have approached a hundred and twenty degrees, the door was left open until the very last instant before the take-off, and then shut with some difficulty against the pressure of air. My neighbour, a sophisticate in European clothing, spent the first half-hour trying to take photographs with a new Japanese camera through the dirty window. He then settled down to a Penguin D. H. Lawrence, automatically fingering through his prayer-beads with his free hand. Burma's outstanding actor was travelling with his pearl-festooned wife and children. He was a dark, sullen-faced fellow, who dressed with costly indifference in the old-fashioned style, and wore his hair in a bun on top of his head. Although he made more money than most Hollywood film stars, he seemed to have no fans on the plane. No one took the slightest notice of him. Most of the passengers were too busy with their smelling-salts to care.

CHAPTER SIX

Conducted Tour

BACK IN RANGOON, I set about the organization of the journey to
the interior. Many difficulties suddenly appeared, some of which
showed signs of hasty fabrication, and it was soon evident that the
authorities preferred foreigners to remain quietly in the capital. The
Burmese airline served about a dozen towns, of which only two or
three could be visited without special authorization. Otherwise,
travel so far as Westerners were concerned seemed to have come to
an end since the outbreak of the insurrections, although the Indian
and Burmese merchants I consulted told me that plenty of goods still
went by road, and that it was easy enough to accompany them.

It was unfortunate for me that two Europeans – both journalists –
had quietly left Rangoon without official blessing, in the last year or
so. Their adventures had spoiled the going for future travellers. One,
a Frenchman, had reached Kentung, a very troubled area, and had
there hobnobbed with Shan dissidents. On his return he had
experienced a short stay in Rangoon gaol, before being expelled from
the country. The second journalistic venture had produced more
lasting damage. A representative of a London newspaper had
actually contacted Karen rebel leaders – a sensational scoop to a
newspaper-man, and a piece of flagrant espionage to the Burmese.
Although the classic English traveller is spurred on in almost all
cases by nothing more sinister than an extravagant curiosity, it has
been hard at the best of times for others to believe that he is not an
agent of the Intelligence Service, especially after the occurrence of
such an incident. In army circles there were many who still believed
that the British had not renounced all ambition to return to Burma,
and they thought it quite natural that attempts would be made to
maintain contact with pro-British and anti-Burmese minority groups.

Until I made my application it had been possible simply to go down to the air company's office and buy a ticket for such towns as Lashio and Bhamó; but in my honour, it seemed, new regulations were quickly slapped on. Suddenly no foreigners could be granted permission to visit these towns, even by air, without application being made on their behalf by their own embassy to the Burmese Foreign Office. The matter would then, it was explained to me, be referred by the Foreign Office to the War Office, and finally passed for sanction or rejection to the General Staff Department. It was clear that this formidable procedure offered the maximum scope for pigeon-holing, and I felt that the hidden intention might have been to break the applicant's spirit by manufactured delays. In any case, it turned out that the British Embassy could not agree to intervene, as this was the first they had heard of such a regulation. I was unofficially recommended to extract what comfort I could from the knowledge that others were, or had been, in the same case, including the United States Military Attaché, and the representatives of a celebrated American magazine, who had come to do a picture reportage, and had left after seeing little more of Burmese life than was to be observed in the uncharacteristic public rooms of the Strand Hotel.

After a few days of struggling, ever more feebly, in the tightening snares of red tape, I was told that even Mandalay had been put out of bounds. At the police headquarters, U Ba San also mentioned with deadly casualness that whenever I got my Burmese travel permit, I should have to apply again (through channels) for one issued by the Minister for the Shan States. The psychological effect of these blows was almost decisive, and I was on the point of packing up and going home. As a last resort, and because there was nothing to be lost, I decided to cut across channels, and go directly to the real seat of power. I therefore presented myself at the War Office, and asked to see a high-ranking staff-officer, whose name I had been given. To my surprise he received me. I found that he had a great sense of humour, and after we had laughed together uproariously about my predicament, the permit was typed out on the spot. I went straight to the air office and booked a seat on the plane to Mandalay two days later. At this time my intention was to fly as far north as possible, and work my way back to Rangoon by road and river.

Next day was another public holiday. My Canadian friend, Dolland, released from official duties, suggested a jaunt across the river to Syriam. His previous visit had been a rapid and unsatisfactory conducted tour, and behind his screen of protective troops he had seen very little.

Dolland, a rare eccentric in matters of travel, was moved in all things by a single principle – a determination to get as close to the country as was possible in the course of his three months in Burma. With this creditable purpose steadfastly in view he frequently travelled about Rangoon, clinging to the platforms of crowded buses, and sometimes arrived at the Strand Hotel in a kind of springless pony-trap of the kind used by peasants to bring vegetables to market. It cost more than a taxi. He was also learning Burmese, wore the national costume whenever he could find an excuse, and finally moved out of the hotel and went to live with a Burmese couple he had persuaded to take him as a paying guest.

On this occasion, then, in accordance with his general line, Dolland wanted to travel second-class on the ferry. My attitude to this was that the presence of two foreigners squatting in agony on mats on the deck among the coolies would be interpreted by the Burmese not so much as democratic interest as meanness. Dolland squatted for a few moments and then joined me up on the first-class benches in the stern, which were, of course, equally patronized by the Burmese.

Having landed at Syriam we were about to walk uphill to the town, about a mile away, when our attention was attracted by a great deal of activity down by the water. Female labourers were loading rice from one of the government depots on to lighters. As they were paid by the basket-load, they worked at a tremendous, almost alarming, speed, in great contrast to the languorous movements of the Burmese female who is not doing anything in particular. We went over to the yard and the girls grimaced, and made witty remarks while we photographed them, going in short dashes from the piled-up rice to the boat, with their enormous loads on their heads. We were just moving off when we were accosted by a very polite, sad-faced young man who said he was the overseer, and what could he do for us. There was nothing much he could do, and our hearts sank when he mentioned that as he was just going off duty, he would show us the town. Outside the yard he hailed another young man, who came over and said, as he shook hands, 'What do you want, sir?' This was the township officer, principal citizen of Syriam. A Ford truck panted at the kerbside behind him. It was loaded with his henchmen. There was no escape. The conducted tour had begun.

I wanted to look for any traces that might remain here of the factories of the East India Company, where they had maintained themselves uneasily for a century, selling their hats and ribbons, and understandably failing to sell their English broadcloth; 'we haveing great quantetyes decaying by us'. From this stronghold, too, the seventeenth-century Portuguese adventurer De Brito had only just failed, from lack of Goa's support, to turn the delta area of Lower Burma into a Portuguese colony. Somewhere on the hill, after defeat by the Burmese king, he met his end by impalement. He failed to adopt the recommended posture – to sit quietly and permit the sharpened stake to penetrate the vital organs – and the point passed out through his side. He lingered three days.

Our hosts were determined that we should see their town in the proper fashion. There was no escaping the inspection of public monuments, the hospital, the town hall. Finally, making them understand the nature of our interests, we were taken to a tiny ruined chapel, in which a tombstone commemorated, in most elegant script, the death in 1732 of one Maria Dias. The township officer carefully noted my translation in his notebook.

On the way back to the ferry – we were still confined to the Ford truck – we asked in desperation if we might walk. It was clear that our Burmese friends were dumbfounded at such eccentricity. Further explanation of what we actually proposed was necessary before the driver was ordered to stop. Then the four of us got down and walked gravely downhill in the middle of the road, while the lorry followed, grinding along in bottom gear, about ten yards behind.

CHAPTER SEVEN

Burmese Gaol

THE MORNING OF my departure for Mandalay was nicely filled in by a visit to the Rangoon gaol. U Thant arranged this at a moment's notice. Even if the Burmese were a little dubious about letting people see what was going on in the interior of their country, they clearly had no misgivings about the condition of their gaols. It was casually mentioned, with perhaps a touch of pride, that in England such a request would have to be made through the Home Office and was not lightly granted. Here all U Thant had to do was to get the Director General of Prisons on the phone, and the thing was fixed in a matter of minutes.

It was the Director General himself, U Ba Thein, who called for me at seven o'clock next morning. U Ba Thein was a small, dapper man, with that concentrated, almost ferocious, energy often found in men of destiny. He told me with some satisfaction that he was of humble origin, but I have no doubt that in traditional Burmese fashion he possessed a spectacular horoscope, and that in his youth vultures had been seen to perch on the houses of his enemies. He was also genial in the extreme, even for a Burman, having a sense of humour that was French rather than English, expansive and *spirituel*.

We shot off in a small English car driven by the Director himself, and soon entered the road leading to the prison entrance, which was guarded with barbed-wire entanglements. The atmosphere was a martial one. At the approach of our car there were warning cries, and a guard tumbled out rather too late to present arms. There was much leaping to attention and saluting as we went through the gate, and U Ba Thein, sighing, and quoting Chaucer, said 'God keep my body out of a foul prisoun'. The Director General had a great reputation as a disciplinarian. He also liked poetry, and the English way of life; in particular, he said, kippers and watercress for tea.

The Rangoon gaol was at first sight less forbidding and dolorous than the average prison. During the recent war, I was unfortunately brought into contact with the repressive arrangements of several countries. At the bottom of the scale were the French in North Africa, where colonial dissidents were put in black holes in the ground – living tombs. Above these were the Italians and Germans with their heartless efficiency. There were no gyves or pinions; but solitary confinement, sound-proof cells, rows of steel doors which opened slowly at the throwing of a switch. In these all-electrically operated hells, food was a dosage with calories; a medical measure against death by starvation. A doctor stood by with a stethoscope while punishment was administered, and in the constant blue light bodies turned as white as if they had been drained by vampires.

Rangoon gaol, perhaps because there had been a merciful shortage of funds, had never been able to run to such refinements. It was no more than a great cage; a collection of barrack-like buildings, where no attempt had been made, as in most prisons, to prevent inmates from seeing even the sky. In these barrack-rooms the prisoners lived communally; each occupying an allotted amount of floor space. When U Ba Thein told me that each building was called a 'house' and that the head-warders were 'house-masters' I admit to a suspicion that this might be no more than another of those sinister euphemisms for which the Burmese have such a genius. Occupants of the various houses wore different coloured longyis, and while, I felt, this grim echo of the public-school system might have been wasted on them, it was at least something that they did not wear prison clothes.

They rose at dawn, U Ba Thein informed me, said prayers and then did PT for half an hour. I could have been sure of it. PT had become an oriental panacea for all the ills, both of body and mind. It would have been extraordinary not to have found it figuring largely in the reformative processes of an up-to-date prison. For up-to-date Rangoon was. The bars were made of wood, and, as the Director General cheerfully admitted, very easy to cut through. However they would not be replaced. Such grants of money as they received would be spent in a more positive way. He was aiming, eventually, at a prison without walls. 'That edifice over there,' he pointed to a blackened building, 'was accidentally devastated by fire. A fortuitous circumstance. We can do without same. Now there will be no excuse for the non-existence of a football pitch.' There was no problem here about making the prison too comfortable. He had heard of some place – Mexico, he thought – where this had been done. 'Why, do you know those fellows actually asked to come back when they were discharged!' It was enough to stop a Burman from gambling and dressing up. Liberty was a precious thing.

The influx of prisoners – eighteen thousand passed through their hands in one year – was attributable to the unsettled times and the breakdown of monastic education, with nothing to fill the gap. The present custom, said U Ba Thein, of entering a monastery for a week was useless. In the old days a boy spent at least a year there. Now he got no schooling until he was ten years of age, if at all. Parents wouldn't send their children to boarding school, far from home. 'There but for the Grace of God ...' he quoted. U Ba Thein had been a village boy himself, he told me; and had first gone to school when he was ten. 'For several years they caned me daily, because like uneducated Burmese people I pronounced f as p.' It had been the *pons asinorum* of the Director General's youth. Having in the end surmounted this obstacle he had taken to learning with a zest, and found what remained comparatively easy. He had gone about noting down all the new words he heard, committing them to memory and practising in conversation as soon as he could. Usually he got the meaning wrong. But no matter, it impressed most people. U Ba Thein said it was a habit he had never grown out of. 'You may have noticed that I still use long words in the wrong place? It is a habit I am noted for. People are still continually pulling my leg about it.'

At the end of the war U Ba Thein had visited England to enable him to study the British prison system on the spot. He had been impressed by the kindness he had received, the kippers and the watercress of course, and by the favouritism of people behind the bars of public houses, who had produced cigarettes for him from under the counter. No one had ever guessed that he was a Burmese. It was at a time when all Far Easterners were Japanese, although nobody had apparently bothered to enquire what a Japanese was doing in England at such a time. When, on one occasion, he addressed some Borstal boys, he invited questions at the conclusion of his remarks. He had mentioned Buddhism, and one of the boys asked if it was true that Buddhists could have more than one wife. 'I informed them that that was so,' U Ba Thein said, 'and I must say they all seemed to regard it as an excellent thing.'

As we paced solemnly down the passages, the prisoners stood to attention by their folded bedding. 'Look at those fellows,' U Ba Thein said. 'They are a product of the times. There is no inherent criminality in those faces.'

It was perfectly true. The convicts looked no more vicious than the young fellows to be seen in the streets outside. They were in for robbery, crimes of violence, murder. Fortunately, sexual crimes were very rare. There was no sexual repression in Burma, the Director General said, owing to the freedom practised between the sexes from the age of puberty. Bigamy was not an offence, and charges of rape were rarely brought because the offender in such cases was considered automatically to have married the girl.

In Burma, U Ba Thein said, robbery and violence had always been the problem. He was inclined to trace some of it back to the deliberate policy of the Burmese kings, who encouraged delinquency in a certain restricted area in Upper Burma in order to provide themselves with a reserve of suitable recruits for their armies. The old Burmese kings were, above all, well intentioned. They had none of the cynical disregard for human rights displayed by recent European aggressors. All men were brothers and equally entitled to the salvation which the Burmese kings – who had seen the light – knew that only they could bring. They wanted nothing better than to extend their enlightened benevolence to all humanity; to govern according to the five fundamental precepts, and the four kingly laws, which ordained that the king should content himself with the tithe, that he should pay his servants regularly, lend money without interest to the necessitous, and use courteous and fitting language according to the age and the degree of the person addressed.

It was unfortunate that only by totally non-Buddhistic measures could those nations which continued in ignorance of the Law be gathered into the fold of Buddhist felicity, so that the Kingdom of Heaven on Earth might become a reality. But since all the king's subjects had received a monastic training in the course of which it had been emphasized that of the five precepts, the most important was to take no life at all, how could they be persuaded – even in pursuit of a sanctified end – to enslave, to ravish, and to slaughter all those who persisted in their error? The solution was the delimitation of the area within which, for the Kingdom of Heaven's sake, the five precepts were ignored. From this the king's janissaries were obtained, and from this still come a disproportionate number of the students at this strange public school of Rangoon.

It was reasonable to expect, I thought, that the Director General would have organized this visit with a little window-dressing in mind. We passed, for instance, a block of solitary confinement cells, which, although 'the inheritance of inhumanity was rapidly being wiped out', were obviously still in use. There were three or four prisoners there who couldn't be put with the rest, but no offer was made to show me them. However, when, with a wave of dismissal, U Ba Thein indicated the women's block, saying that he didn't suppose I wanted to see it, I made it clear, as tactfully as I could, that I did. This seemed a good opportunity to visit a part of the prison where probably no preparations had been made. Before going any further we had to await the escort of the head wardress. This lady, a most chic custodian, arrived swinging her symbolical bunch of keys, her face larded with cosmetic. Bracing myself for a vision of screaming harridans in the manner of the women's prison at Naples, I was surprised to find an atmosphere of gentle domesticity.

With a trace of embarrassment, U Ba Thein excused the presence of the women's babies which, he said, while not in keeping with European practice, they tolerated here for the babies' sake. There were toys that had been made in the prison workshop strewn about the floor; wooden horses, lobsters, elephants. Each mother had a prison pushcart. This building was built of air-field metal landing-strip, and the kittens, which the children had been allowed to keep, wandered in and out of the perforations. The women were spruce in their ordinary clothes. They were importunate, too, and, ignoring the wardress, came up to U Ba Thein to ask favours. Most of them were serving sentences for carrying firearms, and one, a delicate, almost ethereal creature, with the face of an Eastern madonna, had organized a huge diamond swindle.

There was one other class of prisoner. We came on a rather tall man, with an unusually gentle expression. He seemed more reflective and less animated than the average Burman, and although some difficulty is found at first in telling the Mongolian peoples apart, I at least realized that the man was not Burmese. He turned out to be a Japanese *kampé*, one of a number who were serving ten-year sentences for war crimes. U Ba Thein said he had no idea what this one had done, but he had heard that some of them were sentenced for burying prisoners alive. A few words had been exchanged in English. Was he short of anything? The Japanese nodded down at his ragged trousers and the Director General said that he would see to it that he got another pair. We turned away. 'Patience,' said U Ba Thein, in parting salutation, and the Japanese smiled with gentle resignation. 'There but for the Grace of God . . .' said U Ba Thein again as we moved on.

CHAPTER EIGHT

To Mandalay

IN THE LATE AFTERNOON, and several hours behind schedule because of the heat-haze, the plane bumped down on Mandalay airfield. The moment the plane door opened I knew that this was a different heat from the Rangoon kind. The horizon was ringed by scorched hills that wavered slightly as you moved your head, as if seen through bad, uneven window glass. The passengers clambered down and took refuge under the wings; sheltering as though from torrential rain. Waves of scorching air rippled from the plane's metal surfaces. Working very slowly, the airport staff dragged out the baggage.

Mr Tok Galé, representative in Mandalay of the British Information Service, was to have met me. The problem of lodgings was supposed to be particularly bad, and it was hoped that this gentleman, who had been warned by telegram from Rangoon, might have been able to find me a room. Outside the airport huts one or two decayed taxis waited for passengers. These soon filled up and went lurching and bobbing away. The various officials prepared to close down for the day. Mr Tok Galé had evidently given up hope of the plane's arrival.

Another half an hour passed and an outlandish vehicle came rumbling up out of the dust. It was, as I soon discovered, a typical Mandalay gharry. This once modish conveyance had a galvanized iron body, decorated with the British Royal Standard, and much fancy scroll-work in brass. Huge glass rubies were dotted about the coachwork, and there were several diamond-shaped insets of coloured glass. Enormous lamps were supported on fancy brackets, and the wheels turned unevenly under high polished metal mudguards. This piece of fantasy, which had clearly been created and maintained with tender pride of ownership, had something ghostly about it. It was like one of those fragile, immensely aged ladies who, clad in the height of Edwardian fashion, still haunt remote London squares. Nothing could have better typified Mandalay.

Seeing that he had a fare the ancient driver climbed down from his seat. He was gripping a bag, and his horse was allowed to mumble a few mouthfuls of the dried herbs it contained, to give it strength for the new journey. The piece of cord which did service as a handbrake was then untied from the wheel and we set off towards the thorny hedges, the stagnant pools, the ruined palaces of Mandalay

Mandalay. In the name there was a euphony which beckoned to the imagination, yet this was the bitter, withered reality. Through the suburbs mile followed mile of miserable shacks; a squalid gipsy encampment, coated with a bone-white dust which floated everywhere, like a noxious condensation of the heat-haze itself. Pigmy pagodas sprouted like pustules. Hideous dogs snarled and scuffled in the streets, which were still rutted and broken from the pounding of war-time traffic.

Mr Tok Galé, whom I found in his office, was a small, quiet-voiced Burman in well-pressed European clothes. He was just about to make another trip out to the airport, which temporarily could not be reached on the telephone. With relentless efficiency, Tok Galé had already worked out the details of a comprehensive sight-seeing programme to fill in my stay in Mandalay, which was to begin, it seemed, the moment I arrived. A jeep had been hired, and awaited us with the driver standing respectfully bare headed in the terrific sunshine. While Tok Galé stood by I washed off a layer of dust. Within five minutes I was sitting in the jeep, lulled by the balm of my guide's gently imparted information, jerked into wakefulness as we crashed through pot-holes.

The most important of Tok Galé's many kindly services consisted of finding a room for me. The Circuit House, he said, was out of the question. It was a mile or two from the town's centre, well inside the dacoit zone. The room was owned by a Chinese merchant. It had been divided by partitions, and he and several tenants slept in beds that had been distributed as evenly as possible about the available space. It was reached by an outside staircase, at the top of which was a platform with a small table, an ancient, filthy but still beautiful pitcher, full of water, and an aluminium wash-basin. Here, at night, a lonely but brilliantly neon-illuminated figure, I performed my toilet, watched incuriously by the Burmese seated at the tables of the tea-shops below. It seemed that Mandalay was without drains. When I asked my Chinese host what was to be done with the waste water, he pointed to the palm-thatched roof of the house below. When I had finally brought myself to accept his implied suggestion there was a sharp exclamation from within, as if the inmates had never been able entirely to accustom themselves to the procedure.

Night in Mandalay called for special qualities of endurance. As the evening wore on, both heat and noise increased. The large, modernistic windows with their westerly exposure had been a sun-trap since the early afternoon, and by the evening the heat was seeping through the walls themselves. At about six thirty the sun went down redly in a glittering haze of dust particles. Immediately the lights of Mandalay came on. A fluorescent tube had been installed for decorative purposes across the façade of our building, providing a pale glare until the early morning hours. The cinema across the road was outlined with flickering fires of neon. Probably as an anti-dacoit measure, because it was left on all night, a large, naked electric bulb was suspended outside my window. This supplied, when other sources failed, a continuous death-cell illumination.

At all times a cheerful hum of café gossip ascended to my window, mingled with the exuberant blowing of motor-horns. In the evening, the cinema came to life, advertising itself with trailer-music broadcast from powerful loudspeakers, and by the pertinacious note of an electrically struck gong, attached to the wall near by. Above this background of confused noise several pagodas sometimes asserted themselves, signalling their religious offices by harmonious and long-echoing sounds struck from the huge triangles of brass suspended in their courtyards.

The windows were open wide in the hope of catching a current of air, and sparrows flew in, and in their fluttering set in brief motion an otherwise static frieze of lizards.

I took my meals at a Chinese restaurant across the way, called the Excelsior. Whenever I went in the proprietor would come out of the kitchen and guide me firmly into the polite solitude of a private room. A moment or two later I would hear a preliminary scratching and the gramophone would begin to play 'Kathleen Mavourneen', followed by 'The Harp that Once ...' The sides of the record were always played in this order. Always the proprietor asked with a hopeful uplift in his voice, 'Eggs and chips?' And always I shook my head, pointing without understanding to some Burmese or Chinese speciality on the wall menu. This was never available, and the dish finally served was fried soft noodles with mincemeat, although it was always given a fresh name. This was sometimes followed by a turnip-tasting fruit, called in Burmese, 'Ice from Russia'. Mandalay Pale Ale could be had here at the source for three rupees, or four and sixpence. You could also buy Fire-Tank Brand Mandalay Whisky at seven rupees a bottle, which was reasonable compared to genuine imported Scotch at the black-market figure of eighty.

Every night I sat in this sallow cubicle, trying to put off the time when I should have to face the oven of my room. Across the road a rank of small covered wagons, decorated with brass cupids, would be drawn up. These had brought peasants to market and now their owners were sitting in tea-shops, gambling away the proceeds of their sales. Once a woman sat on the pavement outside, giving her baby alternate sucks of a nipple and a fat cheroot, and once while I sat there a silent, thickly bearded Indian came in and handed me a slip of paper on which was printed, 'A conjurer will make your party a success'. On another occasion there was a Chinese private party in a booth opposite and, as the door was slightly ajar, I caught a glimpse of one of the ladies sitting on her escort's lap, washing his face after the meal.

*

There was no important reason for Mandalay's existence. It never possessed a strategic or commercial importance, and the whole district had had a detestable climate since, centuries before, pious kings had cut down all the trees to be used as fuel in brick-making for pagodas. At some time in the remote past astrologers had declared the area to be astrally favoured, so Ava and Amarapura had been built. These had finally been deserted, as Burmese towns were, when it was decided that the efficacy of the human sacrifices made at the foundation was exhausted. And then, in Victorian times, the pious King Mindon had been tempted to try his luck again. On the advice of the Brahmin astrologers an exemplary mass-sacrifice was arranged, including that of a pregnant woman. According to the old Mongolian belief the spirits of mother and child would unite in death to form a composite demon of exceptional malignancy. This would be animated by an implacable desire for revenge, directed – with seemingly defective logic – against the king's enemies. As a Buddhist scholar of renown and the leading authority of his times on Pali texts, Mindon probably disapproved of this stone-age practice. If he permitted the woman to be buried alive, he did so in the same spirit as a socialist cabinet minister might dress for dinner – not because he agreed with the principle, but because these things were expected of him; and, after all, there was nothing to be lost one way or another.

These sacrifices probably established a Burmese record for short-lived efficacy. Twenty-nine years later Mandalay fell to the British without the slightest attempt at defence, either ghostly or human.

CHAPTER NINE

Kings and a Prince

As far as the conventional sights went Mandalay was a town to be dealt with in summary fashion. Apart from a gaudy fantasy of a palace, a few monasteries, and the Arakan Pagoda, it had never contained anything worth seeing; and now, after the passing of the bombers, the palace had vanished as completely as if it had never existed.

On the morning of the second day, Tok Galé took me to see the Arakan Pagoda. This was built to enshrine the great Mahamuni image which for so many centuries had been the palladium of the kingdom of Arakan, as well as the most important of the Buddhist sacred objects. The peculiar sanctity of this image lies in its acceptance by Buddhists as a contemporary likeness of the Master. It was cast in brass when the great teacher visited Arakan, at that time a remote Indian kingdom. The work was done supernaturally by none other than Sakra, the old Hindu Lord of Paradise, who had become converted to Buddhism. When completed, the portrait, which was indistinguishable from the original, was embraced by the Buddha, and thereafter emitted an unearthly refulgence, and actually spoke a few words. Naturally, its possession was coveted by many pious kings, in particular the greatest of Burmese historical figures, Anawrahta, who organized a large-scale raid into Arakan with the object of removing this along with sacred relics to his capital at Pagan. The King's purpose was frustrated by the size and weight of the image: the white elephant which accompanied his army, and was regarded as the only suitable means of transport, could not carry it.

It was finally obtained in 1784 by Bodawpaya, who is declared, in an inscription at the pagoda, to have drawn the image to its present resting place by the charm of his piety. In fact an expeditionary corps of thirty thousand men was involved, after elaborate precautions to

379

deprive the image of its magic power had first been taken by Burmese wizards disguised as pilgrims.

I had been told that only in Mandalay would real Burmese works of art, wood carvings, bronzes, and ivories, be found; and that the colonnades of the Arakan Pagoda would be the most likely place in Mandalay itself. As in the Shwedagon at Rangoon, the roofed-over approaches were lined with stalls selling devotional objects; flowers, votive images, and triangular gongs. Such carvings as there were among the trayfuls of toy jeeps and tanks and hideous Buddhas seemed to me the crudest and most barbarously ugly objects I had ever seen. Burma is a land where art has never freed itself from the thraldom of religious or magic motives. The Burmese never grew up spiritually, as did the Chinese, nor allowed the philosophical content of their religion to free itself from its trappings of superstition. As a result their creative energy was diverted into the primitive and unrewarding channels of pagoda-building, from which they expected to derive not mere aesthetic pleasure, but a substantial spiritual reward. As a minor adjunct to this perpetual heaping up of piles of brickwork, there was some skill displayed in wood carving and the application of lacquer; but when it came to the graphic arts no Burmese painter of monastery frescoes could approach the most primitive of the old Italians, just as no worker in ivory could compare with the least of China's anonymous masters.

Nothwithstanding the impressive attribution of the Mahamuni image, the result, regarded as a work of art, is negligible; a mere seated idol, in the lifeless convention which is still adhered to in most parts of the Buddhist world. An attempt at portraiture would probably have been sacrilegious. What we have here is not a divine teacher but the stylization of a fat man, with heavy, inert features which have suffered further coarsening by the gold-leaf applied by the faithful.

The toleration of Buddhists – however debased their particular brand of the religion – is limitless. Anywhere in the Muslim world a *kafir* would have been chased by mouth-foaming fanatics from the precincts of so holy a place. But here, whatever the condition of one's soul, one spread no contamination. A permanent crowd was gathered before the railings of the shrine behind which the twelve-foot-high image brooded somnolently, but they were quite ready to make room for a not completely human foreigner to take a photograph. One sophisticate even questioned the feasibility of getting a result in so dim a religious light. Whatever one's creed or colour the shrine attendants would accept a bouquet of flowers which could be bought at a nearby stall for a rupee. Gold-leaf was sold for five rupees a packet and the purchaser was entitled to apply it himself, clambering as reverently as possible up the sacred stomach to reach the face. Pilgrims of many races waited their turn to perform this illustrious task. Outstanding were a contingent of Thibetans of the kind that wander about Burma selling gems and hideous medicinal concoctions. There they stood in grimy purple togas; their faces unwashed, gentle, set in masks of beatitude, packets of gold-leaf gripped tightly in their hands. Laboriously they had trudged the roads of Burma, selling their rubies, their bezoars, their serpents' tongues and bats' blood. Now they would squander their gains in one unforgettable devotional spree.

Out in the courtyard, stacked haphazardly against a wall, we found the six survivors of the thirty magic images of Ayuthia, captured by Bayinnaung when he went to Siam for white elephants, and took and sacked the Siamese capital. These potent bronze monsters, triple-headed elephants, and snarling, armour-clad demons, were now, at least, put to a useful purpose by Burmese children who played hide-and-seek about their legs.

The brief, routine tour of the capital is incomplete without a visit to the leper asylum. We were received in a large, dim room in the ranch-like administrative building by one of the handful of Franciscan nuns who are left to conduct this work. The sister was a Maltese woman who one day, when she was a girl of eighteen, and living in her native village, had felt the vocation. The call to surrender her life to the hardest of all forms of service was no mere emotional whim. Her first step, on abandoning her family and the comfortable trivialities of her home existence, was to go to Italy to train as a nurse. After qualifying, she came, with resolve unabated, straight out to Mandalay where she had been ever since.

One by one the other sisters came silently into the room. They were all from the Mediterranean countries. All seemed to move in an aura of extraordinary simplicity, of other-wordliness, of embalmed youth. One, who came from Santander, was delighted to be able to speak a few words of Spanish for the first time for years. And then she seemed ashamed of having felt pleasure at this reminder of the world she had renounced and, excusing herself, she left the room. The sisters' lingua franca was French. The oldest of them, a vigorous old lady, had been there for fifty-two years. None of them had ever been infected, although in Colombo two members of their order had died of leprosy. The years had passed quickly for them, filled with hard work. By dint of concentrated prayer their hospital had come unscathed through the war, although bombs had fallen all round. Even the Japanese had respected them, and given them what help they could. Now, of course, things were worse – worse than they had ever been. Dacoits had taken to breaking in, and stole their equipment and even the medicines.

Later we passed in sombre procession through the buildings where the patients were housed; the rooms, empty but for the row of cheerless beds; the leper faces, often contorted by the disease into apparent fury; the whispers of '*bonjour ma mère*' – or sometimes only a voiceless mouthing – as we passed each bed. The children's wards were inevitably the most pathetic. Sometimes the wistful faces were smooth and clean, sometimes frightfully ravaged. 'This one may recover,' said the Maltese sister, in her cool, even voice ... 'this one will not.' Thus we passed along the ranks, hearing, as each pair of childish eyes was raised to ours, the dispassionate verdict, 'death very soon now,' or 'here there is a small chance'. 'Before the end comes,' said the sister, 'we remove them to a separate building, where they will not upset the others. The sight is depressing to those who are not accustomed to it.' The disease seemed to progress in a series of leaps with intervals of quiescence, the sister explained, and it was only in the crisis that accompanied the entering upon a new stage that the patients really suffered ... then, and in the final agony. Thirty-five years of contact with disease and death in its most appalling form seemed to have raised the sister above ordinary emotional sympathy. She had become what was necessary, an efficiently working charitable machine.

The hardest part of these lepers' condition seemed to me the cruel boredom they must have suffered. All day long they lay still, sat up, even walked a little, surrendering themselves without distraction to the slow disintegration. There was nothing to take their mind off this death meted out to them over the years, to be dreadfully consummated in most cases only after the loss of all five senses. Once they had been allowed to stage occasional plays, but these, for some reason to do with the unsuitability of the subjects, had been given up. The cinema, even if possible from the point of view of cost, was unthinkable because of the worldliness of the films.

It seemed that if the leper wished to surrender himself to the efficient care of the Christians, with the accompanying faint hope of a cure, he had also to be ready to submit to that adamantine virtue, the saint-like abstraction from the world in which only duty and meditation were permissible. If the lepers wanted to live like ordinary sinful humanity, there was nothing to stop them from leaving the asylum; but then of course that last tenuous hope of recovery had to be abandoned. Perhaps the sisters secretly believed that the disease had been a blessing in disguise, the opportunity to save valuable souls at the expense of worthless bodies.

The Burmese, of course, are more human about such things – more human, and less responsible. There are forty-two thousand registered lepers in Burma, most of whom continue to live in their villages with their families. Nothing is done for them except by foreign missionaries; probably because at the bottom of the Burmese mind lies the conviction that in this cruel state they are no more than righting an adverse balance of merit accumulated in previous existences. In this attitude is to be found, from the Western viewpoint, the main criticism of Buddhist practice. The performance of acts of charity is praiseworthy, but not nearly so much so as the building, or repair, of a pagoda. There were no public funds available to supply essential medicines or amenities for Mandalay's lepers although seven hundred thousand rupees could be spent a month before on the cremation of a saintly individual called U Khanti whose work of merit had consisted of adding new pagodas to the already congested Mandalay Hill. But for all their deficiencies the Burmese do not in any way segregate or persecute the lepers. No medicines or treatment are forthcoming, but neither are the unfortunate creatures' last years made miserable by an enforced monastic way of life.

Before we left, the sister showed us a remarkable piece of religious architecture. It seemed that when the bombings were taking place the nuns vowed, if the hospital were spared, to construct a miniature Lourdes. Shortly afterwards the war ended. There had been a prisoner of war camp in the neighbourhood, and the commanding officer, when approached, had lent them a number of Japanese prisoners to carry out the project. The Japanese had set to work with traditional vigour and produced a miniature mountain of rocks and concrete, as steeply pinnacled as one in a Hiroshige woodcut. After that, with mounting enthusiasm, they had added a willow-pattern river with an appropriate bridge. The Japanese captain himself had undertaken to carve the statue of the Virgin, and it had been lovingly done, with just the faintest suggestion about it of a smiling, slant-eyed Kwannon, the Japanese goddess of mercy. From where we stood Mandalay Hill could be seen, frosted with its innumerable shrines. Few of them, surely, had been erected in more curious circumstances than this.

Of the citadel of Mandalay and its palace – the Centre of the Universe – nothing remained but the walls and moat. And it was here by the water's edge, before the heat of the day had gathered, that, of all places in Mandalay, it was most agreeable to saunter. The gilded royal barges had gone and the moat was grown over with lotuses, and spangled with flowering aquatic plants. Children fished with bent pins from ruined causeways and girls came down continually with their petrol cans for water. Hoopoes popped in and out of holes in the willows, and fishing-hawks made occasional sallies over the water. Hundreds of small wading birds were emitting cheerful, chuckling cries as they stepped daintily from lotus leaf to lotus leaf. The deeply castellated red walls that formed the background to this genial scene were no more forbidding than the barbican of a Highland hunting lodge; and the gatehouses and defence towers, with their joss-house architecture and frantic profusion of carving, seemed hardly more serious in purpose than the battlemented Chinese bridge erected in St James's Park in celebration of the Glorious Peace in 1814.

When in 1858 the foundations of the wall were laid, three carefully selected persons had been buried alive under each gatehouse, and one at each corner of the wall. Four more were entombed under the Lion Throne, and yet others at strategic points, scattered throughout the fortress. The grand total was fifty-two, a figure considered by the Board of Astrologers to err on the side of parsimony. They were taken from all walks of life, and included the pregnant woman, indispensable to the composition of a satisfactory foundation-sacrifice. While this was happening, King Mindon, a kind of Burmese Edward the Confessor, was probably splitting hairs with his theologians over obscure scriptural passages. There was a comfortable dualism about the state religion as interpreted by the Burmese kings. The population was enjoined to follow the tenets of the purest form of Buddhism, which forbade the destruction of even the most noxious forms of life, but in matters of state policy the king fell back on his Court Brahmins, Indian specialists in statecraft and occult matters, who were always ready to agree that the means were justified by the end.

Why should it have been supposed that those who had died in such terrifying circumstances should be content, after death, to guard the city of their murderers? And did it ever occur to the victims to warn their executioners that they would refuse to accomplish what was expected of them? Every city in Burma and nearly every bridge and weir had its complaisant ghosts who, according to popular belief, were always ready to drive off intruders, human or otherwise. As in the Far Eastern countries the living and the dead are divided by the most diaphanous of veils; the guardian spirits sometimes took on human form, fought with the weapons of their day, and were even wounded. A case in point was observed on the occasion of the annihilation of the Burmese army by the Mongols of Kublai Khan, when the guardian spirits of the Burmese cities, who had gone armed, presumably with spears and javelins, to the battlefield, were put out of action by the deadly archery of the Tartar horsemen. The Glass Palace Chronicle describes the incident tersely:

> ... on the same day when the army perished ... the spirit who was ever wont to attend the King's chaplain returned to Pagan and shook him by the foot and roused him from his sleep saying, "This day hath Ngahsaunggyan fallen. I have been wounded by an arrow. Likewise the spirits Wetthakan of Salin, Kanshi and Ngatinkyeshin, are wounded by arrows."

Perhaps the fifty-two spirit guardians of Mandalay were similarly handicapped by out-of-date weapons when the British gunboats began their cannonading from the river.

The atmosphere of this town in the days just before the British occupation must have been more macabre than that of Moscow under Ivan the Terrible in his madness. There was a ghastly combination of modernity and crazed medievalism. The telegraph had just been introduced and the town was served by the very latest in steamboats; but wizards went mumbling through the streets, and an English official could be seized and threatened with instant crucifixion if he failed to subscribe to the national lottery.

With a sense of inferiority that was engendered in the knowledge of weakness, every attempt was seized upon to humble the pride of the hated foreigners, unless the King felt that there was any hope of extracting from one of them any of the secrets of their regrettable supremacy in certain matters. Shway Yoe quotes a typical dialogue of the kind that took place between King Mindon and any fresh wanderer to arrive in the city. 'What is your name?' 'John Smith.' 'What can you do?' 'May it please your Majesty, I am a sea-cook.' 'Can you make a cannon?' Whereupon John Smith, if he were a wise man, would agree to make the attempt. A lump of metal would be made over to him, and he would chisel and hammer away at it, and draw his pay as regularly as he could get it.

The contempt for Europeans was rooted originally in Burmese cosmogony, according to which the true human race was concentrated in South-East Asia, which was seen as a symmetrical landmass, in the centre of which were located, not unnaturally, the Burmese holy places. To the north were the Himalayas, and beyond them a kind of fairyland containing the jewelled mountain of Meru and the magic lake in which all the rivers of the world (i.e. the Irrawaddy, the Salween, the Menam, and the Mékong) had their source. To the south were dismal seas, and in them the 'five hundred lesser islands' on which dwelt the inferior people from across the sea. Their attitude, with less justice, duplicated that of the Chinese. In the days of Ava they were outraged that embassies should come from the Viceroy of India, and not the Queen of England, and when the envoys came they might be obliged to live, ignored by the court, on an island where bodies were burned and criminals executed. When called to audience they were forced to walk long distances bare footed and bare headed in the sun; to pass through a posterngate in the palace wall that was so low that the shortest man was compelled to bend. For their benefit the carpets normally covering the floorboards were removed, and their feet were lacerated by the nails which were purposely left protruding.

With the death of Mindon the atmosphere of mania thickened. The ministers of state had manoeuvred the supine Thibaw into the kingship in the mistaken belief that he could be more easily controlled than any of the more intelligent of Mindon's numerous descendants. The stage was now set for a traditional and regularly recurrent Burmese drama, but one which, on this occasion, provoked an unwonted flurry owing to the presence of a foreign colony. All the King's half-brothers and sisters who might have been considered dangerous to the succession and had been promptly popped into gaol, were now, according to the current Burmese euphemism, 'cleared'. The English were much impressed by the preparations for this ceremony, which consisted chiefly in the making of a large number of capacious velvet sacks, a piece of exquisite sensibility on the part of whoever was in charge of arrangements. The 'clearing' was completed in a festival lasting three days, in the course of which the victims were placed in the sacks and respectfully beaten to death; princes, by light blows on the back of the neck; princesses, on the throat. The ingenious purpose of the red velvet was to camouflage any unseemly effusion of royal blood, an advance on the method of Thibaw's ancestor Bodawpaya, who burned to death all his surplus relations, complete with children and servants. Thibaw had shown, too, consideration for the modesty of the female sufferers, an aspect of Inquisitional burnings which was never found altogether satisfactory.

The Burmese have always been ready to excuse such methods of state as the lesser evil; and even survivors of the Thibaw massacre told English friends frankly that, placed in Thibaw's position, they would have done the same thing. The trouble is always ascribed to the harem system, and the superfluity of potential heirs that it produced. Burmese apologists find excuses for this too. It was expected by the King's feudatories and allies that he would take their daughters into his household, and not to have done so, in the face of immemorial custom, would have given offence. In this way, too, the Empire was held together. Certainly, history does not show the kings as unduly concerned with family matters. The only concubine who is highly praised in the chronicle for her capabilities is one who knew where to scratch the King's back without being told where it itched. For the rest, the kings are represented as not even being informed of the children born to lesser queens. A principal queen could be returned at her own request to an old lover: the fantastic tests which Brantôme reports as carried out by Renaissance princes to ensure they married virgins would have filled the Burmese kings with amazement. Even when a queen was seduced, the royal reaction reads more like irritation than wrath. It seems that the kings were content to procreate a polite minimum of a hundred or so descendants, and leave it at that.

Mandalay's foreign colony had hardly recovered from this shock, when another unpleasant affair occurred. A smallpox epidemic carried off two of the King's children; and as epidemic disease was always ascribed to demonic interference, the Indian soothsayers were called in. A formal inspection of the jars of oil buried with Mindon's human sacrifices was made. In the remote past a magic correlation had been established between the condition of the oil thus buried and the efficacy of the haunting. In this case only one of the four jars of oil was found to be intact; and at the full conclave of court astrologers which followed, it was unanimously voted that the city must be abandoned. When the King's ministers refused to do this, the astrologers presented their alternative: the sacrifice of six hundred more persons. Five hundred were to be Burmese, most carefully assorted to include representatives of all ages and stations. A hundred were to be foreigners.

Mindon had secured his fifty-two victims with tact, giving lavish public spectacles which attracted crowds, from which an odd spectator could be quietly spirited away without attracting attention. Thibaw, lacking Mindon's solid, meditative endowments, went at the thing like a bull at a gate, and ordered wholesale arrests. Accounts of such Burmese customs by the early travellers had been too much for the reason of the eighteenth century; consequently they had been denied in Europe as fictitious: 'an abundance of monstrous and incredible Relations ... which one would not think could gain credit even with the weakest of their Readers.' But now the Europeans were to see for themselves. A wave of utter terror seized the city, and wholesale evacuation began. The populace crowded aboard the Irrawaddy steamers or stampeded into the fields and hills. The paralysis of the life of the city together with some doubt as to the possible effect on relations with the English of the inclusion of the hundred foreigners necessary to make a success of the sacrifice produced an official *démenti* of the project. A few of those arrested were never seen again and it was concluded that, in his usual ineffectual way, the King had contented himself with merely tinkering with the problem.

*

Beyond the walls stretched a desolation of tumbled bricks and weeds. I found the spot where, according to a scale-model of the palace which had been erected, the apartments of the white elephant had stood. But of these, too, only the foundations remained. This singular beast dominated the imaginations of all the monarchs of South-East Asia; and although regarded as an avatar of Gautama in numerous previous existences – and therefore primarily of interest only to Buddhists – a kind of collector's fever had developed, seizing such non-Buddhist potentates as the Emperor of Annam. This pressure by the uninstructed – the Hearsts of their day – on a limited supply only increased the ferocity of the competition between the Buddhist rulers.

The wars between the Burmese and their Siamese neighbours were usually undertaken – in theory, at any rate – for the acquisition, or recovery, of these picturesque symbols of power. 'The king in his title,' said Ralph Fitch, writing in 1586, 'is called the king of the white elephants. If any other king have one, and will not send it to him, he will make warre with him for it; for he had rather lose a great part of his kingdom than not conquer him.' In spite of the alleged rarity of albinism in elephants one could be relied upon to turn up sufficiently often in the days of imperial expansion to keep both kingdoms in a state of devastation.

The whiteness of the elephant was nominal, and its sanctity depended upon so many esoteric factors, beyond the layman's grasp, that a substantial body of literature on the subject grew up. The pinkness of the outer annulus of the eye entered into this, as well as the length of the tail, and the number of toe-nails. Ten toe-nails instead of the normal eight were required in a successful candidate. Black elephants possessing this number were collectors' items, although not entitled to adoration, and were classified as white elephants debased by sin in previous existences. The final test, when all others had been passed, was the water one. If the skin, whether black, grey or otherwise, took on a reddish tinge when water was poured on it, the animal was conclusively white. It was elevated immediately to the position of first personality in the land after the king, accorded white and golden umbrellas, given the revenues of a province, diverted daily by a *corps de ballet*, lulled nightly to sleep by a sweet-voiced choir, and if of tender years suckled daily by a line of palace women – an honour eagerly contested by those in a position to aspire to it.

But of all these spectacles and splendours, not a vestige remained. Nothing had survived the citadel's devastation but a few antique cannon. The largest of them turned out to be imitations, with great immovable wheels made of brick. In the later centuries cannon assumed for the Burmese a purely magic significance, having taken over the protective qualities of the leogryph. As they were never fired, there could be no objection to their being fakes, with enormous intimidating bores and twenty-foot-long barrels. The kings were usually ready to offer its weight in silver for any piece of ordnance however old or cracked, and the palace of Mandalay, where all the firearms in the country were stacked up, was a repository of strange museum pieces. They were drawn, when mobile, by teams of auspiciously marked bullocks, which were trained at the word of command to kneel and bow their heads to the ground. The gunners' personal kit was stored in the muzzles. Occasionally a cannon would become, like Alaungpaya's three-pounder, the centre of a cult, and receive offerings of flowers and libations of brandy.

By the end of Mindon's reign it must have been clear that nothing could save Burma. The Burmese, together with all the rest of the Easterners, except the Japanese, were the prisoners of a cosmology composed of interlocking systems, all complete and perfect, and founded in error. Everything had been decided and settled once and for all two thousand years ago. No question had been left unanswered. It was all in the Three Baskets of the Law, its commentaries and subcommentaries; dissected and classified beyond dispute: the seven qualities, the five virtues, the six blemishes, the eight dangers, the ninety-six diseases, the ten punishments, the thirty-two results of Karma. Although Burma was a young nation it had inherited a civilization with the hardened arteries of senility. By comparison with the certainties and self-sufficiency of eastern Asiatic thought, the people of medieval Europe lived in intellectual anarchy. When the end came, the Burmese were beaten not so much by nineteenth-century gunners, as by the Galileos of three centuries before.

That day I was invited to Tok Galé's house for lunch. He lived in the sere reflection of an English suburb, in a detached villa with front garden, gate and path. It was about two miles from the town's centre, in the dacoit belt, and two to three miles from the White-Flag Communists' frontier which ran through some low hills to the east.

The Tok Galés were grandchildren of the Burmese ambassador to France under King Thibaw, and there was a faded photograph in the drawing-room of this dignitary in his court uniform, looking rather sullen, as a result, perhaps, of the long period of immobility imposed by the time-exposure. The family had adopted the Baptist creed, in its tolerant and accommodating Burmese form, and had taken English christian names. The youngest sister, mild, sweet, and mysteriously unmarried, was Anne, who, in spite of not being a Buddhist, had recently been accorded the great honour of acting for a short distance as pall-bearer at the cremation of the venerable U Khanti. Although she had the good sense to retain the Burmese costume, Anne was much anglicized by the friendships she had formed in the old days with members of the British colony. She produced two autograph albums full of the familiar unrevealing snippets in which their memory was enshrined. An American officer had called her, unjustly I thought, a yellow Burmese rose, never having noticed, I suppose that the complexion of the so-called yellow races is rarely yellow. In any case, if obliged to employ a floral analogy, I should have found this charming lady's grace suggestive of the lily rather than the rose. Although the foreign colony of Mandalay was now completely dispersed, Anne maintained her Westernization at full strength by correspondence. She was a member of the Robert Taylor fan club, through which she had made many pen-friends, both in England and the United States.

Lunch consisted of various curries, served in the Burmese style with soup, which was supped throughout the meal. The Tok Galé servitors stood behind our chairs, fanning us vigorously, while we maintained a gently platitudinous conversation that was at once both oriental in flavour and curiously Victorian.

After lunch Tok Galé asked me if I would like to be presented to distinguished neighbours of his, the last surviving members in direct descent of the Burmese royal family; children of King Mindon, by different queens, who, in accordance with custom, had married each other.

We found the Prince Pyinmana and the Princess Hta Hta Paya living in what is usually described, with grim understatement, as reduced circumstances. The Prince was much embarrassed because dacoits had broken into the house a fortnight before, and stolen all his clothes. Before I could be received, Tok Galé went home and came back with a jacket for the Prince to wear for the interview.

The old couple received us in their living-room. They looked very fragile, and Tok Galé said that in recent years audiences had very rarely been granted. The villa, which might have been damaged by bombing, was in a state of advanced disrepair. Plaster was flaking from the walls, which had been repaired by sheets of asbestos and iron grilles. The only pieces of furniture were a few worn-out chairs.

Flanked by Tok Galé and myself, the Prince and Princess sat side by side on two of the broken chairs. They were waited upon by a female servant and her husband, who also served as interpreter. Coming into the royal presence from opposite directions, they shuffled along at a surprising speed on their knees and elbows, smoking large cheroots which were rarely out of their mouths. When a respectful proximity had been reached, they dropped into a comfortable kneeling position and awaited the royal commands with the benevolent patience of spaniels. Occasionally the interpreter leaned forward, took the cheroot out of his mouth, grasped the end of the Prince's ear-trumpet, and bawled a translation of my remarks into it. Once, after shuffling backwards a short distance, he turned and made off to fetch some object of interest the Prince had called for, and on returning collected his baby, which was shrieking in a back room, and came into sight still crawling, but this time on one elbow, the baby gathered in the other arm.

In vain I sought in these aged, placid faces some vestige of the magic presence of their ancestor Alaungpaya, the village headman, who had conquered the Burmese throne with followers armed only with cudgels, driven the French from Syriam, spurned the English, waded in the blood of his enemies. It was generally acknowledged that fire streamed from Alaungpaya's personal weapons; that, like the heroes of the *Ramayana*, he fought with fairy javelins and thunderbolts, and that wherever he stopped gorgeous birds and butterflies entered his dwelling. Here his race had come to an end, in these two feeble, affable old persons, subdued by resignation, and possessing no more than the normal dignity of old age.

Occasionally there was a shrewdness in the Prince's expression, inherited from his father, as well as evidence of a sense of humour, inappropriate in a ruling monarch, but which now in lustreless adversity could be given its wings. He was one of four brothers who had escaped the famous massacre, having been considered too young and unimportant for the dignity of the red sack. Later, to avoid the possibility of any second thoughts, he had become a monk. He was clearly well prepared for certain standard questions; particularly when asked for his opinion of Queen Supayalat, commonly considered to have been Thibaw's evil genius. Why did Queen Elizabeth have Mary Queen of Scots killed? asked the Prince, apropos of Supayalat's Borgia-like methods with rivals. The Prince's eyes were twinkling merrily; he was obviously enjoying himself, and had suddenly taken over from the interpreter, and relapsed into fluent English. It was clear that he liked to stagger his visitors over matters of Burmese high policy in the past. 'Supayalat,' said the Prince firmly, 'was as good as the average Burmese lady. If an ordinary woman comes across her rival in love, she'll do everything she can. Supayalat had the power, that's all.'

The Princess was the daughter of a Siamese lesser queen, and was also considered too insignificant for inclusion in the massacre. She was only fourteen when her mother took her by the hand and they went together out on to their balcony to watch the British troops march in. All she remembered of them was the shining helmets and the plumes. The Burmese, who had expected a sack and massacre of the traditional kind, were much amazed at the mildness of the soldiers.

On the whole the Prince and Princess seemed to regret the old colonial days. Perhaps this was natural because, since Burma had become a free nation, their allowance had been reduced from eight hundred rupees each a month to four hundred rupees. The Prince also complained of the lack of intellectual nourishment these days, and asked me to try to send him a volume of Thomas Hood's poems from England.

CHAPTER TEN

Anawrahta's Pagoda

BEFORE COMING TO Mandalay it had been my intention to visit, if I could, the village of Taungbyon. Taungbyon lies only about twenty miles south of the capital, but I now realized that in the South-East Asia of today it might have become as inaccessible as Lhasa in the last century. This village was associated in about 1070 with Anawrahta's attempt to stamp out the indigenous Burmese religion of nat-worship. Anawrahta was a kind of minor Charlemagne of Buddhism. Conducting a crusade against the kingdom of Thaton he captured the unprecedented total of thirty-two white elephants, each of which was loaded with sacred books for the return to the capital. He also obtained, by conquest or negotiation, the Buddha's collar-bone, his frontlet bone, and an authentic duplicate of the tooth of Kandy. As a result of these triumphs he was acclaimed the foremost champion of Buddhism of his day.

Anawrahta's method of combating the older faith was to order the destruction of the nat shrines found, at that time, in every house in Burma, and to limit the practice of the religion to one village only – Taungbyon. Here elaborate arrangements were made for the celebration of the rites. The site was inaugurated by a spectacular assassination. On the pretext that they had failed to contribute a brick apiece towards the building of a pagoda, the King's chief generals, the Shwepyi brothers, were executed by castration. Reading between the blurred lines of history, it may be supposed that the King was disappointed at the failure of their expedition to China which immediately preceded this event. Sent to obtain another Buddha tooth from the chief of Nanchao (Yunnan), they were fobbed off with a mere jade replica, which had been allowed by contact to absorb a trifling amount of virtue from the original. The generals happened also to be popular heroes, victors of numerous campaigns undertaken to carry the light of religion into adjacent countries; and the King perhaps felt they had usurped some of the lustre that was rightly his alone. As twins, and the sons of a well-known ogress, it must have been clear that they had the makings of superior nats, and it only required such a piece of monstrous regal caprice as their murder to complete the process.

The Shwepyi brothers became the most popular and the second most powerful of all the members of the Burmese nat-pantheon. They are still worshipped at Taungbyon, with a corps of female mediums in attendance to transmit their oracles. Their annual festival is the most important of Burmese animistic ceremonies, and draws huge crowds from all parts of the country.

Since frequent reference to nats is inavoidable in any work dealing with Burma, I must attempt to define the nature of these powerful supernatural entities. The word is used in a loose, generic sense to cover all members – whether ghosts, ghouls, vampires, or merely lost and starving souls – of the spectral world. There were nats called into existence by an intellectual effort, such as Alaungpaya's gun nat. This modernistic demiurge was reverenced in the form of the king's first three-pounder, which, scented, coated with gold-leaf, and wrapped in silk, was propitiated with bottles of liquor. But besides this *déclassé* and miscellaneous ghostly riff-raff a category of sentient beings exists, having its own fairly elevated place in the Buddhist hierarchy of souls. These are the local tutelary spirits, whose worship preceded (and in the case of the Vietnamese, actually outlasted and replaced) Buddhism. Of these there are many thousands; although only thirty-seven, the indigenous Burmese gods, are adored – or rather, propitiated – on a national scale.

According to the cosmogony which the Burmese borrowed from India, there are eleven principal stages or levels of the 'corporeal and generating' soul; four being unhappy, and seven happy. Unhappy souls are those confined in hell, or existing as miscellaneous ghosts, or incarnated in animals. Until recently souls imprisoned in the bodies of foreigners were included in this last category. At the bottom of the scale of happiness come human beings, and immediately above them in the soul's evolution are located the true nats. The situation of a nat is preferable to that of the most fortunate human being, although it is still far removed from the felicity of the ultimate heavens. Nats, although exempt from the ills of humanity, are still subject to sensual passion, which sometimes leads them even to form unions with human beings. From such attachments – whether temporary or otherwise – arises the recognized class of nat-ka-daws – spirit mediums or wives – so numerous that it has been seriously suggested that in the forthcoming census of the population of Burma they should be described as a separate occupational class.

The land of the nats, then, is a kind of Mahommedan paradise, whose occupants are able to make the best, such as it is, of both worlds. With the soul's progress upwards, however, the intellectual pleasures begin to assert themselves, and the more typically human distractions to lose their appeal. Finally, after passage through numerous heavens, a formless and incorporeal state is attained when the soul, imagined as an immaterial sun, hovers on the threshold of Nirvana, a strange, archaic version of the Shavian Life-Force, the pure intellect functioning in the void.

From an examination of the attributes of the thirty-seven nats the influence of the thirty-three devas of the Hindus may be suspected; but it is also evident that their legends enshrine memories of Mongol heroes of great antiquity, some of them shared with the Thais, the Cambodians, and even the Vietnamese, and the peoples of southern China. The legends are confused and vary from district to district. U Shin Gyi, for example, the guardian spirit of Rangoon and the lower Irrawaddy, is there known as the greatest harpist of all time, who, having fatally charmed the sirens of the river, was drowned by them. In northern Burma he is no more than the son of a king of Pagan, who was killed by a fall from a swing while at play. To enter this pantheon of the nats, a tragic death seems, above all, to have been essential. Many of the thirty-seven were kings while they lived, but no king who died comfortably in his bed could enter this magic circle. This strange immortality was only to be achieved by touching in some unpredictable way a chord of popular imagination. Of an ancient tyrant's memory nothing remains but the legend of his perfidious handling of a blacksmith, who became the most powerful of all the nats and the guardian spirit of every Burmese house.

Those who became nats died by murder, of grief or fright, from snake-bite, an overdose of opium or the unlucky smell of onions. Among their numbers was a general who took up cockfighting when he should have been leading the armies, and was buried to the waist and left to die. There was also a politician who, when the king's wrath turned against him, tried to get away on a marble elephant, which, however, he failed to vivify by well-tried magical methods. The Burmese people never forgot this picturesquely tragic episode. Nor were they able to forget the grotesque end of King Tabinshweti, the conqueror who united all Burma and left it at the height of its prosperity in the days when the Portuguese first entered the country. Tiring of the panoply of power, Tabinshweti took to drink and was finally assassinated. According to one tradition he was killed while seated upon a close stool, suffering from an attack of dysentery. Of this king nothing has come down to the Burmese man in the street but this one foolish fact. The marchings and the counter-marchings, the sack of towns and devastations of provinces, have all been forgotten. This founder of the Burmese Empire, this scourge of God, is now no more than a man who died ridiculously while on a lavatory-seat, a dysentery nat, who receives offerings of fruit and flowers from sufferers from that disease, and even used to be worshipped in effigy in the ludicrous posture in which he died.

This strange reversing process, that makes clowns of kings, and that in death takes ordinary unlucky mortals and places them in the ranks of the heroes, is no better exemplified than in the case of Nga Pyi, a messenger, a silly man, who while riding, about eight hundred years ago, a bearer of bad news, to the camp of his prince, dared to break his journey to sleep. For this delay he was executed, becoming the Spirit Rider of the White Horse, a national champion, a Burmese Santiago. White horse-puppets are offered at his shrines all over Burma, and he has made frequent historical appearances like the

Angels at Mons, brandishing his sword at the head of the armies, when the issue of the day has been in doubt. Lately he was reported in the Rangoon press to have been in action against the Karens.

Thus Burmese history is seen, dreamlike and inconsequent, in the popular imagination, just as the average Englishman remembers little of King Alfred but the story of the burnt cakes, and nothing of Robert the Bruce but his encounter with a spider.

My friend Tok Galé thought that a visit to Taungbyon could be arranged through the good offices of the Superintendent of Police; so, when in accordance with my instructions I paid a routine call on this gentleman, the matter was mentioned.

The Superintendent was an Anglo-Burman, of a type frequently to be met with, which takes after the English father in an almost exaggerated way. This variation is tall and of military bearing, favours a close-clipped moustache, and possesses a bluff inhibition of manner to be found in England among minor executives of substantial insurance companies, or army officers of field rank. It seemed impossible that a tiny Burmese mother could have produced so stalwart a son as this.

Smiling shyly, the Superintendent held out a huge hand. There would be no trouble in going to Taungbyon. Absolutely no trouble, old boy. Lay on an escort just in case; but actually things were pretty quiet. Touch wood, and all that. The Superintendent was a man of few words, and one felt a habit of understatement might be concealed by these clipped and unemphatic utterances.

A large map of the Mandalay area covered half of the walls. It was patterned with interpenetrating colours, swirling contours and isolated blotches. By reference to the key I learned that Communists, either the 'Red' or 'White' Flag varieties, held the country immediately to the north-east, east, and south-east of the city. The centre of Mandalay itself was described as 'under effective Government administration', which, however, did not extend to the suburbs, where administration was admitted to be 'non-effective'. Across the Irrawaddy, to the west, the situation seemed to be vague, or 'liquid' as the military euphemism usually puts it. This area was left uncoloured. To the north and south a hideous yellow stain was spreading, flecked here and there with a red rash of Communism. Here the 'White' People's Volunteer Organization held sway; the once patriotic force which had been raised to fight the Japanese, and then, with the war at an end, had refused to be disarmed, and turned to banditry. There were also, said the Superintendent casually, a few 'Yellow' PVOs who, after surrendering to the government, had revolted again, and gone underground. In some sectors the PVOs were supposed to have accepted temporary Communist leadership, and in other places they were fighting them. There, where the map was striped so garishly, the 'White' and 'Red' Communists had united, dissolved their association, and reunited again. The present situation was uncertain. The map-makers hadn't bothered to mark in a few villages held by army deserters, who might quite well by now have thrown in their lot with any of the other organizations.

So there it was, said the Superintendent, with a suspicion of boredom. A bit of a mess, and so on, and so forth, but nothing that couldn't be put right in the end. Taungbyon, I might have noticed, was deeply embedded in PVO territory; but nothing was to be thought of it. With a wave of the hand, the map and all it represented was dismissed. An escort would call for us at eight in the morning.

And at eight precisely the escort was there; but instead of the cheroot-smoking private I had expected, a three-ton lorry had arrived with a squad of tommy-gunners and a Bren gun mounted on the roof. A spruce young lieutenant came over, saluted and clambered into the back of our jeep, and we were off. This display of force was in flagrant opposition to the advice I had always been given in Rangoon; never to travel with the police or the military. To do so, said my informants, was to run the risk of falling into an ambush, whereas by travelling alone or with unarmed companions, one increased the possibility of robbery, but very much lessened that of sudden death.

Out through the southern suburbs of Mandalay we went, plunging and bucking painfully, through the dust curtain already raised by the thousand bullock-carts of the morning. Away to the left lay the abandoned pagodas of Amarapura, glinting dragon's teeth sown thickly in a stony plain. In 1857 this capital city was deserted by order of King Mindon, because its luck was supposed to have become exhausted, and also because the king felt himself drawn towards the sacred Mandalay Hill, of which he had dreamed on two successive nights. In a few years all the lay buildings, constructed of wood, had mouldered away completely, and now only these gleaming cones remained.

Our road floundered on through the exhausted earth. This plain had endured ten kingdoms and a hundred generations, and now it was sapped and vanquished. We were encircled by a ghostly decrepitude, roads that lead to nowhere, canals holding pools of brilliant, stinking water, a few nat-haunted banyan trees, grotesque with old muscled trunks and bearded roots. A row of sickly flamboyants wept their blossoms into a swamp, in which a stork waded away, as if through blood, on our approach. Having taken the wrong road many times, we stopped to ask the way from a girl in a green silk longyi who had come down to a canal for water. As she dipped her petrol cans, first one then the other, into the slime, the whole stagnant expanse suddenly boiled into life as frogs went leaping and splashing away. Before turning back she cupped her hands and drank some water from one of her cans.

Two enormous leogryphs guarded the approach to Taungbyon. They were as large as the monsters that stand before the Shwedagon Pagoda at Rangoon, but painted stark white, and eerie and forbidding in these cheerless surroundings. Beyond, reared up Anawrahta's pagoda.

We roared into the village and pulled up by a structure like a roofed-over market-place in an English country town. The soldiers came tumbling out of the lorry, cocked their Sten guns, and formed a widely spaced circle round us and the sacred places. Beyond them we could see the villagers, temporary dependents of the PVO, gathered at the doors of their huts and watching us without either hostility or enthusiasm. It was correct first to visit the pagoda. With our shoes respectfully removed, we were led by a guardian to the entrance and shown the two spaces still left vacant for the bricks of the Shwepyi brothers.

Apart from building pagodas, the ancient Burmese seem to have set extraordinary store by the act of completing them. Just as in biblical times battles were sometimes decided by individual combat between the champions, there are many examples in Burmese history of conflicts being settled without fighting in favour of the side which could first complete a pagoda. The chroniclers relate with relish the obvious and childish stratagems practised by the victors, who usually had a canvas imitation finished while the incredibly gullible adversary was still busy with the foundations of a traditional building of brick. Perhaps, after all, there was something in the nature of high treason about the Shwepyis' defection.

One of the soldiers now brought up the guardian of the nat shrine, which was in a building under the market-like structure. Padlocks were unfastened and heavy double trellis gates slid back. It was like being let into a bank after hours. In an interior lit by strings of electric fairy-lights and behind a bank of flowers sat two gaudy dolls, with high spiked helmets, and drawn swords carried upon their shoulders. They were quite unmartial in appearance, and yet, in some way, sinister. Unlike the Buddha images with their placid, even smug expressions, these golden faces were shrewd and scheming. What a decline attends the mighty after death! These great captains who had fought their way to China and back, and had plagued Anawrahta after their killing by catching at the rudder of the royal raft so that it could not move (a classical Burmese form of haunting), were now a couple of slightly disreputable Don Juans of the inferior heavens. Legend remembered that they had died by castration, and appeared to attach some tortuous and topsy-turvy significance to this. By a kind of logic in reverse the king who is supposed to have died as a result of an attack of dysentery is worshipped by dysentery sufferers, and the castrated heroes become the patrons of sly amours. At their annual ceremony the chief mediums, who are females, dress themselves in the special costumes attributed to the brothers; in waist-cloths with an ornamental border, wide-sleeved jackets, white scarves thrown over the shoulder, and light red helmets on their heads. They are attended by junior mediums dressed as Burmese princesses. The ceremony begins with the chanting of the traditional song in which the brothers' lives and deaths are briefly described. This ends with the words: 'Now all ye pretty maidens, love ye us, as ye were wont to do while yet we were alive.' In this lies a hint of the mild element of the saturnalia that appears to enter into this feast. As the lieutenant put it, on our way back, 'to accomplish this celebration we proceed not with our wives, as there are many pretty ladies assembled there, also not in company with their spouses'.

CHAPTER ELEVEN

By Lorry to Lashio

AT EIGHT NEXT MORNING I climbed into the gharry called Ford, setting in brisk motion its resident gnats, and ordered the driver to take me to the airport. In accordance with my declared itinerary I was to fly to Myitkyina, leaving Mandalay on approximately the third of March and returning, by river, on the eight. On the ninth I was to set out for Lashio by road. One day was allowed for this considerable journey; but the War Office had generously allotted five days to get to Taunggyi, which was hardly farther. There was some vague talk of occasional caravans of lorries plying by stages between these two towns, but no suggestion had ever been made that there was any way of getting from Taunggyi to Mandalay, a section for which three days had been prescribed. Having reached Mandalay again, I was to board a boat, which the General Staff Department seemed to imagine would be waiting for me with steam up – since no delay was assumed in the city – reaching Rangoon seven days later, the minimum taken by the trip in favourable circumstances. It had seemed to me at the time ambitious, when allowing for Burma's condition, to try to draw up an exact timetable, in the way one might have done in preparation for a Cook's tour in the Dolomites. And now at the airport it soon became evident that an immediate break-down in the original planning was likely.

Nothing had been heard of the plane that was due to arrive at nine o'clock. Nor did the airport staff seem in any way surprised. The plane that had been due four days before, on the Monday, had not arrived either. At that season, thick ground mists often prevented the planes taking off at Rangoon in the early hours, and unless they could make an early start there was no time to go to Myitkyina and back during the day. But there was still hope, and I was invited to make myself at home in the picturesque huts which served as waiting-rooms. One of these had a notice across it which said it was a restaurant. Here in surroundings to which a Hindu ascetic would not have objected I seated myself and ordered breakfast. I was soon joined by a police official, who began to probe me in the most urbane fashion, between mouthfuls of eggs and chips, as to my intentions. Refusing, perhaps through irritation caused by the delay and the heat, to enter into the conventions of the game, I silently produced and spread across the table the whole of my many documents. The officer was hurt at such bluntness, and said that he was only trying to do his job in the most reasonable way. There was no gainsaying this; I apologized, put the permits away uninspected, allowed myself to be drawn forth in a civilized manner, and our interview terminated cordially.

Several hours dwindled away. With their passing the excited anticipation drained from the passengers who now squatted, resignation drawn over them like a shabby cloak, in corners of the airport huts. A group of pongyis, released in these days, it seemed, from the prohibition on such mundane forms of travel, had ceased to examine their tickets and relapsed into holy meditation. Only a few crows turned in the grey, empty sky, in the rim of which the far hills flickered and stirred as if about to dissolve. Occasionally a member of the airport staff came cringing past under the sun. At about midday an official went round whispering to the various groups, as if a great man had died, that the flight had been cancelled.

Back at the airport office, they refunded money on tickets, rebooked those who insisted on a hypothetical Monday plane, drove the despondent crowd into the street, and barred the door. A huge barrel-chested Sikh came up and clutched at me moaning, 'I can't stand this heat.' He wanted to go to Bhamó, and knew a man who might be persuaded to hire him a jeep, with a driver, for five hundred rupees. What would I say to splitting the cost? I hadn't intended to go to Bhamó, but it was in the right direction; so I agreed, and in a moment the Sikh had leaped into the nearest gharry, which bore him swiftly away, his head thrust out of the window, beard quivering with excitement and despair, shouting alternately instructions to the driver and counsel to me. An hour later he was back, heartbroken. The man was a villain who wanted to profit from the misfortunes of others by charging twice the price offered. Now he was off again to comb the city for an honest jeep-owner, and with a furious wave to the driver he went rattling away.

It now seemed to me that I might as well, to use an army phrase, 'find my own way', going perhaps to Lashio and Taunggyi first, and working in the Northern Shan States part of the trip at a later stage. I therefore made enquiries in the neighbouring tea-houses and found that a lorry was expected to leave for Lashio next morning. With the aid of an English-speaking gharry driver, this was located. The driver was either working or sleeping underneath it, since only his legs protruded, but after the gharry-wallah had jerked them furiously, he crawled out and admitted that he would be leaving for Lashio early next morning. Still not completely weaned from Western conceptions of travel, I tried to fasten him down to something less vague. Through the ever-present language difficulties there was nothing to be done. Around us swirled a flood of bullock-carts and pedicabs. There seemed no way of fixing this definite point in the chaos of the traffic, but that would have to suffice. He would leave from there, early in the morning – when you could see the veins on your hands.

Back to Tok Galé I went to announce the prolongation of my stay. There was another visit to our Chinese friend who with limitless hospitality immediately offered me his room again. Another night was to be endured in the reverberating no-man's-land between the cinema loudspeakers, the pagoda gongs, and the penetrating Chinese sopranos of the tea-house gramophones. Once again I took my washbowl to the edge of the parapet, silhouetted there against the neon-pink of the sky, and, trying to convince myself that any previous reaction had been imaginary, poured out the water on the roof below. Once again came back the muffled cry. On my way to the Excelsior a pariah dog turned back and followed me. Remembering the Englishman who was nearly lynched for killing one of these creatures I increased my pace, and the dog did the same. When close at my heels it reached forward and without any particular animosity, in a rather detached and experimental manner, it took my calf between its teeth, and bit. Having done so, it turned back and strolled away, while I was still wondering what the onlookers would do if I kicked it high into the air. In the Excelsior I washed the wound in Fire-Tank Brand Mandalay Whisky, and offer as a testimonial the fact that I suffered no ill effects.

But that night there was good news. Tok Galé arrived to tell me that a Mr Dalgouttie of the British Information Service would be arriving next day by plane from Mandalay and then continuing immediately to the British Consulate at Maymyo in the car which would be sent down to meet him. Although Maymyo was only thirty miles along the road to Lashio, it was situated at an altitude of three thousand five hundred feet, and would therefore be a very agreeable place for me to stay for a day or two while making arrangements to go further. I telephoned the Consulate and was told that there would be no difficulty about putting me up.

About ten miles out of Mandalay, the road begins to climb and to wind. There are trees, at first isolated in tangled bush, and then slowly closing in until linked with thinly flowering creepers. According to reliable information, the area through which we were passing was solidly held by White-Flag Communists. Burmese army lorries passed up and down the road and, in doing so, were frequently shot-up; but no attempt was made by the army to penetrate into the jungle where the Communists administered the villages. It was probably not worth while. Even if a major operation could be undertaken to clear every village, the Communists would come back as soon as the troops had gone away. It seemed likely that an unofficial *modus vivendi* had been reached, and for civilians the road was moderately safe, as long as they didn't travel with the police, or with the army. The White-Flag Communists were said not to indulge in acts of terrorism, which sometimes occurred in Red-Flag areas. The trouble was to know who was in control. The traveller's chief security problem was the lack of effective control by one side or the other; because the Communists, no doubt, had the same trouble with dacoits as did the government.

The Consulate station-wagon sped smoothly over the first section of the 'Burma Road' which, still the country's main strategic highway, was in far better condition than the terrible tracks on which I had hitherto travelled. In about an hour we were in Maymyo, the former hill-station of the English, and suddenly it seemed as though we were entering Forest Gate at the end of a dry August. With a hissing of tyres we drove up a well-kept thoroughfare called 'The Mall', across which, before us, passed a long, thin snake with whip-like movements. There was also a Downing Street and several well-spaced villas, with names like Ridge-View. We stopped for a moment at the golf course to chat with members of the Consular staff, and then drove on to the Consulate, which was set upon an eminence, above evidences of landscape-gardening; a sweep of lawns, with coarse, whitened grass; flower-beds in which larkspur and nasturtiums fought against desperate odds.

Here at Maymyo I was offered a splendid chance to compare the English and French methods of adaptation to South-East Asia. In the previous year I had stayed at Dalat, the French equivalent of Maymyo in Indo-China. In Dalat, one knew that one was in the Far East. Although it was neither France nor Indo-China, the French had tinkered with bamboo and carved wood and produced an acceptable pastiche, a compromise that was sometimes gay and well suited to its surroundings. There were hotels and restaurants where you could eat the local food, Frenchified of course, but still of recognizably oriental origin. In Maymyo there seemed to be no compromise. The atmosphere, by contrast, was austere, sporting, and contemplative. Maymyo was very clean, hard working, hard playing, exaggeratedly national, and slightly dull. Here you began to understand the allegation that the English are an insular people.

But if unadventurous and simple by French colonial standards, life in Maymyo was full of solid comfort. It was quite extraordinary to experience the sensations so often associated with the fatigues and discomforts of remote places in these well-ordered surroundings, to lie at dawn between well-laundered sheets, watching the flocks of green parakeets in the tree-tops, and listening to the early jabbering of exotic birds. Fifty yards from the window, beyond the show of sweet peas, the jungle was kept in check behind an iron railing. The jungle was not particularly exuberant, and had been made to look rather like a gentleman's sporting estate in the Home Counties, by the cutting through it of numerous walks and avenues. In the early hours there was a great scratching of fowls down by the fence, and as it seemed unlikely that the Consul, a dashing figure, should keep chickens, I went down to inspect them. I was amazed to find that they actually were jungle fowl, a cock, with mane and rump of copper and glinting blue thighs, with his numerous harem. As no one had ever bothered them you could get within a few yards and watch their bright, busy foraging among the leaves. Duffy, the Consul, said that they were there every day as he had resisted the servants' implorings to shoot them; he knew that as soon as the first shot had been fired, this decorative adjunct to his demesne would vanish for ever.

That evening the Consul gave a party. Besides the shrunken Consular staff, there were a few Indians and Anglo-Burmese, a Burmese princess with her English husband and her daughter, and a British engineer who was at work on the repair of the viaduct which carried the Mandalay–Lashio railway line over the gorge at Gokteik, about forty-five miles further up the road. Officers of the Burmese Army who had been invited did not appear; a reflection, it seemed, of an officially inspired coolness.

The work on the viaduct sounded like a Herculean labour. It had been in progress for three years and every so often the territory would pass temporarily into the control of some new insurgent movement, and high-ranking officers would come and inspect the work benignly, in the conviction that they would benefit from it in due course. Recently the Communists had made one or two official appearances, once requisitioning the typewriter, for which an official receipt had been left. The local Communists, not having had to fight Europeans as they had done in Indo-China and Malaya, show no particular anti-white animus. When they were about to remove some of his personal gear, the engineer made the private ownership clear by pointing to his chest and saying, 'me, me'. These articles were left.

The guest of the evening was clearly the Princess Ma Lat, who, apart from the possession of a vivid personality in its own right, had acquired some additional celebrity by a reference to her in Mr Maurice Collis's book *Trials in Burma*. The passage, which is practically known by heart by the literary-minded section of the local population, deals with the occasion when, some thirty years ago, Mr Collis, who was then a district magistrate, solemnized the Princess's marriage with a local bookmaker. After commenting with great enthusiasm on the Princess's beauty and dignity of demeanour, the author permits himself an expression of surprise that he should have been called upon to perform this particular ceremony.

Ma Lat's party had settled down at the other end of the room, and I found myself engaged with an Anglo-Burman. He was the opposite of the Police Inspector of Mandalay, dark and Burmese-looking where the other had been Anglo-Saxon; unable to throw his lot in with the Burmese, from whom he felt separated by blood, he was permanently wretched as a result. This man clung desperately, pitifully, to the English in him, of which so little could be externally recognized. In some way or other, he and his fellow Anglo-Burmese had been 'abandoned', left to some kind of nameless fate under the pure Burmese whom they so clearly despised. Such unfortunate people are, of course, always followers of some nonconformist Christian sect, which further impedes their comfortable and happy absorption into the human mainstream of the country where they live.

As the man was becoming lachrymose I was much relieved by the approach of Mr Bellamy, Ma Lat's husband, a man of genial and confidential manner, who still occasionally makes a book. Mr Bellamy said, 'If you want to talk to my mem-sahib, you'd better come over now, because we're going in a moment.'

The Princess Ma Lat was at this time fifty-seven, although in the way of many Asiatics who do no manual labour, she looked much less than her age. She was dressed in conservative Burmese style, and her still handsome features were continually enlivened by an expression which made one feel she was amused by something of which she did not entirely approve. Since it had been brought up several times in the evening, I had an intuition that a tactful allusion to the famous passage would not be badly received. The Princess's characteristic expression deepened. 'I object to the book,' she said, 'only because of its inaccuracy. Mr Collis said that although a member of the royal family, I could not be admitted to any of the European clubs of Rangoon ... My father was an honorary member of *every* club.' When she had said this, the amused disapproval brightened into quiet triumph.

The Princess's grandfather was brother of King Mindon and Crown Prince – a perilous situation for any Burman to be in. In due course, in the preliminary manoeuvring for the succession, he was murdered by one of his many nephews, and as Burmese liquidations were usually extended to include any members of the family who happened to be about, his son – the Princess's father – escaped, to take refuge with the British. Later he went off to the Shan States where he was recognized as 'King of Burma', and raised an army to attack Thibaw, but was forestalled in this by British action.

In these days Ma Lat had become the moving spirit behind various charities, particularly the local maternity hospital. She is the recognized expert in all matters pertaining to the cinema, and is able quite effortlessly to name the stars playing in any American film shown in the last twenty years. I mentioned my recent visit to her cousins in Mandalay, describing in passing the servants' habit of crawling into their presence. Ma Lat nodded with approval, and said that she could remember the time when hers did the same, but, there – you knew what servants were nowadays. Discovering that we both expected to be in Rangoon in about a month's time, we arranged to meet, and I promised to escort her to see the film of *Cinderella*.

The daughter of the union, June Rose, who was about twenty years of age, allied to the graceful beauty of the Burmese a quite European vivacity. She had recently been co-winner of some sort of competition, and as a result had been invited with the other successful competitor, a Burmese boy called Richard, for a three months' tour in the USA. There they had learned to jitterbug.

When the family were about to leave, in an elderly and ailing British car, June Rose showed much skill in locating a short in the wiring, and much tomboyish energy in winding the starting-handle until the engine fired. On reconsideration of the whole episode I cannot really think that the Princess was any worse off as she was, enthusiastically immersed in the interests of any English or American woman of her age, than she might have been in the old days, living the stifling life of the Burmese royal seraglio, with the shadow of the red sack looming with each change of kingship.

It was now time to think of the journey to Lashio, and the Consul sent his chauffeur with me down to Maymyo bazaar, to make enquiries. We were told that the trucks leaving Maymyo that day were going no further than the towns of Naungkhio or Hsipaw. There might be some kind of transport coming through next day, from Mandalay, but no one was sure.

Maymyo bazaar itself was wonderfully lively. We were already on the edge of the Northern Shan States, and there were swaggering, sword-bearing hill men about the street in turbans and the short pyjama-trousers worn by the Shans. Some of them were tattooed so closely wherever their flesh showed that they might have been wearing skin-tights of knitted blue wool. In the big, walled market they sold a fine selection of the bags the Shans carry over their shoulders, wonderfully woven in colours and sometimes decorated with small cowrie shells. There were piles of enormous coolie hats, some of them finished in a central cone of silver, any number of patent medicines, and towels with 'good morning' on them. Maymyo had many barbers' shops, which had found a use for the waste products of the local 'tyre surgery'. Lengths of outer covers were mounted complete in sections of rims on the bottoms of the barbers' chairs, in which the customers rocked themselves in perilous abstraction while the razors hovered over their chins. There were ranks of gharries that appeared to do no serious business, although occasionally a group of Shans would wake up a driver, bundle into one and go for a quick spin round the bazaar, much as in the old days one took a five shilling flip round the aerodrome in a plane. In Maymyo the exuberant fantasy of the Mandalay gharries was diminished, but I saw a pedicab with three pairs of handlebars, twenty-seven lamps, and fourteen horns, one in the shape of a serpent.

At the Consulate, Duffy thought it a good thing to wait at least another day, to see if I could pick up a truck going all the way to Lashio, rather than run the risk of being stranded for a time in one of the smaller towns between. I felt ashamed of the eagerness with which I seized on this short respite.

In the afternoon we visited the local gardens. There was a small, trim lake, a few well-spaced trees and shrubberies in the English style, and here, said the gardener, in the early mornings passed a gaudy, transient population of hornbills, orioles, and parakeets. But always with the mounting of the sun these exotics vanished and were replaced by the drab, skulking bird-life of the European woodlands. Where peacock and silver pheasant had strutted now only hardy, unabashed thrushes and sparrows hopped. But always the background was dominated by the mysterious calls of birds, aloof and invisible in the jungle; the sad hooting of the Burmese cuckoo, which is the call of the cuckoo we know with the notes reversed; the midnight rendezvous-whistle of the brain-fever bird, which repeated without respite, to the victim raving with malaria, becomes an hallucinatory addition to his torments. In the end these sounds become associated with the Indo-Chinese peninsula, and after being away from them for a time, I found myself longing to hear them again.

Dressing next morning I hid a small reserve of money in a bandage round a damaged ankle. The barometer of Burmese travel had fallen back somewhat, since the news had just come through of the slaughter of two tin-miners near Tavoy – a rare and extraordinary occurrence, as foreigners have not been singled out for attack in

Burma. They had been taken off a truck in which they had been riding with Burmese passengers, and riddled with Sten-gun fire. The truck had then been sent on its way, without any of the other passengers being molested. This was supposed to be the work of Red-Flag Communists, or perhaps local Mon insurgents, or perhaps a combination of both. Fortunately it was believed that there were no Red Flags in the Lashio area.

At seven o'clock the Consul's driver was sent down to the bazaar to find out if there was any news of transport. Soon after, he was back again to say that a truck was just about to leave, but that it would wait ten minutes for me. I said goodbye to Duffy, who gave me the usual advice about non-resistance and a smile when dealing with Burmese bandits, and we were off.

But at the bazaar there was no sign of the lorry. Backwards and forwards we went, from the tea-shop to the tyre-surgery, from the tyre-surgery to the petrol filling point. The lorry had vanished, and while we were combing the back-streets of Maymyo, it might, of course, be already putting the miles between us on the road to Lashio. Finally the driver decided that it was no use looking further in Maymyo, and we went sprinting off, down the Lashio road. After a mile he pulled up to make enquiries from a man who was sitting outside his workshop, making a coffin. Only a minute ago, said the man, such a lorry had gone past. But to one engrossed in creative labour time's relativity is very real; a minute may be an hour. On we went, full speed ahead; the last bullock-cart dropped behind, the jungle closed in.

It is well known that the natives of all races who have only recently been introduced to mechanization drive in emergency with special *élan*, but my driver was handicapped by a mysterious ailment of the jeep, a dysfunction which I have never met before or since. We would accelerate, sometimes to nearly fifty miles an hour, and then suddenly the car would be seized by a violent convulsion, whose epicentre seemed vaguely located in the gearbox. Once in the grip of this palsy, the driver would be obliged to bring the jeep practically to a standstill, before the tremors died away, and we could accelerate once again. This rebellion of the mechanism could be avoided by keeping, say, at a steady thirty-five miles an hour, but it was clear that if we did this the lorry might be gaining upon us.

On we went in this way, mile after mile, over hills and through valleys inundated with a frothing, vernal vegetation and filled with the odour of newly watered ferns in a glasshouse. We had been travelling for half an hour when I was alarmed to see that the needle on the petrol gauge had fallen nearly to zero. This I pointed out, but the driver shook his head reassuringly. He had probably laid some kind of wager with himself, and had become seriously interested in the out-come of our chase. Along we hustled, taking full advantage of the rolling downhill slopes when the speed could be kept up with relatively low engine revolutions, which did not bring on our mechanical ague. To me, it was incredible that the lorry should have covered such a distance in so short a time. Whenever we turned a bend, I expected to see it trailing its billows of dust along the next straight, but all we saw was an armoured car with tyre trouble, and a couple of the crew covering with their rifles a third man, while he got on with the repair. The petrol gauge now said empty and I gesticulated at it dumbly again; but the driver had become possessed by his purpose and paid no attention, leaning away out of the car to sweep round a right-hand curve. Down a hill-side we dropped through half a dozen hairpin bends, while large, winged insects, seemingly sucked up out of space, struck us in the face. We swerved wildly to avoid a rotten tree trunk that had fallen half across the road. Again we were stricken of our palsy, slowed down, re-accelerated, and there, at last, were the few huts of a hamlet, with the lorry, lying at an angle in the road's camber, outside a tea-shop.

The third of the Three Great Works of Perfection prescribed by the Buddhist faith is a benevolent disposition towards all sentient beings, and I believe that apart from unfortunate incidents arising out of dacoity and warfare this is much observed by the generality of the Burmese people. But until one comes to know them better, there is sometimes a lack of expansiveness in first contacts, which tends to mask this. A number of faces looked down at me inscrutably from the lorry. Wishing to hear a confirmation of my driver's assurances, I asked if they were going to Lashio. There was a long silence, and then a young man who had been scrutinizing me from between narrowed lids said, 'This car will go to Lashio.' I then asked when it was expected to arrive, and there was another long pause. When I thought that my question had been ignored, the reply came, with slow and clear enunciation: 'We do not know when it will get to Lashio.' There was something about the spokesman that set him apart from the rest of the passengers; a piercing, speculative gaze, a quality of rather sinister deliberation, of the kind which might have been observed in the originals upon which Hollywood film directors modelled their Chinese generals. With slight nods and gestures he controlled the disposition of persons and baggage in the lorry. A lifting of the finger and a few murmured words, and I found a place made for me up in the front, but one place removed from the driver. Before we started off, I hid my two cameras in tool-filled cavities.

The road now became steeper. Painfully we ground our way up the hill-sides, or lurched down them, never travelling fast enough to sweep the engine-heated air from the cabin. In these virgin forests the bird-life was more distinguished than at Maymyo. There were many bee-eaters, hoopoes, and swallows with iridescent blue backs. Jungle fowl scuttled across the road with the foolish panic of barnyard chickens. Vultures wheeled in the sky, and in alighting chose leafless trees – perhaps to leave a clear field of vision – about which they spaced themselves with curious regularity. Once when we stopped on a hill, where a precipice rose from the teak woods above us, I heard a thin, staccato shrieking and saw something which I had heard of but never before seen, a peregrine attacking a vulture, which avoided its furious stoops by negligent dippings of the wing. Besides this one heard continually a shrill, bird-like whistling, which was made by colonies of squirrels.

My immediate neighbour in the driver's cabin was a thin, lively Burmese lady, who at frequent intervals raised her longyi to dab at her left leg, which was thickly coated with mud and stained with blood. When we stopped she had some difficulty in getting down,

and sometimes groaned slightly. Encouraged by the general acceptance of my cigarettes, I asked the admittedly chief passenger what
the trouble was and received the astonishing information that she
had fallen off a motorcycle. At one of our halts she washed her
wounds in petrol, but then, although she hunted about and mixed
up a few trial samples with water, was unable to find any suitable
mud to replace the application.

Frequent repairs to the lorry were called for. Minor engine parts
were made fast temporarily by surplus strips of rattan torn off bales
of cargo. All tyres were reinforced by patches of cover, held in place
by nuts and bolts. Occasionally the engine would falter and choke,
and the driver, jumping down and flinging up the bonnet, would
utter the word 'short', which is now Burmese. At that, the chief
passenger would lower himself from his perch on the highest point
of the cargo, and after a brief, judicial scrutiny, point out what had
to be done. Sometimes a screwdriver would be wiped and put into
his hand, and with this he would operate while the driver and his
various mates looked on as if at delicate surgery. This was the
general condition into which Burmese road transport had fallen. I
wondered what would happen when the day came when all these
old ex-army lorries were utterly and finally worn out, when the
ruined mechanisms could no longer be kept revolving by ingenious
patching and by spare parts taken from other crocks which had
completely disintegrated.

We passed through several small towns. They had no particular
character and consisted of no more than a street and a square where
the markets would be held. As we were deep in the Shan country,
there were no more pagodas, but shrines had been erected on the
town's outskirts to the tutelary spirits, and some of them were hung
with votive offerings of puppet-horses. Among the jumble of
Burmese and Chinese lettering on the shop fronts, a single notice in
English jumped out, PICKLE SOLD HERE. At Kyaukme we stopped
to unload a cargo of small green tomatoes. Here there was to be an
hour's wait, and the chief passenger took charge of my movements

and told me that he would show me round the town. He now introduced himself as Tin Maung. As he was then delayed by being called in to consult on more engine trouble, I wandered over to a tea-house. In this tea-growing country, plain tea is considered unbearably dull. It is served with a sediment of some kind of cereal, and many of the Shans, unsatisfied with this consistency, poured it into their saucers and proceeded to make up a kind of minestrone by mixing it with the contents of a small dough pie, for which the tea-house charged four annas.

After a few minutes Tin Maung made a dignified appearance to take tea. There was the usual preliminary silence, then he asked, 'Are you carrying a weapon with you?' I said no, and Tin Maung said, 'That is a good thing. Before the war we used to carry guns for tigers. But now it is not a good thing to carry guns any more. If we carry guns we shoot.' I nodded understandingly. The market here was exceptionally lively. Some of the local tribespeople wore patchwork cloaks in bright colours, with Moroccan-looking hoods. I asked Tin Maung if he thought I could photograph them and he went over, and, to my mind, with undue formality, called for the head of the family. There was a long discussion, followed by a refusal. Since all Tin Maung's utterances were preceded by the intervals of silence occupied by the marshalling and translation of his thoughts, I shall cease to mention these pauses. On this occasion he said, 'They do not refuse from shyness, but from superstition.' Later when I thought the incident had been forgotten, he said, 'Our minds have to be adjusted to the medieval conditions, which are variable.'

Here in Kyaukme there was a legless leper, who propelled himself along on his haunches, with pads fitted to his hands. He was assisted most tenderly in his passage round the market by a small boy, whose arm was round his neck. From experience gained in Mandalay, I judged that the boy was in the first stages of leprosy.

Through the brazen hours that followed high noon, we crept onwards through a tunnel of glittering verdure. Then in the early afternoon came the official stop for breakfast. We were in a tiny hamlet, a few branch-and-leaf huts round a well. A single half-blind pariah dog slunk up to inspect us and was immediately chased away by a pair of lean, hairy swine that came rushing out of one of the huts. A cavern had been hollowed out of the wall of rock that formed the background to the village, and wisps of smoke trailed up through a sort of bamboo veranda that had been built over the mouth of it. This infernal place was the restaurant.

The moment had now come when all European prejudices about food had to be abandoned; all fears of typhoid or dysentery had to be banished resolutely from the mind. Even if I held back now and refused to enter this murky grotto, there was a long succession of others awaiting me, and ultimately sheer hunger would settle the matter. Remote journeyings had their advantages, the occasional sense of adventure, the novelties of experience. They also had their drawbacks, and this was one of them. And as there was no turning back from them, it was just as well to be bold.

In the dim interior – a model of most remote oriental eating-houses – we were awaited by a cook who was naked to the waist. Tattooed dragons writhed among the cabalistic figures on his chest and arms. A snippet of intestine was clinging to a finger, which, shaken off, was caught in mid-air by an attendant cat. Tin Maung gave an order and in due course the head-waiter arrived, a rollicking Shan with shining bald head and Manchu moustaches, carrying a dish heaped with scrawny chickens' limbs, jaundiced with curry, a bowl of rice, and a couple of aluminium plates. When uncertain how to behave, watch what the others do. A few minutes later I was neatly stripping the tendons from those saffron bones; kneading the rice into a form in which it could be carried in the fingers to the mouth. But the *spécialité de la maison* was undoubtedly pickled cabbage, with garlic and chilli-pepper. This Shan delicacy was gravely recommended by Tin Maung as 'full of vitamins'. It had a sharp, sour flavour, for which a taste was easily acquired; I should certainly have missed this and many other similar experiences had I been able to follow the advice given in the *Burma Handbook*: '... there are no hotels, and the traveller, when he quits the line of railway or Irawadi steamer, must get leave from the Deputy

Commissioner of the district to put up at Government bungalows, and must take bedding, a cook, and a few cooking utensils.'

Although Tin Maung had said that it was most unlikely that we should reach Lashio in one day, we found ourselves by the late afternoon within a few miles of the town. We had just crossed the Nam Mi River, where I had admired the spectacle of landslides of the brightest red earth plunging down the hill-side into deep green water, when we were stopped by a posse of soldiers. They told us that Chinese Nationalist bandits had temporarily cut the road, only four kilometres from Lashio, and had shot-up and looted the truck in front of ours. As this had happened several hours before, it was not exactly a narrow escape. But there was a delay until an officer of the Shan police arrived to tell us we could carry on. As we came into the outskirts of Lashio, the sun set. Flocks of mynas and parakeets had appeared in the tree-tops, where they went through the noisy, twilight manoeuvres of starlings in a London square.

In accordance with the recommendations already quoted from the *Burma Handbook*, I asked the driver of the lorry to put me down at the Dak Bungalow, but there appeared to be some difficulty, and Tin Maung told me that it had been taken over by the army. He invited me to come to his house, where I could leave my luggage while making further enquiries. Lashio had been partly destroyed by bombing but, it seemed, rebuilt along the lines of the English hill-station it had once been, with detached bungalows, each with its own garden. We stopped at one of these. It was now nearly dark, and a young man clad only in shorts came running down the path, and opened the gate. Approaching us, he crossed his arms and bowed in a rather Japanese fashion, only partially straightening himself when he turned away. Tin Maung nodded towards the baggage, and uttered a word, and the still stooping figure snatched up both suitcases and hurried away to the house with them. He was not, as I imagined at the time, a servant, but a younger brother.

I was then invited to go and sit on the balcony of the house, where I was met by Tin Maung's father. U Thein Zan looked like a lean

Burmese version of one of those rollicking Chinese gods of good fortune. Even when his mouth was relaxed his eyes were creased-up as if in a spasm of mirth. He had learned, in fact, as I soon discovered, to express his emotions in terms of smiles: a gay smile (the most frequent), a tolerant smile (for the shortcomings of others), a roguish smile (when his own weaknesses were under discussion), a rueful smile (for his sharp losses, the state of Burma, and humanity in general).

In the background hovered the mother. In her case no formal presentation was made. The three of us, father, son and myself, sat there on the balcony making occasional disjointed remarks about the political situation. From time to time the younger brother came out of the house, bowed, and went in. The mother appeared, curled herself up in a chair well removed from the important conclave of males, and lit up a cheroot. There was no sign of stir or excitement. Later I learned that this was the return of the eldest son after an absence of two years, during which time the brother next in age to him had been killed by insurgents. I could have imagined Chinese etiquette imposing these rigid standards of self-control, but it came as a great surprise that old-fashioned Burmese families should follow such a rule of conduct.

The matter of finding somewhere to sleep now came up, and the younger son was sent off to make enquiries about a bungalow belonging to the Public Works Department. He was soon back to say that it was full of soldiers, although there might be a room free next night. Upon this Tin Maung said that I would have to sleep in his father's house, and signalled for my baggage to be taken inside. I apologized to the old man for the trouble I was putting him to, whereupon he handsomely said, 'Anyone my son brings home becomes my son,' accompanying this speech with such a truly genial smile that it was impossible to feel any longer ill at ease.

But before there could be any question of retiring for the night, U Thein Zan said, there were formalities to be attended to. He thought that owing to the unsettled local conditions I ought to be on the safe side by reporting, without delay, to the Deputy Superintendent of Police, and after dressing himself carefully, he took up a lantern and accompanied me to the functionary's house. The DSP soon mastered his surprise at the visit, seemed relieved that I was under the control of such a pillar of local society as U Thein Zan, and found me several forms to fill in. In the morning, he said, I must report to the office of the Special Commissioner for the region, and to the commanding officer of the garrison. The latter obligation was one of which nothing had been said in Rangoon, and I decided to avoid it if possible. With Chinese bandits in the vicinity I could imagine this officer considering himself justified in putting me under some kind of restrictive military protection, or even sending me under escort back to Mandalay. When I brought up the mater of the attack on the truck, the DSP firmly announced that it had been the work of local Shans.

We went back home and sat for a while chatting desultorily and listening to the radio. Two stations were coming in fairly well: La Voix d'Islam broadcast on a beam from Radio Toulouse, and a station which might have been Peking, because the announcements were in Chinese, and the music Western and Evangelical in flavour, with the exception of one playing of a marching song of the Red Army. U Thein Zan was a fervent Buddhist and liked to talk about his religion whenever he could. He was delighted because next day a famous abbot would be preaching several sermons at the local monastery and he was to play a prominent part in the welcoming ceremony.

Soon after this the family retired to bed. The house was a rather flimsy construction raised on piles about three feet from the ground. It consisted of two main rooms and a kitchen, had a palm-thatched roof, and a floor of split bamboo. I was left to myself in one of the rooms, while the five members of the family – another brother had just turned up – were to sleep in the other. Clearly the old mother did not approve of this arrangement, which I gathered, from her gestures, probably went against her ideas on true hospitality. Perhaps she felt that I was not being treated as a member of the family. At all events she protested and was with difficulty overruled by Tin Maung, who probably told her that communal sleeping was not a European custom; and with a shrug of bewildered resignation she let the thing go as it was. Bars were put over the door and a shutter fitted to the window. The younger brother appeared carrying a camp bed which he erected in a corner. By the side of this Tin Maung set a stool with a lamp, a glass of water, a saucer of nuts, and several giant cheroots. Before going into the other room he told me not to put the lamp out. I wondered why.

Taking off my clothes, I put on a cotton longyi which I had bought in Mandalay. It had been recommended as the coolest thing to sleep in. Turning the lamp low, I lay down on the camp bed, and was just dozing off when I heard a slight creaking, and through half-opened eyes saw Tin Maung, going slowly round the room, flashing an electric torch on the walls and ceiling. I asked him what he was looking for, and he said, 'Sometimes there are moths.' He then tip-toed quickly from the room. My eyelids came together and then opened, reluctantly, at a faint scuffling sound. The bungalow consisted of a framework of timber upon which sheets of some white-washed material had been nailed. It was like a very ramshackle example of a small black-and-white Essex cottage. On one wall, just above my feet, was a Buddha shrine, containing a rather unusual reclining Buddha and offerings of dried flowers in vases. From behind this there now appeared several rats, not large, but lively, which began to move in a series of hesitant rushes along the beam running round the room. There were soon seven of them in sight.

I watched this movement with dazed curiosity for a time, and then began to doze again. Then, suddenly, an extraordinary protective faculty came into use. Once during the recent war, I had noticed that whilst my sleep was not disturbed by our own howitzers firing in the same field, I was inevitably awakened when the dawn stillness was troubled by the thin whistle of enemy shells, passing high overhead. Now, on the verge of unconsciousness, I felt in the skull, rather than heard, a faint scratching of tiny scrambling limbs. Something, I half-dreamed and half-thought, was climbing up the leg of the camp bed. Turning my head I caught a brief, out-of-focus glimpse of a small black body on the pillow by my cheek. Then in a scamper it was gone. It was a scorpion, I thought, or a hairy spider of the tarantula kind. I linked its appearance with Tin Maung's mysterious inspection of the room with his torch. What was to be done? I got up, thinking that whatever this animal was, it would come back to achieve its purpose as soon as I fell asleep. I thought of sitting in the chair and staying awake for the rest of the night, but when I picked up the lamp to turn up the wick, it felt light, and shaking it produced only a faint splashing of oil in the bottom of the container. In a short time, then, the lamp would go out, and my scorpion or whatever it was, with others of its kind, would come boldly up through the interstices in the bamboo floor. The next impulse was to spend the night walking round Lashio, and I went to unfasten the door bar. Immediately the pariah dog that lived under the house, where it lay all night snuffling and whining, burst into snarling life, furiously echoed by all the dogs in the district. I thought of the trigger-happy police of Lashio, who would have Chinese bandits on their mind.

The best thing, I decided, was to use my mosquito net and hope that I could sleep without any part of my body coming into contact with the sides. Fixing it up as best I could, I crawled in and tucked the net well under me. For a while I watched the movement, blurred through the net, of the rats; then consciousness faded again. I was awakened by a not very sharp pain in the lip and putting up my hand found myself clutching a cockroach which had fastened there. This was the last disturbance; when I next woke it was to the mighty whirring of hornbills flying overhead, and the daylight was spreading through the shutters.

CHAPTER TWELVE

The Northern Shans

LASHIO WAS TAKING SHAPE in the calm morning light, its roofs and palisades touched with mist-filtered sunshine. Two-thirds of the town lay below U Thein Zan's veranda, clinging to slopes that slid down into a vaporous valley. Sashes of mist wound through the town, isolating hillocks, huts, and clumps of trees. From some distant meadow concealed in the hazy depths arose a thin, pastoral piping. Beyond the valley a tuft of cotton-wool balanced on a thinly drawn line joining the summits of a distant mountain range.

This was the country – as Lashio was the capital – of the Northern Shans, a curious people who provided an example of a huge racial group in a constant state – like some radioactive metal – of fission and degeneration into lesser elements. The name Shan is unknown among the people themselves, and probably originates, as do also Chin, and Kachin, in a common Chinese term for hill-savage, or barbarian. The Shans call themselves Thai, meaning 'free', and remnants of their race are spread right across southern Asia, from Canton to Assam – the greatest single unit being the Siamese. It is their singular passion for freedom which has kept the Thais disunited. In general, those peoples that remain in the mountains reflect in their character the physical division of their environment into hills and valleys. The smaller the tribe the greater the freedom. These arch-republicans of South-Eastern Asia sometimes carried their democracy to a point where there were no chiefs and not even a village council.

Only when such people are driven by some invader from their valleys, and forced down into the plains – as were the Siamese – can they be united, and prepared for civilization, under victorious tyrants. The Burmese, having reached the plains of the Irrawaddy first, turned themselves into a nation of rulers and ruled, organized themselves, increased and multiplied, and bought the latest weapons. In this way they were able to hold the later waves of immigrants – the Shans, and Kachins – back in their mountains.

Surfeited with democracy, the Burmese organized the Shans politically whenever they could, allowing them otherwise to cling to their natural customs. They are notably uxorious, and those who can support them are permitted three official wives. Miscellaneous concubines are styled 'little women'. Divorce is easy, and women retain their property. The democratic principle is followed even in the matter of seduction. An official who seduces the wife of a non-official is heavily fined, and obliged to restore the woman. The non-official in a similar case escapes a fine, and may even keep the great man's wife, if she agrees to forfeit her property. It is curious that there are racial groups which have lived for centuries among the Shans which, far from being influenced by this liberality of outlook, have marriage taboos and restrictions only equalled by those of the Australian bushmen. The Bghai Karens strangle in a pit those who marry out of their station. The Banyangs' endogamous system is so exclusive that it has reduced the tribe numerically to a point when it is no longer possible for a marriage to be contracted within the permitted relationship groups. Having therefore resigned themselves to extinction, the people can only be kept in existence by state compulsion. Once a year an official arrives in the village, a suitable couple are selected, detailed for marriage, conveyed by force to the bridal chamber, and kept there under governmental seal, tormented, no doubt, by incest-guilt, for three days. Meanwhile, the Shans fill the surrounding villages with their children.

The youngest brother was already up, moving stealthily about the garden, watering the snapdragons, geraniums, and roses with the solemnity of one tending the flowers before the high altar. His face was respectfully averted, and occasionally, when forced to pass within a few yards of me, on his way to refill his watering can, he did so in a hunched-up rush. Soon after he left to go off to some kind of clerical occupation. He was dressed in shorts, a kind of alpine jacket, and a Gaucho hat, with a chin-strap, from the bottom of which hung down a three-inch decorative knot. Under his arm he carried a briefcase. Later, U Thein Zan made an appearance, dressed in his best longyi, worn under an American army greatcoat; he was ready for early-morning prayers at the pagoda. Next Tin Maung, about whom the household clearly revolved, came on the scene. He asked how I had slept, and I assured him that I had rarely passed a more peaceful night. After we had drunk tea, he suggested a stroll along to the market.

Although it was no more than eight o'clock, animation was at its height. Every swaggering Asiatic mode was displayed here. A group of Kachin women wore with demure elegance their black Chinese smocks of some good, coarsely woven material, relieved only by spiralling silver links at the neck-fastening, and a few negligently worn strings of amber beads. There were turbaned Palaungs with infantile faces, and teeth and lips blotted out with betel. They were dressed in dressing-gowns slashed with many colours, and gaily woven anklets, and had massive silver rings round their necks, which made their wearers look as if they had been worn by someone at a game of hoop-la. The Taungthus were in shapeless penitents' chemises of indigo sacking and wore with raffish effect a towel wound several times round the head. Shans, slender and willowy in their long gowns, were the sophisticates, the bourgeoises of the market. Until they looked up, they were extinguished by their huge mushroom hats; then sometimes one looked into the face of a severe beauty, with the regularity of feature of a fine ivory carving; primly pursed lips and wonderfully shaped eyes – to a Westerner all the more piquant from the invisibility, when the eyes were open, of the upper eyelids. Besides these groups there were occasional representatives of more distant peoples; a Lisu, with satchels strapped about him like a medieval palmer, and turban wound with intricate regularity; an unidentified pair in waisted and loose-sleeved Cossack coats.Behind their stalls Shan young ladies viewed their clients with the aloofness of haughty sales-ladies of model garments. Tin Maung said that it was better to deal with the Chinese – perfect shopkeepers who held to the principle that the customer was always right.

On our way back, five beautiful Chinese Shan girls, in blue jackets and trousers and wide cummerbunds, came tripping down the street towards us. They were jolly and free in their manner, and pink-cheeked under their slight tan. I asked Tin Maung if he thought I could photograph them, and after considering the question until it was too late, he gave his verdict, with sensibility, I thought. 'In their own village, they will be pleased for you to photograph them. But here, they are visitors.' He then added an odd corollary. 'They are too slow moving to dance the rumba.'

It had been arranged that a friend of Tin Maung's, who was supposed to have some contact with the Special Commissioner, should accompany me to his house. Afterwards I was to return to breakfast with Tin Maung. The Special Commissioner was also the Sawbwa of Hsenwi, the most powerful of the Shan feudal princes in the Northern Shan States, who had now been turned by the Burmese into a kind of exalted civil servant. The Shan, Kachin, and Karen minorities have always been more or less hostile to the Burmese, for much the same reasons that the Irish have not agreed with the English. Lacking the organization, or perhaps even the natural military genius, to defeat the Burmese in the field, they have rebelled whenever they could, allying themselves – with usually disastrous results – with any invader, whether Chinese or Siamese, and suffering in due course the frightful retaliation that has always been commonplace in South-East Asia. The Burmese have always accused the British – probably with justice – of trying to separate them from the minorities, in accordance with the principle of 'divide and rule'. There is little doubt also that the Shans did their best to play off the British against their old enemies. Traditionally the Sawbwa were educated outside Burma, often in Siam, and the Burmese are still said to suspect them of plotting with neighbouring states to the detriment of Burmese sovereignty. There were, for instance, in Rangoon all sorts of rumours – and not from Burmese sources – of machinations aimed at turning over part of the Kentung province to Siam. I was therefore warned that any approach to the Sawbwas would certainly be misconstrued by the Burmese, and might even land me in some sort of trouble. However, although the Sawbwa of Hsenwi was said to have been in difficulties with the Burmese over the Karen insurrection, he was now a Burmese Special Commissioner, and as such it was not only in order but obligatory to call on him.

The Sawbwa lived in a large villa of European type. My sponsor having explained the nature of my visit to a servant, I was shown into a lounge and left to await the great man's pleasure. The walls were decorated with Chinese silk panels of natural history subjects. A large silver cup of the kind awarded for athletic distinction stood on the mantelpiece. Facing me was a partially curtained stairway, and several ladies of the Sawbwa's household took turns to peep at me from behind the curtain. After a reasonable interval the Sawbwa appeared. He was dressed in loose pyjamas of white silk, possessed a handsome, unlined face and a manner of cultivated tranquillity. Shan rulers were clearly modelled on Chinese rather than Burmese patterns. In spite of the conventional British praise for everything to do with the hill peoples of Burma, I must confess to a preference for the easy-going affability of the Burmese notables, well typified by the Premier, Thakin Nu, by comparison with the well-bred Shan aloofness. I have no doubt that every kind of sterling quality is concealed by his habit of reserve.

After reading my credentials the Sawbwa asked me where I wanted to go, and I told him that my intention had been to make my way to Taunggyi. The Sawbwa thought about this for a moment, and said that it would be easier to go north than south. He could give me a letter to his brother, also a Sawbwa, who was now living at Hsenwi, and who would look after me, and pass me on via Mu-Sé to Nam Hkam. After that I could easily get to Bhamó, where there were no troubles of any kind. This was indeed a tempting alternative to my original plan. Such a route would take me for a considerable distance along the Chinese frontier, and Nam Hkam had been described as, ethnologically speaking, the most interesting town in the Northern Shan States, although hopelessly inaccessible in these times. I mentioned the matter of a further army permit to travel in these areas, and the Sawbwa brushed the question aside. 'This territory,' he said, 'comes within my jurisdiction. I will give you whatever is necessary.' I wondered if, in these words, that utterly efficient facial control cloaked a hint of quiet satisfaction. It then occurred to me to obtain an official ruling on the nationality of the authors of the previous evening's incident, and I quoted the DSP's opinion that the lorry had been attacked by Shans. Without emphasis, the Sawbwa said, 'The Shans have never done such a thing. They have never committed an act of banditry. The attack carried out last night was by Chinese Nationalist troops, of whom there are several hundreds in the neighbourhood.'

Old U Thein Zan, however, was very worried about the idea of my going off along the Chinese frontier without additional army sanction. I said that surely a letter of authorization from the chief civil authority in the Shan States was enough, but U Thein Zan said, 'You do not realize. You will encounter ignorant, uneducated soldiers, who will not understand the Sawbwa's letter.' Well, then, I said, if they wouldn't understand the Sawbwa's letter, what use would an army permit be? Ah, said U Thein Zan, that would be different. An army permit would be written in Kachin, which these ignorant, stupid soldiers from the hills could read . . . Very well then, I would have the Sawbwa's letter translated into Kachin. But still the old man shook his head, with the gravest misgivings. For my part, I was quite determined, at all costs, to keep out of the army's clutches. I had found that I should have to wait an indefinite time in Lashio before finding any kind of transport going in the Taunggyi direction, so that the choice lay between pushing on northwards, and an ignominious retreat to Mandalay. There was, therefore, no choice.

On the way back we called on the SDO, who was in charge of the bungalow of the Public Works Department. In the old Burma it was considered ill mannered to call a man by his name if he held any office. Imaginary and unpaid positions were often created by the king – the non-existent glass manufactory with its hierarchy of officials was one – to allow worthy men that kind of satisfaction which inhabitants of the southern states of the USA are said to derive by calling themselves doctor or colonel without the possession of the usual qualifications. This usage is still reflected in the modern Burmese custom of referring to a man not merely by his function but by a series of initials. I could never remember what those mysterious initials stood for, but everyone in government service had them. They became hopelessly entangled in my mind with similar ones in the British army. The letter D for instance, in SDO – what did it stand for, District or Deputy? But in this case it was Sub-Divisional Officer.

The SDO was a southern Indian, cultured and genial, with a thin, home-sick wife, and a pretty doll-like child, with eyes clouded with malaria. He had inherited his comfortable bungalow from an English predecessor, and was obsessed by the fate of the sweet peas that had gone with it. They were still vigorous and profuse of blossom, but since the country had gained its independence had quite lost their colour, all the sharply divided original shades having faded to a wishy-washy pinkish-blue.

With the SDO's permission I went down to the Inspection Bungalow to take over a room left by soldiers who were just moving off. It was like an ample prison cell, with barred windows and scaling walls. There was no light, and the only piece of furniture was a frame raised on legs, recalling some obscure instrument of torture, across which string had been stretched, criss-cross. On to this I flung my bedding, upon which a few minute red insects immediately appeared. Looking up I saw that the ceiling was entirely screened from view by thick, old cobwebs, which I judged to be no longer tenanted. The door was much splintered and repaired about the lock, and appeared to have been broken in on many occasions.

Having completed these arrangements, I went back and joined Tin Maung for breakfast. An omelette had been prepared, and Tin Maung and I sat opposite at the table and dug into it with ladle-shaped spoons which had been miraculously produced. In the background, her legs drawn up on a chair, sat the old mother smoking one cheroot after another. She never took her eyes off me, and sometimes shook her head sadly. Tin Maung said, 'The old woman says that you remind her of her second son. He was killed by the PVOs last year. No question of politics entered into this occasion. He chanced, according to circumstances, to be passing in his car, and being unsuccessful in their desire to shoot ducks, they shot him.'

That afternoon, the surviving second brother, a gay, philandering fellow, turned up with a jeep he had borrowed for my benefit from some government department. This be-ringed young blood, with his gold bracelet and wrist watch, his American cigarettes, and the chic severity of his longyi of grey chequered silk, was the antithesis of his austere and authoritarian elder brother. With totally oriental insouciance we motored out into the bandit-infested countryside. Climate seems, after all, to have little to do with temperament. Here in the Eastern tropics you felt that while swaggering bravado was probably unknown, an emergency would be met with more than Anglo-Saxon phlegm. Perhaps the whole-hearted belief in the immutability of one's horoscope had something to do with it. I found the Burmese imperturbable.

Although Tin Maung was as near a free-thinker as a Burman could be, our country jaunt resolved itself, inevitably, into a pilgrimage to the local holy places. We did not attempt to enter any of the monasteries. It was sufficient to pull up for a few moments within the aura of beneficence that emanated from them and to gaze meekly at the tiered roofs projecting from their shading trees, before moving on from one to the next. In these rustic areas, the 'no foot-wearing' rules were more strictly applied. In the great pagodas of the towns it was considered enough to remove one's shoes or sandals in making an ascent, when the actually constructed part of the pagoda had been reached. Here, the mounds on which the pagodas were built were holy, too, and however high they were it was incumbent upon one to toil barefoot up the roughly hewed-out steps. We climbed one such bell-shaped pagoda and, from the high terrace, spied out the lie of the land. Below us, a caravan of bullock-carts jogged by, with a trotting escort of Shan farmers, sturdy and bellicose-looking agriculturists, with swords carried on their backs, thrust through sashes. In a few moments they had disappeared, swallowed in the belly of a dust-dragon they themselves had called forth, and we were left in an empty landscape chequered with withered paddy-fields, each with its low water-containing bunds, of that from above it was like a vast grey Chaldean excavation. The rare trees that had been left standing were ancient banyans, baleful monsters which had constantly increased themselves by the pathological multiplication of their limbs, till now they were arboreal labyrinths, full of root-screened nooks and recesses from which the spirits look out upon their domain. The pagoda upon which we stood had, in the dim past, marked the Chinese frontier with Burma, and here, as at other selected points, after the line of demarcation had been amicably settled, a selected soldier of each nation had been buried alive, back to back, facing north and south.

A visit was now made, in the manner of a minor sentimental journey, to a spot where Tin Maung had had a memorable experience, some years before. Since no connected account was ever given of his past, I was left to deduce from casual references that he had, at some time, fought with the Japanese Army, probably as a member of the Burma Independent Army, which had thrown in its lot with the Japanese in return for the promise of national independence. This fact had emerged as a consequence of a remark that he liked Japanese girls, because, he observed with one of his rare, half-stifled smiles, they were 'very obedient'. At all events, the Chinese had captured him and here, having with some difficulty found a suitable tree (the banyans were too matted with aerial roots to get a rope over a branch), they set about hanging him. It seemed, however, that his four appointed executioners were extremely weak from sickness and semi-starvation and, with all four hauling on the rope, had the greatest difficulty in hoisting him off his feet. Moreover, they had neglected to tie his hands, and once in the air he managed to haul himself up the rope. As soon as a couple of the Chinese let go their hold to remedy this situation, the others found themselves too weak to keep him in the air. The thing developed into a lurid Disney-like farce, with the Chinese soldiers, who seemed to be squeamish about using their weapons, running backwards and forwards in an ill-concerted and amateurish attempt to pinion Tin Maung's hands while keeping his feet off the ground. Finally they dropped him altogether and he managed to pull the rope out of their hands and run off with it still trailing from his neck. Alas, no evidence remained of this macabre scene. Even the place on the branch which had been bruised by the rubbing of the rope had long since recovered its patina.

On our way back to Lashio we made a detour to visit a hot spring that bubbled up from under a bank to become a stream which, after trailing its sulphurous miasma round several paddy-fields, again vanished. The neighbourhood of this source, too, was of some sanctity, and had, as a result, the ravaged appearance of public gardens in a slum area. A local erosion had been produced by the feet of many pilgrims, and children had torn at the accessible branches of the trees, many of which hung down by strips of bark. Several small caverns had been excavated in the hillock above the spring, all of which contained Buddha images, where presumably less benevolently inclined figures had once squatted. Silently presiding over this scene were many vultures, distributed in a symmetrical composition among the neighbouring trees. Their presence was entirely congruous in this hallowed spot, ranking high as they do, an honourable and superior incarnation within the animal hierarchy, on account of their restriction to a diet of carrion – a limitation believed by many Burmese to be self-imposed.

A Hindu ascetic who, even as a heretic, had gained extraordinary merit in Buddhist eyes by dedicating his body for the use of these semi-domesticated birds, when nature should have accomplished its course, lived at a slightly lower level in one of these trees, brooded over by his future legatees. Mysteriously he had built himself several aerial huts, although, following the nesting habits of the wren, he occupied only one. It was a kind of large kennel of branches and palm-leaves, reinforced with a valuable find of corrugated iron. Above it drooped white prayer-flags, the banners of a spiritual surrender. Standing below, Tin Maung respectfully called on the recluse to appear and give us his blessing. There was, alas, no response.

Before leaving, it occurred to me to test the temperature of the stream, with the idea forming in my mind of a beneficial sulphur-bath. I found it unbearably hot. Tin Maung, who had been watching, supplied the sombre information that immersion for more than a minute meant death, a fact which had been confirmed empirically on several occasions. I wondered how many wretched beings had been parboiled here throughout history for the equivalent of the Kingdom of Heaven's sake.

On reaching the outskirts of Lashio, Tin Maung suddenly decided to look in at the Inspection Bungalow. What he saw there seemed to shock him and, without a word, he grabbed up my bags and took them out to the jeep. While I was in Lashio, he said, I should stay with him. Naturally enough, in view of the previous night's experiences, I viewed this prospect with gratitude, coloured slightly with alarm.

In an attempt to repay some of the hospitality I had received, I invited my host's family out to a Chinese restaurant that night. However, U Thein Zan was keeping strict Sabbath, a term which includes in its definition fasting and meditation. Etiquette did not permit the presence of the mother, and the youngest and self-effacing brother probably felt the honour too much for him. In the end there were four of us: Tin Maung, the dandified brother, and a friend who was a schoolmaster, a sincere and rather intense young man. The main street of Lashio, which lay at the bottom of the hill, had been rebuilt in the style, if film reconstructions are accurate, of an American shack-town in the pioneering years. But although there was plenty of drama to be had in the vicinity, there were no signs here to be seen of the aggressive rawness of the old-time American frontier towns. Instead, the night-sauntering crowds were, as ever in Burma, demure and well conducted. If some of the Shans carried swords on their backs, you felt that it was no more than a habit of dress; and no virtue would be less esteemed than quickness on the draw. If there were tough hombres here, as there probably were, the toughness was dissimulated in a display of the courtesies, and an eighteenth-century turn of complimentary phrase. 'We are pleased that you condescend to pay your visit to Lashio, sir. You find it hard to travel further from this town? That is our great fortune for us. If you will stay here all the longer it is our very good advantage.'

Entering our chosen restaurant, we seated ourselves at first at a table in the general room, within sight of the kitchen, a smoke-blackened gehenna in which sweating fiends practised their arts over cauldrons and griddles. The meats were on display in a kind of jeweller's showcase, a glass fixture fitted with lock and key. To this customers were beckoned by the proprietor, for the inspection of a discouraging collection of pendant objects, cellular, membranous or veined, swarthy from judicious hanging, or startlingly coloured scarlet and blue. But estimating our purchasing power he soon shepherded us away from this depressing revelation of the raw materials of Chinese cooking, into a separate room. This dimly lit cell was of close lattice work. The walls were hung with Chinese pictures of the kind sold in Rangoon under the generic title 'bon-ton'. Eschewing the pin-up girl favoured by the West at similar artistic levels, these have concentrated on the young Chinese matron as their pet subject. She is shown as pink-cheeked, blooming, and usually with a complex hair-style. Sometimes her face is haloed in luxuriant fox-furs, and almost always a modest brood of children sport around her. These are frequently dressed as Little Lord Fauntleroys, or, as on this occasion, they wear sailor suits. One particular young mother was holding a telephone as if inhaling from it a rare perfume. Telephones are a popular motif of modern Chinese art.

Hope, however, was revived when the food was served in the most beautiful bowls, upon which inspired brushes had, in a few strokes of red and gold, sketched a squirming shrimp or a facetious and bewhiskered dragon. This delightful ware was of current Chinese production, and its export from China had recently been revived. As a token of special esteem the proprietor produced his finest glasses for our Mandalay Pale Ale. They were products of the British export drive, which by most devious and mysterious channels – almost certainly via smugglers from Siam – had found their way here. The labels, which said Jacobean Glassware, were still in position, and it was clear that they had been accepted as part of the decoration, since much effort was made to keep them intact. It was evident that these glasses could not be washed. Before setting them on the table, the proprietor carefully wiped each rim with his fingers, an operation which was repeated – special care being taken in the case of my glass – by Tin Maung. There had been a lengthy explanation, accompanied by some descriptive gesturing, of what was to be cooked for us. Evidently a special dish had been ordered for my delectation, and I awaited with resignation the appearance of some formidable Chinese delicacy, the legendary new-born mice in honey, a Himalayan bear's paw served with sweet and sour sauce, a few fish's lips from a bottle imported at immense cost from the remote China seas. But, alas, I had underestimated my friends' cosmopolitanism. My speciality, when it arrived, was two fried eggs in separate bowls, with more bowls of their inevitable garnishing of chips.

Table gossip was concerned with the higher realities. In Burma the condition of the soul replaces that of the stock markets as a topic for polite conversation. Between mouthfuls of fried rice and prawns, the schoolmaster discoursed on the hereafter, passing in brief exposition over all the thirty-one possibilities that await the discarnate entity beyond the grave. As ever, the unpleasant states were presented with grimly detailed realism, while the pleasant ones were vague and insipid. Behind his glasses the schoolmaster's eyes glittered. His expression was invaded by a peculiarly Nordic eagerness, particularly when discussing the pangs of souls in torment. In Wales, he would have been a nonconformist preacher.

By now it was as if scales had slowly fallen from my eyes, and at last I could distinguish the character in a Burmese face as clearly as in a European one. For the first week or two I had suffered to a mild and diminishing degree from the obtuseness which makes

The sinister smile of the Bayon

A corner of Angkor Vat

Free drinks for the bonzes

Laotian dancers amused by the camera

Audience in Angkor

The fantastic landscape of northern Laos

Meo woman

Pagoda at Luang Prabang

Cochin-China: the search for small fish

people say of Mongolians 'I can't tell one from the other'. But now the Mongol physical characteristics which once had seemed to impose a deadening conformity appeared to be vanishing. There was no longer any sense of strangeness, of not being among people of one's own race. People were resolving into types again. Now there were businessmen, politicians, students, farmers, policemen; each class seemed marked in some way which couldn't be exactly defined, by an undefinable stamp set upon him by his way of life. These Burmese and Shan girls in the market were now something more than Mongolian dolls with hardly more expression than the conventionalized beauties of Japanese woodcuts. Now, at last, I was in tune to the expressions that flickered round those eyes and lips; the coquetry, the humour, the contempt. And just as I was beginning to see trousered and turbaned sellers of vegetables who by some trick of expression reminded me of girls I had known at some time or other, Italian film actresses, secretaries or army nurses, so this Burmese pedant was the living double of someone with whom I had been at school.

While occupied with these reflections, I had gradually become aware of an unmistakable reek, usually described as acrid, as definite but indescribable as the smell of burning feathers or any other pungent odour. The lattice separating us from the next private room was pierced with dimly glowing points of light. Now a murmur sifted through the chinks in the wall; there was a tinkle of laughter, a silence, the sound of a bow drawn tentatively across a single string, producing no more than the rising and falling drone of an insect. This was followed by a rustling, then more laughter. The odour became sharper. An alarmed silence had fallen upon our company. I asked Tin Maung if it was not opium I could smell. After a moment he said, 'I am perplexed.' 'There are Chinese-Shan ladies,' said the schoolmaster, averting his head in deprecation from the offending quarter. 'These ladies are not serious.' The word was used in exactly the way a central European would use it, in harsh condemnation of one who is not right-thinking.

*

439

Our waiter had been a small Chinese boy of about twelve, with all the urbanity of a trained hotelier. He was quick to sweep the scattered rice from the table to the floor, where rats of extraordinary tameness made frequent sorties to deal with it. He was swift and merciless in his annihilation of cockroaches which ventured on the table, despite the wincing of the schoolmaster. Having presented the bill – a sheetful of cavorting ideographs – he astounded me by refusing a rupee tip. I tried to press it upon him, but the rejection was no mere form, although as he retreated before us, bowing, to the door, he was clearly delighted. 'He does not take money, as a sign of respect,' Tin Maung said. 'It is sufficient that you have honoured him by offering it.' A delightful bartering of compliments, I thought, and I practised it on several further occasions. In the end I stopped trying to tip the Chinese, to whom the idea seemed alien – at least, when they are not sufficiently far from their homeland for the old customs to have quite changed. Tin Maung also informed me that in that part of the country, a Burmese, when he is obliged to accept money to which he does not feel entitled, will mark the note or notes in such a way that he will be able to identify them, and give them in alms as soon as he can.

Lashio's main street was in pitch darkness as we strolled back. Chinks of light showed through the tea-house doors, but the only sound to be heard came from a Chinese party in an upstairs room somewhere. An orchestra was playing with spasmodic frenzy, but the undertones were suppressed by distance. The only sound which reached us with rhythmic regularity was that, as it seemed, of an iron saucepan being thrown from a height into the street; a hollow and staccato thud, doubtless to be achieved only after infinite practice at whatever the instrument was.

U Thein Zan had just returned from the monastery and was awaiting us, dressed, as usual, for the evening, in a sailor's blue sweater, which he had put on over his shirt. He had been both chastened and inspired by his visit to the monastery, and it was soon evident that we were to receive a substantial paraphrase of the sermon. First, however, a bottle of rum and two glasses were put on the table, a truly remarkable sight in such a devout household. I felt, indeed, most dubious about committing in the old man's presence what amounted to a deadly sin. But filling up the glasses and raising his in my direction Tin Maung said that if his father wanted an audience, he would have to put up with its wickedness. Shaking his head in fond reproof, U Thein Zan said, 'I do not renounce my son's salvation. Foolishness and laughing is the age and lack of experience. Soon he will come to tell me, "Old man, you were right."' With sandals removed, our legs drawn up on the seats of our chairs, and our pernicious glasses before us, we resigned ourselves to U Thein Zan's exhortations. Since in the Orient no one is distracted by mere noise, the Radio Toulouse programme was left at full strength, although on this night the reception – a concert by the Chasseurs d'Afrique – was fitful and gusty.

Buddhism, as I had gathered from various sermons printed in the Rangoon press, had suddenly become injected with evangelical fervour, a rare phenomenon in the history of the religion. And perhaps with the notion of making the message more palatable to the West, great emphasis was now being laid on its 'scientific' character. Having held back, in the way of religions in which the final and perfect revelation is given once and for all, until it has seen itself in danger of being left high and dry by the times – a survival of medievalism – it has now come forward, almost as if an intolerably compressed spring had been released, with something of a jerk. Buddhist sermons now feature such topics as atomic fission, and the Buddha is sometimes referred to as the first atomic scientist. Even before having been subjected to such propaganda, one cannot have helped noticing that primitive Buddhism, in its rarely found, untainted form, could loosely be described as scientific in its attitude, and in its conception – a feat of great intuitive power on the part of its founder – of the soul's slow evolution through countless ages from lower to higher forms. This foreshadowing of Darwinism is now belatedly exploited by his followers. It is much stressed by the organizers of the Third Missionary Movement – the only previous movements recognized being those of Buddha, and the Indian king Asoka. U Thein Zan's reconstruction of the sermon was a thick soup; a conventional stock of Buddhist mysticism into which much

Freud and Einstein had been stirred. Afterwards he produced a pamphlet by the Venerable Lokanatha of Hong Kong, the leading spirit of this movement, of whose previous announcements I had acquired copies in Rangoon. This worthy monk, described as being in the truth-exporting business, was on his way to the United States, where the construction of an 'incomparable Skyscraper Pagoda in New York, dedicated to World Peace' would be the crowning achievement of his work.

As in many Buddhist sermons, there was an earthiness, a downright manner in the attack. This was strong stuff for the squeamish. There were no airy abstractions here. Briskly the venerable monk settled down to a classification of the body's 'thirty-two filthy parts'. He seeks to shatter the image of fleshly beauty and does so in a few shrewd blows. The body is 'a foul latrine on two legs' he begins, then, warming to his subject with the relish of an Aldous Huxley, he invites our attention to a dead body,

> an excellent subject for meditation. The swollen, stinking corpse, bluish-black, with swarms of worms issuing from the nine holes is enough to make anyone disgusted with the foul nature of the body. We should sit down and identify ourselves with the horrible corpse, with the following reflection: "As I am now, so once was he; as he is now, so shall I be." By thinking in this way the idea will finally dawn on us that our body is a corpse bound to our neck. And we shall loathe and hate our body and the bodies of others. This is the way to destroy lust for ever.

But in case this exercise in meditation should fail to work we are presented with a monkish technique of taming this disturbing and disgusting machine. It reads a little like one of those slightly repellent chats about fitness and the body beautiful in a sun-bathing journal – the note of obsession is common to both – except of course, in reverse. All you do is take as little sleep as you can – four hours at the most, avoid nourishing food, and above all, never relax. In this way you can be sure of building-up the body unbeautiful in a reasonably short time.

But as the Reverend Lokanatha's appeal is directed above all to the citizens of the New World, he feels it necessary to put in a word about how to get rich. 'Men are born poor because they were stingy in the past. Men are born rich because they were generous in the past. Therefore don't be jealous of the rich man driving in a fancy limousine car. Give as he did, and you too will become rich ...' A yard-stick for calculation is thoughtfully provided in a quotation from the Master's words: 'Herein Ananda, the yield to be looked for from a donation to an animal is a hundred-fold, to an ordinary non-virtuous man a thousand-fold, to the Saint, incalculable and beyond all measure.'

It is extraordinary how the fascination of America is felt equally by Burmese bobby-soxers and venerable monks. There is no doubt that the USA has become the Cathay of our times. 'The scientific American will readily embrace Scientific Buddhism. They are eagerly awaiting for our Atomic Bomb of Love. Our incomparable Skyscraper Pagoda in New York dedicated to World Peace will surely crown the world. The year 2500 (AD 1956) will see the rise of Buddhism, and we must start now by preaching in America ...' The wheel has turned a full circle and now the Marco Polos and the Francis Xaviers of the Orient set out for the Hang-chow of the West, on Manhattan Island.

That night, I dealt with the sleeping problem more efficiently, tucking the mosquito net under the bedding so that it was under a continuous even strain all round. Shoulders, ankles, and outsides of arms, where they might touch the net, were smeared with insect-repellent cream, which I now used for the first time. A few baffled cockroaches soon appeared, silhouetted like coracles on the outside of the net, but after mooching about for a while they went away. Rats rustled behind the shrine and ran squeaking along the timbers. From all quarters of the night horizon came the muffled hallooing of owls. In pleasant anticipation of the next day's journey, I fell asleep.

But the next day brought no hope of leaving Lashio. At the market we learned that the only movement signalled was the return of a lorry to Mandalay. The trouble was that there was nobody who could be approached for definite information, no set point of departure. If a driver got a load, he was likely to move off at short notice, and only those who hung about the market continually could be sure of a seat. Then again an owner might announce his intention of going to a town on my route, and then for any one of a number of reasons, suddenly change his mind, and go off in the other direction. This happened in the case of an Indian who had to make the run to Nam Hkam at some time, to pick up some goods there. But there was a rumour that the Chinese bandits had cut the road; so he said, with a kind of jellied smile, that the Nam Hkam trip could wait for another day. The only offer I got that day was of a ride on a bullock-cart going to Mong Pang, about twenty miles along the road. I was warned that although Burmese bullock-carts are a rather more rapid form of transport than one would imagine, this journey might take two days.

At this moment the market was full of rumours. Without particular excitement the knowledgeable hangers-on who forgathered there spoke of heavy fighting to the south, where a Chinese Nationalist division had been split up by Burmese forces, supported by planes. To lend colour to this account, we had at one time, with the stirring of the breeze, heard a distant thudding which might have been the sound of falling bombs. The incident on the Mandalay road came back to us in thunderous and distorted echoes of slaughter, rapine, and destroyed convoys. More ominous was the fact that the post-lorry from Nam Hkam was long overdue, and it was generally assumed that the driver and guard were lying somewhere in a ditch, with their throats cut. Merchants are most phlegmatic and enterprising people, but it was clear that their present attitude to journeyings was tinged with unwonted caution. Into such a state had Burma, and indeed most of South-East Asia, fallen! Travel had become almost as slow as in the days of Marco Polo, and probably more hazardous. Certainly the security of the roads under the Mongols' dominion, when the Venetians made their great Eastern journey, was much superior to that of twentieth-century Burma.

And now as the days passed a pattern of life in Lashio began to evolve. There were the hours immediately following the dawn, when the town emerged from mist like the image on a photographic plate, and when I was now permitted to assist the youngest brother in the serious passage with the watering-can from plant to plant. Then would follow the morning walk down to the market to interrogate drivers on their intentions, followed by a ritual drinking of tea, with its accompanying saffron-cake, undesired but bought out of decency because plain tea was always free of charge. Before midday a shower bath was taken in a shed in the garden. I was attended by the youngest brother, who brought the pitchers of water. At this point I learned the prim Burmese methods of bathing with longyi in position and then releasing the knot in the wet longyi and stepping out of it when the dry one was in position over it. Such douchings were frequent and obligatory. The Burmese bathe as often as possible, and also use water for their most intimate sanitary toilet, relating as a cautionary tale the fate of one of their kings who, because in his immediately previous incarnation he had been an ogre, scorned these matters of hygienic routine and was in consequence deserted by his principal queen.

At high noon we would relax on the balcony before glasses of lemonade, while a sporadic snow of white butterflies drifted across the now sharply defined landscape. This was the time for the collections of snapshots to be produced, and on looking through them I felt that the camera had confirmed, perhaps more convincingly than anything before, the brotherood of mankind. There were Burmese parties on a social outing to the pagoda, just as Europeans might visit a road-house. They halt on the way to be photographed against the blurred background of a waterfall, the girls in the group holding their heads at studied angles, their mouths set in the rictus of the film-star smile. And then there were records of more intimate occasions, such as the canoeing trip with the pretty Shan lady, a shorthand typist, by whom 'pleasant expectations were aroused, but with vain outcome'. A Sawbwa's daughter, whose face contained a suggestion of the forceful characteristics of Edda Mussolini, seemed to have been kinder, since Tin Maung's lips were pursed at the memory – so much so that I almost expected a whistle to issue from them.

In the afternoon I would take up a book, while Tin Maung dismantled the wireless set and prepared it with dextrous tuning for the evening tussle with Radio Toulouse. The evening meal was taken in one of the Chinese restaurants, the opium-smoking and non-serious one being virtuously avoided; on our return, U Thein Zan would be ready with a homily. In a moment of mild exasperation Tin Maung gave away the reason for the present phase of religious fervour. 'It is time now that the old man should die. If he should continue too much longer in this existence all the monetary resources will be vanished away.' U Thein Zan's face cracked into a crestfallen smile. It seemed that he had recently fallen into his old vice of gambling, and having staked heavy sums as an outcome of a fatal blunder in the calculation of his horoscope, his losses had been tremendous. 'You should die, old man. You should die,' said Tin Maung relentlessly; a verdict with which U Thein Zan seemed, humbly enough, to agree.

A day or two later, there was another report of a lorry going to Nam Hkam. It was said to be loading in the market – news which sent me hurriedly packing my things. When I was ready I wanted to go straight down and take my seat, and not leave it for a moment until we were on our way. But Tin Maung would not hear of this undignified procedure. A message would be sent for the lorry to call for me, and I could wait in comfort and propriety where I was. It might be hours before it was ready to depart. I wanted to photograph the family before I left, so they all retired for a few minutes to prepare themselves. U Thein Zan appeared dressed with flamboyant conservatism in a taung-mathein, a long white coat, a sartorial survival of the last century equivalent to a frock-coat. His paso had been wound tightly round the waist and tied in front with a fine, impractical ebullience of material. The made-up turban was replaced by a scarf, tied with the swagger of a buccaneer. It was a fine turn-out, combining the maximum of difficulty of manipulation with good taste. By him stood his wife, wearing all the jewellery she had left to her after U Thein Zan's gambling losses, flowers in her hair, her face powdered ghastly white. The youngest son was dressed as usual for the pampas; the second son with his everyday buckish elegance, whch in any case could not have been improved upon; while Tin Maung, undaunted by the heat, had put on an army pullover. I photographed the little group in colour, amongst their flowers, having promised U Thein Zan to give him some lasting record of the rather pallid glory of his snapdragons and sweet peas. This was all done rather hurriedly, with an eye on the road, and my bags standing by the garden gate. But as the shadows lengthened and the hills across the valley began to gather about them their drapings of mist, there was no heartening cough, rattle, and thump of well-worn mechanism coming up the hill. In the end, I went down to the market again, where I heard that at the very last moment the lorry had been requisitioned by the army.

Early next morning, without heralding, salvation came. A post-wagon was taking mail to Nam Hkam, or as far as it could go along the road, and someone had told the driver about me. There was a scramble to get my things out. When I said goodbye to the others, the old mother was missing, and just as the lorry was moving off she came rushing out with food for the journey tied up in a palm-leaf bundle. She tried, without success, to persuade me to accept also the contents of a handkerchief, which appeared to be several precious or semi-precious stones – another reminder of the fact that, to the Burmese, liberality is the chief of the ten great virtues, and the second of the three works of perfection.

The post-wagon was undoubtedly the most decrepit, the most exhausted vehicle in which I had ever travelled. It was a phantom from a breaker's yard, something which had been unearthed from a bombed building. The treads of all four tyres displayed a rippling pattern of canvas. There was no spare. Before the steering-wheel could influence the car's direction, it had to be spun through half a turn. Gaping sockets showed where all the instruments had been wrenched out of the dashboard. The floor-boards above the engine had been removed, releasing a furnace heat and the rattling vibration of a million nails being shaken in a metal box. Above this pit sat the driver, stabbing like a frantic organist at the control pedals, which in some way had lost their normal independence of each other, since the application of the brake slightly opened the throttle, and the engine had to be switched off, or the accelerator held back, whenever this was necessary. Whenever he wanted to blow the horn, the driver, reaching out as if to catch a butterfly, seized two dangling wires and held them together. The body was insecurely fixed to the chassis, but settled down on a straight road to a steady see-sawing motion to which one soon became accustomed, although the sudden opening of the doors as we took corners continued to surprise.

Our first stop was at the market-place again where two Shan policemen, armed with swords, arrived in company with a Burmese woman. The woman was singing in a penetrating voice, and the policemen looked embarrassed. All three climbed into the back. The policemen unbelted their swords, laid them down beside them, and settled themselves. Two or three onlookers gathered; the woman waved gaily to them and started another song. One of the policemen picked up his sword, leaned over, and tapped the driver on the shoulder with it, nodding to the road ahead. The driver screwed up his face, but said nothing. More onlookers strolled up and stood about, their faces amazed under their turbans while the Burmese woman serenaded them. Another policeman appeared, and checked the travellers' passes, and then, as with a resounding crash the driver engaged bottom gear, our musical passenger broke into 'I put my money on a coal-black mare, doodah, doodah', and away we went.

Within minutes the last of Lashio's cottage gardens was behind us. We were going down a gradient with a steep, flowering slope on our right, and then my heart sank. There was another lorry in the middle of the road, clearly in trouble. From it swarmed like troubled bees a colourful collection of passengers, Kachin women with a chain-mail of silver coins over their breasts, Palaungs with hips swathed in metal bands, and betel-stained holes where their mouths should have been. In the Far East, the courtesies of the road are observed with punctilio. We drew up alongside and immediately a team of experts from the post-wagon was formed to investigate and pronounce upon the break-down. Petrol lines, pumps, carburettor were dismantled in a leisurely manner, fiddled with, and re-assembled. The engine started, wuffled for perhaps ten seconds, and stopped. Meanwhile our singer had reached a number in her repertoire which seemed to give her special pleasure, and was singing that simple tune, 'Happy Birthday to You', for the fifth or sixth time.

A moment later it became clear that the driver of the post-wagon had made a generous decision, for there was a sudden rush of whirling skirted forms in our direction, and in a few seconds we had taken on a jingling cargo. There was something miraculous about the compression involved. A young Indian girl of distracted Pre-Raphaelite beauty joined us. Jewels dripped from a nostril, and round her neck she wore a large iron key. Passing by an act of levitation over the crowded forms, she subsided in a ballet posture among some vegetable marrows. The Palaungs, a compact racial heap, stared around them with the frightened eyes of children in the presence of violence. The singing Burmese woman had been driven by the invasion into a position immediately behind me, although slightly higher. Every time she moved she struck me with her knee in the back of the neck. Forced thus into close contact, I took in the details of her dress, the grubby, flowered longyi, the unbuttoned blouse, and, rather alarmingly, the necklace of beer-bottle tops.

We moved off down the hill, the overloaded post-wagon wallowing with a nautical motion. Whenever we went over a bump there was a sound from the interior like the clashing of circus accoutrements. Having covered a mile or two, we reached a gradient that was too much for us. Everyone got out, and while the passengers trotted by its side the lorry made a groaning, faltering climb. At the top of the hill there was a pause to let the engine cool. The Burmese woman, still singing, leaped suddenly from her perch, easily cleared a low hedge into a field, where, producing a clasp-knife, she hacked down a sugar-cane and began to tear at it with her teeth. I thought this extraordinary because I could never remember having seen a woman run in the Far East before. I got out my notebook and started to write and a young man dressed with striking formality came worming his way through the baggage, pulled my sleeve, and asked courteously, 'What are you writing, sir?' I told him I was writing poetry and received a brilliant smile from under the brown trilby hat.

It occurred to me to comment on the behaviour of the Burmese woman, who was now coming towards us, her sugar-cane held in her hand, in a series of leaps. He said, 'This lady has bad nerves, sir.' I had begun to suspect as much, and now something else struck me. In the Burmese theatre the insane are always shown as Ophelias, distraught and wildly eccentric. Although their condition is pitiable, and sorcerers are called in to heal them by the medieval equivalent of shock treatment, they dance and sing in an absurd fashion, and adorn themselves ridiculously with such things as condensed-milk tins. This then was the recognized pattern of Burmese insanity, and it looked as if the Burmese went mad along accepted lines. It was curious to consider that an element of pose probably lurked beneath the authentic state of derangement. I asked what had been responsible for the woman's misfortune, and my friend, who introduced himself as Seng, said, 'This lady has lost all her children. For this reason her nerves have become bad.' But there was no way of discovering the circumstances of her children's death; my further enquiries only producing flashing smiles of incomprehension. Later he told me that the woman, who had caused a disturbance in Lashio, was being removed under escort to her home village. And where did she learn all these extraordinary hymns, carols, negro spirituals, bawdy army choruses? The answer, when the question had been repeated several times, in different ways, was unconvincing. 'They teach these songs in the schools, sir.' Seng was a Kachin who had been down to Rangoon for his education and was now on his way home. Gradually and rather painfully our conversation expanded. At first there were long pauses while the thoughts in Kachin were translated into English via Burmese; but after a while the sentences began to come more readily, and with their proper Anglo-Asiatic injection of rotundities, euphemisms and prudery.

Our road wound through low hills clothed in formless scrub, and the slow re-animation of secondary jungle, where cultivation has long been abandoned. Occasionally there were patches, ragged in shape as Hebridean islands, which had only recently been given up and where the self-sown maize and the tea-bushes spread in increasing dilution through the ferns, the creepers, and the thorns. In this desolation we passed a single human form, a Shan who wore gauntlets of tattooing and a ring of tattooed dragons leaping up from his waist as if to devour his torso. He stood motionless by the roadside, his arms curled inexplicably round a slender tree trunk, looking, somehow, against this seething background of curving fronds and tendrils, like a capital in a richly illuminated manuscript.

Near here, the Indian girl left us. She was accompanied by an ageing man, who now struggled up from the depths of the baggage, and the pair of them set off down a thorn-lined track, bound, under the relentless sun, for who knows what strange haven of domestic bliss. At Mongli, which although marked on fairly small-scale maps, seemed to possess only one hut, there was a halt for refreshment, and the post-wagon discharged its passengers like seeds exploded from an over-ripe pod. I found that the package Tin Maung's mother had given me contained raw onions and fried meat balls, beautifully done up in banana-leaves and then the locally made, tough, translucent paper. I shared this with Seng, who gave me some tea out of a section of bamboo fitted with a neat wooden cap. It was here for the first time that I noticed the beautiful baskets carried by the Palaungs, who had gathered in a ball-players' huddle.

Being without anthropological training I do not know whether one is entitled to form theories on so slender a basis of evidence, so I only place on record the fact that although regarded as a Mongolian people, the Palaungs possess beautiful woven and lacquered baskets, of a quite extraordinary shape, which are identical with those made by the Indonesian Moïs of Central Annam, which, as the crow flies, is about fourteen hundred miles away. These baskets, which I have photographed in both countries, are not owned by any of the peoples by whom the Palaungs are surrounded. Their construction is very complicated, and they are beautiful on the score of shape and texture, as they are not decorated in any way. I think that the possibility of coincidence is ruled out. It is, by the way, curious that the handicrafts of a people so remote, so neglected, and apparently so low in the cultural scale, should be so much superior to those of the relatively sophisticated Shans and Kachins who are their neighbours. The Palaungs speak a Mongolian language, and I believe that on this linguistic evidence they, as well as so many of the Burmese minorities, have been classed as Mongolian people. From a cursory and superficial study of their features, as well as those of many other obscure racial types I encountered in my travels, I should guess that although these people may have adopted the language of powerful neighbours, and have intermarried with them, they probably also possess pre-Mongoloid Indonesian blood. Many of them have the Caucasian type of eye and thick, wavy hair. The French, who have carried out intense ethnological studies in Indo-China, produce a map showing enclaves of Indonesians clustered along the western frontier of that country, where it is contiguous with the Southern Shan States of Burma. It would be unreasonable to suppose that these cease to be found as soon as one crosses into Burma, when the frontier is, of course, a purely political one. Perhaps if instead of the linguistic classification which has hitherto sufficed, a study were made of the laws, ceremonies, legends, religious customs, and the traditional designs of weaving of these peoples, an entirely new light might be thrown on their origins and racial affinities.

Certainly the Palaungs' legend of their origin sounds a Mongolian one, although it may have been adopted in recent times along with the language. The founder of the tribe was hatched from a serpent's egg – a hint of totemism which is echoed by the women's habit of encircling their hips by forty or fifty narrow cane hoops, which rest one on another, to a depth of about a foot or eighteen inches, and provide a suggestively undulant motion as they walk. Such an ancestry is considered utterly reasonable in the Far East, and the existence of a naga in one's pedigree would have caused no comment, at least until recently, in the gravest of academic circles. The Glass Palace Chronicle – a collation of records combined with historical criticism – written in 1829, goes into the question of 'egg-born kings' at length, but the learned commentators are concerned only to establish their reasonable opinion that a certain Burmese monarch –

Pyu Sawhti – could not have been born of an egg laid by a naga (a female serpent-god) *as the result of her union with a spirit*, and that since the king was human, one of the parents, at least, must have been human too. However, instances are given, and approved, of the oviparous birth of human beings where only one of the parents was supernatural – a naga, or a fabulous lion.

Hsenwi was an incrustation of huts where, in a bare plateau, the road was joined by another from the east. We crossed a rush-choked river, over which shaven-headed children in blue smocks held their fishing rods. There was a small lake with white ducks on it diving through the reflection of a bare mountain, and storks going round in circles overhead. Horsemen, their feet almost trailing on the ground, came charging through the grass to the verge of the road, and as we passed cavorted like movie-Indians and waved their yellow scarves at us. We passed a line of shops with the shopkeepers outside flying fish-shaped kites. A caravan of ponies, piled high with what looked like beansticks, panicked at our approach and, turning, stampeded through the village in a charge like that of the bulls driven before Morgan's pirates at the sack of Panama.

This was Kachin country, although there were still plenty of Shan enclaves. The Kachins, comparatively recent arrivals in these highlands, have always been regarded by the Shans, whose country they invaded, with a kind of superstitious aversion. Their exceptional ability as hunters was apt to be ascribed to the works of the devil. This charge had some slight basis, because the Kachins had the unusual advantage of the protection of a powerful spirit called Kyam, in a country where the most that could be hoped for from the average nat was neutrality, bought at a cost of frequent sacrifices. Kyam led the Kachins to their game, which he fascinated, while the hunters shot them with their crossbows, using aconite-tipped arrows. The service was performed without any question of return, and not even a priest had to be paid.

As far as the Shans could, they kept the Kachins back in their mountains, often burning the villages of those who tried to establish themselves in the more fertile Shan country. But the Kachins were under constant internal pressure to emigrate, the result of the destructive type of cultivation they practised, and of their custom by which the youngest son inherited all his father's property, thus compelling the elder sons to set out to found new settlements. When the Kachins reached the stage when they had to expand or burst, they did so explosively, practising a form of warfare rarely known in the West since biblical times. All living beings were exterminated in the territory taken over. The operation was carried out without animosity, and the ghosts of the victims – who received a decent burial – were placated with inexpensive sacrifices.

In their mountains, the Kachins live in long-houses, which are often occupied by several families. The dead are buried under the floor, where it is felt that they will be less lonely. Up to the time of marriage the women enjoy unusual freedom, and often try a succession of lovers before settling down. They then become chattels, descending to a man's heir with the rest of his property.

Beyond Hsenwi we mounted a hill, entered a stockade, and drew up outside the local military headquarters. The driver expected to find the Sawbwa here, but we were redirected to his haw, a mile away on a hillside among a belt of trees. The haw, or palace, as the Sawbwa's residence is usually known, was a substantial, single-storeyed building of plaited bamboo, with a formal, roofed-over approach, and a kind of exterior waiting-room where Seng and the driver were left, while a servitor conducted me up the steps to the entrance to the haw itself. Here the Sawbwa appeared. We had arrived rather unfortunately in the siesta time, and he showed signs of having dressed hastily. Like his brother, he was polite but without affability. Reading my letter he invited me to be seated at a table in his barely furnished reception room. He then gave an order to one of his sons, a boy of about twelve, who went away and shortly reappeared with cigarettes and air-mail paper and envelopes, which, kneeling respectfully, he handed to his father. The Sawbwa then wrote out an open recommendation to any official I might encounter on the road to Nam Hkam to be of all possible assistance. He advised me to continue with the post-wagon as far as I could go, as it might be some time before another opportunity of transport offered itself. I should have liked to stay a day or two in Hsenwi, but although I made it clear that I did not wish to inconvenience the Sawbwa in any way, this delay was not thought advisable. The village had been thoroughly destroyed by bombing during the war and accommodation was very limited. My interview lasted five minutes. Perhaps the Sawbwa had given up all hopes of the English.

Kutkai was another Hsenwi, except that it was twenty miles nearer the Chinese frontier, and in that distance a marked increase in Chinese influence had taken place. I was surprised to see Chinese women with bound feet pegging along the single street, as if picking their way across a surface strewn with invisible eggs. In one's schooldays one was told that this practice had long been abandoned, and that examples of it were only to be seen in the case of old women, survivors from the Imperial days. At about the time this information was imparted, these women must have been undergoing the minor tortures which had finally moulded their feet into the lotus form. It was an extraordinary quirk of taste that could see the image of a symmetrical bloom in this deformation of the foot-bones.

The village was in a low hollow of the hills. They were covered with whitened grass, a tough, austere growth heralding the vegetable dark age, when the soil has been utterly exhausted by primitive cultivation. We could see Palaungs converging on the town, moving down from the hills in Indian file, loaded with green grass for use in feeding the animals; grass that every year, one supposed, would have to be brought from a greater distance. Here, at Kutkai, the post-wagon gave in. After its long, arduous and useful life, it had chosen just this day of all days to attain the Nirvana of final disintegration, or so the driver thought. The radiator had boiled steadily all the way from Hsenwi, emitting thin jets of steam and water through various perforations, and lately the even, almost rhythmic clatter of loose tappets, bearings, and pistons, and the whine of worn gears, had been invaded by new, irregular, and compelling sounds. Suddenly the power had faded away, absorbed in mechanical convulsions preceding the ultimate coma. We had limped into Kutkai at a slow walking pace. Now a line of turbaned heads was bowed, under the bonnet, over the smoking, reeking mechanism, and a murmur of advice in several of the Thibeto-Burman and Thai-Chinese languages arose. And then, the driver produced his diagnosis. A connecting rod had snapped and it was supposed that a macerated piston had dropped into the sump, where it had been ground into fragments by the crankshaft. If parts could be found a repair would take about four days. Otherwise the post-wagon would never travel further. Sadly the passengers dispersed towards the various caravan-serais of Kutkai. With them went the crazy Burmese woman and her guards. She was still singing and gambolling with the inexhaust-ible vitality of her despair.

I was just about to look for a tea-house myself, speculating on whether Kutkai could provide even one-star accommodation by local standards, when Seng, who had gone off as soon as we stopped, reappeared in a bullock-cart. It was a vehicle of a kind I had not seen before, high wheeled and rakish, and having about it something of the chariot. It was drawn by two fine and almost spirited-looking animals, constrained only by a light yoke. They approached in a quick, shambling gait. Directing the driver, a tattooed and muscled Asiatic Ben-Hur, to put my baggage in this contraption, Seng invited me to accompany him to the house of his brother-in-law, a Kachin headman, who lived only a few miles away. Here I could put up in comfort while enquiries were being made about transport for the next stage of the journey. Accepting this very welcome suggestion, I climbed in and sat down with Seng in the bottom of the cart, the driver cracked his whip, and the bullocks moved off at a sharp pace.

A few miles out of Kutkai we turned off the Burma Road into a rough, rutted track leading up into the hills. Within minutes there was a change of scenery. It was like the escape from a concreted highway with the flat boredom of its surroundings into the sanctuary of the undisturbed woods. The dazzling white deadness of the grass was broken by sere but florescent bushes and thickets of bamboo, and among these the trees, pipuls, banyans and flamboyants, massive eruptions of verdure, became increasingly frequent. Huge rollers flew strongly among their branches, their wings flashing with Aegean blues. 'The foolish bird,' said Seng, following my gaze of admiration. 'This is its designation in the Kachin tongue, because it eats its own faeces.' As we penetrated into these high forests, the butterflies threading among the trees had already lost the pallor of those of the tropical steppe-lands and taken on a wash of colour, a token of the magnificence that awaited us in the deep undergrowth ahead. Palaungs, gowned like pantomime witches and bent under their bundles, flitted away into the trees until we had passed.

The headman's house was on a bare hilltop. It was as big as the Sawbwa's haw, an important construction of stone and corrugated iron, which had been smashed in the passage of the war, and half rebuilt in woven bamboo. Two or three rifle-armed soldiers of the headman's bodyguard were hanging about outside, and a jeep painted with a vigorous, primitive design of tigers and deer was drawn up outside the door. Seng directed our driver to continue round to the back of the house, where we found a kind of tradesman's entrance, surrounded by much domestic actitivity, cooking on outside stoves, and babies sitting in the dust eating rice out of bowls. Here also was the headman's private lock-up, a species of chicken-house strengthened with thick timber bars, in which three inmates were sitting, whom from their blue cotton clothing I took to be Chinese. The door was unceremoniously opened by the headman himself, a short man of almost theatrical inscrutability, dressed like a Soviet official in a plain loose tunic and trousers. He greeted his brother-in-law without surprise or effusion, and invited me to enter. We went in and sat down in chairs placed against the wall, in a room furnished like the waiting-room of an old-fashioned poor persons' dispensary. The headman took my collection of permits and letters in English, Burmese, Shan, and Kachin, and began to read them with extreme deliberation, his lips silently forming the words.

While this process went on, my eyes wandered round the room, passing over the repetitious bamboo pattern of the walls, then arrested by a crudely coloured picture of a number of figures in vaguely Palestinian dress, who were peering into a cave, which they were prevented from entering by a stern-faced, white-robed form. Under this was printed the legend: 'He is not here, but is risen.' The aristocracy of these parts, it seemed, were Baptist converts. Beneath this picture hung a gong, and when the headman had finished perusing my documents he reached up and tapped it lightly with his knuckles. Immediately a soldier came in. He was dressed in a British battledress, was barefooted, and carried a rifle slung on his shoulder. The headman muttered something and the soldier went out and came back almost immediately carrying a tray loaded with three cups of tea and basins of sugar and salt. In the Burmese hill-country, tea-leaves are grilled, and the addition to the brew of salt as well as sugar produces a result which differs greatly in flavour from tea as drunk in the West. The headman passed the tea, having adding the sugar and salt with this own hands. This courtesy accomplished, he was called away to other duties. I could not make up my mind whether I was welcome or not, but resigned myself to Seng, who showed me to a bare chamber leading off a central room, and told me to make myself at home. It was part of the original stone construction, and there was an attached cubicle with a stand, a pitcher, and a hole in the floor, where a shower could be taken.

No sooner had I put my bedding down in a corner than a Kachin girl came in. She had a wide Thibetan face with bright pink cheeks which seemed to continue right up to her eyes, which were narrow, black and glinting. She was smiling with abounding good humour, and bounced round the room in a kind of brisk tour of inspection, skirts swirling and hawser-like pigtails flapping on her back. It seemed as though she wished to assure herself that all the non-existent furniture had been properly dusted, and that the towels had been put out. Finally satisfied with the good order of the void, she withdrew with a slight bow, indicating, as she did, the cubicle, where I found a bowl of hot water had been placed. Five minutes, perhaps, passed while I was unpacking a few things; then I heard footsteps in the cubicle, to which there was also an outside door, and looking up I saw that another handmaiden had arrived with a second steaming bowl. The first was removed. Next the beaming Seng arrived with a chair to put my clothes on. Having arranged my wardrobe on this, and laid out my mosquito net ready for use, I made for the wash-place, just in time to see the water being changed for a third time.

I washed and hung up my mosquito net, and was wondering what to do with myself when there was a tap on the door and Seng was back again. 'Do you like rum?' he asked. I said that I did, and followed him into the central room, where the headman was staring severely at several bottles. We sat down and the headman took three half-pint tumblers, half filled them with rum, and topped them up with the now familiar Mandalay Pale Ale. One of these he handed to me. The headman and his brother-in-law raised their glasses in my direction. Seng smiled brilliantly; he said, 'Chin-chin.' The headman managed a faint grimace. Two heads were flung back and two glasses drained. The headman looked up with faint reproach while I gulped painfully, fulfilling at enormous effort what was expected of me. Immediately the two bottles were raised, threateningly, and I realized that the abstemious and puritanical Burma of the plains was now behind me and that I had fallen among a race of hard-drinking hill-folk.

The headman spoke a little now, groping for words, about local conditions. In recent years they had seen plenty of fighting. When the Japanese had finally gone there had been a plague of Chinese bandits, and then a Kachin insurrection against the Burmese led by a self-promoted Brigadier Naw Seng, who when defeated had escaped with his adherents to China. The headman supposed that he would reappear one of these days in the guise of a Chinese-backed liberator of the Kachin people. He was not disturbed at the prospect. 'We Kachins lack education,' he said. 'We like to fight and to drink country spirit.' If the Chinese Communists ever came over the frontier it would be a good scrap while it lasted, although he was the first to admit that it wouldn't last long. Up to the moment there had not been a single instance reported to him of the violation of the frontier by a Communist soldier, although waves of fleeing Nationalists kept coming over. The road ahead, between this and Nam Hkam, had been closed for a week now because of the attacks they had made on traffic, and in the near future he would have to go and drive them out of the area. He had a two-pounder gun that hadn't been used since the war, and now he was hoping for the chance to fire a few rounds. The headman's voice when he said this lacked the ring of conviction. It was more of the sportsman's gesture to a convention of optimism than a matter of serious hope.

I asked for news of conditions over the frontier. Were, for instance, land reforms being put into practice? Land reforms! the headman echoed scornfully, it wasn't land reforms the hill-peoples wanted. The people over the frontier were Shans, Kachins, and Palaungs, just as they were on this side. If they wanted land, there was nothing to stop them clearing the bush and cultivating it. What the Kachin people wanted was not land, but education. That, he understood, their new masters in China were going to give them, although he had heard that the first samples to return from the school in Kunming had soon shown, to the scandal of the villagers, that they had lost respect for their parents. One of the worst things about the present situation was the closing of the frontier to ordinary respectable people. If you were dressed up like a hill-savage in turban and strings of beads, nobody said anything to you – you could cross backwards and forwards as much as you liked. But if you wore decent clothes – a pair of trousers and a hat bought in Rangoon – they arrested you as a spy. Draining his glass sorrowfully to the memory of departed liberties, the headman reached over and struck the gong. There was an almost immediate irruption into the room of domestics carrying dishes of food. Along with them came the headman's wife – Seng's sister – a strapping Ludmila of the remote Asiatic mountains, who, relieved of the headman's necessity for high-minded seriousness, giggled frequently, especially when in difficulties with the serving of the food. There was a continual coming and going of flouncing pigtailed forms, until the table was closely covered with dishes, scarlet curries with surface currents of ochreous oil, three varieties of what looked like seaweed (inevitably recommended as abundant in vitamins), a paste made of ground beans and chillis, pickled tea-leaves, great bowls of red rice, cups of tea with a container of salt by each. Having brought in the food, the female staff bowed, and one by one withdrew. Their place was taken by soldiers, who took up position behind the chairs and helped with the dishes, into which they sometimes let ash fall from the cheroots they were smoking. In between their duties, they kneeled down to play with several of the headman's young children who had escaped from the nursery to take refuge here, and were crawling about on the floor.

Later that day, I found out from Seng that his brother-in-law had just received definite information of the location of the Chinese band. They were in a jungle village, about five hours' ride to the north, and next morning the headman would lead a party of his men to attack them. By this time Seng and I were on such good terms and I felt able to ask him to persuade the headman to take me with them. The headman, too, had suddenly thawed out with a revelation of charm that was like the unexpected appearance of the sun on a dull day. We talked about such things as education, particularly the flashier subjects like psychology, to which provincial Asiatics are often specially attracted, finding that the transition to such studies is not difficult after a grounding in, say, horoscopy or in the art of making oneself bullet-proof. In the cool of the evening all the able-bodied household, including the womenfolk, were chased out to do physical jerks in the courtyard while the headman, himself, rapped out the orders in Kachin – knees bend, knees stretch. This ritual was thoroughly enjoyed, especially by the women, who usually over-balanced while in the knees bend position. Nothing was said, one way or other, about the next day's expedition.

However, soon after dawn, Seng followed the pigtailed serving-girl into my room, and said, 'The horses are ready.' He was trying to buckle on a Kachin dah, a weapon of monstrous unsuitability, over his Rangoon clothes. Seng was manipulating the dah – a heavy bladed affair, half-sword and half-axe – with a civilized lack of enthusiasm. 'If I do not carry this,' he said, with an apologetic smile, 'the headman will think I have become soft. But I have lost the habit of the strokes.' The soldiers were armed with Sten guns or rifles, but the headman and his brother-in-law were by tradition invulnerable, and carried dahs for reasons of prestige alone.

I am a plain horseman, content to keep my seat, and unfamiliar with equestrian refinements. The pony provided for me looked well shaped enough and there was nothing unusual about it, except a certain sheepish quality about the head, and a drooping of the muzzle that reminded me of some other animal, perhaps a tapir. The stirrups were too short, and could not be lengthened enough for comfort. I mounted, and found myself, in this position, nearer the ground than I had ever been since on a donkey on the sands as a child. The short, fat back sagged springily as it took my weight, and I half expected the animal to collapse. Once firmly in the saddle I kicked experimentally at the pony's sides, and it instantly threw me backwards, over the tail, with an irresistible oscillation, like that of a dog shaking the water out of its coat. One of the Kachin soldiers caught it by the rein, passed a caressing hand over its face, then smacked it fiercely with the flat of his dah. I mounted again, and sat there quietly. The soldiers went off, stringing out into a thin column, with the headman leading them. Behind him rode a soldier, steering a pony which had nothing but a large ceremonial drum strapped to its back. Then came the straggling column, with the soldiers in their British battledress, with waistbands tied over them, and dahs stuck through the waistbands; so that they looked like Japanese swordsmen. Seng and I brought up the rear. My pony started when the others did, and stopped when they stopped. Without any urging on my part, it broke, when it was required to keep up with the rest, into a kind of scrambling gallop, but would tolerate no interference on my part; it danced about and tossed its head angrily if I tried to give it any encouragement other than a shake of the reins, or to influence its course in any way. But it was the smoothest animal to ride I had ever sat on, and Seng later told me that a Kachin pony was unsaleable until it could be put through all its paces, with its rider holding a full tumbler in one hand, without spilling the contents.

That morning I had awakened with a vague sense of indisposition, and now as a growling malaise concentrated and defined itself, I realized that I was in for a mild bout of malaria. The fever soon cushioned the edges of sensation, and simplified things wonderfully. To me the jungle itself has never offered the brilliant variegation of the jungle as it appears in an air-terminal mural. It has never been a matter of orchids and black panthers; and now even the few modest highlights that this forest could have offered were suppressed by two or three degrees of fever. The impression remains that from the outside, as we rode through the wide clearings, it was like the trimly arranged asparagus of a bouquet from which, unaccountably, the flowers had been omitted. But as soon as we rode beneath those delicate awnings of fernery we passed into a seedy vegetable disorder, with many sallow broken grasses, and moulting bamboos; and the sun showered its spears on us through a ragged armour of leaves. There were no serpents, nor startled fawns; not even, in fact, birds of sufficient presence for my fevered eyes to record them. This was a well-worn track, which wild animals had probably learned to avoid. Tribesmen, like any other travellers, are careful to keep out of the virgin jungle, and this narrow path probably carried as much or more human traffic than the metalled high road.

We rode by the verge of swamps, over bare hilltops, and down into the untidy jungle again; and thus on and on. Some time in the early afternoon the soldiers ahead broke into a gallop, and a few minutes later we rode into a miserable Palaung village. The soldiers sprang from their horses, crawled into the huts and came out with a few women. They were half-naked, and all had goitre. The Chinese had gone off the day before, they said, but they had left two sick men behind. They took us to a shelter of leaves and branches, under which the two deserted men lay on the ground, half-conscious, and with their bare feet grossly swollen. The Kachins sat them up, tied their hands lightly, and tried to stick lighted cheroots between their teeth; but the Chinese were past smoking. It appeared that the band had gone off down the trail in the direction of the border, so the headman, leaving a man behind with the prisoners, gave the order to ride on.

We rode out of the village, with the half-clothed, goitrous women standing by their huts looking after us, and down into the jungle, which was exactly as before. The thumping behind my eyes deepened, and with it, the monotony of the ride. Hours later we came down to a river. From our position we could not see the water, which at this time of the year was very shallow and split up by islands and sandbanks. There was a fording-place here, and China was on the other side. We could just make out a village, with an insect-movement of humans and buffaloes among the huts. The headman sent soldiers in various directions to make enquiries and, after a long wait, one of them came back with the news that the bandits had been seen crossing the ford. It was evident that the Kachins did not relish being checked by the purely political barrier. Seng explained that the people across the river were not Chinese, but Shans and Kachins; moreover, he said, 'The actual border is in dispute. Every year the river changes its course.'

But the headman was against further action. There might be Communist soliders on the other side. Not that he was prepared to cross, in any case. To satisfy the men, the big drum was beaten vigorously; and a few seconds later the reply came, a bugle-call, practised, unwavering, and definite. That settled it. A new, unsympathetic authority had announced its presence.

Although I had no idea of it at the time, we were at this point actually within a few miles of Nam Hkam, having in the course of our expedition cut across the base of a triangle of country enclosed by the motor road. In a few days I should be passing once again down the roughly metalled track running parallel with the river.

That night we slept in a jungle-clearing on the way back. There was a remnant of a hut perched on stilts ten feet high, and into it the headman, Seng, and I climbed. Every time one of us turned over, this construction swayed a little. Beneath us, the soldiers thudded with unflagging energy at their drum, and sang a soldiering song with endless verses and an extremely monotonous air. The end of each verse would be signalled by howls of laughter. In the end, as

464

the first wave of fever slowly spent itself, I relapsed into rambling, oppressive dreams. I was soon aroused by a discharge of shots. But it was only a soldier who had been tinkering with his Sten, which was loaded, and had shot off one of his toes.

CHAPTER THIRTEEN

Protective Custody

THE LOCAL SECTION of the Burma Road having been declared open to traffic, the headman took me down in his jeep to the point where the hill-track joined it, and where he had established a road-block, guarded by his men. Seng had come down to see me off, and here we parted most cordially. The soldiers had already stopped a jeep. In it were two Chinese merchants on their way from Kutkai to Mu-Sé. This town was not marked on my map, the production of a very well known map-making firm, which was vague – and, as I later discovered, inaccurate – about this frontier area. The Chinese spoke of Mu-Sé as if it were a considerable metropolis, a local nerve centre from which well-organized transport services left regularly in all directions. This pernicious optimism in informants is one of the traveller's worst enemies. They said there were lorries to Nam Hkam 'plenty often'. More than once a day? Oh, sure, more than once a day. Would we get to Mu-Sé early enough to catch one? Oh, sure we would, sure thing.

The Chinese spoke English better than the Burmese perhaps because they had escaped the schools run by religious institutions, with their hallmark of tedious and involved archaism. By comparison the Chinese made it snappy, and cinema-argot ran like a rich vein of fool's gold through their speech. Their Americanisms are, of course, dated, and as the cinematographic diet of the Far East is largely composed of gun-toting epics, they are drawn largely from the dialects of the cattle-raising states. 'Well, I'll be a son of a gun,' said the driver in amazement, when he learned of my hitch-hike from Mandalay.

The Chinese jeep reflected in its purposeful, surging acceleration, its efficient steering and brakes, and also in certain additional equipment, such as fog-lamps, the tastes and calibre of its owner.

Wherever a plain black handle or knob had existed, it had been replaced by one of sky-blue plastic. Badges in the dashboard announced membership of motoring associations in places like Hong Kong and Cuba, and would have appeared to be of little service to the Chinese member. Sometimes when approaching a corner, round which the odds of an approaching vehicle being hidden were several thousand to one, the driver would touch a button, and a tremendous fanfare of trumpets would flush from the undergrowth an unsuspected population of pigeons and quails.

This landscape was the wild natural reserve common to most frontiers. Exposed to endless incursions of bandits, it had not been thought worth while to build villages, or to undertake any settled cultivation. From the absence of trees on the low hillsides you could see that the Palaungs or Kachins had moved through at some time, set fire to the forest and snatched a crop of 'dry' rice or maize. The road had been cut, a red whip-lash round hillsides and through valleys filled with a dense low tundra of tropical vegetation. We saw few signs of animal life here, except some lizards in the red dust, one of which was carried off from beneath our tyres in the talons of a hawk, which missed annihilation by inches. After perhaps two hours of shattering the savage peace of this wilderness with our heraldic approach, we dropped down into a long valley running north–south, and beyond the end of this, their bases laced with an immediate foreground of tree-fern, loomed portentous and pallid the bare mountains of Yunnan. At the valley's end we passed out into the unchallenged sunlight of a plateau, soon reaching a crosroads with a police post and a knot of harassed sword-bearing travellers. From this point the Burma Road went on to cross the Chinese frontier, at Wanting, about three miles away. The road to the left went to Mu-Sé, and down this broken, calamitous track we plunged, after a cursory inspection by the Kachin frontier police.

Mu-Sé was a place of importance and animation. We pulled up in a considerable square with a market to which a row of Chinese tea-shops with outside tables had given a faintly Parisian atmosphere of graceful leisure. Banners, which might have flown at the fiat of a dictator, were found to advertise the practices of dentists, and were usually adorned with enormous sectional diagrams of the jaw, the danger-spots filled in in savage colour. There was a Shwebo Motor Store with an Indian-Gothic façade in red brick, complete with castellations. Combined grocers and tea-shops had their shelves well stocked with such commodities as nougat and Wincarnis. At one of these the two Chinese and I took tea together, while glossy, blue-black crows hopped about our feet or dived under the chairs to pick up crumbs of cake. Women with bound feet, and conservatively dressed Chinese in long gowns and Phrygian caps, passed by. As in Hsenwi a few of the shopkeepers were combating the tedium between customers by flying kites from the doors of their establishments. This was done with much expertness and the use of the best equipment, the string being wound on expensive-looking contraptions like fishing-reels. In one case some kind of competition seemed to be in progress between an Indian executive of the Shwebo Motor Store and a dentist, some hundred yards away, at the other end of the square. Their kites, flown at such a height that they were no more than white slivers in the sky, were going through the most complicated evolutions, feinting and thrusting, swooping and ducking. It seemed a most convenient kind of game that one could play with opponents in different parts of the town without neglecting one's business.

Enquiring in the market-place, I found that there were no lorries going to Nam Hkam that day. This did not surprise me. I had learned no longer to expect a dovetailing in such travelling connections. Mu-Sé was said to possess a circuit house, but supposing it to be in some exposed position, outside the town, I decided that I might as well stay in one of the Chinese places in the square. Returning to the shop where we had had tea, I managed with some difficulty – since the Chinese are not a gesticulatory people – to make the waiter understand what I wanted, and was led into a dim, lattice-screened interior, where, upon a board raised a few inches from the earth, I put down my bedding. Mu-Sé was a hot town, and outside an ardent breeze had sprung up, carrying processions of whirling dust-genii through the streets.

I decided to take a siesta, and had just settled down when a form darkened the doorway, which in this room was the only source of light and air. In obedience to a silent beckoning, I got up and went out. My visitor – who had shrunk somewhat in the light – proved to be an elderly Kachin police officer, with a flat, sensitive face. He was dressed in khaki-drill shorts, a grey woollen pullover, and a forage cap, worn, after the fashion of all Asiatics, on the top of his head. His manner was apologetic and discouraged, as with a slightly sad smile he led me to a jeep and motioned me to get in. The Indian who had so recently been flying a kite outside the Shwebo Motor Store, and who was a mildly interested onlooker, now moved towards me and said, 'He is taking you to the police station, sir.' Owing to the complete absence of everything that might have been described as autocratic in the police officer's attitude, I could not decide whether I was under arrest or not. I got into the jeep and we drove away, turning off the main square into a side street, which emptied its dust and ruts after a hundred yards into what looked like a neglected playing field. At the end of this was a long, low bamboo construction, raised on piles. This I judged to be the police barracks, as uniformed Kachins were lounging about, or sitting on the steps leading up to the several entrances of the long-house. The distant prospect was splendid. Behind the barracks the ground rose gently, scored with paths like intersecting lines drawn idly with a compass. Gradually the groves of trees, the bamboo thickets closed in, till summits of the low hills were covered with frothing vegetation. Somewhere beyond came the dividing line, the true frontier, where the forests of Burma shrivelled and expired on the slopes of the mountains of Yunnan. With this rampart of pyramids the horizon was closed; golden and glowing slag-heaps, other-worldly in the purity of their utter desolation.

Policemen took my luggage out of the jeep, and carried it up to the lieutenant's room. My bedding roll was laid out on the bamboo floor next to the lieutenant's. Between them was a soap box, on which the lieutenant's washing kit was exposed in military style. A tommy-gun leaned against the box. A tinted photograph on the wall showed my host, or gaoler, dressed as a Buddhist novice. While I was examining it I felt a light tap on the arm and turned to find myself now also provided with a soap box, on which stood a bowl of hot water, a neatly folded towel, and a tablet of some much advertised brand of soap. The lieutenant smiled as if at the memory of secret pain, and went out. I washed, got out a camera, and followed him, noticing as soon as I had reached the bottom of the steps that a policeman had appeared behind me, carrying a chair. When I stopped, he stopped, and put the chair down. As soon as I moved on, he picked the chair up and followed me. It seemed to me that I had better fall in with the inference and sit down. I did so, and in a few minutes the lieutenant came up and squatted beside me. He put a tumbler in my hand. It was a brand new one, just unpacked, and was lightly coated with straw-dust. The manufacturer's label was in position, bright and unsoiled. Raising his pullover, the lieutenant groped underneath, found the breast-pocket of his shirt and brought out a pinch of dried herbs, which he dropped into the tumbler. A waiting policeman now approached with a kettle, and filled up the tumbler with hot water. At the bottom, the herb stirred with sudden impulse, and blossoms uncurled like moths newly released from their chrysalises. Petals unfolded and straightened, stamens thrust forth, until the bottom of the glass was gay with daisies. While the lieutenant looked on eagerly I sipped, for the first time in my life, an infusion of camomile.

I was still unable to make up my mind whether this was protective custody, or no more than strangely spontaneous hospitality on the police's part. After a few moments, therefore, I decided to define the position if possible. Gesturing vaguely in the direction of a neighbouring belt of trees, and incidentally of China, and at the same time smiling inoffensively, I tried to convey the idea that I proposed to go for a walk. This produced no obvious symptoms of disapproval, so I got up, smiled again, and strolled away in a casual manner. Having taken an aimless and wavering course for a couple of hundred yards, I bent down to pick something up, at the same time glancing behind. The lieutenant was no longer to be seen, and as no one was following me, I quickened my pace. On the edge of the level open space was a cemetery with perhaps a couple of hundred mounds. The recent ones were covered with elaborate miniature palaces made of white paper, stretched over a framework of cane. A few of these were intact, minor works of art; and there were others in all stages of disintegration until, on the old mounds, only a few sticks lay strewn about. Beyond the graveyard, the houses were reached again. A street of bamboo shacks led almost to the edge of a chasm. Standing on the edge of this I found myself looking across a valley. From where I stood, steep banks dropped away to the bed of a wide river, riven by numerous islands and sandbanks. This was the Shweli River, and the opposite bank was China. Peasants with their buffaloes were cultivating strips of land left by the recession of the waters, both in Burma and in China and on the islands that lay between and came under who knows what jurisdiction. From across the river came the sound of cocks crowing, and most strangely, what sounded like the ringing of church bells.

That evening a lorry went to Nam Hkam, but, for the first time, I learned that even in the Orient a vehicle can be crammed to a degree when not a single passenger more can be taken. Bales had been piled high into the air, so that, in order to reach their perches, the passengers had to scale sheer precipices of merchandise. And either the weight had been unevenly distributed or a spring had given way, because the load tilted most dangerously. Here it was that I began to long once more for a smattering of Chinese, that valuable lingua-franca of all who travel or have affairs in the backwoods of the Far East. It was laborious and a little ridiculous having to keep up this patrol round Mu-Sé bleating hopefully, 'Car' – now a Burmese word – 'Nam Hkam?' Finally an Indian appeared with a polite, 'What is your destination, sir?' And from him I learned that there was no hope of getting to Nam Hkam until the next day.

There was a permanent market-place in Mu-Sé where a nucleus of traders sold such essentials as liver salts and Vaseline, and a tooth-drawer publicly removed teeth with astonishing speed and address. The market was served by a Chinese restaurant, a grim, open-sided booth with a kitchen in its centre, where the sinister routine of a low-class Chinese eating house was practised without attempt at concealment from the patrons. Here I resolved to tackle the language problem – at least so far as eating went – and persuaded the proprietor, who was grubby as usual in vest and slacks but anxious to help, to accompany me on a tour of his pots. From him I acquired the basic smattering to deal with gastronomic emergencies, and this carried me through Burma. The only adjective that really mattered was *chow* – fried; from which, of course, the American Army slang for food was derived. By keeping to fried dishes, I could reasonably hope most of the bacilli had been destroyed. *Mien*, which is usually associated with *chow* in the Chinese restaurants of the West, meant noodles, although here it was pronounced 'myen'. Chicken was *chi*; eggs, *dan*; rice, *fan*; pork, *youk*. If you wanted the pork chopped up and mixed with vegetables as well as fried, all you had to do was to precede *chow* with the onomatopoeic and memorable adjective *tok-tok*. Strangely enough, this system worked, in spite of my repudiation of the notorious tones which are supposed to be so baffling to the Westerner, in Chinese. No restaurant owner ever failed to understand my order or even had to have it repeated, and one even went through the complimentary farce of asking me in what part of China I had picked up my knowledge of the language. The word for salt, *yem ba*, was very important. This always seemed to be a rare commodity, only produced grudgingly, on special request. Warm Mandalay Pale Ale was sometimes forthcoming at the average price of a bottle of medium quality wine, by uttering the magic words *ku dziu*. Tea, *sha*, was always silently placed on the table as soon as you sat down.

At this restaurant I was hardly surprised to find the police lieutenant sitting, with eyes modestly lowered, at one of the tables. I went over and joined him and tried to buy him a meal. After a great deal of explanation in which the restaurant owner and several customers joined, I was finally made to understand that my host, or keeper – whichever the case might have been – was a strict Buddhist and was observing some kind of penance, or sabbath as it is known locally, involving a semi-fast and some meditation. He could therefore only be prevailed upon to accept a little plain rice.

While we lingered over tea the day was declining. Children came down from the crest of a bare hill, from which a diminishing cone of light had finally disappeared, dragging at their kites which shone like minute fish against the blue depths of the Yunnanese mountains. The tooth-extractor packed up, unhitching the strings of his trophies from the frame on which they were exposed, and lowering them string by string, as tenderly as if they had been matched pearls, into a bag. The last bullock-cart was driven away, producing with its greaseless axle a plain tune consisting of four notes of the pentatonic scale repeated *ad infinitum*. Suddenly the square of Mu-Sé had lost a dimension, the wooden shop façades, splashed with their vigorous Chinese characters, had become a backcloth, dramatic and even menacing, before which a band of posturing actors with pikes and lances might soon present themselves in the nocturnal scene of such a play as *Stealing the Emperor's Horse*. As the twilight deepened, the restaurant owner went softly from table to table, placing on each a tiny oil-lamp. Over the kitchen he hung a lantern providing a sympathetic illumination for the tapestry of viscera. From various directions came a soft, tentative strumming as if plucked from single-stringed instruments hung in space. Three or four distant voices were raised quaveringly, as if to exorcise this Asiatic mood, in the chanting of a revivalist hymn, a tune to which the words usually sung are, 'Jesus wants me for an angel'. Occasionally, when these sounds subsided, a bugle could be heard, very faintly, being blown in China.

We went back to the police barracks and turned in. The lieutenant dimmed the lamp till there was just enough light for him to be able to pick up his tommy-gun without groping for it, and lay muttering his prayers. Beyond the window ebbed and flowed all the sweet sleep-inducing night sounds. The monotonous grumbling gossip of the Kachin policemen was woven through with a silver thread of monochordic music. This was blown away by the rush of wind through the bamboo thickets, and into the following silence fell a dribble of nightingale notes. The Kachins took up their topic again, and now the subdued rattle of monosyllables was coagulating and shaping itself in the rising tide of drowsiness into odd English phrases. As I fell asleep, someone said quite clearly, 'a shortage of timber'.

The chief was up when I awoke soon after dawn, but shortly appeared with a pot of tea. Both of us were wearing, like the insignia of some exclusive club, those popular oriental towels which bear the words, 'Good morning', and in the language of smiles and signs we passed with each other the time of day.

Afterwards I took a brisk stroll over to the border, noticing, as I had done on the previous day, that within a few minutes a Chinese appeared, wearing semi-transparent white pyjamas, and pedalling very rapidly on a gaily decorated but much under-geared cycle. Separated by some twenty-five yards, the Chinese and I stood, two solitary and insignificant figures poised over the grandiose setting of this natural frontier, while beneath us the peasants of Burma and of China were to be seen leading out the buffaloes to their morning tasks in the fields. When I turned away and made for the village through the lanes of cactus, whose leaves were covered in elegant Burmese script with what I supposed to be amorous inscriptions, the Chinese was still there, but soon he overtook me, legs whirling and garments streaming. By the market-place I was met by the Indian of the previous day. 'What are you interested in, sir?' he asked. 'Rubies and jade,' I told him. 'But there are no rubies or jade at Nam Hkam.' The tone contained a mild reproof. He was clearly hurt at an unfalteringly clumsy attempt at deception. He had a fine sensitive face, with that brooding nobility of expression one often finds in Indians, even when in mediocre occupations. As he always appeared, to put some new, straightforward question whenever I visited the market, I supposed that he was the informer assigned to the area, just as the flying Chinaman was probably in charge of the frontier proper.

He must have found my explanation unsatisfactory because after our third encounter a new kind of policeman arrived and signalled me to follow him. I soon found myself in some kind of military headquarters where a Burmese officer, handsome and dapper in his well-pressed British uniform, grilled me with extraordinary suavity, while butterflies fluttered in and out of the open door and a blind beggar collected alms from the guard. It seemed that I had fallen into the hands of some kind of frontier force. The Burmese officer's smile became glazed when, in answer to his probings, I told him I had spent the previous night in the barracks of the Kachin police. My lieutenant was fetched to testify, a rustic and self-effacing figure in these polished military surroundings. A little reluctantly, but with charming resignation, the Burmese officer declared himself satisfied. I could go on to Nam Hkam. A pass and an accompanying letter to the Amat were typed out, to be added to my now bulky collection of official documents. Meanwhile, said the officer, there was no point at all in wandering about the streets of an unattractive place like Mu-Sé. I could wait comfortably in his office until transport was found. Glasses of lemonade were brought in, and then the officer excused himself and went off in a jeep. When I sauntered to the door I found a soldier with a fixed bayonet there. He gulped nervously when I eyed him.

An hour or two later, the transport for Nam Hkam drew up outside. It was a Fordson, externally battered but intact, and scientifically packed with ageing Kachin ladies, who, I later learned, had organized a kind of Mothers' Association outing to the bazaar of Nam Hkam, which was to be held on the next day. They were all dressed, with the sobriety of their years and station, in navy blue, and wore tall cylindrical turbans in which their hair had been severely constrained. As usual, I was allocated a dignified position in the front. I found myself pinned firmly against the door-handle by the two dowagers wedged in between me and the driver. Unhappily the engine in this particular vehicle is set back and occupies much of the space in the driver's cabin, from which it is only isolated by a housing of metal plates. Owing to the external temperature, plus the terrible roads and the decayed state of the engine, this housing soon became blisteringly hot, so that both my neighbour and myself squirmed and struggled endlessly in our efforts to avoid contact with it. The nudging and kneeing provoked by these conditions probably struck my companion, who was about fifty years of age, as improper, because at the first opportunity she changed places, providing a substitute of not less than eighty.

The journey to Nam Hkam, then, although a matter of only nineteen miles, took several hours, and was endured in the most excruciating discomfort. After the first hour numbness spread from the feet to the waist. Only then could I begin to enjoy the scenery through which we were travelling. A mile or two away to our left across a cultivated plain were low ranges of densely forested mountains, while to the right the land slipped away, down to the Shweli River, an unimportant tributary of the Irrawaddy, which here, mysteriously, for no more than thirty miles, swelled into a shallow, much-divided flood, as wide as the Salween. Terraced paddy-fields came down the mountainsides like the ceremonial stairways of a race of giants, lapping the plains in mighty rippling waves. Hundreds of buffaloes slogged through the mud and stagnant water, and egrets crawled about them. The villages were screened behind the matting of roots hanging down, almost to the ground, from huge old banyans. Wells had stone covers like miniature pagodas – sometimes with horses carved on them. The pagodas themselves were on the Chinese joss-house model, with up-swept eaves, often involving much ingenious joining of corrugated iron, which had been artfully hammered and bent into the traditional shape of wooden logs. Tombs continued to carry their ephemeral palaces of paper. Sometimes we passed a tumulus. Under such mounds the Kachins buried the victims, man, woman, and child, of the unlimited warfare they practised whenever compelled by dearth to migrate in force. There were a few isolated houses which advertised the wealth of their owners by the addition to a plain bamboo construction of a carved balcony or some fretwork embellishment of the eaves. Over the Shweli hung a golden mist, composed of particles of sand swept up from the uncovered bed of the river and held in suspension by the wind sweeping down the valley. Just outside Nam Hkam three Chinese Nationalist soldiers in blue cotton uniforms appeared at the roadside. I recognized them from the others I had seen in custody. They seemed to be unarmed, and were probably on their way to Nam Hkam to give themselves up.

CHAPTER FOURTEEN

Nam Hkam Bazaar

NAM HKAM, in the white, dusty haze of the afternoon, was a less concentrated Mu-Sé, a sprawling collection of bamboo huts. The driver pulled out of the main street with its emptiness and aching light, and found the Amat's compound. There he put me down, shook hands, and departed, refusing to accept a fare. Almost collapsing as my legs touched the ground, I waited a moment for circulation and strength to return before picking up the iron bar provided and striking the gong suspended by the gateway. Apart from the medieval grandiosity of this gesture there was nothing impressive about the circumstances of my arrival. The compound consisted of three sides of a square of mean huts, surrounded by a broken fence of the kind which sometimes encloses a surburban allotment. A wrecked two-pounder gun, with wheels askew, stood in the centre of this space. It was attended continually by a guard armed with a rifle. I was led into the presence of a man with a mild, empty Kachin face, whom I felt instinctively to be a clerk. And a clerk he was. The Amat was away but, said the clerk, I could stay in his haw.

The haw proved to be the biggest of the huts. It was raised on piles, about five feet from the ground. I was installed in one of the two large bare rooms, which, when I arrived, was occupied by a circle of soldiers playing cards, and some children who were annoying them. The soliders left, one by one, although the children returned later to watch me as I washed. Shortly afterwards four soldiers staggered in with a massive mahogany table and two chairs. When the table was put down, the bamboo floor sagged beneath it. The soldiers went away, and the clerk appeared in the doorway. He was carrying a bottle of shoum, or country spirit, as it is politely called by the Kachin bourgeoisie. This was not the ordinary market stuff, he assured me, but a bottle from the Amat's reserve, of special potency and flavour. He was right. A judicious sip roughened the lip membranes before passing in a scorching trickle down the throat. It tasted like vodka. Before withdrawing, the clerk asked me at what time he should arrange breakfast for the morning, adding that there would be various curries to order. I asked what was the usual time, and he said about eight o'clock. In Mu-Sé it had been eleven-thirty. It seemed that in the nineteen miles I had run into a new breakfast-time zone.

There was no way of closing the door except by tying it, which would have been churlish. It sagged perpetually eighteen inches open, a circumstance which gave endless pleasure to the clerk's children, who lived in a kind of dependent hut, just across the bamboo landing outside. In this causeway they settled down, a sober, well-behaved group, to learn what they could of my way of life, absenting themselves only for an occasional bowl of rice. In the late afternoon a Kachin soldier arrived. He seemed to have been attached to me for some unknown duty, as he unstrapped a long, heavy-bladed dah, and propped it with an air of finality in a corner, before laying out his kit beneath it. To find out whether this incident involved supervision or control, I went out and ploughed through the dust down to the dismal main street, where, having discovered a Chinese eating-house, I employed my recently acquired knowledge to order a meal. I was waited on by the owner's Burmese wife, who carried a baby in a shawl upon her back. A dog lay curled in a shallow depression scraped in the earth under each table, and a huddle of Thibetans, wrapped in their togas, slept in a corner. Later, as a mild yellowness seeped into the waning sunlight, they awoke and tried gently to arouse the interest of the customers in their dried lizards and coloured stones. All the Thibetans, here, as elsewhere in Burma, carried these treasures in British Army haversacks. The senior member of the party, who wore a purple beret-shaped hat of plaited and lacquered osier, was the possessor of a jar of black unguent which caused some excitement. This I gathered was an extract of the organs of several rare animals. The restaurant owner licked it with connoisseurship, and made an offer, which was smilingly rejected. Someone bought a piece of glass which looked like a ruby for eight annas, one of which the vendor immediately gave to a beggar who was sipping a cup of free tea. The wares were then re-wrapped in their grimy rags and put back in the haversacks; after which the Thibetans settled down to sleep again.

Meanwhile the streets were astir in the cool of the evening and the eating-house was filling up. Customers lined up before the meat show-case where one of the proprietor's virgin daughters, acting as saleslady, was producing delicacies which passed from hand to hand, to be dangled and pinched, before being returned to their hooks. When a sale took place the sliver or collop was passed to another daughter whose headdress proclaimed her knowledge of the world, and, working with a pair of scissors, she snipped the purchase into fragments manageable with chopsticks. These she arranged in neat piles to await free space in one of her father's frying pans. All this activity was abnormal and was due to the influx of visitors and merchants to the celebrated bazaar to be held next day. My arrival at Nam Hkam at just this moment was the only lucky piece of timing in all my travels in Burma. I had been warmly recommended in Rangoon to see the Nam Hkam bazaar, if at all possible; it was said to be one of the most important and colourful in the Far East, serving western Yunnan as well as the Northern Shan States. Since it would be in full swing less than an hour after dawn, and I was tired, I went back to the haw as soon as it was dark. I found my bodyguard sitting at the table, looking into space; but when I got out the country spirit he soon cheered up.

I was up and about by seven, trying to prepare myself by a vigorous walk for the threatened ordeal of the breakfast table. Irregular, sporadic feeding and strange provender were beginning to take their toll, and I felt queasy at the thought of the 'various curries' the Amat's clerk had promised for the first meal of the day. At this hour Nam Hkam benefited from a background of mountains, cloaked in a mist which separated hill from hill and range from range. On these grew towering clumps of bamboo, pale, feathery eruptions in a landscape of smoking precipices and ravines. Below this ethereal panorama the town's profile seemed stunted and broken: this is a normal feature of provincial cities of the Far East and due to an ancient Mongolian prejudice – a racial memory perhaps of the nomadic tent – against the erection of buildings of more than one floor. Sumptuary laws, too, have operated against imposing architecture, except for religious ends. It was perhaps to be expected of the relatively democratic Mongolian order of society – democratic in that its rewards have always been attained in the main by merit and effort, rather than birth – that office and status when acquired should have been hedged about with so rigid a protocol. The position which a man had won was advertised by all the adjuncts of his existence, by the size and materials of his betel-box and spittoon, by his clothes, his animals, his house. It was all laid down. There was no question of living beyond one's means to impress the neighbours. If you had no official position you lived in a single-roomed shack with a palm-thatch. When you became a headman you were allowed something more solid, with teak pillars supporting a log roof. Myozas, or governors, were privileged to shelter beneath a roof of two storeys. Only the Sawbwa could aspire to the glory of a spire, to go with his gold umbrella, his velvet sandals, and his peacock. Nam Hkam, then, was flat and straggling, with a few liquor and opium stores, tailors' establishments and inns, but very few shops to face the annihilating competition of the bazaar. There were a few small, uninteresting pagodas, one of which seemed to have been struck by a bomb. A heap of broken masonry in the courtyard contained several hundred Buddhas, some unusually well carved and coloured, but although they seemed to have been abandoned there, I doubted the propriety of taking one away. By the wall a buffalo lay abandoned to die. Several sprightly crows were already pecking at the soft, accessible parts of the body; the anus, the nostrils and lips. Occasionally a lid slid slowly back, disclosing a terrified eye, the head rolled sadly from side to side, and the crows hopped back. To have attempted to put the animal out of its misery in this consecrated spot would have caused grave scandal, if not a riot.

*

Breakfast was all I had feared. It was preceded by a stiff aperitif of country spirit; then followed an inexorable succession of dishes, vegetable soup, red rice with spring onions, the promised curries, pickled vegetables, tea, poured from a great pot with a chain as handle – two cups at a time for each person. With forthright Kachin hospitality the Amat's clerk ladled out my portions, perplexed and disappointed at the size of my appetite. Feeling that only a twenty-four hours' fast could help, I staggered down the steps of the haw and made for the market. I could not have hoped for a more brilliant spectacle.

Beyond ranks of innumerable pack-animals, bullocks, and ponies, tethered with the regimented discipline which characterizes the parking of cars at a sporting event in the West, the scene might have been taken from a lavish stage production of *Prince Igor*. The first English administrator to reach Nam Hkam reported in 1889 that about six thousand people visited this market every five days, and this number had certainly not decreased. From Burma, I could identify various Shans, in their enormous hats; Kachins with their strings of coins and skirts woven in the colours and zigzag motifs of the Indians of Central America; Palaungs, and occasional Lishaws, who looked like untidy Cossacks in their belted tunics and shapeless trousers. But there were visitors from Yunnan who escaped identification; strapping maidens in voluminous white turbans; spirited groups which scattered and dispersed at the sight of a camera, flouncing away with flashing back-cast glances, and a swirl of long skirts, pigtails and sashes.

The Palaungs of Nam Hkam were particularly elegant in dashingly cut ankle-length coats of cotton-velvet panelled with light and dark blue and with purple inserts at the elbow. They wore made-up cylindrical turbans of dark blue material, from the back of which tumbled, in medieval European style, a veil or panel, reaching half-way down the back. Jewellery was plain: a double or triple collar of silver beads. One patrician figure, who out-topped her neighbours' average of four feet nine by at least three inches, wore a turban that had developed into a kind of busby, its upper edge decorated with a looped chain of beads to match her necklace. Beside this majestic ensemble most European folk-costumes would have looked trivial and doll-like. It appears from the reports of the first administrators that such finery was previously restricted to the use of certain clans: it has now spread as one beneficial result, at least, of the degeneration of tribal organization. One can imagine the horror of the ladies of the senior clan, the Patorus – there was only a handful of them – when the whole of the female section of the Palaung nation took to wearing their exclusive model.

It is said that the Palaungs are the most peace loving of the Burmese minorities. Peoples become in the first instance 'warrior peoples' by using up or outgrowing the resources of their habitat. As soon as the economic origin of their bellicosity is forgotten, it tends to be regarded as inherent martial virtue; to be secretly respected whether one approves of it or not. The Palaungs are an example of a people who through efficient adaptation to an environment do not need a regular fresh supply of *Lebensraum*. They live in harmony with each other; crimes of violence are rare, and murder unknown. Clearly, they make bad soldiers and they were much despised as recruiting material in the British colonial army, whereas the turbulent and aggressive Kachins were the darlings of their British commanders and 'proved themselves magnificently' against the Turks in the 1914–18 war.

The Palaungs are terribly afflicted by goitre. I estimated that twenty-five per cent of the older women I saw were sufferers. Sometimes the head was no more than a promontory upon a mass of shapeless flesh, reaching as far as the breasts. One poor woman I saw had to go about supporting her goitre with her hands.

Like so many hill-peoples the Palaungs have a dislike of the plains which is strongly tinged with superstitious aversion, an attitude found in reverse among the plainsmen of the Far East, whose awe of heights causes them to locate their most sacred places on mountain-tops.

The bazaar of Nam Hkam, where the first British administrator noticed that much Manchester cloth and haberdashery was sold, had not lost its enthusiasm for all the West had to offer. Local products included crudely carved and vilely coloured Burmese toys, bearing only a token resemblance to the owls and alligators they were supposed to represent, coarse pottery, exquisite Chinese crockery, stiff Mandalay silk used in the making of longyis, and artificial flowers. Indian influence showed itself in plastic models of the Taj Mahal. But two-thirds of the market space was allotted to the West – toothpastes, patent medicines, beauty products, cigarettes – even the well-known beverage claimed to possess extraordinary soporific qualities. There were tins of condensed milk, too, valued as much for the container as the contents, empty tins having become a recognized Burmese measure. Thus two *let-kut* (the quantity which may be heaped upon the surface of two hands joined together) equals one condensed-milk tin – originally a *Kônsa*, or the amount of rice required by one person for a meal.

A demand had been produced for all these products by advertising in the Rangoon press; and the Rangoon agents would ship a proportion of what they received out to such markets as Nam Hkam, assuming that whatever the nature of the goods, their place of origin would sell them. Sometimes it was clear that the purpose of the product was not understood. A cheroot-seller, for instance, would, on request, smear a little Vick Vapour-rub on the mouthpiece of a cheroot, before handing it to his customer.

There is no doubt that the East – such of it as remains open to occidental enterprise – is a certain and inexhaustible market for all that can be sent there. When one sees what orientals can be induced to buy it is hard to believe that the East India Company had trouble in disposing of its broadcloths. Above all, the exporter cannot go wrong with patent medicines, to which people who have been brought up in an atmosphere of horoscopes and alchemy surrender themselves naturally. All that is necessary is to find some way, by loans to be used in establishing industries or by the gift of agricultural machinery, of increasing purchasing power. The consumption of branded laxatives, stomach powders, and cough cures would then be colossal. At the present time a Palaung has to put in a week's labour in his opium field before he can buy a packet of aspirins, or a fortnight before a tube of halitosis-averting toothpaste comes within his reach. If only science could find some way of increasing his production he might eventually become a consumer of shirts with non-shrinkable collars, ball-point pens, and electric shavers.

In the mean time the hill-peoples will go on doing what they can to combat by the traditional methods the ninety-six diseases recognized by orthodox Burmans. These methods are most comprehensive, and include dosing with the remedies – most of them fearsome – contained in a vast *materia medica*, with arsenic, soot, and excrement, and with the scrapings of meteoric stones. They include treatment by the exhibition of pictures of peacocks and hares, by semi-strangling, by probing with gold and silver needles, by beating with rods incised with cabalistic figures, by burning and scalding, by inhalation of perfumes and fetid stenches, by the playing of music, martial, strident, or sympathetic, by the laying on of hands, the muttering of spells and prayer. Some of these methods have received belated praise from Western doctors, particularly that of acupuncture, which, dignified by a medico-scientific jargon, has something of a current vogue in France.

The contribution of the Shans to the science of healing is therapeutic shampooing. This is a form of massage, applied chiefly to the head, and here in Nam Hkam, between the tooth-pullers, a specialist was at work upon his victim, who writhed and groaned slightly under the manipulations of the iron fingers, while other patients, stripped to the waist, squatted in uneasy silence awaiting their turn. Shampooing, like all the other treatments, if given with proper regard to the patient's horoscope, is regarded as a panacea, except in the case of venereal ailments, which are thought to be of supernatural origin and produced by the nocturnal bites of nats. It is all very funny, in a way, and yet many Europeans living in these remote parts of the world go secretly for treatment to such practitioners, excusing themselves, if discovered, by saying that at least it can do no harm. When we remember the renowned and highly gifted English authoress who in recent years tried to arrest her fatal malady by inhaling the breath of cows, we realize that in medical matters, the more extravagant the treatment, the greater its appeal, even to the most intelligent of us.

Like all fairs, the bazaar of Nam Hkam had something special to offer in the way of holiday diet. This consisted of thin, buckled cakes, like large chapattis. Something similar in composition was produced in fancy shapes by squeezing maize-flour paste through machines into vats of boiling oil. Cooks were producing by a kind of legerdemain vast, swelling, edible creations, which developed on immersion in the boiling fat from the most insignificant beginnings of paste. Plunging a few thin white strings into the liquid they would slowly withdraw portentous, inflated shapes, which finally resembled the bare ribs of a mighty ox-carcass. The Palaungs, having sold their country spirit and their opium, bought great quantities of those unsubstantial fairings, departing to their eyries with panniers stuffed and ponies piled with fragile mountains of the Shan version of potato-crisps.

For the Shans themselves there were more solid refreshments in store. The killing of cows, which is illegal in Burma, and only carried on as a scandalous, black-market activity, is tolerated in the Shan States, where the brand of Buddhism is less strict, and does not prescribe a largely vegetarian diet. In a discreet corner of the market a buffalo was tethered by a rope round the horns, carried over a beam. A muscular and elaborately tattooed Shan, drawing his dah, advanced and struck the outstretched neck a practised blow that was more an accolade than a mortal wound. Going closer, he examined the gash laid open by the straining muscles; repeating the blow, almost as an afterthought. At this, the buffalo, which had remained passive, seemingly unconcerned, began to lash out with its hoofs and a mighty flexing of the hindquarters, and then to slither, legs momentarily spread-eagled, assisting by its strainings the outgushing of its life. Finally it sank down, its rear legs sliding beneath it, and then, gathering its strength and kicking out furiously, it half rose, before slipping back again. The butcher waited with patience, a long cheroot held in his teeth. Presently he produced and tried the edge of the short knife with which in a few minutes he would open up the belly, hack off the hoofs, and skilfully release the tension of the hide at certain points, before stripping it off like an overcoat. Meanwhile the buffalo fought silently with huge muscles against the lethargy that was dragging it down.

Picnicking Shan families began to gather, laughing happily. In the background, fires had been built, and braziers were already heating. Not a Burman was to be seen.

Thus the bazaar continued through the daylight hours, a good-natured and convivial assembly of half a dozen races, some of whose members could only speak with each other through the common medium of a few words of Shan. Such gatherings, every fifth day, are the mountain people's genial equivalent of the Sabbath, and even when feuds or warfare are in progress, the bazaars are recognized as neutral territory. There are no loud-mouthed disputes, scoldings, or imprecations. The buying and selling, eating and drinking are all carried on with true oriental gentleness and forbearance. In the afternoon, when most of the serious business was over, the bottles of country spirit came out, and the shy, elusive beauties of the morning were to be seen taking unconcealed nips from their flasks – without, however, noticeable effect. Happy, slightly tipsy groups went wandering through the streets, while the mountains sank back into the haze, and a blue twilight settled on the town. The yellows and the greens drained out of the curving roofs so that it was no longer possible to distinguish the skilful metal counterfeit from the authentic original. A twinkling centipede twisted up the nearest hillside – a Palaung family, with their lanterns, going home in Indian file. The traders who were staying the night retired into the opium and liquor stores, and light burst in a thousand spearpoints through the wide chinks of the bamboo constructions. The drivers of fifty worn-out three-ton lorries climbed up into their cabins, and went to sleep. And now the Kachin garrison issued from its barracks to guard the sleeping town.

A Kachin patrol was a cheerful affair, more social than warlike. Fires were lit in the streets in various parts of the town, then the main body of men split into small groups, who visited each fire in turn. Each group carried with it an elaborately carved rectangular frame in which were suspended five gongs of different sizes, all beaten simultaneously by clappers attached to a single bar operated by a lever. As soon as the party reached a fire the frame was set down, and one of the soldiers began to work the lever at an even, rapid tempo, producing a sweet, high-pitched and penetrating sound. When the beating of the gongs ceased, a member of the group would step out from the circle formed, sing a single verse and, taking two swords, while the gongs began again, break into a vigorous, posturing dance. This performance was repeated by each soldier in turn. One of them was old enough to have served under British officers, and remembered a few words of English. I asked him what the songs were about, imagining that they dealt with warlike exploits, but he said that they were 'funny stories about ladies'.

CHAPTER FIFTEEN

Circuit House, Bhamó

THE AMAT'S CLERK said that he had reserved a place in a jeep bound for Bhamó at seven in the morning, so that when seven thirty came and the jeep had not arrived, I became a little nervous. One after another, the merchants' lorries went thundering out of town, until only one was left, which was jacked-up to await the repair of a tyre. It seemed ungracious not to wait for the jeep, when an arrangement had been made, and yet if I allowed the last lorry to go and the jeep failed to appear, it would mean a five days' wait in Nam Hkam, until the next bazaar. Just as the wheel was being put back and I was about to begin negotiations with the driver, I heard the sound of a familiar burping acceleration, and the jeep arrived. The usual maximum of passengers was wedged in among the luggage and petrol cans, from which sprouted like exotic plants in a rock-garden an awkward bundle of umbrellas, as large as those to be found in continental cafés. In spite of my protests a polite re-arrangement took place for my benefit, so that I found myself seated in front, in relative comfort, with the one leg which could not be contained within the car supported on the front wing. We then set off through the fresh morning forest, alive with the movement of lizards and small birds, and strongly perfumed as if by unseen lilies. What was the origin of this fragrance, which in the imagination streamed from white, immaculate blossoms? In my jungle experiences I have never encountered flowers of the often repellent splendour described by tropical botanists, and here in the Shan uplands the flora, which was sparse and even trivial, bore a disappointing resemblance to that of Europe. In this area flowers a gigantic wild rose, and a species of honeysuckle, with corolla seven inches long, which is by far the largest known. But in these forest clearings I saw nothing but a few shrinking primroses, violets, and anemones; and further on, when we made a short stop and I could explore further, clematis, agrimony, convolvulus, and willow-herb, none of which dispensed the mysterious bouquet, which now, as the sun rose higher, was swiftly fading.

At Man Wing my companions stopped to buy country spirit, which was better and cheaper here, they said, than anywhere in the country. This high-grade product was kept in motor-oil cans, while lesser distillations were supplied from ordinary jars. At Man Wing it was bazaar day, intelligently timed to catch traders returning from Nam Hkam. It was a much smaller affair than Nam Hkam had been, and conducted almost exclusively by Kachins, who appeared in a great variety of costumes, woven with the designs by which, in a stylized, dream-like, and semi-conscious fashion, tribes sometimes record the few bare facts of their history – a serrated pattern of mountains crossed in their migrations; the yellow of the desert sands. Some of these Kachin motifs were indistinguishable from others I have photographed among the Maya Quiché Indians. I attribute no more to this than that such simple designs occur naturally to all primitive weavers. Their artistic value seemed great to me, and I should say that apart from occasional articles of silver jewellery, woven cloth is the only article of artistic interest produced in the mountains of the Indo-Chinese peninsula. Unfortunately such cloth, or the garments made from it, are not on sale in any of the bazaars, for at present every woman weaves the material for her own clothes. As soon as printed cottons come within her means, she will, as most Siamese girls have already done, renounce with contempt the gorgeous creations of her own hands, which are the result of the communal artistic imagination of her tribe throughout the centuries, delightedly substituting for them graceless, ready-made models. Art is sometimes protected by poverty, and civilization can be the destroyer of taste.

Soon after midday we arrived at Bhamó, which lay stifling and somnolent in the plains by the Irrawaddy. The jeep dropped me at the administrative buildings – a long, divided bamboo hut – and the driver accepted with a show of protest the modest ten rupees which is the recognized price for long distance de luxe travel in Burma. Here, according to my instructions, I reported to the DSP and the Deputy Commissioner, and was relieved to find that, although I was expected, no comment was made about my arrival from an unexpected direction. With the Commissioner's permission, it was arranged that I should put up at the Circuit House and, finding a decayed gharry, I drove there, at a cost of half that charged for a journey of a hundred miles.

The Circuit House was a forlorn structure in the English half-timbered mood, but of shell-like fragility. No sooner was I inside than in taking a kick at a hornet I put my foot through the wall. This bungalow was presided over by a functionary called the butler, an ancient and dignified survival, living in a kind of monastic seclusion with his memories of the Imperial days and the splendid personalities they had delivered into his charge. Almost before I could look round he produced, with the manner of one displaying an illuminated breviary, a vistors' book in which a number of the great had written their comments and testimonials. The last English one, dating from 1947, by a distinguished lady said, 'A dear old fellow – one of those old-fashioned Burmese servants who are so fast disappearing.' Subsequently there had been a few Burmese contributions, all of which had accorded genteel commendation on English models.

It was about two thirty when I arrived at the Circuit House, and the butler, on his mettle, and anxious to show that none of the old traditions had been forgotten, said something like 'Ih – a – eh?' He repeated this several times before I realized that he was one of those Burmese who do not believe in the existence of English consonants, which are unemphatic compared with those in the Burmese language. Having discovered that I was being offered tea with eggs, I accepted with pleasure, settling down to the enjoyment of my room, for which, after about two weeks in bamboo huts, I felt quite an affection. By normal Burmese standards, it was choked with furniture. There was an iron bed, a chair, and a table, on which stood a mirror and a toilet-roll. Hornets with long trailing stings sailed about the room, and when one came too close, I batted it away, using a book as a tennis-racket. Within ten minutes the tea arrived, formally arranged on a tray, with a bowlful of white sugar, real milk, and two hard-boiled eggs rolling about and crashing heavily into each other with an appetite-provoking sound. When I thrust a spoon into the sugar, ants boiled out of it. I stirred among the crystals and still the ants came, till it seemed that hundreds had scrambled over the bowl's rim to swarm away to the edge of the table along the spokes of an invisible wheel. I ate and drank with enjoyment and relaxation. When I went to sugar the second cup of tea, the ants were back again. It was clear that they located the sugar by its smell, because wherever I perched the bowl, there would be ants in it within ten minutes. There were plenty of other insects about, particularly medium-sized spiders that scuttled off in a panic if I moved in their direction and then hid under the table legs or behind projections of the wall, leaving a hairy leg sticking out.

At about three thirty, just as I was ready to take a siesta, I got a shock. There was a tap at the door, and the butler was there again, announcing with dignity, what, although shorn of its consonants, was unmistakably, 'Breakfast is served.' In came two trayfuls of honest, English food, more eggs – fried this time – fish with chips, bread and butter, jam and tea. Waving away this collation, I went into the cubicle attached to the room, threw jugfuls of water on the cockroaches crawling about the floor, and took a shower. The water splashed on the concrete floor, spread across it like a stain, and began to dry at the edges. Outside, the trees and the earth with its spears of whitened grass were glazed under the sun, and the gilded bell-shape of a pagoda, surmounted with a cap like a Burmese crown, glittered painfully. A barbet, known as the 'coppersmith', invisible adjunct to the Burmese landscape, hooted once every two seconds, and the brain-fever bird added its hallucinatory shriek to this ensemble of heat and fatigue.

With the evening came slight relief, and I walked a dusty mile into the town. Turning into a street of shops I looked up and had a vision of a monumental shape, the mighty torso of a man standing at a first-floor window, his arms raised in the arrangement of a complex hair-style. It was the Sikh from Mandalay. I went into his shop, which was an ironmonger's, but which, with a certain elasticity in trading matters, also sold air-mail envelopes. I bought a packet, and his wife, a Burmese lady, gave me a cup of tea. The Sikh told me that he and his friends had finally managed to hire a jeep, and after a complicated and exhausting journey of four days they had reached Bhamó. They had met with no dacoits, although after what he had seen and heard, he had decided to stay quietly in Bhamó until the troubles were over. The Bhamó–Myitkyina areas were the only ones completely free from bandits or insurgent armies. Here, he said, if the heat would only let you, you could relax and be almost as happy as in a civilized country like India. Avoiding the direct and vulgar question why he didn't go back there, I enquired into his reason for remaining in trouble-torn Burma. India was the better place to live in, he said, there was no doubt about that – more civilized, more cosmopolitan. But Burma was the better place to make a living in – if I saw the difference.

The Chinese restaurateur of the evening's meal was more complimentary to the country of his adoption. He owned one of the half-dozen lugubrious eating-places along the Irrawaddy shore, and was busy, he said, four days in the week – the days when the two boats from Mandalay arrived, and when they left again. The cavern in which he conducted his business was distinguished from those of his competitors by a yard of fluorescent tubing, whose clammy light was an indication of enterprise in such a place. Although he had never formally learned English, he spoke it with the efficiency demonstrated by his race whenever a project is seriously undertaken. He came from Szechwan, he said, and one of his remote ancestors had been an Imperial cook. He delighted me by referring to his 'unworthy' restaurant and his 'humble' food – traditional self-deprecations which, until then, I had been convinced were to be found only in the speech of the Chinese of Ernest Bramah. His family had emigrated to Burma in his youth. He loved the country, had married a Burmese wife, and nothing would tempt him to return to China. In a few glowing words he summed up the Burmese character. The people were franker and more outspoken than his compatriots. 'If I am hungry in Burma, I will say so, and any man will give me food, without thinking anything about it. In China I must not ask. I must wait to be offered, or people will say, "This is an ill-mannered fellow."' My informant was also shrewd enough to suggest that in China conventions were stricter and hospitality more confined because the Chinese could not afford hospitality on the Burmese scale. In Yunnan if there were five members of a family, they could only live by all five working. In Burma, in a similar family, only one worked, and then, he said, not too hard. And how were things in China? I asked. It was evident that I had found at last a Chiang Kai-shek supporter. They were doing fine, he said, if only they hadn't gone just a little too far in the matter of squeeze. And now the Communists were carrying out a house cleaning on a big scale. They were very strict, and people who couldn't believe that things had changed were suffering. In Bhamó alone there were about a thousand refugees, poor people who had been chased out of their country over trifling matters which in the old days would have been beneath the government's notice.

CHAPTER SIXTEEN

The Jade Country

At Bhamó there were other aids to civilization to go with that yard of glimmering fluorescence. I was able, for instance, for thirty rupees a day plus the cost of petrol, to hire a jeep with its driver; and next morning in the dawn and with the frantic whistling and shrilling of birds in our ears, we took the road north, to Myitkyina. It was a great luxury to be travelling at last with the power to stop whenever I wanted to, to linger as long as I liked over the most charming parts of the journey. By the time the heat of the sun could be felt we had reached the Tapeng River. A track from the main road, passing under a bower of orange flamboyants, followed the bank for a way, and up this we went in search of a clear stretch of river in which to swim. Down the narrow valley – most fateful of all the ways of entry into Burma – the water came, frothing among the white boulders, plunging in polished cascades of marbled green into profound pools, where a resistant bubble or a gyrating insect were the only indications of movement and direction.

Over the river hung a cold, sweet smell, carrying with it a sharp association of the shock and the delight of a plunge into opaque depths. Bamboos and tall blond grasses with feathered tops had decayed at their bases and fallen across the rocks, where, roasting in the sun, they gave off a concentrated scent of hay. Here river perfumes poured through and washed aside those of the forest. Small dun birds – brown dippers – bobbed and flitted from rock to rock; and sometimes pied kingfishers passed, hanging for seconds in motionless contemplation above a pool, before darting away. Down by the water there was nothing flamboyant, mysterious, or repellent. It was all familiar and nostalgic. There could have been no better place in Burma than this to study butterflies. They seemed attracted by the damp boulders, on which they alighted in infinite variety, wings spread and gently pulsating. There was no display here of garish colour, no exaggeration, but a rather subdued elegance and sombre good taste, like the *grande tenue* of a nobleman at the Court of Philip the Second.

During the rainy season the level of the water was much higher; now boulders had been left uncovered in which deep basins had been scooped by the action of the water. Some of these contained water, the colour of medium sherry, in which a few small, lethargic fish miraculously survived, a feat which only lost in stature when one remembered that this was the country of climbing perch and of lung fish, which, when their native pools dry up, undertake long overland treks in search of water.

Until 1769 all the area had been Chinese territory, and down this narrow, unimpressive valley the Mongol host had come riding, in 1284, to avenge the slaughter of their envoys by the Burmese king. Somewhere in the plain, within fifty miles of where I stood, at a spot which is now unknown because of the changing of the place-names, the spirits conjured up by the Mongol shamans – favoured perhaps by the reflex bow with its one hundred and sixty pounds' pull – shot the Burmese guardian spirits full of arrows, and the Burmese army was annihilated. For full three months, according to the Burmese chronicle, they, the Burmese, slew the enemy and spared not even the feeders of elephants and horses, but when ten myriads were dead, the chief of the Mongols sent twenty myriads, and when the twenty myriads were dead, he sent forty myriads. The conflict seems to have made less impression on the Mongols, and Marco Polo speaks more of a punitive expedition carried out by a frontier force, a march of 'gleemen and jugglers' with a 'captain and a body of men-at-arms to help them' – a notable lack of agreement upon the fable of history.

Five hundred years later and, once again, at the mouth of this valley, the Burmese handsomely vindicated themselves. First of all there had been a dispute over a Chinese merchant who had wanted to build a bridge over the river for his ox-caravans. Just as in the case of the Mongol envoys, the Burmese found that disrespect had been shown, and they flung the merchant into prison. Shortly afterwards another Chinese merchant was killed in a brawl in Burma. In the comparatively primitive Burmese law manslaughter was a trivial offence, compoundable by the payment of compensation. The Chinese, however, had arrived at the eye-for-an-eye stage, and demanded the handing over of the killer, or a substitute, for execution by strangling. To their great credit, the Burmese, although menaced by a nation they knew to be infinitely more powerful than themselves, refused to give the man up – a resoluteness which shows up particularly well against the weak-kneed conduct of the British, in the next century, when, in similar circumstances, a British seaman was surrendered at Canton. However, the Chinese, under the Ch'ing emperor, were in the mood when wars like that of Jenkins' Ear are fought. The refusal by the Burmese to comply with their demands was thought outrageously unreasonable, particularly when, as it was pointed out, execution by strangling was not to be regarded as more than the just settlement of a debt, involving no stigma for the sufferer.

Several Chinese armies poured into Burma, the main force passing once again through this valley. In a war lasting four years they were completely out-generaled and finally defeated, and, by an act of magnanimity without parallel in Far Eastern annals, allowed to march back once more by the cool waters of this riverine Arcadia, to China. This time the disparity in armaments was reversed, because of the artillery which the Burmese had purchased or seized from the Europeans, with which they shot the Chinese stockades to pieces. By allowing the defeated survivors to return to their country, the Burmese brilliantly avoided what would have become a war *à outrance* with all the resources of the Chinese Empire thrown into it. The Chinese were allowed to save their faces by conveniently forgetting the whole thing, without even a formal treaty of peace being negotiated between the two countries. After a few weeks, trade was silently resumed, and no further reference was made to the affair. No allusion is made in Chinese official histories to the Ch'ing invasion of Burma.

*

Seen from without, the jungle had more variety, more mystery, more charm, than the forests of the north. In the woodlands between Bhamó and Myitkyina there was none of the monotony to be observed elsewhere in the Indo-Chinese peninsula, where a particular tree had adapted itself so perfectly to its environment that no others could take root there, thus producing the regimented boredom of a plantation. Here there was infinite variety of shapes, of sizes, of colour, of degrees of luminosity, with each tree separated from its neighbours by a subtle variation of aerial perspective. There were some that raised themselves to impose upon the sky a symmetrical, trimly contained silhouette; others that exploded raggedly in anarchic confusion of branches; others which struggled up dripping with epiphytic plants, parasites, and creepers, as if emerging weed-laden from the sea. There were trees that looked as if they were composed of moss, which soaked up the light in velvety absorption, and others that scattered the sun's rays in cascades from their metallic leaves. At the road's verge the trunks were screened by ferns, through which, as if in the arrangement of a gigantic bouquet, pale blue and lemon convolvulus flowers were threaded. Sometimes a scarlet carpet of let-pet, the edible blossoms of the cotton tree, had been laid across the road. The total effect was always one of brilliance, and freshness, and even gaiety.

Once, as we rumbled along, a school of gibbons dropped from the overhanging boughs, and avoided us with languid athleticism. We chased a baby wild boar that worked up such a speed that when it finally hurled itself into the jungle it left a noticeable hole in the screen of leaves. Here we saw many jungle fowl. They were almost as tame as the barnyard variety and just as stupid, running in demented zigzags in our path before taking to an easy, floating flight, their tails streaming out behind. Sometimes, in the rare clearings, we saw a most immaculate white harrier, with black wingtips, flapping low over the ferns. The most common bird along this forest road was the bee-eater, both the species which is almost indistinguishable from the European one, and the Burmese green variety, birds with an outright tropical panache. In flight the most streamlined of avian shapes, they were silhouetted like supersonic planes in the long, gliding interval following a few quick wing-beats, as they swept from the branches after their prey. Green and golden-backed woodpeckers glinted at the mouths of flute-like rows of holes in the stumps of dead trees. Butterflies hovered in dark swarms over the buffaloes' droppings, and we were obliged to stop twice, when the engine boiled, to brush a blanket of them, an inch thick, from the radiator.

The Kachin villages we passed through had geometrical shapes in bamboo erected on posts at their outskirts, perhaps to mark the parish limits for the benefit of the tutelary spirit, whose shrine, or cage, was suspended near by. In one case a typical nat-shrine had been put up over a water-pipe which had been enterprisingly built to collect the water from a spring, and, perhaps, to imprison its presiding demon. The feathers of hoopoes and eagles – usually an arrangement of their tails and wings – were flown from masts. There were spirit-shrines too, built far from the villages in the jungle itself, wigwam-shaped constructions of leaves on a framework of branches, which looked as if they should have contained something, but which proved to be empty.

When we came out into open fields, buffaloes were wandering about, each with half a dozen tick-eating egrets perched on its back, and a retinue of others accompanying it on foot. On one occasion, when we had stopped to clean the butterflies out of the radiator, we happened to witness a buffalo fight. We had noticed, without paying any special attention, two bulls standing facing each other, about a hundred yards away, on the edge of a stream. In the background a few cows were grouped, and the bulls watched each other with the introspective air natural to these deliberate and lumbering creatures. I had looked away and then back again just at the moment when both animals moved towards one another, breaking, to my surprise, into a rapid, shambling run. The hollow crash as they met must have been audible a mile away; and startled by the sound a cloud of egrets, and several previously unseen cranes, launched themselves on the air. The fight developed into a pushing match, the buffaloes straining away, with front legs planted widely apart, and heads lowered until their muzzles almost touched the ground, the thick bosses of bone between the horns in continual, grinding contact. Unless one of the beasts could succeed in cracking the other's skull with the first impact, it seemed a harmless sort of conflict, as the horns were swept back in such a way that their points could not be brought into use. In the end, after fifteen minutes had passed, and neither animal had gained an inch, one suddenly gave way, and allowed itself to be shoved into the river, thus providing itself with the excuse to break off the battle by swimming away. Having followed it into the water as far as honour demanded, the victor waded back to the unshared responsibility of the waiting cows.

Myitkyina lay in a scorching plain across the Irrawaddy, to be reached by ferry, a leisurely, time-wasting service run by the Burmese Army. The ferry-boat, its shape blotted in the glare, was tied up under the opposite bank, indifferent to the croakings of our horn, and a yellow, half-mile-wide flood ran between us. We pushed the nose of the car into the speckled shade of some willows, and plucked the heads off the yellow daisies that cut off our view of the river. There was a hot, sweet smell of water that had baked in the sun on the mud-flats all day.

We had discovered an Indian in a yoga pose by the track leading down to the ferry, and now he unfolded his legs and joined us. He was an engineer, working on a bridge-reconstruction job near by. He had been marooned in the jungle for eighteen months and, after endless days of silence – he never troubled to learn more Burmese than was necessary to give his instructions – his speech was beginning to slow down, coming when it did in gushing releases, to be checked again as if by a troublesome airlock in his throat. With despairing tenacity he clung to such of the English rites as he could. It was Saturday evening, and he was going to Myitkyina, he said, 'to paint the town red'. It was difficult to imagine this sad, earnest, fevered man giving himself, even in homage to tradition, to the debauchery he hinted at. This strange, distorted echo of things English was renewed when the ferry, having finally noticed us, dawdled over; a pair of linked Viking boats, opening behind them a fan of glittering reflections in the sallow water. 'Bad show to keep you waiting, old man,' said the Burmese officer, slapping me sharply on the back. 'Why didn't you blow your horn?'

The town of Myitkyina I saw only by night, as after an early-evening lunch at the Circuit House – a replica of that of Bhamó – I lay quietly awaiting the sunset before venturing out. Myitkyina was the last town of size before the Indian frontier, and there was a corresponding increase in Indian influence. Here there was an active and prosperous business community, and the long, single main street was radiant in the tropical night. Flickering myriads of winged insects filled the neon haze, and a man in flowing white robes went up and down playing on a pipe sweet, wild Pyrenean airs, of the kind you might have expected to hear in the Sierra del Cadi. I sat in a tea-shop and drank plain tea. There was a mosque across the way, a sort of two-dimensional Taj Mahal, the main structure and the flanking towers being cut out of flat metal, suitably painted, and supported on a framework. When viewed from the side, the whole construction vanished, as if subjected to enchantment, leaving only a minaret, like an ornamented oil-derrick. From its summit the muezzin was announcing at this moment, in a voice of exceptional quality, the truths of his religion, to the guitar players sitting in the rows of jeeps parked beneath. The radio in the tea-shop was tuned in to a Chinese station, which was broadcasting a slightly re-arranged oriental version of 'The Lambeth Walk', a current favourite in Chinese South-East Asia.

Myitkyina was the starting-point for the great and tragic trek of the refugees who fled from Burma through the Hukawng Valley, before the Japanese advance, in the summer of 1942. Why should this mass flight have turned into a disaster, in which it is estimated that twenty thousand persons lost their lives? On the map the distance from Myitkyina to Margherita, the first town over the Indian border, does not look great. It cannot be over three hundred miles, and the first hundred of them – to Sumprabum – were covered in many cases in motor vehicles. No hostility was shown to the refugees by the tribesmen inhabiting the thinly populated hills through which they passed. How was it, then, that so few escaped? A few extracts from the diary of my friend Lee, who was caught up in this exodus, may help to explain.

His original party of eight – which was later swollen to twenty – consisted of his wife, Ma Pyo, a Burmese girl, their eighteen-month-old son, their servants, a junior officer, and his batman. They arrived at Myitkyina on May 4th, 'organized' and hid vehicles on the west bank of the river, and spent the next three days ferrying civilians and a few wounded soldiers across, using the ferry-boat which had been deserted by its regular crew. On May 7th the Burmese steersman ran off, Japanese fighters strafed the last of the transport planes on the Myitkyina airfield, and the Japanese ground troops were reported very near the town, coming up the Bhamó road. The last party of refugees was therefore ferried across, and Lee and his people set off in their three cars and reached Sumprabum – where the motor road comes to an end – next day. A great multitude of bewildered refugees were encamped here, trying to find coolies before setting out on foot. No one had any idea of what lay ahead, and a usual estimate of the distance to be covered was ninety miles. Lee notes that thirty-eight schoolgirls from the Baptist school in Moulmein had got thus far. A few months later, in hospital in India, he met one of the two survivors.

At this moment, things did not look too bad – at least, to an old mining prospector. Lee knew that they had a long walk in front of them, but he had no doubt that by keeping good discipline, and by covering reasonable daily stages, they would get to India in two weeks at the most. The chief drawback was Ma Pyo's condition. She was six months pregnant, and Lee was furious when she turned down the offer of a female missionary to take her and their baby son, and to keep them safe with her in the Kachin hills, where the missionary had great influence, and proposed to hide out. With an outburst of wrath which establishes the Old Testament mood of their expedition, he assured her that she would be shot if she held the party up by going sick. 'But,' he says, 'I should have known better than to doubt the stamina of a Burmese girl. They are small

The Shwedagon Pagoda

Night at the Shwedagon Pagoda

Clown actress at a puè

The last of the Burmese puppet shows

Clown actress at a puè

The last of the Burmese puppet shows

The Arakan Pagoda: guardian figures taken at the sacking of Ayuthia

By the walls of Mandalay

Old man (race unknown) met in Maymyo market

and dainty, but mighty tough. At one time or another every man in my party lost heart and gave trouble, so that I had to drive them like animals; but Pyo calmly carried on. She did more than her share.' There are further references in the diary to the superior resistance of the womenfolk. 'We met a hugh Sikh woman with her six children, the eldest about ten years and the youngest a few weeks old. She had no one else with her, no food, spare clothing, or bedding. She was worried about her milk lasting out for the baby, but was otherwise cheerful, and too proud to ask for assistance. We did what we could, and left her plugging steadily along, carrying two kids, with the other four helping each other.'

So they had started out confidently enough, with Lee, the professional backwoodsman, at their head. But that night the Wet Monsoon broke, and without their knowing it, twenty thousand had been condemned to death. With the first showers, the mosquitoes came out, and it rained without stopping for ten days. Ten days happens to be the incubation period of malaria, and by the end of that time most of the refugees had it. A few who were taken with cerebral abscesses died within a few hours. Others lay down in the wet jungle, and shivered and starved. A few, like Lee and his party, kept staggering on through the rain, fever or no fever. Lee, who had it worse than the others, became half-blind. When his head cleared a little he remarked that they were passing the first of the dead bodies, and learned, to his surprise, from the others, that they had passed many dead during the previous two days. It was particularly bad in the outskirts of the villages, where the semi-domesticated pigs hung about to feed on the dead – and on the dying. After that Lee gave up trying to shoot pigs for food, finding that his people would no longer touch their meat.

From this time until they crossed the frontier of India, a month later, they were never out of the sight and smell of death; and at this point the refugees dropped, as if with loathing, their civilized poses and pretences. Civilization provides a whalebone corseting, and when this is unfastened, the individual either turns to jelly or begins to flex unsuspected muscles. From now on Lee found something exaggerated in people's conduct, including his own. They had turned into ham actors in an old-fashioned movie, either heroes or villains. It was a study in black and white, with no half-tones.

The gregarious instinct survived these apocalyptic conditions. 'The godowns were crammed full of refugees; with smallpox, cholera, dysentery and malaria rampant,' but decency was the first casualty, '. . . they would not even leave the camp and go into the jungle to answer the call of nature.' And colour prejudice persisted to the bitter end. 'We found an Anglo-Burmese boy of about thirteen years, calling, "Aunty, Aunty." When we asked him what he was doing there all alone, he replied, "My legs will not work, so my Daddy and Mummy have gone on with my sister, who is very white and not dark like me."'

They kept on coming upon camps which the Tea Planters' Association had been operating, but which had been abandoned, and were like water-logged graveyards, with unburied corpses everywhere. Lee, as something of a connoisseur of death on battlefields, was offended by the incorrectness of these civilian postures. They were all undignified. People had died while defecating, or drinking, and had polluted the water supply with the corruption of their bodies. 'The only person I saw who died in a dignified manner was an elderly Mohammedan gentleman. He was a wealthy man, as he had a number of servants with him. When he could travel no further and knew his end was near, he had his servants spread rugs of good quality under a shelter, and then had them stretch him out on them. He crossed his arms and told his people to spread the last rug over him. They did so.'

As for himself, Lee noticed the rapid growth of a protective shell of callousness. To illustrate this, he mentions that on May 24th – the second day of his recovery from malaria – they found a Chinese, unable to walk, but sitting with a happy grin on a pile of rice he had found in a shed. A mile further on they came upon another, lying face downwards, in the last stages of hunger and exhaustion. Lee rolled him over, and sacrificed a little of his precious store of brandy to bring him round. After a while they got him on his feet, cut two walking sticks for him to pull himself along with, and told him how to join his countryman on the rice heap. 'At that time I felt sentimental,' Lee says. 'Had this incident happened three weeks later, I would have passed the man, and left him to die without a second thought.'

On June 8th, after floundering for a fortnight along tracks that were knee-deep in mud in places, they reached the Nam Yung River. It had been converted by the rains into a roaring torrent. Within an hour and a half of their arrival, they saw nine men in succession who tried to cross it torn from the guide rope and drowned. One Gurkha woman, on seeing her husband carried away, gave birth to a premature child. It was born dead, and thrown into the river. That night the guide rope gave way and they were stranded. There were four hundred and fifty demoralized refugees at the crossing and several thousand on the way. Lee found a place up-stream where the river split into two arms, the nearest of which was only sixty feet wide. All they had to do was to drop one of the large trees growing on the bank across it, use it as a bridge, and repeat the manoeuvre on the further bank. But of the four hundred and fifty waiting to cross only twenty-two would volunteer to help cut down the tree. They were all so weak that they could only peck at it with their dahs for a few minutes at a time. 'We nibbled at that tree like so many woodpeckers.' In the end it fell in the wrong direction, lengthways along the stream. Then when another day had been spent in felling a second tree, which had dropped into the correct position, it was suddenly noticed that the water was falling, for it had stopped raining in the upper reaches of the river. At this moment a party of Oorias turned up, ex-fishermen from the Puri coast of India. They were all expert swimmers. It was then decided to repair the guide rope, which the Oorias agreed to swim across with, and to reattempt a crossing of the main stream. Six or seven orderly batches, five at a time, made the crossing, with Lee covering the rope with his pistol from the northern shore. Then the crowd panicked. About thirty at once rushed the rope. It broke under the strain, and they were all swept away. Lee and his party went on without looking back.

Immediately after this came what were for Lee the two worst moments of the whole journey. His old Chinese servant was in a very bad state. He could not keep down any food, and had lost the use of his legs. They were obliged to leave him to die, an action for which he assures me he has never been able to forgive himself. About this time it seemed clear that his baby son also would not survive. He had carried the child on his back for the whole journey, and now it seemed to be in the last stages of dysentery; it was in a state of coma, and constantly oozing blood and pus. As there appeared to be no hope, Lee decided to put him out of his suffering and administered a lethal dose of morphia tablets, 'enough', he says, 'to kill ten men. To our astonishment he immediately recovered; and later on, when he had dysentery again, I repeated the morphia treatment on a minor scale, again with success.'

And so, at the end of June, they came finally into India. Most of the males in the party collapsed utterly as soon as they reached safety, and several nearly died. Lee's normal weight of one hundred and fifty-five pounds had been reduced to ninety pounds. Ma Pyo was the only one who had not lost weight; but she was covered with sores. About eighteen thousand refugees coming this way had got through before them, but most of these, by starting earlier, had avoided the worst rains. There were very few to follow.

The centre of the Burmese jade industry was at Mogaung, near Myitkyina, and next morning I asked the driver to take me there. But it soon appeared that the direct road marked on my map no longer existed, and as Mogaung could only be reached by an enormous detour, the driver said that he would take me to a small jade mine which was more easily reached. We drove perhaps ten miles out of Myitkyina, walked for half an hour up a valley, and there was the mine, a series of small caverns in the hillside, only one of which looked as if it might have been excavated in recent times. The driver assured me that these, as well as some pits to be seen in the half-dry bed of the river, were being worked. To a question as to the miners' whereabouts, I received the astonishing reply that they had gone to chapel. Judging perhaps from the tone of my voice that an affirmative answer was expected, he also assured me in answer to a further question that the traditional method of 'fishing' for jade by paddling bare-footed in the stream was still followed here. It is one of the many picturesque fallacies with which the jade industry is beset, that the best pieces are always found, by touch, in this way. Outside the caverns, a few dirty pieces of rock were strewn about. These, the driver said, were jade of inferior quality, and having observed that precious stones are usually without attraction in their unprepared state, I was prepared to believe that this was so.

The history of jade provides an interesting illustration of the creation by a refined and luxurious society of its symbol of wealth. The white nephrite chosen possessed all the qualifications required. It was beautiful and rare; it could be obtained only with immense trouble – the original Jade Mountain was at K'un Lun in south-east Turkestan – and its fashioning into jewellery, owing to its extreme hardness, called for the expenditure of infinite labour and much technical skill. In the original quarries in Turkestan a certain small amount of green jadeite was also found. By virtue of its rarity this green stone became practically priceless. With a kind of dim recognition of the influence of metallic oxides in establishing the jade's colour, many attempts were made to fake this valuable green by such ingenious methods as burying copper in contact with blocks of white nephrite. With the adoption of jade symbols for the State worship of the Heaven, Earth, and the 'Four Quarters', jade assumed for the Chinese the prestige associated with gold in the West; and it is safe to say that had one of the biblical Three Wise Men of the East come from China, jade would have been his gift.

The discovery by a thirteenth-century Chinese prospector, at a moment when the K'un Lun mines had reached exhaustion, of great quantities of jadeite in the Kachin States of Burma, caused a sensation in the Celestial Empire, and Mogaung became the El Dorado of many Chinese expeditions, the members of which mostly perished, after horrible privations of the type suffered by their Spanish counterparts in their search for gold. Finally the trade was established, and it was found that, most happily, although jadeite of pure translucent green existed, it was rare, compared to the colours produced by the action of metallic oxides, other than copper, upon the silicate. There was plenty of green jadeite at Mogaung, but most of it was the wrong green, or it was too opaque, or was variable in colour, and thus succeeded in one way or another in defeating the demands of finicky connoisseurship. The undermining of Chinese values was averted. Otherwise, one suspects, it would have been necessary to combat the threatened devaluation in some way, perhaps by the disappearance, for reasons of State, of all those concerned in the mine's discovery.

As things were, the Chinese economy remained unshaken. Some sort of a jade-rush took place. Laden caravans set out for China, and were regularly ambushed and looted by jade-thirsty freebooters, although the majority got through safely, to swell what was believed to be the wealth of the nation. Remembering that in their war with Burma the Chinese forces made a bee-line for Mogaung, which they occupied, it may be surmised that the ends in view by those who provoked the conflict were less pure than those of justice.

Prices were kept inflated and production restricted by the fact that all the jade mines were located in the Kachin tribal area. The Kachins insisted on working the mines in their own way, steadfastly declining all offers involving leases or contracts. In their search for the stone, the Kachins relied upon divination. Quarries were opened with elaborate sacrifices and feasting, and then only after the omens had been consulted to decide whether or not the stone was to be allowed to 'mature', it being a Kachin opinion that the colour improved with keeping. Even so the workings might be held up over some dispute about the sharing of the proceeds, a punctilious matter in which every member of the clan, whether present or absent, was taken into consideration. Work was carried on only in March and April. After that the mines became flooded by the rains, and took the rest of the year to dry out. Meanwhile the Chinese buyers sat by, twiddling their thumbs in impotent exasperation, unconscious of the fact that by great good fortune the incompetence of the Kachins worked in their favour and cancelled out the disadvantage that Burma was nearer the cities of China than were the mines of south-east Turkestan. In the last century prices were much enhanced when King Mindon, an enthusiastic monopolist, tried to set himself up as middleman of the industry, and the Kachins retorted by discovering only inferior jade.

The Chinese have never been able to consider jade as mere 'dead' substance; they have always had a rather modern view of the nature of matter. From the earliest times, it was associated with the five cardinal virtues: charity, modesty, courage, justice, and wisdom (one notes in passing the omission from this category of the peculiarly Christian faith and hope). It was also quite inevitable that it should be believed that jade could be taken internally with beneficial results. Once a year, therefore, the Emperor fasted ceremonially, consuming nothing but powdered jade of the most exquisite colour. This was for the good of the Empire; but, in the individual, the liver as well as all the organs in mystical association with it, according to the Chinese medical philosophy, were benefited by homoeopathic doses. The Chinese, in their refined, almost tortured aestheticism, recognize one hundred and twenty colours of jade, some of them baffling to Western amateurs, who find difficulty in differentiating between such shades as sky-blue and the blue of the sky 'after it has been washed by a shower'. Nor can many Western experts claim, as do the Chinese, to distinguish one variety of jade from another by the touch.

At the present time it seems likely that the jade mania may have come to an abrupt end. Production at Mogaung was entirely for the Chinese market, the stone being otherwise valueless. It is difficult to imagine that China's present rulers would sanction this type of import, or that they would approve of so many Chinese man-hours being employed on the production of trinkets, whatever their artistic merit – unless for export. Perhaps, as the driver said so confidently, the open-cast miners in this valley had indeed gone to chapel; or perhaps they had given up waiting for the Chinese merchants to come to the auctions, and had gone back to cultivate their opium, the market for which – if less spectacular – has always been dependable.

CHAPTER SEVENTEEN

Down the Irrawaddy

HAVING LEARNED THAT in the dry season only rare military boats went down the river from Myitkyina to Bhamó, I decided to return to Bhamó by road and to take a river-steamer thence to Mandalay. This stretch of the river was covered by a twice-weekly boat service, and the trip took three days. When I had made some preliminary enquiries about this part of the journey, at the offices of the Irrawaddy Water Transport Board in Rangoon, the information to be had was surprisingly vague. It was known that the boats passed through areas held by both types of Communists, as well as PVOs, and that although they were usually attacked, an escort of soldiers was carried and no boat had so far been lost. What they were not sure about was the nature of the accommodation. The executive I saw thought I would have to sleep on deck and take my own food with me.

At the company's Bhamó office the picture painted was a brighter one, to the extent at least that there was a regular food supply. A butler attended to the needs of first-class passengers, and there was even a choice of Burmese or Chinese food.

At seven in the morning I walked a plank over the shining Irrawaddy mud separating the solid bank from a shallow-draught lighter, one of a number which were hastening with passengers and goods to the steamer anchored in mid-stream. Like most river-steamers it had a romantic and anachronistic air; a flat-bottomed and skeletal construction of open-sided decks, terribly vulnerable, it seemed in its flimsiness, to assault of any kind. The *Pauktan*, of 106 tons displacement and licensed to carry 228 deck-passengers on 2053 square feet of deck-space (when not occupied by cattle, cargo, or other encumbrances) proved, to my surprise, not to be a survival of the last century, but a post-war production.

The show-boat illusion was dissipated as soon as I put my foot on the iron deck, after boarding the ship close by a central redoubt covered by steel plating, from behind which came a cushioned thumping of powerful engines. On one side of this was the deck-passengers' kitchen in which, as I passed, a cook was hacking through a piece of dried fish held on a block. It took two blows of his heavy dah to cut off each segment. Early arrivals had already staked out their claims to deck space. As soon as they arrived they spread out mats or carpets, made tea and prepared bowls of rice and fish which they ate with ready holiday appetite. Before and after doing so they made a constant procession up to a row of sinister iron prison-cells mounted in the stern, labelled in English, Women and Men Wash Place.

After half an hour, an army launch came alongside with an escort of fifty soldiers, each man carrying, besides his rifle and normal kit, an embroidered pillow. A few minutes later there was a second influx of the military, twenty soldiers who were escorting forty-seven Chinese Nationalist internees and five dacoits. The escort party had started out with fifty Chinese, but three had already escaped. They were being taken to an internment camp at Meiktila. The dacoits were going to a prison two days' journey away. Two of them – one a Chinese soldier – had committed murders, and all five, although, as was to be expected, they looked exceedingly depressed, seemed from their appearance incapable of desperate deeds. The Chinese murderer in particular had a gentle and sensitive face.

The military took over the whole of the upper deck, laying out their kit, army-fashion, in neat rows, the embroidered pillows – some with lace fringes – perched squarely on haversacks. Sentries were posted at the tops of the companion-ways. The dacoits, now chained hand and foot, were seated in a melancholy row. To reduce the chafing of their gyves, they had been allowed to wrap rags round the metal. The Chinese formed squatting circles and began to play a game with engraved ivory counters, while their guards looked on with keen interest. A group of pongyis had formed round one of their number who had produced a snapshot album. To my surprise, most of the pictures were of girls, including one combing her hair in front of a mirror. On the deck below barge-load after barge-load of passengers continued to come aboard, alternating with hundreds of bales of dried fish, the odour of which slowly filled every corner of the ship. Most of the passengers, too, had brought with them tough, grey, salt-powdered hunks of fish, and, nervous at first of the promiscuous contacts of voyages, carried them everywhere they went, so that for some hours the decks and approaches of the *Pauktan* were heavy with the intertwining of ammoniacal stenches.

Much to my surprise, in view of the ship's semi-transparent silhouette, there were cabins on the *Pauktan*, containing besides the bed, an electric fan, a wash-basin which emptied out into a bowl placed below, and a placard recommending the Asia Chop-Chop Shop at Katha. A minute triangular saloon was fitted into the bows, where you could sit with an excellent view of the river; and first-class passengers, Burmese and Chinese, who had retired here kicked off their sandals and looked up beamingly at the approach of footsteps, ready to ask politely, 'May I know your destination, sir?' In this room meals were served, presided over by the butler, the Burmese counterpart in dignity and conservatism of attire of the impressive domestic who in England survives chiefly in advertisement descriptions of gracious living.

A good hour after the advertised sailing-time passengers were still arriving. Even when the last of the lighters had cast off, small boats came racing up, with much excited hailing and waving, disgorging fares who for the most part appeared to have come along on the spur of the moment, as they were without luggage. This, in fact, was the case. On making enquiries I learned that these late-comers were members of parties who had been seeing friends off, and then had suddenly felt an urge to join them. On the boat there were many happy and unforeseen reunions. In the end, the captain got tired of this kind of thing; a bell rang and up came the anchor. Leaving in the lurch a couple of boat-loads of impulsive Burmans, we began to slide down the river, accompanied by a dipping, slowly flapping escort of Indian river terns.

All the world's great waterways are scenically uninteresting except in places where the river narrows in its passage through mountains or a gorge. Otherwise, the expanse of water is too great, the banks too far away. Here the Irrawaddy was half a mile to a mile wide, and the monotony of clouded water and the close vegetation of the distant shores was broken only when the pilot, steering a course that wound in great sweeping curves through an unseen channel of deep water, sometimes came close to the banks. The water opened in folds at the bows, carrying a broken, dusty sparkle, and although the sun was high the water had a cold, breath-catching smell of stagnant pools. The banks had been undermined, laying bare the roots of trees in a pale tracery, like some coral growth exposed by the recession of the sea. We soon passed one of the hundreds of ships that had been sunk or scuttled during the war. It had become an extension of the jungle, a boat-shaped peninsula, from which, surprisingly, a smoke-stack and one paddle protruded. The deck rail embraced a variety of luxuriant grasses, bushes, and one small tree – a vantage point selected by a bittern to survey the waters.

Within a few hours we entered the second or middle defile, where the river, narrowing perhaps to one hundred and fifty yards, was shut in by hills covered by the most luxuriant forest, a multiple volcanic eruption of foliage, beneath which a wall of green lava toppled over upon a foreshore of glistening mud. As we nosed forward, silently cleaving the surface of clouded jade, the channel ahead closed in as if we had reached the end of a dark lake, barred by a cliff rising a sheer eight hundred feet out of the water. Then, as we turned a tree-crowded headland, the water could be seen, going on in glossy patches beyond the black boulders. Most travellers have recorded that they saw elephants here, but there were no elephants when the *Pauktan* passed through, although at a blast on the ship's siren a flight of parakeets broke from the tree-tops and came low overhead, a brief green glitter in the blue.

The defiles of the Irrawaddy are said to be of extreme depth, and I have read that a steamer which dropped anchor here failed to reach bottom when six hundred and thirty feet of chain had run out, and, getting out of control, was lost. The butler told me that Burmese Loch Ness monsters are seen with fair regularity, undulant creatures with the inoffensive heads of asses or sheep, which show themselves at times of national crisis, or when comets are seen. Their appearance has no more than a monitory significance, and without harming passing boatmen, they are content to belch a little smoke before disappearing below the surface. It is an accepted fact that river-sharks haunt some of the bays.

We stopped at the village of Shwegu, where most of the population seemed to have gathered on the sloping bank to sell crude earthen-ware pots, vilely decorated by the moulded addition of glossy ceramic peacocks. The art of Shwegu in particular and Burma in general is a disaster, ranking in the scale of debasement, with the honourable exception of its lacquer-ware, as about level with that of modern Egypt. But the little saleswomen, most of them in sparrow's-egg blue longyis and big Shan hats, were charming, and their pots – however deplorable separately – were arranged in the most effective mass compositions. The passengers were delighted with them, and scram-bled ashore as soon as the gangplank was let down, to buy great quantities of these depressing souvenirs.

Beyond Shwegu a few barren islands appeared, fringed with sand-spits bearing ranks of motionless cormorants, some sunning them-selves with wings heraldically opened. Once we saw an eagle wading majestically in the shadows, thus revealing itself as a suprisingly long-limbed bird. Pied kingfishers hung motionless in the air, their long beaks hanging down like hornets' stings, and sometimes dropped, as if an unseen thread had snapped, upon their insect quarry. In its fishing this bird employed a different technique, involving an extraordinary aerobatic feat – a trick which I had never seen practised before. While travelling at full speed, at perhaps seventy miles an hour, parallel to, and just above the water's surface, it would suddenly – at least, so it appeared to me – spot a fish, and then, unable to turn quickly, would at once lose speed and reverse its direction by purposely striking the water. It did so with wings partially opened, in such a way that the impact actually caused it to bounce back, at the same time allowing it to change direction and then go into a shallow dive after its prey. The whole operation, which I was never tired of watching, took about a second, and I wondered when and how the first kingfisher had discovered the possibilities of this manoeuvre, and whether it was generally practised throughout the pied-kingfisher clan, or only by the Burmese birds.

Towards the evening, while the sun was still fairly high in the sky, the landscape suddenly lost its colours. The creamy-yellows of the water, the gliding of the sand-spits, the infinitely varied greens of the jungle trees, the banks, which were sometimes the bluish-white of water seeping through chalk, sometimes brick red, all relapsed into a leaden uniformity, a flat, photographic monochrome; it was more like a brightly moonlit scene than one viewed by the light of day. As the line of the distant mountains was erased from the sky and a tide of mist began to rise up the jungle tree-trunks, the ship was turned into the shore to join a dark cluster of junks.

This was Katha, where we were to stay the night, but although the town was said to be in government hands, the Chop-Chop Shop, alas, was out of bounds, and a trip ashore was not thought desirable. Bren guns had been set up on both decks, and on the bridge – which was also armoured – and their muzzles thrust shorewards in the gathering gloom, which was suddenly violated by the brusque glare of the ship's searchlight. Extra guards had been posted over the prisoners who, with the failing light, had stopped gambling for match-sticks and were singing those rather tuneless European-type marching songs which are believed in the Far East to instil martial virtue. The opium-smokers among the Chinese had been humanely issued with an opium-ration, and had been sent away into a corner to smoke it. The officer who pointed this out was very proud of the fact that there was no opium-smoking in the Burmese Army. Even the dacoits – two of whom it was whispered would be executed next day – had not been forgotten. Earlier in the day, after some self-examination as to the propriety of the action, and with the officer's permission, I had given them cheroots. Now there was an official issue.

CHAPTER EIGHTEEN

A Mild Alarm

MORNING CAME, accompanied by soft fluvial sounds, the light slap of water on the hull, the creaking of the junks' timbers, the splash of leaping fish. Night evaporated along the western horizon and, with it, a rippling veil of egrets was drawn back from the water. A little red had seeped into the leaden landscape, and presently where sky and water met without division, the sun raised itself on a long, clean-cut shaft of reflection. It was a polar spectacle, an arctic night in midsummer. Soon the ship quickened with the engine's subdued convulsion. Nosing out into the stream, it dragged in its wake ropes of unearthly blue through water the colour of tin. Wherever the water was stirred up, it leaped to life as if brilliant lamps had suddenly been lit below the surface. The sun, which had now broken away from its shaft of reflection, climbed swiftly into the sky, and as it did so the mists passed up out of the jungle, like the plumes of smoke from a railway station where many expresses are about to depart.

Here the river was shallow, and our course wound through a hidden channel. Speed was reduced, with the clanging of bells, and one of the Malabar crew stood in the bows taking soundings with ritual cries and the flourishes of a temple dancer. Whenever a satisfactory depth was reached he gave a triumphant shout of 'Allah akbar!' a pious equivalent of 'All's Well'.

Tigyaing was in insurgent hands – what brand of insurgents was not clear – but by virtue of some kind of live-and-let-live arrangement, we were allowed to anchor there, a little off shore, to discharge and take on cargo. The river-barges here were the most handsome boats I had seen in the country – in fact, in any country. They were built of rich, red teak, providentially left unpainted. By keeping the deck free of any encumbrances but a single, elegant deckhouse, placed well back, and with the curved line of its roof exactly repeating that of the high, carved stern, an extraordinary purity of outline had been achieved. There was an element of what is now known as stream-lining in these flowing curves, which undoubtedly reflected the tastes of Burmese boat-builders of bygone centuries. I hoped to have the opportunity to study one of these boats at leisure in Rangoon, but later found that they were a speciality of Upper Burma, and not to be found on the lower reaches of the river.

A few miles below Tigyaing there was some excitement. The river's course was divided here by a large island, and the right-hand channel we took was a narrow one, obliging us to approach sometimes very close to the bank, which was thickly wooded. We passed a village in a clearing, which might have been the objective, previously, of a government landing party, because only the framework of the houses remained. The place had not been burned. The people had just moved elsewhere and taken their portable sections of bamboo walls with them. A red flag still flew from one of the roofs.

Further down we passed the sister steamer, making the journey up-stream to Bhamó. She signalled that she had just been attacked. This news was received with the utmost phlegm, and was passed on to me, without sign of emotion, by the butler. The soldiers of the Kachin Rifles set about organizing the defence, settling themselves comfortably in a row of chairs along the lower deck, with muzzles of rifles and Bren guns supported by the deck rail. A few others lay down behind the funnel, on the corrugated-iron covering to the top deck. From this position they were soon driven out by the escape of smoke and fumes produced when the engines were driven at full speed. The passengers' behaviour was equally restrained. The young people took refuge, without excitement, behind a flimsy barricade of bales of fish. The Chinese prisoners showed amused interest. The old people and the convicts were indifferent. Only the pongyis paraded in the open, secure in the armour of righteousness, and peered and pointed into the green tangle, which sometimes came so near that we passed almost beneath the branches of the largest jungle trees.

But no signs of aggression were forthcoming at the spot where the other ship had been fired upon, and soon the soldiers put their guns down: the Chinese, who had gathered at their backs with professional interest, went back to their gambling, and the ordinary well-behaved tumult of the shipboard life started again. There had been no official declaration of a state of alarm, and now no responsible person decreed that the emergency had passed. The passengers just got tired of waiting for something to happen and decided to go on playing cards, or cooking their food.

I had just gone down for a shower, when there was a sound, muffled, yet amplified in the iron sounding-box of the bathroom, like the rattle of a distant anchor-chain going down. Immediately the room began to jar and vibrate under the hammering of the Bren guns above. I ran up on deck, but there was nothing left of the action but a smell of cordite. The gunners, lolling back in their chairs, were slapping fresh magazines into the breeches, and taking leisurely aim again, and as they did so the crowded cloisters of the jungle suddenly slipped away as our course took us into midstream again. There were no casualties, a fact which convinced me that such attacks are without terroristic intention, and aim only at compelling the Burmese government to divert the maximum number of troops to escort duties. It would have been impossible to empty a machine-gun magazine into such a crowded ship, at twenty yards – even at random – without killing and wounding a number of people.

We had been delayed, so that the sun set while we were still some way from our destination for the night – Kyaukmyaung. At the approach of dusk, the terns, absent since the morning, returned, drifting past us up the river in groups, flapping languidly just above their reflections in the water. All round us dark smoke rose up where the Shans were firing the jungle before sowing their rice, and when the dark came the mountains were ringwormed with fire. The ship's searchlights stabbed out, and swung from side to side, illuminating stark boulders fringing the water's edge as we neared the third cataract, and patches of floating weed streamed past like silver plaques, stars and medallions. Soon brilliant motes appeared in the beam. These thickened until, with speed reduced, we appeared to be pushing forward into a blizzard. The flakes composing this singular storm proved to be winged insects, half fly and half moth, which soon filled the ship, flapping softly in the face and hair, churned by the electric fans into glittering whirlpools, deadening the footfalls in the carpet of their fallen bodies. There was no way of escaping them. When the cabin's windows were shut they spurted, as if under pressure, beneath the door, toasted themselves on the electric light bulb and fell into the wash-basin and drinking glasses. Had they possessed the power to sting, we should all have died, but they were quite harmless, though evidently suffering from some mass dementia. Curiously enough, they were all at the point of death, because after whirring round the room for a few moments they dropped to the floor, and lay still. Within twenty minutes it was all over, the air cleared and the ship's decks, passages and companion-ways were covered with a layer, half an inch thick, of small, feebly moving shapes.

The Kyaukmyaung shore, as we came in, twinkled with a dancing, firefly illumination. This was produced by a night market, held on the deep, sloping bank, to coincide with the boat's arrival. The water's edge and a path leading up to the village were lined with stalls, each lit by a wick standing in a cup of oil. Villagers coming down to meet the boat swung torches as they walked; hence the flickering effect. Most of the passengers went ashore to stretch their legs, and to buy the soup, rice, eggs, or members of chicken offered by the stall-holders. A speciality of this place was yard-long tubes of bamboo, filled with a much sought-after variety of sticky rice. These cost six annas each. All these edibles were sold by the village beauties, silk-clad and be-flowered. It is not considered demeaning in Burma to keep a market stall, and in this way marriageable girls present themselves discreetly for the inspection of prospective husbands. The market at Kyaukmyaung performed, in fact, a double function.

Kyaukmyaung, too, was for the dacoits the end of the road. Here the irons of each man were joined to a long chain, and thus they were marched away with the clinking of anklets of earthbound dancers, up the bank and into the darkness.

Dawn again showed us a landscape engraved in steel, ragged ardent clouds stirred into the sky, a river coldly ensanguined.

Immediately below Kyaukmyaung, we entered the third and lowest defile of the Irrawaddy. It was less impressive than the second, but still sufficiently a wonder of nature to be surrounded with its magic aura. Here there was an island, and it was quite inevitable that a monastery should have been built upon it. The monastery of Thihadaw, now seemingly ruined, long possessed an engaging reputation because of the monks' skill in taming fish. In Burma, fish suffer from their position on the fringe of animal creation, and are victimized by the cunning sophistry which sees no harm in eating them if they happen to have died when taken out of the water. For this reason they have always evoked a special compassion in the breasts of the gentle Buddhist brotherhood, and many monasteries have tanks where fish, saved from the nets by these holy men, lead a pampered existence, sharing with their protectors the alms of the pious. At Thihadaw the monks had tamed the resident population of the Irrawaddy for half a mile around, and it was a favourite tourist spectacle to see them calling up five-foot dog-fish, to feed them and stick honorific patches of gold-leaf on the backs of their heads. These fish were intelligent enough never to wander far from their sanctuary. It is said that the arrival of the English had a deplorable effect on such pleasant customs. Unhappily, the fish which were most readily tamed were also the most appreciated for the table by the barbarous newcomers, and the prices offered tempted the cupidity of the fishermen. To combat the slaughter, the monks adopted many extraordinary measures. Once, at the mouth of the Irrawaddy, a canal was dug at immense labour, joining the river to a monastery tank, and the fish were trained upon a danger signal given vocally or by the beating of the banks, to swim up into the monastery enclosure, where the good men stood guard over them, cudgel in hand.

Below the defile the river spread out, its surface broken by wooded islands and rippling with shallows, where groups of fishing adjutants and herons waded. The banks were steep but shallow, and as the boat's wash reached them, parched earth showered down, and floated like powdered chocolate on the water's surface. Here there were more villages, the grey of their low bamboo shacks pierced by the fierce green of the river's edge grass. There was also more traffic; in particular, barges going upstream, poled forward smoothly and swiftly by teams of men – usually three on each side – who, laying their weight on their poles, marched with languid precision from stem to stern, returning endlessly to repeat the manoeuvre. Small steamers also began to appear on the river. They were flying white flags.

Just above Mandalay the skyline was sharply broken by what looked like one of those freak hills which are a feature of the Moulmein area. For several miles I had watched the growth of this small, isolated mountain, which, as we approached, loomed from the tall trees surrounding it, to overtop a low range of distant hills. Noticing my interest, the butler told me that this was an unfinished pagoda, and only then I remembered the notorious Mengun, which, however, I had not expected to find by half so huge.

The Mengun Pagoda was the work of King Bodawpaya, one of the many oriental princes who at one time or another set out to put up the greatest building in the world. The work was started in 1790, and occupied most of the labour force of the country, which was conscribed and organized on military lines for seven years. At the end of that time a prophecy became current – it had been heard before during the pagoda-building mania which preceded the Mongol invasion: 'The great pagoda is finished, and the country is ruined.' There was something in this, because in a roundabout way this lunatic enterprise certainly accelerated the downfall of the

Burmese kingdom. When Burmese manpower seemed insufficient, Bodawpaya recruited thousands of Arakanese, none of whom returned home. The Arakanese belief that the King considered their nation expendable brought about a revolt followed by mass emigration across the border into Assam. When the Burmese went after them, they clashed with the British and thus, eventually, the first Anglo-Burmese war came about. The Mengun Pagoda, when work on it ceased, had reached one hundred and sixty-five feet of the proposed height of five hundred feet.

Bodawpaya, a kind of Burmese Ivan the Terrible who never slept twice in the same bed, affected a monkishness commonly found in a certain type of tyrant, and it must have made him all the more sinister to his people. He was much concerned with works of merit, of which the Mengun Pagoda was to be his greatest. Believing that it would ensure his apotheosis, he went so far as to anticipate the work's completion in announcing his divinity. In much the same way a modern Burman will adopt the title *paya*, pagoda builder (one entitled to enter Nirvana without further incarnation) as soon as the first instalment-payment on the building has been made. To their eternal credit – since the King thought nothing of burning a few pongyis to death in wicker cages – this claim was immediately contested by the Buddhist priesthood, whose particular glory it is, like the prophets of old, and unlike many of the spiritual leaders of our times, that they have never been ready to sell their religion for the state's support, nor afraid to stand up to a tyrant. From the time when Narathihapate, fleeing before the Mongols, gave the order for his concubines to be drowned, and his chaplain warned him that their murder would entail as a consequence the king's reincarnation as an animal, Burmese history is full of such instances.

By all accounts the ferocity of this king startled even the Burmese, accustomed as they were to ruthlessness in the affairs of state. At his accession, when surplus members of the royal family were eliminated in the usual way, they were burned alive, including the previous king's four principal queens, who were accorded the privilege, however, of dying with their babies in their arms. This monster was diabolically efficient in most of his undertakings and led a charmed life. He built enormous public works, including reservoirs, destroyed his enemies, forbade drinking alcohol on pain of death, captured a perfect specimen of a white elephant, and was the first Burmese monarch to obtain a Buddha tooth from China. He died full of years and honour, and was survived by one hundred and twenty-two children.

Into the relic chamber of the Mengun Pagoda – the first of its kind to be lead lined – went, in addition to the Buddha tooth, all the most exquisite things produced in his day, Buddha images, models of pagodas and monasteries in gold and silver, European clocks, clockwork toys, and the very latest child of European inventive genius – a machine for making soda-water.

This was the last attempt but one of a Burmese king to storm the Kingdom of Heaven by pagoda-building. The final fiasco was left to King Mindon, who, determined to outclass even the Mengun, had a whole hill cut into blocks to furnish stone, and dug canals several miles long for the huge lighters which were to carry the materials to the selected site. After four years of mass labour the pagoda had only risen four feet, and a French engineer who told the king that it would take eighty-four years to complete narrowly escaped crucifixion. Then the king died, and the thing was immediately abandoned.

We tied up on the Mandalay shore in the middle of a sweltering, dust-laden afternoon. A line of gharries, as bizarre in their ornament as properties from the Russian ballet, waited at the top of the slimy bank. I got into one of these and went off in it to see my friend U Tok Galé, and within half an hour was back in my old room over the cinema, suddenly realizing, as I heard them again through the mechanical blare and racket, that in the country of the Shans and Kachins I had missed the mild, sweet sound of the triangular pagoda-gongs of Burma.

Having reached Mandalay after hearing no more than a few shots fired, as a matter of routine exercise rather than in anger, I was now ambitious to continue the journey to Rangoon otherwise than by air.

The Burman rarely raises obstacles to such a project on the score of mere danger. At the police headquarters, the DSP said that naturally no one ever travelled by train, unless it was to reach a town not served by air; but the fact remained that the Mandalay–Rangoon line – the only one operating in the country – was open, more or less. The train service was, in fact, a fairly regular one, only held up from time to time to repair bridges, or remove wreckage from the line. As far as he was concerned there was no objection. He didn't see that there was any point in running the trains if people were forbidden to travel on them. He suggested that I should apply to the station master for more details.

The station master was most helpful. The Rangoon express would be running the next morning at six fifteen. He had just received news that the previous train, that of March 15th, had been dynamited at a place called Yeni, but as the dynamiting had taken place several hours ago, the wreckage should have been cleared in time to let tomorrow's train through. It would be a piece of unheard-of bad luck, he added, if they lost two trains in succession. And at what time would it get to Rangoon? ... Get to Rangoon? The station master was slightly surprised. Naturally, it wouldn't. It was called the Rangoon express because it went in the direction of Rangoon, and it might travel five, ten, or fifty miles before the line was dynamited, or a bridge blown up, or with good luck it might even reach Tatkón, which was about one hundred and fifty miles away. After that it would turn round and come back, because between Tatkón and Pyinmana, sixty miles or so, much of the permanent way had been removed. The railway, said the station master – incorrectly as it turned out – furnished transport to get travellers across this gap; it might be lorries or it might even be bullock-carts. These were held up pretty regularly by dacoits, but even if passengers were robbed – and it was very stupid to carry more than a few rupees – they usually got to Pyinmana safely enough in the end. At Pyinmana, with reasonable luck, a train would be found waiting to leave for Rangoon. The DSP, he said, had been misinformed in the matter of the military escort. There was none. In fact, the only hope of the trains getting through was to run them without military escorts.

He promised to keep me a good second-class seat – not over the wheels.

On our way back, Tok Galé asked me if I believed in ghosts. 'I ask you,' he said, 'because they say that this is the worst thing about travelling by train.' He kept an open mind on the matter himself, mentioning that although he had been passing a well-known haunted banyan tree every day for a number of years, he had never seen anything unusual. However, the fact was that travellers by train complained that they suffered from supernatural molestation. The ghosts came crowding up at night, headless and handless, and all the grislier and more menacing for this deprivation. Tatkón was the worst place for them; and Tok Galé thought that a possible reason for this might be the large number of unburied corpses left lying in the jungle near by, after the insurgent troubles. It was on this warning note that we said goodbye.

CHAPTER NINETEEN

Rangoon Express

THE LONG TRAIN was made up of converted cattle-trucks, marked second or third class. In the second class there were two benches running the length of the ex-truck, but in the third class the space was divided up into sections, so that twice the number of people could be squeezed in. Until six fifteen the phlegmatic crowd on the departure platform was split up into nearly motionless social groups, as if before the performance of a première which nobody particularly wanted to attend. Then a man called the platform superintendent took a handbell from under his arm and shook it, and the train gave a lurch. The passengers who were already in their seats fell on top of each other, and picked themselves up, smiling with dazed pleasure. Those on the platform dashed for the doors. The platform superintendent pushed me into a second-class compartment which he had insisted on keeping empty for me, and which was not over the wheels. 'Remember,' he said, 'in Burma there are no Communists, only people who want a change of government.' The train then moved away from him, and he turned and sank back from sight among the drifting groups of those who had come to see friends off, and in a moment the melancholy ringing of his bell was swallowed up in the clashing steel concussion of the wheels.

I found myself confined in a compartment measuring about nine feet by seven. There were glassless windows which could be covered by pulling down wooden shutters. The door, which had no handle, was fastened by an inside bolt. Passengers were asked to pull the chain in case of emergency, and in the lavatory, which smelt very badly, a notice invited them to depress the handle. But there was no chain and no handle. The electric light came on when two wires were twisted together. Mosquitoes lived in the dark places under the benches and streamed out in such numbers that they seemed to move in rough formation. A few large cockroaches crawled aimlessly about the floor.

Outside, the suburbs of Mandalay, caught in the sallow light of the rising sun filtered through strips of indigo mist, went lurching past. And then, almost immediately, the bungalows and the African huts merged with the mouldering pagodas of Amarapura, with mighty, broken walls, brick-choked moats, headless Buddhas, and a zooful of fabulous monsters, all strangled with cactus and scrub and flowering weeds. Here, with the city's abandonment at a monarch's whim, had been squandered the labours of ten thousand lives. Among the nearest pagodas lay the twisted and charred wreckage of rolling-stock where it had been thrown clear of the line, and left.

I was about to change carriages at the first station at which we stopped, when a smart, bespectacled young Burmese put his hand through the open top of the door, even before the train had come to a standstill, and unbolted it. He then jumped in, looked round the compartment, smiled quickly in my direction, took out a clean handkerchief, unfolded it, and wiped the opposite bench. After that, he jumped out again, and held the door open for another man to enter. The second-comer was an elderly man, tall and dignified, with a stubble of grey hair, and an extremely dark complexion. He came in, walking with some difficulty as if at the head of a procession, and sat down facing me. He wore a longyi, and a white sports shirt, neatly repaired in several places at the neck; two fountain-pens protruded from the breast pocket. Having seated himself he made a slight gesture to the young man who had come in first, and he, in response, trotted over to a group of women and children gathered in the background. From them he obtained a garland of flowers, which he came in and placed round the old man's neck. He was backing respectfully away when an uplifted hand halted him. 'Have you got your notebook?' the elderly man asked. The young Burman said he had. 'Good,' said the other. 'Make a note of these requirements.' And in an old, precise, and rather harsh voice, he dictated a memorandum. The Burman, whom I now supposed to be his secretary, shut the notebook, put it away, and was dismissed.

528

Now two children entered the carriage, a boy of, I supposed, twelve, followed by a girl of about ten. They were handsome and grave, and dressed in Indian style. Falling to their knees, one after the other, they placed their hands together as if in prayer, and touched the floor of the compartment three times with their foreheads. While this ceremony was going on, the old man looked out of the window. As soon as the boy and girl had gone, he opened a suitcase, producing a small pile of *Reader's Digest*s and a biscuit tin commemorating the Coronation of Edward VII, upon which had been screwed a plaque, with the inscription, in English, 'God is Light, Life, and Infinite Magnet'. Turning his attention now to me, he suddenly smiled with a charm for which I had been unprepared, displaying in his dark face fine white teeth and the tip of an extremely pink tongue. 'I am Mr Pereira,' he said. 'I am usually known as Uncle.'

Mr Pereira, despite the patriarchal aloofness of his manner towards his staff and his children, proved to be a genial travelling companion. I judged him to be an Indian, with possible Burmese, and even – as his name suggested – Portuguese blood. Within a few minutes of the train's starting off again, he told me that he was a Buddhist monk, on a kind of sick-leave from his monastery. I gathered that his intense interest in religion had been a recent development and, owing to certain qualms and doubts he had experienced over the Buddhist non-recognition of the eternal soul, he had voluntarily accepted a year's penitential discipline, called tapas, which involved meditation and strict fasting. He had just been released from hospital, where he had spent six weeks recovering from the effects, and was now on his way to Rangoon for further treatment. Fortunately his intellectual capacity had been strengthened along with the depletion of his physical reserves, and now he found no difficulty in the calm acceptance of the personality's extinction in Nirvana. So much, indeed, had he come to crave this release that he had ordered the building of a pagoda on the Sagaing hills. It was to cost fifty thousand rupees, of which sum he had been able to raise a half, thus exhausting the family's capital. But the sacrifice was well worth it, he was convinced; he added suddenly, with the kind of smile that usually goes with a wink, 'I have assuredly purchased a ticket to a higher plane of existence.'

He opened the biscuit tin and took out a photograph of his unfinished work of merit, in the relic chamber of which, he mentioned, had been placed a quantity of earth from the spot where Buddha preached his first sermon. There were other photographs – some of religious objects, such as the Buddha-tooth of Kandy – but mostly of railway disasters. Mr Pereira was an old railwayman, and his affection for his former career had not been obliterated by his subsequent religious preoccupations. At the next station several railway officials joined us, and he entered with vivacity into the technicalities of their shop-talk, while the snapshots of derailed engines and smashed carriages passed, with cries of admiration, from hand to hand. English was the chosen language of these men, who were Burmans and Anglo-Burmans, and they spoke it with pleasure and exuberance. Sometimes they lapsed for a few sentences into Burmese, but even then it was a Burmese studded with English words like 'emergency', 'reconstruction', 'insurgents', 'those sods'. And then the Burmese sentences would fill up with English technical jargon, the Burmese words become rarer and rarer, and once again they would be speaking English.

The indifference displayed by the generality of the passengers towards the hazards of the journey was replaced here by a posititve zest for danger. The railwaymen were eager to display inside information about such alarming topics as the sorry state of the bridges we were passing over, most of which had been blown up several times. It was clear that from their familiarity with the structural weaknesses, of which no layman could have a knowledge, had been bred a kind of possessive affection. Some bridges had been patched up in makeshift ways which flouted engineering theory, and they were proud and happy about it, waiting impatiently for the bridge to come, trying to make me understand why a repaired main-girder could not be expected to withstand the strain we were about to impose, claiming heatedly to feel the bridge – when we had reached it – sway under the train's weight. 'But don't worry,' said a merry little Burmese Deputy-Inspector of Wagons, 'trains don't fall into the river. They blow into the air.' He threw up his hands, made an explosive noise with his lips, and laughed gaily.

In the insurgent areas, as they were called, he also explained, it was usual to economize on materials whenever possible. For instance, as they were always having to replace rails, they used only two bolts to secure them to the sleepers, instead of the regulation four. A colleague now chimed in with the information that the telegraph wires had been cut on the previous night, which always meant an attack; so the engine driver had been given a red ticket – 'to proceed with caution'. But what was the use? The guard, a Mr Brummings, was bound to bring bad luck. He was a regular Jonah, and some drivers refused to have him on the train, although the drivers themselves were no better. They fancied themselves as speed-kings and went so fast that they didn't notice a small gap in the rail. The speaker mentioned that he had jumped a twenty-inch gap in his 'petrol-special' the other day. They were like infantrymen who derive a perverse comfort from exaggerating their sorrows, and it was almost with satisfaction that they acclaimed, just after we had passed Myittha, the violent application of the brakes.

We all got out and walked up to the front. About twenty-five yards from the engine, a small charge had exploded under a rail. The rail had been torn by the explosion, and one of the jagged ends thrust up into the air. Round this the passengers gathered reverently, under their bright display of sunshades. The dull journey had been leavened with incident, and although unexcited they were appreciative. Left to themselves they would have settled down here, as at a pagoda outing, to a picnic. But the engine's imperious whistle called them away, and the train began to back slowly towards the station we had just left, jolting to a halt after covering about a hundred yards, as another mine exploded in its rear.

We were stranded in a dead-flat sun-wasted landscape. The paddies held a few yellow pools, and buffaloes emerged, as if seen at the moment of creation, from their hidden wallows. About a mile from the line an untidy village broke into the pattern of the fields. You could just make out the point of red where a flag hung from the Moghul turret of a house which had once belonged to an Indian landlord. A senior official, going on leave somewhere, had his contribution of pessimism to make. He knew this village from past experience. It was the headquarters of about three hundred Communists. The government was going to have to burn it, he said. And what might the Communists be expected to do now? Nothing much, the official said, with perhaps a trace of regret – at least, judging by previous experiences. At the most they might send a squad of men to look over the passengers, in case there were any political hostages worth taking. With the diffidence which I felt was expected in such unemotional company, I asked what was their attitude to Europeans. The official said he didn't know, because Europeans didn't travel by train. In any case, he would have taken me for a merchant from some vaguely Middle Eastern country, an Iranian perhaps.

The suggestion gave me an idea. My sun-tan had reached a depth which made me darker than some of the Asiatic passengers, and I had got into the habit on journeys like this of wearing a longyi and sandals. Sandals were really essential, because you were always having to kick off your footwear when entering a habitation of any kind – and this included a second-class railway carriage made out of a railway truck. The longyi would have looked like a ridiculous affectation and have been out of the question had there been any Europeans about, but there were none, and in this heat and dirt it had great hygienic advantages. I had two, keeping a clean one in reserve. They could be washed out and dried very quickly, and in this way I managed a change almost every day. It was now agreed among my travelling companions that should insurgents search the train, it would be safer – in view of the Red-Flag Communists' attitude towards imperialist exploiters – for me to be an Iranian. But, said the senior official, nothing whatever would happen – we should see.

His conviction seemed to lack solidity after the account of a similar incident I had just been reading in a copy of *The Burman*, bought at the last station. 'It was 10 o'clock in the morning,' stated the account in the consciously literary style favoured by Burmese reporting, 'that the Special left Shwebo. Twenty-five minutes later it reached milestone 439 3–4 and struck the mine. With the detonation the ill-fated train was subjected to heavy rifle fire. Insurgents then came forwards towards the train to loot ... The exchange of fire quickly drew Township Officer Wetlet, and a squad of UMP (Union of Burma Military Police) on the scene. After a brief engagement the insurgents were routed.' Mr Pereira was quite convinced of his ability to defeat any such assault by the sheer weight of moral authority. At all events, if the insurgents attempted to approach our compartment, he would throw them into utter confusion by the preaching of the Law. For himself, he was quite imperturbable, for besides the other advantages of being a pagoda-builder, he was assured of release from the earthly effects of the Three Calamities: Starvation, Plague, and Warfare.

But there were no signs of life from the village. Time passed slowly, and the old man entertained the company with the resumé of a paper he had read to the Rotary Club of Rangoon. The subject was Charity, and it was illustrated by many instances, some of which were difficult to appreciate in the grotesqueness of the guise the virtue had assumed. There was the story of King Mindon, which I heard for the first time. In a previous existence the king had been a female demon, inhabiting Mandalay Hill, who had sheltered the Buddha, and, cutting off her breasts, had presented them – 'in a devotional ardour', as Mr Pereira put it. This act of merit was rewarded in the next incarnation by a change of sex, as well as the dignity of the Dragon Throne. He also recounted two familiar instances of the Buddha's all-embracing compassion, in his previous existences. On one occasion, when as a human being he had come across a starving tigress with two cubs, he had surrendered himself to be eaten. In the other instance, happening to be incarnated as a jungle-fowl at a time of famine, he had sought out a pilgrim and saved the holy man from death from starvation by the supreme sacrifice. There was nothing in these stories which his hearers would have found difficult to believe. They were not even particularly amazed when the Deputy Inspector of Wagons described a camera he had seen. Persons when photographed with this in their normal attire came out in the nude.

Two hours passed in this way, and a gloominess began to infect the company. The way things were going, it looked as though we should be four days in getting to Rangoon. The train was not allowed to travel at night, and we should be stranded in some God-forsaken spot, with nothing to eat. The exhilaration of escaping a major danger having passed, the smaller inconveniences and imponderables now loomed disproportionately. Mr Pereira began to fret, and to plot alternative courses of action. He had important friends at Thazi, which we might reach in an hour after we started off again, and he wondered whether they could be persuaded to hire us a car to go as far as Yamethin. Or we could leave the train at Thazi, spend the night there in comfort, and then look round for some way of carrying on next day. But supposing we took this chance, and then found that his friends were away? That meant that we might be stranded high and dry for days. No, Mr Pereira finally decided, this was not a good idea. It was too risky. But what were the chances, he wondered, of persuading the station master at Thazi to put a 'petrol special' at the disposition of four distinguished travellers? We could then dash ahead, full speed, in front of the train, and be sure of getting to Yamethin that night. There might be something in that. Once at Yamethin, he could pull strings in all directions to get transport to Pyinmana – even Toungoo. Thus it appeared that even his year's meditation on such themes as futility and evanescence had not entirely cured Mr Pereira of a habit of vain hopes and vain illusions.

Somebody then told him that there was a gang of workmen on the train, going on leave to their homes, and Mr Pereira emitted a scandalized cry. Why had he not been told before? We were carrying spare rails; so let the foreman or senior workman be called into his presence and he would exhort them, with all the weight of his moral influence, to replace the torn rail. Mr Pereira's suitcase was opened in the middle of the carriage floor, and there displayed on the top were his neatly folded yellow robes.

Someone had just gone off for the men, when a distant rattling was heard, and all the passengers were suddenly looking in the same direction. It was a 'petrol special' from Myittha, and it carried not only a breakdown gang, but vendors of samosa (fried minced meat and onion patties), fried chicken, and Vimto – a non-alcoholic beverage which sometimes takes the place of Coca-Cola in soft-currency areas.

Immediately the picnic atmosphere revived. Ladies fluttered from the carriages like unsuspected butterflies from the shadows of a wood; someone began to pluck at the strings of a guitar, and a conjurer gave a free show by the side of the track. Mr Pereira ate heartily, although restricting himself to putto rice, baked in a length of bamboo. Afterwards he spotted my bottle of Mepacrine. 'What are those tablets? Pray give me two to try.' I assured him that they did not contain the vitamins by which he was mildly obsessed; but there was no way of dissuading him from taking the tablets, which he put in his mouth, and sucked with contentment and appreciation.

Soon after we were on our way again. At the next station we collected another permanent addition to our party. This was a junior station master, an Anglo-Burman who was inoffensively drunk for the whole journey. He carried with him a bottle of country spirit, retiring with it to the lavatory from time to time, to avoid Mr Pereira's censorious eye. His Burmese wife and his children were travelling third class, and whenever the train stopped, the numerous family was re-united in our compartment. The degree of this man's befuddlement was uneven, following the curve of an irregular graph which rose and fell gently, dependent upon the maintenance of fresh supplies of country spirit in the villages we stopped at. When he was in a semi-sober condition, he seemed, like most Anglo-Burmans – although they swarm in official positions – to be unhappy with his lot; but soon after the bottle had been refilled he became expansive, in a quite unBurmese way. As this was happening, his opinion of me steadily increased, till by the time he reached the top of the manic curve he believed I was the American Ambassador, and presented me as such to various friends travelling on the train.

At Thazi we met the up-train, returning – six hours late – from Yamethin. It reported the impossibility of reaching Tatkón, as three bridges had been demolished on this side of the town. Bridge-guards had been mortared, and a railway repair-staff kidnapped on the outskirts. Hearing of this, the junior station master, who had promoted himself, in a happy fantasy, to an executive position, decided to go and confer with the engine driver. By this time we were already on our way again, doing thirty miles an hour, and escaping the restraining hands, he got the door open, swung out into space and back again, collapsed on the floor, and went to sleep.

For a short time we had a companion who was not a railwayman but an officer of the Military Police, a thickset fellow with an unusually brutal face. From him I learned a sinister fact which explained the insurgents' war to the death with the UMP, and also, perhaps, threw some light on Tok Galé's ghost story. 'When we take insurgents,' said this man, with a ferocious leer, 'we cut them.' Cut them? – I did not follow. 'We cut them with our dahs,' the fellow said, bringing down his arm in a ferocious swipe. 'In our country there is a belief that the spirits of dead men will guard the bridges.' So that was it, and I wondered how many misguided peasants had been sacrificed to the river spirits in this way.

The bridges were without number. All the important ones were guarded by slit trenches and machine-gun nests, and we stopped to give water to their defenders. Near one was a recent wreck with what looked like a brand-new American locomotive, still shining and well oiled, lying on its side so that we could study its complicated internals. The guards had comfortably installed themselves in 'basha' huts, put together quickly with branches and palm-leaves in a couple of the trucks which had landed upright. The record number of bridges to be blown up in one night in any one administrative area was five, said a member of the repair staff. It was raining 'like the dickens' at the time, and he had to issue fourteen quarts of country spirit to the men, to keep them on their feet and to get the work done. 'By the morning, the trains were speeding on their way. Then my chief sends for me, intending, as I suppose, to bestow a compliment. But this is not so, and all he wants to know is, who is going to pay for the country spirit?' And the man, fat and cheerful, roared with laughter at the memory of his disillusionment.

Listening to such stories I could not help feeling that the keeping open of the Mandalay–Rangoon line must be almost the outstanding example of tenacity in the face of appalling obstacles in the annals of railway history, and that it illuminated a side of the Burmese character which had received little recognition in Colonial days. The speaker had often run up against insurgents, but found them easy enough to get on with if you didn't make the fatal mistake of associating with soldiers. 'They observe us at our labours without hindrance. Sometimes a warning shot rings out and we get to hell. That, my dear colleagues, is the set-up. From running continuously I am rejuvenated. All appetites and sleeping much improved.' Only the other day his 'petrol special' had refused to start after he had been out to inspect a sabotaged bridge, and while he was cleaning out the carburettor a couple of White-Flag Communists had come along and taken him to their headquarters. They took his watch and pocket-book and, after questioning him about the number of government troops in Toungoo, told him that he could go. They expected him to walk home seven miles, although it was after dark. Naturally, he refused, saw to it that he got breakfast next morning, and then asked to see an officer, told him about the watch and pocket-book, and got them back.

CHAPTER TWENTY

Rival Parties

CONFOUNDING all the pessimistic prophecies, we got into Yamethin at nightfall. It was announced that the train would stay there for the night, and return to Mandalay next day, and that passengers might sleep in the train. While Mr Pereira stayed on guard, the junior station master, or JSM as he had better be known, a young Indian wagon-inspector called Nair, and myself, went out to buy our evening meal. There was actually a shop licensed to sell beer. It was tucked away in a side-street, and customers went in under the eye of two or three of the kind of people who gather when an accident has happened, and drank with furtive bravado, standing at an ordinary store-counter. Ice was sent out for and charged separately. We ate curried chicken in an Indian shack where the dust settled so quickly that we covered our plates with palm-leaves in the pauses between eating. Afterwards we chewed betel – in my case for the first time. The taste was at first sweet and sharp, and afterwards slightly soapy, with a faint childhood recollection of the taste of bath water on a sponge. At this point the JSM announced that he was going in search of 'the fancy' which was to be found on the edge of the jungle, and with a cry of 'cheery-bye' reeled happily away into the night. We found out later that he was driven back, without having achieved his purpose, by a government patrol. There was a great deal of military activity in the Yamethin area. The Communists had a stronghold ten miles away at Aingto, and penetrated to the outskirts of the town, where, as I learned from a newspaper when we reached Rangoon, they had held a people's court on the night we were in Yamethin, and executed a prisoner.

A curfew was imposed at nine o'clock, but this did not seem to apply to the precincts of the station where the town's nocturnal activities were concentrated. The water-supply, turned on for a few minutes daily, had been cornered by the enterprising and re-issued here in the form of slabs of ice-cream on sticks. It was also possible to buy a cup of tea, the sale being conditional on the consumption of pyagyo – a fried ball of ground peas and curry. With traditional magnificence a burgher of the town had chosen to celebrate some windfall by offering a free theatrical show – also in the station yard. It was a well-known piece, with a plot about a queen's love for a legless dwarf, that Anouilh himself might have been proud to have invented. For several hours I watched the leisurely unfolding of the story, with its numerous interruptions by slapstick and dancing. About a third of the way through the play I gave up and went back to the carriage.

The others were already there and Mr Pereira, who had just decided to get up and go for a stroll, was told of the curfew. 'Curfew,' he said dreamily, a little later, 'a curious word. Have you ever thought of its origin? I read something about it in a *Reader's Digest*.' He lay stretched out along one of the lower benches, and above him a plank had been let down on a chain to form an upper bunk. Upon this Nair reposed, uncomfortable at the thought of the disrespect involved in sleeping above a venerable pagoda-builder. An argument had raged for some time before the sleeping arrangements had finally been settled and anyone could be induced to occupy this position, left vacant by the fact that Mr Pereira was incapable of the physical effort involved in climbing into the upper bunk.

As it was, he was wakeful and restless. 'I am unable to sleep, Mr Nair,' he moaned. 'Lacking my glass of Wincarnis, I cannot relax. The heat, too, is unseasonable.' Then I found myself waiting for something, a further development of Mr Pereira's discourse, which, as I seemed to have stumbled on a key to his thought-process, I knew must follow. I had only a few moments to wait. 'Psychology has shown us, Mr Nair,' the harsh, pedagogic voice began, 'that there are different levels of sleep ...' The JSM woke up with a groan, sat up in his bunk and said, 'From the jungle's edge, ravishingly she came out to me, like the actress of the screen – Joan, is it? – I do not know her name. But we were restricted by impediment, and – ah ...' He fell back, and his voice trailed off into snores. Out in the yard, the orchestra banged and squealed in endless, zestful improvisation. The wall of the carriage held the heat where the sun had struck it, and an invisible sheet of cellophane across the window prevented any air from entering. Passengers still clung to the platform in unhappy groups, and from the grumbling of their voices an uneasy pattern of dream was forming. A voice murmured, far back in the brain, it seemed, 'Forty-two degrees. Multiply forty-two by nine, and divide by five. Now add thirty-two. Yamethin is the hottest place in Burma. But it is opinion that next month it will be hotter.'

With every morning, at the hour of setting out, came an unfailing exhilaration, when the perfume flowed steadily from the invisible flowering bushes in the forest, which – itself unseen – was there somewhere, beyond the low hills, or, as in Yamethin, crowding at the threshold of the town.

In the early hours Mr Pereira had got up, switched on the light and gone into the lavatory for the scrupulous and lengthy ritual of his toilet. The best time to concentrate, he explained later, was between the hours of four and six, before the bustle of the world destroys the emanations of the higher sphere. 'The brain, Mr Nair, may be likened to a radio machine, of highly tuned receptivity.' And so we lay and struggled weakly on the edge of consciousness, while Mr Pereira splashed about, recited his mantras, and acquired spiritual strength to face the day.

By six thirty, when we stood in the station yard, waiting for lorries, some of this intake of magnetic power had already been expended, and there were even signs of nervous irritability. Besides a following of temporary associates – occupants of other carriages, with whom we were on terms of only slight familiarity – our party consisted of the four of the night before, plus the JSM's wife and three children. Contrary to assurances, no arrangements had been made by the railway company to get passengers to Pyinmana. This was left entirely to their own ingenuity. And although Mr Pereira had several times mentioned powerful friends in Yamethin, who could be relied upon, if the occasion arose, to put transport at our disposal, they were no longer alluded to. Instead, having found that among my many documents was a letter of introduction to the DSP of the town, he urged me to call on this official and endeavour, on the strength of this letter, to have a lorry placed at the disposal of our party. There were several objections to this proposition; the chief being that I saw no reason to appeal to the official unless in a case of genuine emergency. In any case – and this was the argument that carried the weight with Mr Pereira – it was to be supposed that the DSP would not be available before eight, or nine, and by that time any lorry going southwards would most likely have left.

His hopes in this direction having been shattered, Mr Pereira now ordered Nair into action. Within a few minutes Nair was back to say that he had found a lorry that would shortly be leaving for Pyinmana. It was a three-tonner, engaged at that moment in taking on a load of five tons of lead, a few hundred yards from where we stood, down the railway line. It would complete its load with a ton of potatoes, and fifteen passengers, and their luggage. Shortly afterwards it appeared, but Mr Pereira shook his head. He had produced a small handbook on numerology, by an author with the pen-name of Cheerio; it was a best-seller in Burma, although this was the first time I had seen it put to practical use. The number of the truck, he said flatly, was not propitious, and he would not travel by it. His disfavour quickly spread, and the other members of the group also turned away. Happily, another lorry arrived a few minutes later, and its number, 7101, was judged acceptable. It also stopped to take on an immense load of potatoes, upon the towering summit of which we perched, with a splendid but swaying view of the country.

For some reason – probably connected with its supposed vulnerability in case of attack – Mr Pereira refused to accept a seat of honour in the driver's cabin, and had to be lifted, by a kind of alpine rescue feat, to a resting place among the peaks. At intervals of almost precisely five minutes our lorry stopped, while a member of the crew got down, partially dismantled the petrol supply-system, and blew air through it with a foot-pump. Mr Pereira, who had brought out a sheaf of notes dealing with a lecture he had given on the comparison of Buddhism with Christianity, and was about to hold forth, became exasperated with this and even rapped sharply with his stick on the roof of the driver's cabin, whenever the tell-tale spluttering started.

It took us two hours to cover the twenty miles to Tatkón, and here we stopped for lengthy repairs, since, besides the trouble with the petrol supply, the front brakes had seized and had had to be disconnected. I went over to the station and raised the matter of the ghosts with an unemployed ticket collector. He roared with laughter at the absurdity of the rumour. 'Why, anybody knows that it's not everyone who can see a ghost. It's a matter of psychology; therefore they can't frighten *all* passengers.'

After Tatkón my friends were able, with relish, to renew their pessimism. The stretch of road between Tatkón and Pyinmana, they assured me, was the most dangerous in all Burma. The conversation turned naturally on descriptions of atrocious events that had taken place in these hilly and pleasantly wooded surroundings. We were passing through what might have been the Wye Valley, in the exhaustion of late autumn, yet lashed by a strange sun, with a river meandering among the rocks, and eagles flapping overhead. The woods had been patchily and inefficiently burned back from the road, so that there was cover for an ambush only at intervals of about a hundred yards. All the many small bridges had been blown up, and replaced by temporary structures of wood or metal. Sometimes these secondary bridges had been demolished too, so that we were obliged after all to ford the stream in a lurching, swaying rush. Battles had been fought along this main north–south axis. It was a graveyard of 'soft' military vehicles, and there were a few burned-out tanks lying about. Some of these wrecks, bowered in ferns, probably dated from Japanese days, and small dun-coloured birds had taken possession of them and were popping in and out of the shell holes. This drive was a memorable torture. The craters of shells and mines had only been loosely filled in, and the surface had been deeply rutted and macerated by armoured traffic. Sprawled out like fakirs across the protuberances of our potato sacks, we were tossed from side to side and shot into the air as the lorry's wheels crashed into the holes in the road. A few square feet of tarpaulin had been rigged up on a crude frame over our heads, and the sun struck at us through its many openings. Groaningly Mr Pereira implored me for more Mepacrine to help him to endure the ordeal.

We reached Pyinmana by the early afternoon, entering the town by streets where dentists, as if in celebration of a great victory, had hung out many banners, upon which fleshless jaws grinned in ecstasy. The lorry dropped us at the Hwa Sein Store, a wooden-framed building from a Wild Western film, where we fell into chairs round a table, while Mr Pereira, on the verge of collapse, refreshed himself with an Ovaltine. We sat there for half an hour, afraid of what the effort to move might cost us. Sweat glistened like powdered mica on our skins. A Thibetan, vaguely outlined against the sun as if seen in a floodlit aquarium, floated up out of the street. His eyes glowed through the strands of hair hanging down over his face. Untying the yak's-hair knots that secured a paper packet, he showered gems on the table top. The JSM bought an emerald for eight annas, and tenderly presented it to his wife.

A gharry took us to the station, where we found the train that would leave for Rangoon next day already standing at a platform. Here Mr Pereira came into his own at last. Formally presenting himself to the station master, he had a second-class carriage reserved for our party, and a notice was hung on the door to say that it was occupied by railway officials. At the same time, he learned an important piece of news. At Pyinmana, the senior railway staff occupied a small block of flats near the station, and this possessed the splendid amenity of a communal bathroom. The station master recommended us to present ourselves there, precisely at four o'clock, when the water would be turned on for half an hour. He gave us a chit of introduction for the man in charge of the bath.

We went there and found a small group of railwaymen waiting

in reverent silence as if for the performance of some fairly dependable miracle, such as the liquefaction of the blood of St Januarius. The man in charge of the bath stood with his back to the door, of which he held the key. A few years before, the bathroom must have been a showpiece, and even now it was luxurious and sybaritic in the desolation of Pyinmana, which, as an important marshalling yard, must have been bombed on numerous occasions. A few tiles survived on the floor, like a broken Roman mosaic, in an amorphous surface of cement. The bath had a huge chromium-plated tap, which someone still went to the trouble of polishing, although it had been swivelled round until it hung over the floor, and the daily blessing of water was delivered, not through this, which had become no more than a symbol, but from a cruelly naked pipe, which jutted directly from a hole in the wall. Just as the hour of four clanged somewhere in the town, moisture gathered at the rim of the pipe, and the first drops began to splash in the stagnant lake at the bottom of the bath. Any natural desire a Burman might have felt to be the first to assuage his skin's prickly heat, was easily outweighed by considerations of the merit to be earned by deferring to a stranger. I was merely asked not to splash on the floor any of the precious fluid more than I could help. The water was amber-coloured, but, as the man in charge of the bath had proudly claimed, clear. Although quite warm by ordinary standards, it was indescribably refreshing after two scorching, waterless days.

Over the top of the broken door could be seen the remains of a baronial folly in the oriental style, a gabled red-brick house, of which only the façade remained, flanked by two machicolated towers. In the other corner of the view was a pseudo-Renaissance building in the Portuguese style, to which had been added four Moghul turrets, and two towers terminating in onion-shaped cupolas. This, too, had been burned out.

As I stood at the door of the bathroom, while the water evaporated like alcohol from the skin, the whole panorama of the marshalling yards came into view. There was a background of palms partially screening the ruined gothic and Asiatic fantasies, and a few trees with lacquered foliage, from which hung down black beans. Beneath

544

the trees were long lines of goods trucks, most of which would never run on their own wheels again; and distributed about the yards were step-pyramids of railway sleepers, which were in constant demand to prop up temporary bridges. Along the tracks, and round these obstacles, sauntered parading crowds, the girls in longyis of bright silk, and carrying parasols, the men wearing sun-helmets which, being enamelled green and blue, looked like chamber-pots. A dozen Indian labourers were cooking their food, each, for fear of contamination, at a separate fire. There were two sounds, the occasional deep purring of a pagoda gong of rare quality, and the shrieking of kites in the sky. In this scene there were no clear, sharp colours. It was overlaid by yellow light, as if seen through a shop-window over which a sheet of yellow cellophane had been stretched to prevent the goods from fading. To me, coming out of the damp coolness of the bathroom, it was like plunging into warm milk.

Pyinmana had previously been the headquarters of Thakin Than Tun, leader of the White-Flag Communists. (Three months after I left they re-entered the town and fought a battle with government troops in its streets.) From this stronghold, which was later stormed by government troops, he directed the insurrection which broke out on March 6th, 1948; it was the first of a series of revolts directed against the Socialist government by a number of racial and political minorities. Of all the insurgent movements, that of the White-Flag Communists in combination with the Karen National Defence Organization was the most serious. It started off with a succession of victories. Towns were captured all over Burma, until finally, a year after the outbreak, Mandalay itself fell; and Rangoon, and the government's survival, were threatened. After this the tide slowly turned. The insurgents were beaten by shortage of ammunition, their internal divisions, and by the tenacity of the government forces. Mandalay was recaptured shortly after its fall, and all the large towns in insurgent hands occupied one by one. The Karens withdrew into the mountainous area known as Karenni, lying between the towns of Loi Kaw, Papun, and Thaton, while the Communists, the

PVO, and the army mutineers took refuge in the small villages and the jungles, where they still carry on their fight. The Communists appear slowly to be absorbing their competitors, with a consequent accretion of strength.

The Burmese insurrections have a formless and bewildering complexity that make them almost incomprehensible to the Westerner who has not studied their history on the spot. To an outsider the programmes of all the insurgent groups seem identical. They are all apparently of the extreme Left, and resolved to extirpate landlords and capitalists, permit freedom of worship, distribute the land to the peasants, and smash fascism. Each body accuses all the others of failing to respect these ideals, and all accuse the AFPL (Anti-Fascist People's Freedom League) government of being no more than a sham behind which the brutal exploitation of the country by foreign interests is permitted to continue.

Behind the façade of anti-government 'democratic fronts', and the barrage of allegation, one suspects on examining the facts a clash of power-hungry personalities, from which some have emerged defeated to become the relentless opponents of those who have reached the top. The departure of the British from Burma left a yawning vacuum of governmental office to be filled, and offered in the army the prospect of immediate promotion for thousands of officers and men. Many were hurt in the scramble. As an illustration of the attitude of the disappointed place-hunter – and of the real motive behind a political coup – a better example could not be found than the two leaders of the army mutiny who, after announcing their intention of abolishing feudal landlordism, offered to surrender if they were guaranteed the portfolios of Defence and Home Affairs.

The PVOs (People's Voluntary Organization) were originally the Burmese equivalent of the Maquis, formed after the war into this body in an attempt to keep its members under disciplined control while the process of post-war resettlement went on. The resettlement of the rank and file of peasants was a simple matter, but the officer class, having tasted power, refused to return to the banality of its pre-war existence, and quietly refilled the ranks as fast as they were emptied with any restless spirits who cared to join, irrespective of military or resistance services. They then drew up their political programme, but since it had to be Leftist, and there was nothing they could think of to add to that of the Communists, or of the government, they amalgamated these programmes, but dropped from one the expropriation of foreign concerns, and from the other, the land reforms. The PVOs revolted in July 1948, when the Communist insurrection was well under way, and for a time joined forces with them. Later they fought each other with particular ferocity, and the PVOs split into two groups, white and yellow, the whites remaining underground and the yellows joining the Government to fight their erstwhile comrades.

The formation of the Red-Flag Communist organization, as an off-shoot of the original Burma Communist Party, appears likewise to have been a matter of internal politics and of political rivalry between the two principal figures in the movement. Thakin Than Tun, who headed the party before the split occurred, served as a minister during the Japanese occupation, while Thakin Soe, leader of those who broke away, spent most of the war as an underground fighter. It was his contention that as the Communist Party was a party of struggle, only those fashioned by struggle could give correct leadership. He also accused Thakin Than Tun of misappropriation of party funds, and the latter retaliated by an attack on Thakin Soe's morals, which were said to be lax even by the easiest of Burmese polygamistic standards. After the break each side gave priority over the other political tasks in hand to the other's extermination. Thakin Soe, however, by the severity and ruthlessness of his methods has continually lost the support of the Burmese peasantry, while his White-Flag rivals by their relative mildness and strict discipline have extended their influence, and have even attracted middle-class cultivators – whom Thakin Soe would be inclined to extirpate as Kulaks – into their fold.

It is interesting to study the phrasing of the manifestos produced by these various parties. The language of political censure, monotonous and repetitive as it is at any time, is further enfeebled here by a very special Burmese problem. It seems that at some time, perhaps at the turn of the century, when the Fathers of the Western Left were relaxing with their families at the Berlin Tiergarten, they were much impressed by the appearance, and by what they read of the habits, of certain animals; and on the basis of this composed a short lexicon of execration, which unfortunately their political inheritors in all parts of the world have taken over. In a Buddhist environment, however, such animals as hyenas, jackals, and vultures, eaters of carrion-flesh, and not killers in their own right, occupy a highly honourable position. Much strain is therefore put upon the remaining clichés of political abuse. The Karens, who would probably be reactionary enough if ever they could seize power, call the present government 'collaborators and stooges'; the Burmese Army is ineptly described as the 'handmaid of the imperialists'; while the system is 'dominated by adulterers, thieves, dacoits, self-seekers, and those who are extremely vicious'. The PVOs propose to wipe out 'such opportunists as bad-hats, landlords, counter-revolutionaries, and deviationists' – deviationist having become here a meaningless term of abuse, since the PVOs subscribe to no Party line. They themselves, in fact, are described as deviationists by the Communists, who accuse them in their manifesto entitled 'Why we are fighting the PVO' of 'sucking deliciously' the freshly spilt blood of fighters for freedom and democracy. Each party and movement reviles the others, and the government in power, as 'fascists' – another word from which the meaning has drained. All speak of the activities of their own side as an expression of that mystic entity, 'the people' – the people's government, or the people's will.

To have completed this almost utter chaos, it would have been necessary only to introduce the warring religious factions, now endemic in Indo-China, but in Burma excluded by the universality of Buddhism. In the situation of this unfortunate country there is an element of grim Wellsian prediction come to fulfilment.

CHAPTER TWENTY-ONE

The Buffalo Dance

STANDING ON a high place in Pyinmana – the balcony of the railwaymen's flats – and looking out across the derelict rolling-stock, the scorched brick and twisted girders, one saw a glitter of fire, an encrusted brilliance of towers and turrets, that arose shining over at the edge of the town. Even at a mile's distance there was no doubt that this was some gaudy pretence, but of such a magnitude that a visit, even in this murderous sunshine, was not to be avoided.

Mr Nair agreed to come with me and, cautiously picking our way through the woods of shadow, we made towards this lustrous illusion, through mean lanes scavenged by dogs which disease had clipped into grotesque poodle shapes. We found a field full of Chinese pavilions with streaming banners, joss-houses, pagodas with many-tiered roofs, Tartar tents, huge kiosks with façades of peacocks and dog-faced lions. It was a city that might have been built by an Imperial army encamped for a lengthy siege, and in it had been assembled all the glorious beginnings of fair-ground architecture and carnival floats. It was extraordinary what opulence had been achieved merely by the endless variegation of colours – mostly metallic – and decorative shapes with which every surface had been closely covered. In their erection of this dreamland of wood and paper, the people of Pyinmana seemed to have reacted in an understandable way to the drabness of civic reality. There was something defiant in its spurning of the realities. At night-time there would be theatrical shows, and boxers would dance in their corners before butting and clawing each other behind the peacock façades; but in the mean time, the place was deserted with the exception of a small crowd gathered at a booth in a corner to watch a nat-pwè.

The booth was roughly built of woven bamboo, its floor covered with matting. There was a shelf running round three sides, and on this the images of the thirty-seven nats squatted moodily. They were a poor collection of idols. Reflecting the fall in dramatic pitch of Burmese life, such god-like attributes as a dozen arms, each raised to flourish a sword, had disappeared, discarded in the nat evolution as something now as useless as the tail in humans. The convincing malevolence of some of the images to be seen in collections, carved in the days when the nats presided at human sacrifices, inspired spectacular dacoities, and bullied kings, was missing here. These were the mean faces of black-marketeers, of usurers calculating percentages and premeditating foreclosure. Among the images was a gilded buffalo mask, also unimpressive as a work of art. The horns were entwined with leaves and sprigs of herbs.

At the moment of my arrival two stout, middle-aged Burmese women were weaving about in a dance in the cleared space before the images. The dance had no particular form; there were none of the symbolical hand or head movements imported from India into the South-East Asian dance, and none of the painfully learned acrobatics of the Burmese. These were the spontaneous gyrations of the devotees of a West Indian revivalist cult, preceding, perhaps, an orgy of testifying. The shapeless robes went with the dance. There was an orchestra of drums, gongs, and a squealing hnè; and its members, playing with a zest bordering on fury, kept the dancers in a continuous whirl. Before the dancers had set themselves in motion helpers had bustled round them carefully adjusting their turbans, but these immediately became untied, allowing their hair to stream from them like black comet tails. With eyes closed they collided with each other and went spinning away in new directions. Cheek-bones and foreheads took on a polish of sweat; foam bespattered their chins. The women helpers dashed after them with bottles of beer, which the dancers sucked at sightlessly and showered back through mouths and nostrils. The audience remained strangely untouched by this frenzy. They laughed and chatted sociably, and gave the breast to their young babies. Although all were drably and poorly dressed by Burmese standards, there must have been some who were socially important, because acolytes kept coming and presenting them with sprigs of greenery. Suddenly there was a stir of interest. The dancers,

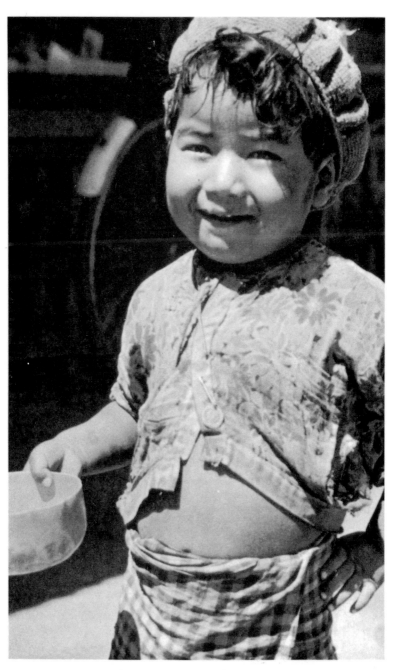

Child beggar in the market at Maymyo

On the road to Lashio; a Shan beggar

The Kachin headman's womenfolk

A corner of the Nam Hkam market

Pot-sellers at Shwegu

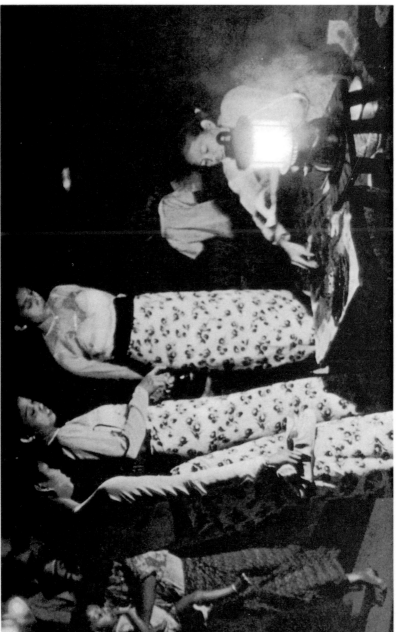

Night market at Kyaukmyaung

Nat-ka-daws – wives of the spirits

Possessed by the buffalo-spirit

Rangoon: at the Shwedagon Pagoda

colliding once again, had fallen to the ground. Now they writhed on their stomachs towards the nat images, and having reached them remained to pray convulsively.

The priest was tall for a Burman, and I could not help fancying that he bore a facial resemblance to certain of the nats. There was an impudent self-possession about him. He was quite clearly a powerful person, a stork among the frogs. I was struck once again by the extraordinary similarity between professional counterparts of different races. I had seen this face, this confident and slightly contemptuous manner, in Haiti; but that time it had been a voodoo houngan. Before beginning his part of the ceremony the priest sent one of his assistants, who was importantly dressed in a threadbare British officer's uniform, to tell me to remove my sandals, and not to take photographs when he danced. Although I was not actually inside the booth, and therefore technically showing no disrespect, I decided to acquiesce in the first demand, and to ignore the second, although with discretion.

Taking up a spray of leaves in each hand the priest went into an easy, swinging dance. He waved the leaves about as a Jamaican obeahman might have waved a pair of maracas. After a time he stopped and signalled gropingly, eyes closed, for the buffalo mask to be brought. At this the crowd stiffened. The amiable gossip died away. Spitting out their cheroots, the members of the orchestra struck out in a new, purposeful rhythm. The mask was handed to the priest by one of the fat dancers. She held it at arm's length, and he took it from her, and keeping it about a foot from his face, began another stage of the dance. This consisted in mimicking the actions of a buffalo charging, turning away, charging again; directed at first one section, then another of the shrinking crowd. He then stopped, put on the mask, and immediately fell down. The drama of the moment was much heightened by the crash of drums and gongs. These barbaric and wonderfully timed musical efforts jarred one for a hair-raising fraction of a second into a sensation of the reality in the performance.

'The buffalo-priest lay writhing on the ground. At the end of the convulsion he raised himself painfully to his knees, and then charged, head down – with remarkable speed in view of his posture – into a group of children, who fled screaming from the booth. He was restrained from following them, and from charging in other directions, by the prayers, the entreaties, the strokings, of several of his female followers. Finally, quietened down, he was led, still on hands and knees, to a large enamelled basin, in which floated bananas and green herbs. Thus the ceremony culminated in the man's making a ritual meal – of buffalo food. Pushing his face beneath the mask down into the bowl, he caught a banana in his teeth, and emerging, ate half of it complete with skin. After that, the buffalo mask was untied and put back on the shelf, and while the priest was led away into the background to recover, the female dancers prepared themselves once more to go into action.

What was the meaning of this ritual? Clearly the women were nat-ka-daws – spirit wives, and professional prophetesses, whom I had read all about in a little booklet on the subject, published in Burma. Nat-ka-daws prophesy publicly on such occasions, and by private arrangement on the payment of a small fee. It is a regular and recognized profession, of which there are so many members that it has been seriously suggested that they should be classified under their own occupational heading in the forthcoming census of Burma. They differ from spirit mediums in most other parts of the world in that they are considered as married to the insatiably polygamistic nats who possess them, and who through them convey their wishes and decisions to animistic Burmese humanity. Such a relationship usually begins with the nat falling in love with the woman. According to my Burmese authority, he visits her at night, well perfumed and 'dressed in up-to-date clothes' (and one quails before the vision of a Mongolian folk-hero in an American-style flowered sports-shirt and a plastic belt). When actually in possession of his lady-love, he can be expelled by a saya – an expert in white magic – or (in the Colonial days) by an officer of the Crown in full uniform. Nothing is said in the booklet about a nat's reaction to Burmese republican officials. Normally, however, a woman's relations or friends would not interfere, because, just as possession by a lwa carried social prestige among the Haitian adherents of the voodoo cult, it is a paying proposition in the lower strata of Burmese society for a woman to become the bride of a nat.

The union is regularized at the bridegroom's expense, with mystical entertainments on a lavish scale, the nat usually being represented by another wife, to whom the bride is solemnly given away by her parents or guardians. The occasion is one for rejoicing. The girl has been recognized by the powerful guild of nat-ka-daws as one of themselves. From that time on she earns an easy living by fortune-telling, or, if she decides to go into business, the capital is put up 'by the nat', that is to say by the wealthy and powerful association of his wives. Nat-ka-daws, owing to their prestige and power among their neighbours, prosper in all their enterprises. The principal drawback to this arrangement appears to be that a girl who has married a nat cannot remarry without his permission, which is rarely given. But a most fortunate aspect of the matter lies in the fact that the nats are said to prefer spiritual to physical charm, and that women whose lack of attractions has kept them single are often married off in this way. The union is supposed to be far from platonic, and the nat's visits, in incubus shape, are said to be more frequent than those of a normal husband.

Here as elsewhere the phenomenon of possession is accompanied, according to medical evidence, by some physical change; the heart's action is increased, cheeks are flushed, respiration is shallow and of the thoracic type; the subject sweats profusely, reaches a kind of cataleptic state with complete insensibility to pain, and, when questions are answered, often replies in a masculine voice. These and other signs are closely observed by experts, who decide whether possession has taken place, and who are also able to decide by variations of manner and expression which nat is involved. It is particularly interesting that a nat-ka-daw when possessed by Shwe-Na-be, the dragon nat, writhes and wriggles in snake-like fashion, in exactly the same way as do devotees of the voodoo cult when possessed by dumballa, the West African serpent-god. After learning something of the nat-ka-daws, I now realized for the first time what the Jesuit Borri had meant when he had said, writing in the seventeenth century, that it was considered highly honourable in

Indo-China to become the wife of the devil, and that such unions were much indulged in by upper-class Annamese women, who sometimes produced eggs as a result. It now seemed clear to me that at one time formal matches with the spirits were arranged by other Mongolian peoples than the Burmese, and that it might have been – and might still be in remote parts of the Indo-Chinese peninsula – a fairly widespread custom, linked up with the legendary oviparous kings.

It remains to offer a possible explanation of the buffalo dance, to hazard a guess at the legendary or even historical occasion that had inspired it – since other animistic ceremonies, and in particular the one at Taungbyon, re-enact in dramatic form some tragic story that has become ineradicably fixed in folk-memory. I had never heard of a buffalo-nat before, and it is certainly not included in the exclusive original circle of the Thirty-Seven. The only explanation, therefore, that I can offer is based upon the remark of an onlooker, who said that the ceremony commemorated the ravaging of the country in ancient times by a buffalo.

In my superficial studies of Burmese history, limited to what has been translated into English, I have been able to find only one noteworthy mention of a buffalo. This occurs in the description of the great King Anawrahta's death. Although the Burmese kings in their lifetimes conformed sometimes to the prosaic pattern of history, as we understand it, the manner of their deaths – particularly that of Anawrahta – was often Arthurian. The king had been returning from a profitable expedition, during which he had built monasteries, dams, channels, reservoirs, and canals, and was just entering the city gates of Pagan when a hunter approached to report that a wild buffalo called Çakkhupala was ravaging the countryside. On hearing this the king turned back, with the pious intention of ridding his people of this menace. He was surrounded by seven thousand ministers, and at the head of four armies, but, says the chronicle, 'the moral karma of the king's former acts was exhausted'. The buffalo, which had been an enemy in a previous life, charged and reached over the back of the royal elephant, and gored the king to death. So the king's ministers and his hosts, his queens, the fifty hump-backed women and the fifty bandy-legged women who served him wearing livery of gold, the women to sound tabors, the women drummers, harpists, and trumpeters, all broke up and scattered in confusion.

What are the facts that have been transmuted here into a dream? Did the nation, symbolized in the person of the king, undergo a tragic experience, suffering perhaps at this time – or even centuries earlier, since the annals are very confused – defeat the hands of invaders whose totem was the buffalo? An interesting speculation. Burmese written history, which speaks of a succession of five hundred and eighty-seven thousand kings, and omitted from the records events which failed to conform to sacred predictions, is not necessarily more reliable than the legends of the people. But, at all events, it seemed likely that here was all that remained in the popular memory of an ancient tragedy, whatever it was: a piece of self-hypnotic mumbo-jumbo, and two fat women who believed themselves to be the brides of a demon.

Night, which lay like a stifling cloak upon Pyinmana, brought no relief from the heat. In the station precincts, there was a curious gathering of passengers, and of those who used the station yard for their social promenadings, in a long line on each side of the train which would leave next morning for Rangoon. The JSM came teetering up to explain. He was sucking an American Cream Soda through a straw in the belief that it was country spirit, and his expression, as the beads of perspiration formed and followed regular channels down his face, was of a man bravely enduring torture. The people, the JSM explained, were waiting for the water-truck. At any moment an engine would draw it along the rails past our train, stopping at each carriage to fill up the small cistern carried in the roof. Usually there was an overflow from each cistern, and those who were waiting would catch the surplus, or as much as they could of it, in their cups, or just wet their clothes with it.

Shortly afterwards the water-tanker came along, with an

entourage of well-dressed citizens, who, as the water streamed down the coaches, pressed themselves tightly against the woodwork, or even got down on the track and crouched by the wheels to allow the water to trickle on their upturned faces, their chests, their backs. Some of the men stripped off their shirts, soaked them and put them on again.

Finding that while the passengers luxuriated in momentary dampness our compartment had been left empty, I went in to begin the stealthy massacre of the mosquitoes and cockroaches, a task which I had carried out in several furtive instalments on the journey from Mandalay to Yamethin. This time I was less successful. All the cockroaches, which were as tame and trusting, and as fat in their way as monastery catfish, were disposed of in a few seconds, and I was quite absorbed with mosquitoes, which could be caught in the air, sometimes two at a time, and squashed by closing the fist, when I heard a sound like a slight groan. Mr Pereira had hoisted himself silently into the carriage, and was standing behind me, his eye fixed on the corpse of a cockroach, lying feet uppermost in the middle of the floor. Did I realize, he asked me, as soon as he could get command of his voice, that this poor, assassinated creature might quite well be my grandfather in another incarnation? The obvious answer to this was that had my grandfather indeed been reincarnated as a Burmese cockroach, I should have regarded it as an act of kindness to release him from what seemed to me – and would probably, from what I remembered of him, have seemed to him – an unsatisfactory existence. This only produced a sermon on Kan and Karma, on cause and effect, into which the matter of merit-acquisition, and thence pagoda-building, inevitably entered. Rebellious at last, I asked him if he didn't think that in his own case, it would have been equally, or even more, meritorious to have given his money to the Mandalay leper asylum. The classic answer would have been, not at all, because the lepers were working off in their present unfortunate condition the adverse balance of their karma, created through misdeeds in previous existences, and there was therefore nothing much to be done about it. But by this time Mr Pereira had recovered himself completely and, remembering the need for Absolute Tolerance, however mistaken a point of view, mildly agreed that it might have been a good thing – the soft answer that turneth away wrath, which, in his case, meant one more mark on the credit side of the balance.

Thus the dreadful night wore on. Since the departure platform of the Rangoon train had become also the town's social centre, there was an enduring babel, in which the keynote was sounded by a mad woman who stood in a clear place for many hours, haranguing the crowd. She was well dressed and cared for, and whenever her hair, which was crowned with cornflowers, escaped its bounds, someone would rearrange it for her. Because of the dry quality of the heat, the temptations and pleasures of life had been simplified, and reduced to the alleviation of thirst. The devil presiding over the delights involved was a dreaming, white-bearded Hindu, who kept a stall with bottles of Vimto and American Cream Soda. His stock, besides these, consisted of a block of ice, and an ordinary carpenter's plane. When a drink was ordered, he would get the cap off the bottle after a long struggle, take a glass out of a slop-pail full of dirty water, and pour in the contents of the bottle. Then he would unwrap the block of ice from its grimy sacking, plane off a sliver, crumple it and put it in the glass, when it would instantly vanish, as if plunged into boiling water. He was agonizingly slow, and as these bottles of branded mineral waters are supposed in any case to contain a quantity nicely calculated not quite to quench the thirst, the only thing to do was to keep a standing order. Once the ice ran out, and there was a long delay while another block was dragged by means of a pair of clamps and a chain along the platform.

At about midnight, I carried away what remained of the old man's bottles, went back to the carriage and climbed into my bunk. Mr Pereira, although not asleep, seemed pleasantly relaxed. 'This evening, Mr Nair, I was able to obtain my customary Wincarnis. I believe that I shall pass a good night.'

The JSM by ransacking the town had found a supply of country spirit and was occupied by delusions of grandeur. A rumbling Johnsonian undertone had entered his speech.

'Yesterday was it? – No, of course, it could not have been

yesterday – but no matter – I encountered at the residence of a friend of mine, where I was taking food, the ADPW (Assistant Director of Permanent Ways). After saluting him, I broached the matter of promotion.'

'And what response did he vouchsafe?'

'My dear colleague—' (the voice faltered, with a sudden alcoholic change in the wind's direction) 'he invited me to get to hell.'

'The dickens he did! These buggers are all the same.'

The next day was passed among the parched greys and yellows of harvested paddy-fields, which now awaited the rains. From this dun wilderness arose nothing but a skyline serration of pagodas, and the low, formless silhouettes of towns which had once been dynastic capitals, the greatest and most glorious of South-East Asia in their day. '...The streetes thereof are the fayrest that I have seene ... the lodgings within are made of wood all over gilded, with fine pinacles, and very costly worke, covered with plates of golde.' Thus wrote Caesar Fredericke of the capital of the kingdom of Pegu, now dissolved in anarchy. The names of these towns were now, as we passed through them, the motive of a melancholy commentary. Ela. 'That was a nice place. It was a cooling station, but it has been burned several times, also recently. Steel Brothers' saw-mill, also burned down.' Toungoo. 'These are territories dominated by the Karens. Much damage has been done. I do not think they can rebuild. It is stated that the leaders have offered ceremonial food to the monks who will present a petition for amnesty. Also these men's leader Saw Tapu Lay is observing daily Sabbath. I do not know. But still shooting continues with all modern weapons, and the dropping of bombs.' Pegu. 'Mostly there are Communists who will not agree that food shall come into this town. Therefore all the paddy remains in the villages, and the farmers cannot eat so much rice. They would like to sell this paddy to the government who will pay rupees two hundred and eighty-five per hundred bags. But this rice they may not sell and they cannot eat it. In this town the people do not eat. It is very ruined.'

CHAPTER TWENTY-TWO

The Shwedagon

IN RANGOON the great annual pagoda festival was being held, that of the full moon of Tabaung, which coincides with Easter in the West. The Shwedagon Pagoda is the heart and soul of Rangoon, the chief place of pilgrimage in the Buddhist world, the Buddhist equivalent of the Kaaba at Mecca, and, in sum, a great and glorious monument. 'The fairest place, as I suppose,' thought Ralph Fitch, 'that is in the world.' Fitch had seen the splendours of the Mogul Empire, and it is a consolation to think that as the Shwedagon has been, if anything, improved since Elizabethan days, there still exists one tiny oasis, in a desert of pinchbeck modernity, where the prodigious glamour of the ancient Orient endures.

The special sanctity of the Shwedagon arises from the fact that it is the only pagoda recognized as enshrining relics not only of Gautama, but of the three Buddhas preceding him. Those of the Master consist of eight hairs, four of them original, given in his lifetime, and four others, miraculous reproductions generated from them in the course of their journey from India. These, according to the account in the official guidebook, flew up, when the casket containing them was opened, to a height of seven palm trees. They emitted rays of variegated hues, which caused the dumb to speak, the deaf to hear, and the lame to walk. Later, a rain of jewels fell, covering the earth to knee's depth. The treasure buried with these relics was of such value that, centuries later, the report of it reached the ears of the King of China, who made a magic figure in human form, and sent it to rob the shrine. This creature, says the chronicle, was so dazzled by the pagoda's appearance that it hesitated, and while in this bemused state was attacked and cut to pieces by the Shwedagon's spirit-guardians. It was the habit of the Burmese kings to make extravagant gifts for the embellishment of the Shwedagon, diamond vanes, jewel-encrusted finial umbrellas, or at least their weight in gold, to be used in re-gilding the spire. The wealth that other oriental princes kept in vaults and coffers was here spread out under the sun to astound humanity. Two of the three greatest bells in the world were cast and hung here. Both were seized by foreigners – one by the Portuguese, and one by the British – and both, causing the capsizal of the ships that carried them away, were sunk in the river. Shinsawbu, Queen of the Talaungs, won so much respect by building the great terrace and the walls that the most flattering thing the Burmese could think of to say about Queen Victoria was that she was a reincarnation of this queen.

Early on the morning of Good Friday, when the festival was at its height, I took a car out to the pagoda to gather a few last-minute impressions of the Burmese *en fête*. The Shwedagon lies three or four miles to the north of the town. The last quarter of a mile I covered on foot, while ahead a volcano of gold rose slowly up from among the trees, into the dusty blue of the sky. Pilgrims, when afar off, prostrate themselves in the direction of this cone as it comes first into sight. The road was lined with shrines and monsters. Streams of jeeps went past, taking early-morning worshippers. A few of them were disguised with a carnival decoration of cardboard peacocks, and were carrying boys, about to enter the novitiate, to pray at the pagoda before the ceremony began. The boys wore expensive imitations of the old Burmese court dress, with gilt helmets and epaulettes like sprouting wings, and their attendants struggled to hold golden umbrellas over their heads.

I left my shoes with a flower-seller at the entrance to the covered stairway, bought some flowers from her, and began to climb the steps. There were two or three hundreds of them, left purposely rough and uneven – like the *pavé* in a French village – to ensure a slow and respectful approach. All the way up, there were stalls selling flowers, gongs, votive offerings, and ugly toys. Barefooted crowds were climbing and descending the steps with the murmuring of hushed voices, and the rustle of harsh, new silks. The air was full of the odour of flowers standing in vases. From somewhere above, light was spreading down the dark shaft, and from its source, too, the sound – like a deep, melodious breathing – of gongs.

Coming out of the cavernous approach on to the wide, glistening expanse of terrace, I plunged suddenly into the most brilliant spectacle I had ever seen. Fitch, a merchant adventurer, who had surveyed without comment the splendours of the Venice, the Ormuz, the Goa and the East Indies of his day, had stood here in admiration, although unable to refrain from a sour aside on the vanity of consuming gold in such a way. The terrace is flanked by shrines, with a press of guardian ogres, fabulous beasts, and mild-faced, winged gorgons squeezed in between and behind them; and then, in the immediate background, rises a golden escarpment, a featureless cliff of precious metal, spreading a misty dazzlement, in which the crawling shapes of pilgrims, sticking on their gold-leaf, are black, vaguely seen insects.

The innumerable foreground shrines were banked with flowers, and decked with the votive parasols which usefully protect an image from the sun in a tropical country and often replace the candles necessary to light its cavern in the north. Round the glittering pyramid went Rangoon's Easter-parade of the gay and the devout. When they wanted to pray – which they did most poetically, with offerings of flowers held between the clasped palms – there were hundreds of images to choose from, of gold, of silver, of marble or wood. (Like most peoples who incline themselves before images, Buddhists insist with the gravest emphasis that they are not worshipping the material object, but the great principle it represents.) People worshipped individually, or in groups, in the large shrines or out in the hot sunshine of the terrace, prostrating themselves vaguely towards the spire of the pagoda. Year-old babies were lowered tenderly into the ritual position, where, often unable to straighten themselves, they sprawled in adoration, until recovered. On this day there were many ways to acquire merit: by buying water (in petrol cans) from the sellers and pouring it over the images that sat in the hot sun; by re-lighting candles that had gone out, and re-placing parasols that had fallen down; by taking up the deer's antlers provided, and striking a gong, and then the ground beneath it, to call the attention of the nats of the earth and sky to the worshipper's prayers.

Until the recent troublous times Buddhists from all over the East, journeying as freely as did European pilgrims to Santiago de Compostela and Monte Sant' Angelo, visited the Shwedagon for this festival. Now, apart from the Burmese, there were only Thibetans, whose tenacious piety nothing could daunt.

A few hundred yards from the foot of the pagoda, the government had organized a secular festival, a combination of a pwè and industrial samples-fair, that was not quite successfully one thing or the other. At night it came to vociferous life beneath the golden symbol of renunciation shining in the moonlit sky above it.

There was an open-air theatre with an actress and two clowns, but it was not very good. Perhaps the atmosphere was wrong. The formal organization seemed to have stripped the thing of its spontaneity. Although the loudspeakers poured out a tremendous babel of noise, and the lights hurt the eyes, this could not compare for authentic quality with the pwès got up by the neighbours of the various districts of Kemmendine.

I spent half an hour watching the boxing, noticing that pongyis were allowed in to see this ungodly spectacle without charge. Half the audience were members of the yellow robe. The boxers came out and prostrated themselves, foreheads touching the ground, to their corners; the obeisance was returned by their seconds. The challenger then executed a very slow war-dance to the music of drums and flutes, stopping occasionally to beat himself on the chest in the Tarzan manner. After that the opponents advanced towards each other with ballet steps, like *Ramayana* champions about to hurl fiery javelins. Suddenly they went into action, leaping into the air like fighting-cocks. There was much initial flurry, an exciting spectacle lasting a few seconds, when both men tried to floor each other with flying kicks. But this exuberance soon died down, as it does in fighting-cocks too. A clinch followed with unrestricted use of knees, fists, and elbows. The winner is decided when, as a spectator explained, 'the first blood oozes out'. With typical regard for foreign susceptibilities this man was kindly doing his best to outline the rules governing the contest, when he was roughly interrupted by a forthright Westernized fellow who said, 'Nothing is debarred to them. They may even kick each other in the sensitive parts.'

At midnight a straight theatrical show started in one of the tents, and I sampled an hour of a performance that would go on all night. The first scene showed a young Burman engaged in the hopeless courtship of a girl who, it was made clear, led him on, only to spurn him cruelly. At first she smiled, but the moment he approached, her smile turned to a grimace of contempt. These tactics were repeated several times. It was most baffling. But then the scene changed and we were whisked back in time a hundred years or so, to be present at a function of the court, with our hero in a previous existence as a prince, and the lady who had first been treating him with such unexplained malice in the role of a minor lady of the palace. By their gestures it was evident that the prince had trifled with her affections, and was now casting her off in favour of one more suited to his station. The scene changed again ... and so did the epoch. What an aid to a flagging plot, to be able to extend the device of the flash-back, not only to the characters' pasts, but to their previous incarnations! But also, alas, how it holds up the action!

Much of the industrial section of the festival could not have been more boring. As most native Burmese industries are still in the planning stage, there was little to see. One booth gave a soap-making demonstration; another tried to extract drama from the workings of an automatic self-photographing machine; a third displayed a revolting collection of Kewpie dolls, under a banner which said, 'Burma makes fine rubber toys'. But there was one exhibit – and it was the main one – which amply compensated for the dullness of the rest. This was the pavilion the government had taken for its anti-corruption campaign. The Burmese have no objection at all to the washing of dirty linen in public, and at this time Burmese newspapers were full of stories of the various rackets practised by government officials. The current scandal was over import-licences, in which, it seemed, a great trade was going on. They were usually obtained by persons who had no experience whatever, and no capital, but who happened to have a friend or relative in the government. Sometimes such shadow-firms, with accommodation addresses, turned out, upon investigation, to be conducted by the wives of the high officials themselves. In any case, the licence when granted was sold to a firm of established reputation, usually at a price equal to the landed value of the goods – ninety per cent of which, however, was paid by the intermediary, or shadow-firm, as a bribe to the official granting the licence. As an immediate result of this system, the prices of the imported goods affected were enormously increased, usually to double the normal figure, or more. What was more pernicious in the long run, from the national point of view, was that although in a desperate financial condition, Burma found itself importing all kinds of useless luxuries upon which this toll could be levied. One of the letters published in the press instanced the licences granted to import silk from Japan, which Burma, as a silk producer, does not require. The importers turned out to be a timber-cutting company and a flour mill.

In the Anti-Corruption Pavilion, these manipulators were dealt with, with a hint of defeatism, perhaps, as far as this life went. Seeming to resign themselves to the wicked man's prosperity in this world, the Burmese government had set themselves to show what awaited him in the next. For their illustrated fable they had chosen a mild fellow of average virtue and weakness, lifted from a comic-strip or toothpaste advertisement, and his downfall was ascribed to the promptings of an ambitious wife, a fact which drew much protest in the Rangoon press from feminists.

In the first of a series of pictures he is shown relaxing from departmental cares in the surroundings of a modest home, listening thoughtfully to the pleadings of his wife, who, seated on the arm of the sofa, bends over him to pour the poison of covetousness into his ear. In Picture Two, he has already sold his soul to the devil. The furniture has been modernized, and there is a big radio set on the table. The honest mediocrity of his appearance has been rectified. He wears a made-up turban. His wife – since the dress of Burmese women has reached an apex of taste which no mere access of ill-gotten wealth can assail – is as before; but there is a twinkle of gems at her throat. Picture Three. Having over-eaten, the husband dies of an acute attack of indigestion. His soul is seen leaving his body. In a vertical position, and respectably clothed, it floats upwards, and is about to pass through a modernistic candelabra. Four. A judge of hell receives him, in appropriately Dantesque surroundings; a rocky area, where huge vultures perch at intervals. The judge is dressed, with the solid conservatism of the last generation, in the Burmese equivalent of a morning suit and top-hat. Picture Five. It now comes to light that the young man has only once accepted a bribe and, most fortunately, it is also discovered that the link connecting soul and body is not quite severed. He is to be given another chance. But to make sure the warning has not been lost, the judge first takes him on a brief, conducted tour of hell, which is organized, on Gilbert and Sullivan lines, to make the punishment fit the crime. Thus arms-traffickers are chased by ravening hounds across a landscape set with bayonets. Corrupt Public Works Department officials are run over by ghostly replicas of their steam-rollers. Excise men who have succumbed stagger blindly through a ravine seething with the fumes of noxious liquors. Co-operative officials who misappropriate rations queue up, ration card in hand, for molten silver to be poured down their throats. Railway executives who sell privilege tickets and take bribes for freight priorities are flogged by demons with lengths of rail. Meanwhile, as the final vision reveals, the unfortunate young man's wife has already remarried, and is busily engaged in spending his loot with her new husband.

First reaction to this morality; if a Burmese evil-doer could really be deterred by such propaganda – and the government evidently thought he could – it showed that heaven and hell were nearer to a Buddhist than I had ever suspected. Secondly, I found it hard to think of the Burmese woman, outwardly so tranquil and so demure, in the role of a Lady Macbeth.

*

The organization of such a show struck me as a praiseworthy and heartening attitude on the part of the government of Burma, which, whatever its failings, possesses in full measure the politically saving grace of self-criticism. They knew that their administration was riddled with corruption, and instead of trying to hush it up, they gave it all the publicity they could. And that, it seemed to me, was the quickest way to mend matters.

No one could have been more cheerfully frank about their shortcomings and their failures than the Burmese. Were things better in the British times? Nine out of ten of them laughed out loud at the absurdity of such a question. 'Better?... Why even bring it up? Everyone was well off then. We didn't know how well off we were.' The Burmese seem to be above nursing old scores, and they either forget or pretend to forget the other side of the picture – the disdains and exclusions by which it was made clear to them that they were regarded, in their own country, as an inferior people. The Burmese never bitterly remind the British visitor of this, and he is freely welcomed by them within the portals of those institutions from which they were debarred.

But in any case these were the minor irritations of the skin, which did not amount to much, except as symptoms of a deep-seated ailment. What was really wrong was that under colonial tutelage the Burmese or any other people lost – or as in this case were in the process of losing – their national character. The only culture they could rebuild for themselves was never much more than a poor, provincial imitation of that of the occupying power. Colonies – and Burma was an example – were sometimes prosperous, but colonial prosperity is a wretched substitute for lost nationhood. Before they could be real Burmese again, and not – at least, so far as the upper classes went – imitation Englishmen, the Burmese had to stand on their own feet, and left to fend for themselves. Whatever the temporary material consequences, I regard it as the greatest possible good fortune for them that this has happened.

*

And now on the eve of my departure from Burma, I re-gathered my impressions in an attempt to form some kind of personal estimate of this fascinating country's prospects. From my record of the present-day somewhat chaotic travelling conditions, the reader may have deduced a pessimism which would not be altogether justified. The Burmese nation stands upon foundations, both economic and psychological, of peculiar solidity. These provide a resilience which has pulled it safely through several historic crises of the gravest kind.

To deal with the psychological aspect; Burma has, in the first place, the extreme fortune to be entirely free from the damaging myths of colour, race, and caste that bedevil the internal relationships of so many nations. Secondly, it has freed itself from Western domination almost with the ease of removing an unwanted garment. As a result, no trace of bitterness remains, and a Westerner can travel with at least as much safety as a Burmese from one end of the country to the other, meeting, as I did, with nothing but the most genial and touching hospitality. Then, once again, owing to the nation's background of Buddhist indoctrination it is free from the delusion – the bane of the West, and much of the East – of the supreme value of material accumulation. There is some corruption and money-grubbing in high places, but real prestige in Burma – and it is very real – lies not with the millionaire, but with the penniless monk. On the national scale this means that there is no reason why the Burmese should not avoid or by-pass that grim interlude in human development heralded in the West by the Industrial Revolution, and rest content to live within their present very adequate means, leaving Tennessee Valley Projects and their like to those who believe that the Kingdom of Heaven on Earth will be here when every family has its refrigerator, as well as two cars in the garage. I state here my sincere belief that the average Burmese peasant working his own land lives a fuller and happier life, and is a more successful human being, than the average Western factory hand or office worker. His work is creative, free of clock-punching and deadly routine, and allows him an enormous amount of leisure, which he consumes with expertness and relish. From the leisure aspect only, it is the difference between filling in coupons, and keeping one's own fighting-cocks; between standing in the four and sixes on Sunday afternoon, and the full-blooded pleasures of a three-day pwè.

As for the material basis for Burma's future, it is excellent. The country is wonderfully fertile, and reasonably populated. That is to say that without much effort enough food can be grown for everyone. Even in the present state of tragic disorder the Burmese can still export annually several million tons of rice. All that is necessary, then, is to cure the people of their infantile craving for manufactured trash from overseas that fills their markets, and to import only essential medicines, hospital equipment, means of transport, and agricultural machinery. If necessary a little teak could be cut, and oil pumped to help pay for this. While the population stays at its present level the Burmese need neither kolkhozes nor Boulder Dams (nor, since they cannot afford an atomic pile, do they need armaments); and there is no mysterious natural law which compels a country to produce a greater population than its own soil can support. Above all, they do not need the glittering baubles described in the advertisement sections of American magazines. The Burmese way of life has never been based on unnecessary consumption, and there is no reason why it ever should. It is as good as any, as it is.

It now remains for the Burmese to compose their differences, to cease to be intoxicated by reach-me-down political formulae and to split doctrinal hairs while the dismemberment of their country goes unheeded. If this can be done (and as yet there is not the slightest sign of it), all that remains is to avoid as the plague all alliances that may lead to their country's being crushed between the millstones of the East and West, and to settle down to the carrying out of those just agrarian reforms upon which all political parties seem to be agreed. Herein lies a simple blueprint for Utopia.

A GODDESS IN THE STONES

Travels in India

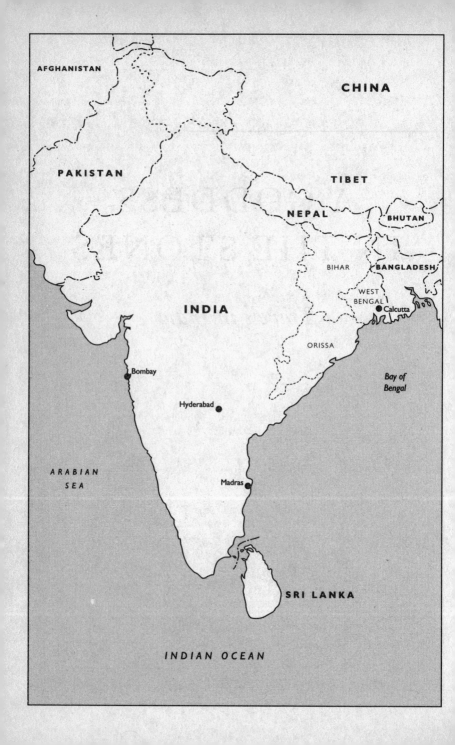

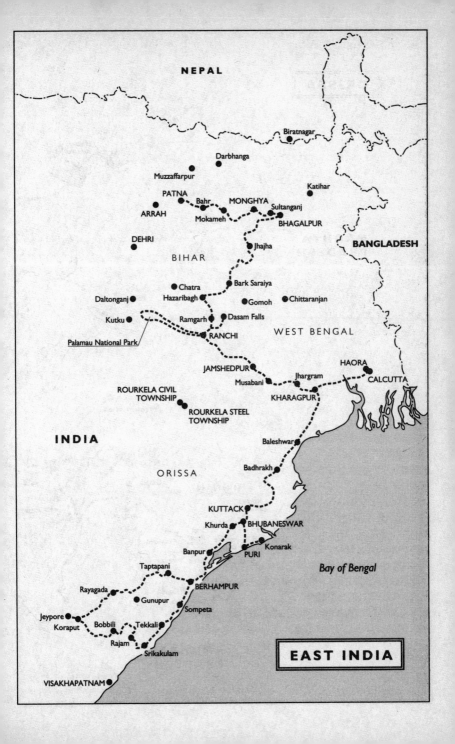

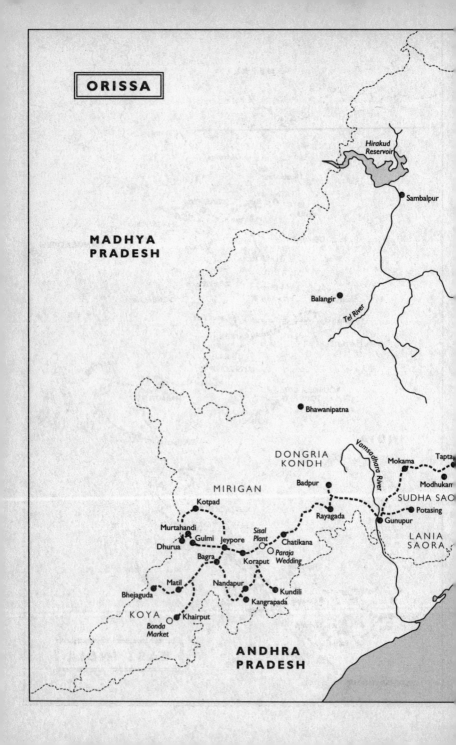

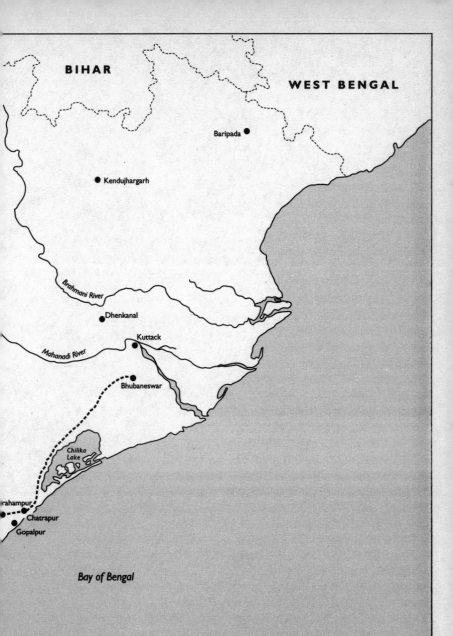

Contents

Preface

It was not the best of years in which to explore the attractions of what may appear to many of us as the most glamorous of the countries of the East. India, these days, is frequently referred to as 'the greatest democracy on earth', but immediately prior to my arrival greatness had been diminished by general elections conducted in an atmosphere of extreme violence and fraud. Paramilitary forces had to be called upon to ensure the safety of electors in the regional elections that followed.

The density and darkness of this metaphorical jungle was deepened in 1990 by a worsening caste-war in the north. Religious fanaticism was on the upsurge, and ten thousand fundamentalist zealots, manipulated by a political conspiracy, set out to destroy a Muslim holy place, the ancient mosque of Ayodhia. They were repelled by the police, but two hundred died in the fighting, thus touching off nationwide reprisals, largely against small, isolated Muslim communities. Death by fire is an all-too-frequent feature of these ultimate acts of violence. Burnings have become part of the ritual of Indian dissent, as in the case of the protesters angered by governmental support for the 'untouchable' cause who set themselves alight.

The worst of these atrocities took place in the State of Bihar, strategically chosen as the starting point for the journey that lay ahead. In Bihar feudalism in its most blatant form remains, nevertheless it is an area of supreme beauty and outstanding historic interest. Little is written about it apart from depressing newspaper reports. It is far away from the well-beaten itineraries of the north offering the justly famous attractions of Agra and the monumental towns of Rajasthan.

Through a shortage of information about the accessibility of regions, my journey was of necessity loosely planned. Moving on southwards from Bihar, I proposed to travel in what were once known as the Central Provinces – now largely Orissa and Madhya Pradesh. Certainly, very little

577

had appeared in print about this area in recent years, although it was of great interest to me since it contained the greater part of the Indian tribal population, numerically exceeding that of any other region of the world. Astonishingly, according to accounts furnished largely by anthropologists, many of these tribal groupings, despite all the pressures put upon them by the times, had been successful in retaining much of their aboriginal culture.

According to the latest census, seven per cent of India's total population of seven hundred and seventy-three millions – roughly fifty-four millions – comprises tribal peoples. These are spread in innumerable pockets all over central and northern India, largely in mountainous areas into which they withdrew following the Aryan invasions from the north immediately preceding the Christian era. Some are classified as Proto-Australoid, having a supposed racial affinity with the Aborigines of Australia. Others, the Dravidians, are regarded by the anthropologists as of Asian origin. In addition there are Mongoloid tribes who have reached India by way of Burma and China. Although a proportion of them still carry bow and arrows, it would be a very great mistake to label them primitive, for their culture, although strikingly diverse from that of the Hindu minority, has developed its own forms of sophistication, notably in the widespread practice and appreciation of the arts. Above all, the descendants of the original inhabitants of the sub-continent are free of the burden of caste.

When, shortly after the war, I travelled through Indo-China and Burma, I went there spurred on by the convictions that much of what I would see and hoped to record was shortly destined to vanish for ever. In *A Dragon Apparent* I discovered that, despite the fairly recent French occupation, a most refined and ancient culture had survived in Indo-China in which magnificence was tempered by good taste. Prestige went to the composer of acceptable poetry. People dressed not according to the dictates of fashion but to be in harmony with their environment, and there were mass excursions to admire the effects of moonlight on lakes, or to paint flowering trees, or simply to admire them. It was a country whose miracles of grace I felt impelled – almost from a sense of duty – to chronicle as best I could, so that not all memory of them should be lost. Burma, too, was heir to a great and little-known civilization, doomed, as I saw it, to effacement through incurable civil war. In *Golden Earth* I attempted once again to put on paper what I could of scenes and ceremonies so soon to be obliterated.

In India – reservoir of endless colour, pageantry, and interest – the pace of transformation, by comparison, has been slow, but it is happening, and at an increasing tempo. India, once dependent upon agriculture, has become a major industrial power, and the unhappy processes accompanying the drive for growth are only too familiar. Here, as elsewhere, the forests are vanishing – in India almost as fast as in Brazil. Hundreds of miles of river valleys are being flooded to provide more water for industries, and tens of thousands of once self-sufficient tribesmen, thus displaced, now furnish low-paid labour for factories and mines. Thirty years ago there were elephants and tigers within a few miles of the centre of Bilaspur in Madhya Pradesh. This is now the scene of the largest open-cast coalmine in the world, which is said to employ one hundred thousand miners. All round, the industrial wilderness stretches to the horizon.

The great palaces, the monuments and the tombs of the north will endure. India's jungles and all that they contain are to be swept away. It was a thought that increased my feelings of urgency in writing this book.

Norman Lewis, 1991

Through the
Badlands of Bihar

Chapter One

MY RICKSHAW joined the stream of traffic at the end of the airport road and turned in the direction of the city of Patna. The scene was one not to be forgotten. Three taxis from the airport bumped through the pot-holes and the fog into the distance and out of sight. After that we were part of a great fleet of rickshaws, of which there were possibly fifty in view, all keeping up with each other, while the pullers – as they were still called – pedalled along as if under the orders of an invisible captain. No sound came from them but the dry grinding of bicycle chains, the rattle of mudguards and the horse-like snort with which they cleared dust and mucus from their nasal passages. Muffled against the cold and fog, the pullers looked like Henry Moore's shrouded shelterers in the wartime tube, or like Ethiopian refugees with only their stick-thin legs showing below their tattered body wrappings, or like Lazaruses called from the dead. The single change in this prospect wrought by modern times was the presence of towering advertisement hoardings, closing off both sides of the road to form continuous ramparts for mile after mile. Floodlit faces radiating joy through the twilight and thickening fog praised Japanese stereos, Scotch whisky, wise investments, luxury footwear and packaged food. Nearing the city the gap left between the bottom of the hoardings and the earth provided glimpses of the homeless, scattered like the victims of a massacre, singly and in groups, who had claimed these uncontested spaces to settle for the night. In the Indian context there would have been nothing exceptional in this apart from the advertisements, and it was these that added a brushstroke of the macabre.

A power failure had cancelled out the city's centre and added it to suburbs glutted with shadows, with sleepers picked out by the headlights who had dumped themselves among the rubbish, and the stealthy inscrutable movements of those who chose to remain awake. From this obscurity the Mauriya Patna Hotel, rescued by its generators, stood apart in an oasis of light. Patna had fallen into a coma. The Mauriya overbrimmed with almost unnatural vivacity. There were big events afoot. WELCOME TO THE BALLOONISTS said a large notice in the lobby, and a small one on the reception counter warned that, since the next day was a public holiday, the hotel palmist would not be on duty as usual. It regretted the inconvenience that patrons might suffer. In the absence of separate public rooms a small area to the rear held two long opulent settees upon which rows of guests sat facing each other in a kind of expectant silence. While waiting for the reception clerk to cope with the lengthy formalities involved in checking in I took my seat here. Indians are not necessarily outgoing with their own people, but often fall spontaneously into an easy and informal relationship with foreigners. It came as no surprise to be asked by the man sitting next to me, quite courteously and without preamble, who I was, where I was from, and what were my immediate plans. 'I am Mr Mandhar Chawra,' he said, 'Inspector of Works. You will be here to see the balloon?'

When I said I was not, he was surprised. He was a small, neat man with a pleasant expression and thick black hair, and nostrils drawn back as if to sniff the odour of cooking of which he approved. 'It is an event,' he said, 'to break the monotony of our life. Something we are all looking to. Have you ever been in Patna before?'

I said I had not, and Mr Chawra said, 'Oh, you will like it. In our country we call it the City of Kings. It is having a bad press, but do not believe half you hear.'

The key was handed over and Mr Chawra and I parted company in the hope, as we assured each other, of watching the arrival of the balloon together on the morrow. I went up to my room for a shower in a lift that warbled soft Hindu music at me as soon as the door closed. The view through the bedroom window was of a swimming pool lightly feathered by fog and with what appeared as a dark bulk afloat in it. Accounts of happenings in this town during the recent election made this at the time seem a little sinister, although by morning it had gone.

584

The fog was slow to lift next day. The neighbourhood people were still swaddled voluminously in African style, or wearing ragged ponchos like those to be seen in the depressed cities of Latin America. I braced myself for a reconnaissance. The hotel had been built with an optimistic vista of the park, Gandhi Maidan, but, turning with some reluctance away from this in the direction of the business centre, I was plunged instantly into a slum. Patna is the capital of Bihar, unanimously recognized by Indians as the most atrociously governed of the Indian states, thus the metropolis of civic abuse. A minor official in Delhi had mentioned that one-fifth of the population slept on the streets, and at the moment of my arrival the mass daily resurrection of these multitudes was in progress, although those with any reason to get up were already pitched into the business of survival.

Perhaps the medieval warrens of Europe were like this. This was the place where an empty beer-bottle had its price, where a worn-out lorry tyre provided material for a dozen pairs of shoes, and tea in the bottom class of tea-shop was swilled from hollowed-out gourds. Men practised their crafts in workshops like enormous rabbit hutches raised upon wooden posts above the cluttered one-man factories at street level. Every square foot of earth was put to one commercial use or another, with occasional lanes patrolled by cows splashed liberally with their dung. The cows fascinated me; clean, sensitive, delicately stepping animals that dealt so effortlessly with the maelstrom of traffic and coped with all the imperatives of urban civilization. I had observed in India before how easily they fall into a routine. Here they were doing the rounds of the town in search of food, gobbling up windfalls of wood-shavings, packaging materials and old newspapers, although quietly nuzzling aside the plastic.

Families lived under sheets of plastic stretched in every angle of the walls, in burrowings among collapsed masonry, on the roofs of houses about to crumble, in dried-up wells, sections of drainpipes (although there were no drains), and in the husks of crashed cars after every utilizable part had been stripped away. There was no room here for the luxury of privacy in the movement of the bowels. Men defecated candidly, without effort or concealment. Five citizens stood in line to piss on or around the feet of the film actor Ramarao, shown in a large poster in the part of a god who looked down with aversion as the yellow trickles joined a black mainstream drawing its tributaries of fermenting liquid from the piled-up rubbish. Perhaps the men did this in token of their displeasure at his performance – there was no way of knowing.

The advertisements were everywhere: great, gloating faces adding their surrealism to those scenes of famine, barely contained, of bodies like cadavers, awaiting dissection, of excrement, urine, mucus, and phlegm. ALWAYS A STEP AHEAD WITH LIBERTY SHOES . . . FOR THEM ONLY THE BEST . . . THE TRUE FLAVOUR OF THE GLEN . . . LET'S PLAY THE FUTURE TOGETHER. On whom were these inducements and appeals targeted?

A Mr Singh, an insurance claims adjuster down on a flying visit from the capital whose acquaintance I had made in the hotel bar, was happy to reveal what he believed was the trickery involved. 'The people who are spending their money in this way may be under the misapprehension that they are buying prime space in Delhi,' he said, 'where it happens that there is a street of the same name.'

Back in the Mauriya, the news was disappointing. A notice had gone up:

WILLS CIGARETTES BALLOONING
ACROSS INDIA EXPEDITION 1990
The Wills balloon 'Indra Dharnust' will take
off between 14.30 and 15.30 hours subject to
favourable weather conditions instead of
11.30 hours as announced earlier.

Mr Chawra was at my elbow. 'I see we will be wasting time,' he said. 'This is problem of weather. We must only hope that there will be no further delay.'

The balloon was to take off from a spot marked by a small circle of whitewash on the grass of the Maidan about two hundred yards from the hotel, all of whose rooms overlooking the scene had long since been reserved. The last of the fog, still adhering here and there like tufts of wool to the grimy façades of the city, was clearing away, and the sun shafting through the clouds haloed a patient group of early arrivals. I would have expected a crowd of those who had not been notified of the postponement to have gathered by now, but the Maidan was surprisingly empty. I mentioned this to Mr Chawra, who said, 'Actually many are not attending in the belief that they have nothing suitable to put on.'

Suddenly the hotel staff seemed to have disappeared. At the reception only the lurking figure of a man whose sole job appeared to be to hand out and receive keys was to be seen. The travel bureau was closed. The porter had slipped away. At the back of the lobby two lines of guests faced each other on the settees, and no one stirred. An out of order notice had been fastened to the lift door. A card left on the palmist's desk held promise. 'On this day the horoscope for all of us is favourable.'

'The thing is what to do with myself,' I said to Mr Chawra.

'Understandably so,' he said. 'Normally in Patna there are many things to occupy the time. When we are holiday-making it is different.'

He was from Gaya he told me, describing it as a provincial hole, and seemed to be happily stimulated by the mere knowledge that he was now in the capital. 'Patna', he said, 'is the centre of my little world. There are people who come to Patna to drive over the bridge to the middle of river. Here they are stopping to make a wish. This is lucky.'

'Isn't there a museum?' I asked.

'There is none better. It is famous for its archaeological sculptures from Maurya and Gupta periods.'

'In that case I may as well give it the once over.'

'Today it is shut,' Chawra said. 'There is also the famous Khudabaksh Library containing many unique volumes. This, too, is closed for holiday. Continually I am arguing that all these places must remain open when there is opportunity for the public to see them.'

'What about the famous grain store?'

'You are referring to the Gholgar built by your Warren Hastings? It is a must, but unfortunately at this moment the only view is of outside as the interior is under reconstruction.'

'Any suggestions, then?' I asked.

'Yes,' he said. 'You should visit the burning ghats here. This is my word of advice. They are very interesting.'

'In what way, would you say?'

'Because they a natural sight to be seen. In Gaya also we have such ghats, but in Patna they are more select. Today is Sankranti, which for us is first festival of the year. Many people will be coming to immerse their bodies in river, also there will be many burnings. As a foreigner this is interesting for you to see.'

The driver of the taxi I took had no more than four or five words of English. Mr Chawra, who had decided to stay in the hotel in case some freak of the weather brought the balloon in to land earlier than expected, told him to take me to the ghats. The driver nodded in confirmation. 'Crematorium,' he said. 'This is a new word they are all using,' Chawra explained. 'He will take you to the ghats.' At the end of the short ride, nevertheless, I found myself shoved through a gate into a dismal shed. This was the new electric crematorium which, had I known, could have been avoided by a nearby path leading down to the river. Here a scarecrow human figure materialized in the gloom, signalling to me with desperate gestures to accompany him. I found myself staring up at what appeared to be a bundle of rags stuffed into a niche in the wall. This was some funerary goddess. An offering was clearly expected. I handed over five rupees, had paste smeared upon my forehead as equivalent of a receipt, then, taken off my guard, found myself peering through an oven door which had suddenly been flung open to reveal a shapeless carbonized mass. Seconds later, reaching daylight and fresh air once again, I found myself holding a leaflet in Sanskrit characters and in English. LOW-RATE BURNING FOR FAMILIES. DISCOUNT SATISFACTION. ASHES FOR RIVER IN 45 MINUTES.

What was on offer was a cut-price although ritually unsatisfactory passage through the portals of this life into the reincarnation appropriate to the state of the dead man's karma. All those who could raise the money saw to it that they were burned with proper ceremony on a pile of freshly cut and fragrant wood at the edge of the great river into which their remains would be most carefully stirred.

At Patna the Ganges, fed by important tributaries, becomes very wide, a placid unruffled flood, green and opaque in the shallows, then lightening to the milky aquarelle of the distant shore, with its line of palms, on this occasion, sketched in on a ribbon of mist. I noted that a few patches of pinkish scum floating at the water's edge were mixed with straw and ash from a recent burning. On the ghat the scene was a lively one devoid even of token solemnity. Children in their holiday best romped noisily up and down the long flights of steps to the water. A few dogs, even, had slipped past the guards posted at the gates to discourage intrusion by persons of the scheduled castes, previously known as untouchable. Funeral parties entered the enclosure by a separate gate and thus, distanced from the holiday crowd, carried their bier to the music of horns and flutes down to the readied pyres they had been allotted. A hundred or two yards upstream those who hoped to refurbish their spiritual lives by a simple process poured water over their heads, torsos, and arms, before immersion. These operations conducted with some grace appeared almost as a ballet, in slow motion. Midway between the groups concerned with this life and those with the next, a man who had arrived on a bicycle unstrapped a large vacuum flask from its carrier, and clambered down the slope to fill it with holy water, evidently for drinking purposes.

The most notable burning that afternoon was of a man whose impressive cortège included a portly Brahmin priest and a photographer with an assistant carrying a battery of cameras. The dead man could have been in his forties, and such had been the mortician's artistry that the semblance of a face flushed with health suggested a man taking a nap after a good meal rather than one that would never rise again. A bed had been made up on piled tree-trunks and on this the corpse dressed in white pyjamas was laid. A flowered coverlet, brought along seemingly as an afterthought, was removed from its plastic wrapping and spread in position. An English-speaking mourner, spotting a European face, came over eager for a chance to speak well of a friend. 'We are all admiring this man for his positive attitudes,' he said. 'Yesterday he announced that he proposed to depart this world on this day, and this he did.' The English speaker was called away to take his place in the group gathering at the head of the bier. The photographer crouched, Pentax levelled, the priest raised a hand to signify that all was ready and the shot was taken. With this, to my surprise, the party broke up, turned their backs and began to walk away. Someone snatched off the coverlet and pushed it back into its plastic envelope. The body was covered with light, combustible material and the dead man's son, abandoned by the rest, approached to apply the match.

On the circuitous stroll back to the centre I paused to study the work in progress on a new building going up at tremendous speed. The building was destined to become a block of flats, and when finished was certain to be outwardly indistinguishable from a similar construction in any city of the West, yet at first glance it was no more than an enormous example of cottage industry.

Although elsewhere in the city all work appeared to have come to a stop, here this was not the case. The first floor, unfinished, sprouted a forest of spindly tree-trunks upon which the one above would be supported, and this teemed with busily occupied figures. A load of bricks had been dumped by the roadside and a team of girls who appeared to be between fifteen and eighteen years of age were carrying these into a position within easy reach of the bricklayers. Each girl, assisted by another, stacked eleven bricks on the platform on her head – a burden which she carried with unfaltering step and even a kind of absent-minded dignity for twenty yards or so to the waiting bricklayer, before returning to be laden as before. I picked up a brick and estimated its weight as at least five pounds. Thus the total load would have been over fifty pounds. I knew that it was one

I could never have carried. These tribal girls were contract or (illegally) bonded labourers recruited in all probability from destitute families who had lost their land and were now prisoners of a system to which many millions of Indians are subjected and from which there is no escape. There is no secret about the abuses to which they are exposed, and the current number of the *Illustrated Weekly of India*, reporting on a seemingly immutable situation, revealed nothing that was new. 'They are ruthlessly exploited,' said the newspaper, 'by labour contractors who are hand in glove with officials. Men are paid 12 rupees [42p] and women 10 rupees [35p] for a 10-hour day.'

The feudal state of Bihar is the principal source of supply of female and child labour. In this case the choice would have been the building site or starvation, and the girls endured their fate with customary stoicism.

Some hours later I arrived back at the Mauriya where Mr Chawra awaited me in a state of consternation.

'Mr Lewis, where have you been missing? The balloon has come and gone. I am sorry for you. It has been an experience of much joy to us all. We were all on the look-out for you, but you were nowhere to be found.'

'I'm sorry. I got rather held up.'

'And you were interested by the burnings?'

'Very much so.'

'I am glad. There has been a press conference given at the hotel by Mr Gupta who is leading the expedition to outline his objectives. I have kept for you one press-release.'

I took the paper and read.

Soaring above the Gangetic plains of Bihar and West Bengal, Mr Gupta asseverated that the Wills Balloon Indra would sail into the clouds amidst the Himalayan heights of Darjeeling and Gangtok before crossing the rolling hills of Assam prior to touching down in the plain of Padman in Bangladesh. Explaining his choice of Patna as the expedition's starting point, Mr Gupta said it would help popularize this adventure sport in this part of the country. 'Anyone who is willing to set up a ballooning club here is welcome to get in touch with us. The Ballooning Club of India will extend all possible help.' Asked to sum up the philosophy behind the sport, Mr Gupta said, 'Sky is the limit, press on regardless.'

'For me the philosophy to be included is that sport is an instrument of peace,' Mr Chawra said.

Chapter Two

NEXT MORNING Mr Chawra went off to spend the last day of his holiday with a party of friends visiting a nearby shrine where there was a spring and a pool in which they would swim; the water being most beneficial, Chawra said, for the condition of the skin from which he suffered.

In his absence Mr Singh provided companionship. The two men were poles apart. Where Chawra was on the whole sanguine, Singh was invaded by doubt. He was tall, lantern-jawed, and one day would be cadaverous. 'I have chosen the wrong profession,' he said. 'It is not good to lose faith in one's fellow men, and in the insurance business this is possible.'

Most of the people who had come to see the balloon had gone home. The travel bureau was open, and the pretty girl in charge was polishing everything in sight for the second time. A woman was discussing her problems with the palmist, who had used a magnifying glass to examine the fine creases of her hand. She looked up at my approach to inspect and evaluate me with her fine oracular eyes. The fog was back, and according to the weather forecast could not be expected to disperse before mid-morning.

'May I know the nature of the business you are conducting?' Mr Singh asked.

'I'm not in business,' I told him.

'But clearly you are not a tourist,' Singh said. 'There are no foreign tourists in Bihar. Did you come here of your own accord? Willingly?'

'It was largely a matter of curiosity. There was quite a lot about Bihar in our papers at the time of the election. It sounded like a place not to be missed.'

Singh shook his head in amazement. 'No one is wishing to come to Patna. I am only here because I am the victim of office politics. In Bihar there are always problems for us, but in my office in Delhi they are ganging up on me so that I am the one who is sent.'

The explanation I had given Mr Singh for my presence was not the whole truth. In the autumn of 1989 my friend John Hatt had visited the great annual fair at Sonepur, just across the Ganges from Patna, in which many hundreds of elephants change hands, most of them being bought by zamindars – the feudal landlords who outside industrial areas or cities are in reality in control of the state. John took tea with one of these, who had an elephant for sale. 'Two gunmen attended him on either side,' he wrote in *Harpers & Queen*. 'When being photographed, he insisted on adjusting his dress in order to ensure a clear view of the pistol at his waist. When I asked my host if his elephant had ever killed anyone, he replied, "Only three mahouts and a labourer." One notorious animal is known to have dispatched eight of its mahouts ... at last year's fair one of these killed a visitor. Life in Bihar is cheap indeed.'

John thought that there was a book to be written about this state alone, although far too much of it would be little more than a relation of atrocity. 'A large number of persons', said the *Indian Express* in a leading article, 'die in police custody ... the favourite police excuse is suicide, or that they run away.' News of the abundant trivial violences of India rarely filters through to the foreign press. Although several years back the methods used by the police of the terrible town of Bhagalpur in east Bihar to deal with recalcitrant bonded labourers proved an exception. A dozen or so were blinded in the police station there by thrusting bicycle spokes into their eyeballs, after which pads soaked in acid were applied to the wounds. Considerable international coverage was also given to the autumn elections in 1989 in which numerous voters were done to death, and in some cases buried in mass graves. In Bihar a television team arrived at a village where an unexpectedly large vote had been polled by the Congress Party and the zamindar who had conducted the polling explained, 'First we bribed them, then we beat them, and after that we killed them.'

'Welcome to hell,' was the greeting of a newspaperman when

Trevor Fishlock visited him in Patna. A few days later this man, too emphatic in his defence of the freedom of the press, was beaten unconscious.

On his outward journey from Delhi Mr Singh's plane had left five hours later than the scheduled departure time and now on the return flight there was a long delay with talk of cancellation. At worst he was faced with another day in Patna, where the hours passed slowly.

We sat in the bar over slightly scented soft drinks of local manufacture while Singh spoke of the reason for his presence in the city. Head office in Delhi had been subjected to a spate of claims arising from what was described as accidental and flood damage to the largest of the housing estates, which consisted of three thousand flats and was one of the biggest in the country. When Singh was packed off down to Patna to go into the case he had an inkling, he said, of what he would find. His suspicions were confirmed by an interview with the company's local agent, who for all that he was a Bihari, Singh said, was a very nice man. Mr Patel, the agent, showed his cuttings from a local newspaper; he had checked on the report and found it to be accurate.

The story was that the Bihar State Housing Board had designed the flats for occupancy by deserving and respectable applicants of middle and low income groups, and a majority of these had been on the waiting list for up to seventeen years. Ninety per cent of the accommodation was found to have been taken over by persons who had been able to grease the palms of officials of the board, or secure the backing of what the newspaper described as unscrupulous politicians. Many tenants possessed criminal records, and Mr Patel, who had thought fit to take bodyguards when he went to inspect the building, concluded that the claims of accidental damage arose through the wilful stripping away for sale of fixtures and fittings of every kind, even of cisterns and doors, and the flooding had been caused through the removal of lengths of piping and damage to the mains. The report added that there were three thousand illegal power connections in the colony and the number of genuine consumers was only one hundred and fifty. Patel had arrived to find a complete breakdown of the sewage system, with night soil everywhere afloat in the shallow lake surrounding the colony. There was no secret about these facts at any time, Singh said. They were common knowledge, provoking laughter rather than indignation.

Singh had an idea. We had been talking about zamindars. 'If you are interested, Patel is the man you should see,' he said. 'He is knowing everybody. Maybe he can take you to see one of these people.'

'Wouldn't it be an intrusion?' I asked.

'An intrusion?' he laughed. 'All these men are looking to find someone to talk to about themselves.' He got on the phone and in a few minutes Mr Patel appeared. He was small and lively, and full of over-energetic movement, reminding me in a way of Mr Chawra, and I was surprised that he should be wearing a battle blouse, muffler, and gloves.

'On account of a vitamin deficiency I am feeling the cold,' he explained. 'Mr Singh tells me that you are wishing to see Mr Kumar. There is no problem. Mr Kumar is very happy to welcome any visitor we may bring to his house. This is a nice man. He is our very good friend.'

Singh excused himself from accompanying us, feeling unable to leave the hotel in the absence of news of his flight, and we set out in Patel's Ambassador, arriving in a matter of minutes at the zamindar's village up a side-turning off the Gaya road. This was a cluster of hutments, appearing as hardly more than the outbuildings of the house of many architectural styles in which the zamindar and his family lived. Basically this was a grey-stone porticoed dwelling based upon early Victorian English models to which had been added a cast-iron first-floor balcony, recently sprayed with aluminium paint, and later ground-floor extensions of concrete, having typical factory windows. We crossed a courtyard full of bullock carts and stunted, scuttling little men, strangely like Brueghel peasants, to reach a flight of steps at the head of which in a doorway flanked by stone cobras with numerous heads, the zamindar waited to greet us.

He was an imposing figure, a good head and shoulders taller than any of the members of his work force in sight, with a fine up-sweep of moustaches divided by a great aquiline beak of a nose. There was something to be learned of him from his attire: a respect for tradition illustrated by the dhoti, the expansive individualism of the Edwardian fancy waistcoat, the devil-may-care confidence of the Astrakhan cap worn at a jaunty angle, and the in-step-with-the-times display of the big wristwatch with over-complicated dial. Above all, I took note of the easy, good-natured, immutable smile that advertised peril in the land of the straight-faced.

The zamindar led the way into a roomful of blurred family portraits from the beginning of photography. An enormous grandfather clock let out a single sonorous chime as he kicked it with a bare foot in passing, and a jolly papier-mâché Ganesh stood enthroned in a corner among frangipani blossom, its trunk dangling in a wisp of incense smoke.

We settled ourselves side by side on a wide divan. The zamindar drew his feet up under him, and Mr Patel, who up to this point had been vigorously chewing a vitaminized betel substitute (which he either disposed of, or managed to swallow), did his best to explain an acceptable purpose of the visit.

The zamindar nodded agreeably, rolling his head from side to side at whatever was said. There was a quick outpouring of Hindi. When this was directed at me the zamindar's eyes bulged in emphasis, and he spoke more slowly and in a louder voice, as if in the hope of demolishing the language barrier.

'Mr Kumar is saying that his family is living here two hundred years,' Mr Patel said. 'His great-grandfather was in this place with two goats and one cow. He was very much liking hard work and made a whopping amount of money. Mr Kumar is also liking work. If other people will work in this manner they also may be rich.'

A door opened on a not unpleasant farmyard smell, mixed with the waftings of curry. A little man shuffled in carrying three glasses of tea on a tray held at shoulder height, as if to lower it in the manner of a yoke over the necks of his oxen.

'Mr Kumar is a very religious man,' Patel said. 'Each morning he is going with offerings to the temple. One teaspoonful of his own urine he is drinking. With his own hands he is feeding cows with vegetables gathered in his garden. In this house no meat may be eaten.'

The zamindar's eye was constantly on me. He gave the impression, perhaps through a kind of animal instinct, of following what was being said, appearing at one moment to be illustrating Patel's account of his pieties with hand movements like those of a dancer. I sipped the milky, spice-flavoured tea and the zamindar nodded and smiled his encouragement.

'Does Mr Kumar own all the land in the village?' I asked.

The question was put, and the zamindar laughed musically.

'He says that is not possible. The government's maximum is forty acres. He laughs because this is no problem. His family is very numerous. Between all members they are cultivating much land. Here they are very grateful to Mr Kumar because he is giving work. Rice, lentils, and crops of many kinds he is growing. All these he is sending to market in Calcutta where prices are better.'

'Can I ask about rates of pay?' I asked.

'You may ask him, but I can tell you. For a strong man he is paying ten rupees [35p a day]. If he is weak he will be asking eight.'

'Is that a bit lower than usual?'

Mr Patel translated, and Mr Kumar replied with such theatrical fluency of gesture that Mr Patel's help was almost superfluous.

'You see he is paying not only with money,' Patel said, 'but with kindness. If a man comes to him to ask for a bag of grain he is giving him that grain. Mr Kumar is the father of all these people. When a daughter must be married he will tell some boy who has no job, "Take this girl and there will be work for you on my farm. This is my dowry for her. Treat her thankfully."'

There was a moment of silence. In the guise of scratching his nose Patel had managed to sneak fresh vitaminized betel into his mouth and, with a sidelong glance at Mr Kumar, was chewing surreptitiously behind his hand.

'Who do the people here vote for?' The question caught him off guard, and he replied from a corner of the mouth. 'They are voting for Congress Party.'

'All of them?'

'All. Here there are no problems with voting. "I am your father," Mr Kumar is telling them. "If you vote for Rajiv Gandhi you are voting for me." They are one hundred per cent thankful for his fatherliness, and this they do.'

The meeting was at an end and Mr Kumar dismissed us with a graceful wave of the hand. On the way back to Patna I asked, 'Does everybody in Bihar vote for Gandhi?'

'No, not everybody. Some are refusing to give their vote.'

I put the point-blank question. 'Do you?'

'What you are asking me is very much a secret,' he said. 'Perhaps better not even to tell my wife. I only tell you because you are a foreigner and tomorrow you will be going. No, I do not vote for this man.'

Chapter Three

MUCH OF INDIA'S wealth is drawn from the mining and steel towns and the industries of a black country extending five hundred miles through Bihar. Yet quite a short distance to the south of this, in the mountains of Bastar and Orissa where there are no minerals to be mined, the old India precariously survives. In 1947 the anthropologist Verrier Elwin, who had spent ten years in the field in the region, published a book about a tribe living in Bastar which, in so far as any scientific book could, produced a stir among the general public.

The Murias Verrier Elwin lived among and described occupied – and still occupy – an area only just over a hundred miles south of the steel town of Bhilai. It remains purely tribal, with sixty-five per cent of forest cover, and mountains hardly even surveyed. *The Muria and Their Ghotul* describes the complex and artistic lifestyle of an exceptionally interesting group, 'the most beautiful and most interesting of all the people of Bastar', Elwin called them, adding, 'it was always with heavy heart that I bid farewell to these children of the foothills.' In those days he thought there might have been about one hundred thousand of these Proto-Australoid aboriginals, established in this location long before the Aryo-Indian invasion from the north. They were short in stature; their skin colour was dark chocolate, their hair and eyes black, and they were vivacious and poetic in temperament. The Murias, Elwin reported, would eat almost anything: monkeys, red ants, even crocodile. They amused themselves with theatrical performances, dancing, marriage games, cock-fighting, falconry, quizzes, riddles, folk tales and recitations, and ceremonial hunts. They used eighteen musical instruments, and a man's prestige depended to some extent on his ability to perform adequately on one or more of these, to sing and to compose poetry. The Muria brewed forty or so kinds of alcoholic liquors from the juice of sago-palm, rice, and many forest fruits, savouring and blending these with expertise. Their brass ornaments, often taking the form of elephants, horses, or bulls, are now sought after as museum pieces. Elwin said that, despite a certain amount of well-regulated ritual drunkenness, 'to visit a Muria village is to receive a general impression of tidiness and cleanliness'. Mother Earth was their principal goddess, worshipped often, in the form of a pile of stones. As the Muria saying went, 'If you believe, it is a God. If not it is a stone.'

What probably stimulated the exceptional interest in this book was Elwin's account of the ghotul – the dormitory in which, beyond the reach of parental interference, adolescent Murias were schooled in the complexities of tribal conduct and ritual, as well as introduced to sex. There was nothing new in the institution, still existing in rare cases among certain African tribes, in Papua New Guinea and the Philippines, and in India, with little publicity, among the Naga, in Bihar, Orissa, and Madhya Pradesh.

It was an institution, Elwin says, devoted to the problem of infertile pre-marital promiscuity. In his day there were a large number of ghotuls. He counted a total of three hundred and forty-seven among the Muria, and many had survived in the neighbouring states. He devotes several hundred pages to the complexity of their organization. There was nothing left to chance in an education in which the rites were as severe as those of any monastic institution. The rules covered every aspect of social conduct between the sexes, personal attire, cleanliness, eating and sleeping habits, the polite formula to be muttered after accidental farts, and of necessity all that pertained to the sexual act. In this matter it became clear that the Muria view of what was right and proper simply turned conventional Western morality inside out. 'Here everything is arranged', Elwin writes, 'to prevent long-drawn-out intense attachments, to eliminate jealousy and possessiveness, to deepen the sense of communal property and involvement. No boy may regard a girl as "his". There is no ghotul marriage, there are no ghotul partners. Everyone belongs to everyone else, in the very spirit of *Brave New World*. A boy and girl may sleep together for three nights, after that they are warned, if they persist they are punished.' Again: 'Sexual romance is not the best preparation for a life-long union' although 'strong and lasting attachment to a girl in this pre-nuptial period may lead to elopement and irregular marriage'. At Kotwal, a populous village to which the Muria looked for example, only the leaders of the ghotul, who might be described as the head-boy and head-girl, enjoyed the privilege of remaining faithful to their partners. The rest were committed to a sternly conformist promiscuity. Out of two thousand cases he examined Elwin found that only one hundred and sixteen ghotul couples had broken the rules by eloping. Despite such weakness and immorality by Muria standards they could eventually expect to be forgiven, and after self-criticism and atonement could apply for readmission into village society.

How much of this libertarian Arcadia, I asked when in India, had survived the miners, the logging companies, the dam builders, the labour recruiters, and the missionaries? Very little, was the general opinion of my Indian friends, although none had been to see for themselves. Even the experts in such matters like Dr S. S. Shashti, the author of several books on tribal India, to whom I spoke in Delhi, held out little hope. Yet even in 1982, when Christoph von Furer Haimandorf published his book *Tribes of India: The Struggle for Survival*, it seemed that all was not lost. Two years before the book's publication he had paid a final visit to the area he had covered before.

The change has been mainly for the worse, few of the tribes I studied in the 1940s have been able to preserve their economic and social independence. The strong emotional ties which linked me with such communities made it hard to observe the turn in their fortunes in a spirit of detachment. Indeed I often wished that I had preserved the memory of the far happier tribal life which I had known in earlier years.

There was an exception to this sombre picture.

I had the unexpected opportunity in 1980 of revisiting a tribal area not far from Andhra Pradesh which had been saved from the ills afflicting the tribes of that state. It convinced me that there are still regions – rapidly shrinking unfortunately – where tribal people live a life in accordance with their own traditions and inclinations ... In the Muria villages I visited there was a relaxed atmosphere indicative of well-being and prosperity, and in my conversation with the villagers no cases of harassment by officials or moneylenders were ever mentioned. There is still enough cultivable land to go around ...

Perhaps to von Furer Haimendorf's surprise he was also able to announce the survival of the Muria ghotul.

The cohesion of the village communities also finds expression in the persistent vitality of the institution of the ghotul. In Nayanar the ghotul was not only well maintained but had been enlarged by annexes, which had not been there in 1948 ... In Malignar village I was able to observe the preparation for a triennial feast in which the boys and girls entertain all the villagers ...

The tribal south beckoned, but the choice of destination and therefore the route to be followed remained in doubt. A question mark, too, hung over the significance of the stamp applied to all tourist visas by the Indian government: Not Valid for Protected or Restricted Areas. No one at the consulate could specify what these areas were. Informants were agreed that there were also 'sensitive areas'. All tribal areas were sensitive – and understandably so when one read of mass evictions everywhere, in the style of the infamous Highland clearances, before flooding valleys to provide more water for towns. A sensitive area might or might not be protected or restricted, besides which any area could become protected or restricted at a moment's notice in case of emergency. It was all very much a hit and miss affair and the best way of tackling it, I was advised, was simply to go and hope for the best. To seek to obtain official advice or sanction was a waste of time. Permission to visit a restricted area – even if eventually granted – might take up to five years to obtain. In the matter of obstructive bureaucracies India continued to lead the world.

Strangely enough, too, with the Cold War about to end, Indians were nervous of the possible presence of agents and spies, in particular the CIA. They had a phobia about missionaries, apart from the Lutheran and Catholic inherited from the past, suspecting the computerized and airborne Evangelists from the West of possession of a stronger allegiance to the policies of their country than to the gospels of Christ.

The choice of objectives was Bastar, about three days away by road to the south-west, or Orissa, lying directly to the south, which could be reached in about half that time. As only the vaguest information was to be had of what was to be expected in Bastar and very little more could be discovered about the interior of Orissa, I decided to put off any decision until joining forces with Devi Mishra, who had been recommended to me by a friend, and was on his way up from Ranchi by car.

Chapter Four

DEVI ARRIVED at the Mauriya, a handsome young man in a dark suit exuding a city aroma of entrepreneurial confidence and worldly wisdom. We settled to breakfast and waited for the weather to clear, while a small crowd gathered round the Contessa car he had come in – an inflated Japanese monster that inspired the veneration of the hotel staff and enhanced my status for the final half-hour of my stay.

Devi ruled out the journey to Bastar, of which he had little more news than I. Almost certainly restricted throughout, he thought, with the kind of roads that could only be tackled by a jeep. In Orissa the roads might be better and the restrictions less. In neither case would he be able to accompany me. There were too many imponderables and he did not want to risk his car. He thought it better to return to Ranchi, the de facto southern capital of the state, and there take further advice. I agreed. When I broke the news that I would like to return by a circuitous route through the notorious and sinister town of Bhagalpur, he showed neither reluctance nor surprise. 'This is a dangerous road,' he said, but with no more excitement than if he had been describing its pot-holed surface. I asked him why, and he said, 'There are some Naxalite armed bands. It is not permitted to use this road by night.'

This piece of information came as a surprise. According to the official history, the Naxalite uprising which had broken out in May 1966 at Naxalbari, a suburb of Calcutta, had been instantly drowned in blood. It had started as a peasant-style revolt, supported by the Communists, against what was generally admitted as the intolerable oppressions of the feudal landlords of that area. A few landlords had been lynched and a large but never disclosed number of Naxalites either shot on the spot or taken to police stations and killed. Nevertheless, despite this instant and crushing blow directed against the original stronghold of the movement, it seemed from later reports that a few small guerrilla groups had managed to elude retribution and pursuit to carry out action of a desultory and sporadic sort in the backwoods of Bihar and Andhra Pradesh. After vigorous government action against them it was announced in 1972 that all Naxalite resistance had been crushed; when I made mention of this Devi laughed. 'There are many armed bands,' he said. 'They are kidnapping landlords. Sometimes they are killing them by cutting off their heads.'

'Are we likely to have problems? That car of yours seems rather conspicuous.'

'It does not matter. We are not policemen or landlords. Naxalites recognize their enemies. They will give us no trouble.'

Devi was easy in his confidences, and had no objection to talking about himself. He was a junior partner in a thriving family business which sold – and proposed to manufacture – computers. There was evidence of a personal conflict here. His family belonged to an upper-crust sub-division of the merchant caste traditionally attracted to the professions, or government service as administrators or civil servants. Now they were no more than successful merchants and he seemed a little sad about the decline. He was exceedingly frank in his admission that business exercised a fascination over him, too. My feeling was that to come away on a trip like this in which there was no money for anybody was an act of resistance, a spiritual last-ditch stand undertaken against the guilty pleasures of mercantilism.

After an hour or so it was clear enough to make a start. The enormous and taciturn driver, who had been away filling up with petrol and checking the tyres, was back with the car, and we drove out following the road along the south bank of the Ganges in the direction of Bhagalpur and Bengal.

Ten miles of suburban muddle and mess separated us from the countryside, and then suddenly at Fatwah we were in a country town streaming with cows and cattle being taken to graze, and here I observed a novel aspect of the Indian pastoral scene. It would have been improper to employ an unclean and aggressive animal such as the dog to discipline the movements of the sacred cow; instead goats had been educated to undertake this duty, their task being to control the cows, who were seemingly indifferent to traffic, and gently nudge them out of harm's way in a maelstrom of bicycles, rickshaws, bullock-carts, and thundering lorries. When I commented upon the phenomenon, Devi said, 'Yes, there is positive co-operation. Both these animals are thinking what is best to be done, and are finding a solution.' At about this time the sun broke through with surprise outbursts of colour everywhere. Ramshackle rickshaws were seen to be bespangled with medallions and flying multi-coloured flags. Burnished lions' heads jutted from each side of a temple entrance through which a man in a yellow robe made an appearance carrying a large green parrot in a cage. Twenty or thirty excess passengers fastened themselves to the sides of a departing bus painted with clownish faces and emblems of good luck, and the driver of the lorry was fixing a fringing of tinsel – a ritual repeated daily in the Patna area – to the top of his windscreen before taking to the road.

Many of us carry an image of the Indian landscape tinctured with a certain austerity, and now, even after three previous visits to that country, the beauty of the Ganges valley at this season came as a surprise. Vivacity and grace formed a background to indelible poverty, yet the eye was lured constantly away from immediate dearth and its consequences to the enchantments beyond. The river was out of sight, but the shapes of its great valley, its hollows and hillocks and its scattered groves of palms were caught in brief brushstrokes of saffron, lavender, and grey. Occasionally, a brick yard drifted into sight, with its millions of bricks arranged like a child's game in innocent, symmetrical piles. A village we approached was raised in a scintillation of mist. We drove into it past the landowner's great house covered with stone figures of demons and gods. The house overlooked the tank in which the villagers doused their bodies among the water lilies. At the back of the tank a tree was so full of white herons that at first glance I took them to be blossom. Along the near bank wigwams of bamboo and reeds had been crammed into every yard of available space, and here it was that the untouchables lived.

So these were the traditional outcasts of the village, portrayed in so many books describing the Indian scene. In this case they were neat and trim enough, and if anything a little more cheerful in appearance than their touchable neighbours. It was hard to believe that they would be debarred from drawing water from the village well lest pollution leak like a baleful electric current from their fingers down the well-rope into the water. Gandhi had done what he could for them, insisting on renaming them *Harijans* – 'Children of God' – and the government with its infallible bureaucratic touch had turned them into 'members of the scheduled castes'. Untouchables, nevertheless, they remained, perpetual victims of the Aryan invader's trick at the beginning of Indian history which divided Hindu humanity into four castes: the priestly Brahmins, the warriors, the merchants, and the peasant cultivators. There remained a faceless, voiceless, powerless multitude, the untouchables, to perform the menial and degrading tasks, the sweeping and cleansing, the disposal of excrement, the slaughtering of animals, the washing of soiled garments, by which activities they were rendered unclean.

In the anonymous city crowds the untouchable may escape notice, but in the country he stands out. Even now in a few ultra-conservative rural areas untouchables are prohibited by custom from wearing clean clothing. They may still be required to keep a certain measurable distance from their superiors: one hundred feet in the case of a Brahmin, twenty-four feet from a lesser caste dignitary. For the untouchable there is nothing to be done about such humiliations in this life. The Hindu scriptures preach that he is no more than reaping the reward of misdeeds in a past experience. Salvation lies in the uncomplaining acceptance of his lot, and the respect and service rendered to his superiors, in the hope of moving up a caste in his next reincarnation. It is a system that has been uniquely successful in keeping the underdog in his place for over two thousand years, and only now faces challenge. In the beginning, with only the four castes, it was simplicity itself. Now, with all the divisions and accrescences that the centuries have added, a staggering total of five hundred and twenty sub-castes has been reached. Thus, in modern times, the system has become unmanageable.

*

From this beautiful, misted village, with its spruce untouchable, the road passed over the crest of a low hill from which the view was of the marvellous geometry of new paddy-fields in spring. So brilliant – almost unnaturally green – were the paddies it seemed as though lamps had been lit beneath them. The scene was full of graceful, archaic, laborious human activity; men transplanting rice seedlings, ploughing with bullocks in the shining mud, ladling water with wonderful old wooden contraptions from one ditch to another. Minute quantities of water were transferred in this way after every dip of the big spoon. The operation was so apparently inefficient and so slow, Devi said, because in this way it was easier for a hidden onlooker to keep tally on the amounts used, which would be noted down and paid for in cash.

This was the traditional heartland of bonded labour, in brick-fields and on the farms. It is an aspect of the Indian rural scene with which the Anti-Slavery Society for the Protection of Human Rights and a United Nations convention on the abolition of slavery have occupied themselves for some years with little result. The convention defined bonded labour – a speciality in labour relations which Indians share with Peru – as a system operating where loans in cash or kind advanced by a creditor are cancelled by the debtor in person – or members of his family – by labour service. Some of the facts presented to the United Nations seem hardly credible. For example: '14 moneylenders in Rakshi Village, Bihar, held about 90 people in surrounding villages in debt bondage. For a loan of Rs 175 [currently about $5.50] one man has been working for 12 years; for Rs 105 another for 10 years and for a loan of 22½lbs of barley another has been bonded for 35 years.' 'Bonded labourers commonly work for 16 hours a day,' the report continued. 'In many areas [in Bihar] children are given into bondage by their parents at a very early age. In some instances [to keep up with the debt payment] bonded labourers are forced to sell their wives and daughters into prostitution.' When a man died his bondage was inherited by his heir.

Mrs Gandhi, who campaigned against bonded labour, succeeded in putting through an act to outlaw it in 1976. Those convicted of keeping bonded labourers were to be punished by heavy fines and imprisonment. In the fourteen years that have followed, only a single case has been brought to trial and the offender was sentenced to three months. Mrs Gandhi believed there were tens of millions of bonded labourers throughout India, and it is unlikely that there are less than a million in Bihar at this moment. Sometimes we read of one trying to escape and of what was likely to happen to him if recaptured. 'Fadali will never be able to work again,' reports *India Today*, May 31st 1990.

> Last month the 30-year-old tribal had his left hand chopped off (he is left-handed) by the man whose farm he has worked for the past five years. Fadali's crime was that although he was a bonded labourer, he had refused to work for his master and run away from his farm. According to the terror-stricken youth the master told him: 'If you work, you work for me, or you don't work at all.' Fadali's master, Narenda Singh Kauran, was described as general secretary of the local Congress Party. He was arrested, but released 'on bail'.

On arrival in Bahr, first of the Naxalite towns, we pulled up outside a bedraggled tea-shop called the City Chic, to give way to a number of small boys riding on enormous buffaloes that slouched by, swinging their heads from side to side and testing the air with sensitive nostrils. Music wailed and banged from loudspeakers over the front of a cinema which Devi said was the largest in the district. This place of entertainment gave Bahr a totally misleading whiff of prosperity, and Devi took me behind the scenes.

There were many brick-fields in the vicinity, he said, exploiting rich deposits of exceptionally suitable clay along the river-banks. Although these enterprises received frequent press castigation for the conditions in which their labourers worked, for those who could stand the terrific pace there were always jobs to be had. Moreover, the brick-fields paid fifteen rupees a day – nine or ten rupees in the case of an energetic child – whereas the going wage on a zamindar's estate was twelve. Thus in Bahr there was money in circulation.

To benefit from this financial surplus motor rickshaws dawdled along the road passing through the brick-fields. They were licensed to carry three passengers, but by miracles of compression and rearrangements of human torsos and limbs twelve persons as a maximum could be taken on board. The fare was one rupee each way to the cinema and back, and the rickshaw driver could expect to pay a bribe of two rupees to the policeman waiting at the door. The cinema put on no regular programme; the continuous show instead consisted of a miscellany of old trailers and lengths of film discarded in cutting-rooms, for which the patron was charged a half rupee for an hour's entertainment. At the expiry of this period the cinema time-keeper would be waiting to drag him from his seat, if necessary, and throw him into the street. The news of the Naxalites was that they had ordered a surviving handful of tenant farmers round Bahr to cease to pay rent. Thus, said Devi, they were between devil and very deep sea: threatened with beatings by the landlords' thugs, and warned against betrayal of the class struggle by Naxalites armed with M14 rifles. At Bahr, Devi said, there were girls in the Naxalite band.

Suddenly we were in cow-country, of the kind I had never seen before. Cities like Patna were full of cows which had to fend for themselves. They fed exclusively on rubbish and were in consequence stunted and skeletal versions of the species. In the country, however spartan the conditions, things were quite different. The countryside conferred a certain dignity upon its inhabitants, whether human or animal. This became very apparent in an unnamed village past Bahr where we overtook a stately perambulation of thin, upright men escorting a magnificent and immaculate cow – on its way possibly to preside at some festival – which was being most carefully groomed as it plodded along by two attendant boys, one on each side. Children went running ahead flying blue kites. It was clear that this episode set the scene for what was to come.

Despite the penury, the police harassment, and the real fear of the zamindars' private armies of thugs, the villagers were friendly and kind. We stopped at a house to ask for road directions and were immediately invited in. We found a resplendent white cow occupying a stall just inside the door, which took up about one-third of the total space, while the family of five were left to do their best with what was left. Surprisingly, the normally ammoniacal smell of a byre was absent, the impression I received being that more time was spent by the family in smartening up the cow than their own living quarters. When asked what they fed this animal upon the answer was, 'All the things it likes. When there's any rice left over, it gets that too. Just the same as us.'

In this village we noticed for the first time that the country folks were an inch or two taller than the natives of Patna, and that the countrywomen were more to be seen in the open, more independent and statuesque in bearing than their sisters of the town. In each village the women wore saris of a typical local colour. Here on their way to early morning temple, they were all swathed in kingfisher blue, a shining procession against a background of stained grey walls and ragged thatch. Every woman, however poor, wore a smart sari for temple-going, along with an armful of plastic bangles and, if by village standards she were rich, a little gold stud through the nose.

As we headed eastwards the ratio of cows to men increased. For peasants who had lost their land, threatened on one hand by the landlords and on the other by floods, they offered a final safeguard against starvation, and I began to understand why they should have been regarded as sacred. In the rainy season the separate beds of the Ganges united, then overflowed and the flood water poured through the streets of these villages, leaving the black tide marks still visible on the walls of the stone houses. For four months in the year all land to the north of the villages was under water, and the zamindars claimed the land above the flood level to the south. In this period of dearth the villages fell back upon their cows, and it was by grace of their cows that they survived.

In these narrow villages of a single street squeezed between feudal estates and the no man's land of the floods the cows lived in scrupulously kept courtyards, in which the human presence concentrated in sty-like outhouses was clearly of secondary importance. Once a week or so the herdsmen passed through the villages to collect the cows and goats, sometimes numbering a thousand of each animal, then drove them to one of the landlords' fields requiring fertilization. Watched over by the herdsmen they passed the night in the fields, grazed on the residue of the harvest crop, deposited their dung, and in the morning were returned to their owners, who regarded the outing as beneficial to the animals' health, in addition to which they could usually expect a small payment for services rendered.

The cows provided those supremely valuable products in the economy of such villages, milk and dung. The dung not only stoked cooking fires and was used in making walls and floors, but combined with earth formed the lining of baskets in which grain was stored. It was an ingredient of ointment and salves for the treatment of skin conditions, piles and sore eyes, and went into paint. A family with cows producing more dung than required for their own needs might offer the excess to a wholesaler with a pyramid of it in his backyard, where the untouchables – most useful members of any village community – earned six rupees a day, plus free dung, moulding the basic product into flat circular cakes, about one and a half inches thick and ten inches in diameter. These were to be seen everywhere, stuck on the walls to dry, sometimes in neat rows, sometimes in attractive patterns. There were varying qualities of dung, and experts, assayers, and connoisseurs existed to test it and fix a price. A hundred cakes of inferior quality might fetch ten rupees, but the finer grades employed for medicinal or cosmetic purposes could fetch ten times the amount. An enquiry as to whether buffalo dung had any place in this market was countered with an emphatic no. Attempts at adulteration, Devi said, which sometimes happened, were regarded as a social crime.

Devi was observant and informative, drawing my attention to the fact that at intervals of roughly thirty miles we passed out of one cultural zone and entered another different from it in almost every respect. These differences, he said, reflected their occupation in ancient times by invaders or settlers of different races. In one area villagers were different in their physical appearance and in their clothing from the next. To this he added that they spoke different dialects, ate different food when given the choice, and whenever it was possible to escape from basic labouring tasks on the zamindars' land, busied themselves with traditional skills and handicrafts.

We passed through a village where irrigational methods were the speciality. At some time in their half-forgotten history these people had found themselves settled on land subject to drought. In bringing water down from a mountain lake they had acquired skills in the management of water for which the zamindars could be persuaded to pay a few rupees above the rate for ordinary labour. In one village they wove enormous baskets, using a technique elsewhere unknown. In another a clan of hereditary physicians made an infusion from the extravagant beaks of the great Indian hornbill to cure all afflictions from tuberculosis to broken hearts. Each of these areas stood apart from the rest, above all in its style of temple architecture. In and around Patna temples were hardly more than a private house or even a cinema. In an attempt to inspire awe an often grotesque entrance had been built, somewhat in the manner of the old fairground tunnel of love. A few miles down the road temples became red brick pyramids with or without the addition of fantastic gods, demons and animals. Later they were pure white cones without decoration of any kind.

Outside the towns, apart from the lorries thundering down the country roads, there was no traffic to be seen. The lorries, laden with bricks and building materials for the steel towns of West Bengal, and for Calcutta, kept up a steady 70 m.p.h. They were fantastically painted with good luck symbols, stylized flowers and beasts. Images on dashboards sniffed at constantly relighted joss-sticks, and in a few cases a small shrine to Kali – the goddess of destruction, although paradoxically also the protectress of travellers – had been fixed to the outside of the vehicle above the windscreen. Legally the companies employing the drivers had to ensure they got a ten-minute break every three hours to rest and drink tea, but, as Devi admitted, such legal provisos had little meaning in India.

Once in a while there were spaces where the lorry drivers could pull off the road. Here, inevitably, dhabas had opened for business. They were long, thatched cabins where tea cost one rupee a glass, and a ladleful of boiled rice with a puddle of dhal was served on a leaf plate for three rupees. A row of string beds was provided on which drivers could lounge after a meal, and of necessity sleep at the end of the day, without extra payment. Following the drivers' example we stopped at a dhaba from time to time, but only to drink tea. Possibly for caste reasons Devi refused to eat in such places, and we subsisted on biscuits.

It seemed extraordinary to me that the drivers of these exceedingly cheerful-looking lorries should be unsmiling and taciturn, as was our own driver, who always seated himself on such occasions at some distance from us, showing only a strong but somewhat melancholy profile, notably devoid of expression. When I commented to Devi on what seemed his excessive seriousness, the reply was, 'He is happy, but like all these people he is unable to express his happiness. This man is a Munda and he is always appearing in this way.'

So Price was a tribal. This came as another surprise. There was an explanation, too, for the unusual name. Some time in the last century the Mundas had staged a revolt against the British, and those imprisoned after the suppression of the revolt were kept there until they agreed to be converted by Lutheran missionaries. They were then given English names as part of the deal. I asked Devi if he thought Price understood the doctrine of the Trinity, to which his reply was, 'He is not comprehending these things.'

Price was a superb driver, as were most professional Indian drivers, I was soon to decide. Many Western visitors to India form a mistaken impression that Indian traffic responds to no rules and is wholly chaotic. This is far from the case. On the whole Indian drivers are both courteous and considerate, and if they appear to the foreigner to take impossible risks, this is only because their reflexes and their ability to judge speeds and distances are developed to a degree that, however much a catastrophe seems inevitable, when vehicles hurtle towards each other with only inches to spare there will almost always be a hair's-breadth escape. But this only applies to the city. On the open road it is very different.

It was on this occasion, coincidentally, that a further mention of the Mundas came up. Among the usual assortment of poverty-stricken shacks in sight from the dhaba, I had noticed several small, poor, but unusually neat houses, set in fragments of garden, with a painted door and even tiled roof. These belonged, Devi told me, to Munda villagers. They were the aboriginals of Bihar and, although overwhelmed and dispersed by ancient invasions and early British howitzers, eight hundred thousand of them survived tucked away in the holes and corners of this and other states, still distinguishable from the Hindu multitudes among whom they lived.

He was well versed in the tribe's recent history, having been born and bred in Ranchi, a Munda stronghold until the 1960s. The latest Nelles Verlag map calls it a hill resort, with a spa and temples, and the latest guide-book finds it quiet, and notes its possession of an enormous mental asylum – probably the best known in India. Since publication, this once peaceful scene had suffered change due to the discovery of valuable mineral deposits in the area and the consequent building of a satellite town devoted to heavy industry. According to accounts in the Indian press, ten villages were 'acquired' for the actual town, six more for a dam, four more for an extra factory, and five for the railway complex. In this way two thousand two hundred families, mostly composed of Munda peasants, were displaced, finding themselves without homes or land. 'People cleared from one village were installed on the arable land of another, whose inhabitants in turn became landless.' It was a situation generating a limitless supply of unskilled labour for employment in the factories – indeed such a surplus that the wages of one and a half rupees (5p) a day must have come close to the lowest in Indian history. Devi, who readily admitted that his own family had been much benefited financially by the great change, mentioned that all the innumerable rickshaw cyclists of Ranchi were now Munda tribals. In the face of protests, he said, the municipality had given them preferential treatment in the allocation of the licences required.

Late in the afternoon we approached Bhagalpur, most tragic of all the towns of Bihar, where the riots originating in the general election of November 1989 had continued almost without interruption for a month, with the latest published death-roll of over two thousand. In mid-January outbreaks of violence were still a matter of almost daily occurrence. Hardly one of the outwardly pacific villages through which we passed had escaped the slaughter. Voters arriving at polling stations had been forced to hand over their slips to be stamped by mafia gangs in control. This is known as 'booth capture'. Where the landlords' gangs had not been able to capture the booths, voters known to be unsympathetic were kidnapped, beaten, or killed, their bodies thrown down wells or into the Ganges – or the polling station might be demolished by hand-grenades, or blown up.

On 27 February an Assembly election would be held, and the prospect filled the underdogs of Bihar with gloom. The *Times of India* reported pessimistically on the likelihood of a criminal takeover of the democratic process:

> A matter of even greater concern is the character of some candidates. In over 60 constituencies known criminals have entered the fray under the banner of different political parties. This is causing a lot of concern to the police administration. In a violence-prone state like Bihar the presence of so many trigger-happy candidates may turn wide areas of the country into a vast battlefield ... The state government has been frantically seeking additional companies of the BSF and CRPE [para-military forces], but the imported force may not be of much use since the local constabulary is used to obeying the orders of one or other of the local dons, all of whom are in the fray. Indeed, quite a few of them may not ony win, but may also become ministers.

Beyond Monghya, with Bhagalpur now only thirty miles away, a sudden calm fell on our surroundings. It was early evening and the sun in decline spread a saffron light over a landscape in which the animals kicked up feathers of dust as they came streaming back to the villages over the fields. Behind us the Ganges, having turned away sharply to the north, had swung back in a wide, dazzling loop to the rear. At the small town of Sultanganj the river was beneath us, close by the road. A line-up of cranes in the shallows appeared in the rippling air-currents as fishermen in white smocks. Here many lorry drivers who seemed disinclined to go further that day sat hunched morosely over their tea in the dhaba. The scene was a supremely pacific one. A group of spotlessly robed old men who might have been conducting a religious ceremony stood hands clasped together near by in the manner of an old-master adoration of the Magi. A woman passed cradling a new-born calf in her arms. As soon as we stopped a brace of chuckling crows alighted on the car. It was hard to believe that hereabouts only weeks before, in such homely, rustic scenes, men could have been beheaded, hacked to pieces, or dragged to their deaths roped to the backs of cars.

We drank tea in the dhaba and took to the road again. Here there were trees: robust mangoes with polished terracotta trunks and limbs by the roadside. Sacred groves had survived, and enormous banyans dangled their curtains of roots. A rising mist threatened to become a fog and the sun went down behind thick foliage in flashes of green jade. We were quite alone on the road, and within a half-hour night closed in on us. We drove, lights off, over the pot-holed surface at hardly more than a walking pace, picking our way by the faint glow of a misted half moon. Devi said, 'It is better we agree a story for our presence in Bhagalpur. No tourists are visiting this place. If we must go to an administrative centre they will be questioning our motives. What must we say to them? They will not believe we are visiting from curiosity.'

The outskirts of Bhagalpur, deserted and in darkness, revealed rack and ruin when Price switched on the headlights. There had been raging fires and explosions. The charred mess of a lorry lay on its side in a gutted filling station, and beyond it we saw a fog-bound scrap-yard of battered shapes. A pile of rubbish sprouted the shafts of wheels of tangled rickshaws. The fronts of a row of booths had been ripped out, leaving one with the still legible sign MOGHUL THRONE. Once this had been a wretched little tea-shop, and such grandiose titles exemplified the self-delusion (or humour) of the poor. In Bhagalpur only one in ten could read such descriptions, or the claims by Horlicks or Wills cigarettes whose exultant poster faces looked down from the hoardings on what so recently had been a sea of blood.

Here through the scarves of mist we saw only the fringe of an area of devastation in which silk mills which provided half the town's working population with employment had been destroyed. At Sultanganj a Muslim who had lost members of his family said that ten thousand people had been killed in Bhagalpur and the surrounding countryside. This we did not believe. The figure given until now had been a vague 'several hundred', but on this very day the *Times of India* quoted figures from official sources, putting the death-roll at approximately two thousand five hundred, with the partial or total destruction of two thousand eight hundred houses.

A generator provided the wan illumination of the Rajhans Hotel, a self-effacing walk-up in the town's fitfully lit centre, where no trace of the disturbances that had ravaged its outskirts was to be seen. Our arrival took the reception unawares. Much rummaging in drawers followed before the necessary forms were produced. An additional form with many questions had to be filled in by foreign visitors; it seemed likely that it had been a long time since one of these was required. Two silent, troubled men went carefully through the details supplied, comparing them in my case with those furnished in the visa and making painstaking adjustments to the entry in the register. In the background hovered a third man I took to be the manager, ready with a third opinion when uncertainties arose. He seemed full of suppressed nervous excitement, with fluttering fingers and eyelids; whenever he looked in my direction he gave a quick mechanical smile.

Devi and Price, whose formalities took less time to accomplish, had disappeared, and as soon as I was free from the paperwork I went up to my room to tidy up, then wrote down a few notes. I suspected that we were the hotel's only guests. It was very quiet. There was no sound of footsteps on the uncarpeted stairs, no distant voices or banging of doors. The view through the window was of a narrow, misted street. Opposite in a row of shuttered shops was a medical hall in typical Indian style, with a spot-lit plaster torso from which the casing on one side had been removed to display the organs beneath. A policeman went by on a Japanese motorcycle, and at the edge of the field of vision a soldier, rifle slung, stood on guard at a street intersection.

I went down to look for the restaurant, pushed through a door into a dim room containing several tables set for a meal. Having seated myself at one of these, I waited for perhaps five minutes, then got up and went to the door I took to be the entrance to the kitchen. There was no one there. I went back and sat down again. After a while the kitchen door was cautiously opened, a face came into view and was withdrawn. With that Devi appeared. There were times when he could be inscrutable, and this was one of them.

'No problem,' he began – meaning, as I had come to realize, that some hitch had occurred. 'We are all receiving food in bedroom. This food is now being cooked. Soon it is coming.'

I climbed the stairs to the bedroom again, glanced through the window where the medical hall was now in darkness and the soldier had gone. I settled again to the notes; half an hour or so passed, there was a knock at the door and the manager was there at the back of a boy carrying a tray. The boy set the tray down and went, but the man hovered, his brow creased in a troubled smile. I transferred the contents of the tray to a table: Black Label beer ready to be poured into a glass ornamented with lotus flowers, a small-boned chicken complete with long, jungle-fowl neck, and a heap of chips. My first guess was that he had taken advice in the matters of Western culinary preferences and been told chips with everything, but this proved not to be true. 'In Glossop,' the manager said, 'they are eating chicken with chips.'

'Glossop?' I asked. The piece of information seemed strange.

'Very close to Manchester,' the manager said. 'I was in business in this town.' He dropped into the nearest chair. By now having accepted a further example of Indian informality, I took a mouthful of chicken and waited for the polite questioning to begin. 'Your impression Bhagalpur?' the manager asked.

'I only got in an hour ago. It's a terrible mess. Can you tell me what went on here?'

'You are meaning the communal disorders?' he asked.

'The riots. The killings.'

'Everyone is telling you something different,' he said.

'You live here. Surely you know?'

'Partly, I know, but I have not seen with my own eyes. Actually there was a ramshila procession for Hindu people. Those people were collecting money for holy bricks for temple of Ayodhia. When Hindu people are going in procession, they are very noisy. Always there is much beating of drums. You have seen these processions?'

'Wedding ones,' I told him. 'They are certainly noisy.'

'The Muslim people were in their mosque. They sent a message requesting to delay procession until after call to prayer. This the Hindu people are refusing to do. Then followed stone-throwing. The Muslims had guns and bombs already hidden in their houses. They rushed out and started to kill these Hindu people. Many of them they have killed.'

'And you believe that?'

'I am believing it because my brother was among these people. Still the doctor is tending his injured leg. He has paid for and given one sacred brick.'

'So the Muslims started it all?'

'That is my opinion.'

'But the papers say there were many more of them killed than Hindus despite all their bombs and guns.'

'That is because the Hindus are fighting back very strongly.'

It was a discussion I wanted to continue, but at that moment Devi came in, and the manager went off. 'The story they are telling here,' Devi said, 'is that one hundred boys in the Hindu college have disappeared.'

'I read about it somewhere,' I said.

'When their parents went in search of them because they did not return to their houses, all had vanished. There were many blood-stains on walls and floors.'

'And were they ever found?'

'No one is setting eyes on them again.'

I showed him the day before's *Hindustan Times*. 'Did you see this?' I asked.

'Newspapers are saying whatever is suitable for them to say.'

'This is a report of the debate in the House. The Opposition claims the riots were organized by policemen. No schoolboys were killed. It was an excuse to burn down one hundred and fifty villages where they refused to toe the line.'

'It is possible. The mouths of political men are full of lies.'

Devi wanted to discuss the plans for the next day. 'Between Bhagalpur and Ranchi the roads are bad,' he said. 'It is long driving and there is nowhere to stay. We must either be leaving at dawn or remain here another day.'

'I should like to see the famous police station and ask a few questions.'

'It will be wise to refrain from putting such questions.'

'You think so?'

'It is the custom of the police officials to make all questions. "Are you a spy?" they will be asking. "What for are you doing in this place?" Better it is not to display interest in the affairs of those in power. As we are saying in India – better to keep nose clean.'

'You don't suppose we could see a refugee camp?'

'They will not be happy for you to do this. Tomorrow in the morning the hotel people will be sending the forms to the police office, and maybe they will be wishing to see us. Better it would be not to be in this place. We shall be seeing many burned villages on the road to Ranchi. Nothing is to be gained by asking questions when you will not receive a truthful reply.'

We started shortly after dawn, plunging into a fog so thick that we could hardly grope our way through and out of the wreckage of Bhagalpur. To avoid the risk of losing the way we turned back along the main road to Sultanganj, thereafter taking the southerly turn off through Kharag, past a ghostly teak forest, and into the wide and sunlit plain of Jamui, where a tributary of the Ganges curled through brilliant fields. Here the sun sparkled like hoar frost in the sprouting crops. Grey and white strands of mist were rising twisted together in the background. Quite close to the road men in conical hats like those of Vietnam peasants were ploughing with buffaloes, and huge kingfishers flashed up and down the waterways.

Devi stopped to enquire the way. Here at the limits of the rioting, violence had it seemed struck haphazardly in an unsensational and unpremeditated fashion. Half the people were Muslims and half Hindus, but they were all jumbled together and one village escaped while its neighbour suffered. This place, said our informant, had been attacked back in November, but the wounds inflicted on mud walls and reed thatch had been healed by the survivors in a few days, and no sign of calamity remained. What had been worse than the ruin of property had been the looting of food stocks and the destruction by the feudalist gangs of standing crops. 'Do the people here have any religious problems?' I asked. 'Sir, these things are beyond their comprehension. The taste of rice is sweet in their mouths.' One man's buffaloes had been killed by the invaders, so his neighbour shared the ploughing of his field.

The absence of signposts was a problem complicated by the presence of new roads not marked on the map; this made the going slow. Leaving the wide valley behind, we moved into the dry uplands where poverty increased. Possessions were reduced to a scrawny cow and a goat per family and an acre of land cluttered by immovable rocks to be scratched round by a primitive plough. Poverty, apart from its abject version in city slums, generates its own brand of virtue ('Poor people give you good regards', as Devi had put it). Here, too, it disguised itself in gracious forms, in the classic faces of the people and their dignified bearing and the splendidly archaic processes of husbandry. There was a deceptive semblance of leisure in the ancient methods of threshing, winnowing, and grinding the grain, and the carrying of pots to the well. Where there were swampy areas the peasants had been able to grow rice. This was dried on the hard surface of the road, and a bottleneck through which traffic was obliged to pass was marked out by stones.

Oases of cultivable earth and occasional water were spaced through bleak landscapes by De Chirico, of polished bedrock and dry culverts and outcrops of metallic ores, productive not even of weeds. There were strange intrusions. Outside a deserted village, once a Lutheran missionary enclave, a row of white crosses projected from the earth. Lutheran communities were scattered through the badlands of Bihar, where they had rescued their converts from the caste system, ordered them to bury their dead, and recommended the consumption of meat, which in most cases the converts were unable to afford. A cigarette advertisement stuck up at a crossroad, miles from anywhere and with no building in sight, assured the literate ten per cent: 'Nothing comes between you and the flavour.'

Here and there were sizeable patches of mixed forest, of teak, sal, mango, pipal, and many valuable hardwoods, interspersed with lesser and greater explosions of blond and rufous bamboo. I had expected the Indian jungle to be a repetition of the great forest of the Amazon, but there was no resemblance at all. To a European there was something about the jungle here that was familiar and comprehensible. These trees with their massive trunks, the symmetrical outthrust of their branches, their compact shape and unexceptional foliage, suggested no more than flamboyant versions of familiar European species. The trees of the Amazon, by contrast, were alien and mysterious. Their roots spread over an acre of the thin skin of soil to anchor slender trunks soaring to extraordinary heights: they were part of an environmental conspiracy, fertilized often by a single species of bat, moth, or bird, defended by insects they rewarded with pseudo-fruit to keep such predators as leaf-cutting ants at bay, as well as engaged in other vegetable–animal alliances for mutual survival. When the Amazonian trees are cut down the environment dies with them. In the Indian jungles the ecosystem may survive. When one tree goes another can be planted in its place.

An intruder enters the Amazon forest with caution. The Indian jungle on the road to Ranchi seemed to encourage inspection. 'Any tigers or elephants hereabouts?' I asked Devi.

'Certainly they are existing. It is no more than one in a thousand chance if you are encountering one such animal.'

I went for a walk. It was not quite Surrey, but devoid of any obvious threat. In north Bihar it was early spring, with the unfolding everywhere of springtime buds, an occasional inconspicuous flower, a bird twittering on a branch. It was a very tidy wood, giving almost the impression that the trees had been clipped into shape. There were no orchids to be seen, no lianas, aerial roots, or fungus of startling colour. I have only once in many such walks encountered a deadly snake, and no snakes of any kind were to be seen here. There was a disappointing absence of visible birds, although doves that had positioned themselves out of sight in the leaf canopy kept up a powerful and persistent moaning. Devi, who had followed me, was pointing down to hoof-prints in the soft earth. 'Bisons,' he said. In these calm surroundings it seemed hard to believe. 'Very large animals,' he added, 'but not interfering in any way. It is a pity we are not seeing them.' We went back to the car, and started off again for Ranchi.

A huge grey smudge across the southern horizon was the first sign of India's great industrial belt, which we should shortly be entering. At first I took it to be a distant storm, although this would have been unlikely at the time of year. From being quite alone on country roads going nowhere in particular we found ourselves among lorries in increasing numbers, and slowly the grey smudge spread across the sky towards us, and at the bottom of it the first factory chimneys pumping out smoke came into sight. They were the outposts of the industrial belt extending almost from the frontier with Bangladesh to Raipur, which comes close to the centre of the sub-continent, almost five hundred miles. It contains large deposits of coal and iron, as well as every conceivable metal, and the steel towns to the west and south of Ranchi probably resemble England's Black Country of a half-century ago. There have been attempts to invest these melancholic surroundings with tourist appeal, evidenced by the description of Jamshedpur, first of the steel cities, in *Bihar Land of Ancient Wisdom*, issued by the Department of Tourism. 'Though the skyline is dominated by enormous chimneys, fumes of copper oxide, and dunes of coal and limestone, the city is an environmentalist's dream come true.'

By nightfall we were running the gauntlet of chimneys now feeding a false sunset with variegated smokes. The road surface, pounded and ground by monstrous wheels, had been blown away into the sky and, imprisoned in an endless procession of lorries, we burrowed into choking multi-coloured dust. The fumes were all the Tourist Office had promised.

Some hours later at the entrance to Ranchi we came upon an unusual sight. A cow damaged by a collision had been left in the road, evidently with a broken leg. Whatever the mishap befalling a cow, it is unthinkable in India to put one out of its misery.

'What will happen to it?' I asked.

'Soon the owner will come,' Devi said, 'and bring it away.'

'And after that, what?'

'If this cow can be cured he will cure it.'

'And if not?'

'Then he may sell it to a man who is buying animals that cannot be cured.'

'So he will slaughter it for the meat?'

'This we are not asking. It is possible. He will pay the owner a very small sum. After that I do not know.'

In Ranchi I checked in at the government Ashok Hotel, catering largely for commercial travellers and foreign technicians from the city's industrial complex, who came there rather despairingly for a change of scene and spent most of their time speechless with boredom in the bar.

The check-in procedure at any Indian hotel can be lengthy, but at the Ashok it occupied a record-breaking half-hour while my passport was passed up through the chain of command and back, advice was taken and heads nodded in agreement. When I enquired why I was being kept waiting the reception clerk who had taken me over said that this was the first time he had seen a tourist visa in a passport, and there had been some delay in unearthing the necessary form.

The Ashok, with its polished empty spaces and its inconsequential happenings, reminded me of one of the old Marx Brothers films. A whiff of institutional austerity was diluted with outbursts of a poetic impulse by which surfaces of the lobby furniture were freshly decorated every morning with patterns of frangipani blossom. Service was well meaning but muddled, and to attempt to put through a long-distance telephone call was to expose oneself to unpredictabilities of success or failure rivalling those of the gaming table.

At dinner a menu decorated like an illuminated manuscript promised fish under eleven guises, each described in hyperbolical terms. The Chef's Choice was grilled pomfret, 'flown to you specially from the Goan Sea'.

'Today we are not serving pomfret,' the waiter said.

'In that case I'll take the snapper.'

The waiter shook his head. 'No snapper, sir.'

'What fish have you, then?'

'On this day we have no fish, reason being that all fish in Indian Sea severely infected by disease.'

The menu listed nine chicken dishes. I ran my finger down the list and the waiter butted in, 'Tonight the Chef is recommending fried chicken, sir.'

'With chips?'

'Oh, yes, sir. Always we are serving chips.'

'Can I have some beer?' I asked.

'Beer only served in bar, sir.'

The bar was immediately behind, its open frontier a yard from where I sat. It was permanently tenanted by silent and lugubrious German technicians separated from each other by an empty stool, and seeking oblivion in Indian whisky. I went into the bar, ordered a beer, and stood it on a table in the bar area within reach of my arm, hoping that the waiter would go away, but this, as he had no other customer to serve, he clearly had no intention of doing.

The following morning, I breakfasted on the balcony of my room where looking down on the flower beds and lawns of the hotel's spacious gardens I was furnished once again with an example of the

627

Indian nervous distrust of independent action. Three gardeners were at work planting young trees. The senior man carried only a ruler with which he measured the diameter of a hole already dug and waiting to receive the tree. This achieved, the second man placed the tree in position and, after slight adjustments indicated by his chief, the third man stepped forward, dug with his hands into the earth piled beside the hole, and began to scoop it handful by handful over the roots. The gardeners had been joined by a small collection of onlookers and when after what seemed a long time the first tree was satisfactorily planted the party moved on to where the next awaited them a few yards away. Here, too, in the context of the industrial sweatshop of Ranchi, was illustrated the Indian paradox of travail and inaction.

In Delhi I had been given an introduction to a man said to be one of the Ranchi mafia dons. I called on him in his office in the city's business centre where he sold cars and road-making machinery, although he was happy to tell me that he had 'irons in many other fires'. Reputedly he was head of a somewhat specialized branch of the Indian version of the Honoured Society controlling the supply of sand used to fill in the cavities left in mines, which otherwise frequently led to dangerous earth subsidences.

We sat in deep, soft, body-enfolding chairs – also made in one of this man's factories – and sipped spiced tea from bone china cups. The view through the window was a busy one. Dispossessed Mundas pedalled their rickshaws frantically; a fleet of lorries, painted in the local manner with rising suns, jockeyed for position at the crossroads; an agile beggar hopped through the traffic, a withered leg slung from his neck. The don – if such he were – was amiable and confiding. He was in his forties, bold-eyed and handsome in the style of a prince in a seventeenth-century Moghul miniature, depicting perhaps a hunting scene among peacocks and gazelles. Kicking off his shoes he revealed small, dimpled feet. He wore a number of silver rings set with pearls which showed to advantage on his dark, smooth hands. A newspaper Sunday supplement on the coffee table was devoted, it said, wholly to astrology and horoscopes.

'So you are enjoying Ranchi?' he said. 'It is very exciting. All the time we are experiencing something like a play. Like the *Ramayana*. So full of excitement is my brain that I cannot sleep. Did they tell you our growth is the second largest in India, with forty thousand now employed in our new town? Here we are making, in maximum security, components for the bomb. Every one of our factories carries on its front our civic motto: "The beauty consists in the purity of heart".'

Chapter Five

I HAD A FREE AFTERNOON. 'Can we see the asylum?' I asked Devi.

'There is no problem.'

For once there was none.

'This is a very famous hospital,' Devi said. 'You will be welcome.'

I was surprised that the visit would be as easy as he suggested. None the less, so far as I could gather after a week's acquaintance, he meant what he said.

My previous experience of Indian treatment of mental disorders had been at the unpublicized Bhagavati Temple of Exorcism in Kerala where patients were put through an energetic form of psychotherapy based upon song and dance. I had been present the year before when a dozen or so girls in their late teens or early twenties, usually kept locked up for most of the day in windowless cells, were placed in an enclosure within sight of the doll-like image of the goddess Bhagavati, and encouraged or compelled to dance. Each girl had her own attendant with his fingers entwined in her hair, and each rotated her body and jerked her head backwards and forwards to the tune of a four-man orchestra. The hold on her hair prevented a girl from damaging her head on the enclosure walls or the ground. A doctor claimed that two-thirds of the girls subjected to this therapy were eventually cured – as testified to, he pointed out, by large numbers of nails protruding from the trunk of a neighbouring tree. Each of these nails represented a cure; the cured patient had used her own forehead to hammer it into the wood.

Such, occasionally, were the mysterious ways of the East, but when I gave Devi a description of this somewhat eerie experience he said, 'You will be finding this hospital a different kettle of fish.'

Application for the visit had to be made to the Chief Medical

Officer whose office was in a pleasant, Georgian-style house located among a complex of single-storey buildings of which only the roofs were visible behind high walls. It came as a surprise that no previous request had been made for an appointment with Dr Bhati, and that it was apparently quite in order to walk into this busy and powerful man's office, and at a pleasant nod from him seat ourselves at his desk while a small queue of staff waited at his elbow for his signature on innumerable ledgers, documents, and chits. The office itself gave an impression of clutter. At the moment of our entrance Dr Bhati shoved a motorcycle helmet aside on his desk to make space for untidy sheaves of papers. I found it interesting that all the pictures in this room – several of Alpine scenes – should be markedly askew and that all the staff members wore lavender pullovers. Having done with his signing the doctor greeted us with great cordiality, picked up a telephone to order tea, and then listened to Devi's explanation, given in Hindi, of the reason for our visit.

'Normally application should be made in writing,' Dr Bhati said. He smiled broadly. 'You may have heard of, or even experienced, our national bureaucracy. In cases where written applications are made you will expect to wait weeks, even months, before receiving a reply. This visit will be strictly unofficial. I will now ring my superior, and if he is agreeable I will call somebody to show you round.'

Dr Bhati rang through to his superior and nodded his agreement with whatever was said. People came and went without ceremony and the flow of documents for signature continued. A woman with a baby slipped into the file of orderlies and male nurses and uncovered its face to display a sore. This the doctor examined with every sign of sympathy and interest, muttered words of counsel, and, having found the baby a biscuit, shoved them away.

There was a pause in the queue of petitioners. 'As you can see, we are kept busy,' Dr Bhati said. 'This hospital is a legacy of the British presence, and although there are many more patients now we have been unable to expand.' He seemed happy to discuss his work. 'In our psychiatric wards we have six hundred and forty-three beds of which one-half are suffering from minor illnesses requiring little treatment. The rest, in most cases, are suffering from schizophrenia or manic depression.'

I asked him whether wealth or status was reflected in the incidence of such mental disorders, and he replied that low-caste patients were more likely to suffer from schizophrenia and higher-caste ones from manic depression. It was the same with poverty and wealth. In these days serious disorders and minor illnesses arising from hereditary factors or chemical imbalance were treated with chemicals. For the rest occupational therapy and keeping the patient interested in life was the chosen solution. He was ready with a listing of small gains, of tiny advances into the boundless *terra incognita* of mental illness. 'A hard slog, but we seem to be getting results,' he droned on gently. 'Life expectation increased – that's certainly a feather in our cap ... pulse and blood pressure consistently down ... increased resistance to infection ... reduction in self-induced amnesia ... Happ's Syndrome a thing of the past ... fissularia well within bounds ... libido – well, just ticking over, as is only to be expected. All in all not too depressing a picture.'

A social worker came to show us over the occupational therapy unit, lodged in a number of barracks in a park-like setting of lawns and flower beds. Such places are quiet, and we had arrived at the time of the midday meal. The patients, who were very orderly, had been released from their therapy to make their way to the dining-rooms. They gave little indication of mental disturbance; perhaps because the suspension of the stresses of everyday life had produced an unnatural tranquillity. I was reminded of the children of my childhood on their way to church, a little bored by the knowledge of what awaited them.

'And now let us take a peep at our production of art,' the social worker said.

He led the way into a large room with a number of paintings on a row of easels. There were unfinished pictures of other pictures, the models available being portraits of Gandhi, Nehru, and some insipid colour prints of episodes from the life of Christ. In addition – and these had been chosen by every copyist – there were British works of art surviving here from the beginnings of Indian independence, when the hospital had been handed over, lock, stock, and barrel, to the new incumbents. These included cricketing scenes at the Oval, 1946, and a number of photographs of the British royalty: of King George VI as Admiral of the Fleet, of his wife and of the two young daughters at Balmoral, Windsor, and the Palace. This is what the psychiatric patients seeking to heal their troubled minds had painted over and over again for forty-three years: thousands and thousands of these trite, smudged, and hardly recognizable icons, to be placed on display on the walls of this and other buildings, commented upon, praised, criticized, awarded major or minor prizes, certificates or compensatory recognition before – after the lapse of years – being stored away in sandalwood chests, each made to contain a quarter of a ton of important documents and inscribed according to custom with the image of the monkey god Hanuman, protector of public records.

Turning away from the pictures I was approached by a handsome, rather puffy-faced man wearing a blazer with club tie. 'Do forgive me for butting in,' he said. 'I gather you're English. It was nice of you to come. I am happy to see you.'

'Are you a doctor?' I asked.

'Unfortunately, no. I'm a patient. My name is Prabhakar. I'm a film actor. Not very well known in your country, I'm afraid. I've played in a number of films, but naturally you won't have seen them. Perhaps I should write the name. It will be unfamiliar to you.'

He took my notebook and pen and wrote down his name. Devi said, 'Mr Prabhakar is very well known. In India we are all enjoying his acting.'

'I am here because I do not sleep well, and this affects my head. All went well until I fell in love with Mrs Hema Malini.'

'Mrs Malini is very famous,' Devi said.

'She rejected my suit. This produced intense depression, which can only have made me less attractive to the lady of my dreams. A vicious circle in fact. With each rejection my state of mind worsened. So you see how it is.' His hand went up to his chin. 'Bad shave this morning. I must get a grip on myself.'

Mr Prabhakar studied my face anxiously. I raked in my mind for a suitable comment. Lamely, I said, 'I hope the problem resolves itself.'

'It will,' he said. 'In fact it has. All goes well that ends well. We plan to marry this year.'

We shook hands and the film actor made for the canteen.

'Do you really believe this man will be marrying Mrs Malini?' Devi asked our guide.

'He will never marry her. This is a delusion. Mrs Malini is a very great actress. Mr Prabhakar is in many films but he is playing bit parts. This man has been with us now ten times. He is happy to think that he will be marrying this beautiful woman, but this will never be.'

On the occasion of a single previous visit to a mental hospital in Burma I had been bewildered by what seemed to me the normality of the patients, but after my experience with Mr Prabhakar and his ingenious concealment of a disturbed mental state, I was in a cautious frame of mind as we approached the female compound of the Psychiatric Centre. This, too, seemed well ordered and supremely tranquil. Looked after by inmates who may have been enthusiastic gardeners in the outside world, the herbaceous borders were colourful and trim. Neatly dressed ladies sat chatting over their needlework among the flowers. One strummed softly on the local version of a guitar for the entertainment of an encircling group. The Centre's splendid trees provided a haven for singing birds. This was the setting of an Arcadian scene from an early miniature.

A Miss Banerjee who had taken charge of us drew our attention to many facilities. There was a pleasant picnicking area where ladies inclined to do so could entertain visiting friends. The Centre encouraged sport: tennis, badminton. Although we saw no one engaged in these energetic pastimes, it was evident that they existed. We were taken to a spacious concert hall, furnished with colour television and a music system. Once in a while, she said, the patients put on a theatrical show here, and beneath the stage a magnificent grand piano awaited the next production or display of the musical talents of an inmate. I congratulated her on this impressive piece of furniture and she smiled with pleasure. A moment later she was called away, and idly lifting the lid over the keyboard I was faced with the fact that the piano possessed no keys. It was a discovery which at that moment seemed of extreme symbolical significance.

For all this intrusion of anti-climax I felt bound to admit that the Centre was an unexpectedly pleasant place, providing all too probably in the case of many patients a haven from the sad domestic case-histories so often reported upon in the Indian press. I wondered if many of the women we saw here might feel inclined to do what they could to prolong their stay. Miss Banerjee agreed that this was inevitable. A further problem for the Centre, she said, arose because there were cases where families had been able to send female relatives here with the intention of putting them out of the way while they employed legal subterfuges to strip them of their possessions.

Leaving the concert hall we found our way barred by a pretty girl with the face, dress, and slightly imperious manner of a Spanish dancer. There is a strong and fairly substantial theory in India as elsewhere that the gypsies of Europe originated in tribes driven out by Indian population displacements of the remote past. Everywhere in the tribal areas of the country these dark, handsome, and slightly predatory faces were to be seen, and at this moment these frilled sleeves and skirts among the saris encouraged the flicker of a theory that something like a traditional flamenco costume might survive in the recesses of the sub-continent. The girl made a grab at us, got a grip on Devi, and was able to thrust a hand into his pocket before Miss Banerjee dragged her away. She ran off. 'Could she have been a gypsy?' I foolishly asked Miss Banerjee. 'Oh, no, sir, this lady has been seeing the film *Carmen*, and now she is identifying with the part.' It was the only flamboyant episode of the morning, and with its conclusion the somewhat sub-normal calm of the Centre was restored.

As we started off down the path towards the gate a group of women came out of a building. They were of mixed ages, and almost certainly mixed castes, and now I was coming to realize that there was something in the atmosphere and methods of the Centre that suppressed individuals, resettled them in groups, smoothed over differences of age and caste, creating slowly a sheep-fold of displaced persons, sedated by the withdrawal of stress and the exclusion of conflicts by these walls. For once, even at a distance of twenty yards, there was one here who stood out from the crowd. We walked past and this member of the group who had remained an individual detached herself, came after us, and caught up. This time certainly a doctor, I assured myself, but with that, doubt set in. She had a fine alert face, smiling slightly and with a briskness of expression and movement that had fought off the lassitude of the place. Such encounters in India set off a barrage of questions which are accepted as polite. 'You're a doctor, aren't you?' I asked.

'No, of course not. I'm a patient. Would you like to hear about me? I'm interested that you should have taken me for a doctor. I did four years' medical school at Patna before having to give up. My name is Mubina Thapar, my father is Dr Prasar Thapar. My uncle's a doctor, too. He raped me when I was four or five. That may have been the start of my trouble. I suffer from OCD. Obsessive Compulsion Disorder. They've found a name for it now. I'm a compulsive. I do silly things.'

Set in what I would have described as a serene face, she had fine, large, rather staring eyes of the kind given to the tragic peasants of Haiti by the gifted primitives who paint them on that isle. 'They treated me for years in Bangalore, then they sent me to Bombay where they have a different specialized treatment. My father thought I ought to get married because he'd been told the love of a husband helps in such cases. It didn't work for me, and I was divorced. Do you know what an obsession's like? For me everything is dirty. Food is dirty, flowers are dirty, everything, everything. They tell me to plant white flowers in the garden but when they bloom they are dirty. I can't touch people because they are dirty. I never stop washing myself, but I stay dirty.'

The hospital was the temple – the kingdom – of purity imposed from without. It prescribed an environment of bodies scoured from taint, of close-clipped lawns, of disciplined flower beds, of wardens who tidied away scraps, and of feeding, sleeping, and therapeutic occupations in an aroma of scrubbed wood. Perhaps subjection to unspotted exteriors only made things worse for this girl. Perhaps it only emphasized an isolation that I was sure hid behind the obsession. At that moment Miss Thapar seemed one of the loneliest persons I had ever met, suffering as much, I suspected, from a sense of abandonment as from imaginary pollution, and I was deeply sorry for her. She trailed along after us at an increasing distance, waving forlornly until we turned the corner and she was lost to sight.

Chapter Six

FACED WITH A GAP of two days to be filled in while awaiting news of the feasibilities of further travel, we decided on a side-trip to the Tiger Reserve at Palamau, some three hours to the west of Ranchi by road. The reserve, one of many throughout the country, had been a product of conservatory zeal following the news back in 1970 that there were practically no tigers left in India. It was believed, too, the nature reserves could be offered as a major tourist attraction, and this proved to be true. The number of tigers and elephants was steadily on the increase, as were those of tourists ready to pay for expensive Shikari holidays. By this year many reserves had waiting lists for those wishing to visit them. Fortunately for us, as there were no tourists in Bihar, this did not apply. Devi assured me that no advance booking was necessary. He suspected that we would be the only visitors, and this proved to be the case.

The Tiger Reserve at Palamau, according to the booklet, comprises most of the Daltongali South Forest Division, about four hundred square miles in all. However, entering its boundary, it came as a surprise to see that a great deal of deforestation had gone on and was still taking place. Villagers were emerging from what was left of the wooded area carrying great bundles of firewood on their heads, and where trees had been left standing by the roadside we saw girls busily hacking away the lower branches. The ravaged landscape where the forest had been seemed to contain earthworks, mounds, and trenches. These, on closer inspection, proved to be no more than deep and final erosion where nothing more than subsoil and bedrock remains. Nevertheless this was the scene of the world's first tiger census, and one of the first reserves to be included in Mrs Gandhi's Tiger Project. The booklet says that it is one of the best developed parks in India, 'catering to every class of visitor, from jaded city-dwellers seeking forest recreation ... to serious students of the plant and animal life of Bihar'.

Elsewhere in newly created reserves there have been instances of the summary eviction of the human population to make room for the animals. A point in favour of Palamau is that a number of small villages continue to exist within the reserve, although the kind of life they offered seemed miserable. Palamau is cruelly poor; the poorest district of what is accepted, outside its industrial belt, as India's most backward and poverty stricken state. According to the Indian press and the 1988 Anti-Slavery Society report to the United Nations, it is the hunting ground of slavers kidnapping children between the ages of five and twelve for supply to the carpet-making industry. 'India today', according to the Anti-Slavery report, has 'at least one hundred thousand juvenile carpet-making slaves', mostly taken from the Palamau region.

The central village of the reserve is Belta, where there is no reason why a tourist should not be able to spend a few days in forest recreation withdrawn from the nastiness of the world. Since the attraction in any case lies in the animals to be seen, isolation is not only acceptable but offered as a feature, and the tourist lodge is sited on a low hill a few hundred yards from the village, where it commands in fulfilment of the brochure's promises a splendid view of the wild life of the area. We were warned that we should see little but spotted deer in this particular area. They were there by the hundred, forming large, static, but gently inquisitive groups.

Taking into consideration that the lodge was empty, without electricity, and that there was no food to be had, we opted for the life of the village, to be seen from the newly built, and also empty, Hotel Debjon. This proved to be a collector's piece of its kind. On arrival on January 18th we were presented with a Christmas card apiece by the manager. The staff were all stony-faced tribals – 'They are smiling in their hearts but their pleasure does not appear on their faces,' Devi said. In their determination to be of service they frequently burst into the rooms, which were unprovided with locks, and wherever we went in the vicinity of the hotel they followed us closely in the hope of being commanded to do something. The hotel's prize possession (and wonder of Palamau) was a model in polystyrene, salvaged from packaging material, of the Victoria Memorial in Calcutta. Despite the great difficulty in working with the soft and friable medium, the creator, over a period of five months, had carved out, sculpted, and glued together nine hundred and twenty-four components. A book contained the names and admiring comments of the visitors who had flocked to see it. An MP had written, 'I am at a loss for words. This is art.'

The hotel garden was quilted with marigolds through which strutted and scuffled the most marvellous cockerels, raised from eggs collected in the jungle, with combs like red sealing wax, scintillating plumage, and enormously long legs. There was very little to do in Palamau and a kind of Mexican lethargy had fallen upon the men, who squatted for hours on end in the angles of walls, wide-brimmed hats pulled down over their narrow eyes. The tribal boy who did all the odd jobs about the place took my attention. 'How old is he?' I asked Devi, who spoke to him in Hindi.

'He does not know.'

'Tell him to have a guess.'

'He thinks maybe eight.'

'What do you suppose they pay him?'

'Very little. He is not working very hard. Maybe three rupees.'

'I'm curious to see whether these people ever smile,' I said. 'I'm going to give him five rupees and watch the reaction.'

I called the boy over and gave him the note. He stared at it for a moment, and nothing moved in his face. Then he backed away.

'No effect whatever,' I said. 'Does he understand the value of money?'

'Yes, he understands it.'

'Then why doesn't he look pleased?'

'This boy is feeling great happiness at this moment. His heart is singing. It is something he cannot show.'

The villagers were listless in appearance and sluggish in their movements. Even young men walked very slowly, a few yards at a time, and it was hard not to suspect that they might be suffering from malnutrition, and under the necessity of conserving whatever energy they possessed. The feudal lord of Belta heard I was there and came to see me followed by three of his bodyguards. He was a head taller than the rest, a man with fine patrician hands and an overshadowed expression who had spent some time in Coventry and hoped that I knew that city. He dispatched flies unerringly with the fly-swat he carried and spoke of his friendship with Gandhi's successor, Vinoba Bhavi, who had passed this way accompanied by his disciples in an immensely prolonged symbolic walk round the country. His object had been to induce landlords to give away a tiny proportion of their land to landless labourers, many of whom were dying of starvation at the time. 'Not an acre was donated,' he smiled sadly. 'I was wholly in favour of his movement, and if there had been a proper response I would most willingly have chipped in.'

He got up to go, extended his hand, then remembered. 'Should you be needing an elephant at any time while you're here,' he said, 'don't hesitate to take mine.'

Missionary campaigns had been very welcome to the dispossessed of Palamau. There were three groups in the field, all in strenuous competition with each other in the battle for souls, all offering inducements to conversion. The Jesuits and the Lutherans bid against each other, rewarding converts with food and medicine equal in value to the exceedingly low wages paid by the zamindars. It was normal for the beneficiaries to sell these medicines for cash. A year or two before our visit the Muslims entered what now became a three-sided contest. Not only medicines were on offer in this case, but the Muslim paradise with lavishly described pleasures compared to which the Christian version might have seemed intangible to some. To outwit the local practice of inflating income by belonging to three religions at a time the Muslims insisted that converts grew tufts of beard 'of a religious kind'. This left the locals, apart from attending prayer-meetings and readings of the Koran, with very little to do. 'They are bored,' Devi said. 'Now they must not gamble or drink, and these religious people are not permitting them to play noisy games.'

Despite the missionaries' precautions he reported that a few of the villagers had managed to benefit from all three religions, satisfying the mullah that they were unable to grow the regulation beard, while kidding both Christian contestants along, and even secretly visiting the Hindu temple to keep on the right side of the prominent goddess Durga, where the priest, although comparatively poor, was accustomed to bribe them with sweets. For all that, the stress-free life had become a little dull, a matter of a long linger in the dhaba over a glass of tea, mosquitoes, ritual ablutions, prostrations, and prayers.

But, as Devi put it, the zamindars of the whole region were batting on a sticky wicket for the redoubtable and mysteriously all-knowing Naxalites – avengers of ancient peasant wrongs – were drawing nearer and nearer, killing and being killed in and around Daltonganj, only nineteen miles away. Here the peasantry had supported them in a pitched battle with the gangs employed by the zamindars, who had been driven off. Now the Naxalites were more or less in control of the sixty-mile stretch of road to Auranagar, along which landlords had ceased to be able to collect their rents. It was clear from the absence of tourists at the reserve that the news had got round.

Evening approached, and it was time to go in search of the animals: since the most interesting of these are nocturnal in their habits there is very little opportunity to see them after the hour following dawn or before that immediately preceding sunset. In its booklet the reserve laid claim to a wide range of beasts and birds, most of them described in spirited terms. There were fifty-four tigers, forty-six leopards ('most effectively cryptic in bush or grass'), herds of 'significantly robust bison', eighty-three elephants ('it is wiser to retreat than to show courage'), 'quite exclusive wolves', India's only hyenas, the Indian wild dog, the sloth bear, two species of monkey, and four of deer.

The suggested car-tour of the Reserve was an expedition I embarked upon with no great expectations. A mild pessimism as to the outcome of all such ventures has been based upon a long experience of anti-climax. I am probably the only person having had the good fortune to have known Laos – Land of a Million Elephants, as it called itself before the carpet-bombings – without seeing an elephant. Despite travels in countries where tigers once abounded, I had never seen a tiger, either, or for that matter any wild animal of a spectacular kind. Since the great forests of South-East Asia had failed to provide such excitements, I found it hard to believe that the tiny patch of woodland representing the Palamau Tiger Reserve would do so.

Nor was the central area of the Reserve, described in the booklet as 'carved out of virgin forest', as impressive as I would have hoped. Although reprieved from the final catastrophe of commercial felling, I could not help feeling that in the denuded and impoverished surrounding area the local people would have helped themselves to a tree here and there whenever they could. The fact that such reservations could exist at all was probably only due to the British mania for killing large animals, adopted as a matter of prestige by the rich Indians who followed them. So closely aligned was shooting to status and power that as late as 1955 a 'privileged hunter' was allowed to wipe out half the tiger population in the Kanha National Park.

Using Devi's pride and joy, the Contessa, we were accompanied by a ranger on a short but uneventful tour of the roads. The ranger then suggested we should visit the prime viewing area, leave the car and go for a walk. Despite the three villagers who had been killed by a 'mad' elephant, the Reserve's attitude to such 'regrettable incidents' was nonchalant. The best place, the ranger said, to see animals – once in a while even to run into a tiger – was on a high bank overlooking the Kamaldah Lake, and there we went, parked the Contessa, and set out on our walk. Reasonably enough the ranger was extremely anxious that our time should not be wasted, and he was delighted to be able to point out a slide in the mud where a group of elephants had come down the bank. This was the moment for a word of caution. Should an elephant suddenly appear, you either took cover behind a dense bush – relying on the animal's poor eyesight – or you ran for it. In the latter case you had to run downhill – something an elephant could not do, although on the level a male in top form could reach a speed of up to twenty-five miles per hour. Should the danger have presented itself here, the only way of escape would have been down the bank into the lake.

We waited for the elephants but nothing in the forest moved. Kamaldah Lake spread its green, shimmering waters, a mile across, fringed with peach-coloured reeds and small bright explosions of bamboo. Black, streamlined trogons criss-crossed its surface, chasing after flies, and above fishing eagles circled contemplatively, stacked at varying heights. All round, the trees resounded with the ventriloquial squawking of birds – then came the moment that redeemed the day. A clump of bamboo parted its fronds for two peacocks in flight. They balanced delicately in the air currents immediately below before dropping to earth at the water's edge. They were both males and indulged in a brief posturing display, followed by a competitive spreading of plumes. They advanced strutting upon each other, sidled away and returned, at once both stately and skittish. Suddenly, as if a button had been pressed, they both took off at the same moment, winging away at great speed within inches of the water.

At this moment the ranger made an excited return. He had discovered bisons' hoof-prints in the mud near by, an evidence of the small herd's recent passage within yards of where we were standing. Splendid animals, he assured us, and likely to be close by. The Indian bison (*Bos gaurus*), said the booklet, was the 'tallest, handsomest and most peaceful perhaps, of the world's wild oxen'. The ranger thought they would return; meanwhile he guided us to a clump of randia trees bearing small fruit which, although when crushed were used to poison fish in shallow pools, were irresistible to deer. If we concealed ourselves within sight of these he was sure the deer would eventually come.

A half-hour passed. The sun was on the point of setting, with no sign of bison or deer, and we started back. As we did so a small tree went down with a crash near by. It was wiser to retreat, as the booklet advised, and this we did. The car was close and we ran for it. Both Devi and the ranger claimed to have seen a patch of grey elephant skin in a stirring of leaves. I did not, but I was quite prepared to take their word for it that the elephant was there.

There was an attempt on my part that evening to experiment with minor social adjustments, which met with little success. I have always found it uncomfortable to travel in a group in which a member, whether a driver or otherwise, is excluded at mealtimes. In India with its complex caste separations the situation was more tricky than in England, for people who seemed to mix easily enough when working together sometimes appeared to withdraw into a strange dietetic purdah when mealtimes arrived. I had already noticed that when we stopped for tea at one of the dhabas, Devi refused to eat and our driver immediately disappeared from sight. This reminded me of the scene in Burma when the Indian railway-repair staff, normally united in the stresses of the Burmese Civil War raging round them, formed three separate and exclusive circles at midday to consume their rations.

Dinner at the Debjon was to be served at 7 p.m. I found a table with a spotless cloth, a bowlful of zinnias, and a little printed notice that said 'Good Morning. To salute joyfully the day.' The table was laid for one. 'Won't you be eating?' I asked Devi.

'On this day I am fasting,' Devi said. 'I will take a little rice before retiring to bed.'

'Where's the driver?'

'He is busy with the car. He will be coming later.'

I ate alone, went up to my room, read for an hour or two, then went down for some bottled water and saw Devi and the driver seated together just in sight at a table round a corner. Their backs were turned to me and I quietly withdrew.

There was a mystery here, and behind it what appeared as an unusually complicated situation. The Indian railway staff in the threatened town of Pyinmana in Burma had been playing the caste game properly, according to the rules to avoid pollution of their food. The pollution they feared was entirely spiritual. If one of the railwaymen squatting round the food had not been entirely successful in scouring the oil-stains from his fingers before plunging them into the common rice, this would not have mattered. The contaminating presence of a non-caste-member would.

It was a feature of Hindu society that has never ceased to amaze the foreigner. Friar Navarrete who chose to travel in India on his way back to Spain in 1670 did so because the religious community of Canton had assured him that it was a pleasure not to be missed. And so it turned out to be but for a single incident when his servant accidentally brushed against a pot in which a fellow traveller was carrying his food. This, although it was wrapped in protective cloths and carried in a sack, was held by its owner to have been defiled and instantly taken out and smashed to the ground. So intricately complicated is this matter of spiritual cleanliness that a successful and affluent restaurant owner who happens to be of low-caste origin may frequently seek to boost his turnover by employing an impoverished and sometimes physically dirty Brahmin to do the cooking. In such cases stresses may arise when the Brahmin seeks to defend the ritual purity of his food by debarring the immaculate although ritually unclean employer from his kitchen.

The sub-divisions of caste are endless, and Devi, although bracketed with merchants in general, had forebears who were in government administration, a circumstance that had edged him towards the top of that division. He prided himself on his liberal attitude in such matters, and I believed that he was justified in doing so. In an earlier conversation that day he had described city life as the great demolisher of caste. How, for example, he had asked, could a big city office be expected to run a half-dozen separate canteens? The thing became absurd.

Devi was prepared to sit down at table with a tribal, who had no caste at all. Would he have shared a meal with an untouchable? Giving some thought to it, I felt sure that he would. So where did I come in? I can only assume that he knew his Englishmen, and believed that my class prejudice might be stronger than any inhibitions imposed upon him by caste. It was a saddening thought.

*

Next day's programme was for a morning trip to another part of the reserve where the presence of a sloth bear had been reported with what I would have put at an infinitesimally small chance of seeing it. It was arranged that this would be followed by the investigation of some Moghul ruins of importance recently uncovered in the jungle. Just as we were about to set out, the plan was thrown into disarray by the surprise arrival of a bus full of factory workers with their families on a three-day holiday break from Calcutta. No one at Belta claimed to have heard anything of this although a paper was produced by the party's guide confirming that a visit to the Reserve was included in the deal. So far, said the guide, the holiday had been a disaster. At the end of the first day's long journey from Calcutta they had been promised unspecified urban excitements, which had turned out to be a tour of a Ranchi steelworks, and tea and stale cake in a factory canteen. On this day they were hoping to see the full range of animals advertised in the Reserve booklet, and the mad elephant whose fame had even reached Calcutta.

The ranger said that there was no alternative but to take them round in their aged, battered bus. It would be a short run because the bus could only be driven over a mile or two of the wider tracks, but this ruled out any possibility of our seeing the sloth bears. He was upset because the children were very noisy, and the animals would take days to get over it. The bus, which had lost its silencer, sounded like a plane about to take off. A trip would take an hour or so, he thought, after which he hoped they would go. The bus was parked some hundreds of yards from where we stood, and from it arose the hootings, the whistlings, and the jubilance of children released from the grey prison of the Calcutta streets. A firework exploded with a loud crack overhead, and the ranger shook his head miserably.

We found another driver to take us to the ruins, which included a sixteenth-century fort of the Choro kings. It once must have been an imposing Moghul building, but was now a tropical ruin wrenched apart by ingrowing trees and parasitic vines. Of the profusion of decorative tiles that must have covered its walls nothing remained but a fragment under the battlements about thirty-five feet from the ground. There is something claustrophobic and oppressive about Moghul ruins, which with their small, secretive windows in vast areas of blank wall depended at the best of times upon an abundant source of artificial lighting in brilliantly decorated interiors.

The fort offered another example of the sexual mania of the rulers of those days. On a visit in the previous year to the Mattancherry Palace I had been impressed by the cruel absurdity of the roughly contemporary Cochin Rajah who had arranged for the numerous members of his harem to spend their lives in one low-roofed room, from which the view through a lattice was of three or four yards of pavement crossed only by female servants. Here at Palamau a well about twelve feet in diameter and thirty feet deep had been constructed outside the walls of the fort. This was reached by an underground passage from the women's quarters, opening at a point just above the water level about twenty-five feet below the surface of the ground. The purpose of the underground passage was to ensure that no one apart from the King could ever set eyes upon the ladies of his household on the way to, or coming from, their ablutions. What a sad fate awaited a pretty girl who caught the eye of a Cochin rajah or a Choro king – and how much better off were village women, safe in the homeliness of their features, exposed only to hard labour, deprivation, and hunger.

Chapter Seven

ON THE RETURN JOURNEY we made a side-trip to the Dasam
Falls, twenty-eight miles from Ranchi. This was believed originally
to have been a sacred spot and place of pilgrimage of the Munda
people. Now fewer Mundas were to be seen; for it had been
discovered by Indian tourists. Suddenly, at so short a distance from
Ranchi with its web of roads, its cuprous fumes, its vigour and
squalor, this was another world, peopled by natives who dressed as
Indians but were not. Here there were narrow and winding lanes,
patches of ancient woodland, and Munda peasants going to their
fields carrying wooden ploughs on their shoulders. Here for the first
time I saw a wild animal of any standing, an emaciated jackal that
came through a hedge, loped across the road, and disappeared into a
thicket. I was surprised that it should be so long-legged and lanky.
Devi, cheered that we should have shared this small-scale experience,
claimed that jackals were more aggressive than I believed them to
be, and exceptionally dangerous to children.

Tourist buses on the way to the falls tore through these lanes. The
tourists, full of the holiday spirit, shouted and waved to the Mundas,
who returned the usual Munda blank looks. Munda tribals were
bigger men and women than those on the buses, benefiting, so long
as they remained in the mountains, from a better and more varied
diet than that of the towns, and perhaps from their less complex
religion. The Hindu women, in particular, in contrast with the free-
striding Munda girls, appeared like passive wraiths.

When Devi had first driven through here the people were still
naked, armed with bows and arrows, and likely to shoot at anyone
who laughed at them. These Mundas still kept to their villages at
the tops of the mountains and little was known of their customs.
Every twelve years the women of the tribe dressed as men for a

single day and went hunting. Now *that*, said Devi, would be something to photograph, although as far as he knew no one had done so. Nearing the falls we saw a stranger riding a horse. This, said Devi, was an Imli, a member of a tribe of hereditary moneylenders, tolerated by the government although seen as the worst scourge, after the feudal landlords, of rural India. The Imlis battened on tribal people without understanding of commerce and finance, and tricked them into accepting loans – usually to buy useless consumer goods. Rates of interest up to ten per cent per month were levied.

Arriving at the waterfalls we were astounded to find that the same Calcutta trippers who had gone rattling away from Palamau the previous evening were in uproarious possession, their children leaping about like goats on the surrounding crags, lighting fires on the hillside and slashing ineffectively at the branches of hardwood trees, while the adults played their transistors and gurgled down beer from the bottle. The best view was to be had from a flat top over a gorge. Immediately below ran a small, calm river, bordered by silver sand. A quarter of a mile upstream this river had plunged one thousand feet over a cliff's edge into a wide pool enclosed by cyclopean rocks. It emerged from this area of compression as a great spouting of water some two hundred yards above the point over which we were poised. In the rainy season the view must have been of a great aquatic tumult and even now, although in sedate fashion, it was impressive. The great attraction for the adventurous was the pool at the bottom of the cliff. Many people felt under compulsion to swim in it. A notice, in English, said BATHING IN THESE FALLS IS VERY DANGEROUS AND MANY PRECIOUS LIVES HAVE BEEN LOST. It was no exaggeration. There had been an endless catalogue of drownings. On the occasion of Devi's last visit he had taken part in a failed attempt to rescue a swimmer sucked in the outfall of water through the rocks. What was it, he wondered, that had drawn so many men, here, to their deaths? Could there be any substance in the Munda belief in a tribal god who demanded sacrifice?

A few yards away some Munda girls squatted with the alcohol made from the flowers of their sacred sarhul trees which they had brought for sale. Of all kinds of country spirits, this was the most highly esteemed. The men from Calcutta bargained in sign language for the alcohol, transferring their purchase from the elegant clay pots of the Mundas to empty oil cans they had brought in readiness. Their womenfolk watched from a distance. They were neat in their factory-made, over-bright saris; the Munda girls were unkempt although they had style. Back at the end of the century the Mundas had made fine jewellery and copper amulets now sought after by collectors, but contact with civilization had artistically neutered them, and nothing remained of the accomplishments of those days but the finely shaped pots. Now they sold alcohol to the Hindus, and the cash thus obtained bought tawdry bangles and rings.

On the natural platform overlooking the gorge a tea-house had been built where Hindus sold special tea and millet cakes deep-fried in oil. We settled there after a laborious climb down the steps cut in the rock face part way to the river, to a point where the steps ended. Here we found ourselves chatting to a Munda, indistinguishable to me from an Indian, up for the weekend from Ranchi.

This man's history, in Devi's translation, was an extraordinary one. Like most tribal people he was hazy about dates, but some fifteen years earlier when he seemed to have been in his late teens, his family had been involved in one of the early Ranchi evictions, in which they had been reduced to outright beggars by the loss of house and land. Money allocated for relief had been embezzled, as so frequently happens, by government officials. His parents died, and he – the only child – had migrated to the slums of Patna. The change in his fortunes had happened a year or two later after his rescue of an old moneylender attacked by robbers. The old man died shortly afterwards; he inherited his house and in the course of clearing it out the Munda had uncovered a box containing a considerable collection of jewellery taken as pledges. Munda superstition did not permit him even to touch this. Instead he called in an agent who valued the articles, wrapped them in a cloth used to wipe a temple image – thus proof against the evil eye – and took them away to negotiate an exchange deal for land. The Munda received about five acres, on which he planted rice and lentils.

For three years all went well. He bought more land and took on

Hindu labourers, then the Naxalites moved in and sent him the usual warning.

'Why did they do that?' I asked.

'They accused him of exploiting his workers.'

'And did he?'

There was an exchange of questions and answers in Hindi.

'He does not understand this question. I cannot make him understand what is exploitation. With tribal people he would have shared this land. These were not tribal people.'

'So he thought it wiser to come back?'

'Yes, it was wiser for him to do this.'

That, in brief, was the story, and now the Munda was safe back in his own country, where so far, at least, the Naxalites were under control.

Through the window of the tea-house I saw that a woman had just arrived carrying on her head a large jar of alcohol from which the small pots of the liquor-saleswomen were about to be replenished. The Munda smiled approvingly. 'He is saying that here women are the real bosses,' Devi said.

'And do you agree?'

'For the tribals, yes. This is true.'

Among the Hindus, the Munda went on, women were nothing. Their fathers bought husbands for them, and a man with many daughters was ruined. I would have expected Devi to come to the defence of his own culture at this point, but he stuck to translating without comment, nodding agreement to the claim that the Mundas had to buy their wives and were often obliged to pay their future fathers-in-law dearly for them. Even when the couple set up home together the wife in practice owned everything.

Our Munda friend gestured in the direction of the scene through the window where the tribal menfolk, having finished playing a game like five-stones, were now sharing a bowl of liquor pushed by one of the girls in their direction as if to keep them quiet. That, the Munda suggested, was a typical tribal setting. The men played silly games, drank, chatted, and lounged about, while the women did the work. There were two things to be said in their favour. One was that they played hockey so well that there was a Munda player in most of the big teams. Other than that they had a passion for tidiness, and while the women got on with the hard work in the fields they were useful to keep the place clean.

At that moment three men staggered past us and out of the door carrying bins full of rubbish to be tipped into the ravine.

The Munda turned away his head in disgust. This was something, he told us, that could never happen in one of their own villages because it was offensive to tribal religion. We followed his eyes in a moment of silence to the rumble of water bursting through the bottle-neck in the gorge. The Munda growled his criticism. 'He is saying the gods are angry to look down on such a mess,' Devi said.

The question of sati, the ancient Hindu practice of the burning of widows, came up following a discussion on the subject of dowry murders, itself prompted by a headline in a newspaper, 'Victims of Dowry Hungry In-Laws', picked up on the drive into Ranchi. The article reported that Karmiki – a women's voluntary organization – charged the police with often refusing to file complaints arising out of wife-abuse or dowry deaths. In reply the police spokesman mentioned that in Delhi about four hundred cases of dowry deaths or 'Eve-teasing' (maltreatment including torture) were dealt with every month. The suggestion was that, with the number of such offences constantly on the increase, there were not enough policemen to go round.

What was the situation in Ranchi, I asked Devi, to which his answer was that although he had not given much thought to the matter, he assumed that it was much the same as in the north. Offhand he could only think of a couple of recent dowry deaths. He could not remember the details of the first but thought that it was a routine kitchen-stove killing. In the second case a young man had ordered his wife to put pressure on her parents to supplement the amount in cash already paid by the gift of a new motorcycle, and on their refusal had pulled out a pistol and shot her through the head. Both cases were 'under investigation', he said.

Sati was barred by the British over a century ago. Although rare these days, Devi said, it was most certainly still practised. When the 'honourable' woman's sacrifice was occasionally performed it might receive a great deal of publicity, or more likely be hushed up. In the case of Mrs Rupkandar there had been no such conspiracy of silence. Although a Ranchi girl by birth, Marwari Rupkandar's family were from Rajasthan. When the time came to look round for a suitable husband the father wrote to members of the Rajput merchant caste there – to which the family belonged – to ask for their help. At that time Marwari, aged eighteen, attended the local high school, and Devi, who remembered her well, said that she was both exceptionally lively and pretty.

An acceptable husband, of roughly the same age, was found, the marriage arrangements went through, and Marwari left for Rajasthan. In due course a wedding photograph of the radiant young Mr and Mrs Rupkandar was published in the Ranchi newspaper, soon after which silence fell. About three months later the father assembled his friends to make a simple announcement: 'My daughter has gone sati.' The facts were that Marwari's husband had died of a heart attack, and Marwari had been persuaded to join him on his funeral pyre. Pilgrims, said Devi, came in numbers to scramble for handfuls of the ashes, and the most prominent of them were given copies of Marwari's photograph taken in the last minutes of her life. The 'holy event' was whole-heartedly supported by the local population. Marwari had since become a goddess and the place where the sati had taken place a centre of pilgrimage. 'I think', Devi added, 'that the police are still busy with their investigation. Soon there may be arrests.'

A friend who had visited Rajasthan on a number of occasions and knows it well said that due to the increasing influence of the Rajputs there – the practice of satis is strongly embodied in their traditions – this form of ritual murder is on the increase in the north. In all parts of the world and throughout history women have lived longer than men. Bearing this in mind it seems evident that in the period of two thousand five hundred years or more in which sati has been practised, Indian widows by the million must have died by fire.

The standard explanation for a public spectacle which startled so many foreigners in India in the past fails to convince. Here is the Venetian traveller Caesar Fredericke, writing in about 1585.

> It was told me that this law was of ancient time to make provision against the slaughters which women made of their husbands. For in those days before the law was made, the women for every little displeasure that their husbands had done unto them, would presently poison their husbands and take other men, and now by reason of this law they are most faithful unto their husbands, and count their lives as dear as their own.

Among the reading material I had brought with me was the third volume, issued by the Hakluyt Society, of the *Travels of Ibn Battuta*. It dealt largely with his journeys through central Asia and India, in the course of which he spent some time in the years 1334–6 at the Court of Sultan Muhammed Ibn Tughluq at Delhi. Leafing through the pages of volume three back in Ranchi, I found, as was to be expected, his account of a sati of his day. Such events appear to have been as commonplace as weddings, and in the early stages of the procedure hardly differed from the noisy and jubilant wedding processions of our day. 'I used to see in that country', says Ibn Battuta, 'an infidel Hindu woman [on her way to the burning], richly dressed, riding on horseback and preceded by drums and trumpets' – going, as Caesar Fredericke puts it, 'with as great joy as brides do in Venice to their nuptials'.

Ibn Battuta, a humane man, clearly appalled by what he saw as barbaric practices, would have felt compelled to include a description of them in his meticulous record of the life of the countries through which he travelled. In this instance three widows had agreed to burn themselves after the death of their husbands fighting in the Sultan's army against the guerrilla resistance of the day. It was regarded, he says, as a commendable act by which their families gained prestige, but was not compulsory.

> Each one of them had a horse brought to her and mounted it, richly dressed and perfumed. In her right hand she held a coconut, with

which she played, and in her left a mirror, in which she could see her face ... Every one of the infidels would say to one of them, 'Take greetings from me to my father, or brother, or mother, or friend,' and she would say 'yes' and smile at them. After travelling about three miles with them we came to a dark place with muddy water. They descended to the pool, plunged into it, and divested themselves of their clothes and their ornaments, which they distributed as alms. Each one was then given an unsewn garment of coarse cotton. Meanwhile a fire had been lit in a low-lying spot. There were about fifteen men there with faggots of thin wood, while the drummers and trumpeters were standing by waiting for the women's coming. The fire was screened by a blanket held by some men in their hands so that she should not be frightened by the sight of it. I saw one of them, on coming to the blanket, pull it violently out of the men's hands, saying to them with a laugh, 'Is it with the fire that you frighten me? I know that it is a blazing fire.' Thereupon she joined her hands above her head in salutation to the fire, and cast herself into it. At the same moment the drums, trumpets and bugles were sounded, and men threw on her the firewood they were carrying and the others put heavy balks on top of her to prevent her moving. When I saw this I had all but fallen off my horse, if my companions had not quickly brought water to me and laved my face, after which I withdrew.

Written two and a half centuries later, Caesar Fredericke's description fits that given by Ibn Battuta almost to the detail. Even the blanket held to screen the vision of the blazing fire is still in use.

Before the pinnacle they are used to set a mat, because they shall not see the fierceness of the fire, and still custom demands that its succour be rejected by the victim ... yet there are many that will have it plucked away, showing therein a heat not fearful, and that they are not afraid of that sight.

And that, until nearly three hundred years on, when the British stepped in, was in all probability more or less the way it went.

The lot of Hindu women, on the whole, has been a sad one

throughout the history of India: reduced so often by an arranged and loveless marriage to the status of a menial in the husband's house, to feed as a widow the fires roaring through the centuries, or in our days to contribute to the vast statistic of young women dying from usually uninvestigated causes, few being of sufficient interest to warrant press comment. ('State prosecutor Mr Lao said there was nothing peculiar about this case except the mode of burning – the bride having been doused in whisky.')

A TV programme at the Ashok that evening offered the possibility of a clue as to the reason why Hindu civilization should have offered its womanhood so low a promise of fulfilment and happiness, so great a likelihood of the intrusion of contempt and pain. The programme was entitled *Women's Right to Salvation*, and took the form of a discussion by a panel of savants of a book by a Canadian scholar, Dr Katherine Young, whose speciality was the study of women in Hinduism. In her perusal of the Sanscrit scriptures, the author had discovered that major commentators of the past on spiritual themes had held the view that women could rightfully opt for sanyasa, the path of renunciation of fleshly desire, and thus attain salvation. In making this assertion it seemed that Dr Young had broken new ground. According to the members of the panel taking part in the discussion the doctor had stirred up great controversy. She had said in her book that some orthodox Hindu thinkers of these days still see women as irretrievably lost. The *Bhagavad Gita* contains many references to them as 'those of evil birth', at most conceding a temporary state of 'heavenly bliss'. Dr Young nevertheless had uncovered a more liberal view of Hindu femininity in the *Bhagavad Gita* commentaries of the tenth and eleventh century championing the rights of women to take the path of renunciation and thus attain salvation.

The three learned pundits of the panel in their impeccable cottons were impressive indeed, rising easily above the trivialities too often imposed by the media in such encounters. These softly purring ecclesiastical voices were armed to extinguish doubt. Listening to them I could appreciate how hypnotic suggestion by television was a proven fact. One, the gentlest in his gestures and smile, ruled out the possibility of the female soul in paradise. The second seemed to give it a more than fifty-fifty chance. He admitted to having been swayed by recent re-interpretations of the *Gita*, which he accepted as being the central scriptural authority of modern Hindus. Renunciation was the theme of the third. If salvation were to be attempted in the case of a woman it seemed to him to rule out marriage, which provided as he saw it opportunities of indulgence likely to damage the karma. His point of view seemed to reflect that of St Paul – that (at most) it was better to marry than to burn.

How does Hinduism define salvation? For the layman of any faith it is a nebulous and even arguable concept, but whatever it may signify in the Hindu religion, women's exclusion according to the orthodox stigmatizes them as the inferior sex, and has served at one time or another to subject them to every form of indignity and abuse.

It became evident in Ranchi that restrictions and probable prohibitions on travel in Madhya Pradesh made an approach to the area that interested me impracticable through south Bibar. The general opinion was that the southern part of the state, and the district of Bastar, would be more conveniently reached by travelling south from Calcutta to Bhubaneswar and then heading in a westerly direction through southern Orissa into areas of maximum tribal concentration. It was arranged with Devi that he should drive me as far as Calcutta. We decided to break the journey and spend the night at Jamshedpur, India's first planned industrial city, so warmly recommended by the Department of Tourism for its environmental attractions.

Leaving Ranchi we ran into intense industrial traffic, with an endless succession of heavily laden lorries charging in both directions. We passed the wreckage left by some of the most spectacular crashes I have ever seen, where monstrous vehicles travelling at 70 m.p.h. had sometimes been in head-on collision, literally exploding and scattering cargoes, demolished bodies, engines, axles, and wheels all over the road. In one case an eight-wheel leviathan had impaled a small house and charged with it into a field. 'Often they are trying to make up time,' Devi said. 'There is a fine for lateness. They must keep to schedule.' There were deviations to avoid insecure bridges, bottle-necks, and hazards of all kinds, and often the lorries had opened up new rights of way simply by driving through the fields, creating an anonymous, churned-up, dust-clogged landscape devoid of signposts, in which it was easy to lose the way.

It was on this wasteland that we encountered our first Indian motel, an establishment of the kind in which ambitious beginnings are betrayed by a shortage of funds, and perhaps a secret belief that nothing will last. This could have belonged to a Turkish beach-development scheme, with pseudo-marble cracking from concrete surfaces, naked wiring sprouting from walls, and door-handles that fell off. In the restaurant area the atmosphere was frantic with bellowing Indian film music and victims of a crash being sponged free of blood and bandaged up on the floor. Outside in the garden all was calm. Here a procession of strikingly robed tribal women, with the faces of temple carvings, brought cans of water collected at a dribbling spigot to top up a bath from which three languid gardeners filled pint-sized bottles to water the flowers.

I joined a group of German technicians from Jamshedpur, drinking beer at the edge of the kidney-shaped pool. They were here for a swim and for lunch, and had mistrustfully brought with them their own pool chemicals, but seemed to have overestimated the quantity required, as the water gave off a tremendous odour of chlorine. The meal that was to follow was of a rather special kind – beef-burgers, to which they had been introduced by an American colleague at the factory, who had come here in missionary spirit to instruct the kitchen staff in the art of cooking them. It was a secret and expensive operation, involving smuggling and bribery, as the slaughter of cows for meat is illegal in most parts of India. The unvarying curries provided by Jamshedpur's only restaurant, said the Germans, made the high cost of the black-market Indian equivalent of the Big Mac well worth it. They had been in India for periods of up to a year, and had developed a kind of protective holy indifference to deal with the boredom inevitably generated by a situation in which nothing was of interest but work. None of them had travelled more than a few miles from Jamshedpur. They received the same inflated salaries here as in Saudi, and there was slightly more to do, but the climate was worse. One had enrolled himself on an embroidery course; another had tried yoga and given it up. This, it was agreed, was like an open prison; still the money was good.

This was Ho territory, and the Hos were brilliant irrigationalists. We found ourselves in a wide plain with soft mountainous edges; there were occasional clumps of feathery trees, and neat, tiny villages of a half-dozen or so huts, all of the same shape and size, rather like a conscientiously constructed scale model in an anthropological exhibit. The Hos, perhaps over the centuries, had dug out innumerable ponds, linking them with ditches, so that although we were already in the third month of the dry season water abounded. They cultivated rice and various pulses, but spent much of their time scooping up tiny fish in their nets. Where a hard, clean road surface was near at hand they had marked off segments with stones and spread out their rice to dry. It struck me as remarkable that the harassed lorry drivers should be prepared to tolerate a practice by which they were so much slowed down.

The site for the construction of the dam on the Subarnarekha River lay at the edge of the plain under the misted shape of a sugar loaf mountain. It was one of the two dams in the Jamshedpur region which are to submerge thirty thousand hectares of land and fifty-two villages, thus displacing up to one hundred thousand tribals – the majority Hos – settled here since before the Aryan invasions. When served with notice to go there were cases of villagers armed with bows and arrows raising a protest. Police 'firings' followed, and a few 'extra-judicial encounter killings' – the current euphemism for the death of arrested persons while in police custody.

Many dams have been constructed in India since independence, and many more are in the making. Hydropower projects – despite many doubts as to the ultimate benefits conferred – are fashionable and make the fortunes of numerous bodies and individuals involved in the construction. A whole-hearted and fairly powerful resistance based upon pragmatic, ecological, and even humanitarian grounds is a feature of Indian politics, despite which such undertakings assume ever more and more fantastic size. The Narmada Valley Project – the largest in the world so far – will include thirty major dams, one hundred and thirty-five medium dams, and three thousand minor dams, and since there is no previous experience of the problems involved, experts are even worried over the possibility of seismological effects. One argument raised in parliament is that it may inundate more land than it will irrigate. Dealing with the humanitarian aspects of the case, it is noted that up to seven hundred villages are to go with possibly one and a half million people displaced. Never has so much land, so many homesteads, so great an area of virgin forest been planned to disappear beneath the waters of sterile lakes, and whatever the promises made, experience teaches that for the dispossessed doomsday awaits.

We stopped at a small dam near Jamshedpur which had been completed some years before and was now a place where people went for an hour or two's escape from an overwhelmingly industrial scene. It provided a recreation area where men were playing cricket, a car-park with water laid on for the washing and polishing of cars, a children's cycle merry-go-round, stalls selling assorted nuts and pictures of tigers and gods, and a portrait photographer stalking disconsolately with his Polaroid.

There was an injection of something quite new to me in this otherwise normal holiday-making Indian crowd, for the recreation area was suddenly invaded by a band of local hippies calling themselves love children. Since they were involved in protest, this had to be demonstrated first by the clothing they wore, but here a problem arose. The first hippies of the West had been deeply influenced by Indian fashions, as was evident by the trailing skirts and clinging drapery. To distinguish themselves from the phlegmatic multitudes of Jamshedpur their Indian counterparts had to reverse the order of dress. Where the originators of the cult had favoured concealment, they chose physical display, with sleeveless jerkins and shorts and close-cropped hair. Where flower power had trod softly, they bustled, sprinting here and there to cover the walls with graffiti: *God is my love*.

The cows climbing the steep slopes of the dam in search of fresh grass made this otherwise a wholly Indian scene. A flight of steps led to a narrow path along the rim of the dam, and there families promenaded to enjoy as best they could the lifelessness of an artificial lake that it would take fifty years for the landscape to accept. Fish had been introduced and ingenious wicker traps were offered for hire in which several, not exceeding two inches in length, had been caught and transferred to tins full of water. These were being examined by a pretty and expensively dressed little girl, who I was to learn had never seen a live fish before. 'And what will they do with them?' she asked her father. 'They will eat them,' he told her. She seemed to turn pale with horror, and be on the verge of tears. The father explained smilingly, 'She is very gentle by nature. You see, we are Brahmins. We do not eat living things.'

Jamshedpur disappointed. We arrived after dark to find the five square miles of the renowned steel city closed off like a vast prison camp, surrounded by a high wall topped with barbed wire. The skyline was indeed dominated by enormous chimneys, and the sky itself illuminated in a fitful although theatrical fashion by outpourings of multi-coloured smoke. Perhaps the wind was in the wrong direction for the advertised copper oxide fumes, instead pollution was by noise, an infernal roaring not entirely excluded by winding up the car's windows. Tours of many of the complexes had been offered as 'a rewarding stop on a sightseeing trip', but we were warned that these might take a day or two to arrange due to industrial disputes which had had to be quietened down by the army's intervention.

The hotel was rather dark and sad. There was a huddle of worried men at the reception who had been called upon to cope with a sudden influx of guests taking part in a seminar on disaster management. At this critical moment the wind had changed and the cuprous fumes were being blown in our direction. Someone had been called to spray the lobby with a fragrance of that antiseptic kind used to squirt the cabins of planes stopping at airports in Central America. A cow that had thrust its head through the hotel door was persuaded to back out.

Next day we took the road to Ghatsila for Kharagpur and Calcutta. Now we were in Santal country, where women were in the forefront once again. Although Devi discovered that missionaries had combed the area with hand-outs of 'seemly clothing', a hundred yards or so back from the road the girls went topless, and many of them in roadside villages wore tribal-style short skirts which, upsetting as they may have been to the religious eye, were supremely suitable for work in the fields or for riding pillion on a motorbike. Some of these villages were prehistoric Venices built along canals and on the banks of omnipresent fish ponds, with water everywhere. Every Santal village was a hive of Brueghelesque activity; people were ploughing with oxen in waterlogged fields, making carts, building or pulling down houses, cockfighting, or just running up and down to work off energy. Often the roads had been broken to pieces by the traffic, and lorries were blundering through the ruts and tremendous pot-holes like a herd of elephants in flight. At the entrance to one village they – and we too – had been held up by Santal boys demanding contributions for the festival of Saraswati, goddess of knowledge and education, and there had been a long and surprisingly good-natured wait while money was counted and receipts given.

Santal villages were immaculate although status required the headman to build a house of corrugated iron in which he lived surrounded by dwellings of beautifully woven bamboo and carved wood. The Santals had little understanding of commerce and when we stopped at a tea-house we found that the management had been handed over to a non-tribal Hindu. It was a filthy, relaxed, and somnolent place. Before filling the glasses the boy smeared them with a grimy rag, then squatted in a corner to go back to sleep. Twenty yards away the lorries went raging past. Right in the middle of the village, one had suffered ultimate catastrophe, moulting a great collection of parts all over the road. Another involved in the collision had landed up in a pond where it lay on its side garnished with lilies. We took our glasses round to the back of the tea-house to escape the worst of the exhaust fumes. Here the scene was pacific indeed. Santals clothed in the white shirts and shorts they favoured squatted in a row along the edge of a brilliant square of paddy, where – although engaged in transplanting seedlings – they might have been weaving a carpet. Further out, more men were fishing with nets, an operation they seemed to turn almost into a dance. A beautiful Santal girl with skirts over her knees went past, leading her old, blind father by a stick. She laughed at something he said. Wherever there was a bush a bird warbled. A lorry driver brought his tea out to talk to us. He was grumbling about the collection for Saraswati. With a few minutes in hand he had asked to see the shrine, which he found unimpressive. It was a crudely made bamboo hut containing a Communist Party election poster, and an image of the goddess which turned out to be a fairground doll dressed in Santal style. 'What do you think they want that money for?' he asked Devi. 'Don't believe it's for education – they vote Communist. It's for dope.'

We reached Calcutta in the late afternoon, stiff and a little dazed after a drive over bad roads that had started at dawn. Smog hung like a delicately tinted gauze curtain over the city, muting, I suspected, a rawness that might otherwise have been apparent. A tremendous concentration of traffic had filled the sallow streets with smoke which billowed through the bottle-necks as if from a railway tunnel. Long-distance lorries were jammed in one behind the other – sometimes driven in an erratic manner as if the drivers had been overtaken by intense fatigue. In among them were squeezed a large variety of local vehicles, all of them fantastically overloaded, with adiposities of cargo spreading over the footpath on one side and into the road on the other in such a way as to cut off the vision of following drivers. The noise of open exhausts, horn-blowing, and advertisements bellowed from loudspeakers suspended over the streets produced in the end a stunning, almost soporific effect. I had hoped to change a booking made for me at an over-luxurious hotel, but by the time we arrived I was too tired to care. We pulled into the forecourt and immediately a queue of arrivals formed behind us. Devi was anxious to be well out of the city before dark, so the leave-taking was short. It had been an excellent trip, and I was sad to see him go.

Chapter Eight

CALCUTTA INSPIRES the respect and even the affection of many of those who know it well. Victorian grandeur often relieves the monotony of mean streets. Its people are intelligent, imaginative, and kind, and the fact that the city has failed in my case to awake enthusiasm is probably due to an episode dating from my first visit in 1950.

I had arrived there in the company of Gautam Chautala, the Reuters man in Saigon, who had covered the French war in Vietnam and was on his way home for a month's leave. Gautam was one of the most engaging human beings I had ever met. We had shared a number of minor adventures in Vietnam, and now I was delighted that my first contact with India should be in his company.

The circumstance of our meeting had been in some way enlightening, providing as it did a first glimpse into the mysteries of caste. We met at the Continental Hotel where, through the intense demand for accommodation arising from the war, the manager felt obliged to ask us to share a room. It was a very large one, he said, and so it turned out to be, but what he did not go on to explain was that it contained five beds, three of them tenanted at the time of our arrival. In the event we shared with two French officers – one of whom raved in his sleep – and a young couple who had been bombed out of their house and were in the queue for plane seats back to Paris. Gautam led me to the capacious bathroom to define the problem that had arisen. 'I am a Brahmin,' he said, 'and I would like to ask you as a great favour not to use my towel. This is one of these religious things.' He gave a self-deprecating laugh. I told him I quite understood and would see to it that no unintentional defilement took place. Some time later there was another embarrassed request. Would I have any objection to his bringing in a prostitute? None whatever, I told him, but what about the others? 'There's a war on. They'll understand,' he said. 'And the defilement?' I asked. 'I repeat a few mantras. There's no problem.'

In Calcutta we put up at the Great Eastern Hotel, which came as an experience. Five waiters of varying degrees of responsibility stood behind our chairs, although, greatly to my disappointment after the austerities of Vietnam, only English food of the most uninspiring kind was to be had. At this time I received my second insight into the workings of caste. Returning to my room for something I had left behind I disturbed the sweeper tidying up the bathroom, who covered his face with an arm as if to ward off a blow, then scuttled almost bent double from the room.

We finished our meal, ran the gauntlet of bowing and scraping, and made for the street. A row of rickshaw-pullers were lined up at the doors, and Gautam got into one. 'This man is taking me to see a nurse,' he said.

I walked on, plunged in a matter of hours from the limited misery of Vietnam at war into the unlimited misery of the streets of Calcutta. The wide, stained pavement ahead stank of urine, and all over it were strewn what at first seemed bundles of rugs but which on second glance were transformed into human forms. Small stirrings from some showed signs of life, others were quite inert – dying or dead, there was no way of knowing. A man on hands and knees struggled dreadfully to draw breath; another, face down, added dribbles to a puddle of blood. A woman who had covered her face with a scarf so that none of it was visible lay legs apart, vagina exposed. I stopped, more shocked probably than ever before in my life. The war in Vietnam had imposed instant anaesthesia. There I accepted what could not be avoided. The battle scenes were part of the protocol of the circumstances: the flies on the human fat, the neat package of brains blown from the head of a tied-up prisoner. I had permitted a hardening of the tissues of sensitivity. This was different. The exposed vagina within twenty yards of a doorman dressed like a maharajah in turban and scarlet coat was no part of the protocol of peace. I was not ready for Calcutta. I had stopped, at a loss for a moment to know what to do, and thus had caused passers-by hurrying home to slow down and turn their heads in astonishment. They had long since trained themselves not to see the grim scenes such as this that surrounded them. Men and women dying on the pavement was something to be overlooked; the spectacle of a man who stops to observe these things was not.

I described the episode to Gautam.

'Of course they were surprised,' he said. 'What do you expect? They must have thought you were some sort of nut-case.'

'Was that really a nurse the rickshaw-puller took you to see?'

'We call them that,' he said. 'Often they are. It's a poorly paid profession.'

This time I found myself staying at the Oberoi, once known as the Grand. This was largely by accident since I normally avoid luxury accommodation, which notoriously isolates the traveller from the life of any country, and is unlikely to promote adventure. In this instance efforts to make a change were frustrated by the fact that Calcutta's telephones no longer worked and personal attendance was called for to settle all the details of onward travel. This, in India, can be a time-consuming affair.

Nevertheless, the Oberoi had its advantages, for it was centrally located in Chowringee, where all my business had to be done. Five-star hotels can be brash, pretentious, and noisy. The Oberoi had shown respect for its inheritance from the days when it was a Victorian boarding house and was still pleasantly sedate, free from intrusive music, and provided an environment that calmed – almost in a churchy fashion – the human voice. Guests wandered stealthily through wide corridors over green marble floors. A bowl of tuberoses had been placed in every alcove and a single, perfect red rose (five hundred were delivered to the hotel every morning) in a vase on each table. The walls were covered by fine reproductions of late eighteenth-century aquatints of Indian scenes by Thomas and William Daniell. The restaurant offered dishes based upon meat imported from New Zealand, praised on the menu with occasional outbursts of bad poetry. Its staff were most interesting to talk to, obviously college graduates to a man. An average tip left for a waiter in the bar would probably have equalled the average Calcutta family's income for a week.

The entrance to the Oberoi is in a forecourt with a drive-in from the Chowringee Road, now renamed after Jawaharlal Nehru. A scattering of onlookers sometimes form at the junction to the private drive-in and road simply to stare at the hotel. No one waves them away. They seem like the party guests in Buñuel's strange film *The Exterminating Angel*, held back by an invisible force at a threshold over which they cannot pass. Their view is of a hundred square yards or so of inviolable territory, and here they stand, silent and motionless while the minutes pass, with their backs to the vociferous and squalid city. Of this a high percentage of the hotel guests will catch no more than a glimpse through the windows of the car that picks them up at the hotel door. A minority of the curious must venture out on foot: the macabre pageant of the handicapped taking place a half-dozen paces from the frontier of this tranquil world can only have been staged for their benefit. The central figure is a man spread-eagled face downwards – a prey to constant convulsions which increase in violence at a foreign tourist's approach. From these he suffers in public for a long working day, with the assistance of a species of manager who occasionally scoops up the few coins of tiny value that have accumulated in the tin dish. The man on the ground almost exactly fits the description of a similar unfortunate to be seen in or near this spot in Geoffrey Moorhouse's *Calcutta*, yet it is hard to believe that the same man – whose appearance gives little clue to his age – can have pursued his fearful profession for the twenty years that have passed since the book was written.

My hope had been to stay in Calcutta only long enough to clear up one or two details of travel and book the first available seat on a train either to Puri or Bhubaneswar in Orissa, these cities being separated by a relatively small distance. I had gathered that the matter of a seat on a train might not be so simple in India as elsewhere. Foreigners who tackle such arrangements unaided often discover unsuspected complexities that may take hours or even days to solve. It is better to leave these things to be dealt with by one's hotel, and the Oberoi being what it was I foresaw no difficulties. Its impressive tourist bureau, however, had no truck with railway travel and I was referred to the porter's desk where a smiling reassurance was forthcoming that a first-class ticket on the next day's night express to Puri would be obtained. As the telephones did not work, a boy would be sent over to the station, the porter said. We chatted about Indian politics and one thing and another until a minute or two later he went off duty. The news some hours later was discouraging. All seats on the Saturday night express had been sold. Would I care for the boy to go back and try to book a seat for the Sunday night? I was handed a substantial bill for the cost of the taxi to the station.

This, from a traveller's point of view, was a cloud in the sky no larger than a man's hand, but in the light of both my own experience and that of many others it was one that could expand into its meeting with the horizon. I was sure that there were seats to be had on this train, and it was only a question of knowing who to approach.

I was given the name of an agent, went to see him, and took to him at first glance. Travel on Saturday he assured me could be ruled out. Sunday was more promising. He drifted away into a back office to ask somebody's advice and left me to admire the charm of the environment: the narrow, ill-lit room cluttered with wonderful ethnic trappings, grainy, faded Alpine photographs, a dust-covered fragment of an erotic carving, an outdated calendar, a dancing Krishna with one of his six arms broken off and badly stuck on again, a cigarette advertisement showing a pretty girl, 'For the Gracious People'.

He returned with two assistants, all of them with mild smiles and the saint-like faces of men who engaged in ascetic practices. 'We are agreed', he said, 'that there can be a seat on Monday morning six a.m. Super-Fast to Bhubaneswar.' The kindly smile was lost momentarily as he winced, perhaps with embarrassment. 'The price', he said, 'will be extra ... I am sorry,' he added, and I'm sure he was.

*

Calcutta is the filthiest of cities, although its filthiness is largely a matter of habit and a caste-system-induced attitude of mind. It is generally admitted that Indians are unequalled in their obsessive personal cleanliness. Within the city endless ablutions go on behind closed doors and the tanks and ponds of the countryside have their permanent population of washers and scrubbers in public. Yet such bodies of water where the search for cleanliness is all must be approached with caution to avoid haphazard foulings by human excrement. Poverty and overcrowding are often offered as an excuse, although many of the cities of the Far East are as poor and as overcrowded as those of India, while remaining as clean as those of the West. In Calcutta the bhangis (scavengers) still go about carrying baskets of human excreta on their heads, and when Gandhi sent India's first health minister to investigate them in 1947 she reported that the delegate members who accompanied her vomited and returned without completing their study. The caste system is to blame. In the case of the bhangis a lifetime of degradation is to be cheerfully endured, for if you are an efficient and uncomplaining cleaner-up of other people's messes your karma may be so benefited as to reward you with promotion in your new incarnation. This will give you the right to leave your own messes for others to clean up. V.S. Naipaul, in *India: A Wounded Civilization*, speaks of the Shiva Sena movement in Bombay in which the dispossessed had decided to take over their own destiny, with the construction of a squatter settlement dedicated to self-help and run by idealistic committees. This largely failed because no sweepers were brought into the community. There were no untouchables to clean up the mess. 'It was unclean to clean; it was unclean even to notice.'

In Calcutta it was a dangerous exploit to turn right out of the hotel, walk a hundred yards down the city's principal thoroughfare, then cross the road to reach what appears to be a wide verge close to the entrance to the underground station – for this is used as a public latrine. Yet there are areas of Calcutta that are as spruce as any other city, in particular the settings of lawns, gardens, and ornamental ponds of the Victoria Memorial, face to face with which I found myself when all the trivial negotiations of the journey had been settled. This was the inspiration of so many lovingly constructed imitations in polystyrene, such as the one I saw at the Hotel Debjon – Britain's answer to the Taj Mahal. Some of those who attended its opening ceremony had been reminded of the Taj, others had found a resemblance to St Paul's and various London railway stations. Mussolini, one of its latter-day admirers, on being shown a photograph of this shining marble mountain, and believing it to have been of recent construction, is reported to have declared, 'We, too, will do this.'

It was a public holiday and families, brightly attired for the occasion, were streaming across lawns and up to the pathways dividing the trim flower beds in the direction of the entrance, where an immensely long and very slowly moving queue had formed. Something in this imperial prospect seemed to impose upon these pilgrims a truly Victorian propriety and restraint. No child plucked a flower, whistled, whined, or so much as let drop a toffee paper. In Bihar people from Calcutta were notorious for their noise. On their home ground all was modest stillness and humility.

Inside the great building the presence of so much embalmed imperial paraphernalia may have been daunting. Here were lined up the stern-visaged, confidently posturing viceroys and generals, their jutting faces, beetling brows, and protruding eyes in some way exaggerated by the marble: Cornwallis and Warren Hastings in Roman togas; Clive in the attitude of a man about to carry out a physical assault. Through gallery after gallery the quiet crowd wandered, gently shoving their way, softly treading. In voices that fused in a multitudinous velvet murmur, they commented on the weapons in the armoury and Zoffany's paintings of pride and prejudice, of royal and aristocratic Victorian faces marked as indelibly by their epoch as they might have been by mental or physical ill-health. They were engrossed in the spectacle of all those things gathered here and put on show to impress or dismay.

A single episode stands out in the memory. A woman had placed herself, holding a child of about three in her arms, under a bust on a pedestal of a particularly fierce-looking general. After waiting for a few moments to make sure she was not attracting attention, she held up the child to allow him to smooth the distinguished features with his hands, in the hope, no doubt, that he would absorb some of the power and spirit they emanated.

Temples and Goddesses
in Orissa

Chapter Nine

AT 5.30 A.M. ON THE DOT my friend the agent called as arranged to take me to the Howrah Station to catch the 6 a.m. Super-Fast for Bhubaneswar. It had seemed to me to be cutting it fine, but he replied, 'Long waiting at the station is to be avoided. There will be time.' He was a most likeable man; a worrier, overburdened with responsibility, bearing the marks of strain in his face that seemed to have deepened since our last meeting. His work, he said, put him under constant pressure. With travel – especially in India – you never knew. The planes were always late and sometimes flights were cancelled, putting more strain on the railways. Booking a seat on any train was essential but it did not always mean that one would travel, besides which sometimes there were invasions by passengers who took possession of seats to which they were not entitled, and it was impossible to eject them. He was worrying now in case something of the kind happened to me, and would not be able to relax until he saw me safely in my seat.

Howrah Station at 5.40 a.m. seemed even more remarkable than its formidable reputation had promised, and it was hard to imagine how an unescorted foreigner could have found his way in the semi-darkness through these seething multitudes to the place where, with some luck, his train awaited. Apart from the travellers, the station had its own resident population of the homeless, and in it, according to the books, some of them managed to spend a fair proportion of their lives. Here they were asleep, huddled in family groups, sprawled out singly, lying on their sides, knees drawn up almost to touch the chin in the posture of pre-historic burial, or with the approach of dawn had raised themselves on their elbows, faces turned, like sarcophagus figures in Etruscan tombs. There was something in the vast claustrophobia of the station and of its earthy cavernous odour that recalled a necropolis, a sensation heightened by the presence of a circle of men who sat facing each other absolutely motionless and, as far as it was possible to see, eyes closed, in chairs with no legs, which, said the agent, were seats wrenched from wrecked buses.

The train, suddenly bursting into this scene, came as a surprise, for it was encrusted with grime – as though it had come straight from a siding in which it had lain, exposed to the weather, for several years. From long experience the agent had chosen a position on the platform exactly facing the first-class entrance when the train stopped. There was a wait for the conductor to arrive with the key, followed by a rush for the door, composed to my surprise largely of beggars who placed themselves in strategic positions to await boarding passengers. The operation had been a successful one. The agent exchanged secret greetings with the conductor, who found my name on his list and showed me to my seat, knocking its back into an upright position with a blow of the fist. I thanked the agent, and shaking hands with him I noticed that the lines anxiety had carved at the corners of his mouth had lost depth. Settling in my seat I found myself confronted with a beggar incessantly banging on his bowl with the stump of a fingerless hand. Besides him waited a man who was clearly quite blind and could only have been attracted to me by a foreigner's unfamiliar odour. The faces of both men were contorted with anger. In a street situation I could have escaped, but this was a prison, and however much small change is accumulated in readiness for such occasions, it is soon exhausted. After that the only remedy in the face of whatever fury it may provoke is to strive after the holy indifference of Calcutta. In this case the problem was rapidly settled, for in five minutes, and exactly on time, the train began to pull out.

This was a dirty train, and it was a relief to remember that the journey was unlikely to last more than seven hours. The moquette upholstery was grimed with filth, and innumerable hours of bodily contact had left a dark polish on the seats. What had once been a white holland cover drooped in greasy folds from the back of each seat, and the conductors's first and last service so far as I was concerned was to grab at the one I was faced with, and rip it away. The windows had probably never been washed, although by luck a brushing contact with some external object had left a transparent fissure about two inches in length in the encrustation of dirt level with my head. Through this opening a smeared and narrow vision of dawning day was to be had. Thirty years before, crossing India in the clean and well-run trains of those days, I had seen a Brahmin defend himself from defiling contact by placing his hands to cover the vacant seat at his side. When, nevertheless, I took the seat it was with the obvious disapproval of other passengers who preferred in the circumstances to stand. How did Brahmins travel in these days?

The passengers were a mixed bag of families accompanied by jubilant, clambering, scampering children, young men in American peaked caps on their way to the beach at Puri, and commercial travellers in dark suits. A rich little girl with a bejewelled and elegant mother cuddled a blonde doll. A European couple, probably just released from a four-star hotel to come on this journey, seemed out of their element in these surroundings where nothing worked, struggling with faulty light switches, jammed windows, and ruptured seat-backs. The advertised air-conditioning was supplied by electric fans which either did not work or provided uncontrollable draughts.

Gloomy-faced attendants wearing football scarves came through bringing food in battered receptacles: semolina cakes, samosas, biscuits, fruit, much of it in wrappers which were to be dropped with peelings on the floor. Tea came in little earthenware bowls which, as a gesture to hygiene when emptied, went through the nearest window that could be persuaded to open. Many passengers had provided themselves with paper tissues, which after use were screwed up into small balls before letting them drop.

Lights streaked past the clear patch in the window and I pressed my eye to the glass to watch the city's grey, cardboard shapes jogging by at dawn. The wasted profiles of Calcutta shrank away. The sun's burgundy disc came bobbing up through the smog, then trees appeared among the gaunt buildings and the shacks, and the city's hold upon the countryside was broken.

The Super-Fast picked up speed, rattling in style through the flat countryside. For a while the chaos of Calcutta was in hot pursuit: villages like excerpts from the Bara slums, the wreckage of ancient disasters, bogies and twisted iron at the bottom of an embankment. Then the countryside's victory was complete, and the transfiguration stunned. This was a vast country aquatint of utmost delicacy, at worst softened and romanticized by the thin screen of dust adhering to the glass. It was a part of India surely that had been able to free itself from the landlords and the moneylenders and the politicians who provoked civil conflict in order to increase their power. Untrained peasant art and good taste in the blood had created the clean, cool geometrical patterning of these fields, the cutting of waterways and the siting of villages and ponds. Time after time remote West Bengal presented its flawless old-master compositions: flaxen hamlets set in the soft colour-washes of early spring, glossy buffaloes dragging the plough, kite-flying children, mathematical displays of bright washing laid out at the water's edge, a flight of cranes, a man repairing a thatch.

The train stopped at Baleshwar almost within sight of the sea amid the explosive excitement of a crowd for which the arrival of the Calcutta Super-Fast would have been the event of the day. Since only a handful of passengers joined the train, there could be no other explanation than this for the platform throng; people dressed as if for an audience with a cabinet minister or a party with a film star, outbursts of uncontrollable laughter, the exaggerated exchange of greetings when friends bumped into one another, the unruly conduct of children who had been brought along. A great collection of food-sellers advertised what was on offer with an assortment of musical cries, blending sometimes into what might have been an intentional chorus. One man sprinted down the platform carrying a black crab and thrusting a single enormous claw in the faces of potential customers. A brace of wonderfully robed and painted holy men paced up and down; a few beggars of the more presentable kind had put in an appearance; a horoscopist sought to draw attention by ringing a bell, and a porter having delivered packages into the care of the guard stripped himself down to his underpants for a wash in the drinking fountain.

After Baleshwar came Badhrakh with more station-platform light opera, more messy titbits for the travellers, and more paper wrappings and cellophane to be trodden underfoot. By this time the farms and the glowing fields of West Bengal had slipped away taking with them the sparkle and the last of the thin mists of early spring. Now in Orissa, summer was installed. I had managed to prise open the window, and the overhead banks of electric fans were in action producing small flurries among the many crisp bags littering the floor. We rattled, one after another, across the iron bridges over the tributaries of the Brahmani River, which was then entering the great Mahanadi Delta. The view was of one of the loneliest places of India: a great blond billowing amalgam of desert and marsh, with temple ruins overwhelmed in sand, and a great refuge of birds and beasts choosing to live by the sea.

The yellow refulgence of sand here seemed to have drained colour from a sky spread with the small summer clouds that gave no shade; they streamed out like soap bubbles from a child's pipe. The train rocked us away past dunes that had been licked into extraordinary shape by the wind. There were goats all over them, prospecting the hollows for edible wild marigolds. By far-off patches of sedge men burnt as black as negroes were working on a patch of land reclaimed from the sand which they would cultivate for a few months before its obliteration by the monsoon storms. According to the guide-book there are stretches of this coastline where at low tide the sea goes out three miles. It is so dangerously shallow and full of uncharted sand-banks that commercial fishing fleets are held at bay, leaving wonderful catches for the local fishermen to make in their prehistoric boats.

Thirty or forty iron bridges separated us from the green and pleasant fields of Bhubaneswar, but despite the Super-Fast's deliberate rumbling progress across them we finally drew into the station on time almost to the minute. The train emptied here. Most of the passengers were on their way to Puri – ranking fourth in the holy cities of India – and they were committed to a thirty-eight-mile journey by road, for which normally only taxis were available. A racket was inevitable. Taxis charging extortionate rates bribed porters to capture the luggage of arriving travellers, and this inspired conflicts on the platform in which it was possible for one's property to suffer. A fellow passenger had warned me what to expect and how to cope with the situation. Before the train came to a standstill it was boarded by struggling porters who did their best to tear the luggage from passengers' hands and escape with it through the doors. 'Let us remain seated,' said my friend, 'and pretend that we are not leaving the train. Soon they will go.' They did. The tumult died away, and we followed cautiously in the rear of the scrambling multitude, only to be spotted as soon as the collector had taken our tickets. There was a concerted rush by empty-handed porters and our baggage was wrenched away. The holier the city the worse the problem for the arriving traveller.

The extortion was scrupulously organized. One man controlled his gang of three. A taxi was allowed to approach. 'Give me the money,' said the boss. 'I will distribute it.' I gave him a quarter of the large sum demanded and was amazed that he should take it so well. Probably he had asked for ten times the usual tip.

Chapter Ten

AFTER THE STRENUOUS morning the policy when it came to the choice of a hotel was, better the devil you know, and I settled unhesitatingly for the Bhubaneswar Ashok. I would not have expected the appearance of this to have attracted extra business for it contrived to resemble a picture of a strongpoint in the Maginot Line of old. Apart from the self-assertive exterior it proved saturated with the familiar Ashok atmosphere. This gave the impression that, however austere the building and fundamental the appointments, behind it all was a small, hard-working, and basically pious Hindu family, liable occasionally to make mistakes.

Here, once again, were the morning arrangements of frangipani blossom, although by the time of my arrival they were strewn on the floor mixed up with screwed-up chits and telephone messages to await the coming of the sweeper. Here, too, were the three gardeners who, since there were no important operations such as tree-planting to occupy their time, picked up fallen leaves by hand, one by one, occasionally sprinting like greyhounds to catch an airborne leaf as it came floating down. As at Ranchi, the restaurant featured chicken and chips, but the waiter in his recommendation stressed a radical difference, confiding with a screwing up of the face that enjoined secrecy that this was a black-market version of the Colonel Sanders secret formula. In small matters nothing worked too well, as advertised in the behaviour of the large electric clock over the reception which was always exactly a half-hour fast or slow. This caused more amusement than confusion among the guests.

Where the hotel at Ranchi had been frequented by glum foreign technicians the Ashok was crammed with sales managers and vice-presidents, being a great place as I was told for conferences and conventions due to the proximity of Puri with its excellent beaches.

At this time there was a strong contingent from the Parke Davies pharmaceutical group on a seminar. All these Indian businessmen were exceedingly genial and friendly. It was enough to go up in a lift with one and suffer the small but regular frustration of being delivered to the wrong floor to be given a large and handsomely engraved card and an invitation, 'If you're ever in Bangalore give me a ring.'

The amazing thing was they meant it. This was no mere engrained sales approach. The company was giving a party that evening (this was what had sent the gardeners scurrying to tidy away the leaves), and on the basis of a two-minutes' acquaintance I was invited to attend, plied with imported Scotch, and treated to the most exciting performance of the dancers of Orissa.

Inevitably, for the assembled company men this was the sugaring of the pill of duty to be swallowed, and inspiring speeches by top executives were to follow. I slipped away but listened perforce through my bedroom window to the long and resoundingly amplified eulogies of the triumph of commerce; of sales targets reached and surpassed, of increased market shares captured, of new products to be launched, of new expansion foreseen. This was received with dutiful applause. In the planning of such speeches some respite from solemnity is usually recommended, but notwithstanding an up-to-the-minute theme of scientific advancement and the triumphs of modern technology there was something strangely out of date about the light relief when it came. The speaker produced an old-style off-colour joke which had the effect of provoking a wave of obedient titters. In the calm of this transparent, perfumed, and otherwise silent night the witticism could have been overheard by a listener a half-mile away. It was sad, stale stuff, and here very much out of place.

The agent in Calcutta had given me the name of a man he thought might help in the matter of travel in the interior of Orissa. By this time I was beginning to know the ropes, and that agents are indispensable to the traveller in India. I found Subrath Bose in his office tucked away at the back of a down-town development, a small, gleeful, twinkling man, to whom, as in the case of his counterpart in Calcutta, I took an immediate liking. He was in travel in a small way, concentrating inevitably on visitors in town to do the rounds of Bhubaneswar's formidable collection of temples. Bound as he was to be a source of inexhaustible information on the subject of religious monuments, he gave the impression of yearning for involvements of a more venturesome kind.

He had been attracted into the business, he said, by the call of the far-off places, and at first there had been journeys of zestful exploration. 'In Orissa we have sixty-two tribal groups, making up one-third of the population,' he said. 'I must tell you about nomads living on the mountain tops that few people have seen. If permission can be obtained I could send you to a village where only one single European has been. Many of these people have retained their ethnic identity.'

One exploratory adventure stood out from the rest in his mind. It was in the last year before office drudgery and the onset of middle-age had dragged him back to Bhubaneswar. He had found his way into the Bonda country in the far south, drawn there by lurid accounts of the Bonda lifestyle and the reputation of this small tribe for casual homicide, and a detestation of interference of any kind.

The principal Bonda market was at the village of Khairput. Bose had been driven there in a jeep, incautiously pressing on up a narrow and precipitous road towards the nearest hill village when he and his driver found they had reached a point where they could neither go forward nor turn back. It was here that a swarm of tribals, bows in hand, had come out of hiding and hustled them away. They were placed on a platform and held there all night, guarded by Bondas aiming their bows at them. At one moment, believing that they were about to be sacrificed, Bose fainted away. In the morning they were given roots to chew and alcohol to drink, after which he vomited. At that point, inexplicably, their captors underwent a change of heart – possibly, Bose thought, due to some oracular pronouncement by the village god. After demonstrations by the Bondas of something approaching affection, the jeep had been manhandled into position facing down the hill, and they had been released. 'Those people are still there,' Bose said. 'You can see them. They are much the same as ever.'

There were a dozen more tribes in southern Orissa, he said, who had managed to hold themselves aloof from our times. Police permission to travel in restricted areas was required but he believed that this could be obtained. A question mark hung over some areas infiltrated by Naxalite extremists of the People's War Group who had acquired sophisticated weapons and were said to be supported by subversive elements in the local population. He would make enquiries. Above all, I would require the services of a guide who could not only find his way into the hills, but who had some knowledge of tribal languages. He knew of a suitable man, and hoped that he could contact him.

'How long would all this take?' I asked.

For the police permit and finding the guide – if he was still to be found – he thought about a week.

'And meanwhile what is there to see and do?'

'Very much. Your problem is not to find things to see and do but how to compress all of them into one week. Not only is Puri a holy place, Bhubaneswar also is holy. Once there were many thousands of temples. Even now we have five hundred, although some are in ruins. Pilgrims come here with maps and are very happy to spend days and weeks hunting down the shrines. A foreigner may take a taxi and see perhaps fifty in one day, finding that enough.'

'And after the temples?'

'I would recommend a visit to our zoo. This is the largest in India. I am told that methods have been developed of reconciling animals to their captivity.'

'That should be interesting. I'll certainly take a look at it.'

'You must not fail to see the Sun Temple at Konarak with its many erotic carvings and it is impossible to stay in Bhubaneswar without a side-trip to Chilika Lake which is the largest brackish-water lake in the east, and reputedly very fascinating, although I have not seen it personally. If that is not enough it will amaze your friends if you tell them you have been in Bhubaneswar without visiting the battlefield on which the Emperor Ashoka gained the great victory following which the Buddhist kingdom was established. There are very many other things to hold your interest. Believe me, you will be kept busy. There will not be enough time for you.'

I made a start with the largest zoo in India. All zoos are depressing to the animal lover, but Bose had spoken of scientific methods employed here to increase the animals' general well-being, their resistance to disease and even their life expectation. Encouraged by these assurances and my own belief that Indians are more compassionate than most in their treatment of animals, I went along. I hoped to find Bhubaneswar less cruel and depressing a place than the equivalent in the West, but did not. There were certain native animals, such as the sloth bear, that I wanted to see, but these and all other such rarities had taken refuge from the crowds and skulked out of sight. The great apes, more likely than other imprisoned animals to die of broken hearts, seemed if possible to be in an even more pitiable condition than usual. What may have been the principal attraction of the whole zoo was a chimpanzee in an open pit that seemed to have gone off its head. It was shambling, head slumped between its narrow but massive shoulders, its back to a crowd – largely of youngsters – who were throwing stones intended to provoke it to what was quite frenzied action. No stone hit the chimpanzee – they were probably not intended to – but when one fell near the animal it would spin round, run a few skipping steps, strike the rock surface with great force with its huge open hand, then throw the stone back. Its aim was poor, but the performance caused great delight.

The zoo possessed a unique collection of 'white' tigers which although a great rarity looked bleached out and much less impressive than specimens of the usual colour. A notice on the enclosure furnished the astonishing information that in 1967 a wild tigress climbed the fence and jumped in to mate with a male in captivity. The union continued for a number of years until the tigress's death. Replying to my comment upon what appeared to me as these animals' listlessness, my guide explained that this was a Monday when Hindus fasted, and that the animals, too, were not fed on this day. 'Let us return tomorrow,' he said. 'We may look forward to witnessing some activity.'

A short distance from the zoo I noticed an open-air pavilion featuring an exhibition devoted to India's YEAR OF THE YOUNG GIRL of which I now heard for the first time. I went in and found that it was depressing stuff. Indians have little hesitation in displaying their communal wounds and many of the photographs on show, and the facts and figures accompanying them, would certainly have startled the first-time visitor with no previous knowledge of the country. There is a lively public in India for exhibitions of all kinds and this one was well attended, mostly by families with numerous children tailing along who received low-voiced explanations of such of the miserable scenes depicted as they might have failed to understand.

The main feature of the display was a series of large photographs of Indian girls, striking and attractive as they always seem, engaged either in the hardest of labouring work or in routine tasks of evident monotony. There were the usual lugubrious processions of young women carrying on their heads piled up baskets of ore from where it had been blasted out of the mountain-side down to the waiting trucks. There were girls pictured in Kerala seated by the roadside breaking stones. The very young ones, who might have been seven-year-olds, clutched tiny hammers weighing only a few ounces, while their older sisters wielded four-pounders, with which they reduced granite rocks to piles of chips for use in road-surfacing, thereby earning some ten rupees a day. 'Contributing to the Family Kitty' was the general caption applied to this section of the exhibition.

The enduring scandal of child marriage was illustrated in a photograph from Rajasthan of a girl bride aged ten, on horseback, riding pillion in all her wedding finery, in which she appeared hardly more than an enormous doll behind a large husband with rouged cheeks and flowing moustache. Such marriages were illegal, insisted the caption, punishable in the case of parents arranging them by fifteen days' rigorous imprisonment; nevertheless, up to one hundred thousand took place each year, and so far no one had gone to prison. No more, so far, than has anyone – as mentioned elsewhere in the show – illegally employing girls of eleven or twelve years of age in hard labour on the building sites or on the roads.

These were no more than the commonplace excerpts of the Indian scene, strange and disturbing at first to the visitor, but as familiarity increased almost overlooked. Having skipped through the common-places of Indian misery, however, the visitor moves on to graver things, and is confronted with facts which in some instances it seems hard indeed to believe.

Female infanticide is commonly practised, said the social investi-gator in Rajasthan, where traditional anti-feminism is more solidly entrenched than elsewhere. In other northern states including Uttar Pradesh, Haryana, and the Punjab girl children were permitted to survive, although with reluctance. Dr Surander Jaitly of Banaras Hindu University, who questioned a number of village women, found a sinister predominance of women who had lost daughters through accidents ('they fell down'), but never a son. Lakshmi Lincom of the Tata Institute of Social Sciences found that if a girl avoided outright infanticide she could expect discrimantion right from the cradle, being weaned before a boy and liable to suffer from malnutrition. She would be taken out of school and introduced to child labour much earlier than her brothers, and was four times likelier than them to be employed in the rural hard-slogging labour that comes so close to the definition of slavery. When in the past there have been famines, the girls have been the first to die.

The most horrific of the information published here – and presumably in innumerable similar exhibitions throughout the country – prompts the question of what is to become of an India shown as prepared to debauch its culture by the diversion of newly invented medical techniques from the aim of the preservation to that of the destruction of life? The photograph this time was of a seedy house in Bombay bearing a signboard 'The Healthy Boy–Girl Guide Centre'. This was one of numerous squalid little back-street clinics, set up to employ amniocentesis tests, used elsewhere to identify genetic disorders in the foetus but misused here, according to the text, to ascertain its sex and procure abortion should this be unacceptable. Almost incredibly, the Tata Institute ascertained from data collected from six Bombay hospitals that of eight thousand foetuses aborted following such tests all but one were female.

The Indian young girl who has managed to surmount all the obstacles placed in the path of her early life by a male-dominated society faces at the entrance to womanhood the supreme handicap of marriage to a husband, of whom in nine cases out of ten she knows nothing, and who is hunted down for her by her parents through the agency of marriage brokers with whom the all important matter of the dowry is worked out. A system in which a girl's husband is in effect bought for her in the manner of a market transaction involving haggling of the most prolonged and resolute kind goes against the grain of many Indians, yet the young victim is likely to see to it when the time comes that the same humiliations are imposed upon the wife chosen for her son. It was hard to find an Indian among those I met with anything good to say for this routine degradation of their womenfolk. They proclaimed the intention – whatever their parents' wishes might have been – of having nothing to do with arranged marriages, choosing instead some girl with a similar background and tastes that they had happened to meet at an office get-together or some such function, in Western style. But would they, when their time came? That was the question.

Progress in India in the matter of social custom moves at the speed of a sprightly tortoise, but a study of the matriomonial pages appearing in the Sunday issues of Indian newspapers suggests the beginnings of an infinitely slow post-ice-age change of attitude. 'Bride wanted. An irreligious or moderately religious beautiful girl for secular-minded graduate government employee. Caste no bar. No dowry.' The advertisement would have been unthinkable thirty years ago, and even now could only appear in a provincial newspaper – the *Kerala Sunday Express* – drawing its readership from the population of a notoriously eccentric state. It is doubtful whether the august *Times of India*, which has two tightly packed pages of matrimonial ads on Sundays, would agree to print it. The *Times* readers are more traditional in their aspirations. Boys whose fathers are in a good line of business, or army officers, or in the government, detail their requirements in the way of bride, who should be extremely beautiful, slim, fair, a graduate, and convent-educated. With the flush of dawn somewhere on the social horizon, up to one advertiser in seven has decided that the time has come to rid himself of the incubus of caste. Thus the formula 'no bar' is included in the insert. Dowry – by consent in India the most crippling of its institutions – would appear to be a very different thing. Only three advertisers in the issue of the *Times* I studied specifically disclaimed interest in cash, property, motorcars, etc., to be passed over with the bride, and one of these, clearly conscious of his relatively low marketability, mentioned that he had lost his right leg. One advertisement was clearly in search of substantial financial induce-ment. It was by a government officer on behalf of his only son, and worded in such a way that it was clearly money that mattered: correspondence was invited, with full bio-details and horoscope, from rich families of 'little-educated girls'.

Even after the initial haggling, the prospects for the candidate seem dreadful. There may be long and traumatic delays while 'bio-details' are checked, horoscopes submitted to the experts for scrutiny and interpretation, the girl's habits reported upon by persons specializing in the supply of such information – even a medical certificate if proof of virginity requested. If the qualifications in the matter of beauty, status, and education are sufficiently high an acceptable husband may be picked up at a bargain price. But for each slim, fair, graduate convent-educated beauty there are a dozen (according to the advertisements) who are homely, sweet, serene, traditionally sober, wheatish in complexion, meritorious, and perfect in household affairs. These are the descriptions applied to the second-rate, for many of whom the conjugal future is likely to be bleak. It is sad to contemplate the eventual fate of the little-educated girl from which nothing is expected but the possession of rich parents.

Chapter Eleven

Bose had been insistent that I should on no account fail to do the round of Bhubaneswar's unique collection of temples. On taking further information on what this entailed the prospect seemed a daunting one. Bhubaneswar possessed a tank – an artificial lake – of exceptional sanctity. The Bindusagar, or Ocean Drop, was reputed to contain holy water collected from every suitable source in the sub-continent, and its power to cleanse away sin was still kept up to proof by additions of water provided by pilgrims returning from the Ganges carrying as many bottles as they could manage.

The Ocean Drop is accepted by devout historians as once having been ringed by seven thousand temples. One looks at the space available and wonders how this could possibly have been. There are still temples galore, some recognizable as such, others no more than vestigial shapes sticking up like decayed teeth from jawbones of rock. A Friends of the Temples society has pinpointed the location of a hundred or two, although some of these holy buildings seemed to be little more than ruins, and the Friends had classed three of these near-ruins, built one on top of the other among the brambles in a back garden, as three separate temples in their determination to inflate the tally.

Five major temples remained that were in good shape and current use. The Hinduism of this area of Orissa had come under the influence of fertility cults, and this was reflected in the phallic inspiration of their lofty towers, and in the frequent presence in the chambers at their base of the god's image in the form of a lingam, projecting from three to ten feet from the ground. The walls of most of these edifices were richly decorated with erotic carvings, some of which had suffered defacement at the time of the sixteenth-century invasion by the Moghuls, who failed to appreciate their purely religious significance.

Every traveller to Bhubaneswar is expected to make for the Lingaraj, accepted as one of India's most outstanding temples. In this case the deity is represented as a block of stone which, according to rumour, is bathed daily with hashish steeped in milk. Some fifty small temples are crammed into the Lingaraj enclosure alone, from which soars a tower carved with motifs of great interest. None of these nor any of the internal details of the temple can be inspected by the foreign visitor, who is invited to make use of the viewing platform outside the walls erected for the use of Lord Curzon who, as a non-Hindu, was equally debarred from access, although granted leave to inspect the temple through his binoculars. When I climbed the tower I was accompanied by two temple servants, one of whose duties it was to ask for a donation, the other to enter the amount along with my particulars into a book he carried. All the previous donations, considering the sparseness of the visual experience offered, seemed very high.

Of all the temples in Orissa a visit to the great Sun Temple by the sea at Konarak sounded likely to be the most rewarding, there being no prohibition of access. It was at the centre of an area containing many other features of interest – above all Puri with its Car of the Juggernaut. I had decided to put up in Puri for a day or two while awaiting news from Bose, but before moving, a trip to nearby Khandagiri, with its Jain cave temples and its swarming pilgrims, seemed a pleasant diversion.

The Khandagiri caves were a few miles down the Kuttack road. Although a Jain pilgrimage centre, they were equally popular with Hindu pilgrims doing the rounds of the holy sites. About the time of my arrival, depending on certain astrological calculations, Jain priests were expected to arrive – imposing in their total nudity, with gauze covering their mouths to prevent the sacrilegious inhalation of winged insects – and thereafter take up residence in the upper caves.

The Jains had not yet appeared, but the hill and its surroundings swarmed with religious devotees and holy men of various categories who had arrived to attend what might have been seen as a religious version of an insurance brokers' convention at the Ashok. Khandagiri is on the itinerary of long-distance-travelling saddhus. Some of those who were here would have undertaken the great Narmada River pilgrimage – a journey of eight hundred miles through the legendary forest so soon to be extinguished beneath the waters of the great hydropower scheme. Two years were normally devoted to this karma-strengthening exercise, but some never returned. Where almost every tree provided fruit of a kind, and caves by the hundred offered shelter all along the banks of the sacred river, there was no better place to practise the holy idleness enjoyed by a complete surrender to religion, and in the end almost to overlook the reality of the world.

It was hard to know what saddhus lived on when in town. At Khandagiri there were no begging bowls in sight, unlike elsewhere in the east. I was never approached by a request from one for money or food, nor were obvious offerings made by members of the Indian public. Affluence and success here are generally indicated by bodily size. A successful businessman is large, doomed to eventual coronary failure or other organic collapse. The holy men of Khandagiri, with their dazed smiles and aroma of mild religious dementia, were, by contrast, as thin as rakes, yet they scampered like mountain goats up and down the hillside paths. To be just on the right side of malnutrition seemed not a bad thing.

On a natural platform halfway up the hill a party of Jain ascetics had gathered to chant mantras. They were led by a precentor with a tremendous voice, wearing twenty or thirty shell necklaces and his abundant hair dressed in exuberant style. He held a volume almost as large as a chained Bible, from which he read the text, nodding occasionally in the direction of the accompanists on single-stringed fiddles and drums when their participation was required. A scout had been placed to warn women pilgrims to keep their distance to avoid spreading potential defilement. Overlooking this scene at the entrance to a rock temple was a rare sight indeed – a woman priest in a red robe, with the heavy, powerful features of a male politician. At her back a group of acolytes similarly dressed, one wearing tinted spectacles, had taken up deferential attitudes. Presently they turned to join forces and melted into a narrow pathway to become a thin flame licking up the hillside.

Khandagiri is a picnicking site of the religious kind, much suited to this purpose by its high therapeutic reputation and the innumerable caves with which it is furnished, available for childish exploration. To eat well and in a relaxed fashion in the presence of the gods is seen as a form of piety, and a number of well-disposed divinities are thought to frequent the area in order to partake of the spiritual essences of the food. Nevertheless in this devout environment a greater than usual preparational effort is called for. Ideally, new cooking pots will be bought for the occasion, failing which existing ones are burnished to a high level of brilliance. Woods of the better kind, producing a fragrant smoke, are brought along to make the fire, and women with a little money to spare may lash out for a new sari. Some thought in such cases is given to the choice of a colour to go with the surroundings – at Khandagiri terracotta earth, and the dark foliage of pines. The culinary processes at such times can assume a certain theatricality – this is no more or less than an open-air performance, abetted by the exhibitionist antics of the holy men in the background. The women encircle their cooking pots like the players in a Greek drama: all the gestures of fire-stoking, food-tasting, and the adding of condiments are ceremonial. Actions are premeditated and hieratic. At Khandagiri the onlooker should take up a position in which such family groups are back-lit by the streaming morning sunshine, muted and diffused by wood smoke in such a way that the frontiers of colour of the saris, the purples, pinks, and blues, spread to merge a little.

Everyone buys something from a souvenir stall which offers carved wooden pheasants in all sizes with arrogant, matriarchal expressions, crests like Spanish combs, and feet equipped with the talons of falcons. In addition there are gaudy little cabinets housing the effigy of the Lord Jagannath, seen – despite his notably liberal temperament – in dehumanized form with black face, a narrow beak of a nose, and huge, staring owl's eyes. The cabinet in which he is supplied fulfils a purpose, for at night the doors are closed cutting off the all-seeing divine scrutiny which otherwise might trouble human sleep. In another climate of faith folk art of this kind may be seen as whimsical and Disneyish. Here, a residue of belief in such objects saves them from this fate. They are good fun, but they are also invested with secret power, and to be treated with respect.

Pilgrims to the hilltop Jain shrine are accustomed, having completed their devotions, to seat themselves out in the open on stone benches under the trees. Here they are joined in orderly fashion by monkeys who accept their presence as a matter of course, seeming to have adopted not only human postures but also human attitudes in such matters as their apparent appreciation of the view. The Jains provide themselves with packets of nuts upon which, together with rice, they largely exist, and these they share freely with the monkeys. When a monkey's allocation runs out he will frequently nudge the donor gently in the hope of a further contribution.

The oldest caves on neighbouring Sunrise Hill are of Jain origin. Preceding by a thousand years the routine eroticisms of Konarak and Khajuraho, these carvings are devoted to familiar non-religious subjects, to the scenes of wild life, elephants, tigers, and recognizable birds that inspired the art of the day. Sometimes a scene will be purely anecdotal – such as the ladies of King Karavela's court showering blows on a family of elephants caught devouring the lotuses in their pool. Few of the crowds attracted to the Sun Temple at Konarak come here, but there cannot be many of the ancient sites of India where the rough and tumble of pre-history is glimpsed so well.

Chapter Twelve

IN THE MATTER of good advice Bose failed me only once. Everyone in search of accommodation in the Puri area will naturally turn first to that nostalgia-saturated local relic of the Raj, the South Eastern Railway Hotel at Puri, spoken of with gratitude by all seasoned travellers in this part of the world. Thus, naturally, I did, only to find that it was full. This was a disappointment. After accidental and reluctant exposure to what is described in the travel guide as the 'top end' of tourist accommodation in Delhi and Calcutta, and otherwise to the perfectly straightforward and pleasant commercial atmosphere of the Ashoks, the South Eastern was clearly what I had always been looking for. All the faces had changed, but these were the settings of a book with a faded Victorian cover; silent, spacious, embalmed in time.

The ambience was also faintly enigmatic. A reception clerk appeared only to say that there were no vacant rooms, then vanished. Otherwise there was nobody to be seen. The South Eastern was devoid of intrusive music, there were no footfalls, no doors slammed distantly. It was hard to imagine the Oberoi being the scene of unusual experiences, less so here. I went out and seated myself at a table on a wide, empty veranda overlooking a lawn, with a line-up of bedrooms behind me having all blue doors closing over French windows. The interiors of several bedrooms were visible, featuring large chandeliers and beds draped in the snowy folds of enormous mosquito nets.

A waiter had come up from the rear, a silent, immaculate, and almost spectral presence, bringing, as if an order had been communicated by thought-transference, tea, toast, and jam. He added sugar as directed to the tea, then went on to stir it. A tiny green bird flashed out of a flowering shrub and hovered with obvious intent until he cuffed it gently away.

Afterwards I wandered into the reception area, then into a sitting room to examine some of the cupboards full of vintage English books: Pearl S. Buck, Mrs Henry Wood, Harrison Ainsworth, Frances Parkinson Keyes. Hidden clocks chimed softly from ambush; a polished gecko slid into sight from behind a Victorian landscape after Constable. I would have liked to settle down in the South Eastern for some days, but since it was not possible, Bose's choice of the Marina Gardens, six or seven miles away down by the sea, seemed the next best thing.

The change was extreme. I was confronted at the reception by a notice announcing checking out time at 8 a.m. On querying this I was told that arrangement could be made for guests to leave somewhat later than this if prepared to accept the charge for a half-day. I spoke to the charming and sympathetic Mrs Panda, the manageress, and learned with some alarm that she had just returned after completing a course at a London business school. Mrs Panda assured me that she would make an exception if necessary in my case, but it became evident in later transactions that traditional Indian hospitality at the Marina Gardens had been vanquished by the philosophy and methods of the Western hard-sell. Mrs Panda's mantle of enchantment was stripped away in the end by the knowledge that at the Marina Gardens you paid a little more but got a little less, and what would otherwise have been a pleasurable experience was soured by smiling extortion.

A bad mistake, but not so bad as had first appeared, for the hotel bus advertised as available to take guests to the beach was not in evidence: the alternative was a fairly expensive taxi on hire through the Marina which most guests seemed reluctant to afford, and those electing to walk found that although the beach was described as being within easy walking distance it was some three miles away. All in all this, from my point of view, was no bad thing, for in one way or another the beach had been left as it always was. When I went there the fishing fleet had just come in: big, extravagantly painted boats with the staring eyes of idols, and a few smaller ones made of planks slotted together, which could be taken apart as soon as beached and the planks carried away.

To me the catch was a phenomenal one. The sand in the vicinity of the boats was littered with splendid fish for sale, some of which still leaped into the air, twisted and shuddered. With their arched backs, snapping jaws, bulging eyes, and sail-like spread of fins they reminded me of the decorations added to old nautical maps. Puri, with it shallow waters and sand-banks and shoals, was too remote and chancy to attract the commercial fishing from the north which would so rapidly demolish the richness. A procession of statuesque girls were carrying the fish on their heads up the road to be loaded into trucks. A twenty-pound monster fetched about the equivalent of 50p, and you could buy as many as could be crowded into a motor rickshaw for five pounds.

The hotel's real attraction was its garden, which had probably been laid out in a matter of weeks at a cost of so much per square yard by a firm specializing in such undertakings. There might have been three acres of it, and more was in the course of construction. A bulldozer came along, tore the original sand away and replaced this with topsoil in which seedlings were planted of showy annuals such as dahlias, calendulas, and marigolds, which grow like weeds and sometimes emulate them in climates where frost is unknown and there is abundant sun. Above these great spreads of colour hovered butterflies by the hundred, and I was struck with the fact that they were almost the first butterflies I had seen in India, where every inch of the cultivable landscape is devoted to filling empty stomachs and therefore devoid of flowers. In all probability they were a local, permanent population, attracted to a reserve brimming with nectar from which no reasonable butterfly would ever be induced to depart.

Although lacking the sombre splendour of the morphos of the South American rain forest, many were large and coloured with a subdued magnificence. Above all their extraordinary tameness gave rise to speculation. They could be touched carefully without flinching. Very gently, I picked one up, released it, and it flew back to the flower. Why should this have been? The possible answer was that in a country where priests were prepared to go to such pains to avoid the accidental death of insects, no one has ever collected butterflies to be pinned in rows on a board. They had nothing to fear from humans.

Nor, seemingly, had the flies. There were not many about, but they were quite fearless, and having settled on the skin refused to move unless they were brushed off. Nobody swatted a fly. A notice by the pool said, enigmatically, 'Guests are requested to refrain from inhuman acts'. Guests came here to take their breakfast but there were no signs of inhumanity. A number of the most elegant long-tailed crows waited stealthily in the casuarinas to clear away the vestiges of the meal – including the napkins – which they did instantly and with wonderful skill as soon as a guest got up from his seat, and before he had had time to leave the table. Perhaps from reasons of caste few people used the pool. The exception was a mother and her grown-up daughters who circled endlessly and very slowly, following each other in a clockwise direction. They appeared to be well-educated and conversed in loud, clear voices in nothing but English. Workmen were doing something to the men's changing room and the mother was afraid that a man might be tempted to use one reserved for the ladies. 'It's not important, Mother,' one of the daughters said. 'You will not be there.' 'Yes,' said the mother, 'but a man might see my clothes, and I should be very embarrassed.'

I was virtually under orders to visit Konarak, and as soon as I had put in an hour or two's butterfly watching, and investigated the immediate vicinity of the hotel, which turned out to be a nature reserve, I did this. The temple of the Sun God, built close to the shore, had appeared hardly more than a pile of ruins until 1904 when, after clearing away the sand and debris, most of the original building was uncovered. Because the temple had been protected from the weather since its abandonment it was found to be in almost perfect condition.

The first thing that impressed was the grandiose and imaginative concept that had inspired its building. It represented the chariot of the Sun God, drawn upon twenty-four colossal wheels by seven huge, straining, and wonderfully carved horses. As was to be expected in India, hidden meanings and symbolism were attributed to all aspects of the building. 'The wheels', explains the Tourist Board's leaflet, 'represent time, unity, completeness, justice, perfection, and movement, and all the measurements were found to be of astral significance.' What struck the men in the street was the nature of the many thousand carvings themselves – safely concealed from view in all probability by the sand at the time of the puritanical Moghuls coming upon the scene. The description in the government pamphlet touches on this aspect of the subject lightly, offering what sounds like an excuse. 'The temple was conceived as a total picture of the world, and without mithuna or union in love which is the fount of creation, it would not have been complete. A great part of the temple is, therefore, covered with erotic art.'

The fact is that the picture of the world presented in the carvings at Konarak is narrow and specialized. India abounds with temples belonging to roughly the same period devoted whole-heartedly to erotic statuary. It was a purely religious art form and therefore almost certainly in olden times less than exciting in its effect upon beholders in general. Christian doctrine of the day frowned upon sexual activity and decorated the cathedrals with images of elderly saints in the attitudes of prayer. In both cases the postures were largely standardized and repetitive. All the bearded saints of the medieval cathedrals look roughly the same, and so do the girls in the arms of their lovers in the innumerable carvings on the walls and the wheels of the Sun Temple at Konarak. In both so widely sundered civilizations the boredom of a sculptor, deprived of all outlet for invention and condemned to the mass production of almost identical figures, must have been extreme. Of the thirty-two amatory postures catalogued by the *Kama Sutra* only six or seven were represented here, the rest being too complicated for the carvers. No wonder that in both cases the most interesting work appears in the scenes of everyday life – of scolding fishwives, men playing cards, cheating in the market, a child playing with a dog, carved in some corner of the edifice, out of range of pious eyes.

In the old days worshippers would have been drawn to Konarak, just as they were now to Jagannath Temple in Puri, to improve their fortunes in this life and their prospects in the next. The erotic statuary is likely to have been taken for granted and passed by with hardly a glance. The most devout of the males among the crowd might have responded to the impulses of religion by coitus with a temple prostitute, the carnality of the act diluted with its devotional ingredient. Nowadays, since the temple no longer functioned as such, it was the carvings that attracted.

Pleasure may have been spiced with guilt. After long contact with the British the Indians have become a puritanical people. This was illustrated on the Marina Garden Hotel's beach, where the only visitors I saw were a mixed party of young Indians who had at least been able to free themselves of the supervision of their elders. Nudity, or anything approaching it, is banned from the productions of the Indian cinema, but some sort of breakthrough in the direction of liberation happened a few years back when public opinion was induced to tolerate shots of girls who through some accident had received a dowsing and were portrayed in wet and clinging saris. The great sport on this particular occasion was to encourage the girls to wade, fully dressed, into the sea, then emerging to exhibit forms coming close to nudity in slightly provocative postures. No wonder after all this suppression that three crowded planes fly daily from Delhi alone to Khajuraho, where the many temples display their erotic masterpieces by the acre. Inhibition is the spur.

At Khajuraho the scene must have resembled Konarak. Trippers bussed in for an hour's scramble over the terraces here, and were waylaid at the entrance by potato-crisp sellers and touts offering watches and rings they claimed to have picked up on the street. At the temple, photographers awaited to snap them against backgrounds of intertwined bodies, and postcards were proffered with pretended although quite unnecessary secrecy. Mothers and fathers brought their children along, perhaps as part of the duty of keeping up with the times. Mums speeded up a little, eyes front, to pass the danger spots. A few dads risked quick, sidelong glances, then turned away to continue conversations with young members of the family, undoubtedly on educational themes. In certain sensitive areas ropes had been stretched about a yard from the wall, possibly to prevent close-up photography of the ingenious love-making of the thirteenth century. These sections of wall were under observation by a guard, and when someone with a camera ducked under the rope and started to focus-up, the guard would blow his whistle and wave a stick.

The ladies featured in action on the walls of the Sun Temple were known as devadasi, 'handmaids of the god', and although playing a lesser part perhaps in the rituals of Church and State in later centuries, they were still in action at Puri in the Jagannath Temple in 1818 when R. Ward, a Baptist minister, wrote furiously in his book *A View of the History of India*: 'It is a well-authenticated fact that at this place a number of females of infamous character are employed to sing and dance before the "god".'

Although there may have been some decline in the quality of temple prostitutes by the time the Reverend Ward came on the scene, they were originally selected by state functionaries with the greatest possible care, and the 'noble maidens' occupying the highest of the seven grades were treated with great honour. They held highly paid posts at the court of King Chandragupta, taking turns to hold the royal umbrella and carry the King's golden pitcher. Punishment for rejection of the royal advances was one thousand lashes, although it is supposed that this was rarely administered. Apart from sexual services provided for members of the court and generous contributions to temple funds, the ladies spent much of their time fanning idols. They were traditionally secret-service agents, and besides fulfilling the most exacting criteria of beauty they were expected to be well-educated and witty, with conversational standards 'much better than those of the chattering housewife'.

The stunning fact is that what is known as the Devadasi System still exists in a clandestine and wholly criminal form, acting as a vehicle with which the brothels of the great cities, in particular Bombay, are continually replenished by fresh and innocent young victims from remote country villages. It has always been there, easily foiling any attempt to repress it. The passage of the Karnataka Devadasi Act of 1981 has failed to have any effect upon a practice by which large numbers of village girls, either tribals or from the

untouchable castes, are persuaded by local priests, with the conniv-
ance of parents, to allow themselves to be dedicated to the goddess
Yellamma in mass ceremonies performed each February on the night
of the lunar eclipse at a number of villages in Maharashtra and
Karnataka. Pimps lie in wait, the police turn a blind eye, and the
young girls are spirited away to Bombay or Pune, never to be seen
again.

The attractions in the past for the poor, ignorant and priest-ridden
families were substantial. The profession of the devadasi was, and in
some cases still is, seen as an honourable one. Until recently a
devadasi by law had the same inheritance rights as a son. She could
perform the religious rites denied to other Hindu women, and –
since in theory she was 'married' to a goddess – the family would be
freed from the dowry burden. The new law has, in theory, put an
end to these small inducements. Otherwise it has done nothing, for
the situation has remained unchanged, and although hundreds of
devadasis are known to have been dedicated in the years since the
passing of the act only a single case has been brought by the police
resulting in a conviction. The Indian film masterpiece *Salaam
Bombay* fails to make it clear how the young girl preyed upon by a
pimp in Bombay has fallen into his power, and one can only suppose
that its makers may have been under some compulsion to hush up
the facts. The *Times of India* reporting on the situation comments
bitterly upon the irony that in the Year of the Young Girl such
terrific abuses should seem unable to touch the national conscience.

What is almost incredible is that there is really no mystery about
these regular brothel recruitments. Everyone who reads a newspaper
must know that the Temple at Saundati in Belgaum district has
always held the principal shrine of the Yellamma cult, that every
February a festival there attended by many thousands of religious
pilgrims takes place, and that in the past numerous dedications of
girls who were to become prostitutes took place; if the traffic has
momentarily been halted at Saundati it carries on as before in many
smaller temples in that area. The fact is that there is money in this
for everybody: for the girl's parents and relatives, for the priest, for
the pimp, and for the police. There is a waiting list of rich debauchees

in the city ready to pay up to the equivalent of five hundred pounds for the privilege of deflowering a young girl. The police are corrupt, say Indian friends, because they are underpaid. This may be so, but in the end in matters of custom, even of criminal custom, India appears incapable of reform.

Chapter Thirteen

WHILE I WAS AT KONARAK I could not resist a little diversionary pilgrimage to the mouth of the Devi River, flowing through sandbanks to the sea some three miles away. I had been an avid reader of the travels of Sebastian Manrique, the Portuguese missionary, and one of the great travellers (and adventurers) of history. It was here in August 1640 that Manrique landed on his way back from the Far East to continue his peregrination overland, through India – the Indian section of the journey largely by bullock-cart – back to his home in Portugal. His wanderings had taken nearly fifteen years.

The first point of land they identified from the ship, Manrique says, was the Jagannath Temple, but they arrived at Puri a month too late for him to have witnessed in person the great Car Festival of that year of which he provides in his book a lively and fairly accurate description. He was never a one to miss such an occasion, and was probably delayed by bad weather. There is a routine report on the subject of sati, seen by travellers in general as the most dismal of the rites of the Hindu religion, and an extraordinary account of sacrificial rites practised in his time on Sagar Island at the mouth of the Hugli, in which devotees of a local cult, both men and women thrown into a state of ecstasy, offered themselves to the sharks.

As soon as they have made this vow they enter the sea up to their breasts and are very soon seized and devoured ... and since they [the sharks] are accustomed and thus encouraged constantly by tasting human flesh, they become so bloodthirsty that they rush up fiercely at a mere shadow. Yet at other times they are either so satiated ... that they reject the offerings made by those unhappy idolators. They then look upon this escape, which they should consider as so much happiness and good fortune, as an event full of ill luck, and hence leave the sea weeping and lamenting loudly, believing that owing to their sins they were not considered worthy to have their sacrifice accepted by their false and diabolical gods, and henceforth they look upon themselves as forever damned and doomed.

Much of the interest in Manrique's narrative lies in the fact that he travelled in areas (such as Arakan in north-western Burma) never visited by Westerners before his day and by hardly any since. His editors speak of his 'uncompromising religious zeal' but, although his writings abound in the conventional pieties of his time, he is by temperament more of a merchant – as described in his passport – than a man of God, and is not above trying to smuggle the goods he carries through customs, or in one case, in India, using silk bought in China to bribe an official when he becomes embroiled with the law.

On landing in India Manrique immediately fell in with an Englishman called John Yard, of the East India Company, who lived upriver in or near Bhubaneswar, which they visited by boat. The river 'was covered over by great, pleasant, shady trees, whose thick branches here and there interlaced so as to look like an artificial avenue. This was full of most beautiful peacocks, of green screaming parrots, pure shy doves, simple wood-loving pigeons . . .' The change since then has been a dramatic one, for with the trees long since gone the view from the low reaches of the Devi River is of sand.

Yard, with whom Manrique got on extremely well, would appear to some to have been a typical Englishman. He carried a gun wherever he went and on this occasion shot at everything in sight, so that by the time they finished the river journey he ended the day, as Manrique puts it, laden with the results of his toil. He was spellbound with admiration. After that Manrique, well supplied with funds, bought a horse, hired a number of servants, and set out for the north. It was a journey to which he looked forward. India under Moghul rule was prosperous and peaceful. Rest-houses for travellers were provided at frequent intervals along the main highways, and Manrique noted that they offered all the amenities of the day, and were clean and cheap. Friar Domingo Navarrete, who followed him exactly forty years later, was enraptured by a similar experience.

'There is no such easy and restful way of travelling in the world. We always lay quiet and safe. There is no enemy here to be found.' In the seventeenth century there was no fear of dacoits or of encounters with corrupt and brutal police. Nevertheless the Moghuls kept a tight rein in their dominions and, as Manrique was to learn, their justice could be severe.

Despite fifteen years in the East Manrique could still be amazed and a little scandalized by the treatment of animals in India, which struck him as contrary to God's purpose. 'There are some', he says, 'who go to such lengths in showing this consideration that they give dogs wadded cotton coats in winter. In the Kingdom of Gujarat I saw cows and calves clothed in fine coats of this kind, buttoned and tied over their chests and round their bellies.' Even if Manrique could bring himself to tolerate such absurdities in the case of household pets he firmly drew the line with wild animals taking 'every advantage of the ample privileges accorded by that heathen sect [Hinduism] to wild animals which thus become tame and enter their houses'.

It was the season of monsoons, with roads turned to mud and much of the country under water. On one occasion the travellers took refuge with a Hindu farmer who fed them and let them sleep in his barn. Here they were found by peacocks sheltering from the weather, 'accustomed', as Manrique says, 'to being petted on other occasions', and therefore caught quite easily for their necks to be wrung. The birds were cooked and eaten, but thereafter doubt set in as Manrique and his Muslim servants remembered Hindu prejudices in such matters. As a precaution they buried the remains of their feast, but a few small feathers were overlooked. Next day, after they had left, these were discovered by the farmer, who raised a hue and cry which was followed by hot pursuit. There followed a running battle for several miles with the Indians showering them with arrows, and Manrique turning back twice to fire off his musket at them. Luckily the English marksman had been left behind for no one suffered a scratch. But the alarm had gone ahead, and at the next town they were arrested and thrown into gaol. Having to deal with the Muslim authorities, Manrique put forward the plea that according to both Christian and Muslim faiths animals were created by God for man's use and that it was lawful to eat them. With this the governor was in emphatic agreement, pointing out, nevertheless, that the Moghul Emperor had guaranteed his Hindu subjects the right to live without interference under their own laws and customs. It was a law he was bound to uphold although he proposed in this case to show leniency by punishing the perpetrator of the offence by no more than a whipping and the loss of his right hand.

This was an emergency of the kind where all Manrique's aptitude for manipulation came to the fore. Possibly as an ecclesiastic he had been freed and was in a position to make his enquiries. He undoubtedly knew his man at a glance and had been able to pick up enough of the case history of his wife to decide how the situation was best handled. 'After mollifying him [the governor] by the usual inducements on such occasions, I sent through him a piece of green flowered Chinese taffeta, worked with white, pink, and yellow flowers, to this lady. It was a sufficiently rich and pleasing gift, and being such the lady gave as good a return, to show her gratitude, and did her best with her husband to get him to send me secretly to set the prisoner free on the pretence that he had escaped.'

It was to Manrique's credit that he would not settle for an alleviation of the punishment by which only the fingers of the offender's hand were to be amputated, but kept on with his bribery and cajoling until he was released. The episode illustrated not only the characters of the protagonists but that of the civilizations that formed them. Only John Yard the Englishman is missing from the tableau.

Chapter Fourteen

A PHONE CALL to Bose produced reassuring news. Police clearance for the journey to the interior had come through. The expedition he had in mind would cover up to some one and a half thousand miles through most of those parts of south-western Orissa accessible by road. He had found someone to go with me familiar with the area, who spoke three of the principal tribal languages, and who would be ready to travel in three days' time. He quoted the approximate cost involved, which seemed extremely reasonable.

Traveller's cheques had to be changed to meet the bill so I went to Mrs Panda. Tourists in India soon learn to steer clear of bureaucratic institutions such as banks, in recognition of which hotels are empowered to change money at roughly equivalent rates, and they are under obligation to display a notice showing what those rates are. I found it a little ominous that the Marina Gardens should fail to do this, and when after preliminary blandishments Mrs Panda got down to brass tacks I could understand why. Nothing changed in the seraphic smile when I told her that I preferred to save money by going to the bank in Puri. This was a Saturday, she pointed out, and the banks in Puri were closed. She wheedled: if a large sum of money were involved she might be able to do a little better.

An Indian fellow guest who had hovered within earshot while these transactions were taking place took me aside to assure me that whatever Mrs Panda said, the State Bank of India at Puri remained open until midday. However, there was some delay in obtaining a taxi, and by the time it arrived I knew that it was touch and go whether I would get there before the bank closed. The taxi was old and slow, we were held up by road-mending operations and then a procession, after which resignation took over and I adjusted to the fact that what had started as a rush to a bank about to close for the weekend would end as a leisurely tour of the sights of one of India's most fascinating cities.

Puri was five miles away down the coast. My taxi drove into its heart down the wide street built to allow the lumbering, hardly controllable passage of the Car of the Juggernaut blundering through multitudes entranced by the presence of the god. Scarlet flags flared from the icy-white pinnacle of Manrique's landmark, the Jagannath Temple tower, which thrust into the sky. Holy men overtook us and passed pedalling furiously on garlanded bicycles. Pilgrims had bought conch shells and filled the air through the tinkling of bicycle bells with their melancholy hooting. Beside the shells the stalls sold pilgrims' souvenirs saturated in the imagination of the buyer with magical force; images of the Lord of the Jagannath, bold-eyed ceramic cockerels, squares of tin-plate punched with patterns of sunflowers, mystic birds, and the footprints of Lakshmi, goddess of poverty and wealth. The crooked side-streets running back from the temple were full of pilgrims who washed themselves endlessly. The suds trickled down to join a mainstream from their ablutions finding its eventual way into a black gutter.

The cows of Puri were quite unlike those anywhere else. They were the best organized in India, going in single file and orderly fashion the round of the streets, pausing only for a moment to collect an offering from a regular contributor before moving on. They were calculating, nimble and sleek.

This was the Chaucer's Canterbury of eastern Indian. People had always come here out of the natural delight of going on pilgrimage, or to profit spiritually or physically from the proximity of holy things. Letters in the local press attested to the benefits to be derived. A stay in Puri, it was claimed, with frequent visits to the temples, promoted sublime visions, strengthened transcendental consciousness, and improved digestion and the elimination of waste products. Someone had developed a highly sensitive piece of electrical equipment which measured the strength and direction of divine influences radiated from the Jagannath shrine. A correspondent wrote that his friends had detected a current flowing from his body on his return from pilgrimage and that for the first few days physical contacts with him sometimes produced slight shocks. Many such experiences transmitted by word of mouth had added to the reputation of Puri over the centuries. Nowadays in season buses delivered and collected up to five thousand pilgrims a day. At the time of the Car Festival in June or July the town's population was swollen by several thousand, with pilgrims bedding down in lodging houses ten or twenty to a room, covering the rooftops at night with their recumbent bodies, and lined up row after row under plastic sheeting all along the beach.

The Lord Jagannath, usually depicted in naive childlike imagery, is senior member of a family trio including a brother Balabhadra, and sister Subihadra, and replaces Durga (Kali) of neighbouring West Bengal as the most popular deity of Orissa. This partiality is derived, it is said, from his accessibility to worshippers of all castes. Nevertheless the cult is exclusive. Only Hindus are allowed to enter the temple, even Mrs Gandhi's application being turned down through what was seen as her unorthodox marriage. Foreigners wishing to see something of the temple beyond its external walls are invited to view it from the roof of a library across the road, gaining little from this although paying a charge.

The religious activities of Puri are on a grand scale. The temple itself is enormous – a city in miniature. Within the compound six thousand men are permanently employed in temple duties, many engaged in the construction of the famous cars, always destroyed following each annual festival and taking a year to rebuild. It takes four thousand pullers to haul the processional cars down the street. The leading car in which Lord Jagannath rides is fifty feet high, weighs over one hundred tons, is carried on sixteen wheels, and once started is virtually unstoppable, although the distance covered is exceedingly short. In the past instant admission to paradise was assured for those who threw themselves under the wheels. The supposed hypnotic effect produced by this pre-eminent local god featured largely in the schoolbook histories of old, and descriptions of mass immolations under the car of the Juggernaut were insepar-able from the Indian scene. They may have been based upon such second-hand accounts as those given by Manrique: 'They voluntarily offer up their wretched lives, throwing themselves down in the centre of the road along which the procession passes with its chariots full of idols. These pass over their unhappy bodies, leaving them crushed and mutilated. Such men are looked on as martyrs.' Even now devotional frenzy may demand a lesser sacrifice. A friend, a native of Puri and witness to a number of processions, saw a man cut off his tongue and offer it to the image. Onlookers, even in these days, were sometimes roused to a pitch of fervour, he said, causing them to slash their throats, although in symbolic fashion, producing spectacular, although non-fatal, results.

With nearly half the day still in hand this seemed the opportunity for the excursion to the site of the battle between the Emperor Ashoka and the King of Kalinga for control of a sizeable portion of the ancient world. It is in the delta area of the Devi, the Kusha, and the Bhargabi Rivers, up one or other of which – most likely the first named – Manrique travelled through such enchanting sylvan scenery after his arrival in India. Now whatever trees have been spared by the woodcutters must have been carried away by the annual floods consequent upon deforestation. With all that, and despite the change, this riverine landscape retained its own kind of inoffensive beauty – at least in the dry season, although it was hard to imagine the furious inundations of the monsoons. A sweep of fields down to the water's edge had been patterned like a patchwork quilt with brilliant geometrical shapes upon which the spring's snatch-crops were being grown. Where the receding waters had left stagnant pools a little amateurish fishing was going on and children were sailing boats knocked together by their fathers in a few inches of water rippling over white, polished stones at the river's edge. Three hundred and fifty years ago, Manrique had written of parrots and peacocks. Now there were glossy black crows pecking over the mud at the edge of the pools. This was a calm vista – there was nothing of tropical extremism in the scene.

It was fertile soil too, enriched a little annually, in the style of the Nile Valley, by silt deposited by the river in spate. There were many small villages, and in most years at monsoon time the floods poured over or through them. This being so, only a clear six months were available to till the soil, sow and harvest the crops, and attend to all the other matters of production, growth, and defence against annual near-catastrophe. Everything in these villages seemed to be over-shadowed by the short-term passage of time, in the certain knowl-edge that by a set date the shallow river-bed would fill, overflow, and the water released would be lapping against the makeshift walls.

Hirapur was an enchanting place, devoted to the making of temple bells – a form of cottage industry carried out in so many hut-like buildings scattered through the village that the tinkling musical concussion of hammers on brass came from every direction, and was never out of the ears. It began at close quarters as a peremptory blacksmith's chink of hammer on anvil, but distance transformed it so that the hutments at the far end of the village seemed to conceal aviaries of excited birds. The work was done in hectic fire-lit gloom; an infernal chaos of noise and heat in which order must have been concealed, round an open furnace on the floor. Bellows were pumped to flush darting sparks into the air. Men groped with tongs in the flames to pull out fiery ingots, dropping these on metal slabs by which specialists waited with their hammers. The hammers clanged down, jarring the eardrums and flattening the brass. Experts at shaping took over. The bells were dowsed in water and hammered again. Metal workers had always been the highest of the artisan castes. By local standards they made good money – fifty rupees, the equivalent of £1.60, a day – and could afford to send their daughters by rickshaw to a nearby school, a valuable precaution in a society in which female mobility comes under suspicion, and is the subject of strict control.

In Hirapur monkey gods keep an eye open for people who walk over thresholds without removing their shoes – a major solecism in this village – but their principal occupation is to keep watch on floods, and for this purpose they are placed at strategic points along the perimeter. The goddess Lakshmi also helps with flood defences and almost every house was decorated with the most elaborate symbolic designs to enlist her support in keeping out the water. This attractive custom has spread through the villages of Orissa, although I was never to see examples of the art form quite to equal those of Hirapur. These designs are created by the womenfolk of the village. Originality of motif is sought after, and the very best work is said to be inspired by dreams. Otherwise the women take their inspiration from the bustle of everyday village life: its traffic of bullock-carts and jeeps, worshippers at the temple, a political rally, a procession with loudspeakers and flags.

In the best specimen I found at Hirapur, all the walls including those of a large courtyard had been densely covered with stylized flowers, butterflies, and musical instruments, painted in white on an ultramarine background. Most Indian village people – as all the travellers of the past have recorded – are extremely hospitable. It was only necessary to show interest in the paintings for doors immediately to be opened, with a hearty invitation to come in and look round. In the villages of the interior such Lakshmi paintings, executed under various local names, are painted and repainted with some frequency while those carried out in the street on the threshold of a house to invite the goddess to enter will be repainted every night. The Hirapur masterpieces are renewed every year, on the eve of the feast of Lakshmi ... otherwise, as the lady of the household explained, the goddess would be bored. She added that it had taken her about five hours to carry out this major piece of creation, fitted into what time she could spare between the household tasks. When I complimented her on the unusual design she said that the goddess, famous in the locality for her musical tastes, had put the idea into her head. She felt sure that the result had met with divine approval. So far it had been a good year.

Hirapur is full of interest. The large tank permanently fringed with children splashing among the lotuses and aquatic plants is not only an indispensable convenience but saturated with beneficial influences, for a large number of images illustrating the carver's art over many centuries have been recovered from the mud. Near by is the sixth-century open-air temple of the sixty-four yoginis, one of the four of its kind existing in India. The yoginis are lesser goddesses enabled by their not too exalted status to interest themselves in the solution of minor human problems, and consequently highly popular among ordinary working folk. All sixty-four of them are splendidly carved on the temple's circular wall, shown in the style of the period in vigorous action of the kind associated with their special powers. A few arms and legs were broken off at the time of a Muslim incursion, but as the stone employed is exceptionally hard, religious vandalism was no more than symbolic. Few people seem to know of the temple's existence.

Dhauli Hill overlooks the river a mile or two upstream, and on both banks immediately below took place one of the decisive battles of the ancient world – the encounter between the Emperor Ashoka, who by 250 BC had conquered almost the whole of the sub-continent, and the King of Kalinga. The forces of Kalinga were annihilated, and an imperial inscription speaks of several hundred thousand battle casualties, followed by the deportation en masse of the survivors. At this point the Emperor is supposed to have been overcome by remorse, and to have embraced the Buddhist philosophy of non-violence, thereafter succeeding in the tricky task of conducting the affairs of the empire while turning to ascetic practices and becoming himself a monk. There were family precedents for adoption in later life of extreme forms of belief, for Ashoka's grandfather Chandragupta, who campaigned successfully against the Hellenic Greeks in north-west India, followed his victory by becoming a Jain and entering a monastery. Here he deliberately starved himself to death in orthodox Jain fashion. The turnaround in Ashoka's case was almost equally dramatic, for the Mauryan Empire was based on a successful espionage system with spies working in the guise of recluses, householders, merchants, ascetics, mendicant women, and prostitutes. From this unpromising ethical start, and with the final battle behind him, the Emperor moved on to his formulation of Dhamma, the universal Law of Righteousness, of which much is made in the Ashoka rock edicts carved at many sites throughout the length and breadth of the country.

It is assumed by many Buddhists that it was following the great victory that what had up to this time been no more than the credences of an Indian sect were carried forward on the impetus of imperial backing to become the religion of much of the eastern world. This was the belief motivating the Japanese who arrived on the spot in 1972 to erect a Buddhist Peace Pagoda on the summit of Dhauli Hill. This stark white building, shaped in a way that recalls a medieval samurai's war helmet, is highly unsympathetic to the environment.

At the foot of the hill India's earliest rock-carving, taking the form of an elephant, surmounts one of the Ashokan inscriptions – in this case a collection of edicts which, although for the most part perfectly legible, were not deciphered until 1837. They are accompanied by an atrocious translation into English.

There is no way of knowing whether the edicts ramble on in the original Brahmi in this muddled and sometimes incoherent fashion. Here we are presented with a mixed assortment of imperial pronouncements – copied in style it is supposed by some from those of Darius – random moralizing, and philosophical asides, interspersed with detailed instructions to the Emperor's morality police, created some twelve years after his reign began. The Emperor apologized for a course of actions that departs from the principles of non-violence, but explains with extraordinary frankness, 'It is difficult to perform virtuous deeds.' At this juncture Ashoka's Dhamma was beginning to take shape, some aspects of it being revolutionary indeed.

In the earliest of the edicts – which in their entirety cover a time-spread of fifteen years – Ashoka concentrates, remarkably enough, on the welfare of animals. It suggests a rapid and compulsory conversion of his subjects to vegetarianism, and the Emperor refers with distaste to the previous gluttony of the court. 'Formerly in the royal kitchen many hundreds of thousands of animals were killed daily for the sake of curry. But now only three animals are being killed, namely two peacocks and a deer, and even this deer not regularly. Even these three animals shall not be killed in future.' The sacred cow was well established in the third century BC, for the second edict is concerned largely with its welfare. Medical treatment was established by the Emperor for his subjects, but also for cattle. 'Wherever there were no herbs that are beneficial to men and cattle, they were imported and planted. Roots and fruit were also planted. On the roads, wells were dug and trees planted for the use of cattle and men.'

Twelve years followed the Emperor's anointing before the Maha-matras of the morality force received their orders, which were repeatedly emphasized in subsequent edicts. They were to ensure proper courtesy to slaves and servants, reverence to elders, abstention from the killing of animals, moderation in spending and possessions, and liberality to the religious poor. 'All men are my children,' said the Emperor. 'I desire that they may be provided with happiness in this world and the next.' The morality officers were to furnish prisoners with money, and in the case of those with 'bewitched children' or aged parents to support, to free them from their fetters.

The Dhamma of Ashoka had something about it of the New Man political philosophy of the South American revolutionaries of the sixties. Both failed to some extent through the impossibility of defining and setting bounds upon the idealism motivating the struggle. It was hard to conceive of the principles of Dhamma enshrined in a state institution, and non-violence and imperial administration were badly matched. A sort of priesthood evolved to defend the Emperor's growing obsession with virtue, becoming in the nature of things a self-protective orthodoxy resistant to change. For a few more years slaves were treated kindly and prisoners with aged parents or bewitched children freed from their shackles, but with Ashoka's death India returned to the cast-iron rule of certainty and submission.

Chapter Fifteen

BOSE'S RECOMMENDATION of a visit to Chilika Lake was one of his suggested side-trips that interested me most. Over the years I had done a fair amount of sporadic and disorganized bird-watching, and never missed on any journey an opportunity to look at birds. It was an outing, nevertheless, that I approached with certain reservations. I had actually heard of Chilika before coming to India, remembering that it had been spoken of by ornithologists as one of the most interesting bird sanctuaries in the world. For all that I had reason to consider myself as hardly more fortunate in the business of sighting rare birds than impressive animals. I went on such forays armed with hope but armoured by the unexciting experiences of the past against disappointment.

Chilika Lake is enormous, having an area of four hundred and twenty-five square miles. The first view of it from a hilltop was remarkable, for there was no way of knowing that I was not looking down on the open sea, although the unruffled shallow water over a bottom of white sand appeared as a sea of milk, and its great luminosity imparted a sullen purplish tinge to the sky. Island shapes were sketched in here and there on the surface, and a number of fishermen's boats in thin black silhouette seemed to intensify the whiteness of the water.

The foreshore under Barkul village had been left to its own devices. It was edged with mud, and contained a number of boulders and unidentifiable masonry half sunk in rock pools. In this setting a great assortment of small sea-shore birds, black-winged stilts, avocets, ruffs, and coursers of the kind now rare in Europe scuttled from pool to pool. A hundred yards out on the lagoon a raft of pelicans drifted by, and beyond them ducks of all kinds bobbed about. This promised well, but someone to do with the hotel was quick to dispel illusions as to the possibility of any really exciting avian encounter.

'I am afraid you have arrived just a week or two too late,' he said. 'Now the nesting season is at an end and the birds are about to depart. At the beginning of the month you would have seen black storks from the position in which we are now standing. On the far side of the lagoon you will still be seeing rare cranes. Also I am told up to one thousand flamingos including some of the lesser variety. To view them you would require to take a boat, one hour and a half in each direction.'

'I would be very happy to do that,' I said.

'Alas, today that would not be possible. All the boats have been booked by parties wishing to visit the shrine of the goddess Kali Jai on one of the islands. There will be many people, but as you may imagine, no birds.'

If I wished to take lunch at the hotel, the man warned me, it might be a good thing to do so forthwith, otherwise with the press of business there might be a long delay. Several buses had in fact just arrived and were disgorging numerous passengers, largely fraught and excited parents accompanied by their many phlegmatic, self-possessed children. This was clearly to be another Indian family occasion. Charming as it was the hotel was singularly ill-equipped to deal with multitudes on pilgrimage. By way of a lavatory it offered a large single room containing several brooms, cans of paint, rope, an outboard engine, a pedestal in a corner and a cistern that could be induced to release a brief drizzle of water. With the arrival of the buses a long and, in parts, agitated queue formed at the door, and it was some hours before this entirely dispersed.

The boats mustered to carry the pilgrims to the island awaited at the water's edge, long, low in the water, rather frail-looking, painted with all-seeing eyes and naive representations of lake birds, and possessing a single square sail. They were perfectly adapted to the fishing requirements of a calm, shallow lagoon, and I suspected that apart from the recent addition in each case of a small outboard engine they had remained as they were now for thousands of years. I joined a boatful of visitors which puttered slowly towards Kali Jai

Island where the goddess had been installed in her cave. An Indian sitting next to me told me what it was all about. At some time in the far past a local girl was to be taken by boat to her marriage in the village of her husband on the other side of the lagoon. Last-minute difficulties arose through the non-availability of any male member of the family except the girl's father to escort her to the wedding, and for the father to do so was a serious breach of custom. Nevertheless the family, father included, boarded the boat and set out, but halfway across the lake, at the moment of passing the small island for which we were bound, a sudden retributory squall blew up, the boat was overturned, and the girl seen no more. The search for her was continued by the father until sunset, when his daughter's voice spoke to him from the water. 'I have left this world to become a goddess. Now I am Kali Jai. Make a shrine for me on this island.' The village girl is now accepted as having been an incarnation of Kali, and although hardly known in other parts of the country, her reputation in Orissa and West Bengal – including Calcutta – where she is worshipped as goddess of family troubles is enormous. 'People do not come here to see the lake, nor are they interested in the birds,' said my informant. 'It is this goddess who interests them, who is very close to their hearts.'

The story of the girl drowned on her wedding day who becomes a goddess is typical of the East, and one of the genre based upon hope turned through breach of custom to despair that crops up in various forms in the countries of eastern Asia, and to a lesser extent halfway across the world. Can it be a matter of spontaneous generation, or is there some mysterious breeding ground from which such legends spread? Take for example the principal item of a Welsh myth, located in an actual village, Myddfai, in Dyfed. The story is that in the eleventh century, a fairy emerging from the waters of a nearby lake was persuaded to marry a village boy, providing him with an ample dowry of cattle summoned by her from the lake. Stipulations were imposed. Should he in the course of this marriage strike her three times she would leave him. This, inevitably although largely by accident, he did, and the lady, taking her cows with her, vanished again under the waters. By tradition there were offspring of the marriage. A local doctor of half-fairy origin is commemorated in a stone set at the entrance to the village church, being one of a clan of medical men of mixed human and fairy antecedents known as the physicians of Myddfai, the last of whom, having abandoned medicine, kept a shop in a nearby town and died about thirty years ago.

It is a legend repeated almost to the last detail throughout the world. In 1944, engaged in the lugubrious duty of escorting Asiatic prisoners back to Russia, I was entertained, almost nightly, by recitations of Uzbek folk tales. Among them was the story of the girl drowned on her wedding day who becomes a demon. Among them, also, was the supposedly Celtic Lady of the Lake with hardly a detail changed from the Welsh version. The Myddfai story, too, features in Indian mythology except that she abandons her human lover, vanishing with her flocks beneath the waters as soon as she is pregnant, and there is no talk of a subsequent birth. Thus, perhaps, in shadowy folk-memory are recorded the sorrows of pre-history.

While on shore the pilgrims had seemed to keep their distance from one another, to remain isolated in self-contained families and groups, and there was a certain formality in the air. From the moment of setting out on the water, wedged often precariously in position on the swaying, overloaded boats – sometimes even obliged to clutch at a stranger for support – they were suddenly infused with holiday jollity and high spirits. The grown-ups chatted happily with whoever they found themselves squeezed up against, laughing at whatever was said, and sometimes even did their best to clown a little, while their previously sedate children were as jubilant and obstreperous as they were expected to be.

So sudden, unexpected and complete was the transformation that I suspected it was part of the protocol of the pilgrimage. Those who consume the ritual meal they prepare for the god are supposed to exhibit a satisfaction to be transmitted in essence to the deity, and it was reasonable to hope that Kali Jai would enter into the spirit of a joyous occasion. Whatever the ancient tragedy the festival may commemorate, the custom of the East is to dress in new clothing, to be effusively companionable, to eat the best food that can be produced, to play inspiring music, and let off noisy fireworks if this is permissable. Kali Jai is a scaled-down version of the Kali of Calcutta who, despite her fearsome reputation, was created by the gods as destroyer of demons. The original Kali is a valuable ally in the battle against major catastophe, against cholera, the floods, or even the Naxalites. Kali Jai, who inspires no fear, helps out with the lesser predicaments such as stomach ulcers, bad examination results, or the loss of a job.

Incense floating in clouds from the island reached us when we were still fifty yards from the shore. The island was dense with smoke from the charcoal fires lit by picnicking families who had arrived in such numbers that it was difficult to chart the way over the rocks round them. Feeding operations, as usual, were conducted with immense ceremony, and the use of a great variety and size of pots. Some families had brought along elaborate barbecues, which had to be put together before the cooking began. A number of stalls selling the usual sweets, nuts, and souvenirs were jammed into a minute square of tableland at the top of the island, to one side of which steps led down to the narrow entrance to the cave containing the goddess. A small statue of her as a pretty young girl had been built into the wall of the little temple, but, dehumanized by design in the cave below, she was little more than a head wearing a sexless mask, and a featureless bodily shape draped by a patchwork of brightly flowered materials that represented a dress. This rag-doll effigy was seen through a curtain of dangling votive offerings of human bodily parts, cockerels, and goats, cut and hammered out of tin.

The visit was a homely procedure. For once a foreigner was accepted, seemingly even welcomed, in a queue at a shrine. I rang the bell at the entrance to announce my presence, made an offering, accepted the ritual sliver of coconut from the priest, exchanged congratulatory smiles with the women who followed me, and went out. Outside children had clustered to eat rice cakes scalding from the pan while others tried rather hopelessly to play hopscotch in the few spare feet of vacant space among the stalls. Several transistors tuned to the same station softly brayed film music.

I was found by the friend I had made on the boat, who hauled himself up through the crowd, roaring with astonished laughter. His eyes glittered with euphoria and the upswing of his luxuriant moustaches seemed to have developed a lighter curl. He had paid his respects to the goddess, and had a feeling that everything had gone well.

'But how are we to cope with all these pilgrims I am asking?' he said. Now, with the increase in people's troubles, and therefore the increased following of the goddess herself, the problem was how to pack all the visitors on to the island. At the feast of Makrar Sakranti, celebrated earlier in the month, the boats had circled for hours waiting to disembark passengers. Once ashore they had been jammed together in a static mass so that many pilgrims had had difficulty in reaching the shrine. There was some talk of increasing the size of the island by concrete blocks of the kind used in sea walls. But opinion was divided, some saying that it would be unsuitable if not actually sacrilegious. 'On this matter,' he said, 'they will never agree.' If only a decision could be left to Kali Jai herself, he thought. That would be the ideal solution.

To the Tribal Heartland

Chapter Sixteen

ON MONDAY there was a phone message at the hotel saying that Bose would like to see me as soon as possible. When I tried to ring back I was told there was a delay of uncertain length, so I decided to check out. That, since there were bills to be paid, called for a second trip over to the State Bank of India at Puri.

Up to this point I knew Indian banks only by repute, and while it could not be said that I particularly looked forward to the visit I was prepared to write it off as an episode of travel that might add a few sentences to the account of a country in which such institutions are perfectly adapted to the environment.

At first glance the bank of Puri was like any other large bank, with the air-conditioning breathing out its faintly conventual odour of stale paper, and the meek, bovine queues of customers unmanned by the terrific indifference of the staff and the uselessness of protest. The bank had established its autocracy by a large, curt notice framed with small marginal decorations like an imperial Russian ukase.

COMPLAINTS DAYS
CUSTOMERS OF THE BANK HAVING COMPLAINTS ARE
INVITED TO SEE THE ASSISTANT-MANAGER ON TUESDAYS
AND THURSDAYS

I noticed a long, narrow bench of the kind on which visitors to Spanish model prisons are seated to await their turn to be admitted, and this was crowded with customers anxiously eyeing a large clock which, like those in British taverns – and presumably for the same reason – was ten minutes in advance of the correct time.

The long wait I was prepared for at the currency exchange took place while the counter clerk dealt with the huge monetary transactions and the paper-work of those ahead of me in the queue. Finally my turn came, and the clerk took my passport and traveller's cheques and, having subjected them to a long scrutiny, signalled me to countersign the cheques. This I did. He examined the result, but was clearly dissatisfied. 'Please sign one more,' he said. It was evident that the second attempt was unsatisfactory, too, for he went away to discuss the matter with a superior seated at a desk, who followed him back to the counter. 'The signatures do not tally,' the superior said. 'We must go to see the assistant-manager.'

All these men including the assistant-manager wore watches of exceptional quality; the higher the position with the bank the better the watch, and the better the watch the more sympathetic its wearer. To the counter clerk I was no more than a face in an obscure multitude. His superior, who saw fewer people, was reasonably polite, and the assistant-manager, emerging from the comparative solitude of his office, went so far as to apologize for the trouble to which I was being put. Nevertheless he felt obliged to ask me to produce a few more examples of my signature, and when this had been done shook his head sadly. 'Every one is different,' he said.

'But surely, all signatures are,' I protested.

'Yes,' he said. 'If the counter-signatures appear as identical a suspicion of forgery may even arise, but in this case the disparity is very great.' He glanced at his splendid watch and clucked exasperation. 'We are bound to refer this to the manager, but most unfortunately he is out for a short time. I am sorry. Perhaps you would not object to going to the waiting-room? I am sure he will not be long.'

The waiting-room was the bench along the wall and it was here that I happened to sit next to James Womack, a man with a soft voice and a slow weepy smile who had not the slightest objection to spending the better part of a morning on a narrow bench in an Indian bank.

'Been here long?' I asked him, not realizing this.

He considered the question. 'I suppose I have,' he said. 'Quite a while.' He told me he was waiting for a call to Bangalore about a bank transfer that should have come through and had not. 'It'll take an hour or two,' he said. 'What does it matter? This is India. Everything here takes three times as long as anywhere else. So what? All you do is adjust your sense of time.' His tone suggested that delays were part of the charm of the country. He was an Australian from Sydney, a member of a group-practice specializing in homoeopathic medicine, and had come to this country to advance the scope of his studies, where he had based himself in Bangalore. Now he was in Bhubaneswar for a short stay and a course in herbal remedies, for which it was a centre – well known even in Australia.

Where was he staying in Bangalore, I asked, and he told me at an ashram, not far from the town.

'Boiled rice, meditation, and Vedic mantras?' I suggested.

He laughed softly. 'Well, not quite,' he said. 'Something like that, but you can have a lot of fun. Have you ever stayed in an ashram?'

'On one occasion, yes.'

'Which one was that?'

'The ashram of Sri Aurobindo at Pondicherry,' I told him. 'A long, long time ago. My second trip to India.'

'That must have been a great experience,' he said, but by the way he looked at me I was not sure that he was convinced that this had really happened.

Everybody on our bench had been given a ticket with a number on it and when this number lit up on a grille under the clock it meant that the holder was wanted at the counter. After ten minutes or so Womack's number was flashed. He got up, but soon came back smiling as though someone had made him a present. 'False alarm,' he said cheerfully. 'Just to say there's another hour's delay. I was wondering, when you were at the ashram, did you have any contact with Sri Aurobindo himself?'

'He was dead by then. The Mother had taken over.'

He nodded. 'Did you see something of her?'

'Most evenings at the nut-giving ceremony. I was allowed to touch her sari at the first ceremony I attended. The secretary who took charge of me told me how it was done. She might speak to me, he said. Then I could take a fold of the sari between the first and middle finger of the right hand. He told me I might experience a discharge of power passing into my body.'

'And did you?'

'No,' I said.

His disappointment was clear. 'Maybe you were not ready for it,' he said. 'Tell me how she looked.'

'She looked like a little old Frenchwoman, which she was, although she was always dressed in Indian style. Her face was covered in make-up. She wore platform shoes with silver buckles and she had very bright eyes, like a lizard.'

'I have a book about her,' Womack said. 'She drew people to her like a magnet.'

'Yes,' I said. 'She did that. There were five hundred or so in the ashram when I was there, about seventy or eighty English of the upper classes. She took their possessions into her care and set them to work in the orchards. They did it for their food. That was enough. Nobody complained.'

'Would you expect them to?' Womack asked. 'Money would have been no concern to them.'

'I'm sure it wasn't. I got to know a man called John. He used to teach at Oxford and he was there with his wife. He was keen on photography and one day he asked the Mother if he could buy a camera. "Wait, my son," she told him. "The opportunity will come" – which it did. A few days later a Frenchman came in and turned over his belongings, among them a camera. She gave it to John. He saw it as a kind of miracle.'

'It wasn't, though,' Womack said. 'There was a natural causation. Happenings like that are of a daily occurrence at Bangalore. You might find them strange, but they're not. What mystifies me is how you managed to get into Pondicherry. I wonder if you're quite the type.' He laughed pleasantly. 'Excuse me for putting it like that.'

'I ran into some rich Americans who were staying there. They poured money into the ashram and were put up in its rest-house which was quite luxurious. Their idea was to make a disciple out of me and they got a secretary called Mr Padu to show me the ropes.'

The mere mention of his name was enough to remind me of every detail of his face and voice. 'Please to wash most carefully in preparation for the meal. One piece of bread only. You may ask for sugar. If you cannot be seated with comfort on the floor I will bring you a table.' The hollow-eyed English disciples squatted there in the background of memory, scrabbling with their fingers in the vegetable curry. Some had been at work in the fields since dawn, and this meal had been preceded by gymnastics and meditation. They were always eager to be allowed to explain why they had exchanged the middle- or upper-class way of life for the present one, which came close to that of a coolie. 'You see, there are no problems, no doubts. Mother knows what is best for us.'

There was a confusion, with lights flashing on and off over the grille. Womack, accompanied by several of our neighbours on the bench, went to see what it was all about. They returned, with Womack's cheerful exception, gesturing exasperation.

'We're into regular flower-distribution in Bangalore,' he said, 'but your nut-giving ceremony is something new to me. Was this an important aspect of the ashram routine?'

'*The* most important,' I said. 'The idea was based on an army parade. We had an ex-regimental-sergeant-major from the British Army. The Mother sat on a throne with a halo painted on the wall at the back of her head, and when the sergeant-major called us to attention she climbed down from the throne for her inspection. He walked beside her with a stick under his arm. After that came one of the secretaries carrying what they called "the book". He was supposed to note down cases of slackness, like they do in the army. Behind him was the man carrying the bowl of nuts.'

'You're kidding,' Womack said. He seemed to be laughing more at me than at what I was telling him.

'That's how it happened,' I told him. 'Every evening at six on the dot.'

'I only wish I could have been there in your place. Didn't this have any effect on your outlook?'

'A slight one. I used to watch John who had taught at Oxford weeding beans, and wonder.'

'Why shouldn't he?' Womack asked. 'It was good for him.'

'I'm sure it was. The Mother never weeded beans. She looked after the investments and drove in a big limousine.'

'That was good for her.'

'Mr Padu said he had worked with me in a previous incarnation,' I told him. 'All the ashram members had worked with each other. They had come there drawn along lines of magnetic force from all over the world to link up again. The ones I talked to about it had spent what they could remember of past lives in interesting places. John thought he could remember something of the court of the Moghul Emperor.'

'He was to be envied,' Womack said. 'He may have reached a spiritual summit most of us have still to climb.'

'Yes, but I stayed where I was, down at the bottom of the hill. Padu wouldn't give up. He put me through a few yoga exercises and tried to teach me how to stop thinking for a few minutes at a time, which was a big step towards developing consciousness.'

'But it was no go?'

'Not in my case, no. I bought a set of Sri Aurobindo's works and we parted on good terms. The books came in handy as souvenirs for friends. Some seemed grateful and even impressed, but I could make very little of them. Perhaps it was impossible to express his thoughts in straightforward English. Whatever it was, they were Greek to me. I just couldn't understand.'

Womack said he expected to be back in Bangalore in a week or two's time, and would there be any chance of seeing me there? He was very keen to hear more about the Mother, whose reputation so far as he was concerned had not suffered from my account. Above all he wanted to introduce me to his ashram, where no one had to work, or even pay for their food, and their were no gurus riding in big cars, and maybe one of the near miracles regularly performed might be arranged for my benefit. It was left that we would meet again in Bangalore if that proved to be possible. Within minutes my light showed up and I was called to the counter to be told that the manager was back and agreed that the cheques might be paid. The operation had taken not quite an hour.

I took a taxi to Bose's office in Bhubaneswar, arriving just in time to delay his departure for his siesta.

'Everything is fixed up,' he said. 'The police permit has come through, and the man I told you about will be available to accompany you.'

'The one who speaks tribal languages?'

'Three of them. This is important for you. He has also spent a long time among the Saoras, who are the largest tribe in this vicinity. He will be showing you something of the Kondh, who were accustomed until recent years to perform human sacrifices. Also if there are no problems he will take you to the Parajas, the Godbas, the Mirigans, and the Koyas. You will remember the story of my trouble with the Bondas. You will go there, too. By the latest news I have received they are not very much changed, and for you that is interesting.'

I asked if an itinerary had been worked out and he said that was not possible. There were security difficulties in some of the areas which could change from day to day. There was a cutting ready on his desk from a recent issue of the *Illustrated Weekly of India*. It was a very long report on the current state of Bastar with a number of passages underlined:

> officials are deeply concerned that Naxalite extremists belonging to the People's War Group whose main base is in the adjoining districts of Andhra Pradesh have now spread to Southern Bastar and who have acquired sophisticated weapons like AK-47 rifles ... these squads have been held responsible for various violent actions like gun-snatchings, burnings of bases and trucks ... They are suspected to have indulged in at least 7 murders .. to have led a mass dacoity ... released 3 under-trial prisoners from Jagdalpur jail ... 1,400 troops are stationed in various villages ... it is significant that most of the activists killed by the police are tribal themselves.

'I remember that on the last occasion, you were wishing to go to Jagdalpur,' Bose said. 'It is not certain that this would be permitted. Frequently the problem is with the police. Where there are such happenings they are worried by the presence of supposed spies. If there are incidents, they do not wish them to be seen. This may be declared a prohibited area.'

He brightened as a consoling possibility struck him. 'What is wrong with an excursion along the Bastar border? This is possible for you, and really there is no difference. To see the country is the same, and the Kondh tribal people are the same on either side. There is one village where an Italian went to study tribal medicine, but no other foreigner I think. You may see this village. To go to the Bondas you must pass by Koraput. This, too, is full of Naxalites. Last week they kidnapped five policemen, but so far there is no prohibition if you have a permit.'

Thus the journey into the deep south of Orissa and the north-eastern corner of Andhra Pradesh was arranged, planned as an easy run through hilly, fairly frequented countryside for the first three hundred miles or so, to be followed by an exploration as far as the roads existed of the labyrinthine mountain valleys of the south where, I was assured, the main interest of the expedition lay.

The young man Bose had found to accompany me, Ranjan Prasad, and the driver, Dinesh, presented themselves at the Ashok Hotel at 7 a.m. the next day. Ranjan was dark, with strongly featured good looks, an extremely enthusiastic man in his late twenties, a back-sliding Brahmin who both ate meat and drank alcohol, and a history graduate specializing in temple architecture. His father was a school teacher, now retired to a smallholding, having sold much of his land to provide dowries for his three sisters. His interest in tribal peoples stemmed from his birth in a village on the edge of tribal territory. This had made him familiar with their many problems. He lost no opportunity, he said, to revisit the tribes. There was an underlying hint that there had been a romantic adventure.

Despite the vagueness on the part of the suggested itinerary, Bose had provided a fairly positive schedule which Ranjan seemed to wave aside. He was also sceptical about the packed lunches suggested for the journey. In Bhubaneswar, yes, packed lunches might be considered reasonable – but after that, what? Where were the sandwiches coming from in the Orissan back of beyond? Better to be realistic, he thought, and be ready to live off the land. At this point he mentioned that the driver, Dinesh, was a strict vegetarian, and unable to tolerate even the spectacle of others eating meat, including ham sandwiches. Despite his nonchalant attitude in the matter of provisions, Ranjan agreed that bottled water was essential, and a large reserve of this was at that moment being loaded into the car. This was an Ambassador, an Indian version of the 1954 Morris Oxford with slightly more power than the original accompanied by the asperities to be expected in what was in effect vintage motoring.

At the moment of setting off there was a surprise in store. Two thousand years before, in his ninth edict, Ashoka turned to the task of cutting out unnecessary ceremonies. They were to be restricted to a maximum of four which he saw as too important to be abolished: those connected with birth, the marriage of a daughter, illness, and setting out on a journey, and here was Ranjan, wholly a young man of his times, hoping that no objection would be raised to a visit to the temple of Kali to solicit the goddess's support for our enterprise.

The temple was sited among a row of shops on the outskirts of the town. We found cars lined up outside, including some of the better kind such as recent Toyotas, while their owners popped in and out as though calling at a post-office to buy stamps, to give the goddess details of their trips and solicit a blessing. The temple's exterior was half concealed by a complex structure decorated in fairground grotto style, full of allegorical violence. A heavily moustached plaster demon, villainous-looking and near naked, sprawled like a defeated wrestler on the pavement, having suffered an attack by a snarling lion upon which Kali was mounted. She was sternly beautiful, one arm upraised in victory, like a Hindu Britannia. This was the triumph of good over evil.

On its inside the temple was less impressive: a trim, suburban courtyard with a small wall-opening in which a faceless image was embowered among artificial flowers and tin-foil cutouts. At this opening a small queue of obviously busy men had formed to transact whatever business they had with the goddess in the minimum possible time. Ranjan placed himself in line to wait his turn, head bowed, to rattle off a brief account of the purpose of our journey and the itinerary to be taken. The priest materialized, eyes averted, for a contribution taken like a swallow snatching up an insect in flight. With this the encounter was at an end.

The journey began with a straighforward hundred-and-eighty-mile stretch of the NH5 Highway down through the coastal plain to the south with the Ambassador wedged in an endless train of thundering lorries. Once in a while a village had stretched an imploring banner across the road: HELLO DRIVER – WE LIKE YOU NOT TO PUT TO YOUR SPEED. Such appeals had had small effect. Lorries had plummeted down embankments, toppled over bridges, and, in one case, leaped one upon the other, like a praying mantis devouring its prey. Those judged not to be recoverable were in course of dismantling by breakdown gangs swarming over the wreckage like leaf-cutter ants.

A halt was called somewhere about midday at a roadside dhaba decorated with hundreds of paper flags and a single garlanded bottle of Old Tavern whisky – which although not affordable by any customer was regarded as diffusing good luck. Apart from the dusty inferno of passing lorries this was a supremely rural scene. Down the side-turning opposite, a cow-minder was collecting a beast from each house, for a rupee's worth of exercise and grazing on a rubbish tip. A few yards further on where the fields began, three girls dressed traditionally in blue and green saris for the particular task were spreading and turning rice to dry with the rhythmic gestures and steps incorporated in an ancient dance called the dhemsa. Here, too, the aerial roots of a vast banyan tree were used by the village children as a swing. In this, and all other villages of the neighbourhood, reserves of rice to last two months were stored in sunken repositories by the roadside with the earth raised in mounds over them, to give the appearance of vast newly heaped-up graves. I was reminded otherwise of the scenery of the Mexican mesa: brilliant blue houses under black rocks. There was something here of Mexico, as well, in the nasal-membrane-tingling odour of toasting chillies, the peons asleep with their hats pulled over their eyes, the fighting cocks, and the silent, evasive dogs.

We opened the first and last of the packed lunches. Dinesh got up and moved to the other end of the dhaba and sat with his back to us. Crows that had settled like a coverlet on the next bed but one were galvanized into readiness, unfolding their wings and hopping about in an excited fashion. The owner of the dhaba avoided disturbing them to bring sweet tea flavoured with caraway seeds. Dust-covered drivers came reeling in from the road, drank tea, scooped up a plateful of rice with their fingers, then fell back on their beds for an hour's sleep, while the crows flapped down to clean up the plates.

Pseudo-Mexico with its black rocks, its blue houses, circling buzzards, and flowering trees was with us until Berhampur, where the road narrowed, turned off into the hills, and lost most of its traffic. The forest closed in. In the early evening we reached Taptapani on a steep hilltop, a local spa of some renown and famous, says the government brochure, for the wild life to be seen by overnight visitors from the tourist rest-house. Here we stayed, and no halting place could have been better chosen. The animal viewing once again disappointed. Ranjan was enchanted by the sudden flashy appearance of a roller on the boughs of a tree at the edge of the rest-house terrace. This, he assured me, augured good fortune for the trip. Apart from this there was little to report. A few deer were kept in a paddock at the bottom of a hill, and a local boy who came roaring up on a motorbike mentioned seeing elephants a few weeks before from the position in which we sat, but at this moment we might well have been in Surrey. Shortly after this an aged man wandered into sight and seated himself to admire the view. In response to my query, Ranjan asked him how old he was. 'He does not know,' he told me. 'He is a tribal man. All he can say is that the

Prince gave them sweets three times. Sweets were given every twenty years. That makes him maybe seventy, but he is looking older than that.'

The matter of the roller's encouraging advent came up again. Ranjan appeared to have been emboldened by the auspice and went on not only to confirm Bose's hint that he had involved himself with a tribal girl, but to admit hoping that the opportunity might arise to contact her once again during the course of our journey. To my extreme surprise, he added that an eventual marriage was not beyond the bounds of possibility, and he was reaching the point when a decision had to be made. I assured him of my approval, and co-operation if required. Indeed nothing could have been more welcome to me than participating as a spectator in such an interesting development.

Taptapani was famous for its hot spring inhabited by a mysterious god of fertility who appeared not to possess a name. The sulphurous water issuing at nearly boiling point from a crevice in the mountain-side was piped down to a pool in a clearing above the rest-house. By the time it bubbled up in this the temperature was just bearable for a quick dip by those who came here to benefit from a range of curative effects. A notice on display near by warned bathers of the requirements of modesty and illustrated correct bathing attire for use by both sexes. At the time of our visit there were no men in sight except a priest and his assistant, but mooching about the place were several dispirited-looking ladies who had come from an encampment a short way up the hill. Ranjan, who had been here before, told me these were barren women, in the course of treatment, which could be arduous and prolonged. People suffering from such complaints as arthritis and bad backs simply waded into the pool, stayed there splashing about for a few seconds, and climbed out. A barren woman was required to inure herself to high temperatures by increasingly long immersions, and it might take several days to prepare her in this way for what seemed to me the ordeal that awaited her. Seed pods dangled from the branches of a tree overhanging the pool, and the pods upon opening dropped seeds into the water which sunk to the bottom. The cure for barrenness was to enter the exceedingly hot water, grope about in the mud, and recover a seed.

While we looked on a woman attempted this. The priest's assistant took a coconut from his supply, split it open, mixed basil with the milk it contained, then handed it to the priest who rang a bell to alert the god before pouring it into the water. At that point the woman waded in, and with the water reaching her waist, bent down to grope for a seed. The assistant switched on a transistor radio which tinkled an appropriate tune, lit a number of joss-sticks, and the air was full of incense, anxiety and hope.

The attempt – the woman's fourth – failed. This, Ranjan said, was normal. Eventually she would get her seed, and return home with it to face life with renewed confidence.

'And was the treatment successful?' I asked.

'Yes,' he said, 'of course.' A doctor had written about it in a medical journal, and this had led to a mention in the press. Unfortunately, only tough tribal women like those we had seen seemed to be able stand the scalding involved, and an attempt to modify the treatment for the benefit of the average Hindu wife had not met with success.

Apart from spectacular treatments to be watched, Taptapani offered the huge inducement to the travel-weary of a species of private mini-spa adjacent to the main bedroom. This, in effect, was a colossal bath in which a swim of a few strokes was possible. The water that gushed from the faucet was reduced by fifty yards of piping down from the pool to exactly the right temperature. In such arrangements the curative reek of sulphur fumes is psychologically as important as near-scalding water and here the fumes were concentrated enough to catch at the throat. Only the confirmed hypochrondriac could have resisted the benefits of the experience. Commenting on it later to Ranjan over a dish of the inevitable chicken and chips that had sent Dinesh racing from the table into the night, I said I felt better than I had for years, although accepting that it was all in the mind. 'It is all in the mind,' he agreed, 'but if you believe, then it becomes real. It is a pity we cannot return to this place at the end of each day.'

Taptapani was the frontier with Saora territory, homeland of about four hundred thousand members of one of India's most populous and successful tribal peoples. They had been spread through Orissa since before the Aryan arrival, although continually pushed back out of the fertile plains, first by outright invasion and conquest and later by various forms of expropriation masked by legal skulduggery of the kind still generally practised. They were notable for their collection over the centuries of innumerable gods (a principal one being the earthworm), and for complication and cost of their ceremonies. It is their custom in the case of death to conduct two funerals, the second of which, a protracted affair known as the Guar ritual, had bankrupted many families.

The ladies we had seen in search of fruitfulness at Taptapani were Saoras, and the unnamed fertility god, too, was in all likelihood from their vast collection. The local girls from nearby villages belonged to a division of the race known as Sudha Saoras – sudha meaning clean – in recognition by their Hindu neighbours of the fact that they no longer ate the meat of the cow. At the far end of the Saora country where the high mountains had discouraged Hindu penetration, the Lanjia Saoras clung wholeheartedly to the old ways and Ranjan said that the opportunity would arise to see them too.

We left Taptapani at dawn, climbing among misted forests into and over a low mountain range, held up for a moment by another of India's great vistas, with yellow morning light flooding the plain streaked with the brushstrokes of shadows cast by the tall palms. The first Sudha Saora village gathered shape by a stream curling through glowing fields, and we stopped, left the car, and walked to it.

It was another page of an atlas turned. On the road to Taptapani India had imitated Mexico; here were laid out the softer splendours of one of the countries by the China Sea. Here were the sago palms, first sighted from above, now seen to have pots fixed to their trunks below incisions from which dripped the sweet sap in which fermentation would begin on the same day. Something of the kind was to be seen in Indo-China of old where as here no serious obligations could be undertaken, no troth plighted, and no contract sealed without ceremonial imbibings. Generally among the Saora the bride-price includes twenty pots of wine, and none of their innumerable ceremonies can be completed without libations. The theft of alcohol is their most serious crime, resulting sometimes in mortal retribution.

At this hour in the morning the village was the scene of intense activity, with men, women, and children at work doing odd jobs and tidying up round the houses, or out in the fields pumping up water, weeding, hoeing, grinding millet, twisting sisal fibre into rope, cleaning out irrigation ditches, and bringing in bundles of long, feathery grass with which to make or repair thatches. The place swarmed with animals, with puppies, piglets, and bantam chickens, kept – since the Sudha Saora were vegetarians – as pets.

The villagers showed their excitement at the sight of new faces, and were eager to show us round. One thing about their village stood out – its spruceness. Being outside the caste system had left the Saora with no alternative but to clean up for themselves. It was a cool place in a hot country. Unlike the Hindus, who being basically migrants from the north, had only been on the scene for two thousand years, the Saora, having been obliged from time immemorial to defend themselves from the sun, had learned how to do it. They built themselves windowless houses with thick walls of wooden trellis plastered with mud, and two doors in line at the back and front kept open to pass the air through. The thatch came as low as three feet from the ground, and was deep enough to accommodate a spacious veranda on which the family spent much of the time. The Saora took pleasure in pointing out and explaining the merits of these architectural features. They were proud of their decorative skills, leaving their walls coloured the rich maroon of the local earth and free of ornament, but carving woodwork, doors, door-post, and lintels in lively animal shapes: rampaging elephants, peacocks in flight, strutting roosters, and an occasional whimsical and inoffensive-looking tiger.

The village Gomang – the headman – now trotted into sight, a pleasant, twinkling little man who, said Ranjan, had taken time to slip on his ceremonial gear: a hat with white plumes, tunic, tasselled loincloth, training shoes, and a species of silver codpiece, worn in this region perhaps as a badge of office. He had a frank and ready answer for questions. Modhukamba, he said, contained twenty families, totalling two hundred people. They lived on cow's milk, various pulses they grew, and the income from the sale of tussore silk cocoons – all such production being equally divided in the presence of the village god. The elections at the end of last year had provided a small cash windfall, for he had been able to negotiate a fair price for the community votes. When I showed surprise that such a transaction could be openly discussed, Ranjan explained that vote-selling was the normal practice in all such backward areas, and a vote cast without receiving a cash reward would be unheard of.

Nodding his agreement the Gomang added that the settlement in this case had been unusually generous, for the candidate who had visited the village in person had even presented him with nine pots of mohua flower wine, considered much superior to the liquor of their own production. This would be utilized in a big Guar ceremony, to be held as soon as enough funds had been collected to buy a buffalo for the sacrifice. I raised the question of the Sudha Saora's vegetarian diet, and the Gomang said that this was a rare case when departure from the rule was tolerated. The village priest, a Hindu, would abstain from the ceremony, to be performed instead by a kudan, or shaman. It was by the performance of such rituals, he pointed out, that the village's health and prosperity were maintained. On the topic of health he added that the Hindu priest dealt with minor ailments with considerable success. As for the rest, he capped his ears with his hands in what Ranjan said was a gesture of resignation. Most of the villagers, he said, had never seen a doctor. The nearest town was many miles away, for which reason no child went to school. The whole village was illiterate.

The Gomang was suddenly surrounded by women who made it clear by their gestures that they had a serious problem to discuss. It turned out that they were suffering from the attentions of officials operating the Incentive Tribal Development Programme and, said Ranjan, had at first assumed that we had something to do with the scheme. The programme starts off from the premise that tribal people's unsatisfactory existences can only be improved by government interference. This often takes absurd forms. V. S. Naipaul recalls a project designed to provide farmers of India, whether tribals or not, with bullock-carts fitted at unimaginable cost with pneumatic tyres and ball-bearing wheels. Bastar, along with Bihar, is considered as being one of the most exploited and wretchedly backward areas in the world, yet the *Illustrated Weekly of India* reported that a start had been made to improve the situation of the region by the installation of solar lights in some villages, 'which of course do not function'.

In Modhukamba the government Micro-Project seemed even more lunatic in its inspiration. In such communities cow dung is as highly valuable as we had found it to be in Bihar, above all as an ingredient in an ointment applied to sores and for mixing with vegetable dyes. The ITDP had turned up, built a large underground concrete chamber, ordered the villagers to fill it with their precious manure, and closed and sealed the lid, through which a number of copper tubes led into the village houses. The villagers were told that this arrangement would supply gas for their cooking fires – they only had to turn on the tap. This they did, but there was no issue of gas. 'None of the projects worked,' said the magazine article. 'Every programme is ill-conceived and found to be utterly irrelevant in a particular context.' In the case of Modhukamba there was no wood to be had in the neighbourhood, the women said. No other fuel but dung. What were they to do?

Chapter Seventeen

EVERY EXPERIENCE OF this journey contradicted the picture of rural India as presented by the films. India has always been shown as overbrimming with people. Here it was lonely. Having left the main coastal road with its unceasing procession of lorries, there was no traffic at all, and on this and succeeding days we drove all day without encountering, except in an occasional small town, a single private car. The fact is that there is virtually no travel in the interior of India. There is nowhere to stay, nowhere to eat, and it is not particularly safe.

We were now making for the area of Gunupur on the Vamsadhara River close to the border with Andhra Pradesh, where the main concentrations of so-called primitive Lanjia Saora are found in high mountains and thick patches of forest. Once again the scenery had undergone an almost theatrical change; a harsh Indian version of the Australian outback: red rocks tumbling through a wood, the black, bustling untidiness of hornbills in the high branches of trees with sharp, glinting leaves and orange trunks, terracotta earth, the copper faces of Saoras cutting wood with the sound of metal striking metal in a forge.

A dhaba in this isolated spot offered no alternatives for the midday meal: a narrow hut with crows fluttering over the scraps at the entrance, and a three-legged dog licking at something splashed on the floor. This possessed its own landscape in miniature of eroded hills and dales – even a river in the form of a black dribbling from the kitchen area. Plates made from leaves stitched together with something like toothpicks were stacked on a shelf and a man in a dirty singlet with a bad skin condition of the forearms took down three of them, and wiped away the red dust using the rag with which he had just pushed the sodden rice left by the last customer from the table top. On to each of these leaf-plates he ladled a dollop of rice, then went off to return with earthenware saucers containing fiery mixtures of vegetables cooked with chillies.

The moment had arrived once again, after so many years of lack of practice, to eat soggy rice with the fingers, an operation never at best elegant in the eyes of the onlooker and intolerably messy until the knack has been acquired. The local method was to pick up and compress the gobbet of rice with the tips of the five fingers, raise it to the lips, then propel it into the mouth with a sharp upward thrust of the thumb. Thereafter – and this was new to me – the diner would dislodge the grains of rice adhering to his fingers with a jerk of the wrist, scattering them about the floor where the three-legged dog awaited.

Discreetly I studied the performance of Ranjan and our driver, watching for fine points. Both, as to be expected, were excellent. The rice I scattered went in all directions; their scatterings were contained within the circumference of a circle no more than a foot across. The meal was conducted in total silence on our part, that of the dhaba staff, and the two Saora woodcutters, with fine, aquiline, slightly predatory faces, seated in a far corner and flicking their fingers free of rice with graceful, patrician gestures. At the door the man in the dirty singlet waited to pour water over our hands. The crows were trying to get at a silver lizard that had taken refuge from them under the Ambassador.

Suddenly we were in an area of Christian missionary effort and conversion. The Indian government had consistently opposed the presence of missionaries in wholly Hindu areas, but tolerated Christian Evangelism in tribal country such as this, persuaded that the integration of the tribals into the national society can best be effected by the demolition of tribal customs and religious beliefs. The Catholics and Lutherans have long shared the harvest of souls and continue, often in fierce competition, to confuse potential converts who find it hard to understand why the same God is to be reached by such widely divergent paths. To its credit the government has banned fundamentalist sects of the kind involved in recent years in Latin American scandals in which they have been charged with forcible conversion and genocide.

The first indications of missionary presence and success were graveyards with large white crosses planted in the red earth on the outskirts of tribal villages. Cremation, said Ranjan, had always been practised except in cases of persons dying from unnatural causes, whom it had been the custom to bury. Burial was thus associated with tragedy, calling for discussion among the elders as to the extra funeral rites required to succour and appease an unhappy soul. In all parts of India, Ranjan said, it was the same. The missionaries bought conversion with food and medicine. They were the only source of anti-malarial pills in the anopheles-ridden mountain villages of the Saora country. If the Saoras were only required to say, 'Yes, I believe in God,' before receiving the hand-out, he thought it would have been an excellent thing. It turned out that much more than that was expected in exchange to complete the deal. The Saora had to convince the good father, or the Christian Evangelist, that he no longer believed in the Earth Mother, the gods of fire and water, the gods and goddesses in charge of the fertility of a whole assortment of crops, in the Lord of Thunder, the Guardian of Roads, in Thakurani, the blackened pole under its thatched roof defending the village, in the goddesses of each individual household, the cobra god to be placated with flute music and fed with rice and milk, and Labusum, Divine Earth Worm and Creator of the World. The Saora saw no objection to adding the Christian deity to the others, but even with the magic tablets within their grasp were profoundly troubled at the obligation of doing away with all the rest.

Back in the rainy season when malaria reached epidemic proportions the Gomang of another Saora village had discussed his problem with Ranjan.

'We Saora have many gods,' he said.

'You do,' Ranjan agreed.

The Gomang, like the rest of his people, was innumerate. 'Could you help me to work out the number of these?' he asked.

Ranjan and the Gomang totted up the various names, adding two or three who were considered too powerful or dangerous to be mentioned by name, and could only be alluded to in a roundabout and placatory fashion. A total of twenty-three was agreed upon.

'Most of them have always been kind and useful to us,' the Gomang said. 'The missionary is asking us to exchange twenty-three for one, plus a month's supply of Nivaquin. It seems unreasonable.'

In Latin America the liberation theology of the Catholic Church has gone hand in hand with a new sympathy and even respect for tribal culture. In India, instead, the Church seems to have moved closer to nonconformist fundamentalism, and there was a whiff of old-fashioned crusading fervour in the air following a recent event in the small town of Mokama, through which we passed.

Despite the bloody communal riots at the time of the last election – now generally believed to have been politically instigated – Indians as a general rule are immensely tolerant of the religious practices of their neighbours, so often mixed together in communities of Hindus, Christians and Muslims. To take an example, the first Indian friend I made while in Kerala was a Christian married to a Hindu wife, and he had no objection to agreeing to the children being brought up in her faith. Indians were devoid of the urge to proselytize. Ranjan, when questioned on this point, said, 'I pay respect to all the gods, including those of the tribal people I visit. These gods do not quarrel among themselves, and what have I to lose?'

At Mokama a procession had been organized by the Catholics for the Feast of the Epiphany, in which their converts from several neighbouring villages led by a band would march in the spirit of 'Onward Christian Soldiers' into the town. Such demonstrations in India are normally part and parcel of electoral campaigns, planned by astute politicians, frequently supported by a strong contingent of club-waving village rowdies, and sometimes under the protection of a venal police. Religious and political demonstrations are completely foreign to tribal peoples who in neither case know what is going on. In this instance the demonstrators would have been no better than a collection of simpletons from the hills, many of whom would have been at the palm-toddy before setting out. They would have straggled along behind the pipes and drums urged by the native deacons accompanying them to shout religious slogans in a language they did not understand, and doing their best to give good value for medical or other favours received.

No two newspapers can ever be found to agree as to what has happened in incidents like this, and where there are deaths the lack of precise information is frequently increased by the secret disposal of bodies to avoid the complication of inquests. Ranjan remembered a report that the procession had been met in the town by a shower of stones and the Saora were dispersed and forced to run for their lives. Shortly afterwards they were back but this time armed with their bows and arrows. In the ensuing battle lasting some hours there had been a number of casualties, and police reinforcements had been brought from a nearby town. Riot Order 144 was solemnly read, followed by a 'firing' in which one person had been killed. Such accounts were normally little better than exercises of journalistic imagination. When we drove into Mokama a bullock-cart had broken down on a bridge and Ranjan stopped to question the three men doing something to a wheel. Yes, there had been a big fight at the time of the Catholic puja. Many people injured. Some undoubtedly killed. One of the men's friends had been struck in the armpit by an arrow. But that was as far as it got. None of the men had personally seen anything of the riot; they had been working in the fields at the time. Eye-witnesses of such events were as difficult to find in India as in a Mafia-dominated area of Sicily. 'I saw nothing. I heard nothing. I have nothing to say,' would be the response, whatever the language.

It was a sad affair, a sad example of the intrusion of religious competitiveness into a rural area where so many faiths have co-existed in harmony for so many years.

Potasing, a Lanjia Saora village built on a hillside thirty miles away, was recommended by Ranjan as one of the least afflicted in the zone by the government's efforts to uplift the tribal peoples and guide them along the paths leading to national integration. He found it – as I did – mysterious that the main targets chosen so far for these endeavours should have been remote mountain villages, most of them difficult to reach. In these areas the teams had made a start by knocking down cool, solid and practical Saora houses and replacing them with rows of concrete cabins with corrugated-iron roofs, located normally without access to water or refuge from the sun.

Incomprehensibly to Ranjan, Potasing, which would have been so easy to reach and demolish, had so far been left alone. It was a village of eighty-five families, one of a group described in a recent government report as 'in a real primitive stage, nevertheless of instant visual charm'. The low houses with their plain, immensely thick walls of red mud had been fitted into the contours of the hill in a way that recalled the harmonies of Taos. As in the case of Modhukamba, doors, door-posts, and lintels were richly carved and painted with flower and animal motifs, and like the lowland village it gave the impression that daily routines of house-scouring and sweeping went on. Here mountain rivulets ran down through the lanes with butterflies by the hundred at their edge, opening and closing their wings as they sucked at the moisture.

Someone had run to fetch the Post Master, who appeared in Potasing to have taken over the function of the Gomang of old. He was pleasant and eager to be of assistance, a young man in well-pressed slacks, a wrist watch with a metal band, a button lettered PM pinned to his white shirt, and a fair amount of English. His official duties, he said, occupied little of his time and left him free to pursue his spiritual studies. He announced that Potasing was now a Christian village, and that he himself in the absence of a resident Catholic priest was empowered to act as deacon in charge of the welfare of the religious community.

The mass conversion at Potasing – so close to the road and the Hindu sphere of influence – had been a major achievement carried out in five years. In other cases where Christians had allowed their guard to drop – 'Christian inspiration slackened' were the words he used – the Hindus had moved in. 'But now we are giving battle on this front,' the PM said. The battle was to be against illiteracy, which impeded access to the Scriptures. We were informed that there were twenty-four places for pupils in the new village school. And how many attended classes? I asked. 'One,' he said, in no way abashed by what would have seemed to me a melancholic truth. 'The teacher is sent by the government. He is to teach in Hindi,' he explained. 'This they are not understanding.'

The Saora were famous for their icons, as they are generally termed, although known locally under the name *anital*. Charming and vigorous examples of folk art of the kind are to be found with local variation among most of the tribal peoples of India. There was a recognizable affinity with the vast paintings with which the housewife of Hirapur covered her walls, although icons were limited in size to a few square feet. In Hirapur inspiration of old had been diluted by custom, and by the sheer necessity of employing space-filling patterns to be finished in a matter of hours in between odd jobs about the house. At Potasing the artist sat alone in silence, and in a darkened place, waiting for a vision to form. Only a few families – the Brahmins of art – were allowed to paint icons, thereafter made available to the general public in exchange for a small gift or service. An icon was painted in commemoration of a recent death, in honour of an ancestor, or to celebrate a festival when, like a magnificent Christmas card, it was often offered by the artist to a friend. It was also employed in the treatment of illness by a shaman who might prescribe the dedication of an icon to the village deity, together with, say, a course of massage and the sacrifice of a white cockerel.

For the PM the icons had become meaningless, and therefore slightly boring. The Church of Christ did not require such paintings, nor, he added, did the new generation of the village. 'They are looking', he said, 'another way.' And the carvings in and around the doors? I asked. Were they to come to an end, too? That was to be expected, he said. The few carvers left would find other things to do. Some were learning to carve toys for sale. People no longer wished for carvings on their new houses. They were a sign of backwardness. And were the new houses to be made with concrete and corrugated iron? When these materials could be had, he thought.

For all that – for all his distaste for those things in which Ranjan as well as I showed what must have been such inexplicable interest – he was an impressively tolerant man, and ready to help us in any way he could. It was at his suggestion that we set out to scour the village for any icons that might have survived. A small hitch arose. Most of the villagers were out, he explained, working in their fields, and nowadays when they left their houses they locked up after them. Even the PM seemed surprised to encounter this sudden intrusion of un-tribal practice. In a land in which, by my experience so far, all doors were open, this indeed was a break with the past. The PM led us to several houses known to belong to notorious conservatives who might have had an icon about the place, while a few villagers who had joined us, including a young man in a Toshiba T-shirt, scampered up and down side-lanes in search of a household that might not have moved with the times. In the end one was found and an elderly lady festooned with bangles and beads invited us in to inspect her icon. It was painted in Saora style in white upon a red background, recalling Aboriginal rock drawings, or palaeolithic hunters on the walls of caves, or even more the figures and scenes woven into the *huipils* of the Indians of Central America. Here Saora manikins pranced and capered in ceremonial hats and under ceremonial umbrellas, rode elephants and horses, pedalled bikes, and were carried by fan-waving attendants in procession. They played the musical instruments of the past but shouldered the guns of the present. Gourdfuls of wine awaited their pleasure, displayed like Christmas gifts on the branches of palms. The flaming sun illuminating this scene might have been copied from an Aztec codex, as might the Saora medicine-men too, who had conjured it from darkness with their feathered wands.

The PM, watching us, smiled at our pleasure. He was happy for us. 'We are lucky to find this,' he said, 'it is belonging to one old lady. I am thinking it is the last.' I tried to match his face with the faces of the Saoras who had crowded into the dark room after us, but they seemed to belong to a different race. 'Can he really be a Saora?' I had whispered to Ranjan. 'Yes, he is a Saora,' was Ranjan's reply, but centuries of evolution miraculously crammed into five years had produced an astonishing metamorphosis. The PM had leaped out of the Stone Age of Saora art and belief, and the change seemed even to have paled his skin among the deep mountain complexions of the men at his back, and to have smoothed and softened the Saora aquilinity of his once Saora face. He had stripped away the credence that inspired paintings and carvings. Life, as he tried to explain, above all had become simple. 'Too many gods,' he said. 'Too many processes. Now one process only.' The concrete and corrugated-iron shack was all part of the process of simplification.

The village of the Sudha Saora had swarmed with people. Potasing, with about three times its population, seemed strangely deserted; as many as four houses out of five were locked up. I asked why this should be.

'They are working in the fields,' the PM said. 'They are very active in employment.'

'But this is an in-between season with not much to do,' I suggested.

'If there is a willingness to work it is always to be found. We shall be growing new crops which now they are planting. One government inspector was here. He is sending us pineapple to try. In the old times people were lazy. They were drinking much wine. Even the young children were drinking wine. That was bad. We have cut down those palm trees which were giving the wine.'

'But what do they do to amuse themselves? Do they drink at all, dance, go to harvest festivals, stage the *Ramayana*, put on cockfights? Surely it is not all work? I know they've stopped painting.'

'Well, we cannot say it is all work, but we are not wishing to do these other things. I am telling you that everything is different now. On Sunday we are attending church. Practising also to sing hymns. They are telling us that soon a bus will be coming on Fridays for the cinema in Gunupur. This is something for which we are all very glad.'

The PM had turned his back on art, and art had forsaken him.

We had hoped to stay in Gunupur in the heartland of Saora territory, but could find nowhere to put up, so were obliged to press on to Rayagada in the country of the Dongria Kondh, where we found rooms at the Hotel Swagati. The façade of this, apart from old

election posters, carried a large notice above the entrance: PILES
WILL BE CURED IN HALF AN HOUR WITHOUT PAIN. SPECIAL
TREATMENT FOR ASTHMA.

After the sluggish pace of the mountain villages Rayagada
provided a small but concentrated dose of the excitements, frustrations, and bustle of the city. Here was re-emphasized the familiar
craving for travel – whatever the conditions – by public transport.
Twelve people, arms and legs ingeniously folded, were crowded into
a small Japanese version of the jeep licensed for four, and passengers
had piled up on the roofs and hung in layers from the outside of
buses. Commercial activity was intense; there were medical halls and
electrical shops galore mixed in with a sprinkling of astrologers'
booths. Men were making chairs and beds all over the rudimentary
pavements. Country medicines were handled by a nicely decorated
kiosk at the far end of the town which sold things like dried bats,
curative snakeskin, and above all hornbill beaks, which were
relatively expensive due to their reputation when administered in
ground-up form as a cure for all the ills to which the flesh is heir.
There was a permanent queue at the kiosk, largely composed of
tribals – some of whom, unable to cope with cash, had brought bags
of rice and vegetables with which to negotiate a deal. The centre of
the display was a coloured action-photograph of Miss Datta, a
gigantic weight-lifter who would shortly represent her country at
the Asian Games in Peijing. 'Take our products regularly,' said the
wording in translation. 'You, too, could be like this.' In Rayagada
they also made excellent toys, and a kerbside vendor had lost control
of a couple of lively plastic dogs which wandered into the street to
be promptly kicked over by scampering goats. A wash of sheer noise
flowed over this town and its car horns brayed from all quarters like
the trumpets under the walls of Jericho.

Here, once again in a prosperous small town, people who could
afford to do so ran to fat. It was to be supposed that they fell prey to
the grosser satisfactions, over-ate and over-drank, suffering also the
consequences of the townsman's conviction that it was mean-spirited,
even eccentric, to walk if it was possible to ride.

We shared the hotel dining-room with five enormous men

slumped round a table bearing a bottle of imported Scotch. When one was obliged to haul himself to his feet it clearly involved a conscious process of calculation of the displacement of weight. Absurd notices surrounded us exhorting consumption and offering remedies for excess ... QUALITY THAT'S FOR EVER ... CHOICE OF THE GRACIOUS PEOPLE ... STAY AHEAD WITH A LUXE SURGICAL ORGANIC CHECKUP ... WHAT A GREAT WAY TO START THE WEEK.

Down in the street a line-up of rickshaws awaited custom, their pullers if Hindus consoled perhaps in the belief that the uncomplaining fulfilment of their destiny in this life might help their promotion to the status of sixteen-stone whisky drinkers in the next.

After several days without access to newspapers we had picked up a collection at Rayagada, one of which, coincidentally, contained an article on the Saora. It was particularly concerned with the problem of bringing them, along with the other tribal minorities, into the mainstream of Hindu society.

'We must turn our back on this talk,' Ranjan said. 'For forty years they are talking but nothing is done. Are they wishing these people to be Hindus? For this they must have caste. A man who is born a Saora cannot have caste.'

One of the rickshaw men down in the street had found a customer. An immensely corpulent man, helped by a small friend, climbed in. The rickshaw man stood up on a pedal, bringing all his slight weight to bear, and they moved off.

'Is that a Saora?' I asked.

'That is a Hindu. When a Saora becomes a rickshaw-puller it is end of road. They speak their contempt for working for pay. "I am a farmer," they will say to you. "I am not a slave."'

I read on. 'It says here that the Saora are exceptionally primitive.'

'Primitive, yes. Backward. Most people are seeing it in that way.'

'But in their villages there is no real poverty.'

'That is my personal opinion. They have no possessions, but no one is hungry. No, they are not poor.'

'Would you say they are devoid of personal ambition, and that crime is unknown?'

'They have no ambition. It is safe to mingle with them. You will not be robbed.'

'Do they work in each other's fields, as it says they do in this paper?'

'This is automatic. They are also helping to build each other's houses. They are very democratic. Not even the Gomang may give them order. He will say, "Let us sit down and talk." Then he will say, "This is my advice."'

'And this is backward?'

'The government says it is. The government tells us it is backward. I am very much liking these people but they are backward in all the things they do. Our national society is requiring from them the opposite of all these things.'

Beneath us another customer – this time of average size – had turned up for a rickshaw, and Ranjan called my attention to the transaction taking place. The slender, boyish rickshaw-puller at the head of the line waved the fare to a grey-haired man waiting behind him.

'This young man is passing an easy fare to the old man who is following,' Ranjan said. 'He is a Saora. I think only a Saora will do this. They have a goddess who tells them they must help, so they are eager to behave in this way.'

'Are they going to survive?'

'If they learn to use money they will survive.'

'How does that affect the situation?'

'Because if they are not understanding money they will be cheated.'

'Who by?'

'Everyone who comes who is making business with them. Always it has been their custom to barter the things they make or grow. They know how many bags of rice to a goat; they cannot handle rupees. If a tribal man cannot barter he must sell to a merchant. He cheats them with his weights and with his money. When the merchant has robbed him it is the turn of the moneylender. Maybe

755

the Saora's crop has failed and he must buy food, but he does not understand what is meant when the moneylender speaks to him about interest. So this man cannot pay and he must give up his land go to be a labourer and break stones or dig coal for all his life.'

'How often does this happen?'

'All the time. Who can tell you? Now we have industries more labour is wanting. Also politicians and landowners are desirous of obtaining more land. This is happening thousands of times every day.'

Chapter Eighteen

WE WERE ON THE ROAD AGAIN with the first light for a detour to the north for Badpur, Ranjan's favourite Dongria Kondh settlement, under that part of the Eastern Ghats known as the Niyamgiri Hills. There may be as many as a million Kondhs, who make up Orissa's most numerous tribe. They are Proto-Australoids, having exceedingly dark skins, and are divided into several sections, according to their degree of development. Of these the Dongria Kondhs are about halfway up the list, as eaters of meat who do not worship the Hindu gods. Remarkably enough, they have retained a large degree of their original culture, although this is under constant and increasing threat.

Once again, as the sun lit up the landscape, we found ourselves back in the dry, metallic, glittering scenery of the Australian outback; red earth, silver-leafed trees – often with scaly trunks – great boulders balanced one upon the other. We passed under burnished, coppery cliffs, by the edge of a scalloped gorge at the bottom of which a river had been scorched away probably thousands of years ago. Fire storms had happened here, leaving trees complete with a meticulous spread of branches turned to carbon as a monstrous, sepulchral decoration of the landscape.

Ranjan said in a reassuring and hopeful way that there were many tigers and hyenas in these forests, but for mile after mile I saw nothing but an occasional scampering squirrel. Once we stopped to examine a shed snakeskin, and then to listen to the broken-hearted hootings of the birds, and here by chance I saw my first and last great pied hornbill. It was much bigger than I would have expected it to be, grotesquely magnificent – something that should have become extinct but had mysteriously survived – awkward in its movements, stabbing at nothing with the huge unmanageable beak,

757

before suddenly appearing to lose its balance and to go crashing with a shower of black and white pinions down through the foliage, out of sight.

Badpur came into view in a great yellow eroded patch where trees had once been. The village had been built by design on an easy slope down from the road and at right angles to it: an enormously wide, single street, perhaps two hundred yards in length. It was possibly the most beautiful tribal village I had seen anywhere. At the top end of the village a pump delivered water through a conduit running down the exact centre of the street, and halfway down a small shrine contained a stone representing Jhankar, the Earth Mother. Following the principle of the Sudha Saoras at Modhukamba, the Kondhs' houses had extremely low, thatched roofs – all joined together – but in this case so low as to make it necessary almost to crawl under the overhang to reach the veranda. It was the custom of the Kondhs to build their villages so that the occupants of a house could stand at its entrance to greet their neighbours face to face across the street with the rising of the sun. This genial and impressive morning ritual must soon come to an end because the government proposes – as soon as it can afford to do so – to rehouse villagers in barracks-pattern army huts. A dispiriting photograph in a publication by the Tribal and Harijan Research Institute shows one of these dwellings, which looks like a white cowshed at the edge of a sun-roasted building site. The photograph bears the title MARCHING TOWARDS PROGRESS. I was told that the actual house was occupied for a week or two, then abandoned.

Just as the Saoras had been, the Kondhs were clearly stimulated and delighted to have new faces about the village. In a comparable Hindu village the womenfolk only too often appear as subservient shadows flitting in the background, but here the women took over and strutted giggling at our sides while the men tailed along in the rear. It was a lively scene indeed. In one house a cigar-smoking travelling medium, face striped with white like a New Guinea tribesman, had dropped in to offer his services on the matter of laying a troublesome ghost. On the veranda of another several jungle-fowls had been induced to sit on eggs contained in ornamental baskets, and a boy crouched near by with a flute ready to soothe them with music if they showed signs of restiveness.

The women – who alone were permitted to carry out such work – had decorated every surface to which ornamentation could be applied. No two designs, they insisted, of birds and butterflies, of peacocks, elephants, and tigers linked by the swirling tendrils of convolvulus, were the same. They had carved geese along the wooden framework of beds, because the flight of geese through the recesses of the drowsy mind was conducive to sleep. The women smoked short, fat cigars, performing what seemed to us the danger-ous feat of drawing on the lighted end, inserted in their mouths. Doing this they managed a half-smile, while rolling their eyes. They drank like fish, stopping frequently for a nip of alcohol offered by a neighbour in a brilliantly painted gourd. I was induced to try this, but found it both sour and sharp.

This female self-sufficiency, this pleasantly arrogant independence, reflected the fact that in Indian tribal society, as a general rule, a woman is accepted as more useful, responsible, and above all more hard-working than a man, in consequence of which her value finds expression in the matter of marriage settlements. In Hindu society one of the greatest strains most families are called on to face arises from the problem of finding tempting dowries for marriageable daughters. A husband is in effect purchased, whereas among the tribals a girl is sold – often, too, in this case, the price may be crippling. As Ranjan wryly pointed out, the dowries for his three sisters had left his family's fortunes in a shaky state. Had they been tribals they would have kept their land and probably even added to it. These women owned most of the property, carried out all the business transactions, and above all were guardians of the all-important alcohol they kept in constantly polished aluminium pots and distributed according to their own severe rules as to when it was to be drunk, and by whom.

Dongria Kondh feminism was again reflected in the fact that they were the only tribe to train and employ female shamans – the Bejuni – who after years of preparation become trance-mediums through which the gods speak their oracular utterances. The Bejunis practise healing and divination, are denied sexual contacts, but enter into life-long 'marriages' with their guardian spirits. It was the Bejunis who conducted the human sacrifices for which the tribe was notorious until their suppression by the British in the middle of the last century, and it was they who distributed the parcels of the victims' flesh about the fields in such a way as most effectively to increase their fertility.

Sacrifices of this kind were likely to have been practised in a discreet and sporadic fashion by a majority of the hill tribes, until the British took action, but it was among the Kondh that they became a systematized and increasingly important feature of tribal life. The Kondh carried out these procedures in the full blaze of publicity, informing neighbouring groups well in advance of the date fixed for what had become a major religious occasion, with subsequent distribution of highly valued parcels of flesh among favoured local communities. The inevitable military campaign to put a stop to this state of affairs was launched in 1851 under the command of Major-General John Campbell, who wrote an account of his experiences and of the ritual killings he had investigated.

The Kondh had convinced themselves of the existence of a mathematical relationship between tribal prosperity and the number of victims immolated. These always remained in short supply, *meriahs* – as they were called – being obtained in three principal ways. Donations of children for what was seen as a supremely spiritual purpose were made by devout parents. *Meriahs* were in effect bred, using a class of women paid by the community for their services, and to make up any short-fall professional kidnappers were employed to capture adults (for which a huge price had to be paid) in other tribal areas. The *meriahs* received considerate, even pampered, treatment while awaiting their eventual fate.

A sacrifice was a spectacular event, attracting visitors who often travelled great distances to be present. The atmosphere was festive rather than solemn, as all participants were piously intoxicated for days in advance and, says the general, the victim was virtually unconscious from the effects of liquor before the end came, death usually from strangulation.

Major-General Campbell appears in this as a humane and tolerant man, somewhat loath, as the British often were, to be forced to interfere with other people's religious freedoms. In the British way, too, he shows evidence of a sneaking sympathy for minority peoples in the areas of conquest. One of the centres of trouble was Jeypore and – once again in imperial style – he does his best to shift responsibility for action to the local rajah. Nevertheless a few obstinate sacrificers hold out and a village here and there has to be burned down. Even then amends are made by a cash contribution towards the costs of their rebuilding. Thus, in the end, the two sides part good friends. To remove any source of temptation the general takes the precaution of rounding up *meriahs*. These he shares out among eagerly awaiting missionaries.

Ranjan had a surprise for me. We had discussed Verrier Elwin's work on the Muria and their Ghotul, and I was informed that the young people's dormitory system continued to flourish among the Kondh. He quoted the opinion of S. Routray, who has dedicated some years to the study of the tribe, that the exceptionally low rate of fertility in Kondh women results from what may be described as ritual promiscuity practised in early life.

Discussion of such matters is probably overshadowed by Hindu taboo. The Kondh are well aware that such sexual practices still existing among a high proportion of the tribes of Orissa and Bastar are regarded with disfavour by the national society, and whereas they were once prepared to discuss them openly – even with relish as it would appear from Elwin's accounts – they are now inclined to shamefacedness and secrecy. The Japanese anthropologist Sugiyama Kolchi, who spent the year 1963 among the Mundas in a village only a few miles from the vast industrial complex of Ranchi, was surprised to discover, for example, that all the young men and women there spent their nights together in the 'sleeping houses' before marriage. Adult villagers criticizing this conduct were ashamed not for their licentiousness, but their backwardness. The opinion of the outside world was what bothered them. It was quite possible that such a youth dormitory existed in Badpur, Ranjan thought, but only the most tactful of questioning would have been likely to persuade the Kondhs to admit to its presence. The Kutia Kondhs, cousins of the Dongrias, tucked safely away from the benefits of civilization in their mountain valleys, would still believe that they had nothing to hide, otherwise it was a subject, he thought, better avoided.

A number of young girls now appeared on the scene. Ranjan explained that as we had been spotted they had all dashed off to titivate, and here they were, each laden most attractively with junk jewellery: up to a dozen aluminium hoops worn as necklaces, ear-rings and nose-rings from the market, twenty or so plastic bracelets on each arm, a cheap little knife stuck into the hair, together with a comb behind the right ear. Examples are to be seen in museums of exquisite jewellery made by the Dongria Kondhs up to forty years ago, but a short step along the road to acculturation has put an end to all that. Nevertheless, whatever the quality of the materials employed and the sad artistic loss, the general effect was charming.

Before leaving the village we had noticed a few ramshackle-looking houses failing to conform to the local style, placed moreover in such a way that they were out of sight of its single street, with its water conduit and its earth goddess. These were occupied, we were to learn, by the Dombs. By the exercise of some wholly mysterious power these untouchables have established a parasitic grip on the Kondh that nothing, including the passage of an act of parliament to curb their activities, has been able to break. Wherever there are Kondh communities the somewhat sinister Dombs are in watchful attendance. The Kondhs, who may have picked up the trace of a caste attitude from the Hindu populations of towns they occasionally visit, have no social contact with them. A Domb – despised as an inferior being – is not allowed to enter a Kondh house or even to be received on the veranda, yet the creative, energetic, and intelligent tribals have allowed themselves to be trapped in a species of hypnotic dependency upon this clan of moneylenders and manipulators.

A partial explanation may lie in the fact that the Dombs first appeared as itinerant traders carrying supplies of goods such as dried fish, sugar, and oil, which otherwise could only be procured at great cost in remote hill villages. From small beginnings they expanded their trade, establishing near-monopolies in the supply of sacrificial animals, alcohol, and various kinds of cloth otherwise not to be found in the neighbourhood. The Kondhs remained stubbornly improvident and illiterate while the Dombs took all they needed of what the school had to offer: enough reading and writing to be able to understand and draw up contracts, and a knowledge of how to work out percentages and keep accounts. They became the barrack-room lawyers of the hills, with the police in their pockets, and ready to go to law at the drop of a hat. They isolated their Kondh victims from their contacts of old, with whom they had been accustomed to practise fair trading in barter deals. Now more and more they were compelled to buy and sell for cash through the offices of cunning, worldly-wise, and unscrupulous go-betweens who fattened on the profits.

It was a strange experience to visit the Domb settlement. In the way of most Hindu villages it was messy, but there was something nomadic about the scattered odds and ends outside the houses that reminded me of a gypsy encampment with its litter left to rust or rot. It had attracted a number of crows, of which Badpur was virtually free. More extraordinary was the fact that the Domb males dressed in such a way as to be indistinguishable, apart from certain physical differences, from the Kondhs. Ranjan said that they did this to be able to come and go among market crowds without drawing attention to themselves. Their womenfolk appeared as average Hindu low-caste women wearing rather dingy saris, and in Hindu village style they spent most of their time in their houses out of sight. Unlike the Kondh women who put on their best clothes and embroidered scarves to flock to any market in the vicinity – sometimes walking all night to be able to do so – the womenfolk of the Dombs stayed at home.

It is altogether astounding that the Kondhs feel under compulsion to buy cloth from their unwelcome neighbours, which they then embroider and sometimes sell back to the Dombs, who are unable to undertake decoration of any kind.

*

Ranjan was determined that I should see for myself the physical force the Dombs were prepared to apply, when necessary, in order to keep the Dongria Kondhs subjected to their domination. This was best to be witnessed, he said, at any local fair, and having learned from our friends at Badpur that one was to be held that day some fifty miles away at the village of Chatikana, we turned back to Rayagada, and took the road to the west leading to Koraput and Jeypore. Immediately we plunged into another climatic region, bringing with it a stark change of scenery. The finely incised clarity and the burnished metallic colourings of Badpur were at an end. Now there were heat hazes and grey misted shapes: volcanic cones and mountain humps floating above the subdued greens of the forest. Scraps of savannah held huge, isolated cotton trees around which birds swarmed like bees. Sometimes we saw a patch of cultivation with a branch-and-leaf hut beside it, and in this a guardian would remain all night, Ranjan said, beating an enormous drum to keep the monkeys and wild pigs away from the crops.

Chatikana had justified its description as a village by a single unfinished building to be constructed of breezeblocks and asbestos. Otherwise it was no more than a crossing of the ways most easily accessible to tribals coming down from the surrounding hills, and here, by the time we arrived, the Kutia Kondhs were present in force. These, however, were no more than close relatives of our friends the Dongrias. Living, as they did, at the tops of the mountains, they were much less affected by what is now often called the process of Sanskritization. The Dongrias and their other cousins, the Desia Kondhs – who have settled in the immediate vicinity of Indian towns – are quite happy to wander in and out of Hindu temples, and buy a sari for their wives to wear to visit a fair. The Kutias do none of these things. In the case of the Kutias, too, the stern laws of the survival of the fittest continue to apply. They are always on the move, wrestling with the poverty of mountain tops, a wiry, athletic people, with – as their appearance here suggested – a touch of controlled ferocity about them.

Every man carried his spear or an axe on his shoulder. Some wore loincloths alone and some were quite naked except for a strip of cloth twisted round the waist and drawn up through the loins. The girls, by contrast, were overdressed in spectacular tribal finery, with multiple ear-rings, nose-rings of extreme complexity covering most of the top lip, richly embroidered scarves, and combs plus a dagger in their hair. They came skipping down the mountain paths in parties, flashing their eyes in all directions, chattering in high-pitched, bird-like voices, then settling themselves in rows, arms linked together – in theory to avoid abduction although, as the Tribal and Harijan Research Institute book informs its readers, 'both marriage by consent and capture are popular'.

The Kutia Kondhs sold jungle berries and fruit, medicinal herbs, grain, and leaf-plates made of sal leaves stitched together, and they bought or obtained by barter dried fish. An interesting surgical skill was on display at the market, for a Dongria Kondh woman – almost certainly a female shaman – was removing thorns embedded in the feet of patients who had walked barefoot anything up to fifteen miles across the mountains to reach the market. In this way, the worst sufferer had picked up eleven thorns.

But there was no intrusion by Dombs in this potentially formidable assembly. To see them in action, Ranjan decided that we should make a side-trip, if necessary, to visit Kundili where the greatest tribal market in Orissa, attracting at least ten thousand visitors, would be held on the coming Sunday.

We took the road again for Koraput, pulling in to the side after a few miles to watch men at work in an extremely primitive sisal manufacturing plant, set up here because it was a convenient place for lorries to dump their loads of the great spiny agave cactus leaves used in the process. Labourers with bleeding hands were feeding these at great speed into the jaws of a machine linked to an old Ambassador engine, which crushed and masticated them, separating in some way the tough, valuable fibre from the mass of vegetable pulp. This done, a team of dejected-looking women took over, using a succession of archaic wooden contraptions to dry, comb, and twist the fibre until in a remarkably short time it was transformed into rope.

All those engaged in this operation seemed close to the limits of exhaustion. As usual, labourers here worked a ten-hour day, the men receiving fifteen rupees (50p), less 'small' deductions, and the women twelve rupees. The men, said the overseer, got a day off once in a while, and went to a market – 'To try to capture women,' he added as if by way of an afterthought.

It was hard to know how to take this. Was it intended to be a joke? Ranjan had translated, and a grim thought struck me. 'Do you imagine these women working here could have been abducted by them?'

'I do not think so,' Ranjan said. 'Many girls are captured at the markets for the purpose of marriage. This is the custom. After the capture an arrangement will be reached with their parents. It is not the custom here to capture the women for the purpose of labour. This man may be joking. I cannot tell. Of one thing we can be assured. No lady will take up this employment of her own wishing.'

Suddenly, within minutes of our arrival, everything had come to a standstill. It was the midday pause. The workers dropped to the ground and went instantly to sleep. The overseer sauntered across to exchange a few words with Ranjan, who told me that a Paraja wedding was being celebrated at a nearby village and that he had offered to show us the way to it. A deputy was left with instructions and we set off together.

The village was only a few hundred yards away across the fields, although obscured from the road by clumps of trees. We were guided to it by the tremendous festive hubbub. The first thing that became quite clear when we arrived was that the whole population, men, women, and children, was drunk – many of them uproariously so. The narrow, shadeless main street was full of musicians traipsing up and down, playing squeaky pipe music and banging drums, and lines of dancing girls colliding with them, and the menfolk staggering about, drinking alcohol from aluminium jugs and bawling noisy choruses.

The fact that the Paraja girls danced together made it clear, Ranjan said, that no boys from other villages had been able to attend. Like the exogamous Kondh, Paraja women may only dance with males born in other villages. The atmosphere so far as we were concerned was hospitable to the point of effusiveness, and, having been subjected to close and speculative examination by a tipsy girl, Ranjan said to me, 'I do not believe there is any shortage of sex in this place. These people are normally strict in their behaviour but they are letting their hair down for this celebration.' He then told me that it was a Paraja in whom he was interested, and described the circumstances in which they had met.

The vast majority of tribal villages in Orissa are only to be reached – usually with some difficulty – on foot. However, someone had told Ranjan about Kangrapada, down near the frontier of Andhra Pradesh, which only the odd government official and itinerant trader had so far discovered, and to which a road of kinds had recently been built. He went there and was delighted to discover an unusual situation in which two tribal peoples, the Parajas and the Godbas, had decided to settle down together, forming a satisfactory mixed community in which they had probably lived for a hundred years. There was an amicable mix-up of circular Godba houses and roughly square Paraja ones, and an open area in the centre of which the goddess Hundi, represented as a pile of stones, was worshipped by both peoples. Ranjan parked his car in this space and went for a stroll round, noticing that a mixture of Paraja and Godba elders had seated themselves on benches round the shrine and were gossiping in exceptionally loud and clear voices. He was later informed that the goddess was expected to listen in to such conversations in which problems were ventilated: it was hoped that she would settle these on the spot without recourse by the villagers to formal offerings and prayers.

Ranjan made a brief tour of the village, took tea with a nice old man, admired the old circular houses and the heavy silver neck rings worn by the old women which could only be removed after death, and struck up a two-minutes' friendship with a pretty Paraja girl. The village was exactly as described to him, saturated with a drowsy calm, free of the presence of moneylenders and labour agents, with its people drinking, dancing, and sleeping on the threshold of an Eden from which they would shortly be driven. He went back for the car and found it ringed by the old men who had previously been seated chatting in their loud, clear voices round the shrine of the goddess. Kindly smiles received him but he sensed there was something wrong. When he made to get into the car the village elders gently restrained him. He had offended Hundi by not presenting himself to her and requesting her permission to be in the village. It would be necessary to sacrifice a buffalo to appease her before he could remove the car. The villagers were hazy on the subject of figures but thought the cost of one might be in the neighbourhood of a thousand rupees.

It was the second time in a year Ranjan had been in trouble with local deities. On the first occasion he had wandered into a remote and nameless village of the Bhunjias, the smallest of the tribes of Orissa, isolated in the Kalahandi hills. The people received him well, offered him food, and were happy to show him round. He was unable to understand a word that was said to him, and for that reason could not be warned not to enter any of the sheds built adjacent to each house which – although quite empty – constituted the sacred and inviolable shrine of the household god. The Bhunjias skipped along at his side, smiling and gesticulating, but were too polite to keep him out of a shed by force. Finally he entered one, found nothing inside, and came out. Instantly the owner, according to the rule in such cases, set fire to it and burned it down. Ranjan offered money in compensation which, as the Bhunjia had no use for it, he smilingly rejected. His parting from the villagers was as friendly as his reception. From their gestures he gathered that the owner would soon build a new shed. 'These country people are making allowances,' Ranjan said.

Once more, at Kangrapada, Ranjan found himself up against a language problem. The Dravidian tribal languages in which he could get by offered no help in his efforts to argue his case with the Parajas, but villagers were forthcoming who knew a few words of Kondh and of Oriya – the official language of the State of Orissa –

and with the aid of these negotiations stumbled ahead. Ranjan was able to make the Parajas understand that the car was not his property and produced a convincing mime of poverty to persuade them that he could not find the thousand rupees to pay for a buffalo. At this point the Parajas, who were clearly very nice people, began to show signs of sympathy for his plight, and it was decided to put the suggestion to Hundi that the cost of the sacrifice should be reduced to a hundred rupees. Further discussion was put off until the following day. He stayed in the village that night, and next morning the Paraja elders announced that Hundi had been kinder to him than expected and had reduced the cost of the necessary sacrifice to ten rupees – this being the price of a large white cockerel.

At the leave-taking, the Paraja girl brought her father along to say goodbye. It was clear that he had made a good impression not only on her, but on the family, for the father made the announcement – unprecedented in tribal society – that if Ranjan wished to marry his daughter he could have her without payment of the usual bride-price. The matter had already been cleared with the headman and the council of elders, and if the offer were taken up the village would build a house for them in a matter of days.

Ranjan thanked all concerned and asked if he might be given a little time to consider the proposition. He was a man of enthusiasms which he made no attempt to conceal, and his genuine admiration both for the girl and the village in which she lived would not have been lost upon the Parajas. I had come to regard him as a bit of a romantic, as well as a rebel against the claustrophobic and caste-ridden Brahmin environment in which he had been brought up. It was a picture of which Kangrapada, overbrimming with freedoms, presented the reverse. Sri R. P. Prusty, writing of the tribal culture of Orissa, had set the scene. 'In cultivation, agricultural work and the construction of a house, group labour is required. A feast is offered to participants after completion of the work. The ultimate incentive is the maintenance of the goodwill. The boys and girls of these villages visit each other on dancing expeditions, and leisure is enjoyed through feasts, dances and music.' It was a place in which any Gauguin of Orissa might have made his escape, and it seemed likely from our discussion that Ranjan had considered the possibility of taking eventual refuge here from our times.

A minor obstacle was his relatively slight knowledge of the Paraja, about whom little information had appeared in print apart from anthropological data hardly intelligible to the layman. Ranjan had grown up in the proximity of the Saora and the Kondh – the nearest of the tribal groups to his place of birth. These he could cope with. He had taken the measure of the Saora with their strange sexual taboos, knew the order of precedence in which alcohol is offered, with whom to exchange ritual jokes, how to reprove a dog in the presence of its master, and when to lose purposely at a game of hazard. With the Parajas, by comparison, he was at sea. They complicated their existences, he explained, by totemistic affinities with animals. Thus, although meat-eaters, under obligation to consume animal flesh on ceremonial occasions, the meat of the totem animal was strictly taboo, and it was therefore desirable for both husband and wife to belong to the same totemic group. He sighed. There were little pitfalls awaiting the unwary everywhere in tribal society. You were liable to commit one solecism after another until you knew the ropes, he said. The only remedy was to watch what other people did, use your head, and not be afraid to ask advice.

My impression was that Ranjan had been turning this episode over in his mind in the year that had passed and that the allurements of Kangrapada and a union with an unspoilt child of nature had strengthened against the background of the urban stresses and strains of Bhubaneswar. It may even have been that he had seen my arrival on the scene, hoping to travel in the area that interested him, as not so much a coincidence as the intervention of the hand of fate in his affairs.

The news in the previous day's paper was that the Naxalites had appeared again, in and around Koraput, where we proposed to spend the night. It seemed very much a sign of the times that in such reports Naxalite activity – while clearly played down in the press – should be mentioned in a way that suggested cautious or even open approval.

The paper in this instance noted that in Bastar tribals had been cheated (the newspaper's word) by contractors who forced them to accept as little as three paese for a bundle of fifty tendu leaves, and that when the Naxalites came on the scene, this price was forced up to a record thirty paese – which clearly struck the newspaper as being a good thing. 'The tribals', said the newspaper with something that sounded like enthusiasm, 'are increasingly turning to the Naxalites for justice.' Government resistance to this slowly simmering rebellion might have been weakening, for Dr Channa Reddy, Andhra Pradesh Chief Minister, announced here that he 'supported the genuine demands of Naxalites and would take steps to meet them. In the crucial matter of tribal lands', he said, 'the government stood very clear, and it wanted to restore all tribal lands to tribals. However, it was not possible to oust all non-tribals [from lands that had been invaded] in one go.'

Despite such wavings of olive branches, well-armed guerrillas, both male and female, specializing in kidnappings and the taking of hostages, had appeared for the second or third time in the vicinity of Koraput, where the atmosphere struck us as apprehensive. Although we had seen few vehicles on the road in a day's journey, some had passed, and here they had been stopped at a road block and lined up for what was clearly to be a lengthy examination. It was a situation to be faced in a casual manner. Fifty yards short of the line of lorries we found a dhaba and went in for tea. Having served us, the owner rummaged among his stock of cassettes for one left in error by a party of foreigners who had passed this way some months before. This was a very Indian scene. A lorry parked near by had lost the oil in its sump and the strong odour of this mingled with that of curry was characteristic of such roadside stops. We were surrounded by ravaged red earth bestrewn with abandoned odds and ends, among which hopped a few alert and elegant crows. Once in a while the bellowings of an enraged policeman reached us faintly, then the music started. It was yodelling recorded in the Swiss Alps. The dhaba owner turned the volume up, and after a while we climbed back into the Ambassador and drove up to and past the road block in the most inconsequential fashion.

Chapter Nineteen

JEYPORE, TWO HOURS further on, captivated us with its charm at very first glance. We found rooms at the Hotel Madhumati where the whole reception area was occupied by guests being shaved by a team of barbers in readiness for a wedding taking place that night. The hotel was infused with homely disorder, and its barely furnished spaces resounded with the outcry of guests and their many friends who had suffered from its inefficiency. The system in such places was to flatter the better-class clientele by addressing them in English, and the staff rushing hither and thither on abortive errands responded with averted eyes and routine soothings to their complaints, whatever the language in which they were expressed. 'Not to worry, sir. Now at *this* moment it is coming. I am sorry for your patience.'

This town was the centre of the arts and entertainments of south Orissa, full of conjurors and fire-eaters, of strolling players, musicians, mind-readers, and illusionists. It seemed impossible without retreat to a bedroom to shut out the nearby sound of someone tuning up a stringed instrument or producing desultory blasts on a horn. Near the entrance stood a cart drawn by two bullocks in which, under paper chains and sprays of artificial flowers, twenty-two musicians, and a harmonium had been crammed. A notice said OUR PROPOGANDA IS TRAVELLING 10 KMS ANY-WHERE FOR YOUR PLEASURE. SAY YES TO LIFE. A man pleaded into a microphone, 'This night we must sing and dance together. We must banish heaviness and care.' Across the frontier of these blandishments, on the far side of the road, the scene was strangely calm – almost reverential. Here at sunset, scrupulously avoided by the throngs of passers-by, the housewives were on their knees decorating the flagstones in front of their doors with the white powder design representing the footsteps of Lakshmi, drawn in the hope of inducing the goddess to enter the house and there spend the night.

At this season of the year, with most of the harvests already in, and the rains awaited before sowing could begin, there was nothing much to be done in Jeypore for those who could afford it but relax and enjoy themselves. People stayed up most of the night promenading in the brightly lit main street, window-shopping, chattering with friends, and drinking tea. Frequently there was a power failure to delight the children. Cars cruised up and down with their radios turned up to broadcast film theme music much distorted with over-amplification. Noise was all part of the fun.

Everyone in the theatrical business had come to this town for their costumes: splendid, tawdry finery, star-spangled jackets, sherwanis, embroidered pantaloons, masks galore, and pleasantly ridiculous multiple crowns hung from the façades of the shops. Such was the local obsession with the theatre that every village in the area had a field set aside for the staging of performances of the *Ramayana* and the *Mahabharata*. Of these two epic Sanskrit poems, dating from about 500 BC, the longer, the *Mahabharata*, contains one hundred thousand stanzas – about fifteen times the Bible's length – and is presented in poetic form as the Great History of Mankind. Both the *Ramayana* and the similar *Mahabharata* have been dramatized in India and the countries of South-East Asia where they have been playing to audiences for at least fifteen hundred years. At Jeypore a short version of *Ramayana* went on all night, but a full-scale production might last a week. The show usually started at ten and lasted until six in the morning, after which people went home and slept for the rest of the day.

'What sort of an audience do they get?' I asked Ranjan.

'All kinds. Everyone is going who can.'

'Tribals, too?'

'Many of them. Most of the actors are tribal people. Their memory is very good for the long parts.'

Some people, Ranjan said, had to have medical treatment to cope with the exhaustion. In addition a mysterious epidemic had broken out – as a result, it was thought, of all-night open-air theatre-going. This took the form of a high fever and a temporary loss of balance, caused by the bite of a noxious night-flying insect attracted to its victim by a faint odour released through the pores by the stress of constant excitement.

There had been a break in the sequence of such performances at about the time of our arrival due to an unsatisfactory confluence of the stars. It was one, however, that favoured marriages, and one or more took place each night, the more stylish of them based upon our hotel. All the rooms apart from those we occupied had been taken over by the male members of a wedding party, with the bridegroom and his guests engaged in dressing themselves in archaic costumes which in most cases did not fit or were short of indispensable parts. The bedroom doors, left open as guests rushed in and out, showed half-clad men tripping over tin swords, or wrestling with enormously long turbans, and the endless buttons of *achkans* made either for fat men or dwarfs. Barbers, cut-throat razors at the ready, groped their way from customer to customer in the half-light.

At 7 p.m. the town's lights went on, and as if to show the citizens' exultation and relief a great, crashing reverberation of drums was to be heard in all directions. Lined up outside the hotel were the vehicles, both ancient and modern, which would convey the bride-groom's party to the bride's house, each of these being connected to a bicycle rickshaw carrying a small generator and an amplifying system. The band had arrived in something like an old-fashioned school brake, with an ear-shattering uproar of drums, fifes, flutes, and horns of various descriptions, and rockets hissed up and exploded with stunning detonations immediately overhead. At this moment the hotel lights went out to an outburst of cheers. It seems to have been expected, something that had developed perhaps into a good-humoured convention for people who had acclimatized them-selves to a situation in which nothing worked for long. This suspicion was strengthened by the sudden appearance of a number of beautiful girls who came scampering up the stairs with lighted candles to be placed in position all along the passages. With that, instantly, the lights came on again and the bellowing of the hotel's television, on full blast, was added to the street uproar outside.

There was no place better in which to imbibe the pure aroma of provincial India than Jeypore's main street. It was very long and quite straight, beginning with the splendid decrepitude of the once Maharajah's palace at the top of the town, and petering out among the bullock-carts and banyan trees and children flying kites on the edge of the tattered vestiges of a jungle. The Maharajah's palace had fallen into decay after the last ruler's death in 1920. This sombre though magnificent building was entered through a gateway thirty-five feet in height to permit the passage of an extremely high processional vehicle resembling the Car of the Juggernaut, and the great width of the street at this point facilitated its manoeuvrings and those of its accompanying elephants among surging festive crowds. The gateway was flanked by lions said to have been modelled on those by Landseer in Trafalgar Square. Facing this grandiose entrance was the lesser gateway of the palace annexe, guarded by green demons and two more lions with black raging faces and crimson manes, both imbued with a ferocity that Landseer's animals comfortably *couchant* across the road quite lacked. The top half of this prospect was always obscured by ranks of sherwanis by the hundred, displayed on their hangers like a headless army marching upon the town. An enormous brass statue of the ruler of old occupied a domed building like a bandstand in the ravaged palace enclosure, gazing with satisfaction over vistas that had long since vanished. It was pointed out to me that his brass boot-caps had been polished by the kisses of his faithful subjects, a few of whose descendants still attended here regularly to salute his memory in this fashion.

The peace and the apparent prosperity of Jeypore seemed remarkable when the miserable insecurity of Koraput, so short a distance away, was advertised by the presence of the Naxalite People's War Group. In Jeypore there were no policemen in the streets and queues of its citizens waited outside the principal cinema to be subjected to the anodyne of the Indian masses. The cinema was showing *Young*

Love Blooms with Monisha Koirala and Salman Khan – both given fashionable mousy hair – and dealt with teenage lovers who keep their innocence.

Another sign of affluence was the presence of many pharmacies, and their blown-up versions known as medical halls. India manufactures and exports a huge range of pharmaceuticals, and these, flooding the home market and advertised with persistence and cunning, are on sale even in the smallest towns, mopping up a high proportion of any spare cash that happens to be about. I read that such is the craze for self-doctoring in search of the improvements of health promised by so many products that clubs are formed of hypochondriacs created by advertising. These spend their spare time discussing the merits of patent remedies, and a hard core have reached the point of devising menus in which a fistful of rice will be supplemented by capsules supplying the necessary minerals, vitamins, and synthetic flavours.

Jeypore appeared to be full of people well-off enough to worry about their health, and medical halls sowed the seeds of fear by window displays showing what could happen to those who tried to bypass the medicinal road to wellbeing. The evidence provided was startling, but since it was accepted that some citizens with spending power might be illiterate, and that most tribals were, the facts and figures were supported by photographs that spoke for themselves of the ravages of disfiguring diseases. The most popular display included a wonderfully convincing working model of a defective digestive tract, with arrows pointing to the zones of malfunction. This was garnished with large colour photographs of abscesses, tumours, and cysts. The exhibit drew a constant crowd, and people stopping to inspect it on their way home from the cinema may well have found it an antidote to the sugary images of *Young Love Blooms*.

The day was passed in pleasant exploration of the oddities of Jeypore. Back at the Madhumati for dinner we found the scene hardly changed from the previous evening. The advance guards of another wedding party had arrived to invest the hotel with its daily quota of confusion, charging up and down the stairs, pressing every bell in sight, and bursting into already tenanted rooms.

Rickshaws bringing the evening contingent of wedding guests waited to discharge their fares at the moment when a sudden and probably brief splurge of urban illumination would do justice to their glittering attire. At street corners musicians carrying ancient instruments stood in silent anticipation, like a bullring band waiting for the procession of the *toreros*. Indifferent to the growing tension and excitement, the women across the road got on with the evening decoration of their thresholds.

The Madhumati gave the impression of being the intellectual centre of the town, frequented by young men of outstanding liberal views, with advanced opinions on such controversial matters as arranged marriages, the dowry system, caste, and the abolition of the inequalities from which the women of India suffered. It was a setting in which it was possible to speak with qualified approval of Naxalite successes.

We were seated in the hotel's somewhat austere dining-room, furnished with a sideboard piled with empty bottles, with pictures of dispiriting Alpine scenes, and plain tables spread with rumpled cloths in preparation for the evening meal. An open serving hatch afforded glimpses of the arriving wedding guests in their coruscating gear, trying one after another to make urgent calls on a phone that did not work. No one in the Madhumati dared complain at the spectacle of beer being drunk openly in one of the public rooms, as it was here by a group of young men at the table next but one – although they had screened the bottles behind a fence of the hotel's large menu cards, offering in reality little but chicken and chips.

Ranjan had been joined by an old friend he had run into here by chance. Anand Gopal, now an inspector in the Department of Works, was from a high-caste background and the possessor of an exceptionally fair skin endowed by forebears who watched over such attributes as jealously as they did their wealth. It was the sight of the public beer-drinkers that sparked off the topic. Anand, now twenty-nine, said that he had only been allowed to drink water up to twenty-five years of age. Tea was banned until then as excessively stimulating, and he had only drunk it in secret and as a guilty indulgence.

'How do you feel about such prohibitions now?' Ranjan asked.

'I am unable to acquire a taste for beer, but I move with the times.'

'Have they arranged a marriage for you yet?'

'I am not permitting it,' Anand said.

'But many years ago there were some discussions. This I remember.'

'Nothing came of them. My father sent many letters to friends and some leads were established. It all fizzled out. I was opposed to anything that was suggested.'

'You are a difficult fellow,' Ranjan told him.

'I am not difficult. It was against my thinking. You see, I am progressive.'

'So now what is happening?'

'Nothing is happening. There is an agency called Life Partners. My father was in touch with them secretly but I would not co-operate. I am as free as the air. They were proposing ten lakhs of rupees as dowry for a lady with eastern features, but I am not prepared to be sold like a calf in the market. If there is a lady with whom I can share an ideal, that is a different matter.'

'I am of your opinion. Absolutely,' Ranjan said.

We were interrupted by a group of hotel regulars who came in carrying a television set. While watching an instalment of a religious epic in the television-room, they had been disturbed by the invasion of the wedding party. The set was plugged in next to the sideboard, and with a garland placed round it out of respect to the spiritual message embodied in the programme, it was switched on.

'And there is no present activity for you on that front?' Anand asked.

'For the moment there is none. I am awaiting developments. This is a problem I may discuss with you, but no decision has been reached.'

'Take your time and consider carefully,' Anand said. 'We are defending principles.'

This being the kind of discussion it was, the enmeshments of caste were bound to come up, and condemnation by these two Brahmins of the system which had favoured them was a foregone conclusion. Had there been any real improvement in this direction since Gandhi had admitted the untouchables to worship in the temples back in 1938? Ranjan thought not much. Now blandly renamed Children of God, they were still condemned by custom if not by force to dismount from their bicycles and wheel them through his native village. In rural areas he knew of they were still likely to be stoned if they attempted to draw their drinking water from the village well, and had to drink from the tank in which clothing was washed and buffaloes cooled their skin in the mud, unless a higher-caste villager could be persuaded to draw their water. Anand agreed with Ranjan. In the past days a television news item from Rajasthan had reported the case of a harijan, determined to ride a horse to his wedding, being set on and lynched by a hostile crowd, along with five of his supporting friends.

Had I seen anything of the recent caste atrocities in Bihar, I was asked, and my reply was that as a foreigner I would not have expected to, but I had talked to people and read the newspapers.

I told them about Mira Kumari, daughter of a high-caste family of Loyabad, Bihar, who eloped with a low-caste suitor, Satyendra Singh, and was secretly married to him. Mira was carried off, and subjected to thrashings in an attempt to induce her to remarry. The family hired four killers to drag Satyendra away to a quiet place and cut his head off.

'And what was the outcome?' Anand asked.

'There wasn't one. The chief of police said, "I don't recognize this marriage. After all, ours is an Indian culture."'

'I am not wishing to visit this place,' Anand said. 'Did they kill the girl, too?'

'No, they just kept up the beatings for eighteen months. In Patna Anita Pandey came off worse. She married out of caste, and her father had her abducted by a gang who broke her arm, scarred her for life, damaged an eye, and bored an inch-deep hole in her back. After that she was shut up in a home for fallen women in Patna.'

'But this is impossible if she has been legally married,' Ranjan objected. 'In that case her husband may set her free.'

'Her father produced a certificate in court,' I told him, 'giving her age as thirteen. This was intended to give him custody.'

'And this was true?'

'No, it was found to be false, so she was released.'

'In that case,' Ranjan said, 'justice was done.'

'With some reluctance,' I said. 'Yes. I read about the case in a magazine which quoted interviews with the people who could see the father's point of view. There was some talk of caste associations which place a ban on inter-caste marriages and imposed sanctions on members breaking the rules.'

'This is so,' Anand said. 'Even now, this is the case.'

The writer of the article seemed to feel fairly sympathetic towards the father himself. 'If he'd accepted his low-caste son-in-law, he said, he stood the risk of being ostracized by his caste-fellowship and being disinherited from the large family property.'

'This is true,' Anand said. 'To give example, even in my case I must move carefully. If I am in open revolt against our custom it is certain that my father will not disinherit me, but it is not so certain that I will be keeping my job. And if I lose this job, where in these times shall I find another?'

Chapter Twenty

WE DECIDED TO base ourselves on Jeypore and make a number of sorties from it into the surrounding countryside where it would have been otherwise hard to find anywhere to pass the night. Next morning we left early as usual, running immediately into thick mists. The only signs of life were the shrouded forms of women on their way to the field, each carrying on her head a burnished pot, which in the grey monochrome of the landscape appeared to emit soft rays of light.

Dense clumps of sugar cane had spread through the fields here and provided refuge for numerous cobras. A lot of people were bitten by them, Ranjan said, but forceful eradication was impossible for religious reasons. Instead non-violent persuasion was traditionally practised. The great event took place every year at the time of the November half-moon when a large contingent of snake-charmers appeared on the scene. The snake-charmers located the ants' nests in which the cobras had taken up residence and played music to induce them to leave their holes. They were then fed with milk, molasses, and the only recently discovered gastronomic inducement, pop-corn, which had become their favourite food. Their ceremony of feeding at an end, each cobra was presented with a new *dhoti*, after which the priest would wish them a happy and successful year and beg them to cease to bite members of his community. Nevertheless some continued to bite as before, and many countryfolk in the neighbourhood died in this way. Victims were carried to the temple, the area surrounding the bite excised by glass, and a tourniquet applied, after which one hundred gallons of cold water was poured over them while mantras were recited. Ranjan said there was a sixty per cent chance of survival, both for the religious who were treated in this fashion, and for the non-religious who preferred to call in a doctor, although treatment in the temple was normally cheaper.

Patches of jungle were beginning to show the effects of the dry season. Flagging blossoms and limp clumps of bamboo lay like a wilting flower arrangement among the trees. The road emptied for two hours before we overtook two men on a bicycle carrying a large image which had flowing red locks fixed to its front. Taking a left fork along the road to Jagdalpur, we shortly arrived in the village of the Mirigan tribe. This small but extraordinary group are believed to have been a branch of the Murias of Bastar, called suddenly to a puritanical form of salvation by the Kabirdas sect, causing them to take refuge in Orissa from the advertised wrath to come. Here, in the plain just across the border, they installed themselves to begin the practice of chastity (ideally sexual activity was restricted to seven occasions in a lifetime), abstinence from alcohol, and strict vegetarianism. Unfortunately, back in the mountains they had lived as hunter-gatherers. Now they were forbidden to hunt, there were no minor forest products such as fruit and berries to collect, and they knew nothing of the cultivation of the soil. Their predicament was crucial and they were only saved from extinction by the pronouncement of a Kabirdas elder that the ibis did not rank as an animal. Many of these congregated in local swamps, and on ibises the Mirigans lived.

Apart from this they were able to gain fame locally as weavers of cloth, using vegetable dyes mixed with cow dung, varying the colours by increasing or decreasing the proportions of aloes or turmeric as required. The abstract designs employed, and low-key colours, seemed to me a little dull, and all too well to reflect the solemnity of the village and its inhabitants. Little girls would go about tittering softly all the time, but after a certain age, as Ranjan said, laughter was frowned upon. Local cultivators gave the Mirigans grain in exchange for their cloth, or sometimes bought a little for cash. The people kept a few sheep for their milk, feeding them – since no grass grew in this area – upon fallen leaves. It was a scene of which Ranjan appeared on the whole to approve. 'They have no desires,' he said. 'All they need of this life is easily obtained. They fiddle with their looms, which cannot be called work; they walk about talking of God in his heaven, they sleep.' Sometimes, he thought, they danced. This surprised me, and in the hour or two we were with them there was no such evidence of merriment.

Kotpad was another weavers' village, and once again sober abstraction was the keynote of the work, which may even have fallen under the influence of its Mirigan neighbours' puritanism and restraint. Nevertheless, there was evidence that Kotpad had been reached by Christian missionary endeavour, for the principal object in the office of the weavers' co-operative secretary was an icon of the Crucifixion.

We skirted round Jagdalpur in Bastar by taking the road to the Dhurua district, seen by Ranjan as the Ultima Thule of Orissa. This was flat country, once thick jungle, and the wind sweeping unchecked across the plain cut silken swaths in the long grass. We used a railway bridge to cross the River Halti, and waiting at the near end was a crippled itinerant musician, with a wife in attendance, playing a one-stringed instrument some four feet in length. For a half-rupee he would play a tune guaranteed to disperse the evil spirits known to lie in wait for travellers at such places.

Dhurua, the last village of any size along this road, had a mixed population. A majority of Kilvas lived side by side with Parajas and Godbas in their separate and widely different cultures, yet in what appeared to be perfect amity. A forest guard – a government official having limited police functions – attached himself to us. He was a low-caste official from Bhubaneswar with a leathery city smell about him, and a habit of calculation that constantly narrowed his eyes. The tribals who had been trying to talk to us backed away respectfully when he came up, and stood like soldiers awaiting the next order. Ranjan translated. 'We all get on fairly well together,' he said with sinister emphasis. 'Sometimes a problem arises over land because no one is really sure who owns what. When this happens I plant a white flag in the field under dispute. No one may cultivate it until the case is settled by law. This can take up to seven years, by which time nobody can pay the costs. The government then takes over the land and sells it by auction.'

Even Dhurua, so far from anywhere, was in the grip of crack-brained advancement, and the first of the beautiful old houses had been torn down to be replaced by atrocious corrugated-iron shacks. Many of the remaining houses were painted on the outside with curiously modern-looking designs inherited in all probability, Ranjan thought, from the remote past. The icons and the wall-paintings of the Kondh and the Saora had been exuberant and complicated, with an intense feeling for pattern. In Dhurua ornamentation was sparse and restrained: here and there a stylized flower, butterfly, or fish; once only a flying jeep isolated among the crows. There was an obsession with abstract mountain shapes which seemed curious as no mountains had been visible for some hours. Were these representations, I wondered, rooted in nostalgic memories of a tribal past in other surroundings, like the Alpine vistas of the Hotel Madhumati? Occasionally a musical instrument had been hung on the façade of a house to supply additional decoration. No attempt had been made to improve the appearance of the stark government shacks foisted upon the villagers. Instead the owner had sometimes ordered a new door carved with traditional designs to break the monotony.

Ranjan had bought sweets in Jeypore for such occasions. We found a central space where people were invited to line up for the hand-out. They were received with acclamation both by children and grown-ups. But sweets were a rare sight in Dhurua, and demonstrations were called for as to the way in which they were unwrapped. Hundi, the Paraja Earth Mother, accepted by all three tribes-people under different names, presided here from within her usual stone-pile, and village councils when in session placed themselves, as recorded by Ranjan in Kangrapada, in a position where she could readily overhear their deliberations. In Dhurua itself the custom was to marry for love but lack of choice of suitable partners and of the opportunity in remote hamlets for young people to meet sometimes obliged parents to apply to the councillors for their help in arranging a marriage. We watched their bland, aged faces unmoved by the urgencies of desire. A wide-eyed child contemplated the miracle of an unwrapped sweet. A musician passed through, playing a complicated tune on a bison's horn. A man in a tiger-mask peered out from cover, before slipping from sight. The forester remembered to tell us about the bride-price which had dropped to a new low. A third of local income depended upon such forest produce as honey, and the local sal forest was being cut down for its valuable timber as fast as this could be done. No one in Dhurua had any money or livestock to spare to finance a marriage. You could pick up a bride for next to nothing, he said.

Murtahandi was almost at the end of the road, a spillage of huts with little fenced-off gardens sheltering the small odds and ends of tribes who had gone to earth here, as they hoped, out of reach of human predators. Among them were a few Muria Vatra, whose name unflatteringly signifies 'non-animal', and the Dumajadi, who wore blue-painted masks believing them to be an infallible defence against bounty hunters in search of bonded labour fugitives, and against the tigers with which some of their villages were said to be overrun.

Small as it was, Murtahandi was celebrated for its possession of the only school for many miles around. There was a rustic calm in this setting of neat little houses around an open space that was not quite a village green which faintly recalled a corner of the English countryside in high summer. The village school stood in a large garden with a picket fence in which innumerable asters and marigolds bloomed in beds divided by a crazy-paving path. The schoolmaster, hastily called, who was young and ebullient, came bounding into sight, rushed up the garden path, and round the back of the building to open the front door and greet us. We found ourselves in a large, clean room in which the only article of furniture was a table upon which rested three books. Squatting all round three of the walls were about thirty small boys, who at our appearance began a prolonged droning which, Ranjan whispered, was a traditional chant of welcome. This stopped when the master held up his hand.

A problem arose, for the master, as was to be expected, launched into an immediate account of the activities of the school. He spoke English very rapidly, in an excited high-pitched monotone that I found difficult to understand and some embarrassment arose when I was obliged to ask Ranjan to help out with what almost amounted to a translation of what he said.

The school had been opened, said the master, as part of the campaign stemming from the Five-Year-Plan for tribal advancement, the immediate target being the defeat of illiteracy, which in the case of males reached about eighty-three per cent. Women were totally illiterate since the ability to read and write appeared to the tribals to serve no purpose. Families were concerned in extracting the maximum bride-price for their daughter. A girl, for example, who could castrate a goat might command a couple of hundred rupees more than one who couldn't, but knowing how to write her name would not add the value of a single hen to the amount a father could reasonably ask.

It was almost as bad with the boys. They had an obsession with manual occupation, with building and making things, and using their hands. They enjoyed rearing animals, cultivating the land, and working as blacksmiths. Part of the government drive was to put an end to the universal practice of slash-and-burn cultivation, which was bad for the environment, but the only way to stop this was through education.

Ranjan asked the teacher if he knew the Kilva language generally spoken in the area, and the man winced and said, 'Not very well.' He had had a long struggle and it was still going on. Small inducements had been made to families to send exceptionally bright boys to school and a few had been made to understand that literacy could change their lives. Companies working to develop backward areas were constantly on the lookout for literate tribals to act as overseers, and there were any number of minor government jobs going for promising young men who could cope with some paperwork. He had to admit that it was still hard to make his pupils see the point of it all.

'What are they being taught at the moment?' I asked.

'Some Oriya,' he said. 'Also we are making a start with English.'

He called a boy up from a row squatting along the wall, who came forward in a hesitant and reluctant manner. The master beckoned to him impatiently to come closer, and the boy placed himself in front of us, swallowing nervously and for an instant showing only the whites of his eyes. 'This boy is very good,' the schoolmaster said. 'His father is an illiterate basket-maker, but he is wishing to become assistant to the supervisor of markets. For this he will be recording the numbers of all animals in a book.' He picked up a ruler from the table and raised it as if about to conduct an orchestra. 'Now he is to speak English to us,' he said.

The boy squeezed his eyelids together and opened them again. 'My name is John,' he said.

'Hello, John,' I said. 'How are you? Can you say anything else?'

'Well come. What iss your name? Where are you going in? My name iss John.'

An effort to prolong the conversation led to blank looks and a little string of gibberish. I congratulated the master on the boy's accent and he led me smilingly to the door and out into the sunshine where someone thrust a marigold into my hand.

Ranjan, an amateur of remote places, had found a dot on a large-scale map denoting a village some ten miles away in what was shown as jungle. He suggested we go there. There was no road but the forester offered to guide us through the tracks made by loggers to take out the timber. The village's real name was Gulmi but it was familiarly known by an expression meaning the end of the world. And what, asked Ranjan, did people do for a living in a place like that? The forester told him that they made the best arrow poison to be found anywhere as well as hand-rearing baby parakeets, taken from the nest, for which there was a strong demand among what he called normal people, i.e., non-tribals.

Both pieces of information fascinated me. 'So they use arrow poison here?'

Not all the time, the forester told Ranjan, but every year just before the rains the people from all the neighbouring tribes got together for a great annual hunt whatever their differences of language and custom and the disputes over one thing or another that might have arisen throughout the year. They would come together to stake out the areas in which as many as a thousand hunters might take part, burn off the underbrush, and move in for the kill. In preparation for this Gulmi people who were possessors of a secret formula sold all the arrow poison they were able to concoct. A small animal like a rabbit, said the forester, would die of the merest scratch and so great was the bag of rabbits and edible forest rats that the only problem was to keep the meat fresh. Some hunters who went without meat for eleven months in the year would gorge themselves on so much that they would blow up like balloons. 'What about the larger animals?' Here they ran into religious prejudice. They were all sacred to one god or another. They killed a few deer, but these had to be prayed to first. A shaman would rub the sap of a certain tree all over his skin to cover up the human smell, then wrap himself in the skin of a hind to attract the stags. The trick always worked but most of the villagers refused to eat the meat.

We bumped on slowly over the branch-strewn tracks. A lacing of dark shadows hung from the trees, and I waited in hope for the metamorphosis of obscure foliage into the shape of an elephant twitching its ears. This part of the jungle, said the forester, remained as it had always been, for no one was allowed to cut timber, not even to remove the dead trees that had clutched each other before falling among the grey castellations of ant-hills. Then, with the hutments of Gulmi in sight, we drove out of the wood into a yellow plain, with the spring grass already razed away by the sun and parakeets glinting like smithereens of glass in the sky.

Things on these travels were never as expected. Gulmi, nestling in the cloak of invisibility at the back of beyond, now appeared as a trim hamlet of four houses, protected (ineffectually) by a tiger fence but otherwise, like Murtahandi, remarkably European in appearance. It possessed twelve adults and seven children. The population of all such places was on the decline, said the forester. It was a decline Ranjan explained through the difficulties in getting the children married off – none of whom by custom could marry within the village. The solution would have been to move to Dhurua, but this would have confronted people with the intolerable predicament of abandoning the megaliths implanted in the village soil linking its people with the souls of their ancestors. It might have been the worst of the traumas, he thought, that the tribal peoples had ever faced, for thousands of families had been driven from their villages to build the dams, provoking innumerable suicides among hopeless oustees.

The pace of life in Gulmi was leisurely in the extreme. The tiny harvests of millet and dry rice had been gathered in and consumed by the time we arrived, and now people tightened their belts and made sporadic excursions, when they felt the need to do so, into patches of jungle where at this season there were trees to be found producing a variety of minuscule and not particularly tasty fruits. Some of these they ate but most went into the making of alcohol – an activity pursued here with the usual tribal enthusiasm. Ranjan said that if pushed to it the villagers would eat almost anything in the way of animal flesh, but their limited meat diet was based largely on small animals – edible rats and an occasional bird. These were shot with bows and arrows.

I asked to see a bow and the man who up to this point had been describing village life here with considerable vivacity showed signs of nervousness at the prospect of having to produce this weapon in the presence of an official. This seemed strange as it was to be assumed that every forest dweller in the state possessed one. However, he went off, rummaged in an outbuilding, and returned with the bow, which could hardly have exceeded a yard in length, and looked like a superbly made child's toy. The arrow, too, was short and light. Through Ranjan I asked the man to give us a demonstration of his skill, and having balanced a small jack fruit on a rock some twenty yards away he took aim and scored a bull. Was that the maximum effective range, I asked, and he said it was. It seemed extraordinary that while Amazonian Indians had developed a bow up to six feet in length, with which once in a while they managed to kill a jaguar, these tribals whose proficiencies had evolved in roughly similar surroundings were unable, except on an organized communal basis, to hunt any large animal.

Creativity, that mysterious compulsion, assisted here by a natural desire to fill in the vacant hours between essential chores, kept these people occupied. At the moment of our arrival two or three men gathered socially round the Earth Mother shrine were carving lumps of wood into animal shapes in an abstracted, almost automatic fashion. They might have been knitters of sweaters who manage to fashion a garment while watching the television, yet every crouching tiger or rampaging elephant was individual and unique. Gourds were used as drinking vessels, and each one, scraped clean of its vegetable content, had been carved with flowers and birds.

From these occupations the womenfolk were debarred. Instead, at this hour they were promenading with their fledgeling parakeets on their shoulders. The birds received considerate, almost ceremonious treatment, being fed titbits taken from their lips. In the matter of their sale a stipulation was imposed. The purchaser was obliged to take the bird away before it could fly, otherwise it could not be parted from its human foster mother. One often saw unsold birds fluttering round the women's heads, the forester said. These in the end were taken back and released in the jungle.

In Dhurua, tribal people of the same stock painted butterflies, stylized mountains, and the occasional jeep – Pegasus of the tribal imagination. Why then in Gulmi this mass production of carved tigers and elephants? This is our way of showing our admiration and respect, was the reply. In recent years the tigers had not taken a villager, but a single bound carried a hungry one over the useless fence, and off he went with a goat. The elephants were a worse problem. Here as in most of the tribal liquor-producing areas they raided alcohol supplies and in the end turned into alcoholics. They sniffed the liquor from afar and came charging out of the forest in a plundering herd. An intake of liquor enraged and incited them to vandalism, and they laid about in all directions tearing off thatches and butting down walls. The only sure remedy against such an invasion was to bury the liquor stores underground. But the workings of the tribal mind would also have suggested an act of propitiation, a token obeisance to irresistible force, the soft answer that turned any wrath. Hence all the carvings.

Chapter Twenty-One

IT IS INEVITABLE that those who have studied the tribals of India should have devoted ample space to their lovelife – so often in contrast not only with Western mores but also those of the Hindu majority still a little encumbered with the legacy of Victorian England. Even the Puritan Fathers with their fear of the human body could hardly have matched the ibis-eating Mirigans in the field of sexual abstinence. The large and flourishing tribes of the Saora regard copulation as offensive to the gods – particularly in woodlands and open fields directly under the divine eye. Engaged couples are thus required by the community to keep their physical distance, to be virgins at the moment of marital consummation, and thereafter remain faithful to each other for life. Intercourse is discontinued after childbirth for a period up to three years.

There are a few other tribals with attenuated sexual activities, but on the whole the tribal is liberal – sometimes outstandingly so. Sugiyama Kolchi, the Japanese anthropologist investigating the Munda in 1968, noted the existence of 'love markets', and that the young men and women of Maranghada, where he carried out his field studies, spent the night together in local 'sleeping houses'. According to Dr N. Patnaik, the Kondh, of whom we had been able to see a little, possess dormitories where unmarried boys and girls pass the night. A brief glimpse of Paraja girls in action at a wedding party had suggested that they were easygoing in their attitude to sex, while Verrier Elwin finds conventional Western morality turned upside down among the Murias, who fine a young man who attempts to confine his passionate advances to one girl.

*

791

To the list of emphatic non-adherents to our standards must be added the Koya, numbering some fifty-five thousand and inhabiting the Malakangiri Hills on the border between south-west Orissa and Madhya Pradesh, who have attracted some renown for their own peculiarity in the matter of marital customs, insisting that a wife should be substantially older than her husband at marriage. The writer P. K. Mohapatra says that marriages are frequently conducted between a boy of thirteen and a woman of about thirty. When we went to their principal village, Bhejaguda – which means 'The House of God' – a happy couple of such a kind were pointed out to us. The Koyas are said to attach little or no importance to a girl's physical beauty when it comes to marriage, the criteria for a coveted wife being her sound health and capacity for hard work. Despite this reported indifference to good looks we found the Koya a most handsome people. In his account Mohapatra goes on to say that the wife has to wait for her husband to be fully grown before sexual intercourse takes place. 'She sleeps with her husband and is expected to remain chaste,' he says, adding wryly, 'but actually it does not happen so.' To this, after a short conversation with our Koya hosts, who spoke quite frankly about themselves, Ranjan added the rider – 'If a woman shows some impatience her father-in-law may be called upon to do the necessary.'

The Koyas had grand manners, and were at pains to put all visitors at ease. The village was a street of yellow houses built on and among the rocks of a hillside and as we came into sight a number of splendid matriarchs in crimson togas appeared at their doors to receive us with expressions of interest and enthusiasm. Next a bed was carried out into the street and covered with a clean mat and we were invited to be seated upon this. It was a signal for what might have been the lesser families to drag out their beds. Upon these more impressive-looking ladies settled in imperial fashion. They smiled and nodded and their gold ornaments clinked. A strapping late-comer arrived with her husband, who might have been fourteen, at her heels. He was left with all the other men, standing meekly in line at the back of the assembly. 'We are waiting for the headman,' Ranjan said. In a moment this dignitary arrived, accompanied by an assistant of sorts who was outrageously drunk. The drunkard was got rid of, and the headman went into his speech. Like the other men he was dressed in a white loincloth, was barefoot and naked from the waist up, and despite his office there was something subordinate about his manner in this context of praetorian women. One eye was half closed and I detected eccentricity in his movements. Two women who had arrived for whom seats could not be found seemed to be swaying slightly. Could they all be drunk, I asked myself. Ranjan explained what it was all about. They had out on a theatrical show and been up all the previous night. 'They've been hitting the bottle,' he said.

The time for sweet distribution had come and once again there was the minor problem of how to set about unwrapping a factory-wrapped product. Perfectly behaved children were led forward to be exposed for the first time to the joy and excitement of synthetic raspberry flavour after the varied mediocrity of those the jungle could offer. One, who must have been about five, had to be deprived of the nipple before he could join the queue. Were some of the children tipsy too, I wondered. It seemed a possibility. Most of the adults also tasted Western-style sweets for the first time, and there were wild guesses as to their provenance, the most conservative and religiously minded taking the view that, like the universe, they had always exsisted, but only recently been discovered.

We were shown over a house, but there was little to be seen. The Koya take refuge from the great heat of summer by doing without windows and putting up with the total darkness – and airlessness – of their sleeping quarters, while spending the daylight hours on shady verandas surrounding the house. At this season – as elsewhere – nothing much happened apart from the search for pleasure. Most nights, said the headman, reeling and hiccuping occasionally, there was a show on somewhere. Work was strictly taboo, and anyone found engaged in surreptitious labour was subjected to reprimand. Only the making of liquor was permissible, and this used up half the time. There was hardly a tree in the vicinity from the leaves, sap, or fruit of which the Koya had not learned to distil liquor. As Mohapatra says, 'Without alcohol the Koya cannot survive. A Koya can carry on without food for a few days, but not without liquor.'

Now was the time among the Koya when their unequally matched marriages took place. Strapping women, valued after much chaffering in terms of cattle, would be handed over to diminutive grooms. Much as they strut and preen in their togas and gold jewellery, with their self-effacing menfolk in the background, there is no economic basis for this swagger: in reality these impressive girls are no more than their fathers' chattels. Nothing makes this clearer than the fact that whereas love marriages are favoured by two-thirds of the tribes of Orissa, here they are out. Instead the father sets out to negotiate the best possible deal for a valuable piece of property, looking forward to being ten to twenty head of cattle richer if a successful bargain is struck. Love cuts across bargaining, and marriages where an infatuated couple elope in the night and in consequence no bullocks change hands are considered self-indulgent and disgraceful.

At a push the Koya settle for marriage by capture, a down-market procedure not without its farcical aspects as the bridegroom is invariably smaller and weaker than the bride, and the violence largely symbolical. In such cases tribal mechanisms exist by which fairly standardized sums are paid out by the family of the abductor by way of compensation. Finally, in the case of poor families unable to pay a bride-price a service arrangement may be agreed by which, in the traditional Old Testament fashion of Jacob and Laban, the son-in-law pays for his wife by working for his father-in-law for a number of months or years.

The Koyas rationalize marriages between mature women and adolescent boys by explaining that their women in early life work harder than men, employed not only in field work and their household tasks, but in bringing up children, and when the time comes to take it easy they need a husband in full possession of his physical powers to come to their support. This is a myth. The Koyas may at times work hard but only over short periods, and their lifestyle offers an instance of the relative idleness of so-called primitive people. Indian tribals work when there is forest clearing, sowing, weeding, and harvesting to be done, enjoying the long work-free pauses in between in a way that Westerners with their noses to the grindstone might find it difficult to understand, just as a set working day of so many hours is inconceivable to the tribal mentality. Almost certainly someone like Mr Mohapatra will have calculated the average of daily working hours put in by the Koyas at their various forms of husbandry: among Amazonian tribes (equally expert in the pleasurable exploitation of what we call waste time) engaged in the cultivation of the market gardens in a similar environment to this, the average can be as low as one and a half hours.

Religious ceremonies and observance are bracketed in the esteem of the Koya with public entertainments of every sort. In addition to the large assortment of their own gods they are quite happy to add those of their neighbours to their pantheon, as these, including a half-dozen Hindu divinities, serve to increase the number of feast days and the opportunities for the villager to have a good time. We noted that the Koyas even had a version of the Car of the Juggernaut, which being too large to accommodate in the village street had been shoved off the road at the bottom of the hill and left until the August festival.

We happened to be at Bhejaguda at the moment of the arrival of the peripatetic team of a priest and two acolytes touring the countryside with an image of Mongola, an up-country version of Kali Jai who watches over depressives and is hugely popular among the tribal peoples. Mongola was represented only by her head and up-flung arms. Her face was that of a startled child, with wide staring eyes and bright cheeks. Beneath the head was nothing but a bunched-up floral dress, and concealed in it was a pad which supported the image when carried on the priest's head. The priest's eyes were wide too, perhaps with the strain and exhaustion of so many miles covered in the burning sun. In token of his standing he wore a white vest in addition to his dark blue pantaloons. His assistants, each of whom carried two tambourines, were clad in loincloths only. All three were bare-foot.

Their presence, immediately following our arrival, set off a new explosion of excitement. All country people living in isolation welcome a new face, and since, as they will often admit, boredom is the enemy, excitement can be distilled from almost any variation of the day's routine. In this case the newcomers offered a dramatic performance of an unusual kind and, throwing off the torpor induced by hangovers and an all-night staging of the *Ramayana*, the villagers braced themselves to enjoy what was on offer.

According to the tribal philosophy, sickness is largely the product of an unsatisfactory lifestyle. The patient has succeeded in annoying one or more of the gods who punishes him accordingly. All villages had a shaman, going by different names, whose principal task it was to decide which god had been offended, and why, and decide upon the appropriate offerings to be made. Although in theory the sacrifice of a cockerel, or the painting of a ritual picture, should have been enough, it was normal to assist the processes of recovery by the administration of herbal remedies based upon a rich tribal pharmacology which has yet to be fully investigated. A dogged empiricism assisted by faith had produced a fairly successful result. The life expectation at birth of a non-tribal Indian is fifty-seven years. A tribal in an optimum situation, comparable to that of the Koya, and free from outside interference, can add five or six years to this figure. The tribal benefits from a diet of fresh and more varied food and an outdoor life, and probably from a more amusing and relaxed existence as well. Perhaps, too, the practice of an extreme form of democracy, unknown in industrialized society, may be of help. Among the Koyas the headman is chosen from candidates presenting themselves against whom there has never been a complaint. His job is to settle disputes with absolute impartiality, to make sure that the village is well supplied with liquor, and to stand up to brow-beating government officials. At the end of a year's tenure of office, the whole village gathers to discuss his performance, and if this is found to be below standard he is replaced on the spot.

It seemed that once in a while people suffered from disorders resistant both to medicines and offerings to the gods. Women whose affairs of the heart had gone wrong – whom nobody had ever wanted to capture, suggested Ranjan – were nearly always the sufferers, and in such cases Mongola could be effective.

The treatment was novel. A party of the sufferer's relatives and friends would be gathered together to accompany the three Mongola men and the image to the patient's house. A dance followed. The priest's assistants beat their tambourines, capered about, and sang a lively song, while the priest danced with the image, in which most of those present would have assumed the goddess herself to have taken up temporary abode. Inevitably, at a certain moment, caught up by the general excitement, the patient would join in the dance. This was the moment to thrust the image into her arms and compel her to dance with the goddess who, according to the headman, was a lively partner despite the absence of legs. The climax came when the goddess, speaking through the image's mouth, counselled the patient as to how she could best be cured. The headman mentioned that she had a strange, squeaking voice. 'A case of ventriloquism?' I suggested to Ranjan. He translated, and the headman said, 'Perhaps, but stones are gods, if you believe. That is all that matters.' A wry evaluation, it might have been thought, of so many doctrines.

Had there been any prospect of witnessing treatment by Mongola we would have happily delayed departure from Bhejaguda, but as no suitable patient could be found we left, making for the Malakangiri Hills. This small mountainous area on the Madhya Pradesh border in south-western Orissa is of exceptional interest. As late as the seventies the hills were covered in dense forests of sal and teak and possibly – despite the ravages of the timber extraction industry – much of this remains. Conservation, as ever, has been favoured by the absence of good motorable roads. Inland there are a few *kachas*, as they are locally called, with terrible surfaces and no bridges, and thus only usable for the six months of the year when it does not rain.

When last reported upon, the animals included almost every species currently recorded in India, together with a spectacular array of birds. These, in particular the birds, are increasingly under siege by collectors employed by dealers, who succeed in exporting them, with or without licence, all over the world. Once their principal customers were zoos, but with the increased demand for exotic pets in the affluent West, pet shops are now the worst offenders. It is a trade which shows no sign of abatement, and one is likely only to be reminded of its existence by an occasional report of an illicit cargo discovered at Heathrow of once live animals which have died before reaching their ultimate destination.

The animals are hunted with great skill by the Koyas and other small groups in the vicinity. They use trap-cages with call birds, or occasionally the sticky substance once known as bird-lime, to capture the birds, having been shown photographs of what is in demand by the sinister Dombs, who act as agents of the trade. Normally the tribals hunt only for food. To catch a sizeable animal, a pit is dug, covered with branches and leaves, suitably baited, and armed with iron spikes upon which the trapped animal impales itself. To deal with the commercial demand for live animals a modified system is called for, and this is based upon a complicated system of trenches and pits always employed in the capture of the sloth bear.

This bear, sometimes spoken of as India's most dangerous animal, and once existing in great numbers in the jungles, is now rapidly disappearing. As in the case of the unfortunate rhinoceros, part of its body is valued as an aphrodisiac in the Far East, to which sloth bear gall bladders have been exported in numbers. More unpleasantly, it can be easily taught to perform. Once captured an iron ring is fixed in its nose, and attached to a rope with which it is dragged about. Despite its natural ferocity the animal is soon disciplined by a hot iron applied to the tender parts of its body. The training begins by chaining it on a metal platform beneath which a fire is lit. When in agony the bear is compelled to raise one foot after another while a simple tune is played on a pipe. After a week or two of this, a Pavlovian reflex is established and the bear is ready to go into its dancing routine whenever the tune is played, without encouragement by fire. Dancing bears are still to be seen all over India, but in south Orissa the Dombs have practically cornered the diminishing supply.

We were making for Bonda country to the east of the Malakangiri

Hills, but since the local verdict was that our Ambassador could never tackle *kacha* roads our only recourse was to turn back through Matil, thereafter branching right for Khairput, administrative centre of the Bonda area. At Matil we stopped for tea in the centre of another idyllic rural scene. The building opposite had once been a temple and was now a ruin in almost classic style. In what remained of an archway a woman in a blue sari was taking bananas – held as if they were precious objects – from a basket having a wide, amphora-shaped neck. These she polished scrupulously with sal leaves before arranging them in a design at her feet. In the background doves and crows, mixed in together, wove slow elegant patterns of flight. An old, nearly nude man whose bones under the tightly stretched skin recalled an anatomical chart, was crouched supported on one elbow, a few feet from the woman, playing a Jew's harp. The faint wheezing of this was obliterated momentarily by the rumble of a bullock-cart, and at the moment of passing its driver, walking by the head of the offside animal, leaned down to whisper something in its ear.

After Matil the road was dead straight, an ochre slash that might have been cut by an axe through a grey wasteland of stubble and weeds, with no houses in view, and the green hump of the Malakangiri afloat distantly in the haze. It was now that for a brief moment we were in contact with the drama of sloth bears. Suddenly a group of women were hurrying towards us down this deserted road. The driver pulled up, and they came clamouring round the car. Their story came out in a Dravidian outpouring mixed with the Oriya that helped piece it together. Three of their menfolk out hunting with their bows had been killed by a single gigantic bear. It had held one in its forepaws and ripped him apart with its claws, while the others held their fire for fear of hitting their friend, after which the bear turned on them and killed them too. Those who die unnatural deaths cannot by local custom be cremated, but must be buried as near as possible to the spot where the death occurred, and these women were on their way to join friends in another village with whom the burial party would be formed.

*

The Bonda, whose territory we entered shortly after this, have attracted great and continuous publicity due to their capacity for sudden and deadly wrath. This has occasioned numerous homicides within the tribe itself, and also the death of sundry strangers who have wandered incautiously into these hills and given unwitting cause for offence. Isolation in a single, relatively small area has deprived the Bondas of the study devoted to larger and more accessible tribal peoples. They are Australoids surrounded by peoples of Dravidian origin; their language is difficult and their origins obscure. A dozen or so anthropological works have been devoted to them, but the outsider consulting them is likely to find himself lost in a wilderness of social anthropology, struggling with hardly comprehensible jargon and expected to derive excitement from such topics as territorial exogamy on two levels, fictive siblings, marital taboos, moities, and joking and avoiding relationships. This may seem as dry as dust when what is likely most to concern the average layman is why the Bondas are ready to kill at the drop of a hat when they are surrounded on all sides by tribal people of exemplary tolerance and pacific behaviour.

In the anthropologist's world political action can play little part. His job is to assemble facts for scientific study. It is possible to find one, for example, gathering such data as the names of the parts of a fish in a language which, because a tribe is about to disappear, will cease to be spoken in a matter of a few years at most. *The Bonda*, published in 1989 by the Tribal and Harijan Research Institute, is the latest book about the tribe. In the main it concentrates as it is expected to on anthropological information, but makes occasional ill-conceived forays into an alien world of opinion in which the authors flounder without direction. Some confusion, too, may be due to the existence of two or more contributors having different, or even conflicting, views.

The first departure from verifiable fact deals with assessment of tribal character. 'The Bondas exhibit', says the contributor, 'a kind of personality which is characterized by aggression and criminal propensity. The village officials do not have any control over such cases of murder, and the tribal political system does not seem to have any responsibilities in the matter of bringing about any reform in the homicidal activities of the people. The general social control works only to the extent that the murderer is excommunicated and handed over to the police for trial.'

This reads like unscientific stuff, but a few lines later the writer is back on course with a discussion of magico-religious rites as an aid to conception, only to fall into difficulties further on with a news item dealing with a government micro-project. As a result of this 'the Bondas have become change-prone and adopted many schemes for their development ... Thus a transformation from the stage of stagnation has come about. Visitors to the Bonda villages can now move about and mix with the Bondas freely and without fear.' The improved security and change in atmosphere, said the book, had been due to changes in the socio-economic life. The Bondas had learned to grow several new crops like potato, wheat, pulses, ginger, and vegetables, and were using improved seeds and techniques of cultivation. Even chemical fertilizers were now applied to the Bonda fields.

More opinions and a whisper of consumerist propaganda follow. The Bondas, enthuses the writer, are to become cash spenders ...

Now that they need this and that [consumer goods] and that they express their eagerness to have them, frequent contacts with outsiders have influenced their religious beliefs and practices. Changes are also taking place in their dress and material possessions. A Bonda woman puts on a sari when she goes out. Similarly the Bonda are now very much interested in giving education to their children. In order to meet this need some schools have been set up.

Perhaps Bonda women do wear saris in token of these advanced times, but we never saw any that did so. Possibly visitors can now move about and mix with Bondas freely and without fear, although it was hard to forget that several who had been incautious in the use of their cameras had been struck with Bonda arrows. After the effusion of so much optimism in the early chapters, can it possibly have been the same man who a few pages further on produces this depressing summation of the Bonda condition and future?

They are no longer self-sufficient as they were in the past, and are in dire want of food and other necessities of life. Excepting a few well-to-do families, most of them need credit in the shape of foodstuff for consumption, seeds and also cash for agriculture, and domestic animals for payment of bride-price.

Following his work with the Murias, Elwin moved on to the Bondas, contributing a chapter entitled 'The Bonda Murderers' to the encyclopaedic collection *Man-in-India* published in 1945. In this and later in a full-length book, *Bonda Highlanders*, he shows himself as fascinated and even perplexed by a tribal society in which homicide, often casual and seemingly unpremeditated, was perhaps the strongest cultural feature. Bonda males suffered from fits of anger provoked by the slightest of offences, or even imaginary grievances, but having killed the offender rarely bothered to cover up their traces. When arrested they co-operated readily with the police because their code of beliefs, which permitted murder, prohibited a lie. Elwin found them completely fearless, indifferent to property, and devoid of sexual jealousy. They prided themselves on their stoicism. He reported an annual 'castigation ceremony' when, in the manner of North American Indian braves, they demonstrate their indifference to various tortures inflicted on them. An extraordinary village institution in the Bonda highlands was the formation by the women of a kind of feminine home-guard to prevent their menfolk from committing murders, or themselves being murdered.

Our only hope of finding beds in the Bonda Hills area that night was at the Block administrative headquarters at Khairput, and we were a few miles short of this on a road winding through low hills when it occurred to Ranjan that we might discover that there was no food to be had when we got to the end of our journey. By the greatest good luck he had hardly mentioned this when the next building – the first sign of human habitation for miles – carried a notice in Sanskrit characters announcing itself to be a chicken farm. It was an extraordinary place, run by a Hindu whose business consisted in the supply to the villages of chickens for sacrificial purposes. Most of them were caught for him in the jungles by tribals

– usually young boys – who imitated the cries made by chickens of either sex in search of a mate and then shot those deceived in this way with small, blunted arrows which only inflicted temporary damage. The Hindu also bred captured jungle-fowl with selected domestic breeds to produce stunningly beautiful hybrids retaining the brilliant iridescent plumage of the wild, although twice the size of birds from the jungle. For these magnificent creatures, which only the richest villages could offer to their god on the occasion of the annual festival, a huge price was asked. The man, perhaps suspecting that Ranjan was acting for such a community, produced the best on offer, a truly splendid cockerel cascading multi-coloured feathers, with an autocratic expression, burning eye, and a flaming spread of comb the size of my hand. When it was brought to us the owner clasped his hands together momentarily as if in prayer. It was only through a hitch somewhere in the mechanism of its karma, he said, that it had been born what it was and not a man. The price worked out at about £20. Ranjan told him we wanted a bird to fry up for the evening meal. The news seemed to stun the owner, and he said something about religious principles. In the end he relented to the extent of indicating a neighbouring market and we went off there and bought a run-of-the-mill chicken for the equivalent of 50p.

Khairput, despite its official prominence and its name on the map, proved to be a nothing of a place, reminding me of a war-time position of no special importance hastily abandoned in anticipation of an attack. It was formless, unkempt, deserted, and a little sinister. In the optimistic assumption that we should find somewhere to put up for the night the first essential was to find someone to cook the chicken. Khairput turned out to possess the filthiest dhaba we had so far encountered, with refuse scattered everywhere over the earthen floor under investigation by a small incontinent dog. Four tribals with obsidian faces, blanketed like Mexicans, their eyes fixed immovably upon us, occupied the next table. The unwashed and taciturn Hindu who ran the place came up as stealthily as an assassin from behind, and when Ranjan asked him to cook the cockerel he said that not only was his a vegetarian restaurant but he had never cooked a chicken in his life. Ranjan then gave him instructions how this was done and he agreed to cook the bird so long as it was eaten off the premises. An untouchable sweeper was on hand to carry out the execution, and grabbing the protesting bird from Ranjan he reached for an old ceremonial bayonet hanging on the wall, and slipped through a tattered curtain and out of sight.

Overlooking this scene was a recently published mass-production picture of Lakshmi, shown as a pleasing, fair-skinned young woman of strikingly Western appearance, who could have been a film star, extending her blessings with four arms. I waited under her indulgent gaze while the hideous outcry behind the curtain began, reached its brief crescendo, then stopped, and the sweeper reappeared, kicked the dog from under our feet, and hung up the bayonet.

We finished our tea and went out. Ranjan had been directed by the owner of the dhaba to the man who kept the keys of what were called Suites Nos. 1 and 2, where officials obliged to visit Khairput were normally lodged. He went off, shortly returning with the keys and slightly disquieting news. Next day, Sunday, the Bonda market would be held as usual about half a mile down the road from Khairput. However, a recent market had been the scene of a violent incident. Outsiders – no one knew who they were, but they could have been Indians or even foreigners – had appeared in the market and begun to take photographs using flashbulbs. Possibly from fear they were under attack the Bondas had snatched up their bows and one or two of the intruders had been struck by arrows. The news was imprecise and shot through with rumour. One person said one thing, and another something quite different. Certainly, though, there had been trouble.

Suites Nos. 1 and 2 were on the far side of the desolated little open space, each forming a half of a low-lying concrete barrack with a pitted front, corrugated-iron roof, shuttered windows, and a goat tearing at shreds of matting on the veranda. Suite 2, first inspected, consisted of a large, dark, tarnished room, empty except for a bed and a mattress sullied with disquieting stains. People had come here to face the night and had left, often scattering unwanted objects on the floor: screwed up election-leaflets and cinema handbills, bus-tickets, a flattened toothpaste tube, a brush that had shed most of its bristles, and the stones, kernels, and skins of a variety of fruits. Large spiders had inhabited this room at a time when the rainy season had provided abundant insect prey. They had draped the gossamer voile of their webs across the windows in such a way as almost to simulate curtains of an exceptionally light material. Now, in the dearth of approaching summer, they had gone, leaving only the desiccated remains of an exceptional specimen dangling like a small overlooked article of clothing from a hook in the suite's bathroom. This cell in total darkness contained a large tub of stagnant water, and the torch revealed a swirling pattern left on its surface dust suggesting that some small animal, perhaps a gecko, might have fallen in and circulated for a while before drowning and sinking to the bottom. Beside the usual hole in the bathroom floor there were a cracked jug for ablutionary use and, fixed to the wall above, a sink. From this hung down a foot or so of piping through which any water, used say to wash the hands, would splash straight on to the floor.

The condition of Suite No. 1, to be occupied by Ranjan, was roughly the same, and the problem now arose of what to do to clear up this very considerable mess. Even in a village like Khairput where a tribal population was accustomed to keeping houses clean, the caste influence of a minority of Hindus was so strong that a kind of shadow of untouchability had developed among the tribals themselves. Ranjan rushed round the village looking for someone to sweep out the rooms, change the water in the bathrooms, and perhaps clean the windows, but although he offered more than a labourer would have been paid for ten hours of the most gruelling work, it was some time before a reluctant and sulky boy could be found to take on the job. Shortly he arrived, treating us to a baleful glance as he slunk past clutching the bunch of twigs and the filthy cloth with which the process of cleansing would be accomplished.

The chicken was delivered steaming and fragrant, and Dinesh, averting his eyes from the spectacle, scuttled away down to the dhaba for his rice with dhal. Ranjan settled to his usual evening lecture. He enjoyed speculation on the subject of the Bonda because at the end of the twentieth century, so little was known about them – in the matter of their origins, nothing at all. They were here, and, said some of the savants, had been here since palaeolithic times. But of course it was all surmise, there was no proof of anything. Their language, it was clear, belonged to the Austro-Asiatic group, which was fortunate for Ranjan, because so did the Saora language, which he spoke fairly fluently. The difference between the two tongues might have been greater than that between English and German, but when a Bonda spoke there were words here and there that Ranjan recognized, and sometimes meanings could be pieced together. The Bondas in Dr Patnaik's scientific account were as stiff and unconvincing as the woodcuts in an ancient treatise. When Ranjan spoke of them from his own experiences they came vigorously and menacingly to life, leaping, grimacing, and waving their bows as they had done a year before when Ranjan had ill-advisedly pitched his tent in the shadows of a wood in Bonda country.

It turned out on that occasion they wanted food. He gave it to them and they danced round him and went away. He had been alarmed, but fascinated, too. They were different in every way. He had never encountered human beings like them before and he wanted to know more about them. He found that they carried everything to extremes. If you tried to cheat a Bonda he killed you on the spot, not because he objected to material loss, but for the lie underwriting the attempted fraud. Visitors to the Koyas were startled to hear that Koya boys of thirteen married women of thirty, but the Bonda went one better, for marriages of boys from eight to ten, said Ranjan, with girls in their twenties were commonplace. Most of the tribals either approved of, or at least permitted, marriage by capture. In the case of the Bondas it became a kind of sport: they not only raided their own villages for suitable brides, but even mounted expeditions for this purpose into the territory of neighbouring tribes. This, too, Ranjan saw as typical excess in a community never short of sexual adventure, with its courting parties of young boys going from village to village to serenade girls compelled by the rules of hospitality to take them to bed in the local dormitory.

Ranjan did not surprise me by expressing his admiration for the Bondas' intense individualism. They refused to take orders from anybody, and it was impossible to induce them to engage in communal undertakings of any kind. He was impressed by the fact that they possesed a great number of different musical instruments, and that every man played one or more of them. More remarkably, he could even find an excuse for their showing no care or concern for their parents or the old people.

What seemed to shock him – reflecting probably his position in a society ruled by strict dietetic taboos – was the fact that even at a time when game of all kinds such as pig and deer was in plentiful supply and jungle trees produced abundant fruit, the Bondas should happily eat rats, mice, crows, and such insects as cicadas and ants. Yet the avoidance of such foods is largely a matter of custom and prejudice. I have never been brought to the pass of having to satisfy hunger with nutriment of this kind, but friends have done so. Marcus Colchester, when working among the Yanomami of the Orinoco, was compelled for a time to subsist on an exceptionally large genus of caterpillar. These, he said, were quite palatable so long as one remembered to discard the heads.

Chapter Twenty-Two

DESPITE THE EXTREME SQUALOR of the dhaba, breakfast there at six in the morning turned out to be a pleasant and enlivening experience. The proprietor and his slatternly wife were shovelling pancakes and doughnuts into pans of boiling oil, to be served eventually with curried beans. All this was delectable. Breakfast must have been the main meal of the day, for cloths were taken down from a shelf, beaten with a stick to remove a caking of whitish dust, and laid on each table. Despite the irremediable filthiness of the place it was full of the frangrance of sandalwood, intentionally created by dropping gum collected under the sal trees into the open fire.

A pudgy minor official of sorts was breakfasting at the next table. Ranjan asked him where all the Bondas had gone, and he said back to their hill villages. He was quite sure that the market was to be held as usual because tribal advance parties had come down at dawn, as they always did, to clean up and prepare the site. The police would be there to keep things under control and impound cameras that might be produced. Any Bondas in Khairput, he thought, could be found at the Lutheran Mission church, to which he directed us.

We rang the bell at the iron gate, and immediately the pastor came out to greet us. He was a pleasant, smiling, rather portly young Indian, who in the instinctive judgement of this first meeting it would have been hard to dislike. He handed me his card, K. Devasahayam, IMST Missionary, Khairput Post, then led the way into his church, which seemed very bare. The Hindu temple at Khairput had been decked with flowers, both artificial and real, and there were paper chains, little coloured flags, odd scraps of flowered material pinned up here and there, and a genial, rather ridiculous picture of Ganesh which had helped to bolster the light-hearted and indulgent atmosphere of the place. But God, as seen by the Protestant sects, was averse to such attempted beautifications and elected, they believed, to be worshipped in surroundings of unrelieved solemnity. To come here after the temple was to enter a kind of vacuum.

I asked the pastor about his work with what he might well have seen as the most intractable heathens of all. 'We have simple rules,' he said. 'Don't go to dormitory. Priest conducts marriage. No polygamy. Not to drink.'

'And is your rule accepted?'

'No,' he said. 'They smile and say yes. They go on as before.' It was impossible not to admire his frankness and also the good humour with which he admitted defeat. Yet I wondered why the notorious Bonda violence should have been excluded from the prohibitions, and why three out of four embargoes were connected with sex.

'Have you made many converts?'

'Seven families have come to Jesus Christ.'

'Out of a population of how many?'

'By latest census this is five thousand one hundred.'

'So it sounds like a long haul.'

'Ah yes, it is a long way to go. We are hoping. We go on trying. We are labouring in the Lord's vineyard.'

'What sort of instruction do you give your converts?'

'That also is very difficult. It is hard to make them understand and we have a language problem. I am showing them a picture of Our Lord walking on the water. This is a picture they are liking very much.'

There was a sudden small outburst from him as if a bitter truth had forced its way out. 'These people we have gathered to Our Lord are very poor. Very necessitous. To keep them we are giving concessions.'

'In what way?'

'We know they are breaking faith with us, but we are looking in the other direction. Very much they are taking drink. If we say them this must stop, they will go.'

The Mission House, Mercy College, was next door. I would have liked to see the converts and asked if they were staying there.

No, he said. One of the strange things about them was they would only live in houses they had built themselves.

'And the church?' I asked. 'Do you hold services?'

'No one will come,' he said. 'They are afraid to be seen. In Bonda country many people are afraid.'

Ranjan had gathered more up-to-date information. The main body of the Bondas, both men and women, were accoustomed to take the direct route straight down to their market, but for some inscrutable reason a number of women, unaccompanied by their menfolk, preferred to reach Khairput by a circuitous approach. These came down from the hills using the same narrow and precipitous track on which, eleven years before, Bose in his jeep had been captured and briefly held prisoner. The Bonda women using this detour, said Ranjan's informant, were quite approachable, and raised no objection even to the taking of photographs.

We accordingly set out in hope and had walked only a few hundred yards when we spotted the first of the Bonda girls on their way down. It was still early morning, with the leaves whitened by a residue of mist, and the sun throwing down taut lines of shadow from the tree-trunks ahead, and once again it was a piece of Indian theatre. The first girl tripped towards us half obscured in dense patches of shadow, then scintillating as the sun winked on jewellery displayed as if in a garish fashion parade. Behind her, fifty yards further away, came a second girl, and then a third, hardly more than a brilliant insect flashing through the sunshine at a distance of a quarter of a mile.

The first girl came close, then stopped, a tiny Ethiopian with a thin Amharic face, a touch of melancholy in the eyes and finely cut features, among the wide cheekbones of tribal India. The cautious wraith of a smile undermined a dignity abetted by ten aluminium hoops compelling her to hold her head imperiously erect.

The Bondas are tradionally a naked people, their enforced nudism being of ancient origin. It followed a curse laid upon them in the times of the *Mahabharata* when Rama and Sita were journeying in the Bonda Hills at the time of their fourteen-year banishment. Sita, cleansing herself in a river after menstruation, provoked the laughter of Bondas who had gone there to draw water. She thereupon laid a curse on them that they should always go naked and be the object of laughter – a punishment which they never cease to resent. To laugh at a Bonda is the deadliest of insults.

It is the purpose of the neck hoops to draw the beholder's attention up and away from the parts of the body deprived by the rigidity of custom from normal concealment. This girl also wore the obligatory hundred long necklaces, a massive glittering bulk extending from the neck to cover the pubic regions. Each forearm carried silver bangles extending almost to the elbow. Sita had stipulated that Bonda heads must be shaved and the bare scalp was covered by a cap of minute beads. Bonda girls were obliged to wear jewellery instead of clothing, but a small concession of recent origin had permitted the adoption of a kilt which, to avoid irreparable breach of custom, is of insufficient width to go right round the waist and thus permits glimpses of bare buttocks.

While we were examining the great collection of ornaments passed by inheritance from mother to daughter, the other girls, one after another, came up, stopped to be admired and photographed, and went on. Presently middle-aged and elderly women began to arrive, always in groups of three and four. These, seemingly, had passed beyond the reach of the taboo from which their daughters suffered, as they had been allowed to cover their jewellery with a mantle of light cloth, reaching to the knees. The question was why had the young and pretty girls of the tribe chosen to walk alone in this area where marriage by capture was an everyday occurrence, while their elders, relieved by the years from such hazards, sought company for the journey, and perhaps the protection of numbers? Could it be that the village beauties who put themselves to such bother with their attire for the trip to market to barter a few pounds of rice for a bowlful of fruit were providing their admirers, well away from interference by fathers or brothers, with an opportunity for romantic violence en route?

We followed them, lurking behind at a respectful distance, down to Khairput's muddle of hutments through which, for their own mysterious reasons, they had chosen to pass on their way to the market. Somehow, on our way back to the suites and to pick up the car, I became separated from Ranjan, and then, a moment later, turning a corner came on him facing the first Bonda male I had seen, who stood in his path holding a bow with an arrow fixed to a point vaguely in the direction of Ranjan's feet. After the surprise of the weapon came the surprise of the size of this man I first took to be a local urchin playing a silly prank. I came up behind and the Bonda glanced back over his shoulder showing the same long, thin Ethiopian nose as the girls we had photographed and a tight, thin-lipped mouth. He stood about four foot ten with no more of a physique than an average Indian boy of twelve but nevertheless exuded a daunting firmness of purpose.

At such times the compulsion is to look round for an ally, but Khairput, empty as ever, offered no support. There was the dhaba squeezed into the edge of the field of vision ahead, but breakfast was over and everyone had gone away. It was a confrontation that lasted no more than a matter of seconds before Ranjan reached out and took the bow away. He handed me the arrow, which was very light and very small, and beautifully made. I found it hard to imagine how a man like this, having the size and musculature of a child, and using a weapon which however expertly made was hardly more than a toy, could actually kill another man in the way that Bondas did.

While this was going on there was no reaction from the Bonda of any kind. He showed no sign of anger, or surprise, and no disposition to argue. Ranjan handed back the bow, but when I held out the arrow the Bonda waved it away with a gesture of rejection, leading me to suspect that I might have damaged its magic by my touch. Ranjan gave him ten rupees, and nothing changed on his face. For a moment I was reminded of the trained imperturbability of a gangster in an old American film. Perhaps what we had experienced was no more than an automatic reponse to any stranger's presence, to be countered only with a show of calm. A moment later he slipped away. Later we saw him briefly again, still mooching about bow in hand, looking perhaps for someone who would start a fight with him.

We found the Bonda market tame and quiet and shrunken by all accounts, concentrated under the trees a mile down the road. We had passed by a police building and the officer in charge, exuding the sinister jocularity often generated by the consciousness of absolute power, came out to chat. The Bondas had put their bows away out of sight and, apart from a certain amount of apathetic bargaining over vegetables, nothing very much was going on. It was the most dispirited of such markets we had attended and after a few moments we left, making for Kundili back in Kondh country. Here on this same day each week was held what was described as possibly the greatest tribal assemblage in eastern India, with an attendance of not less then ten thousand. This was the market at which, Ranjan had promised, we should see the parasitic Dombs in action robbing and fleecing the Kondhs.

We arrived at Kundili after a four-hour drive to find a seething multitude, drawn from a number of tribes, gathered into a mile-wide dust bowl at the conjunction of the main road into Andhra Pradesh and a number of country byways leading down from the hills. Under the hard forthright midday sun it was a sight to guarantee eye-strain and eventual headaches. The sky was bleached white, with drifts in it of what appeared at first as red smoke blowing across, but which proved to be the blood-red dust, which lay a quarter-inch deep on every surface, caught up by the gusting wind. When the dust was blown across the sun it turned dark, swelled up, and seemed to tremble. From all points of the market came the piercing glitter of metal articles for sale, from sheets of corrugated iron, pots and pans, and above all from the rows of polished aluminium receptacles containing alcohol for sale.

Desia Kondh girls dispensed the alcohol. The Desias are the

branch of the Kondhs inhabiting lowland villages which are in close contact with the Hindus, thus they are influenced by Hindu culture to the extent of abstaining from eating the meat of cows. Visits by travelling Hindu film shows have also brought about changes in Kondh fashion, and these girls, although covering themselves with jewellery made by their own silversmiths, and with nose-rings so large as to cover most of the top lip, had taken to wearing saris of strident colours produced in the factories of Bombay. The girls squatted in rows in the red dust, arms linked together, supposedly to impede unwanted abductions. Additional security was provided in the case of each group by a huge somnolent dog. In front of each girl stood a two-gallon container of alcohol which, although now-adays of aluminium, surprisingly retained the classic shape of the old pots long since thrown away. Drinks were served in aluminium pint beakers after the red dust had been scrupulously wiped from their rims. Sales were brisk and productive of much antic behaviour by drunken exhibitionists. One of the customers mentioned to Ranjan that he had walked all night carrying a small pig to market on his shoulders. 'Now I have a right to get drunk,' he said, 'and it is my intention to do so.'

Such terrific journeys at night – always with the risk of attack by animals – produced extremely low monetary reward. A government report published a few years ago said that goods brought to market in this way fetched an average selling price of one and a half rupees per person, and even now allowing for inflation this figure is unlikely to have increased more than four or five times. Besides selling their alcohol, Ranjan said it was generally accepted that these girls were here to place themselves on display. He drew attention to lurking Kondh boys who had renounced tribal loincloths in favour of Hindu dhotis. They would spend the day going round the market studying all the girls, and when a boy saw a girl he fancied he would offer her a bracelet, which while keeping a stony face she was obliged by custom to accept. If the girl was to be seen wearing the bracelet when she appeared at the next week's market it was an indication that the suit might be pursued. In nine cases out of ten – probably more – Ranjan said, she threw the bracelet away as soon as the donor's back was turned. She was choosy, and could afford to be. Only the most eligible of the Desia Kondh girls sold liquor in the market and their bride-price was a stiff one. To stand any chance of success the boy would have to satisfy Hindu rather than tribal standards by having a lighter skin than average, and thinnish nose and lips. It was an ideal difficult to approach by a Dravidian Kondh. Difficult, too, was the growing of a Mexican-style moustache, now all the rage since its popularization by the famous actor Hemamalin, although little suited to the tribal face.

The bracelets were of plastic, more appreciated in these days than the metal variety, and the red earth in the vicinity of the liquor sales-ladies had been imprinted with a patterning composed of hundreds and perhaps thousands of plastic fragments, in evidence of sexual overtures refused.

The market at Kundili offered a huge range of merchandise: sugar sold by the yard in bamboo tubes, specially treated rice for the making of instant alcohol, corrugated-iron roofing, chicken wire, parrots and argus pheasants, herbal remedies in abundance for all known and imagined ailments, medicines to delay – and even hasten! – the menopause, arrow poison, ground hornbill beaks to promote unnatural strength, a sap which painted on the skin ensured invisibility against tigers, charms guaranteed to procure the growth of a serpent in an enemy's intestines or encourage an invasion of his house by hornets, jungle fruit juices to lighten Dravidian skin, philtres to spread or extinguish the fires of love.

All these were no more than the mercantile trimmings: mere fair-ground embellishments along with the thorn-surgeons, barbers, fortune-tellers, and the dozen or so handsome and strapping trans-vestites – many of whom have been castrated – who are a feature of all the great markets and festivals of India. The real business at Kundili was the buying and selling of animals, cereals, and dried fish, and this was the trade that attracted Dombs, whose hold upon the tribal population was so implacable that hardly a sale could be made without their taking a profit.

The Dombs had set up two high wooden tripods supporting their scales along every road at the approaches to the market. Each of these posts was manned by three Dombs: tall men of athletic appearance and dressed in Hindu style. Peasants bringing in their grain or animals such as goats, or baskets of hens, would be stopped at the first post about a hundred yards from the market pitches, and an attempt made by the most aggressive kind of bargaining to acquire what they had for sale. Those who refused to sell found a further and more vigorous attack at the second post, fifty yards further on, where reluctance to be subjected to an enforced sale was countered by every degree of physical persuasion short of outright assault, with Dombs wresting sacks of grain from the tribesmen's hands, tipping the contents into their scales, thrusting a few rupees into their victim's hands and waving them away.

Three or four tribesmen travelling together might have been expected to put up a struggle, and thus escape molestation. Solitary individuals, even couples, were inevitably accosted and, weighted down with their bundles, found it impossible to escape the Dombs, who sprinted after them bellowing blandishments and threats, and waving their arms like great birds labouring to take off.

No woman could escape, and it amazed us that they risked journeying alone. Within minutes of placing ourselves in a position where we could watch operations at one of the scales a woman appeared in sight, saw what was happening, and succeeded despite her load of grain in making a wide detour to avoid the first Domb scales, only to be caught at the second. After a brief and hopeless struggle and mewing protest she gave in, her rice was weighed and she was paid what Ranjan said would normally be about half the market price. All this happened within sight of a number of people who did not attempt to intervene.

How could it be that the Kondhs, who were at the market by the thousand, could have tolerated such spectacular robbery, which had been going on for decades, had been continually denounced in the press, prohibited by an act of parliament, yet continued unchecked as before? A Domb had deprived a man of his goat, tearing the lead from his hand and running away with it, but somehow the man had got the goat back. Now he told Ranjan that the market price of a large goat such as this was four hundred rupees but the Domb had refused to pay more than two hundred and twenty rupees under the pretext that by the new health regulations only Dombs could sell goats in the market. When it came to grain, he said, the Dombs scored on two counts, for they not only grossly underpaid for whatever they bought but, as everybody knew, used false weights.

Why didn't the Kondhs get together and put up a fight, Ranjan asked.

'The Dombs pay gangsters to look after them.'

'Even so, there must be ten times the number of Kondhs in the market.'

'If anyone starts a big fight the police will be called in. They'd call it a riot and bring their guns along. The police are in the Dombs' pay, too.'

'So there's nothing you can do?'

'Nothing. They can do what they like with us.'

Chapter Twenty-Three

THE NEAREST APPROACH of modern times to Kangrapada happened when an earth-moving machine sent in error by officials employed on a tribal micro-project trundled to within a mile or so of the village, chewed a few cubic yards of earth out of a bank, broke down, and was withdrawn. Thereafter the village had been left alone to defend itself by self-sufficiency. A patchwork quilt of vegetables had been spread in the sun at its entrance. These the villagers ate themselves, as they did a meagre harvest of dry rice, and a few rabbits hunted in the jungle. They kept cows for their milk, and from their own silk worms they spun silk, which the girls made into elegant dresses. Not even the silk was for sale. The Parajas and Godbas sharing the village of Kangrapada took nothing from the outside world. They were modest drinkers of one of the better versions of alcohol made from the flowers of marua. In this way moneylenders were kept out, and if one succeeded in worming his way in he might be induced by a warning arrow to curtail his stay. As the villagers incurred no debts there were no bankruptcies, no fields seized in lieu of payment, no contractors offering debt bondage as the only solution. Fifty miles away we had seen girls of fourteen and fifteen working as labourers in the road. None of them would have been from Kangrapada.

This was Ranjan's Eden, everything at first glance as it had been exactly a year before when he had spent a quite pleasurable day bargaining with the headman and his advisers, as well as making friends with the villagers before being required to mollify the village goddess for a supposed offence by the offering of a cockerel. The village was a cool place. Kondh and Saora villagers we had seen scored their partial victories over the sun by living on verandas sheltered by a tremendous overhang of thatched roofs. The Parajas and Godbas were spared such measures by their good luck in living in a patch of jungle in which they had spaced out the trees so as to leave no part of the village uncovered by dappled shade. Yet so cleverly had the use of shade been exploited that not a corner of the village was gloomy or dark.

As elsewhere in our travels we found that here too it was the season of leisurely relaxation – the social art-form, Ranjan said, at which these people were past masters. The village notables were gossiping, much as he had left them, within earshot of the Earth Mother. People, dressed in their best, were walking up and down chatting to each other. A few were taking naps on their verandas. One or two women were occupying themselves with silk-making processes in an uncommitted way – children were playing a game like hopscotch. An occasional male appeared to be inoffensively drunk.

Two things disturbed Ranjan slightly. The first was that as he now remembered the only outsider to have stayed any length of time in Kangrapada had been an anthropologist, who having done field-work there returned to Bhubaneswar to stage an exhibition. For this a party of Godbas had agreed to build a replica of one of their unique round houses, and this – built, as Ranjan remembered, in five days – had produced excited comment from visitors who could not understand how primitive tribals could produce anything having so great an appeal for what were sometimes called 'normal people'.

This was something that had drawn attention to Kangrapada for the first time and there had been articles in the local papers about it. The second matter for concern was that despite the admiration evoked in the city by the Godbas' circular house they were falling out of favour in Kangrapada, where a Godba couple with the assistance of Paraja neighbours had built themselves a rectangular house in Paraja style which in Ranjan's opinion was 'a box with a veranda'. Ranjan's informant, one of the tribal elders with whom he had been involved in the negotiations over his breach of custom in the previous year, said something to the effect that 'we all have to move with the times'. When Ranjan complained that the Paraja houses were less comfortable, the man replied, 'Sometimes we may sacrifice comfort for appearance.'

The lure of modernity had also touched the Godba girls. Ranjan had been relieved to find that the older women still wore the great, solid silver necklaces passed down from generation to generation and which could only be removed by the silversmith after death. At the time of our arrival he was a little surprised to find the girls parading in their best dresses, as if for a festival, although nobody had mentioned one. All the dresses were identical, almost as if uniforms, and made of cream-coloured cotton cloth into which was woven a series of wide diagonal stripes; three of them red alternating with one black. Despite the influence of the Hindu sari the general effect was Western rather than oriental, with nothing about it that we would have labelled 'ethnic'. What was different was that the enormous silver hoop ear-rings, six inches in diameter, which the girls had worn dangling on their shoulders at the time of his previous visit, had been replaced by a standard factory product supplied by a pedlar. When we spoke to the Godba girls about this, they said that that change had come about through unanimous decision. They objected, they said, to the discomfort. For special occasions they would wear the ear-rings hooped over their ears, but not suspended from the lobes. I found them all very beautiful, but somewhat reserved and unsmiling. They would be dancing later that morning, they said, and then they would wear the traditional ear-rings.

The strikingly wrapped sweets bought in Jeypore were now doled out, to the children first – engagingly shy when pushed to the forefront of a respectful encirclement – then the adults of both sexes. There followed a brief demonstration in the method of removing the wrappers, certain to be carefully conserved without damaging them in any way. Within a few minutes half the population of Kangrapada was sucking sweets.

'Nice people,' Ranjan said. 'Very reasonable. I just asked if it was all right to park the car where it is and the old headman said, "You have been introduced to the goddess, and you offered her a cockerel, there is no problem. You are one of the family now."'

820

'They're very poor,' I said.

'We may feel this as poverty, which for us it will be. For them it is not poverty, it is living their life. They feed themselves. They are happy. What else, they will ask, is important? A moneylender who comes here must wear mourning. To lend money he will be asking for a security, and what security can he find? If he asks for a field it must grow rice, and there is no water for this purpose. A field for growing chillies is no use to him. As yet the buses are not coming and that is good ...'

By now every corner of the village had been explored and greetings exchanged with Ranjan's acquaintances of old for the second and third time. The village was full of cordial little pigs with long snouts whose ancestors would have been wild boars. 'They are saying a pig has been killed to be cooked,' Ranjan said. 'They do not know why.' We turned back for another tour of the neighbouring collection of houses. 'We are walking,' Ranjan said, 'because I am looking for that girl.'

'Don't you know where she lives?'

'I know where she lives but I do not understand their customs in this way of visiting, and am not wanting to put my foot in it as has happened before.' He was referring to his misadventure in the Bhunjia country, when the outhouse containing a family shrine had had to be burned down after he had blundered into it out of mere curiosity. 'They were very understanding. No one blamed me for my mistakes. Something like that could happen to me here if I am not careful. This is to be avoided.'

'I agree with you,' I told him. 'Better to play for safety.'

'Soon her friends will go to tell her I am here,' he said, 'and she will come out.'

Somewhere over on the further side of the village drumming had started. We stopped to listen. 'Does that mean they're dancing?' I asked.

'This is certainly the case. In Kangrapada always there are celebrations going on. For the birth of a child they are celebrating, and then again for the first cutting of hair. When the rain comes and when it stops there is a very big dancing. If a man recovers from a sickness all his friends must dance with him. If they cannot find a reason for celebrating they are doing so for no reason at all. In this village there is dancing with any excuse.'

We strolled in the direction of these celebratory sounds, finding ourselves shortly in an open space shaded by splendid old trees in which a man hammering on a drum was being accompanied by another on an exceedingly shrill flute. Nine Godba maidens, arms linked, advanced, retreated, advanced, and kicked, almost in chorus-girl style. With a change in the music's tempo they formed a single file to follow their leader waving a broom in a capering circle round the musicians. Crouching in a shady corner of this scene was a bearded Westerner in shorts, a video camera held to his eye. A second Westerner, clean-shaven, also in shorts, was doing his best to direct the action of the dancers and confine this within the camera's field of vision.

'Those are the girls we were talking to just now. Seems as though they're putting on a performance,' I said.

'For money,' Ranjan said, 'someone is paying them money.'

'It is something you have to expect.'

'In Kangrapada no one is given money to do such things. Money is not necessary. They are dancing all the time for the pleasure of dancing.'

'Our friends have no way of knowing that. Apart from Kangra-pada that's the way things are done.'

'But there is an Indian with them. He should tell them.'

At that moment a young Indian dressed in town style in shirt and slacks had come into view from behind the car that had brought the filming party. 'This is something you have to accept,' I said. 'Even Kangrapada will have to come to terms with money.'

Variations had to be introduced into the dance routine to accommodate the camera's requirements. The girls were halted and called back, led by the broom-waver for several repetitions of their dance. The music was slowed down to give each girl time to provide a separate dead-pan close-up before moving back into line. They had stiffened up. Spontaneity wilted.

'This is not Godba dancing,' Ranjan said. 'When the Godbas dance they are not going for walks. They are staying in one place.'

'I expect the photographer wanted more action, and this is the best they can do.'

'Yes, that may be so. They are accustomed to dance in their own way.'

'Does it matter if it's not authentic? They're trying hard. The man with the camera is getting what he wants. After all, this is not for local consumption.'

'The village has changed. Now everything will be bought with money.'

'Eventually, yes. It was bound to happen. The change has come sooner than expected, that's all. After all one single video camera in a thousand miles isn't too bad.'

The drum thumped out its subtle complexities that had left the dancing-to-order so far behind, and as the flute squealed untamed ecstasy the Godba girls traipsed conscientiously up and down and backwards and forwards. The photographer's assistant gestured to the girl with the broom to wave it more vigorously, and she did so. He pulled at the corners of his mouth, producing a grimace meant to represent a smile, but the girls did not understand. Ranjan had said of another such village, in illustration of tribal temperament, 'When they are dancing no one is knowing when it will end. While they are happy this dancing must go on.' The pity in this case was that it all depended on the running time of the film which at that moment seemed to have come to an end. The cameraman held up his hand and it was all over. The music wailed through a showering cascade of half-tones to silence. The drummer let fall his sticks. The girls, dismissed by the Indian boy's gesture, shuffled off into the background. Their leader threw the broom away, and the crows that had taken refuge from this disturbance in overhanging branches now unfolded their wings and dropped about us from the trees.

'No one came to watch the dancing,' I said.

'They do not come to watch dancing, they come to dance. That is why no one came.'

It was one of the small misadventures of travel, an abrupt debasement of the coinage of experience that I suspected neither of us would forget. The day had flagged. Watched by the village elders with amiable somnolence we recovered the car for a final tour of the village. After a few minutes, and with no sign of disappointment, Ranjan said that we might as well go, and we had reached the last of the houses when he spotted the Paraja girl he had come to see, standing among a group of friends at the top of a slope from which they could keep the road under observation.

We stopped and waited, sitting in the car. The Paraja girl detached herself from her friends and came down the slope, bent down to the window and she and Ranjan began what sounded like a casual chat. She was a pretty, lively girl with a gentle smile. Ranjan had mentioned that, as usual, none of the villagers of Kangrapada knew their ages. I would have put her as being seventeen. Despite the immense effort taken in all these tribal villages to prevent interbreeding there was a recognizable form of beauty shared by these girls, whether Parajas or Godbas. Why should the Parajas smile, I wondered, whereas the Godbas remained straight-faced? The foreigners had chosen badly, the Parajas should have danced for them.

The soft-voiced discussion through the car window ought to have betrayed traces of excitement even if under control – but there was none. 'When I am with these people,' Ranjan said, 'I watch them and I try to behave as they do. Always I play for safety.' This was in reply to my comment that I never remembered seeing a Paraja who was not actually smiling, or who failed to convey the impression that he or she was about to smile. But perhaps this was all part of the protocol of concealment of feeling. The Paraja stiff upper lip. Slowly I was coming to the realization that for all the apparent free loving and living of the so-called primitives they were in reality wanderers under watchful eyes in the labyrinth of custom. Now Ranjan and the girl appeared to be joking together, but I remembered the implacable joking and no-joking relationship imposed by the Kondh and the Bonda. Perhaps this, too, was a ritual prescribed for such an occasion. Perhaps, even, it was all played according to the rules, including the antics at the Paraja drunken wedding we had attended.

Could it even be that this encounter and this setting had been contrived in advance? I had heard Ranjan's story of his proposed marriage with the Paraja girl in which the father had taken the unheard-of initiative of renouncing the bride-price, besides consenting to her union with a caste-member from the city. The question was how had the village taken this? Ranjan may have been deceived by an assumed complacency. He seemed never to have considered the posssibility of opposition, yet surely there must have been a minority of dissenters in a community ruled by a cabal of ancient conservatives under the all-seeing and assuredly critical eye of the Earth Mother in her heap of stones?

At the top of the slope seven Paraja girls, all identical from this distance, the same ear-rings, nose-rings, bracelets, anklets, and smiles, stood in a motionless row to watch what was going on. Were they part of an essential audience? Now I realized that other onlookers had silently placed themselves within the frame of vision: a man with an archaic stringed instrument wearing a long old-fashioned loincloth, whom I saw here for the first time, a man carrying a single peacock's feather held like a staff of office, a man leading a white dog on a length of rope. There was a planned formation in this setting, like that of a scene from *Antigone* when the Fates are about to enter their part of the drama.

The exchange of words faltered, was breached by small silences, which in turn were filled in by what I suspected were repetitions. It was the familiar climate of partings, when there is nothing new to be said. Heads were rocked in Indian fashion gently from side to side to signify acceptance, agreement, conclusion. The Paraja girl straightened herself and moved back; Ranjan touched the driver on the shoulder, and the car began to draw away. Ranjan continued to look straight ahead but after a few yards I twisted round to watch the Paraja girl climb the slope to join her friends, still facing us and in line. The few onlookers had begun to drift away.

Chapter Twenty-Four

WE MADE AN EARLY START next morning on the road back to Bhubaneswar, taking a short cut through north-eastern Andhra Pradesh which extends a closed hand in profile with the index finger pointed northwards along the coast in the direction of distant Calcutta.

I was in no hurry to arrive. As in the case of most pleasurable experiences, time had speeded up, and what was left of the journey was slipping away too fast. When we stopped for tea I got out the local, amateurish large-scale map which tore a little more at the folds every time I opened it, and for which despite its inaccuracies in the matter of place names and distances I had developed an affection. It was full of signs and symbols and little conventional drawings of temples, hot springs, rock inscriptions and paintings, images of Vishnu sleeping under an umbrella, of Buddhist antiquities, and 'Scenic Picturesque Picnic-spots', of forests furnished with tigers and crocodiles in an aggressive stance; and a single sinister ideogram denoted a hydro-electric project with its dam, at the head of a tragically flooded valley.

What I was looking for was excuse for delay, a short detour back into the vanished hinterland, a postponement of the moment when I would face the engrimed Super-Fast ready on the dot to pull out from Bhubaneswar Station, a final truancy to prepare for and soften the impact of anti-climax.

But all roads from this point on led to Bhubaneswar, and from the moment of crossing the state border of Andhra Pradesh an instant change was to be felt. South Orissa had been peopled by thin men; here there were fat men, too. Their faces, demeanour, and even their walk were different. People you saw in these streets were going about their business; no one carried musical instruments. In

826

Orissa we had sometimes driven all day without passing another car. In this right-hand top corner of Andhra Pradesh fed by National Highway NH5, rampaging legions of lorries filled the road. In the small countryfied towns and the vast emptiness we had come through the police had been spread thin. Here they were everywhere, watching, questioning, poking among the fearful carnage of road-accidents waiting to be cleared away, manning check-points through which vehicles preferring to pass without inspection could do so in payment of a standard fifty-rupee bribe. I saw something I had never seen in Orissa, a whole roadside village of wonderfully woven beehive huts occupied by untouchables, with neat and pretty untouchable girls crawling in and out of them. Ranjan said that they had been ordered to build their houses in this way to assist caste differentiation. Further on there were labour gangs of girls of about fifteen or sixteen, supplied by this community to haul stones broken up with hammers into position for road-repairing steam-rollers.

There was a different pulse of life here; different inducements, different goals. Luxury advertisements had appeared to encourage the circulation of money. Film stars displayed their Westernized good looks from every wall, otherwise covered with a scrofula of misleading appeals by candidates for election. The whiff of development and prosperity fostered lapses of taste. An up-to-date temple with parking offered facilities for the better class of traveller. Three over-large factory-produced images of Saraswati, Krishna, and Ganesh, sharing local adulation, had been unappealingly sprayed in shiny black enamel, and one could sit in comfortable chairs and sip superb tea served by the lady attendants while exchanging stares with these. A little way down the road a retired admiral had built a villa in the shape of the front half of a warship, painted in undulations of grey-green camouflage with portholes for windows and a stone five-pounder threatening the surroundings from its deck.

Hereabouts we suffered the first tyre trouble for well over a thousand miles, an occurrence that sparked off a small mutiny in our driver who complained that this was due to our not paying our respects at another shrine which we had overshot, after which Ranjan had refused to turn back. Up until this we had been travelling in the main through the spheres of influence of easygoing tribal deities, but now we were in the territory of Kali, who, as the driver assured us, was less likely to overlook such offences. With that, almost, the tyre went down, calling for an awkward repair. Our hope had been to spend the night at the ashram of Shiva about sixty miles further on. ('The priestess will not even question your religion,' Ranjan said. 'If she is not minding, why should you?') Now, with the onset of darkness, this would not be comfortably possible. We decided to find beds in the local metropolis, Srikakulam, thrusting its flood-lit towers into a sky in which – as if in presage of what was to come – a single rocket exploded to spread a glittering, slowly falling trail.

Srikakulam had half a ring-road, a one-way traffic system, white taxis, and the first traffic lights I had seen since leaving Calcutta. At the moment of our arrival the lights were stuck at red, and the biggest and most unruly herd of buffaloes I had ever seen were stampeding, like a scene from a western round-up, in the wrong direction down the one-way main street, and carrying all before them. Srikakulam, too, was in the throes of its many weddings, with fireworks now exploding all round and insoluble tussles for precedence at the lights between the processions and distraught buffaloes separated from their herd. The Hemamalin Film Star Hotel was bursting at the seams with fantastically attired wedding guests, and marooned among these were a number of regulars, some extremely fat, and one asprawl in an armchair being fanned by one middle-aged woman and massaged by another. There were no rooms, said the reception clerk, adding in a voice that held a suspicion of triumph that we would not find any in the town. Nor, he added, was there any food. Drinks could only be served to guests in their cars, but this – and we agreed with him – was impossible in a street which at that moment was glutted with panicking cattle. He then handed us a leaflet about a local cobra festival to be held in November, for which hotel reservations were required well in advance.

With the buffalo stampede at an end, somebody directed us to a last-chance hotel in the less fashionable part of town, and we drove there under a sky speckled with small explosions and the surroundings fitfully lit by a descending parachute flare as if in preparation for military assault. The General Lodging, as it was called, reminded me of a prison in Madrid where I had once visited a prisoner detained for political reasons. It occupied in this case a floor of an unfinished building long since abandoned. A passage accessible through an iron gate led to a dozen small rooms: well-swept, adequate cells, free of mosquitoes and devoid of dark recesses in which venomous spiders might have lurked, each with a clean sink, small barred windows, and a naked bulb that dispensed waxing and waning light. I had come very much to like the people who owned or ran such places and the roadside dhabas; unsmiling as a whole, the practitioners of extreme if distant courtesy, and free of ingratitude or pretence. I was happy to be where we were rather than at the Film Star Hotel.

The problem of food arose, and it was a little more complicated than usual. On the whole we were committed, like it or not, to a diet of rice and dahl, which suited our vegetarian driver very well. We were directed to the Military Meals Restaurant, a flashy sort of place, where after taking one look at us the doorman pointed at a side entrance leading to an upstairs area set aside for patrons in search of a discreet ambience in which to drink whisky and eat meat. To ensure privacy and anonymity diners were served in booths like oversized telephone boxes, so faintly lit that they must have had to grope for their food.

Dinesh would have none of this. The waiter assured us that pure and unadulterated vegetarian food was served on the ground floor, but the driver raised the objection that the ladles used for the rice might have been contaminated by meat, and made a bolt for the door. Left to ourselves we chose the relatively well-lit main restaurant, simple food and good Indian beer.

Back in the General Lodging I took up position to enjoy the view over the low wall of our passageway, which also served as a communal balcony. The building occupied half a substantial crater, possibly fifty yards across, from which it was to be supposed that sand and gravel had once been extracted leaving a wilderness of a special kind, deeply eroded and fissured, and an occasional small cavern among little pyramids of building materials in its bottom. This, by Indian standards, was a valuable site, since it provided shelter of a basic kind for those who could not afford a roof and walls, and in most cases not even rent. A flight of steps had been cut into the crater's side and these joined at the bottom with a path leading to a settlement improvised in the foundations of the General Lodging itself. This appeared to be occupied by citizens in regular work, who arrived home in some instances carrying briefcases. Tucked away in a far corner of the crater and only partially visible by leaning over the wall was an encampment made from plastic sheeting stretched over a wooden frame, of the kind put up in a single day to accommodate labourers working in the neighbourhood. It was early enough for the shops still to be open in the street running along the top of the crater wall, from which a certain amount of light penetrated into the cavity. Smears of torchlight showed in the interiors of the black plastic shacks, but it was likely that the labourers and their wives had already gone to bed, for there was nothing of them to be seen. Nevertheless their children, still up and about, continued a joyous and jubilant exploration of the crater's fairyland.

Ranjan joined me to enjoy the view, followed by the owner of the place, who had the face of a wolf but who was very kind, bringing us tea. Something in the air made me feel Ranjan's mood had changed. It was hard not to be soothed in this environment. Not a word had been said about Kangrapada since leaving it, and I had found it significant that he had not even marked the village's position on a sketch map of our journey I had asked him to make. Now he suddenly brought up the filming of which he had shown such disapproval, news of which had reached a contact in Jeypore where we had spent the last night. 'These men were Americans,' he said. 'The Indians who took them told them the people were not asking for money. Instead they gave them a pig.'

Since the matter was now in the open, I asked a question. 'Any further thoughts on the subject of marriage?'

'Yes,' he said. 'This has been settled in my mind. I am thinking it will be an arranged one.'

'Traditional style,' I said.

'That is the meaning of an arranged marriage. It means I am saying yes to tradition.'

It came as a disappointment. I would have preferred this romantic adventure and my tiny involvement to have ended on a different note.

This he seemed to have sensed, and there was a touch of consolation in his laugh. 'Unless minds are changing,' he said. 'That is always possible.'

After a moment of failure the town's lights had all come on again, and we sipped our tea and enjoyed the prospect. A night market was held along the road across the crater with the leaves of the shade trees turned to coral by its cooking fires. Shoppers piled their bundles into the rickshaws and struggled to help the pullers drag them up the slope to where the road levelled out. Below us the labourers' children screamed unflagging delight; a husband back from work came scrambling down the crater waving his briefcase to a wife positioned somewhere out of sight beneath. Film theme-music from distant sources had been blended by an ocean of air into a sweet Eastern droning. For me it was the best of India. It was a scene to be included in the album of the journey's memorabilia along with the sad aquatints of Bihar, the blossoming night skies of the steel towns, and the ghostly Australia of the mountains where tribals danced upon metallic ores.

In this context of the immediate past a gallery of faces were called to mind, all of which had made an appearance, however brief, in this experience: Mr Chawra, enraptured at Patna by the balloon, the genial and helpful Mr Singh who liked humanity on the whole but was depressed at the prevalence of insurance fraud, Devi with his swaggering Japanese car fraternizing cautiously with his casteless driver – even the Debjon's manager who was cordiality itself and rewarded me on my departure with two additional Christmas cards, one inscribed 'Well come. Any time to drop in.' Finally there was Ranjan, lapsed Brahmin, and a prey to romantic impulse, but otherwise a man of extraordinary perception who showed me his country in a new light, and with whom I would have asked nothing better than to travel on uncovering together hidden pleasures of India.

He had gone off with the General Lodging's owner and was back with more tea. 'What time in the morning?' he asked. 'Six?'

'Let's make it later,' I said. 'There's no hurry.'

I wondered what the few miles along the coastal road had to offer. 'How long is it to the ashram?' I asked.

'Two hours.'

'I suppose we could stay there if it came to the push?'

'They will be welcoming us, but better it is to stay only a short time. This is a very quiet place. There is very little to catch the eye or occupy the interest.'

'In that case there's nothing for it,' I said. 'It's on to Bhubaneswar.'

Select Bibliography

The Anti-Slavery Society, *Anti-Slavery Reporter*, 1989.

Sumanta Banerjee, *India's Simmering Revolution: The Naxalite Uprising*, Zed Books, 1980.

Ibn Battuta, *The Travels of Ibn Battuta – A.D. 1325–1354*, issued by The Hakluyt Society, CUP, 1971.

Rev. A. Duff, *The First Series of Government Measures for the Abolition of Human Sacrifice Among the Kondh*, Calcutta Review, Vol. VI, 1851.

Verrier Elwin, 'The Bonda Murderers', *Man-in-India*, 1945.

The Muria and Their Ghotul, OUP, 1947.

Bonda Highlanders, OUP, 1950.

Judith Ennew, *Debt Bondage – A Survey*, The Anti-Slavery Society, Report No. 4, 1981.

Trevor Fishlock, *India File: Inside the Subcontinent*, John Murray, 1983.

Caesar Fredericke, 'The Voyages of Master Caesar Fredericke into the east India, and Beyond the Indies,' in Hakluyt's *Voyages*, Everyman's Library, Dent, 1907, Vol. 3 pp. 198–268.

Christoph von Furer Haimendorf, *Tribes of India: The Struggle for Survival*, University of California Press, 1982.

John Jourdain, *The Journal of John Jourdain – 1608–1617*, issued by The Hakluyt Society, CUP, 1895.

John Keay, *Into India*, John Murray, 1973.

Richard Lannoy, *The Speaking Tree: A Study of Indian Culture and Society*, OUP, 1987.

Sebastian Manrique, *The Travels of Sebastian Manrique – 1629–1643*, issued by The Hakluyt Society, CUP, 1927.

Domingo Navarrete, *The Travels and Controversies of Friar Domingo Navarrete – 1618–1686*, issued by The Hakluyt Society, CUP, 1962.

A. R. N. Srivastava, *Tribal Freedom Fighters of India*, Ministry of Information, Government of India, New Delhi, 1986.

Tribal and Harijan Research-cum-Training Institute, *The Bonda*, Bhubaneswar, 1989.
The Kondh, Bhubaneswar, 1989.
The Saora, Bhubaneswar, 1989.

A VIEW OF THE WORLD

Selected writings

NORMAN LEWIS

These twenty articles, written during a period of thirty years, include an interview with Castro's executioner; a meeting with a tragic Ernest Hemingway; a farcical trip to the Chocos of Panama; a description of a fishing community in an unspoilt Ibiza; an extraordinary story of bandits in the highlands of Sardinia, and Lewis's famous report on the genocide of South America's Indians.

I have no hesitation in calling Norman Lewis one of the best writers, not of any particular decade, but of our century.
Graham Greene, The Daily Telegraph

A View of the World will carry Norman Lewis's reputation even higher than it already is. It is a triumph.
Patrick Marnham, The Literary Review

Everything is portrayed with a brilliance which makes all other travel-writing read like the blurb on a brochure.
Time Out

Norman Lewis is outstandingly the best travel writer of our age, if not the best since Marco Polo.
Auberon Waugh

PUBLISHED BY ELAND

NAPLES '44

An Intelligence Officer in the Italian labyrinth

NORMAN LEWIS

Norman Lewis arrived in Naples as an Intelligence Officer attached to the American Fifth Army. By 1944 the city's inhabitants were so destitute that all the tropical fish in the aquarium had been devoured, and numbers of respectable women had been driven to prostitution. The mafia gradually became so indispensable to the occupying forces that it succeeded in regaining its former power. Despite the cruelty and suffering he encountered, Norman Lewis writes in the diary, 'A year among Italians has converted me to such an admiration for their humanity and culture that were I given the chance to be born again, Italy would be the country of my choice'.

A wonderful book.
Richard West, The Spectator

As unique an experience for the reader as it must have been a unique experience for the writer.
Graham Greene

Here is a book of gripping fascination in its flow of bizarre anecdote and character sketch; and it is much more than that.
J. W. Lambert, The Sunday Times

The best single British memoir of the Second World War.
Geoffrey Wheatcroft, Daily Mail

One goes on reading page after page as if eating cherries.
Luigi Barzini, New York Review of Books

PUBLISHED BY *ELAND*

THE HONOURED SOCIETY

The Sicilian Mafia observed

NORMAN LEWIS

Epilogue by Marcello Cimino

Norman Lewis describes how, after Mussolini came close to destroying the Mafia, the U.S. army returned them to power in 1944. Henceforth they infiltrated every aspect of Sicilian life, corrupting landowners, the police, the judiciary, and even the church. In one of the most astonishing chapters, the author tells the story of how an eighty-year-old priest, Padre Camelo, led his monks on escapades of murder and extortion, frequently using the confessional box for transmitting threats.

One of the great travel writers of our time.
Eric Newby, The Observer

This book has not a dull moment in it; it is indeed imbued with that quality of terribilita which Giuliano himself was said to possess.
The Spectator

It is deftly written, and every page is horribly absorbing.
The Times

The Honoured Society is the most penetrating book ever written on the Mafia.
Time Out

PUBLISHED BY ELAND